### Tony Wheeler

Born in England, Tony spent most of his younger days overseas due to his father's airline occupation. Those years included a lengthy spell in Pakistan, a shorter period in the West Indies and all his high school years in the USA. He returned to England to do a university degree in engineering, worked for a short time as an automotive design engineer, returned to university again and did an MBA, then dropped out on the Asian trail with his wife Maureen. They set up Lonely Planet in the mid-70s and have been travelling, writing and publishing ever since. Travel for Tony and Maureen is now considerably enlivened by their daughter Tashi and son Kieran.

### Nancy Keller

Born and raised in northern California, Nancy earned BA degrees in history and social science, working along the way in a variety of occupations. In the '70s Nancy worked in the alternative press, doing every aspect of newspaper work from editorial and reporting to delivering the papers. She returned to university to earn a master's degree in journalism, finally graduating in 1986 after many breaks for extended stays on the west coast of Mexico. Since then she's been travelling and writing in Mexico, Israel, Egypt, Europe, various tropical South Pacific islands, and now New Zealand.

She's now in Central America researching a new LP book, *Central America on a shoestring*. After that it will be back to Mexico, to work on a new edition of LP's *Mexico – a travel survival kit*.

### From Nancy

For their help while researching this 6th edition, thanks to the staff of the tourist information centres and Department of Conservation (DOC) offices all over New Zealand, who were knowledgeable, friendly, and patient in the face of collectively thousands of questions. These local agencies, found in just about every city and town, are a tremendous resource for travellers!

Thanks to the proprietors of the numerous hostels, backpackers, etc, who shared their hospitality and provided travelling tips on their areas. A special thanks to Paul Crooks of the YHA.

Much appreciation to my friend Mrs Tek van Asch of Takapuna, Auckland, who welcomed me into New Zealand, helped me get sorted out to begin the project, and who provided a stable mailing address while I was constantly moving around.

Special thanks also to the folks in Waitomo, who helped to make my stay there one of the most enjoyable, interesting and memorable experiences of my stay in New Zealand.

## From the Publisher

This book was edited by Sharan Kaur and Diana Saad and Trudi Canavan was responsible for the design, illustrations and cover design. Vicki Beale and Graham Imeson drew the original maps which were updated and added to by Margaret Jung.

Thanks must also go to David Meagher for copy-editing, Michelle de Kretser for editorial help, Alan Tiller for proofing and Sharon Wertheim for indexing.

See page 461 for the names of travellers who wrote in with corrections, suggestions and additions.

## This Edition

This book has had a varied history. Tony Wheeler did the 1st edition back in 1977 and the next two were updated by New Zealander Simon Hayman. The 4th edition was updated by Australian Mary Covernton and Tony Wheeler went back again and did the 5th edition. Robin Tinker wrote the Tramping section. This edition was updated by Nancy Keller.

## Warning & Request

Things change – prices go up, good places go bad and bad places go bankrupt – nothing stays the same. So if you find things better or worse, recently opened or long since closed, please write and tell us and help make the next edition better.

Your letters will be used to help update future editions and, where possible, important changes will also be included as a Stop Press section in reprints.

All information is greatly appreciated and the best letters will receive a free copy of the next edition, or any other Lonely Planet book of your choice.

# Contents

# Introduction

Fresh open air, magnificent scenery and outdoor activities are the feature attractions of New Zealand. It's not a big country but for sheer variety it's hard to beat.

New Zealand's got everything, from sandy beaches and rugged coastlines to calm green meadows and ominously smoking volcanoes; from flat plains and placid lakes to high snow-capped mountains and bubbling hot mud pools. There are even icy glaciers that creep right down into sub-tropical rainforests.

There are cities too, but they pall beside the natural wonders. New Zealanders are friendly, easy going and helpful. Getting around is a breeze as there's lots of public transport and hitchhiking is reasonably easy. Finding accommodation is also easy and generally won't empty your wallet too fast,

although it's an idea to book ahead if you decide to go there in the high season. The food is fresh and there's plenty of it and these days even the wine can be excellent. It's a great country for travellers.

## THE BIG 12

There are so many superb physical features in New Zealand that you find yourself taking the beauty of the country for granted after a while. But if I had to pick a dozen 'not to be missed sights or things to do in New Zealand' here's what they'd be:

• Bay of Islands and Waipoua Kauri Forest, Northland. This is the historic meeting point of New Zealand's European and Maori cultures and an area of great natural beauty.

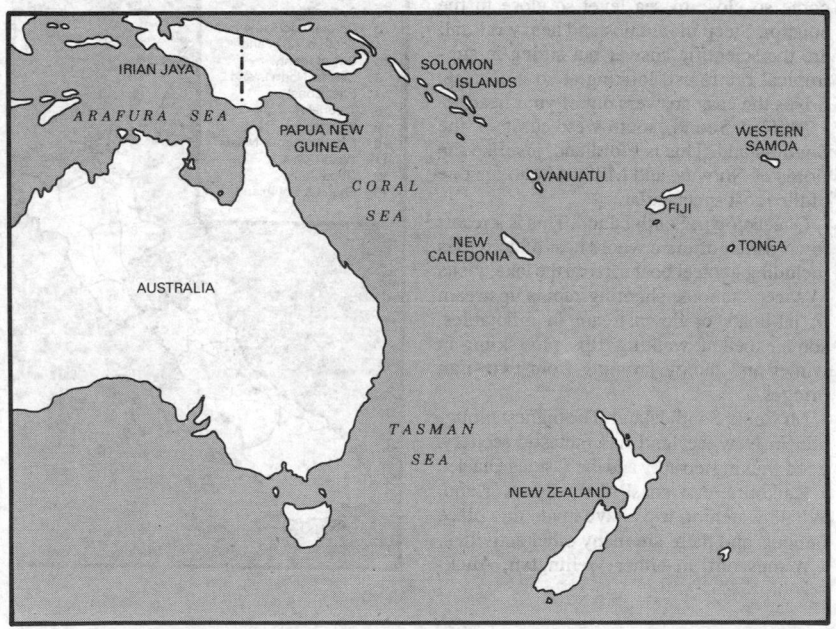

• Waitomo Caves, south of Hamilton. Limestone caverns with stalactites and stalagmites are obvious tourist attractions. There are a few of them scattered around both islands and one is much the same as another but this cave has the unusual feature of a glow-worm grotto. Black Water Rafting is a particular thrill. Visit it on the way to Rotorua.

• Rotorua, central North Island. This is one of New Zealand's most interesting areas. Go there for the thermal activity (boiling water, hissing steam, bubbling mud pools) and the Maori culture (don't miss the night-time Maori concerts or a *hangi*).

• Tongariro National Park, central North Island. This park has some of the best mountain/volcano scenery in the country and excellent tramping tracks. It's a short run south of Rotorua.

• Fox and Franz Josef Glaciers, west coast of the South Island. Nowhere else do glaciers come so close to sea level so close to the equator. Steep mountains and heavy rainfall are the scientific answer but sitting in sub-tropical rainforest, looking at so much ice, drives the easy answers out of your head.

• Milford Sound, south-west coast of the South Island. This is Fiordland, just like the fiords of Norway, and Milford Sound is one of the most spectacular.

• Queenstown, South Island. This is a resort town which offers a whole host of activities including genteel boat trips on the lake, visits to sheep stations, shooting rapids upstream in jet-boats or downstream in inflatables, some excellent walking trips, plus skiing in winter and bungy jumping from two high bridges.

• Mt Cook, South Island. The highest mountain in New Zealand has fantastic scenery, good walking territory and the Tasman Glacier.

• Kaikoura, east coast of the South Island. Whale watching trips have made this place famous, and there are many other activities.

• A museum, in either Wellington, Auckland, Christchurch or Wanganui. While you're in one of the cities, go to a museum and get an insight into Maori culture. The ones listed are amongst the best but New Zealand is well endowed with excellent museums. The Wagener Museum at Houhora in the Far North is most unusual.

• Stay on a farm. Farm life, especially sheep farming, is what rural New Zealand is all about.

• A walk. Somewhere along the line set a week aside and do one of the long walks for which New Zealand is justly famous. The Milford Track is the best known but others are equally rewarding.

## Organisation of this Book
The following map shows how we have divided the country:

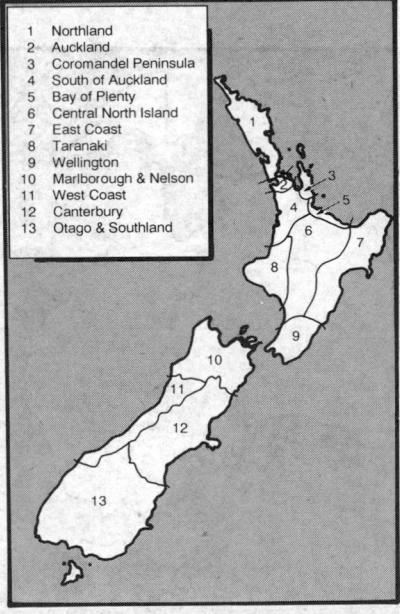

| | |
|---|---|
| 1 | Northland |
| 2 | Auckland |
| 3 | Coromandel Peninsula |
| 4 | South of Auckland |
| 5 | Bay of Plenty |
| 6 | Central North Island |
| 7 | East Coast |
| 8 | Taranaki |
| 9 | Wellington |
| 10 | Marlborough & Nelson |
| 11 | West Coast |
| 12 | Canterbury |
| 13 | Otago & Southland |

# Facts about the Country

## HISTORY
New Zealand's history has two distinct phases – the Maori part and the more recent history since the arrival of Europeans.

### Maori History
The original inhabitants of New Zealand were known until fairly recently as Morioris. Recent evidence now indicates that the Maoris arrived in Aotearoa – the 'land of the long white cloud' as they called New Zealand – in a series of migrations and that the Morioris were in the first wave of Maori migration rather than being a separate and distinct race. It was these early settlers who hunted the huge flightless bird, the moa, both for food and its feathers until it became extinct. Today, the name Moriori refers to the original settlers of the Chatham Islands where the last full-blooded Moriori died in 1933.

Since the Maoris had no written language, their history and culture is recalled through storytelling and songs, which means it's probable that the saga of Kupe, Hawaiki and the 'great migration' has been embellished over the centuries. While it would be unwise to take the legend absolutely literally, there's obviously a good deal of truth in it. One of the heroes of the story, Kupe, a particularly brilliant Polynesian navigator, is said to have set sail from Hawaiki in the 10th century for the 'great southern land, uninhabited and covered with mists', and managed to return to tell the tale.

Centuries later, when things weren't going so well in Hawaiki – overpopulation, shortage of food and all those other familiar problems – the decision was made to follow Kupe's instructions and head south. Despite the similar names, Hawaiki is not Hawaii; experts believe it was more likely to have been an island near Tahiti. The similar spelling and pronunciation, however, suggests that another party of emigrants from Hawaiki settled in Hawaii, naming it after their home island.

According to legend, 10 great canoes sailed to New Zealand in the 14th century, though historians now feel the great arrival may actually have been more than 1000 years ago. The names of the canoes are all remembered, and their landing points, crews and histories also recalled. Today, Maoris still trace their lineage back to one or other of the canoes of the great Polynesian migration. Of course the 'moa hunters' were there and some other Maoris from an earlier, smaller migration, but the new immigrants from the great fleet soon established themselves in their adopted home.

Maori culture developed without hindrance from other cultures for hundreds of years but being warriors they engaged in numerous tribal battles in which the losers ended up as slaves or pot roast. Given the shortage of animal life in New Zealand, enemies must have been a useful source of protein! While they did not develop a written language, the Maoris created a complex art form involving beautifully carved war canoes and meeting houses and intricate tattoos on both men and women. They were still Stone-Age people (in New Zealand it would have been difficult to get beyond that stage since there are few metals apart from gold!) but they produced exquisite greenstone (jade) ornaments and war clubs. Expeditions were mounted to the South Island to find jade but otherwise most of the tribes wisely stayed in the much warmer North Island.

### European Exploration
In 1642 the Dutch explorer Abel van Tasman, who had just sailed around Australia from Batavia (modern day Jakarta, Indonesia), dropped by but didn't stay long after several of his crew were killed and cooked. His visit, however, meant that the Europeans now knew of New Zealand's

sealers (who soon reduced the seal population to nothing) and then whalers (who did the same with whales). They were hardly the cream of European society and they introduced diseases and prostitution, created such a demand for preserved heads that Maori chiefs started chopping off their slaves' heads to order (previously they'd only preserved the heads of warriors who had died in battle) and worst of all they brought in European arms. When they traded in greenstone *meres* (war clubs) for muskets, the Maoris soon embarked on wholesale slaughter of each other. By 1830 the Maori population was falling dramatically.

## European Settlement

The arrival of Samuel Marsden, the first missionary, in 1841 righted the balance a little and by the middle of the 19th century warfare had been much reduced, cannibalism fairly well stamped out and the raging impact of *Pakeha* (White people) diseases and their modern armoury were also curbed. But the unfortunate Maoris now found themselves spiritually assaulted and much of their traditions and culture were destroyed. Despite the missionary influence their numbers continued to decline.

During this time European settlers were arriving in New Zealand and they began to demand British protection from the Maoris and from other less savoury settlers. The Poms were not too keen on further colonising – what with burning their fingers in America, fighting in Canada, and generally messing around in other places, not to mention having Australia to worry about. But the threat of a French colonising effort stirred them to dispatch James Busby to be the British Resident in 1833. The fact that this was a very low-key effort is illustrated by poor Busby even having to pay his own fare from Australia and, once he'd set up shop, his efforts to protect the settlers and keep law and order were somewhat limited because he had no forces, no arms, no authority and was soon dubbed 'the man-of-war without guns'.

existence and in those days of colonialism it also meant that they would eventually want it.

The Dutch, after their first uncomfortable look, were none too keen on the place and it was left alone until Captain Cook sailed by in 1769, discovered that his Tahitian interpreter could communicate with the Maoris, claimed the whole place for Britain, sailed right round both islands mapping as he went, and split for Australia. The good captain made a number of friendly contacts with the Maoris and was impressed with their bravery and spirit and with the potential of this lightly populated land.

When the British started their antipodean colonising they opted for the even more lightly populated Australia so New Zealand's first settlers were temporary ones –

## Clashes with the Maoris

In 1840 the British sent Captain William Hobson to replace Busby. Hobson was instructed to persuade the Maori chiefs to relinquish their sovereignty to the British Crown. In part this decision was made in the expectation that if the government didn't get in there and organise things every Tom, Dick and Harry settler would be buying land off the Maoris for two axes and a box of candles and chaos would soon result.

With a truly British display of pomp and circumstance, Hobson met with the Maori chiefs in front of Busby's residence at Waitangi in the Bay of Islands. It is now known as the Treaty House and the anniversary of 6 February 1840 is considered the birthday of modern New Zealand. The treaty was signed by 45 chiefs (or rather Hobson signed for them) and eventually 500 chiefs from around the country agreed to British rule.

This orderly state of affairs didn't last long. When settlers wanted to buy land and the Maoris didn't want to sell, conflict inevitably resulted. The admirable idea that the government should act as a go-between in all Maori-Pakeha deals to ensure fairness on both sides fell apart when the government was too tightfisted to pay the price. The first visible revolt came when Hone Heke, the first chief to sign the Waitangi treaty, chopped down the flagpole at Kororareka (now known as Russell), across the bay. Despite new poles and more and more guards Heke or his followers managed to chop the pole down four times, and on the last occasion it was covered with iron to foil axe-wielding Maoris! After this final destruction of the pole he burnt down the town of Kororareka for good measure, an action which has since been acclaimed as a sign of his good taste because it was a pestilent place.

In the skirmishes that followed, the British governor put a £100 reward on Heke's head, to which Heke brilliantly responded by offering a matching £100 for the governor's head. This was only one in a long series of skirmishes, battles, conflicts, disputes and arguments, which escalated between 1860 and 1865 into a more or less full-fledged war. The result was inconclusive, but the Maoris were effectively worn down by sheer weight of numbers and equipment.

## Modern New Zealand

Things calmed down and New Zealand became an efficient agricultural country. Sheep farming, that backbone of modern New Zealand, took hold as refrigerated ships made it possible to sell NZ meat in Europe. Towards the end of the last century New Zealand went through a phase of sweeping social change that took it to the forefront of the world. Women were given the vote in 1893, 25 years before Britain or America and more like 75 years ahead of Switzerland. The range of far-sighted social reforms and pioneering legislation included old age pensions, minimum wage structures, the establishment of arbitration courts and the introduction of child health services. The latter included the foundation in 1907 of the Plunket Society, an organisation of nurses who care for expectant mothers and young babies.

Meanwhile the Maoris floundered. New Zealand grew through immigration (a very selective immigration), but by 1900 the Maori population had dropped to an estimated 42,000 and was falling fast. The Maoris were given the vote in 1867, but the continuing struggle to hold onto their culture and their ancestral lands sapped their spirit and energy for some time. In the last few decades there has been a turnaround and the Maori population has started to increase at a faster rate than the Pakeha. Today they number about 9% of the total population, or about 302,000.

New Zealanders are proud of their record of racial harmony; there has never been any racial separation and inter-marriage is common. In *Return to Paradise* James Michener tells of the outraged NZ reaction when WW II GIs stationed in New Zealand tried to treat Maoris like American Blacks. Despite this the Maoris are a disadvantaged race sharing a less than proportional part of the nation's wealth and leadership. It's a problem New Zealanders are wrestling with but without great success as yet.

### New Zealand Today

Today New Zealand is still predominantly an agricultural country but the '70s and '80s were hard. The closure of much of its traditional European market for agricultural products combined with the oil crisis price hikes of many of its mineral and manufactured imports have done no good at all to the country's economic situation. Unlike Australia, New Zealand has little mineral wealth to supplement its agricultural efficiency. Furthermore the inefficiencies of small scale manufacturing that afflict Australia are simply magnified by New Zealand's even tinier population. It's still an affluent, organised, tidy country but things simply aren't as rosy as they once were.

Internationally, however, New Zealand has become by far the most interesting and important country in the South Pacific region. It has taken a strong stand on nuclear issues, refusing entry to nuclear-equipped US warships and condemning French nuclear testing in the Pacific. This brave policy has caused more than a few problems for the Kiwis. The USA has dumped them from the ANZUS treaty agreements and the French have even gone so far as to send government-sponsored terrorists to sink the antinuclear Greenpeace ship, the *Rainbow Warrior*, in Auckland's harbour.

### GEOGRAPHY

New Zealand stretches 1600 km from north to south and consists of three large islands and a number of smaller islands scattered around the two main ones. The two major land masses are the 115,000 sq km North Island and the 151,000 sq km South Island. Stewart Island, which covers an area of 1700 sq km, lies directly south of the South Island. The country is 10,400 km south-west of the USA, 1700 km south of Fiji and 2250 km east of Australia. Its western coastline faces the Tasman Sea, the part of the Pacific Ocean which separates New Zealand and Australia.

New Zealand's territorial jurisdiction also extends to the islands of Chatham, Kermadec, Tokelau, Auckland, Antipodes, Snares, Solander and Bounty (most of them uninhabited) and the Ross Dependency in the Antarctica.

### CLIMATE

It's upside down compared to the northern hemisphere and similar, though a little colder, to southern Australia. The North Island has an average rainfall of around 130 cm, with average maximum daily temperatures from around 10°C to 25°C. Generally, it doesn't get as cold in Northland as it does further south.

Auckland is more or less like Sydney, but not so hot in summer, with average temperatures around 23°C and average rainfall about 130 cm.

Generally snow is only seen on the mountains (Egmont, Ruapehu, Ngauruhoe and Tongariro), though there are sometimes snowfalls in the high country in winter.

The South Island tends to have more extremes in climate, though at any one time there's really not a great difference in the temperature or rainfall throughout the country.

The west of the South Island is wetter than the east and can have an annual rainfall of 700 cm or so, while not far away in Central

## Climate Chart

| | JAN Approx Temp | | | FEB Approx Temp | | | MAR Approx Temp | | | APR Approx Temp | | | MAY Approx Temp | | | JUN Approx Temp | | | JUL Approx Temp | | | AUG Approx Temp | | | SEP Approx Temp | | | OCT Approx Temp | | | NOV Approx Temp | | | DEC Approx Temp | | |
|---|---|---|---|---|---|---|---|---|---|---|---|---|---|---|---|---|---|---|---|---|---|---|---|---|---|---|---|---|---|---|---|---|---|---|---|---|
| | Max °C | Min °C | Hum % | Max °C | Min °C | Hum % | Max °C | Min °C | Hum % | Max °C | Min °C | Hum % | Max °C | Min °C | Hum % | Max °C | Min °C | Hum % | Max °C | Min °C | Hum % | Max °C | Min °C | Hum % | Max °C | Min °C | Hum % | Max °C | Min °C | Hum % | Max °C | Min °C | Hum % | Max °C | Min °C | Hum % |
| Auckland | 23 | 15 | 74 | 23 | 16 | 75 | 22 | 15 | 76 | 19 | 13 | 77 | 16 | 10 | 80 | 14 | 8 | 81 | 13 | 7 | 80 | 14 | 8 | 80 | 16 | 9 | 77 | 17 | 11 | 76 | 19 | 12 | 75 | 21 | 14 | 74 |
| Wellington | 19 | 12 | 79 | 20 | 13 | 80 | 18 | 12 | 81 | 16 | 10 | 82 | 13 | 8 | 84 | 11 | 6 | 83 | 10 | 5 | 84 | 11 | 6 | 83 | 13 | 7 | 81 | 15 | 8 | 80 | 16 | 10 | 79 | 18 | 11 | 80 |
| Christchurch | 21 | 11 | 72 | 21 | 11 | 72 | 19 | 10 | 77 | 16 | 7 | 78 | 13 | 4 | 82 | 11 | 1 | 83 | 10 | 1 | 84 | 11 | 2 | 81 | 14 | 4 | 76 | 16 | 6 | 75 | 19 | 8 | 72 | 20 | 10 | 73 |

Otago the rainfall is only 30 cm. Even in the middle of summer it can be cold and rainy in the West Coast area of the South Island, although when the sun comes out it's as pleasant as you could ask. In the south of the South Island it can get quite cold in the winter (June, July and August), but not as cold as it does in northern USA.

Central Otago has both New Zealand's coldest winter days and hottest summer days. Snow is common in the hills in the South Island in winter, especially in the very south where it occasionally even snows at sea level.

Prevailing winds tend to be westerlies of one sort or another. This explains the rainfall pattern in the South Island, where the 'norwesters' dump their rain in the west as they hit the Southern Alps, continuing across the Canterbury Plains as hot dry winds, often of gale force.

Antipodes, according to the dictionary, is a place 'diametrically opposite' so if you looked for the antipodes of New Zealand you would find a sort of Spanish/North African mix.

### FLORA & FAUNA

As is the case for most Pacific islands New Zealand's plants and animals are for the most part not found anywhere else in the world. And, like other Pacific islands, New Zealand has been invaded by pest plants and animals brought by settlers, mostly in the last 200 years.

Wild pigs, goats, possums, wallabies, rabbits, foxes, dogs, cats and deer have all made their mark on the native wildlife, and blackberries, gorse, broom and the usual crop of agricultural weeds have infested huge areas of land.

Even so, much of New Zealand's flora and fauna has survived, although over 150 native plants –10% of the total number of species – and many native animals are threatened with extinction.

### Flora

The most obvious imports are the massive plantations of radiata (or Monterey) pine, Douglas (or Oregon) fir and Californian redwood, which supply the economically important sawn timber and paper industry.

Some notable flora reserves are Lake Waiparaheka Scientific Reserve in North Auckland; Enys Scientific Reserve in Castle Hill Basin, Canterbury; a portion of Russell State Forest, and part of the North West Nelson State Forest Park. The Department of Conservation (DOC) administers most of the protected areas, although private landowners are being encouraged to preserve important natural areas on their land through covenants administered by the Queen Elizabeth II Trust and the DOC.

The Maoris have given us some marvellous names for the native plants of New Zealand that are almost unpronounceable to Europeans – tawhairauriki, whauwhaupaku, mingimingi, hangehange, kumarahou, kowhai ngutu-kaka, and pua o te reinga, to name a handful. Some of the English names are nearly as colourful, and it's interesting to speculate about their derivations – gum digger's soap, wild Irishman, seven-finger, bog pine, flower of Hades, and Dieffenbach's Spaniard.

**Kauri** The kauri, known to science as Agathis australis, is the king of the North Island forests. Found only in New Zealand and in north-eastern Australia, mature kauris – sometimes as old as 1500 years – can reach a height of 36 metres with a diameter of over 3 metres for the first 30 metres, making them one of the largest trees in terms of wood volume in the world.

The kauri is a conifer, and thus related to the common pine trees in other parts of the world, but it has unusual long, broad and thick leaves, sometimes tinged red.

Before European settlement the kauri dominated 3 million hectares of forests from North Cape to Waikato. It wasn't long, though, before the Pakehas realised the value of the kauri wood, and the wholesale destruction of the great kauri forests began. Today, not much more than 10,000 hectares of mature kauri forests remain, mostly reserved in the Waipoua forest, although another 20,000 hectares of young kauri forest is being carefully nurtured.

The early settlers also found that the white to reddish-brown gum of the kauri could be used to make a high-quality varnish, and a huge 'gum-digging' industry arose. Trees were scarred with long V-shape grooves that oozed huge amounts of gum, and fossilised gum was also dug up from around the old stumps of burned or felled kauris – hence the name 'gum-digging'.

The first gum was exported to Sydney in 1815, and by 1895 it had become New Zealand's chief export, earning more revenue than gold. The kauri gum varnish industry collapsed in 1925 when synthetic varnishes became widely available, although gum-digging continued on a small scale into the 1960s, when gum was worth about $400 per ton.

Of course, the Maoris knew all about kauri gum long before the Pakehas discovered it. They chewed it, tattooed with it, and even made torches with it.

**Other Plants** The variety of vegetation types in New Zealand is enormous. Apart from kauri forests there are the luxuriant lowland kohekohe forests of the Bay of Plenty; the rainforests dominated by rimu, various beeches, tawa, matai and rata, and a great variety of tree ferns; the podocarp and hardwood forests of the lower parts of the North Island with its kahikatea, tawa, rimu, rata, and kohekohe; the summer-flowering alpine and subalpine herbfields; and the windswept scrub of the smaller islands.

In the South Island the vegetation changes dramatically as you climb into the mountains. The lowland supplejacks give way to rimu, miro, and then tree ferns at about 800 metres. Beyond 1000 metres the totara, wineberry, fuchsias, rata and kaikomako are gradually left behind, to be replaced by subalpine scrub. At about 1200 metres the scrub gives way to the tussock grasses and alpine herbfields, and at the extreme heights only some hardy lichens hang on to the rock, ice and snow-bound peaks.

One of the more noticeable plants is the pohutukawa, or New Zealand Christmas tree, which explodes with brilliant red flowers around December, peppering the forests with colour. Another Kiwi favourite is the yellow-flowered kowhai.

Like the Australian species, most of the 72 New Zealand orchids are not large or brilliantly coloured; one exception is the beautiful *Earina autumnalis*, which produces heavily perfumed cream flowers at Easter.

The cabbage tree, found throughout the plains and foothills, doesn't provide cabbages, nor is it a tree; but its swordlike leaves did supply the Maoris with medicines, rope and thatching. It is common throughout the country on the plains and foothills.

The northern rata is a tall tree that begins life high in another tree, sending down aerial roots that join horizontally and gradually enclose the host in a hollow trunk. It's found throughout the North Island and along the north-western coast of the South Island. The kahikatea, or white pine, dominates the lowland forests from North Cape to the Bluff, often having massive buttress roots to support a 60 metre high trunk.

New Zealand's best-known palm is probably the nikau. While it is mainly a North Island species, it also occurs as far south as Greymouth, on the west coast of the South Island.

Two plants to be wary of are the tutu and the ongaonga, or tree nettle, both tall shrubs or small trees. Every part of the tutu is poisonous, but particularly the black berries that hang invitingly in loose clusters. Unless you are a foremost expert on edible native plants, leave them alone. The leaves of the ongaonga are covered in brittle stinging spines. If you brush against them they'll break off and stick to your skin, releasing a poison that makes you groggy and uncoordinated for several days. It's also extremely painful and can be fatal.

The matagouri, or wild Irishman, is a thorny bush of the South Island lowlands. Its incredibly hard thorns were used by the Maoris for tattooing when bones were in short supply.

Another plant that was important to the Maoris was harakeke or flax, which they used to make rope, baskets, mats, fishing nets, and clothing. The British were so impressed with its usefulness that a huge export industry was born in the early 1800s, continuing strongly until its collapse during the depression of the 1930s. The last flax mill was closed at Foxton in 1937.

## Fauna

When animal life is so common in New Zealand (the four-legged, off-white, woolly variety that is), it's kind of curious to discover that there are virtually no native mammals. The first Maori settlers brought some rats and the now extinct Maori dog with them but the only indigenous mammals were bats. So you can imagine how surprised they were, the Maoris *and* the bats, when the Europeans turned up with sheep, cows, pigs and everything else old MacDonald's farm could offer. Today there are several species of deer, rabbits, possums – all introduced and many of them harmful to the environment – and, of course, sheep. In fact, there are so many sheep that after lambing time the sheep population can reach 100 million, 30 sheep for every man, woman and child.

If New Zealand had few animals it had plenty of birds – *had* being the operative word. Seven species of native birds are on the endangered list. The worst affected were the flightless birds like the kakapo and takahe which were easy prey for the introduced competitors and predators. In fact, the takahe was considered extinct until a small colony of them was discovered in the wild country of the southern fiords in 1948. Experts are having some success in breeding takahe in captivity and you can see them at a wildlife sanctuary in Te Anau. Other rare species are the crested grebe, the spotless crake, the black stilt, the fernbird and falcons. The rare brown teal's natural environment is the wetlands which have been affected by continued drainage and reclama-

tion of swamps and the modification of rivers for irrigation and hydroelectricity.

The best known of New Zealand's birds is the kiwi which has become the symbol of New Zealanders. It's a small, tubby, flightless bird and, because it's nocturnal, is not easy to observe. There is a theory that the kiwi became so lazy it lost its ability to fly. Kiwis may have no wings, feathers that are more like hair than real feathers, short sight and a sleepy nature, but the All Blacks (New Zealand's champion rugby team) have nothing on them when it comes to strength of leg! The kiwi has one thing in common with Australia's equally 'cute' national symbol, the koala – a shocking temper, which is usually manifested in giving whatever or whoever it is upset with a thumping big kick. Despite the fact that night-time is when they are most active, they are still fairly lazy, sleeping for as many as 20 hours a day. The rest of the time they spend poking around for worms which they sniff out with the nostrils on the end of their long bill.

The female is larger than the male and much fiercer. She lays an egg weighing up to half a kg, huge in relation to her size (about 20% of her body weight), but having performed that mighty feat leaves the male to hatch it while she guards the burrow. When kiwi junior hatches out it looks just like a mini version of its parents, not like a chick at all, and associates only with dad, completely ignoring mother kiwi. There are several 'nocturnal houses' in New Zealand where you can see kiwis in a good representation of their natural habitat. Although the kiwi is not endangered it is suffering from the destruction of native bush, pig-hunters' dogs, and the use of opossum traps.

Other bird life includes the morepork (mopoke), a small spotted owl, and the raucous kea – a large parrot decked out in the most unparrot-like drab green with a preference, also unparrot-like, for high altitudes and cold weather. The kea has a reputation for killing sheep which makes them unpopular with farmers but they may be just as unpopular with you since they like hanging around humans, tipping over garbage bins

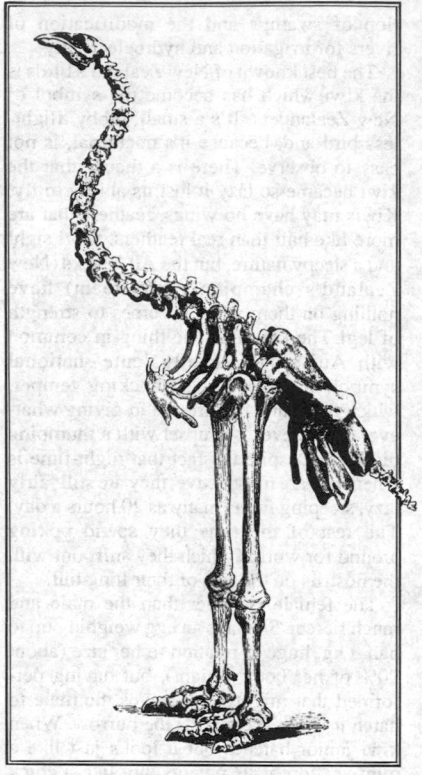

Moa skeleton

and sliding, noisily, down roofs at night. They're amusing, fearless, cheeky and inquisitive birds. Keep a close eye on your gear when they're around since they have incredibly strong beaks and will have a peck at anything, including pulling eyelets out of boots and ripping sleeping bags and tents.

Another amusing bird is the duck-like weka which hangs around camping sites and rushes over to steal things when you turn your back. The weka will purloin anything it can carry in its bill – particularly if it's a nice, shiny object – so don't leave rings and watches lying around.

The NZ bird you won't see is the famous moa, a sort of oversized ostrich. Originally, there were numerous types and sizes, but the largest of them – the huge giant moas – were as high as 4 metres. They were well and truly extinct by the time the Europeans turned up but you can still see moa skeletons and reconstructions in many NZ museums.

Surprisingly not extinct is the tuatara, the sole survivor of a group of ancient reptiles somewhat akin to the dinosaurs. Sometimes mistakenly referred to as a lizard, it is now found only on a few offshore islands and is absolutely protected. New Zealand has no snakes and only one spider that is dangerous to humans, the rare katipo which is a close relation of the North American black widow or the Australian redback.

New Zealand is renowned as an angler's paradise, largely due to the introduction of brown trout, rainbow trout, perch, carp, Atlantic salmon and quinnat salmon to its rivers and estuaries. Native fish include the tenacious kahawai and the moki, hapuku, John Dory, gurnard and tarahkihi. Game fishing for sharks, tuna, bonito, albacore and a few other fish is popular in the North Island, from the Bay of Islands to the Bay of Plenty.

If you hear something croaking during the night in New Zealand, you can be sure it's not one of the three species of Kiwi frogs – they lack a vocal sac, so they can only produce a high-pitched squeak. They're also remarkable in not having a free-swimming tadpole stage, instead undergoing metamorphosis in a capsule. One frog is restricted to the high parts of the Coromandel peninsula, and another to the summit of Stephens Island and remnant rainforest around Marlborough Sound.

## GOVERNMENT

The government of New Zealand is modelled on the British parliamentary system, elections being based on universal adult suffrage. The minimum voting age is 18 and candidates are elected by secret ballot. The maximum period between elections is 3 years, but the interval can be shorter for various reasons, such as when the government of the day needs to seek the confidence of the people on a topic of particular national importance. Unlike in Australia voting in New Zealand is not compulsory, but on average more than 80% of those eligible to vote do so.

The difference between UK's Westminster system and the NZ model is that New Zealand has abolished the upper house and governs solely through the lower house. Known as the House of Representatives, it has 92 member's seats; four of which are held by Maoris. Maoris were admitted to parliament in 1867. The House of Representatives functions primarily to legislate and review the actions of the government in power. No tax can be imposed, nor any money spent until the house has authorised such action. The procedure of legislature is similar to that of the British House of Commons with each bill being given three readings. The first reading introduces the bill, the second involves full-scale debate, followed by the committee stage – a clause-by-clause analysis of the proposed legislation; and the third is usually a formality unless a particular bill contains a contentious issue. Should this be the case, the opposition party can press for a full third-reading debate, to place on record desired changes not achieved during the committee stage.

New Zealand follows a party system; the two main ones being the National (conservative) and Labour parties. Among the others is the Social Credit Party. The party that wins a majority of seats in an election automatically becomes the government and its leader, the prime minister. In July 1984 the Nationals, in office for three terms under the leadership of Sir Robert Muldoon, were bundled out unceremoniously by the landslide victory of the Labour Party led by David Lange. In August 1987 Lange won a second election, a mandate to continue his sweeping changes to the NZ economic system.

In August 1989, after Lange had made bold changes, garnered friends and enemies, sacked and reinstated various members of Cabinet, suffered a heart attack and recovered, he shocked the country by resigning the prime ministership, effective immediately. The next day Deputy Prime Minister Geoffrey Palmer was appointed prime minister. Lange remained in government as an MP and became the new attorney general.

Like the UK, New Zealand is a constitutional monarchy; the traditional head of state, the reigning British king or queen, being represented by a resident governor-general, who is appointed for a 5 year term. An independent judiciary makes up another tier of government. The hierarchy of the courts comprises a Court of Appeal, High Court and District Courts. All three exercise both civil and criminal law jurisdiction, but as its name suggests, the Court of Appeal deals entirely with appellate cases, while the function of the High Court is concerned with major crimes, the more important civil claims, appeals and reviews. The District Courts have an extensive jurisdiction in civil and criminal cases and domestic proceedings. The Family Courts come within the division of the District Courts and have jurisdiction over most family matters including divorce.

## POPULATION

There are about 3,359,000 people in New Zealand. Ethnically, 81.2% are of European descent, 9% are Maoris, and New Zealand also has a large and growing population of Pacific Islanders, now numbering 3% of the total population. Many of the islands of the Pacific are currently experiencing a rapid population shift from remote and undeveloped islands to the 'big city' and Auckland is very much the big city of the South Pacific. It's causing a great deal of argument, discussion and tension and much of it is not between the recent Pacific immigrants and the Pakeha population but between the islanders and the Maoris.

If Pacific immigration were to continue unchecked and the Maori population also continued to grow faster than the population of European descent, the Pakehas would eventually find themselves in the minority. Over the last 10 years the economic situation led to a mass exodus to Australia and further afield. In some years there was an actual population decline but recently the flow has started to slow.

New Zealand is lightly populated by European standards but much more densely populated than Australia with its forbidding stretches of empty country. The South Island once had a greater population than the North Island but now it's the place to go for wide open spaces. Its entire population is barely more than Auckland's. The capital is Wellington but Auckland is easily the largest city. The five largest cities are:

| City | Population |
| --- | --- |
| Auckland | 841,700 |
| Wellington | 325,200 |
| Christchurch | 300,000 |
| Dunedin | 106,600 |
| Hamilton | 103,500 |

## HOLIDAYS & FESTIVALS
People from the northern hemisphere never seem to become completely familiar with upside-down seasons. To them Christmas simply doesn't fall in the middle of summer and how is it possible to shiver in the midwinter cold of August? But it's worth remembering since Christmas, in the middle of summer and in the middle of school holidays, means lots of vacationing New Zealanders, which in turn means crowds and higher prices. If you want to avoid the school-age hordes, they're out of captivity from mid-December until the end of January (the same time as Australian school kids) and then for a couple of weeks in May and again in August.

Public holidays and special events around New Zealand include:

January
*New Year's Day* and the next day (2nd) – public holidays
*Annual Yachting Regatta* – Auckland
February
*New Zealand Day* or *Waitangi Day* (6th) – public holiday; actively celebrated at Waitangi in the Bay of Islands

March
*Good Friday/Easter Monday* (March or April) – public holidays
*Fiesta Week* (mid-March) – Auckland; great fun with some terrific fireworks and the 'Round the Bays' run
*Golden Shears Sheep Shearing Contest* – Masterton (southern end of the North Island); a major event in this sheepish country!
*International Billfish Tournament* – Bay of Islands
*Ngaruawahia Regatta for Maori Canoes* – Hamilton
April
*Anzac Day* (25th) – public holiday
*Highland Games* – Hastings
May
*National Woolcrafts Festival* – Christchurch.
June
*Queen's Birthday* (1st Monday) – public holiday
*New Zealand Agricultural Field Days* – a major agricultural show at Mystery Creek, Hamilton
October
*Labour Day* (4th Monday) – public holiday
November
*Canterbury Show Week* – Christchurch
*International Trout Fishing Contest* – Rotorua
December
*Christmas Day* (25th) and *Boxing Day* (26th) – public holidays

Each province also has its own anniversary day holiday. Local holidays include:

| | | |
| --- | --- | --- |
| Wellington | 22 | January |
| Auckland | 29 | January |
| Northland | 29 | January |
| Nelson | 1 | February |
| Taranaki | 31 | March |
| Otago | 23 | March |
| Southland | 23 | March |
| Hawke's Bay | 1 | November |
| Marlborough | 1 | November |
| Westland | 1 | December |
| Canterbury | 16 | December |

When these local holidays fall between Friday and Sunday, they are usually observed on the following Monday; if they fall between Tuesday and Thursday, they are held on the preceding Monday.

## THE MAORI LANGUAGE
The Maoris had a vividly chronicled history, recorded in songs which dramatically recalled the great migration and other

important events. It was the early missionaries who first recorded the language in a written form. They did this using only 15 letters of our alphabet and ending all syllables in a vowel.

The language is related to other Polynesian languages (including Tahitian and Hawaiian) and has some similarity to dialects found in Indonesia. It's a fluid, poetic language and surprisingly easy to pronounce if you just remember to say it phonetically and split each word (some can be amazingly long) into separate syllables. Few Maoris speak it in day-to-day life now; it is mainly used for ceremonial (and tourist) events, although it is a matter of some pride to have some fluency. Many places have delightful and descriptive Maori names – unfortunately some of the nicest are no longer used. Would you rather have Mt Cook or Aorangi – the 'cloud piercer'?

## Pronunciation

When pronouncing Maori words the main thing is to master the five vowels:

| | |
|---|---|
| a | ar, as the 'ar' in 'farther' |
| e | air, as the sound in measure |
| i | ee, as the sound in seem |
| o | or, as the sound in or or the long o in low |
| u | oo, as the sound in room |

In a Maori word, each syllable ends in a vowel and there is never more than one vowel in a syllable. Thus Maori itself is pronounced Mar-or-ree. The only compound consonants are WH and NG. The nearest in English to WH is F, which is not quite the right sound, softening the F helps. NG is a nasal sound, but used at the beginning of a syllable, rather than the end of it as in English. Thus Ngaruawahia is pronounced Ngar-roo-ar-war-hee-ar, and Whangarei is pronounced Far-ngar-rair-ee. There are no silent letters and each syllable has equal stress.

You can find many Maori-English phrasebooks and dictionaries in New Zealand if you want to have a go. Recently interest in the Maori language has grown enormously in New Zealand and many Pakeha pronunciations of Maori words are suddenly reverting to their correct Maori pronunciation. The town of Whangarei has become something closer to 'Fangarei'! Meanwhile here are a few words to try out:

*atua* – spirit or gods

*haka* – war dance

*hakari* – feast

*hangi* – oven made by digging a hole and steaming food in baskets over embers in the hole

*heitiki* – carved, stylised human figure worn around the neck, usually shortened to 'tiki'

*kai* – food, any word with kai in it will have some food connection

*ka pai* – good, excellent

*kumara* – sweet potatoes, a Maori staple food

*mana* – psychic power or influence

*mere* – flat, greenstone war club

*moko* – chin tattoo on women, not prevalent today but you may still see some old Maori women with them

*pa* – fortified village, usually on a hilltop

*Pakeha* – whitey, European in general

*tapu* – taboo, forbidden

*tiki* – an amulet or figurine, often a carved representation of an ancestor

*tohunga* – priest, wizard or general expert

*wai* – water, place names with 'wai' in them will often be on a river

*whare* – house

*whare runanga* – meeting house

*whare whakairo* – carved house

## Greetings

*haere-mai* – welcome

*haera-ra* – goodbye, farewell

*kia ora* – good luck, good health

## Place Names

Many place names have a clear Maori influence. Maori words you may come across incorporated in New Zealand's place names include:

*anatoki* – axe or adze in a cave; cave or valley in the shape of an axe
*awa* – river or valley
*ika* – fish
*iti* – small
*kahurangi* – treasured possession, special greenstone
*kai* – food
*kainga* – village
*kare* – rippling
*kotinga* – cutting or massacre
*koura* – crayfish
*manga* – branch, stream or tributary
*mangarakau* – plenty of sticks, a great many trees
*manu* – bird
*maunga* – mountain
*moana* – sea or lake
*moko* – tattoo
*motu* – island
*nui* – big
*one* – beach, sand or mud
*onekaka* – red-hot or burning sand
*pa* – fortified village
*papa* – flat, broad slab
*parapara* – the soft mud used for dyeing flax
*patarua* – killed by the thousands, site of early tribal massacres
*pohatu* – stone
*puke* – hill

*rangi* – sky, heavens
*rangiheata* – absence of clouds, a range seen in the early morning
*repo* – swamp
*roa* – long
*roto* – lake
*rua* – hole, two
*takaka* – killing stick for parrot, or bracken
*tane* – man
*tapu* – sacred or forbidden
*tata* – close to, dash against, twin islands
*te* – the
*totaranui* – place of big totara trees
*uruwhenua* – enchanted objects
*wahine* – woman
*wai* – water
*waikaremumu* – bubbling waters
*waingaro* – lost, waters that disappear in certain seasons
*wainui* – big bay or many rivers, the ocean
*whanga* – bay or inlet
*whare* – house
*whenua* – land or country

Try a few – Whanga-roa is 'long bay', Roto-rua is two lakes, Roto-roa is long lake, Wai-kare-iti is little rippling water. All those names with 'wai' in them – Waitomo, Waitara, Waioru, Wairoa, Waitoa, Waihi, and so on – all have something to do with water.

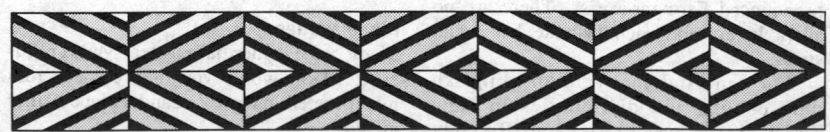

# Facts for the Visitor

## VISAS

Everyone needs a passport to enter New Zealand. Until recently Aussies technically didn't need their little blue book to enter, if they were coming direct from Australia, although they did need it to get home again! However, from November 1987, Australians also have to present their passports to immigration officers on entry. All passports must be valid for 3 months beyond the intended departure date.

Australians do not need visas and can stay indefinitely. British passport holders (who have UK residence rights) do not need visas and can stay up to 6 months. With certain exceptions, if you're from a country of Western Europe, Canada, Iceland, Japan, Singapore or the USA, you do not need a visa for stays up to 3 months.

If you're from another country, or if you wish to stay for longer than those periods or work or study then you must have a visa. Check with the NZ consular offices for more visa information. As with almost anywhere in the world entry requirements are likely to change so always check the situation shortly before you depart. There's nothing worse than arriving at the airport and finding you must have a visa, when you thought you didn't! All visitors must have onward or return ticketing and sufficient funds to maintain themselves for the duration of their stay without working.

## CUSTOMS

The usual allowances of 200 cigarettes, one bottle of liquor, etc apply. Like Australia the customs people are very fussy about drugs. New Zealand has heavy duties on cameras, cars, TVs and other electronic equipment and you can expect customs to be finicky about these sort of consumer goods. Like Australia they are also fussy about animal products and the possibility of animal disease, which is not surprising when they've got 60 million sheep.

## MONEY

| | | |
|---|---|---|
| A$1 | = | NZ$1.28 |
| C$1 | = | NZ$1.41 |
| DM1 | = | NZ$1.02 |
| S$1 | = | NZ$0.91 |
| UK£1 | = | NZ$2.90 |
| US$1 | = | NZ$1.70 |
| Y100 | = | NZ$1.18 |

Unless otherwise noted all prices quoted in this book are in NZ dollars.

New Zealand's currency is dollars and cents. There are 1, 2, 5, 10, 20 and 100 dollar notes and 5, 10, 20 and 50 cent coins. The 1 and 2 cent coins were discontinued in late '89. Yes their coins will fit Australian parking meters and pay phones!

You can bring in as much of any currency as you like and unused foreign currency or travellers' cheques which you brought in with you may be exported without limitations. Unused NZ currency can be changed to foreign currency before you leave the country.

### Banks

Banks are open from 9.30 am to 4 pm Monday to Friday. All the usual brands of travellers' cheques are accepted and they can be changed at banks or large city hotels. Exchange rates vary a few cents from bank to bank; you'll get a slightly better rate for travellers' cheques than for cash. At most banks there's no service charge for changing travellers' cheques, only a 5 cent stamp fee per cheque.

If you're intending a long stay it may be worth opening a bank account. Westpac and Bank of New Zealand (BNZ) are probably the two with the most branches throughout the country, easy to get to on your travels, and you can request a card for the 24 hour teller machines giving you access to your money anytime. PostBank, which was once a part of the post office but has now gone

independent, is another bank with many branches but their services are a bit more limited.

### Credit Cards

Australian Bankcards are widely accepted throughout New Zealand, as are Visa, Mastercard, American Express and Diners Club.

### COSTS

Inflation is a fact of life in New Zealand, although it's slowed down considerably from a few years ago. One cause for the rapid price hikes at one point was the introduction in late '86 of GST. It's a European-style VAT which added 10%, later raised to 12½%, to the price of just about everything. Most prices in New Zealand are quoted inclusive of GST but when you're paying for something beware of any small print announcing that the price is GST exclusive; you'll be hit for the extra 12½% on top of the stated cost. There are rumours that the GST may be

raised even higher, to 15%, which would drive the price of everything up once again.

### TIPPING

New Zealanders do not believe in it. They have an even greater aversion to tipping than Australians. The first sign you see on arriving in New Zealand is likely to advise you that 'tipping is not a New Zealand custom'. So don't!

### TOURIST INFORMATION
### Local Tourist Offices

There are local information centres or Public Relations (PR) offices in nearly every city or town. Almost any town big enough to have a pub and a corner shop seems to have an information centre or PR office. They're usually mines of information on local activities and attractions and have plenty of brochures and maps. Make use of them.

### Automobile Association (AA)

The AA is a very useful organisation to join.

Benefits of membership (many of them free) include detailed info on accommodation, guides, maps and services for motorists including breakdown services, technical advice and vehicle inspections. They also sell auto and travel insurance, make car loans, and members receive discounts to many tourist attractions nationwide. If you are a member of an overseas auto association bring along proof of membership because you're then eligible for reciprocal rights. There are AA offices in all major towns with agents in the smaller ones. Main offices are:

Auckland
    99 Albert St (tel (09) 774-660)
Christchurch
    210 Hereford St (tel (03) 791-280)
Wellington
    342-352 Lambton Quay (tel (04) 738-738)

## Overseas Reps

The NZTP (New Zealand Tourist & Publicity Office) overseas travel offices listed here have information on all aspects of a visit to New Zealand. They also offer advice and in many cases they can book tours, accommodation and transportation within New Zealand.

Argentina
    10th floor, Marcelo T Alvear 590, Buenos Aires (tel 066-4143)
Australia
    Watkins Place, 288 Edward St, Brisbane Qld 4000 (tel (04) 221-3722)
    270 Flinders St, Melbourne Vic 3000 (tel (03) 650-5133)
    Network House, 84 Pitt St, Sydney NSW 2000 (tel (02) 233-6633)
Canada
    Suite 1260, IBM Tower, 701 West Georgia St, Vancouver BC V7Y IB6 (tel (604) 684-2117)
Hong Kong
    3414 Connaught Centre, Connaught Rd, Central Hong Kong (tel (05) 255-044)
Japan
    Toho Twin Tower Building, 2F 1-5-2 Yurakucho, Chiyoda-ku, Tokyo 100 (tel (03) 508-9981)
Singapore
    13 Nassim Rd, Singapore 1025 (tel 235-9966)
UK
    New Zealand House, Haymarket, London SW1Y 4TQ (tel (01) 930-8422)
USA
    Suite 1530, 10960 Wilshire Blvd, Los Angeles CA 90024 (tel (213) 477- 8241)
    Suite 530, 630 Fifth Ave, New York NY 10111 (tel (212) 698-4680)
West Germany
    Kaiserhofstrasse 7, 6000 Frankfurt am Main (tel (0169) 288-189, 988-189)

There are also NZTP offices in New Zealand where they perform much the same function as travel agents. These offices in New Zealand are often not as useful for general information as the local information centres or PR offices.

## GENERAL INFORMATION
### Post

Post offices are open from 9 am to 5 pm on weekdays. You can have mail addressed to you at 'Poste Restante, CPO' in whichever town you require. CPO stands for Chief Post Office.

### Telephones

Most pay phones in New Zealand have been converted to the new card-operated type. In the Wellington region, for example, there are now 400 card phones and only 50 coin phones. The few coin phones still remaining are in the more remote areas where you cannot buy phone cards.

The card phones accept $5, $10, $20 or $50 cards, which you can buy from any shop displaying the lime-green 'phone cards available here' sign, including news-agencies, tobacconists and 24 hour service stations. NZ Telecom has arranged to have at least one phone card outlet in any town where card phones are installed.

To use the new phones, simply insert your card and follow the instructions on the phone. The meter automatically deducts the cost of your call from your card, and tells you how much value your card has left when you finish the call.

As well as making normal local calls, you can use phone cards for making long distance calls from pay phones, including international calls. And because you can dial direct, you do not have to pay for an operator to connect you.

Charges for international calls are divided into Zone 1 (South West Pacific, including Australia) and Zone 2 (the rest of the world). Calls to Zone 1 cost $1.80 for the first minute and $1.60 for each subsequent minute. Calls to Zone 2 cost $3.30 for the first minute and $3.00 for each subsequent minute.

If you intend travelling in more remote areas, take plenty of 20 cent coins to use, as only the old-fashioned coin-operated phones may be available. You usually put your money in, dial the number, and press button A when it is answered. If there's no answer, press button B on the side and your money will be returned.

You can make long-distance calls from Telecom offices, but you will have to pay a surcharge of $2, even if it's only a call to the next town down the road. In some smaller towns where Telecom does not have offices, you may still be able to make calls from the post office.

Another option for long-distance telephone calls is the call-back service. Dial 016 before you make the call and an operator will ring you back immediately after you hang up to tell you how much it cost. This service costs an extra $2 on top of the price for the call, but it means that many hostels, hotels and so on will allow you to place long-distance calls from their telephones, paying on the spot.

To reach the local operator dial 010, for the international operator it's 0170. Directory assistance is 100 for local, 102 for national, and 0172 for international information.

For emergencies in the major centres dial 111 and say whether you want police, ambulance or fire brigade. Emergency calls are not charged.

Telecom is currently standardising all the telephone numbers to seven digits with a two-digit STD code. As it is now, a telephone number may have anything from three to seven digits and an STD code with as many as five digits! Many towns which had, let's say, three-digit phone numbers in the last edition of this book have now added one or two numbers in front of the previous number; for example, '345' might become '66-345'. Telecom says that if you ring the old number you will usually get a recorded message telling you that the number has changed and advising you to check with directory assistance – although sometimes you might just get mysterious sounds over the line.

### Electricity

Electricity is 230 volts AC, 50 cycle, as in Europe and Australia, and the same Australian-type three-prong plugs are used.

### Time

Being close to the international date line, New Zealand is one of the first places in the world to start a new day. New Zealand is 12 hours ahead of Greenwich Mean Time and 2 hours ahead of Australian Eastern Standard Time. In summer New Zealand observes Daylight Saving Time, an advance of 1 hour per day, which comes into effect on the last Sunday in October and lasts to the first Sunday of the following March. Usually when it's noon in New Zealand it's 10 am in Sydney or Melbourne, 2 am in London, 5 pm the previous day in San Francisco or Los Angeles.

## Business Hours

Office hours are from 9 am to 5 pm Monday to Friday. Shops are open from 9 am to 5 pm on weekdays, with a 'late shopping night' to 8 pm one night of the week, usually Thursday or Friday. In most places shops are also open on Saturday mornings. Additionally, there are now many convenience stores open much longer hours. This is a considerable improvement on just a few years ago when the doors clanged shut at 5 pm on Friday and absolutely everything was closed up like Fort Knox until 9 am Monday.

## MEDIA

### Newspapers & Magazines

There is no real national paper although the *New Zealand Herald* (Auckland) and the *Dominion* (Wellington) both have wide circulations. Backing up the city newspapers are numerous local dailies, some OK, some not. The closest to a national weekly newsmag is the *Listener*, an excellent publication which provides lots of info on radio and TV programmes, a weekly guide, plus in-depth articles on the arts, social issues and politics. *Time* and *Newsweek* are available almost anywhere.

### Radio, TV & Film Industry

There are two national noncommercial radio stations and many regional or local commercial stations, broadcasting on the AM and FM bands.

There are two state-owned and one private TV stations, although all have commercials.

Although New Zealand's film industry is even smaller than Australia's, it has recently produced a number of highly acclaimed films like *The Quiet Earth*, *Utu*, *Mr Wrong*, *Smash Palace* and *Vigil*. Other notable films include *The Navigator*, *Ngati*, *The Grasscut-*

*ter*, *Starlight Hotel*, *Bad Taste*, *Goodbye Pork Pie* and *The Flying Fox and the Freedom Tree*. Even the beloved NZ cartoon character, 'Dog', has a film out – *Footrot Flats – The Dog's Tale*. Most video shops in New Zealand have at least some selection of NZ films.

## HEALTH

There are no vaccination requirements. New Zealand is largely a healthy, disease-free country. Medical attention is of high quality and reasonably priced but you should have medical insurance. If you suffer personal injury by accident in New Zealand you are entitled to compensation as a right – irrespective of fault – which means you do not have to sue in the courts for damages. This covers such things as medical expenses and payments for permanent incapacity but note that it covers only accidents, not illnesses. If you simply get ill and require medical attention you'll have to pay for it.

### Travel Health Guides

*Travellers' Health* by Dr Richard Dawood (Oxford University Press) is comprehensive, easy to read, authoritative and also highly recommended, although it's rather large to lug around.

Lonely Planet's *Travel with Children* by Maureen Wheeler includes basic advice on travel health for younger children.

### Pre-Departure Preparations

**Health Insurance** A travel insurance policy to cover theft, loss and medical problems is a wise idea. There is a wide variety of policies and your travel agent will have recommendations. The international student travel policies handled by STA or other student travel organisations are usually good value. Some policies offer lower and higher medical expenses options but the higher one is chiefly for countries like the USA which have extremely high medical costs. Check the small print:

1   Some policies specifically exclude 'dangerous activities' which can include

scuba diving, motorcycling, even trekking. If such activities are on your agenda you don't want that sort of policy.

2 You may prefer a policy which pays doctors or hospitals direct rather than you having to pay on the spot and claim later. If you have to claim later make sure you keep all documentation. Some policies ask you to call back (reverse charges) to a centre in your home country where an immediate assessment of your problem is made.

3 Check if the policy covers ambulances or an emergency flight home. If you have to stretch out you will need two seats and somebody has to pay for them!

**Medical Kit** A small, straightforward medical kit is a wise thing to carry. A possible kit list includes:

- Aspirin or Panadol – for pain or fever.
- Antihistamine (such as Benadryl) – useful as a decongestant for colds, allergies, to ease the itch from insect bites or stings or to help prevent motion sickness.
- Antibiotics – useful if you're travelling well off the beaten track, but they must be prescribed and you should carry the prescription with you.
- Kaolin preparation (Pepto-Bismol), Imodium or Lomotil – for stomach upsets.
- Rehydration mixture – for treatment of severe diarrhoea; this is particularly important if travelling with children.
- Antiseptic, mercurochrome and antibiotic powder or similar 'dry' spray – for cuts and grazes.
- Calamine lotion – to ease irritation from bites or stings.
- Bandages and band-aids – for minor injuries. Scissors, tweezers and a thermometer – mercury thermometers are prohibited by airlines.
- Insect repellent, suntan lotion and chapstick.

## Basic Rules

Care in what you eat and drink is the most important health rule; stomach upsets are the most likely travel health problem but the majority of these upsets will be relatively minor.

**Nutrition** If you're travelling hard and fast and therefore missing meals, or if you simply lose your appetite, you can soon start to lose weight and place your health at risk.

Make sure your diet is well balanced. If your diet isn't well balanced or if your food intake is insufficient, it's a good idea to take vitamin and iron pills.

**Everyday Health** A normal body temperature is 98.6°F or 37°C; more than 2°C higher is a 'high' fever. A normal adult pulse rate is 60 to 80 per minute (children 80 to 100, babies 100 to 140). You should know how to take a temperature and a pulse rate. As a general rule the pulse increases about 20 beats per minute for each °C rise in fever.

Respiration (breathing) rate is also an indicator of illness. Count the number of breaths per minute: between 12 and 20 is normal for adults and older children (up to 30 for younger children, 40 for babies). People with a high fever or serious respiratory illness (like pneumonia) breathe more quickly than normal. More than 40 shallow breaths a minute usually means pneumonia.

Many health problems can be avoided by taking care of yourself. Wash your hands frequently – it's quite easy to contaminate your own food. Avoid climatic extremes: keep out of the sun when it's hot, dress warmly when it's cold. Avoid potential diseases by dressing sensibly. You can avoid insect bites by covering bare skin when insects are around, by screening windows or beds or by using insect repellents. Seek local advice: if you're told the water is unsafe, don't go in. In situations where there is no information, discretion is the better part of valour.

## Medical Problems & Treatment

**Meningitis** The one strange health hazard to watch out for in New Zealand is fortunately also easy to avoid. In natural thermal mineral pools, there's a kind of amoeba or microorganism which, if you put your head underwater, can enter the orifices of your head (ears, nose, etc) and cause meningitis. It can't enter your body in any other way, so the solution is simple – just keep your head out of the water!

**Hypothermia** This condition occurs when the body loses heat faster than it can produce it and the core temperature of the body falls. It is surprisingly easy to progress from very cold to dangerously cold due to a combination of wind, wet clothing, fatigue and hunger, even if the air temperature is above freezing. It is best to dress in layers; silk, wool and some of the new artificial fibres are all good insulating materials. A hat is important, as a lot of heat is lost through the head. A strong, waterproof outer layer is essential, as keeping dry is vital. Carry basic supplies, including food containing simple sugars to generate heat quickly and lots of fluid to drink.

Symptoms of hypothermia are exhaustion, numb skin (particularly toes and fingers), shivering, slurred speech, irrational or violent behaviour, lethargy, stumbling, dizzy spells, muscle cramps and violent bursts of energy. Irrationality may take the form of sufferers claiming they are warm and trying to take off their clothes.

To treat hypothermia, first get the patient out of the wind and/or rain, remove their clothing if it's wet and replace it with dry, warm clothing. Give them hot liquids – not alcohol – and some high kilojoule, easily digestible food. This should be enough for the early stages of hypothermia, but if it has gone further it may be necessary to place victims in warm sleeping bags and get in with them. Do not rub patients, place them near a fire or remove their wet clothes in the wind. If possible, place a sufferer in a warm (not hot) bath.

**Sexually Transmitted Diseases** Sexual contact with an infected sexual partner spreads these diseases. While abstinence is the only 100% preventative, using condoms is also effective. Gonorrhoea and syphilis are the most common of these diseases; sores, blisters or rashes around the genitals, discharge or pain when urinating are common symptoms. Symptoms may be less marked or not observed at all in women. Syphilis symptoms eventually disappear completely but the disease continues and can cause severe problems in later years. The treatment of gonorrhoea and syphilis is by antibiotics.

There are numerous other sexually transmitted diseases, for most of which effective treatment is available. However, there is no cure for herpes and there is also currently no cure for AIDS. Using condoms is the most effective preventative.

AIDS can be spread through infected blood transfusions and by dirty needles – vaccinations, acupuncture and tattooing can potentially be as dangerous as intravenous drug use if the equipment is not clean.

**Cuts & Stings** Skin punctures can easily become infected and may be difficult to heal. Treat any cut with an antiseptic solution and mercurochrome.

Local advice is the best way of avoiding contact with sea creatures such as jellyfish. Stings from most jellyfish are rather painful. Dousing in vinegar will de-activate any stingers which have not 'fired'. Calamine lotion, antihistamines and analgesics may reduce the reaction and relieve the pain.

Bee and wasp stings are usually painful rather than dangerous. Calamine lotion will give relief or ice packs will reduce the pain and swelling. There are various fish and other sea creatures which can sting or bite dangerously or which are dangerous to eat. Again, local advice is the best suggestion.

**Women's Health**
**Gynaecological Problems** Poor diet, lowered resistance due to the use of antibiotics for stomach upsets and even contraceptive pills can lead to vaginal infections. Keeping the genital area clean, and wearing skirts or loose-fitting trousers and cotton underwear help to prevent infections.

Yeast infections, characterised by a rash, itch and discharge, can be treated with a vinegar or even lemon juice douche or with yoghurt. Nystatin suppositories are the usual medical prescription. Trichomonas is a more serious infection; symptoms are a discharge and a burning sensation when urinating. Male sexual partners must also be treated, and if a vinegar-water douche is not effective medical attention should be sought. Flagyl is the prescribed drug.

**Pregnancy** Most miscarriages occur during the first 3 months of pregnancy, so this is the most risky time to travel. The last 3 months should also be spent within reasonable distance of good medical care, as quite serious problems can develop at this time. Pregnant women should avoid all unnecessary medication. Additional care should be taken to prevent illness and particular attention should be paid to diet and nutrition.

## FILM & PHOTOGRAPHY

Photographic supplies, equipment and maintenance are all readily available.

## ACCOMMODATION

New Zealand has a wide range of accommodation and places to stay but to all of it there is one catch: the Kiwis are great travellers. Even Australians fall behind the New Zealanders when it comes to hitting the road – a greater proportion of New Zealanders have passports than in any other country and when they are not jaunting around overseas they'll be jaunting around at home. So during the holiday season you may well find a long queue at popular places. This applies particularly to youth hostels and almost any cheap accommodation in major holiday areas. The answer is to book ahead if you are going to be arriving in tricky places on popular occasions.

Accommodation has been bracketed into several categories. First of all there are hostels – the YHAs, YWCAs and YMCAs, and the private hostels. Then there are the guest houses or B&Bs, hotels and motels followed by camping sites and cabins. Another option is accommodation on farms or in private homes, usually known as 'farmstays' and 'homestays' in NZ parlance.

There is considerable overlap between these various groups. Some hostels may be straightforward bunkroom style while others may have double or even single rooms. One establishment may have both guest house accommodation and motel rooms. Hotels and motels are often very similar and at some camping sites you may find not only areas for camping but also cabins, motel units and perhaps even a hostel-style bunkroom. Farms may offer farmstay accommodation in the family homestead for one rate, but cheaper rates in cottages or shearers' quarters off to one side.

### Accommodation Information

To find your way around New Zealand's camping sites, cabins, motels, motel flats and so on, three books put out by the AA are extremely helpful. The *Accommodation & Camping Guide* covers the South Island, while the North Island is split into two separate publications, the *Accommodation Guide* for hotels, guest houses and motels and the *Outdoor Guide* for tourist flats, cabins and camps. They are revised every year and are available from any AA office. They're not a complete listing but most places are included. Copies are available free to members of the AA or to overseas visitors who belong to an automobile association enjoying reciprocal rights with the AA.

*Jason's* accommodation directories are similar commercially produced guides, but they don't have as many listings as the AA books because it costs the hotel, motel, camping ground or whatever a lot of money to get into *Jason's*. The NZTP also puts out a *New Zealand Accommodation Guide*.

A couple of other publications are useful for the latest rundown on hostels (both YHA and private) and Department of Conservation (DOC) camping sites; see them in those sections.

### Hostels

Hostels offer cheap accommodation in locations all over New Zealand. At a hostel you basically rent a bed, usually for around $10 to $15 a night. Some hostels have male and female bunkrooms for 10 or more people. Others have smaller bunkrooms or even double or single rooms. Double and twin rooms are becoming more available at hostels as they are often requested by travellers. You usually have to provide your own bedding although sometimes this can be rented, and some hostels provide it. There's usually a communal kitchen, a dining area, a lounge area and a laundry room.

To an even greater extent than Australia the hostel scene has gone through a real revolution in the past few years. It's a combination of strong growth, more liberal attitudes and a new commercial approach.

Hostels have always been popular in New Zealand, after all it's a good country for backpackers. But the recent growth in demand has been phenomenal as there are now a lot more travellers. So many more, in fact, that hostels have frequently been booked out far in advance which has, of course, created the need for more hostels – both YHA and private.

The second factor affecting the hostel scene has been a change in the general attitude towards hostelling. The old, strict segregation by sex, lights out early, stay away all day policies have taken a considerable battering. In part it's been because people staying at the hostels have been demanding a more easy going approach, but also because younger-minded people have been running the hostels. The old hostel 'wardens' have even metamorphosed into 'managers'!

A major factor, of course, has been the growth in private hostels, commonly called 'backpackers' in New Zealand. Attitudes have been much more liberal at these new hostels and they've forced the YHA hostels to catch up.

Finally both these factors – growth in demand and the need for more liberal attitudes – have come together in a new more commercial approach. Getting people to stay in hostels has become a commercial decision just like other businesses. If hostel A is better equipped, cheaper or a more pleasant place than hostel B then people will stay in A rather than in B. And running a hostel, many people have suddenly realised, is just as good a way of making a living as running a motel. What's the difference between a motel room for $48 with two people in it and a bunkroom for four at $12 each? Well with the bunkroom

you don't have to provide a TV, telephone or attached bathroom, or launder bedding for starters!

So today hostels, YHA or private, are much more attractive places to stay. If you're a couple you can often manage to get a room to yourself rather than have to separate into male and female bunkrooms. You can often arrive rather late at night. You're much less likely to be locked out if you get back from the pub late at night (but be quiet!) and you won't be pushed out the door because 'the hostel is closed from 10 am to 4 pm'.

Apart from being just about the most economical form of accommodation, particularly if you're travelling solo, hostels are also a great place for meeting people and making friends. They're also wonderful information sources – almost every hostel has a notice board smothered in notes, advice and warning and the hostel managers are also often great sources of local information. Hostels, both private and YHA, often negotiate special discounts and deals for their hostellers with local businesses and tour operators.

YHA Hostels The YHA in New Zealand produces a very useful free annual *YHA Handbook* which, along with general information, also lists all their hostels with a description and photo of their facilities, prices, phone numbers, information on the area and a location map. You may be able to get a copy from your national YHA or you can write to the NZ association. Their national head office address is PO Box 436, Christchurch, New Zealand. It's also available at YHA offices and hostels throughout New Zealand.

The YHA hostels are only open to members. You can either join the YHA in your home country (don't forget to bring your membership card) or in New Zealand at any YHA hostel or at the Auckland or Christchurch offices. There's a joining fee of $10 and annual membership is $24. Membership in the New Zealand YHA also allows you to use YHA hostels anywhere else in the world. Your YHA membership also entitles

you to a host of discounts in New Zealand. Recent innovations are a one-night temporary membership charge of $4 for non-members who just want to spend one night in a hostel, and a 'Kiwi Starter Card' introductory 3 night pass for $12.

Blankets, pillows and pillowcases are provided free of charge at all YHA hostels. You can sleep in your sleeping bag or bring your own sheets or a sheet sleeping bag. If you don't have your own linen you can hire it from the hostel for a small fee. You can make a sheet sleeping bag from a couple of sheets or buy one ready-made for $16 at the YHA shops in Auckland or Christchurch or from the YHA in your home country.

The YHA hostels in New Zealand have considerably relaxed their rules in the last few years and they've never had the 'thou shalt not arrive by car' attitude that some European hostels have. There's usually a time bracket during which you can book in and at some (but not all) YHA hostels you're expected to do a duty every morning. At most hostels there's a 3 night stay limit but this is only likely to be enforced when the hostel is crowded. Most hostel offices close from 10 am to 5 pm, but now every hostel has at least some areas, including the kitchen and common room, open all day. At most hostels you also have free access to your room at any time, with your own room key. All hostels have fully equipped kitchens, hot showers, a common room and/or dining room, and laundry facilities. Most of the hostels have a relaxed and easy going atmosphere.

During the summer extra hostels open up to cater for some of the demand. Some of the major and very busy hostels have overflow facilities which they can call on when they get very crowded. There are also a few Associate Hostels – privately owned premises approved by the YHA as suitable for members' use. You don't need a membership card to stay at an Associate YHA Hostel.

Particularly during school holidays and at popular hostels it is a wise idea to book ahead. You can do this either directly with the hostel in question, through the NZ offices, or one hostel can make a reservation for you at another hostel. Reservations have to be paid for in advance and again the handbook has full details on what to do.

Finally, if you want to make a lengthy stay in New Zealand, you might think about working at a hostel, they often need temporary or long term workers. The pay may be very little but you get free accommodation, plenty of spare time and you'll meet lots of people. Write to the YHA for info.

Auckland Office
    36 Customs St East (PO Box 1687), corner of Customs & Gore streets (tel (09) 794-224)
Christchurch National Office
    PO Box 436, corner of Gloucester & Manchester streets (tel (03) 799-970)

**Private Hostels** The numerous 'backpackers' (private hostels) not only provide many additional hostel beds but they've also been a principal cause of the changing policies at YHA hostels. Like YHA hostels, nightly costs are typically around $10 to $15.

Many of the private hostels operate just like regular YHA hostels with bunkrooms, kitchen and lounge facilities and so on. Some of them are operated by ex-YHA managers so they're fully aware of all the plus and minus points about YHA hostel operations. Some of the private hostel operations are just camping ground bunkrooms or farm hostels but one of the most interesting aspects of private hostels has been the new-from-the-ground-up hostels which have opened recently. The Rainbow Lodge in Taupo, the Thermal Lodge in Rotorua and the Tasman Towers in Nelson are three examples of purpose-built hostels.

A couple of handy leaflets are useful for the latest listings of many private hostels, which are springing up all around the country with amazing rapidity. The *New Zealand Budget Backpackers Accommodation* pamphlet, commonly known as the 'Blue Brochure', is an excellent quarterly publication. The November '89 edition listed 75 private hostels, from Pukenui in the north to Stewart Island in the south. It's published by Budget Backpackers Hostels NZ Ltd, a loose organisation of hostels led by the operators of Rainbow Lodge at Taupo in the North Island and Foley Towers at Christchurch in the South Island. It's available at scores of hostels and information centres around New Zealand.

The Blue Brochure is the most popular guide to the private hostels but there's also the *New Zealand Backpackers Bible*, with listings of other private hostels which for one reason or another are not listed in the Blue Brochure, and other useful information for backpackers and budget travellers.

**YMCA & YWCA Hostels** There are YMCA and YWCA hostels in several larger towns which offer straightforward, no frills accommodation and are generally reasonably priced. A few of them are single-sex only (especially the YWCAs) but most of them (especially the YMCAs) take men and women. Although the emphasis is on 'permanent' accommodation – providing a place to stay for young people coming to work in the 'big city' – they are increasingly going after the 'transient trade'.

Accommodation in these hostels is often almost all in single rooms. They have one extra plus point – they are often less crowded during the holiday seasons, when every other place is likely to be short of space.

**Guest Houses & B&Bs**

There's a wide variation in types and standards in this category. Some guest houses are spartan, cheap, ultra basic accommodation in some cases defined as 'private' (unlicensed) hotels. Others are comfortable, relaxed but low-key places, patronised by people who don't enjoy the impersonal atmosphere of many motels. Others are very fancy indeed and try to give their guests a feeling for life with a NZ family. Because they tend to get lumped into this one category, the 'B&B' places at the top of the heap try hard to dissociate themselves from the rock bottom guest houses at the other end of the strata.

The B&B accommodation in private homes has recently become a fashionable concept in the USA and there are now many New Zealanders offering family-run enterprises of that type. Get a copy of *The New Zealand Bed & Breakfast Book* by J & J Thomas (Moonshine Press, Wellington) for suggestions about B&B accommodation all over the country. This is an excellent book which comes out annually and is available from most bookstores and also from many visitor information centres (the Auckland Visitors Bureau has it).

Another development in this type of travel is that there are now many agencies specialising in booking accommodation in private homes and farms throughout the country. Many of these are B&B arrangements. The NZTP has a list of reputable agencies.

Although breakfast is definitely on the agenda at the real B&B places it may or may not feature at other places in this category. Where it does it's likely to be a pretty substantial meal – fruit, eggs, bacon, toast, coffee or tea are all likely to make an appearance. Many guest houses seem to really pride themselves on the size, quality and 'traditional value' of their breakfasts.

If you like to start the day heartily it's worth considering this when comparing prices. There are several cooperatively produced lists of B&B accommodation. They're usually available from guest houses which appear on the list. A list produced from the Aspen Lodge in Auckland lists only places that guarantee to provide a good breakfast!

Also guest houses can be particularly good value if you're travelling on your own. Most motels, hotels, cabins and so on are priced on a 'per room' basis whereas guest houses usually charge 'per person'. Typically B&B singles cost $25 to $40 but in some of the more spartan breakfastless guest houses the price can drop to $20 or less while a double in some of the country's best B&B can cost $100 or more. Except at the most expensive B&B guest houses, rooms generally do not have attached bathrooms.

There's also the DB&B (dinner, bed & breakfast) plan which is popular with skiers, for example, who like to wake up, have a good breakfast, go out skiing and come back to a hot meal.

## Hotels

As in Australia a hotel essentially has to be licensed to serve alcohol. So at one end of the scale the hotel category can include traditional older-style hotels where the emphasis is mainly on the bar and the rooms are pretty much a sideline. At the other end it includes all the brand new 5 star hotels in the big cities, hotels which are pretty much like their relations elsewhere in the world in facilities and in their high prices. In between, many places that are essentially motels can call themselves hotels because they have a bar and liquor licence. At the cheapest old-style hotels singles might cost as low as $20 while at the most luxurious new establishments a room could cost $200 or more.

**THC Hotels** Scattered around New Zealand are a number of THC hotels. The THC is a government-run organisation whose intention is to operate hotels in tourist areas where it would be difficult for privately run hotels to charge reasonable rates and make a profit. Actually some of the THC places are so expensive it would be difficult to make a loss!

It's difficult to say what the future of the THC hotels will be. As of early '90 they were all up for sale, as part of a massive programme designed by the government to get itself on a better economic footing, selling many of its former services into private hands. The THC hotels have been on the market for several months but until a sale goes through, the government is continuing to operate them.

You'll find THC hotels at some of the most scenic spots in the country and two of them, the Hermitage at Mt Cook and the Chateau at Tongariro, are the most famous hotels in New Zealand. You won't find budget travellers staying at these places (they're expensive) but they're often worth a look. The hotels themselves may be rather attractive (the Chateau), have a bit of history to them (the Hermitage) or have other attractions. They may also serve as the focal point for the area and you'll find their bars crowded and friendly. If the idea of a public-service-run hotel is pretty horrible you're in for a surprise, as they're interesting, well run places.

## Motels

Motels are pretty much like motels anywhere else in the world although NZ motels are notably well equipped. They always have tea and coffee-making equipment and supplies; usually there's a fridge and very often there's a toaster and electric frying pan if you just feel like whipping up some scrambled eggs. Even a real kitchen is not at all unusual, complete with utensils, plates and cutlery. Although long-life milk for your coffee or tea is starting to take over, at a great many traditional motels you'll still find a small bottle of fresh milk by your door every morning.

Sometimes there's a distinction drawn between 'serviced motels' and 'motel flats'. Essentially the difference is that a motel flat has more equipment and less service. You don't get people rushing around pulling the sheets straight every time you turn round – which is just fine with me and probably with you too. They're a sort of indicator of the basic rightness of the NZ way of life – for how long would all that kitchen equipment last in a motel in the USA? Someone would cart the lot out on the second night, right!

A motel room typically costs around $55

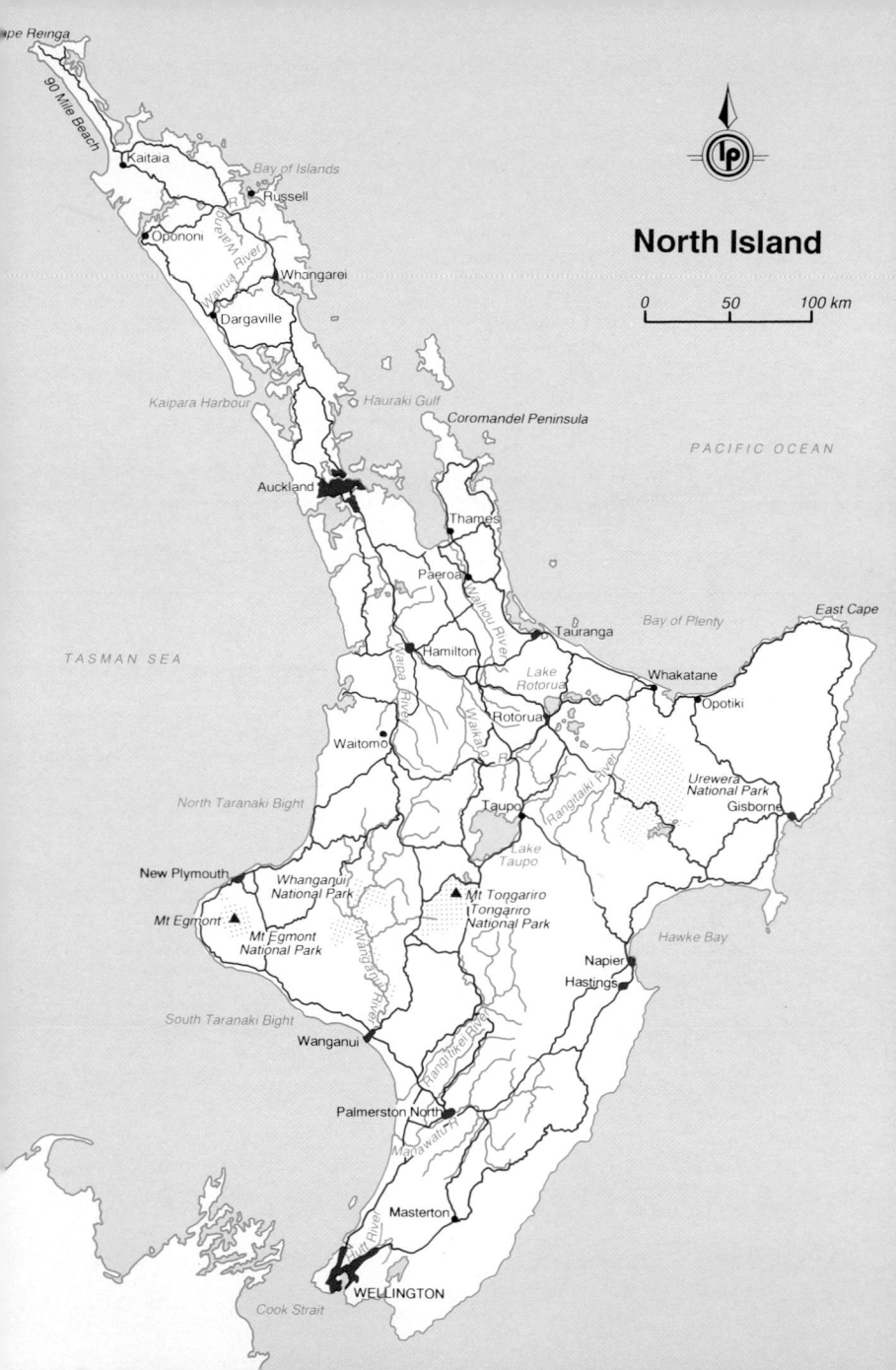

# North Island

0    50    100 km

Cape Reinga

90 Mile Beach

Kaitaia

Bay of Islands

Russell

Opononi

Whangarei

Dargaville

Kaipara Harbour

Hauraki Gulf

Coromandel Peninsula

PACIFIC OCEAN

Auckland

Thames

Paeroa

Tauranga

Bay of Plenty

East Cape

TASMAN SEA

Hamilton

Lake Rotorua

Whakatane

Opotiki

Rotorua

Waitomo

Taupo

Urewera National Park

Gisborne

North Taranaki Bight

Lake Taupo

New Plymouth

Whanganui National Park

Mt Tongariro
Tongariro National Park

Mt Egmont

Mt Egmont National Park

Hawke Bay

Napier

Hastings

South Taranaki Bight

Wanganui

Palmerston North

Masterton

WELLINGTON

Cook Strait

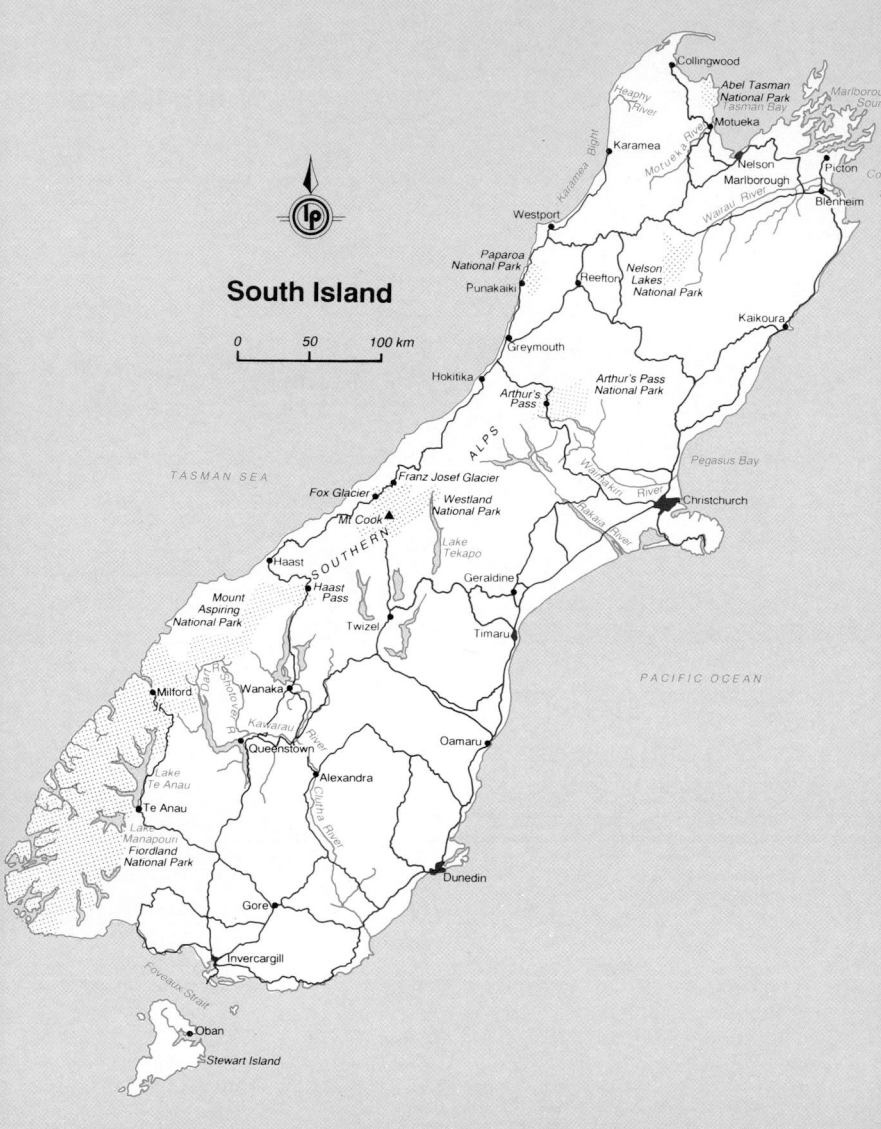

# South Island

0    50    100 km

- Collingwood
- Abel Tasman National Park
- Tasman Bay
- Marlborough Sounds
- Motueka
- Karamea
- Heaphy River
- Motueka River
- Nelson
- Marlborough
- Picton
- Blenheim
- Cook Strait
- Karamea Bight
- Wairau River
- Westport
- Paparoa National Park
- Reefton
- Nelson Lakes National Park
- Kaikoura
- Punakaiki
- Greymouth
- Hokitika
- Arthur's Pass
- Arthur's Pass National Park
- Pegasus Bay
- Waimakariri River
- TASMAN SEA
- Fox Glacier
- Franz Josef Glacier
- Westland National Park
- Mt Cook
- Lake Tekapo
- Rakaia River
- Christchurch
- Haast
- Haast Pass
- Geraldine
- SOUTHERN ALPS
- Twizel
- Timaru
- Mount Aspiring National Park
- Milford
- Wanaka
- PACIFIC OCEAN
- Kawarau River
- Queenstown
- Oamaru
- Lake Te Anau
- Alexandra
- Clutha River
- Te Anau
- Lake Manapouri
- Fiordland National Park
- Dunedin
- Gore
- Invercargill
- Foveaux Strait
- Oban
- Stewart Island

to $65. Sometimes you can find them cheaper, even down towards $40, and there are many more luxurious new motels where $70 to $100 is the usual range. There's usually only a small difference in price, if any, between a single or double motel room.

## Camping

If you plan to camp, New Zealand is a great place for it. You may have tried camping in Australia (where it's OK but would be a lot better if the sites weren't aimed so much at the caravanners) or in Europe (where it's very good, but increasingly expensive and crowded). Well, in New Zealand it's simply better. For the tent camper the Kiwi camping sites are the best in the world – which doesn't mean caravanners aren't catered for as well – just that people with tents get a fair go too.

If you are driving, cycling or hiking around with a tent and sleeping bag everything will be fine – there are a lot of sites, particularly in touristy places, and they are very well equipped. Many of them have kitchens and dining areas where the cooker, hot plates and often kettles and toasters are provided; all you need to bring is the utensils, plates, bowls, etc and the food. They're great places to meet people – you talk with other people while you're fixing your food, you carry on when you share a table to eat it. There are also laundry facilities and often TV rooms too.

How the sites are charged varies fairly widely. Sometimes there's a site charge and then an additional cost per person. Sometimes it's just a straight site charge. But most of the time it's a per person charge and that's typically around $6 to $8 per adult, half price for children. Most sites charge a dollar or two more per person if you want a powered site for a caravan or campervan as opposed to a tent site without power.

At most sites the kitchen and showers are free but you do get a few sites where there are coin-in-the-slot operated hot plates and/or hot showers. At most sites laundry facilities are coin operated.

If you intend to camp round New Zealand but have no equipment you can buy it when you get there. Good, high quality tents and sleeping bags are available, but the prices are also high. If you're coming from North America or even Australia, you can get better prices in those places. Remember it gets cool in New Zealand in the winter, so camping becomes a lot less practical then, especially in the south. If you're well enough equipped it's not quite so bad in the north, although New Zealand's weather is very changeable.

**Sites in the Parks** There are DOC camping sites in reserves and national, maritime and farm parks. Most of these camping grounds have minimal facilities – fresh water, toilets, fireplaces and not much else – but they also have minimal charges, often $5 or less. They include sites on islands in the Hauraki Gulf off Auckland, up towards Cape Reinga, on islands in the Bay of Islands, on the Coromandel Peninsula, on the Marlborough Sounds and at numerous other locations.

The DOC publishes a very useful booklet, *Accommodation and Camping Guide*, with details on all the DOC camping and hut facilities throughout New Zealand. Check with local DOC offices for details on the facilities, what you need to take with you and whether you should book in advance. Many DOC camping sites cost only a couple of dollars, meaning that you could travel throughout New Zealand with practically no accommodation costs with the help of this booklet. There are also some free camping sites, particularly in the North Island, that although are often difficult to reach, are worth the walk if you're geared for camping.

There are also numerous huts which can only be reached on foot. Most of the longer walking tracks have huts, usually spaced about 4 or 5 hours walking distance apart on the more accessible tracks. Once again there are basic facilities only – pit toilets, fresh water and bunks. Cooking has to be done on open fires or gas or wood stoves, and you have to bring your own cooking gear. The fee for a bed in these huts ranges from $4 to $12 (half price for children). See the Tramping section in the Outdoor Activities chapter for more details on huts.

In the more remote areas trampers must be self-sufficient. You need a tent and a portable stove. Contact specific national parks for more details.

**Cabins & Tourist Flats** Many camping sites will also have cabins which are simply equipped rooms where you have to provide your own sleeping gear (a sleeping bag is fine) and towels, unlike a motel where all that sort of stuff is provided. Cabins can be very cheap, often less than $20 for two which makes them even cheaper than hostels. They generally charge per two adults, plus so much for each additional person, but some charge per cabin and some per person. Maureen and I did one trip round New Zealand on a motorcycle where we generally camped but if it was a chilly night (or a wet one) we opted for the comforts of a cabin. Usually you can rent sheets and blankets if you come unequipped.

These days the standards of cabins seems to be rising – the prices too. Often the cabins become 'tourist flats' which seems to mean they're equipped closer to motel standard with kitchens and/or bathrooms. You will still have to do the clean up yourself and bring your own bedding, towels and so on, although at many camps now even the bedding is included. On-site caravans (trailer homes in US parlance) are another camping site possibility. Many camping sites have regular motel rooms or an associated motel complex and hostel-style bunkrooms are another possibility.

### Farmstays (Farm Holidays)

New Zealand has been called the world's most efficient farm so a visit to a farm is an interesting way of getting to grips with the real New Zealand. Farmstays are a very popular activity as many farms take guests who can 'have a go' at all the typical farm activities and be treated as one of the household into the bargain. If you want to know more about it contact the NZTP. It can make recommendations or provide names and addresses of organisations that specialise in booking farmstays. Their *New Zealand Accommodation Guide* lists individual farms and also umbrella organisations that list farms in specific locales or all over the country.

There are all sorts of farms you can choose from – dairy farms, sheep farms, high country farms, cattle farms, mixed farming farms. If you're staying in the homestead typical daily costs are in the $60 to $120 range including meals, but there are also many on a B&B only arrangement where costs may be more like $25 to $40 per day, with an extra $10 to $15 if you want dinner. Some farms have separate cottages where you fix your own food and have to supply your own bedding; these usually charge by the week. Rates can get as cheap as $10 per night in basic sheep shearers' cottages, for example. You'll probably find that the cheapest farm holidays are booked when you're actually in New Zealand, only the more expensive places go looking for customers abroad.

A very economical way to stay on a farm and actually do some work there is to join Willing Workers on Organic Farms (WWOOF), based in Palmerston North in the North Island. Membership of WWOOF provides you with a list of farms in both islands where in exchange for your 'conscientious work' the farm owner will provide food, accommodation and some hands-on experience in organic farming. Once you've made a decision about which farm you'd like to visit you have to contact the farm owner or manager directly by telephone or letter. They emphasise that you cannot simply turn up cold. Write to Janet & Andrew Strange, WWOOF, PO Box 10-037, Palmerston North, New Zealand, or telephone (063) 553-555, for full details. Membership costs vary with the airmail cost to where you live but they're typically about NZ$8, A$10, £5, or US$7.

### Homestays

In addition to farms there are also numerous possibilities for staying in private homes throughout New Zealand, whether in urban or rural areas. Most are B&B arrangements

– see the Guest Houses & B&Bs section for additional details. Several of the agencies which handle farmstays are combination 'farm and home stay' services. Ask the NZTP for a list.

## Home Exchange

If you want to spend sometime in one area, an option is to arrange a holiday home exchange. It works the same way as in other parts of the world: you pay a fee to a matching agency, which arranges for you to exchange homes with someone in the area you want to visit who wants to visit your home area. Once the connection is made, there are no more accommodation costs – it's an even swap, home for home.

Easterbrook Services (tel 596-570), 102B Highsted Rd, Christchurch, has listings for holiday exchange homes throughout New Zealand. There's a $70 booking fee, which is refunded if they fail to come up with a suitable match.

## FOOD

If you're expecting any sort of gastronomic highlights in New Zealand you may be in for a bit of a disappointment. Nowhere does New Zealand's solid English ancestry show through clearer than on the dining table. New Zealand has not had the wide variety of immigrants that has given Australians a healthy liking for 'spicy tucker'. But if straightforward solid, honest fare like steak & chips, fish & chips, roast lamb and the like fit the bill then you won't be unhappy.

Having said that let me immediately add that it wouldn't be possible for the Kiwis to be the keen travellers they are without bringing some of it back from abroad. The choice of restaurants is a lot more cosmopolitan than it was just a few years ago although Chinese restaurants still predominate over any other sort of overseas eateries. Curiously, despite the proliferation of international restaurants – everything from Middle Eastern food to Vietnamese food can be found in the larger cities – there is nothing to be seen from the Pacific Islands, the source of New Zealand's largest number of immigrants.

There's not much of a NZ national cuisine – no moa & chips or Auckland fried kiwi. They're big meat eaters though and a NZ steak is generally every bit as good as an Aussie one. Lamb, of course, is top quality and available everywhere. New Zealand is also renowned for its dairy products and the milk, cheese and ice cream are excellent.

With all that coastline it's not surprising that seafood is pretty popular and there are some fine local varieties of oyster and the now rare and expensive *toheroa* or slightly less pricey *tuatua*. In some places, such as 90 Mile Beach in the North Island, a few minutes of digging in the sand at the beach can yield bucketfuls of shellfish. Crayfish (lobster) is a speciality in some areas.

New Zealand also has good fresh water fish, with incredibly large rainbow and brown trout. The area around lakes Taupo and Rotorua in the North Island is particularly famous for giant-sized trout, but in fact they are found in many places in New Zealand. You can't buy these trout in the shops but there are many opportunities to catch one yourself. There are a number of guidebooks about fishing in New Zealand.

### Kiwi Fruit

New Zealand's most famous fruit, the kiwi fruit, is also known as the Chinese gooseberry. The fruit is fuzzy, brown, and about the size of a small lemon. The skin peels off to reveal its unique green flesh, high in vitamins and fibre. The name kiwi fruit was dreamed up in the 1950s.

Imported from the Yangtze Valley in China, the first kiwi fruit climbers were grown as ornamental garden vines and it was only 50 years ago that attempts were made to grow them commercially. The industry grew very slowly at first; only in the last 20 years has it finally assumed the economic importance it enjoys today. New Zealand now produces about two-thirds of all the kiwi fruit grown in the world.

### Fast Food & Takeaways

Starting from the bottom there are plenty of fast food joints along with those symbols of American culinary imperialism Colonel Sanders, Pizza Hut and McDonald's. I developed a theory on my last visit that the more prominent the big fast food operators were the worse the local alternatives were likely to be. Wanganui, with what must be the poorest selection of sandwiches of any comparable town in the country, is a wonderful example.

Of course there is fish & chips. Unlike in Australia where frying up good English fish & chips seems to be an Italian or Greek occupation, in New Zealand it's very often a Chinese one. New Zealanders are just about as tied to the meat pie as Australians but they probably do make a better job of them. To any Americans or Poms out there, the meat pie has as great a cultural significance to Australians as the hot dog does to a Noo Yorker – and is as frequently reviled for not being what it once was or currently should be.

### Pub Food

If you move up a notch and into the pubs you'll probably find, as in Australia, the best value for money. Counter meals (pie & chips, stews, etc, very cheap) have more or less died out, though some bars still sell pies from a pie warmer. A lot of pubs now have bistro meals – simple but good food like schnitzel, steak, fish or the like with chips (French fries), and a good fresh salad or coleslaw. Average main courses range from $8 to $12 and they are usually excellent value. Cobb & Co restaurants are a chain offering pub-style food in locations all over New Zealand. They're safe, sound and consistent and also open commendably generous hours 7 days a week.

### Restaurants

Up another jump and into the restaurants. As in Australia there's the BYO-Licensed Restaurant split. BYOs (bring-your-own booze) aren't as clearly defined as in Australia but the same basic story applies – you can bring your own bottle of wine or whatever along with you and the food prices are generally a notch lower than in licensed restaurants. Check before you arrive if it is BYO or not. If you like reading about restaurants before you try them *Michael Guy's Eating Out* is an interesting guide to restaurants all over both islands of New Zealand.

One of the real pleasures of my most recent visit to New Zealand was the proliferation of excellent vegetarian restaurants. Gopals, the Hare Krishna-run places, can be found in several locations while in Auckland there are a number of cheap and excellent vegetarian places including Dominoes and Simple Cottage. In Christchurch Mainstreet Cafe is more expensive but the food, especially the desserts, is superb. The best meal, vegetarian or non-vegetarian, I had in either island, however, was in the wonderful Te Kano restaurant in Wanaka – definitely worth a detour. Ditto for the pizza at the tiny Theatre Cafe in Motueka, west of Nelson.

### Self-Catering

Buying your own food to cook yourself is generally far cheaper, of course, and with most camps and all hostels and motels having cooking facilities it's a relatively easy alternative. Shops are open from 9 am to 5 pm Monday to Friday, and on Saturday mornings; supermarkets, of course, tend to be cheapest.

In the evenings, early mornings and weekends the good old corner dairy is the place to go. A dairy is a small shop found on many street corners throughout New Zealand, which sells milk, food, the local newspaper, chocolate and sweets, milk shakes – in fact a bit of everything, but mostly food lines. They're open for longer hours than other shops, are far more widespread, but their selection is usually not as good as a larger shop, and their prices tend to be higher.

### DRINKS
### Alcohol

**Beer** New Zealanders are great drinkers and the beer and pubs are pretty good. Almost all the beer is now brewed by only two companies but down in the deep south you'll see some different labels – Speights, Southland Bitter, Bavarian. Bavarian used to be brewed by a private company, as was much of New Zealand's beer, before it was taken over by one of the two giants. Many a true Bavarian drinker will tell you it's not the same as in the good old days.

Cans aren't very popular and most beer is sold in bottles anyway as they're refundable and cheaper than cans. In a pub the cheapest beer is on tap. You can ask for a '7' which was originally 7 fluid ounces but is now a 200 ml glass, the nearest metric equivalent (it's still called a '7' though – old ways die hard!); a 'handle' which is a half litre or litre mug with a handle; or a jug, which is just that.

Drinks at public bars are the cheapest while lounge or other bars tend to mark their drinks up more but prices vary very widely. I noted half handle prices of $1.20, $1.25, $1.50, $1.70 and $2.30 in various bars around the country.

In public bars you can pretty much wear anything, but lounge bars have a lot of 'neat dress required' signs around. You sometimes get the feeling they are determined that New Zealand should be the last home of the necktie. The bars with entertainment are normally lounge bars, which can sometimes make things a bit awkward for the traveller with his jeans, sandals and T-shirt.

An NZ invention is the Trust-operated pub which started in Invercargill. For some time that stout town was 'dry' and when the prohibition was repealed they decided that pubs should be publicly owned and the profits go to the community. It worked so well that many other pubs around the country are also Trust operated.

**Wines** New Zealand also has a thriving wine-producing industry and many wineries have established international reputations, particularly for their whites. Air New Zealand has been a consistent winner of awards for the best wines served by an airline.

More unusual is kiwi fruit wine. There are lots of different varieties – still and bubbly, sweet and dry – not least of which is a liqueur. You may not like it, but New Zealand's the best place to try it. It's also an interesting way to while away a few hours – taking a look at a kiwi fruit winery and having a free tasting in pleasant surroundings.

## BOOKS

New Zealanders have the same self-fascination as Australians – there are plenty of books about the country's history, prospects, activities and pretty views. Particularly the latter. Almost any bookstore will have a section specialising in books on New Zealand.

The book which has had the most attention and interest in New Zealand in recent years is *The Bone People* by Keri Hulme, winner of the British Booker Prize for fiction in 1985, which made it an international bestseller. It's a book people either love or hate, I'm on the hate side!

Probably the most well-known NZ writer is still Katherine Mansfield, but there are a number of notable contemporary authors too. Big-name novelists include Stevan Eldred-Grigg, who writes historical novels about New Zealand; Janet Frame, whose *An Autobiography* won wide attention when it appeared in 1989; and Maurice Gee. Fiona Kidman's *The Book of Secrets* won the 1988 New Zealand Book Award for fiction. Witi Ihimaera is a major Maori novelist. James K Baxter, who died in 1972, is probably New Zealand's foremost poet.

## MAPS

Excellent road maps are readily available in New Zealand. If you're a member of the AA you can go into any AA office, present your card, and get all the maps you want for free. They also have larger road atlases, which you have to buy. Otherwise the Shell Road Atlas is excellent. The Department of Land & Survey Information (DOSLI), which publishes topographical and other maps good for trampers (see the Tramping section in the Outdoor Activities chapter), also publishes various good highway and city maps.

## THINGS TO BUY

You don't go to New Zealand intending to come back with a backpack full of souvenirs (a photograph of some flawless moment may be your best reminder) but there are some things worth checking out.

If you're planning a camping trip around

New Zealand you can buy top quality sleeping bags, tents, clothes and other bush gear. Unfortunately these days the prices are also in the top bracket. You can also buy stunning woollen gear, particularly jumpers (sweaters) made from hand-spun, hand-dyed wool. Sheepskins are also popular buys. Fashion clothing has also become very competitive and the Canterbury sports clothing label is internationally known.

### Greenstone
Greenstone or jade is made into ornaments, brooches, earrings, cuff links and *tikis*. The latter are tiny, stylised figures (usually depicted with their tongue stuck out in a warlike *haka* challenge), worn on a thong or necklace around the neck. They've got great *mana*, or power, but they also serve as fertility symbols so beware!

### Arts & Crafts
Maori wood carvings are worth checking out, particularly in Rotorua. New Zealanders have a reputation as great do-it-yourselfers and there are a lot of excellent handicraft shops. The quality of the pottery and weaving is particularly fine: they make good presents to take back home and don't take up much room in your pack. Nelson, in particular, is noted for its excellent pottery. The quality of the local clay has attracted many potters there.

### WHAT TO BRING
The main thing to remember about New

Zealand is that while it may be a small compact country it has widely varying and very changeable weather. A T-shirt and shorts day at the Bay of Islands can also bring snow and sleet to a high pass in the Southern Alps. In fact, on those southern mountains you can often meet T-shirt and snow-gear weather on the same day. So come prepared for widely varying climatic conditions and if you're planning on tramping come prepared for anything! Waterproof rain gear and a warm down sleeping bag will help to make your stay in New Zealand much more pleasant at any time of the year.

Come prepared for New Zealand's 'dress standards' too. An amazing number of restaurants, bars, clubs and pubs have signs proclaiming their equally amazingly varied dress rules. I sometimes have the feeling that if you combined all of the rules together (one place proclaims no denim, the next no leather, the next no shirts without collars, the next no sandals, etc) the only thing you'd be permitted to wear was your birthday suit!

Otherwise there are no great preparations to be made. New Zealand is a modern, well organised country and you should be able to find most visitor's requirements from film to pharmaceuticals. Although laundromats don't seem to be as prevalent as in many other countries, nearly every motel, camping site or hostel will have a laundry. The cheaper the accommodation the more they seem to charge for using their laundry machines!

# Outdoor Activities

New Zealand offers visitors many popular outdoor activities, including tramping, skiing, jet-boating, rafting, canoeing, kayaking, scuba diving, surfing and many others.

## Tramping

Tramping, or hiking/walking/bushwalking/trekking as it is known in various countries, is the best way of coming to grips with New Zealand's natural beauty. It gives the traveller the greater satisfaction of being a participant rather than just a spectator.

The country has literally thousands of km of tracks, many well marked, some only a line on the maps. What makes tramping especially attractive are the hundreds of huts available, allowing trampers to avoid the weight of tents and cooking gear. Many tracks are graded so that they are easily covered by those with only a moderate amount of fitness and little or no experience. Many travellers, once having tried a track, then gear the rest of their trip in New Zealand to travelling from one track to another, with side trips to see the 'in' sights. This section should open your eyes to the possibilities of tramping but before attempting any track consult the appropriate authority for the latest information.

### Information

Only brief descriptions of the most popular tracks are given here and pointers to other possibilities. My personal preferences are the Abel Tasman track for coastal/bush scenery, the Routeburn for subalpine scenery and the Tongariro National Park (Ketetahi-Mangatepopo) for thermal/volcano activity.

### Tracks, Huts & Wardens

The following notes on tracks, huts and wardens apply only to the popular 'tourist' tracks. If you venture off these onto any other of the many tracks and areas available, things will be quite different. For example it may take you an hour to cover 1 km, huts may be 8 hours or so apart, there won't be any wardens and you will have to be much better prepared.

- When walking allow about 4 km per hour on easy ground.
- Huts are usually placed 3 to 4 hours apart.
- Huts usually have beds for up to 24 with thick foam mattresses on bunks.
- Huts on the more popular tracks usually have wood stoves with gas burners.
- There is a 2 night limit on huts, if they are full.
- Camping on tracks is, in theory, banned because of the effect on the environment. In practice, if the hut is packed, wardens will turn a blind eye. Check with the warden. The main point is to leave the site cleaner than when you arrived – washing dishes in lakes is a strict no-no.
- Always leave firewood in huts for the next group; in case they arrive in heavy rain or the dark.
- Tracks are administered by rangers and wardens; the former are permanent staff, normally well trained and very knowledgeable. The wardens are temporary; usually employed for the summer season to keep an eye on and maintain the huts, provide track information and first aid, collect hut fees and generally be helpful to trampers.
- Wardens in the national parks collect hut fees, when they're on duty. When they leave, at the end of February or March, payment is up to the conscience of trampers. Hut fees range from $4 to $12 per night (see Back Country Huts).
- Check with wardens for weather forecasts and information about the track.
- Getting into and out of tracks can be a real problem. Having a vehicle only simplifies the problem of getting in. Having two vehicles allows the positioning of one at each end of the track. If you have no vehicle then you have to take public transport or hitch in. If the track starts or ends at the end of a dead-end road, hitching will be difficult. Fortunately with the far greater number of trampers now walking New Zealand's tracks there is also far more transport available.
- Leave excess luggage behind or send it on to a point near the end of the track. Camping grounds

will often hold luggage for free. Bus companies will carry excess luggage at a very reasonable price and will hold it in their offices until it is picked up.

- Surprisingly most people on the tracks are from outside New Zealand. It's quite common to have only 10% Kiwis in a hut although on the Milford Track, of course, it can reach 50%. Kiwis do tramp, but they tend to avoid the more popular tracks, seeking the really wild and untouched regions. To most New Zealanders tramping is still considered to be blazing trails through deep snow over 4000 metre passes, sleeping out in the open during blizzards, then fording rivers neck deep, ducking to avoid the blocks of ice, all done in shorts and T-shirt. In the last 10 years there has been an amazing improvement in the conditions of tracks and huts.

- Citizens of Oz should note that it isn't necessary to carry drinking water in rainforest!

- Once on the track be careful. In good weather most of the tracks are safer than walking around town but what makes them dangerous is New Zealand's contrary weather. A glorious walk in perfect conditions suddenly becomes a fight for survival in a blizzard. An easy 2 hour walk to the next hut turns into a grim struggle against wind, wet and cold over a washed-out track and swollen rivers. Hopefully this won't happen but it has often, and will again, so be prepared and be careful. Weather forecasts should be watched but taken with a grain of salt. New Zealand's prevailing weather comes from the south-west, an area which has no inhabited land and very little sea or air traffic, making accurate reporting difficult. In Fiordland it is considered that the forecast weather hits the area a day before it is forecast.

- The 'season' for tracks is approximately the same as the Christmas school holidays – from 1 to 2 weeks before Christmas to the end of January. The couple of weeks before school breaks up in December can also be bad as many school groups are on the trails. December-January on the main trails is a good period to avoid. The best weather is January to March inclusive. June and July are considered the middle of winter and not the time to be out on the tracks. It's best to time your walks so that the most southerly are done in the middle of summer.

- For an enjoyable tramp the primary consideration is your feet and shoulders. Make sure your footwear is adequate and that your pack is not too heavy. Having adequate, waterproof rain gear is also important, especially on the west coast of the South Island, where you can get drenched to the skin in minutes if your rain gear is not up to the challenge.

## Back Country Huts

The DOC has a network of back country huts in the national, maritime and forest parks. Hut fees are $4 to $12 per night (children half price), paid with tickets purchased in advance at any DOC office or park visitor centre. The tickets cost $4 each (you can buy them in booklets) and are valid for 15 months. Huts are classed into four categories and, depending on the category, a night's accommodation may require one, two or three tickets. On arrival at a hut, you simply date the ticket(s) and deposit them in the box provided. Hut accommodation is on a first come, first served basis.

The best, Category One, huts have cookers and fuel, bunks or sleeping platforms with mattresses, toilet and washing facilities, and a water supply. They may also have lighting, heating, radio communications, drying facilities, and a hut warden on duty. Category One huts cost $12 (three tickets) per night.

Category Two huts have bunks or sleeping platforms with mattresses, toilet and washing facilities, and a water supply. They may also include cooking and heating facilities, but you may have to provide your own cooker and fuel. Cost is $8 per night.

Category Three huts are more basic, with bunks or sleeping platforms (but no mattresses), toilet and water supply only. You provide your own cooker and fuel. These huts are $4 per night.

There is no fee for Category Four facilities, which are usually just simple shelters for getting out of the rain – no bunks or other amenities.

Camping is permitted outside some Category One and Two huts (but not the ones on the Milford, Routeburn and Kepler tracks). Cost is $4.

If you plan to do much tramping, consider getting an Annual Hut Pass. The pass allows you to stay overnight at all Category Two and Three huts on a first come, first served basis, and to camp outside all Category One huts where this is allowed. Cost is $60 (children $30) and the pass is valid for 1 year from the date of purchase.

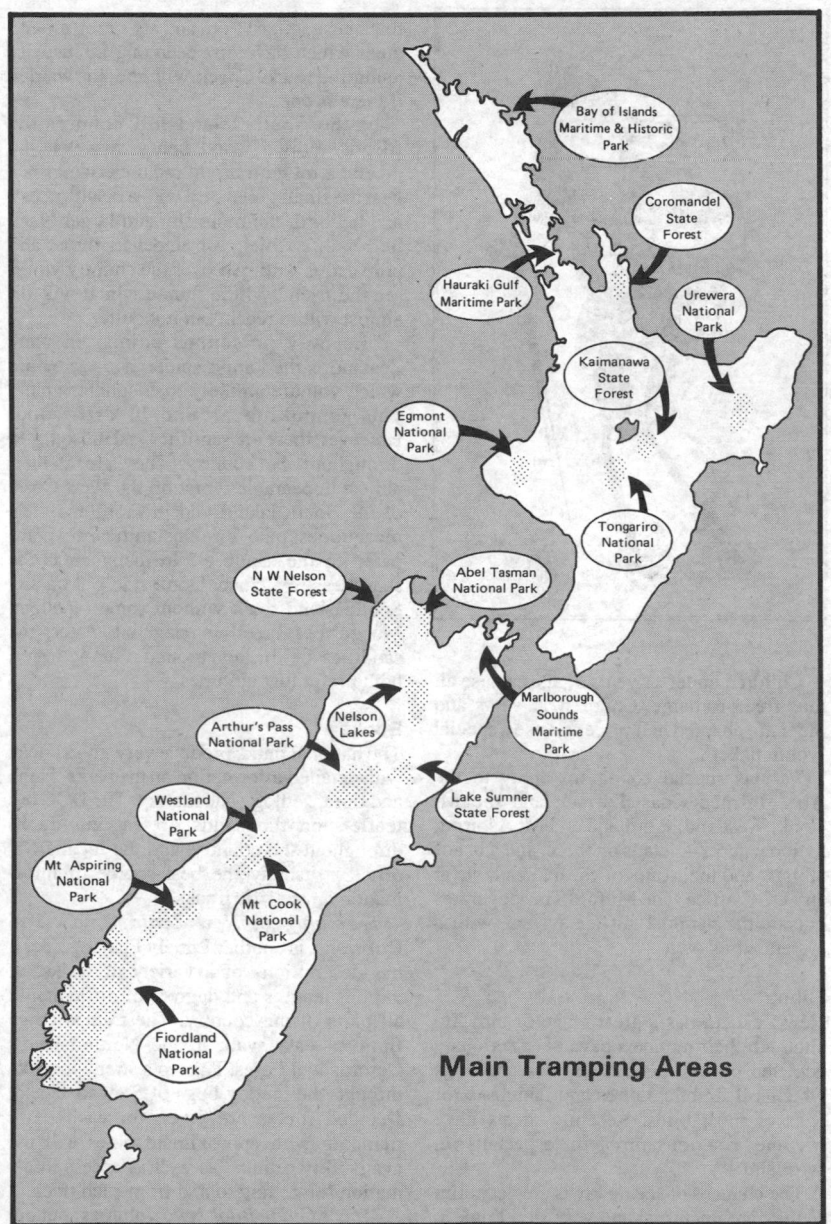

**Main Tramping Areas**

Children under 11 years of age can use all huts free of charge. Children 11 years and older are charged half price and use a special 'youth ticket'.

Various special conditions apply to the Abel Tasman Coastal Track and the Mt Cook, Westland, Fiordland and Mt Aspiring national parks – details on these, and a list of all huts and their categories, are available at any DOC office. The Milford Track operates outside the national hut fee system, with a system all its own.

### Fauna

New Zealand has a great range of bird life although their numbers have been seriously depleted by introduced cats, rats and dogs which kill flightless birds and raid nests for eggs of most birds. Recently, stoats have become a serious problem, especially in Westland.

The chances of seeing kiwis are very slim as they are nocturnal and very shy. Look in thick bush, after 11 pm and after rain, around areas which have just been dug up, usually along the track. Check with the hut warden if there is one.

In the South Island hill country the friendly brown wood hen is a weka; the green parrot with bright red underwings is a kea; the small green bird with a beautiful call is a bellbird; the more shy and larger black bird with a white crop under its throat and pure call is a tui. All over the country you'll see the friendly little fantail which will flit almost within reach, but not quite.

The only poisonous animal in New Zealand is the katipo spider, a shy creature which you are unlikely to encounter unless you go poking around in driftwood. However, there are sandflies and mosquitoes throughout the country. They are at their almost unbearable worst on the West Coast of the South Island and in Fiordland. The mosquitoes pale into insignificance compared to the sandflies. In many areas the sandflies are a curse. Don't start out on any South Island track without some repellent. Mosquitoes breed in stagnant water, the sandflies are thickest around moving water; both prefer low altitudes.

### Books

The national parks produce very good books with detailed information on the parks' fauna and flora, geology and history. The DOC has leaflets on thousands of walking tracks throughout the country, and the local DOC office is usually the best source of information on specific tracks.

*Tramping in New Zealand*, by Jim DuFresne, is another Lonely Planet guide. It has descriptions of a variety of walks, of various lengths and degrees of difficulty, in all parts of the country. The tramps range from an easy walk in the North Island's Coromandel Forest Park to a strenuous hike through the muddy bogs of Stewart Island. Detailed routes are given for each day's tramping with approximate times and the availability of huts, as well as access information for getting to and from each track.

*Moir's Guide Book* (two volumes) put out

by the NZ Alpine Club is the definitive work on tracks in the south of the South Island. There's also a series of *Shell Guides* on the more popular tracks.

## Maps

The DOSLI (Department of Survey & Lands Information) topographical maps are the best, though stationery shops tend to have a very poor selection of them. DOSLI has map sales offices in the North Island in Auckland, Hamilton, Gisborne, Napier, Rotorua, New Plymouth, Palmerston North, Wellington and Whangarei; and in the South Island in Blenheim, Christchurch, Dunedin, Hokitika, Invercargill, Nelson and Timaru. The DOC often has a selection of DOSLI maps for sale on the tracks in its immediate area.

DOSLI has various series of maps for a variety of uses. 'Parkmaps' are produced for various national, state and forest parks and there are 'Trackmaps' for some of the more popular walking tracks. There are also 'Holidaymaker' maps, 'Touringmaps', 'Terrainmaps', 'Streetfinder' maps and larger 'Aotearoa' and 'Pacific' maps covering all of New Zealand and many Pacific islands. The most detailed maps that DOSLI produces are the 'Topomaps' series of topographical maps. They have the best details, but the problem is you may need two or three maps to cover one track. All the maps cost $11.

## Department of Conservation (DOC)

The DOC looks after parks, walkways, tracks, huts and general tramping facilities. It also administers over 1000 scenic, historic, scientific and nature reserves, and wildlife refuges and sanctuaries.

The local DOC office is usually the best place to go for information on nature and outdoor attractions in any area. They produce excellent pamphlets on almost any natural attraction of interest. In some places the information centres will have the same information and a collection of DOC pamphlets, but usually it's worthwhile to pay a visit to the DOC office.

## The Parks

DOC information centres for the various national parks and maritime parks are found at:

Abel Tasman – Totaranui, Nelson, Motueka, Takaka
Arthur's Pass – Arthur's Pass village
Bay of Islands Maritime & Historic Park – Russell
Egmont – Dawson Falls and North Egmont on Mt Egmont
Fiordland – Te Anau
Hauraki Gulf Maritime Park – Auckland
Marlborough Sounds Maritime Park – Blenheim
Mt Aspiring – Wanaka
Mt Cook – near the Hermitage Hotel
Nelson Lakes – St Arnaud
Paparoa – Punakaiki
Tongariro – Whakapapa on Mt Ruapehu
Urewera – Lake Waikaremoana
Westland – Franz Josef and Fox Glaciers
Whanganui – Pipiriki

In addition to the national parks there are state forest areas covering 11,850 sq km. Information is available at local DOC offices.

## New Zealand Walkways

Walkways are a new idea, similar to the American National Trails. The New Zealand Walkways Commission, appointed in 1976, is establishing walkways close to urban centres which are suitable for families, with the intention of eventually linking them into a nationwide network. There are already many walkways open, and many more being planned. They are all 1 day walks and good practice for the real thing. Information is available from the New Zealand Walkways Commission, Charles Ferguson Building, Bowen St, Wellington (Private Bag), or from local DOC offices or information centres.

## What to Take

**Equipment** This list is for someone who will be sticking to the main tracks, staying in huts and tramping during the summer months. It is inadequate for snow country or winter.

- Boots – light to medium is sufficient; it is possible to get through in tennis/running shoes or street shoes, but they make the going much harder and the risk of injury much greater and are not recommended. The boots should be broken in or you'll get painful blisters. Cover your heels with band-aids before you start if you think there is any chance of blisters. Feet are the greatest source of discomfort on a track and therefore should have the greatest care.

- Alternative footwear – thongs/sandals, running/-tennis shoes for strolling around the huts and if the boots become just too painful to wear.
- Socks – three heavy woollen pairs; two to be worn at once to reduce the chance of blisters. Frequent changes of socks during the day also reduces the chance of blisters but isn't too practical.
- Shorts, light shirt – for everyday wear, swimsuits for the immodest.
- Woollen sweater/jersey, woollen trousers – essential in case of cold weather. Wool is the only thing to have when it's wet.
- Raincoat – must be waterproof, although it is unlikely such a thing has yet been made. A combination of wet and cold can be fatal.
- Knife, fork & spoon, cup, plate, soup bowl. (You can cut this back to knife, spoon and bowl – a bowl is multipurpose: you can eat or drink out of it, and mix things in it.)
- Pot/billy (one) – 1½ to 2 litres capacity is sufficient.
- Pans (two) – 15 cm across and 5 cm deep is plenty. The pot and pans are adequate for two to three course meals for two people. Preferably they should fit into each other and be made of aluminium for lightness.
- Camping stove – not essential, but can be handy when huts are full, or the gas runs out.
- Matches/lighter – for cooking and lighting candles. Matches are a bit of a bind as it is difficult to keep them dry.
- Candle – half to one candle per day, depending on how many are sharing the hut. Some huts have lanterns supplied.
- Torch (flashlight) – for nocturnal toilet visits and late arrival at the hut.
- Toilet paper, band-aids, insect repellent (try Dimp or ask a chemist for the active ingredient of Dimp, then water it down). Some people suggest taking vitamin B tablets regularly from a couple of weeks before you hit sandfly country. This is supposed to sweat out through your pores and put off sandflies!
- Small first-aid kit – nothing fancy.
- Small towel – should dry quickly.
- Sleeping bag – light to medium weight, including a light stuff bag for rapid and easy packing.
- Pack of cards – brush up on Crib, 500 and Euchre.
- Pen/pencil and paper.
- Pot scrubber and tea towel – washing up is usually done in cold water making pot cleaning difficult; cloth is for drying dishes and wiping down sink.

**Food** It should be nourishing, tasty and lightweight:

- Breakfast – the most important meal of the day. Muesli/porridge (quick cooking) – good with sultanas (raisins). Bacon & eggs – bacon in vacuum pack will last days. Bread, butter/margarine, Vegemite/honey. Tea/coffee, sugar, instant milk.
- Lunch – it's normally eaten between huts and therefore should not require too much preparation Bread/crackers, butter/margarine. (There are some nice wholemeal crackers available, but 'Cabin Bread' is larger and stronger and so will stand up to being crammed in a pack better.) Cheese – tasty, not bland.
- Dinner – must be hot and substantial Instant soups – help to whet the biggest appetites. Fresh meat – good for the first 2 days. Dehydrated meals – Alliance excellent, Vesta OK, TVP bad. Dehydrated vegetables, instant mashed potatoes – check the preparation time; 20 minutes is the limit. Rice – goes with everything. Dessert – easy to cook, instant such as tapioca or custard.
- Snacks – important as a source of energy while tramping Chocolate – 100 grams per person per day. Raisins, sultanas, dried fruit. Scroggin – combination of all the above; make it yourself. Glucose – in the form of barley sugar, glucose tablets or powder from chemists; it gives almost instant energy. Biscuits – great before bed with tea. Cordial concentrate – powder; great thirst quencher, adds extra excitement to the fresh water of waterfalls and streams.

As all rubbish should be burnt or carried out, ensure that everything is in suitable containers. Extra lightweight metal and plastic containers are available from supermarkets and some chemists. Don't take bottles, transfer the ingredients, such as coffee and Vegemite, into light containers.

This list of equipment is by no means complete but it should get you through the first tramp without suffering from withdrawal symptoms. For a 3 day tramp, one loaf of bread, 200 to 300 grams of butter/-margarine and 200 grams of instant dried milk is sufficient. As so many dishes require milk it is important not to underestimate your requirements.

Everything should be in plastic bags, preferably two, to protect them from the elements. Clothes must be kept dry under all circumstances. The green rubbish/garbage bags are the best available. Put the whole schemozzle into a lightweight, waterproof backpack. The total weight should not exceed 14 kg for a 3 day tramp.

## MILFORD TRACK (4 days)

'The finest walk in the world' is a special track, unique in New Zealand. It is the country's best known track and one which most Kiwis dream of doing, even if it's the *only* track they ever walk. Many overseas visitors also make a special effort to do the track, sometimes planning years in advance, though sadly they often leave New Zealand without realising that other tracks even exist.

For most walkers who have done other tracks, Milford generates a lot of bitterness because of how it is run. It is interesting that a lot of trampers doing the Routeburn, only a few km away, move on to other tracks and refuse to do the Milford because they feel they will be ripped off.

Hassles aside, the highlights of Milford are the beautiful views from the Mackinnon Pass, the 630 metre Sutherland Falls, the rainforest, and the crystal clear streams, swarming with clever, fat trout and eels. The track can only be done in one direction, from Lake Te Anau to Milford, and you need a permit from the Park Headquarters in Te Anau. This allows you to enter the track on a particular day and no other. As bookings can be heavy it pays to book as far ahead as possible – even several months or a year in advance is not a bad idea, especially for December and January. Bookings are made through the THC Resort Hotel, PO Box 185, Te Anau (tel Te Anau 7411).

The track is open from early November to early April although heavy rain can close it sooner. As a party of trampers usually leaves every day during the season, it's only possible to stay extra nights in huts if the following party does not fill the hut. As it is necessary to enter and leave the track by boat, the tight control is necessary to handle the large numbers.

Milford is synonymous with rain: 5½ metres of it a year is only average. However, the number of rainy days is not exceptionally high, so when it does rain in this country of granite the effect is an experience not to be missed. Water cascades *everywhere* and small streams become raging torrents within minutes. A few years ago large sections of the track were washed away, as were several bridges which only hours previously had been standing several metres above the surface. The level of Lake Te Anau rose half a metre in less than 8 hours. Imagine the state of any hapless trampers making their way to the next hut – and remember your raincoat! You should also pack your belongings in an extra plastic bag and send any excess luggage to Milford or leave it in Te Anau.

### Costs

For independent walkers the cost of doing the walk is made up of a $64 (children $54) permit fee, which includes 3 nights in the huts, plus the costs for the launch from the end of the track to Milford Sound, the bus to Te Anau Downs, the boat from there to the track, and the bus back to Te Anau. All of this, including the permit fee, will probably come to around $135 per person (children $80). If you stay at the hostel in Milford add another $15 per night – plus food, of course, particularly at Milford.

In addition to independent trampers, organised parties are taken through by the THC guides staying at a different chain of huts. The THC huts are usually an hour before the 'freedom walkers' huts so there is little mingling of the two. The THC walk – 5 days and 4 nights – costs around $1070, somewhat less for children 10 to 15 years old. Children under 10 are not accepted.

THC's stranglehold over Milford and the Milford Track has been a source of bitterness over the years. There was a stage when

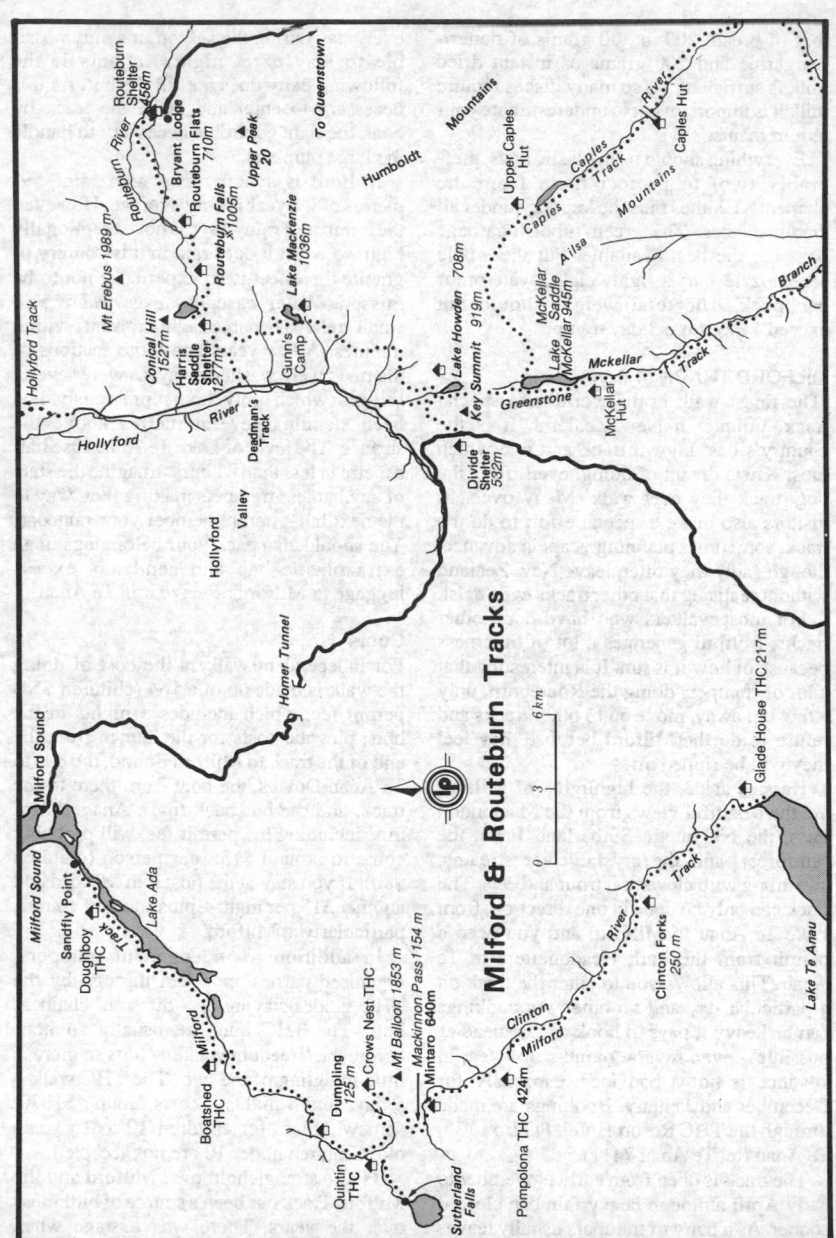

Milford & Routeburn Tracks

'freedom walkers' were not allowed on the track, and you had to go on a THC tour. Until fairly recently the THC ran the boat from the track end to Milford so that it missed the bus back to Te Anau, forcing trampers to stay overnight in the THC hotel or hostel; the nearest camping ground is conveniently several km out of town. The only meals available at Milford are those at the THC's restaurant and pub, and those at the hostel. The THC's public bar is very popular with trampers in the evening! Currently the government has put the entire THC hotel chain up for sale, and no one knows what changes may occur with the change of ownership.

### In & Out

**Te Anau End** InterCity has a bus from Te Anau to Te Anau Downs to connect with the Fiordland Travel boat to Glade House at the head of Lake Te Anau, where the Milford Track begins. Other, smaller operators offer the boat trip cheaper. See the Te Anau section in the Otago & Southland chapter for details on getting to the track. There is a route, very difficult to follow and only for those with climbing experience, over the Dore Pass east of Glade House, cutting out the boat trip.

**Milford End** The ferry to Milford goes from Sandfly Point at the end of the track in the afternoon. Buses from Milford take about 2½ hours to Te Anau, with a stop at the Divide, and there are connections from Te Anau to Queenstown. Hitching out is possible but requires patience. Or you can fly out from Milford to either Te Anau or Queenstown.

### Walking Times
Boat landing at Glade House to Clinton Forks hut: 2 hours, Clinton to Mintaro hut: 4½ hours, Mintaro to Dumpling hut: 6 hours, side trip to Sutherland Falls: 1½ hours return, Dumpling to Sandfly Point: 5½ hours.

### Track Information
The track follows the fairly flat Clinton River valley up to the Mintaro hut, passing through rainforest. From Mintaro the track passes over the Mackinnon Pass and down to the THC Quintin hut and through the rainforest in the Arthur River valley to Milford Sound. You can leave your pack at the Quintin hut while you make the return walk to Sutherland Falls. If the pass appears clear on arrival at Mintaro hut make the effort to climb it, after a hot drink, as it may not be clear the next day. The view from Mackinnon Pass is the exceptional feature of the track.

### KEPLER TRACK (4 days)
This new track was officially opened in early '88 although it could actually be walked even earlier. The track was cut in '86-87 to give access to the Kepler Mountains at the southern end of Lake Te Anau. Like any Fiordland track the walk depends on the weather; when it's wet it's very, very wet.

The walk can be done over 4 days and features a variety of vegetation and terrain including lakeside and riverside sections (good trout fishing!), then climbing up out of the beech forest to the bushline, from where there are panoramic views. The alpine stretch between Iris Burn hut and Mt Luxmore hut goes along a high ridge line, well above the bush with fantastic views when it's clear. Other sections cross U-shaped glacier-carved valleys. It's recommended that the track be done in the Mt Luxmore-Iris Burn-Moturau direction.

The track is top quality, well graded and gravelled, and the three large huts are well equipped, with heating and gas stoves. Hut fees are $12 per night (children $6) and hut wardens are on hand from early November to late April. Camping is permitted at Dock Bay and Brod Bay on Lake Te Anau and at Shallow Bay on Lake Manapouri.

The alpine sections of the track may be closed in winter due to snow and weather conditions; these sections also require a good level of fitness. Other sections are much easier. The first leg from the control gates to Brod Bay makes an excellent easy day trip.

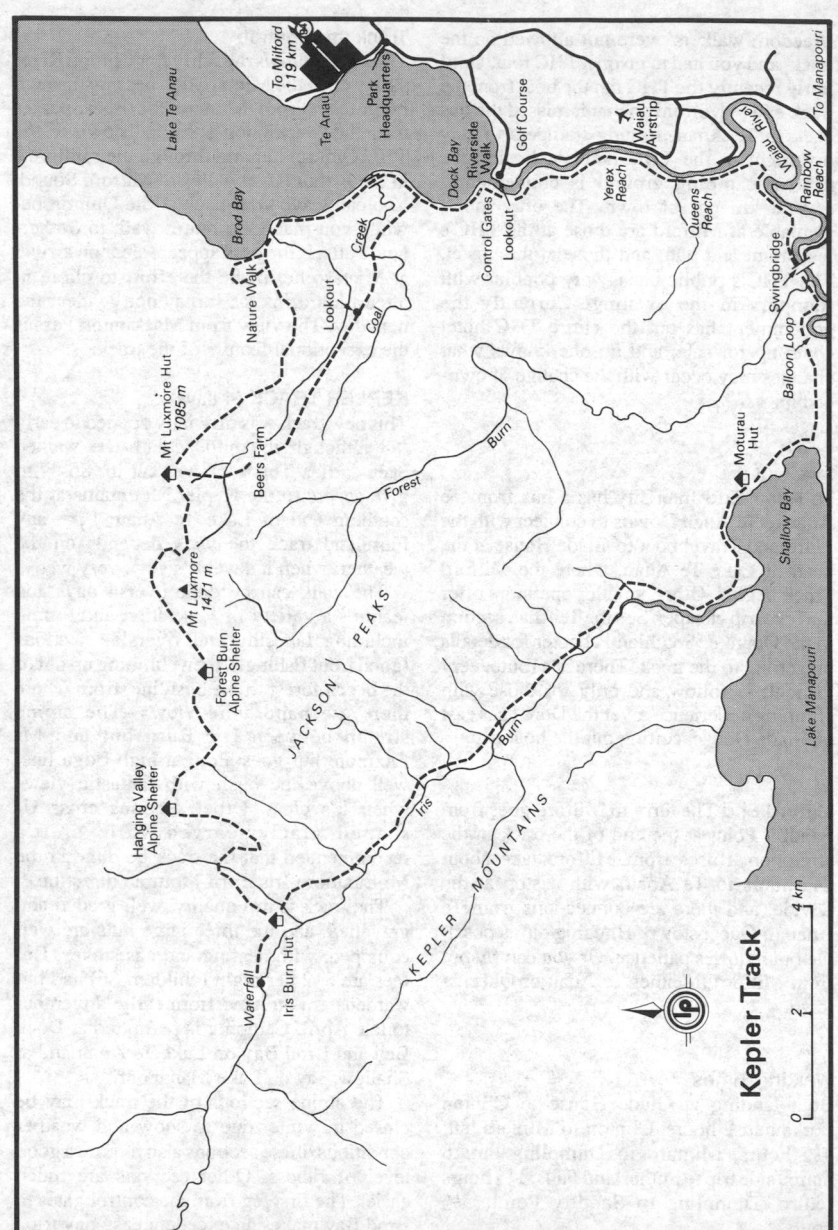

Kepler Track

## In & Out

The track is a loop, starting and finishing from the flood control gates at the southern end of the lake, within walking distance of Te Anau. Another possible start/finish point is about 10 km down the road towards Manapouri at the Rainbow Reach Swingbridge.

## Walking Times

Park Visitor Centre (Te Anau) to control gates: 45 minutes, control gates to Brod Bay: 1½ hours, Brod Bay to Mt Luxmore hut: 3½ to 4½ hours, Mt Luxmore to Iris Burn hut: 5 to 6 hours, Iris Burn waterfall track: 20 minutes one way, Iris Burn to Moturau hut: 5 to 6 hours, Moturau to Rainbow Reach: 1½ hours, Rainbow Reach to control gates: 2½ to 3½ hours.

## ROUTEBURN (3 to 4 days)

The variety of country and scenery makes the Routeburn the best rainforest/subalpine track in the country and only the Abel Tasman National Park coastal track rivals it for sheer beauty.

The track can be started from either end. Many people travelling from the Queenstown end attempt to reach the Divide in time to catch the bus to Milford, connecting with the launch trip across Milford Sound. The highlight of the track is the view from the Harris Saddle, especially from the top of Conical Hill. It is recommended that you stay an extra night at the Falls hut, if the saddle is clouded over, in the hope of better weather the next day. Almost as good is the view from Key Summit which offers a panorama not only of the Hollyford Valley but also of the Eglington Valley and the Greenstone River Valley.

Trampers starting from Queenstown can return by the easy, flat Greenstone track (2 days or 1 very long day) to Elfin Bay on Lake Wakatipu and then walk up the road 10 km to the bus at Kinloch (the same service that you use for the Routeburn), or charter a jet-boat back to Queenstown.

There are guided 4 day walks on the Routeburn which include transport between Queenstown and Routeburn Valley and between the Divide and Queenstown, accommodation, meals and guiding.

## In & Out

**Queenstown End** It's possible, but difficult, to hitchhike. The Magic Bus service up to the start of the walk is probably the most popular way of getting to the trailhead. See the Queenstown section in the Otago & Southland chapter for details.

Up at the northern end of Lake Wakatipu, Glenorchy is a convenient base – it now has excellent facilities – to do the Routeburn, Rees-Dart or Greenstone-Caples tramps. You can stay at the *Glenorchy Holiday Park* and they offer special packages from Queenstown which include transport to Glenorchy, overnight accommodation and then transport to the trailhead in the morning. Again see the Queenstown section for information. You can also organise to be collected from the trailheads if you do the walks in the opposite direction. The cost of transport to or from the trailheads may seem expensive but they're good value considering the state of the roads.

The store at Glenorchy has a reasonable selection of tramping supplies – freeze-dried food, basic trampers' stodge, grains, cereals, dried fruit, a selection of fresh vegetables and fruit, eggs, frozen foods and gear like candles, pots, pans and toiletries, as well as ice cream, milkshakes and pies. There's also a pub, post office – no bank so take enough cash with you – and a ranger station.

**Divide/Te Anau End** It's possible to hitchhike from Te Anau (you must leave in the morning) or Milford (leave early morning or mid-afternoon). Hitchhiking out is much easier, early morning to Milford, mid-afternoon to Te Anau; the object is to connect with people driving up to Milford from Te Anau for the day. Magic Bus does trampers' transport between the Divide, Te Anau and Milford during the summer, with bus frequency scheduled according to the demand. There are also InterCity buses from Te Anau via the Divide to Milford and back every day.

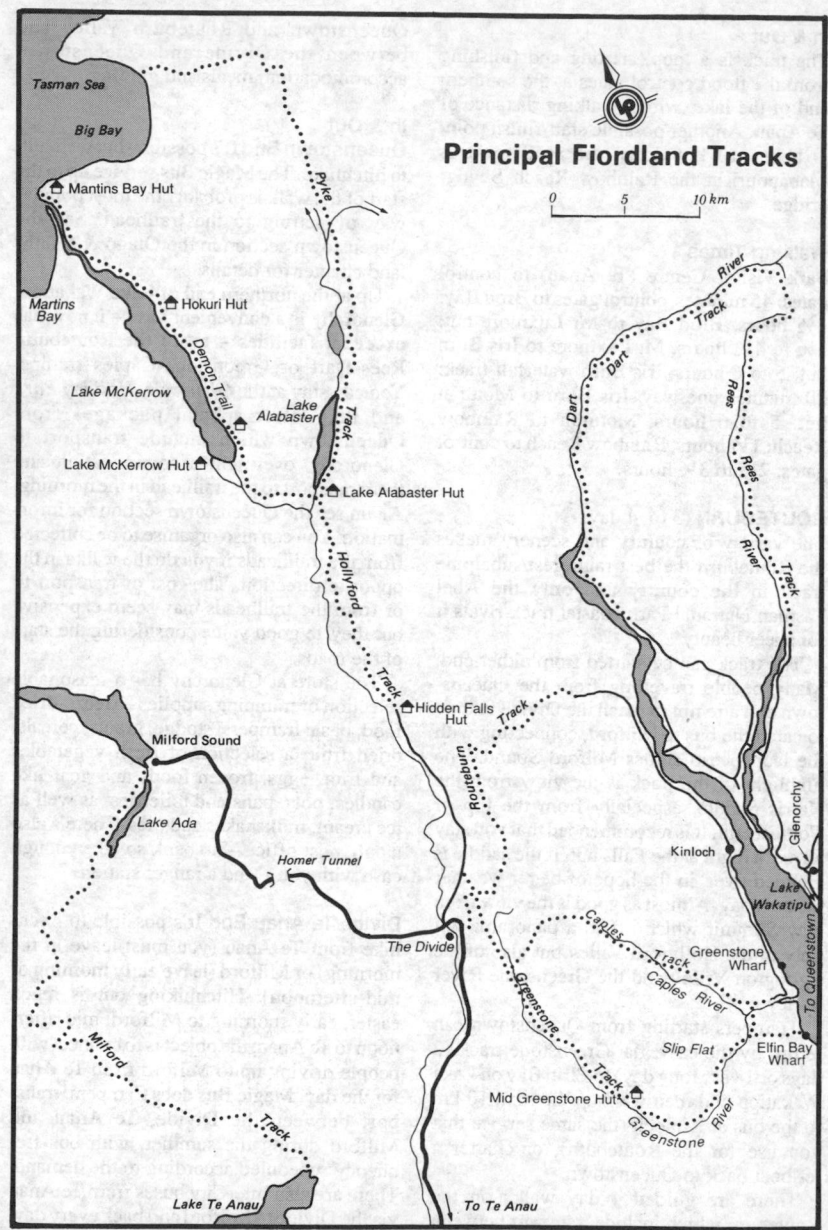

Principal Fiordland Tracks

Check the latest schedule details so you know what time to expect the bus.

## Walking Times

Bryant Lodge/Routeburn Shelter to Flats hut: 2½ hours, Flats to Falls hut: 1 hour, Falls to Harris Saddle: 1½ hours, Harris Saddle to Lake Mackenzie hut: 3½ hours, Lake Mackenzie to Lake Howden hut: 3 hours, Lake Howden to Divide: 1 hour.

## ROUTEBURN-CAPLES

An option on the Routeburn trek is to combine it with the Caples or Greenstone tracks and make a round trip. Access at the Caples and Greenstone end is at Greenstone Wharf. There is now a road from Kinloch to Greenstone Wharf which is OK, though fairly rough in spots as there are some fords to cross. The Caples and Greenstone tracks together form a loop track.

## Walking Times

Greenstone Wharf to Caples hut: 3 hours, Caples hut to Upper Caples hut: 2½ hours, Upper Caples hut to McKellar Saddle: 3½ hours, McKellar Saddle to Lake Howden hut: 3 hours, then proceeding on the Routeburn as mentioned earlier.

Other options from McKellar Saddle include turning off for The Divide before reaching Lake Howden hut, or turning into the Greenstone track.

## Track Information

Most huts have four bunks with gas stoves at higher altitudes, wood stoves elsewhere. Those at lakes Howden and Mackenzie are almost luxurious, with flush toilets, running water and even gas cookers. Huts on the Routeburn, Caples and Greenstone tracks cost $8 per night (children $4). There are some newer huts on the Caples-Greenstone route: the McKellar hut at the southern end of Lake McKellar and the Upper Caples hut, upriver from Kay Creek and not far down river from Fraser Creek, both of which can accommodate 20 people. The latter is particularly well designed and has a good wood stove with coal provided. At either end of the Routeburn track, the Divide and Routeburn shelters are only day-use shelters, with no bunks or fireplaces. The Harris Saddle shelter is similar, for emergency use only.

The Routeburn track is closed by snow in the winter and is extremely popular in January. The record for one night was 44 people in a 20 bunk hut! A stretch of the track between Harris Saddle and Lake Mackenzie is very exposed and dangerous in bad weather. This section has even been closed by snow in the middle of summer, so check with the warden if the weather looks dicey.

## GREENSTONE TRACK

This track is often used as a means of returning to Queenstown from the Routeburn, or as a loop with the Caples track. It is a 13½ hour walk down the broad easy Greenstone Valley to Lake Wakatipu from Lake Howden. You can meet Lake Wakatipu at either Greenstone Wharf (where the Caples track also begins) or at Elfin Bay. There are several huts along the track but only a shelter at Elfin Bay. From Elfin Bay you can charter a jet-boat to Queenstown, from Greenstone Wharf there are minibuses to and from Glenorchy. Guided walks along the Greenstone track are available. There are several tracks in the adjacent more attractive Caples valley.

## Walking Times

Greenstone Wharf to Slip Flat biv: 3 hours, Slip Flat to Mid Greenstone hut: 3½ hours, Mid Greenstone to McKellar hut: 5 hours, McKellar hut to Howden Lake hut: 2 hours. Coming from the Caples side, it's 3 hours from McKellar Saddle to the McKellar hut.

## HOLLYFORD-MARTIN'S BAY-PYKE

This is a well known track along the broad Hollyford valley through rainforest to the Tasman Sea at Martin's Bay and then on to Big Bay, returning by the Pyke River back to the Divide. Because of its length it should not be undertaken lightly. Check at Fiordland Park Headquarters in Te Anau.

There are guided walks on the Hollyford which include the flight out and a jet-boat trip on Lake McKerrow, which avoids the hardest and most boring part of the walk, Demon Trail.

### Walking Times
Gunn's camp to Hidden Falls hut: 2½ to 3 hours, Hidden Falls to Lake Alabaster hut: 3½ to 4 hours, Lake Alabaster hut to Lake McKerrow hut: 3 hours, Lake McKerrow hut to Demon Trail hut, 1½ hours, Demon Trail hut to Hokuri River hut: 5 hours, Hokuri River hut to Martins Bay: 5 hours, Martin's Bay to Big Bay hut: 5 hours, Big Bay hut to Upper Pike hut: 4 hours, Upper Pike hut to Barrier River: 6 hours, Barrier River to Lake Alabaster hut: 7 hours.

### DART-REES (4 days)
This is a circular route from the head of Lake Wakatipu by way of the Dart River, Rees Saddle and Rees River valley, with the possibility of a side trip to the Dart Glacier if you're suitably equipped. Access by vehicle is possible as far as Muddy Creek on the Rees side, from where it is 2 hours to 25 Mile hut. You can park a vehicle at Muddy Creek, or there is transport to and from the tracks available from Magic Bus in Queenstown or the Glenorchy motor camp. Most people go up the Rees first and then back down the Dart. Information is available from the DOC office in Queenstown or from the ranger station in Glenorchy.

### COPLAND TRACK (3 to 4 days)
This well known route crosses from the Hermitage Hotel near Mt Cook right over the Southern Alps and down to the west coast road, 26 km south of Fox Glacier. The actual crossing is only for those with alpine experience in ice or snow and with the right equipment but once over the pass the descent down to the road past the Douglas Rock and Welcome Flat huts is quite simple. The hot springs at Welcome Flat hut is the highlight for many.

The most favourable time of year to attempt the Copland track is from early December to mid-March, although the crossing is always dependent on weather and snow conditions. Be sure to check with the ranger station at Mt Cook before starting out, and to register your climbing intentions there. Heed their advice carefully – this track is not one to take lightly, people have been killed trying to get across!

If you do not have the equipment and experience it is possible to hire a guide who will take your party up and over the pass and then leave you to follow the trail down to the coast. From Alpine Guides in Mt Cook this costs $400 for a one person party, $500 for two people, $600 for three. See the Mt Cook section for more details. Alpine Guides at Fox Glacier will also lead you over from the west coast side but this is more expensive and a lot more difficult. It's best to do the track from east to west.

Another possibility is to go to the hot springs and Welcome Flat hut from the Fox Glacier side. This makes a good overnight trip and it's an easy walk up the valley from the west coast road.

### Walking Times
From the Hermitage it's an easy day walk to the Hooker Hut, from where it takes about half a day over the pass to Douglas Rock hut. Douglas Rock hut to Welcome Flat hut: 2½ hours, Welcome Flat hut to west coast road: 5½ hours.

### ABEL TASMAN NATIONAL PARK COASTAL TRACK (3 to 4 days)
This track is probably the most beautiful in the country, passing through pleasant bush overlooking beaches of golden sand lapped by bright blue water. The numerous bays, small and large, make it like a travel brochure come to life.

Once little known outside the immediate area, this track has now been 'discovered' and in summer hundreds of backpackers may be on the track at any one time – far more than can be accommodated in the huts, so

Abel Tasman National Park

bringing a tent is a good idea. At other times of year it's not so crowded.

### In & Out

A variety of transport services provide access to the track and it's now easy to get in and out from Nelson, Motueka and Takaka. See the Abel Tasman National Park section. Hitching is difficult going to or from either end of the track. There's a telephone at the Marahau parking area to phone for a taxi if you miss the scheduled bus. An enterprising individual has set up a food stand at the

Marahau end with all sorts of delicious goodies waiting for hungry trampers.

### Walking Times

South to north, Marahau to Anchorage hut or Torrent Bay hut: 3 to 4 hours, Torrent Bay to Bark Bay hut: 3 hours, Bark Bay to Awaroa hut: 3 hours, Awaroa to Totaranui: 1½ hours.

### Track Information

Huts have bunks for a minimum of 16 and are equipped with wood stoves. The track operates on a 'Facilities Use Pass' system – cost is $4 per night on the track (children $2)

whether you stay in the huts or camp. You can obtain the pass in Nelson from the DOC, in Motueka from the DOC or the Information Centre, and in Takaka at a number of places including the DOC, the Information Centre, the bus depots, the Shady Rest Hostel and the Pohara Beach Camp. All these DOC offices are sources of track information, and there's also a National Park Visitors Centre at Totaranui, open seasonally from late November to February.

Several sections of the main track are tidal with long deviations during high tides, particularly at Awaroa. As the tidal stretches are all just on the northern side of huts it is important to do the track in a southerly direction if the low tides are in the afternoons and from south to north if they are in the mornings. Check the newspaper, subtracting 20 minutes from the Nelson tidal times. Tide tables and advice are available at the DOC office in Motueka.

If you have the time take additional food so that you can stay longer should you have the inclination. Bays around all the huts are beautiful but the sandflies are a problem, except at the tiny, picturesque beach of Te Puketea near the Anchorage hut. There are some Maori rock carvings on the coast track between the Bark Bay and Awaroa huts. They're in a cave at the extreme northern end of Onetahuti Beach, just north of the Tonga Quarry. You have to ford a small stream to reach the two caves and the spiral, abstract carvings are in the left cave, not the one half filled with water.

Kaiteriteri and Totaranui have large camping grounds; there is a smaller one at Pohara Beach, 10 km east of Takaka on the road to Totaranui. Excess luggage can be sent very cheaply by Newmans bus between Nelson, Motueka and Takaka. There are 4 day guided walks on the track for around $525 (children $465). Or you could do the track by sea kayak! See the Abel Tasman National Park section.

## HEAPHY TRACK (4 to 6 days)
The Heaphy is one of the best known tracks in New Zealand, probably second only to the

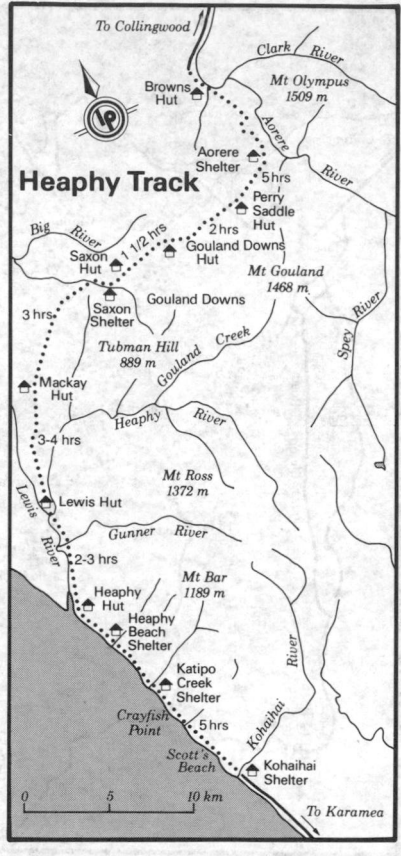

Milford. The track doesn't have the spectacular scenery like at the Routeburn, but it still has its own beauty. Some people find it a disappointment if done immediately after the nearby Abel Tasman National Park coastal track.

The track lies almost entirely within the North-West Nelson State Forest Park. Highlights are the view from the summit of Mt Perry (2 hour walk, return, from Perry Saddle hut) and the coast, especially around the Heaphy hut. It's worth spending a day or two resting at the Heaphy hut, something which is appreciated by those travelling south from Collingwood. It is possible to cross the Heaphy River at its mouth at low tide, but with caution, scramble through a hole in the cliffs and come out to a wrecked Japanese squid boat.

Alternatively, take the very badly marked track (check with the DOC) over the hill to the coast then walk south along the beach. Almost an hour up the coast is a seal colony. Take matches and a billy and have a meal of delicious mussels; only available at low tide of course. To find the best mussels turn over all the large rocks – you'll see them hiding on the underside, and they're often as big as 15 cm. You're only allowed 50 mussels a day per person!

It is possible to return to the Nelson/-Golden Bay region by the more scenic, if harder, Wangapeka Track (about 5 days) starting just south of Karamea. The track now has km markers along its length; the zero marker is at the start of the track at the Kohaihai River near Karamea and the total length is 76 km.

### In & Out

**Collingwood End** Hitchhiking in either direction is very difficult. There's a bus service from Nelson to Collingwood with stops at Motueka and Takaka. From Collingwood you can charter the minibus to take you to the trailhead. See the Collingwood section for details. There's a phone at the trailhead so you can call for the bus. There's also an airstrip nearby and it's possible to fly back from there to Karamea.

**Karamea End** Hitching is very difficult. You can take a taxi between Karamea and the start of the track – it can be called from the end of the track. A bus is also available and it's possible to charter a plane back to the Collingwood end of the track. There is a bus service to Westport from Karamea. See the Westport section for details. There is a rather primitive camping ground at the Karamea end of the track and Karamea has a very popular hostel during the busy season.

More detailed information and maps are available from the DOC offices at Nelson, Motueka, Takaka and Karamea.

### Walking Times

Browns hut to Perry Saddle hut: 5 hours, Perry Saddle to Gouland Downs hut: 2 hours, Gouland Downs to Saxon hut: 1½ hours, Saxon to Mackay hut: 3 hours, Mackay to Lewis hut: 3 to 4 hours, Lewis to Heaphy hut: 2 to 3 hours, Heaphy to Kohaihai River (track start): 5 hours.

**Km Markers** Browns 76, Perry Saddle hut 61, Gouland Downs 49, Blue Duck Shelter turn-off 47, Mackay 36.5, Lewis 24, Heaphy 17, Kohaihai River 0.

### Track Information

Huts are geared to handle 16 people. They all have gas stoves, except Heaphy and Gouland Downs which have wood stoves, and hut fees are $8 a night (children $4). The great majority of people travel west from Collingwood to Karamea. From Browns hut the track passes through beech forest to Perry Saddle (but don't take the shortcut going uphill, unless you are fit). The country then opens up to the swampy Gouland Downs, then closes in with sparse bush all the way to Mackay. The bush becomes more dense towards the Heaphy hut with the beautiful nikau palm at low levels.

The final section is along the coast through heavy bush and partly along the beach. Unfortunately the sandflies are unbearable along this, the most beautiful part of the track. The climate here is surprisingly mild but do not swim in the sea as the under-tows and currents are vicious. The lagoon at Heaphy hut is good for swimming though and fishing is possible in the Heaphy River.

Send excess luggage by Newmans bus between Westport and Nelson, Motueka or Takaka.

### WANGAPEKA TRACK

Although not as well known as the Heaphy Track in the same park, it is a more enjoyable walk. The track starts some 25 km south of Karamea on the west coast and runs 56 km east to the Rolling River. It takes about 5 days and there is a good chain of huts ($4 to $8 per night, children $2 to $4) along the track.

## STEWART ISLAND

The northern portion of the island has a circular track but unfortunately it is long, some 7 to 10 days, and uninteresting for stretches with many patches of muddy bog. However, the section from Oban to Christmas Village Bay contains some very attractive, sheltered bays and bush, ideal for relaxing. The drawback is having to return along the same track. A track has been opened between Port William hut and North Arm, making an interesting circular route near Oban.

### In & Out

See the Stewart Island section for details. There are no roads on the island outside the immediate vicinity of Oban.

### Walking Times

Ferry terminal to track start: 1 hour, track start to Port William hut: 3 hours, Port William to Big Bungaree Beach hut: 3 hours, Big Bungaree Beach to Christmas Village Bay hut: 4 hours. Mud can lengthen these times.

### Track Information

Huts range from the smallish smoke-filled Big Bungaree Beach hut to the relatively new and well-located Port William hut with 24 bunks. The Port William hut is frequently used by school parties who are expected to take tents and use them if others require the bunks. Huts cost $4 (children $2) per night and have wood stoves. From Christmas Village Bay hut it's a 3½ hour climb to the summit of Mt Anglem (980 metres) and an outstanding view of part of the South Island and most of Stewart Island. An excursion can be made to Yankee River (4 hours one way) but the track is very boggy. An old boiler at Maori Bay is a reminder of the timber milling days.

Due west of Oban is the attractive and wild Masons Bay with its extensive sand dunes. The walk between Oban and Freshwater hut is not particularly pleasant though and tends to be boggy. It's possible to hire a small boat to North Arm hut, cutting out the first day. From Freshwater to Masons Bay you're walking on a tractor track, firmer under foot, but it may be under water.

### Walking Times

Oban to North Arm hut: 4 hours, North Arm to Freshwater River hut: 4 hours, Freshwater River to Big Sandhill hut (Mason's Bay): 3 hours. The first two times are subject to mud.

## KETETAHI TRACK & TONGARIRO CROSSING (2 to 3 days)

The Tongariro National Park has a long, circular track embracing the three mountains and requiring some 10 days. Regrettably, some parts of it can be hard, unrewarding walking.

One exception is the Ketetahi/Tongariro Crossing track in the far northern part of the park. The Ketetahi track goes from an access road off Highway 47A near Lake Rotaira to the Ketetahi Hot Springs, at the Ketetahi hut. From the Ketetahi hut the Tongariro Crossing track continues to the Mangatepopo hut. Highlights of the track are the hot springs at Ketetahi, the Emerald Lakes and Red Crater, and the view over hundreds of sq km to the north, including the whole of Lake Taupo. It's an eerie feeling looking over the dormant craters, the beautiful colours of the crater lakes and the smoky majesty of Mt Ngauruhoe. The track is very accessible, as it's only a few km off SH 1, and it's a popular and well-used track. Watch out for one badly maintained section, between the Mangatepopo hut and the Chateau. An ice axe and crampons may be required in winter for the Tongariro Crossing.

### In & Out

Transport to and from both the Ketetahi and Mangatepopo ends of the track is available from Taupo, Turangi, National Park and Whakapapa with Alpine Scenic Guides (tel Turangi 68-392). In Whakapapa the

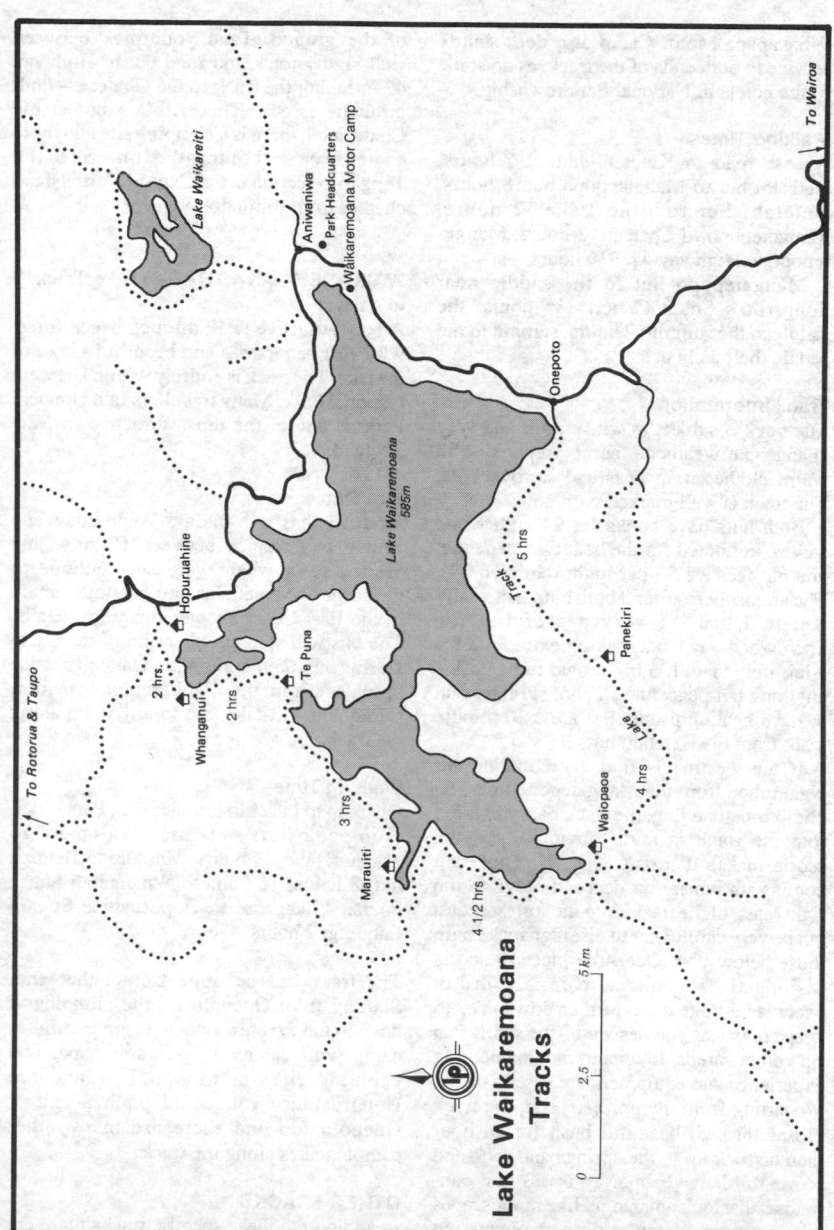

Lake Waikaremoana Tracks

Whakapapa Motor Camp also does shuttle service to both ends of the track, as do some of the hotels in National Park township.

### Walking Times
Access road to Ketetahi hut: 2½ hours, Ketetahi hut to Mangatepopo hut: 8 hours, Ketetahi hut to Blue Lake: 2 hours, Mangatepopo to Chateau: 2 hours, Mangatepopo to Highway 47: 1½ hours.

Mangatepopo hut to the saddle near Tongariro's South Crater: 1½ hours, the saddle to the summit: 2 hours, summit to the saddle: half an hour!

### Track Information
The track is subject to wild storms and very changeable weather – come prepared with warm clothes, rain gear and sturdy boots. The track is well marked with poles.

Both huts have bunks for 24 with wood stoves, not noted for the heat they generate, and hut fees are $8 per night (children $4). The atmosphere around both huts, especially Ketetahi, can be very peaceful if it's uncrowded – consider taking extra food for a leisurely stay. If a big crowd turns up it's anything but peaceful. The hot springs, said to have healing properties, are a 10 minute walk from the Ketetahi hut.

If the weather is fine, try climbing Mt Ngauruhoe from the Mangatepopo hut. The climb is demanding, the track partly marked (but the route is fairly obvious), and the scoria makes it a hard slog. If people are coming up when you descend move to the right (east) of the tracks into the softest scoria but be very careful not to dislodge rocks onto those below you. One little piece of scoria dislodged can collect material until it becomes a huge slide further down. Try to keep control as you descend – the scoria can rip you to shreds. In winter, mountaineering experience and equipment are essential.

Starting from the northern end, the track passes through beautiful bush for an hour then tussock up to the springs and rock and scoria to Mangatepopo. You pass vast panoramas that look amazingly like moonscapes with awesome craters and steam oozing out

of the ground. Take your pick between walking by track and road out to Highway 47 or taking the track to the Chateau – both through tussock. There isn't a hut at the Chateau but there is a camping site and more expensive accommodation. See the Tongariro section in the Central North Island chapter for information.

### WAIKAREMOANA TRACK (Lake Track, 3 to 4 days)
A very attractive walk through beech forest with vast panoramas and beautiful views of the lake. The track is entirely within Urewera National Park. Many travellers rate Urewera Park as one of the most attractive in New Zealand.

### In & Out
InterCity has a Monday, Wednesday and Friday bus service between Rotorua and Wairoa from where you can continue to Gisborne or Napier. See the Gisborne section in the East Coast chapter for more details. The bus will stop at either end of the track. During the summer months, a launch service operates from the Waikaremoana Motor Camp and will take you to any point along the track.

### Walking Times
Onepoto to Panekiri hut: 5 hours, Panekiri to Waiopaoa hut: 4 hours, Waiopaoa to Marauiti hut: 4½ hours, Marauiti to Te Puna hut: 3 hours, Te Puna to Whanganui hut: 2 hours, Whanganui to Hopuruahine Stream Landing: 2 hours.

The track can be done from either end. Starting from Onepoto all the climbing is done in the first few hours. There is a motor camp with cabins at Waikaremoana, and camping sites at Mokau Landing and Hopuruahine. You could pitch a tent at Onepoto too and there are many other camping sites along the track.

### OTHER TRACKS
In addition to these specific tracks there are

numerous possibilities in all state and national parks, especially Arthur's Pass, the Nelson Lakes, Coromandel and of course Mt Egmont – an easy climb in good weather. See Lonely Planet's *Tramping in New Zealand* for more details.

# Skiing

New Zealand is one of the most popular regions for skiing in the southern hemisphere. For Australians it has a number of big attractions, not the least of which is that it's more reliable and cheaper than in Oz. Australia's relatively low mountains mean the snow cover is unpredictable and the season is short, so the costs of skiing have to be high to cover the limited season. The lower lift, parking and hiring costs in New Zealand, however, balance out the extra cost of getting there.

For Europeans and Americans the attraction is skiing 'down under', skiing in the middle of the northern summer, not to mention some unique attractions such as skiing on the slopes of a volcano or the long Tasman glacier runs. Heli-skiing is another attraction of NZ skiing. New Zealand seems to have more helicopters than it knows what to do with and in winter many are used to lift skiers up to the top of long stretches of snow. The cost of these flights is surprisingly reasonable.

New Zealand's ski fields are generally not very well endowed with on-field chalets, lodges or hotels. The places to stay are usually some distance from the slopes, so it's a bit of a drag going back and forth every day. This does however mean that the accommodation, when you get to it, is fairly cheap.

At the major ski fields, lifts cost about $40 a day and group lessons are around $25 a half-day, $35 a full day, or $50 an hour for private lessons. You may as well bring your own equipment if you have it, although all the usual stuff can be bought or hired in New Zealand. The ski season is generally from

June to October, although it varies considerably from one ski field to another.

There are plenty of ski-package tours both from Australia and within New Zealand. The NZTP has brochures on the various packages and can make bookings.

## NORTH ISLAND
### Whakapapa

Whakapapa ski field is 7 km above the Chateau Hotel on Mt Ruapehu in Tongariro National Park. It's the end of the road – known as the Top of the Bruce – and has the most popular ski slopes in New Zealand, including a downhill course dropping nearly 800 metres over 4 km. The normal season is late June to late October.

There are chairlifts, T-bars and ropetows. You can drive yourself up to the slopes or you can take the 'Whakapapa Shuttle' minibus up from Whakapapa Village. There's an expensive hotel, cheaper motel and a camping site with cabins at Whakapapa Village around the Chateau (see the Tongariro National Park section in the Central North Island chapter for details – bookings are very heavy during the ski season). There are also ski club lodges at Iwikau Village on the slopes but these are generally available only to members and friends.

During the ski season there are private bus services to the Chateau from Auckland and Wellington, plus InterCity buses which operate all year.

### Turoa

The Turoa ski field on the south-western side of Mt Ruapehu was opened in 1979. Chairlifts, T-bars and ropetows take you up to the start of a 4 km run. There's also a beginner's lift. The season lasts from June to November. There is no road toll or parking fee and daily ski field transport is available from Ohakune, 17 km away, where there's plenty of accommodation. Skis can be hired on the slopes or at many places around Ohakune.

### Mt Egmont

There's more volcano-slope skiing on the eastern slopes of Mt Egmont. This is a club-operated ski field near Stratford with a T-bar and several ropetows. The season is July to September and accommodation is available in New Plymouth or closer to the snow in Stratford.

## SOUTH ISLAND
### Coronet Peak

New Zealand's southernmost slopes, near Queenstown, are rated the best in New Zealand and comparable to any in the world. There's even talk of running a future winter Olympics here. The season is comparatively short – July to September. Access to the ski field is from Queenstown, 38 km away, and there's a shuttle bus service in ski season. You can hitch it if you leave early in the morning and depart before 4 pm to come down again.

Chairlifts, T-bars and beginners tows take you up the slopes. The treeless slopes and good snow provide excellent skiing – the chairlifts run to altitudes of 1585 and 1650 metres.

The ski field is operated by Mt Cook and it has a licensed restaurant, overnight ski storage, ski repair shop, creche and pre-school ski lessons. For accommodation see the Queenstown section in the Otago & Southland chapter; there are active après-ski possibilities.

### The Remarkables

Like Coronet Peak, the Remarkables ski field is near Queenstown, with shuttle buses running from Queenstown during the season. It, too, has beginner, intermediate and advanced level runs, with chairlifts, T-bars and beginners tows. Passes for Coronet Peak and the Remarkables, including weekend and multi-day passes, can be used interchangeably at either ski field.

Both Coronet Peak and The Remarkables have designated ski school areas, with group, private, and childrens' lessons. The Remarkables also offers a Nordic ski school, Telemark (racing) and cross-country lessons. Snowboard equipment and instruction are also available.

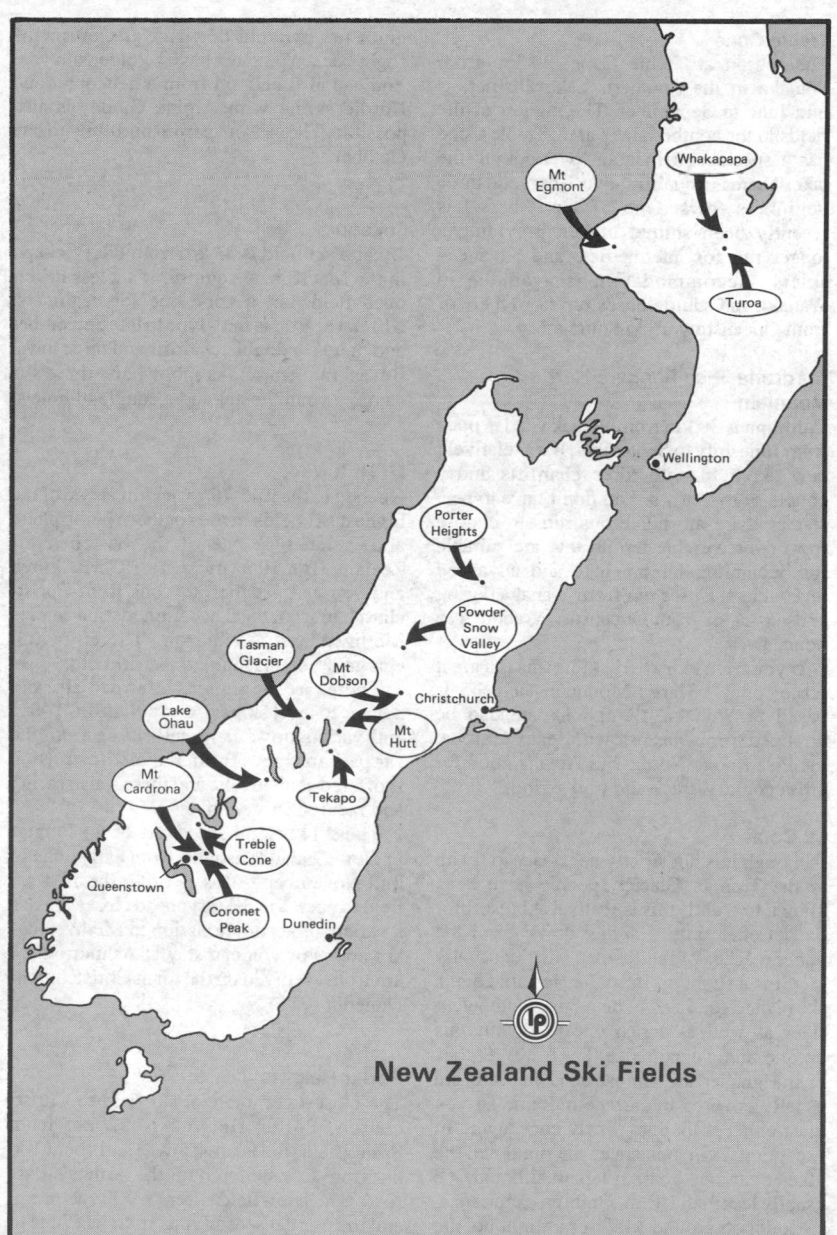

**New Zealand Ski Fields**

## Treble Cone

The season at Treble Cone, 29 km from Wanaka in the Southern Lake District, is mid-June to September. The highest of the fields in the southern lake area, Treble Cone has a spectacular location overlooking the lake. There is a chairlift, two T-bars and three beginners tows. One of the T-bars has recently been shifted higher, providing a longer run for intermediate and advanced skiers. Accommodation is available in Wanaka and shuttle buses run from there or from Queenstown, 1½ hours away.

## Cardrona, Pisa Range & Harris Mountain

Cardrona is 30 km from Wanaka and is open from June-July to September. It's a relatively new ski field with three chairlifts and a couple of rope tows. You don't have to be a star as there are numerous runs to choose from over variable terrain that are suitable for beginning, intermediate and advanced level skiers. Buses run from Wanaka during ski season, or from Queenstown, about 1½ hours away.

If you want to try heli-skiing this is a great place for it – Harris Mountain Heli-Ski is based at Wanaka, though it can also be arranged from Queenstown. Near Cardrona, the Pisa Range Nordic Ski Area is good for cross-country, track and trail skiing.

## Mt Cook

Although it is not strictly necessary to fly up to the Tasman Glacier (people have been known to walk!) this is really a ski resort for the jetsetter only – skiing down from the upper reaches of the Tasman Glacier usually requires a flight up from the Hermitage in a ski-plane. You need to be a fairly competent skier as well as a rich one to savour this unique skiing experience. The lower reaches of the glacier are almost dead flat and are usually covered in surface moraine so you must either walk out – or fly once again. In exceptional circumstances the run down the glacier can be 20 km in length although it's usually less than 10 km. Quite an experience.

Count on around $450 for a flight up, the guide fee, two runs down the glacier and the flight back. You must have a guide with you. You can also heli-ski from a helicopter and Nordic skiing with Alpine Guides is also possible. The season is from mid-July to late October.

## Tekapo

Tekapo ski field is 33 km from Lake Tekapo in the MacKenzie country. It's a less developed field, but a good one for beginners. Normal season is mid-June to late September and there's a double chairlift and three tows. Buses run from Tekapo where there's a camp, a youth hostel and a couple of hotels.

## Mt Hutt

Opened in the mid-70s, Mt Hutt is one of the highest ski fields in the southern hemisphere and is rated as one of the best in New Zealand. It's 104 km west of Christchurch and you can get there by bus from Christchurch or from local accommodation centres Methven and Ashburton. There's a toll charge if you drive up to the ski field.

There are beginner, intermediate and advanced level slopes, with a chairlift, T-bars and various tows, and heli-skiing from the car park to slopes further afield. Instruction is offered at all levels, and there's also racing and racing instruction.

The ski season here is one of the longest in New Zealand, usually from early June to mid-November – this is often the first ski field to open and the last one to close. There's a variety of accommodation in Methven (24 km away) or you can stay at Ashburton, 34 km from Methven on the main Christchurch-Dunedin road.

## Porter Heights

The closest commercial ski field to Christchurch, Porter Heights is 22 km from Springfield (the nearest town) and about 100 km from Christchurch on the Arthur's Pass road. The snowfield offers a 700 metre run and the normal season runs from late June to early October. There are three T-bars and two beginners tows. You can stay on the field but accommodation is limited in neighbouring Springfield.

### Other Ski Fields

There are lots more slopes in the South Island, many club-operated, including a collection of club ski fields off the Arthur's Pass road, some offering all-inclusive ski weeks. In the north there's a club field at St Arnaud in Nelson Lakes National Park. The Rainbow ski field is just outside the park. Mt Robert, inside the park, has a hut to stay in right at the ski field, but it's a 2 hour walk from the car park, 7 km from St Arnaud, to reach it. The Mt Lyford ski field, one of the newest in New Zealand, is near Kaikoura.

# Jet-Boating

New Zealand is the home of the amazing jet-boats, invented by CWF Hamilton in the late 1960s. An inboard engine sucks water into a tube in the bottom of the boat, and an impeller driven by the engine blows it out a nozzle at the stern in a high-speed stream. The boat is steered simply by directing the jet stream.

The boats are ideal for use in shallow water and white water because there are no propellers to damage, there is better clearance under the boat, and the jet can be reversed instantly for quick braking. The instant response of the jet enables the boats to execute 360° spins almost within the length of the boat. All that adds up to some hair-raising rides on NZ rivers.

The Shotover and Kawarau rivers near Queenstown in the South Island are popular jet-boat rivers, with the Dart River less travelled but also good. Just about every riverside and lakeside town throughout New Zealand has a jet-boat company that runs trips, sometimes in combination with other adventure activities like bungy jumping, flightseeing and rafting.

# Rafting, Canoeing & Kayaking

There are almost as many white water rafting possibilites as there are rivers in New Zealand. The Shotover and Kawarau rivers in the South Island, popular for jet-boating, are also popular for white water rafting, as is the less accessible Landsborough River, but there are plenty of North Island rivers, like the Rangitaiki, Wairoa, Motu, Tongariro, Rangitikei and Ngaruroro, that are just as good. And there is no shortage of companies willing to take you on a heart-pounding, drenching, exhilarating and spine-tingling ride down some of the wildest and most magnificent rivers in the world.

The rivers are graded from one to six, with six meaning 'unraftable'. The grading of the Shotover canyon varies from 3 to 5+ depending on the time of year, the Kawarau River is rated 4, and the Wairoa River is graded 3 to 5. On the rougher stretches there's usually a minimum age limit of 12 or 13 years. The rafting companies supply wet suits and life jackets.

Rafting trips take anywhere from 1 hour to 3 days and cost between about $65 and $130 per person. Spring and summer are the most popular rafting times.

Many companies offer canoeing and kayaking trips on the same rivers where rafting is popular. You can go for a few hours of quiet paddling or white-water excitement in hired canoes without a guide, or take longer solo or guided camping trips with perhaps fishing and other activities thrown in.

Canoeing is especially popular on the Wanganui River in the North Island, where you can hire a canoe for days at a time; there are many other possibilities. Kayaking and canoeing are also being done on lakes, notably Lake Taupo.

Sea kayaking is relatively new in New Zealand but those who have tried it rave about it. Popular sea kayaking areas are the Bay of Islands (with trips departing from

Paihia) in the North Island, and in the South Island the Marlborough Sounds and along the coast of the Abel Tasman National Park, where sea kayaking has become a viable alternative to walking on the Abel Tasman Coastal Track.

Yet another variation on the rafting theme is not true rafting at all, but it is very unusual and exciting. Known as 'Black Water Rafting' at Waitomo in the North Island, and as 'Underworld Rafting' at Westport in the South Island. It involves donning a wet suit, a lighted hard hat and a black inner tube and floating on underground rivers through some spectacular caves. An added attraction is seeing glow-worms, those unique NZ insects, glowing away like a Milky Way of stars in the bowels of the earth.

Before you book any sort of water adventure trip, check that the company has a good safety record and that it employs only experienced guides.

# Bungy Jumping

Bungy jumping was made famous by Kiwi

A J Hackett's bungy dive from the Eiffel Tower in 1986. Hackett now operates one of a growing number of bungy jumping companies in New Zealand; his company alone has sent more than 20,000 people hurtling earthward from bridges over the Shotover and Kawarau rivers, with nothing between them and kingdom come but a gigantic rubber bungy cord tied to their ankles.

The jump begins when you crawl out onto the jumping platform, get your ankles strapped up with a towel for padding, and stand out over thin air, ready to jump. The crew shout out 'five, four, three, two, ONE!' and you're off and flying. Likely as not you will dunk head first into the river below before soaring upwards again on the bungy.

After bobbing up and down like a human yo-yo, you finally settle down, grab the pole held up to you by the crew down below, and are pulled into a rubber raft. There you're unstrapped and towed back to dry land. No doubt about it, it's a daredevil sport, and the adrenalin rush can last for days. But it's all very well organised, with every possible precaution and attention to safety.

The historic Kawarau Suspension Bridge,

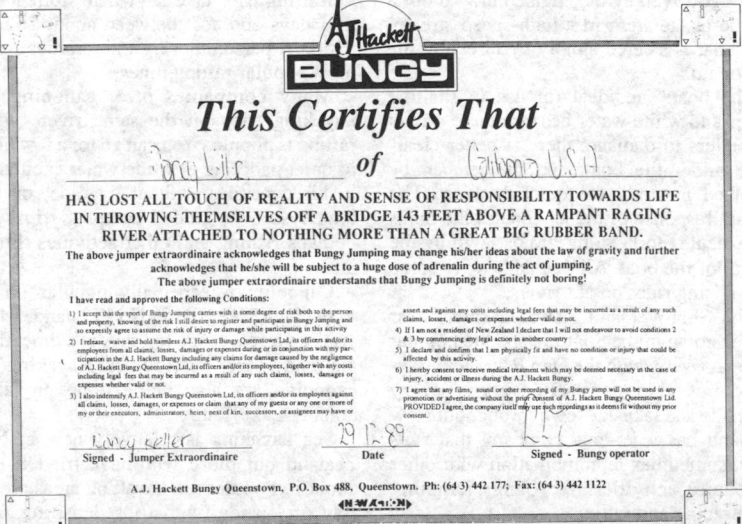

Top: One that didn't get away, fishing at Tongariro River (NZTP)
Left: Virgin snow on the treeless ski slopes of Mt Aspiring (JL)
Right: Bungy Jumping, near Queenstown (TC)

Top: Detail of Maori war canoe, Waitangi (MC)
Left: Carved Posts at Whaka Village, Whakarewarewa Thermal Reserve (NZTP)
Right: Intricately carved gateway to Whaka Village, Rotorua (MC)

near Queenstown, attracts the most jumpers; it's 43 metres above the Kawarau River. The most spectacular dive spot is Skippers Canyon Bridge, 69 metres above a narrow gorge on the Shotover River, also near Queenstown. Jumping is also done from the 45 metre railroad bridge near Ohakune, in the Central North Island, which unlike the other two has no river at the bottom of the canyon.

You'll pay upwards of $80 a bungy jump, which includes a bungy T-shirt that can only be obtained by actually doing the jump. It's even more expensive at the Shotover bridge, but there the price includes transport to the rather remote jump site. You can also arrange for still photos or a video of your jump, to impress the folks back home.

# Scuba Diving

Scuba diving also has its devotees. The Bay of Islands Maritime & Historic Park and the Hauraki Gulf Maritime Park in the North Island, and the Marlborough Sounds Maritime Park in the South Island, are obvious attractions but there are many more diving possibilities around both islands. Even Invercargill has a club!

New Zealand has two marine parks – parks in the water! – which are protected marinelife reserves, interesting for diving. The Poor Knights Islands Marine Reserve is around the Poor Knights Islands off the coast near Whangarei, north of Auckland. This reserve is reputed to have the best diving in New Zealand, and French naturalist Jacques Cousteau rates it one of the 'top 10' diving spots in the world. The Sugar Loaf Islands Marine Park, another interesting reserve, is off Back Beach in New Plymouth, not far from the city centre.

Fiordland in the South Island is a surprisingly interesting place for diving. The diving here is most unusual because the extremely heavy rainfall leaves an actual layer of freshwater, often peaty brown, over the saltwater. You descend through this murky and cold freshwater into amazingly clear and warmer saltwater. The freshwater cuts out light which discourages the growth of seaweed and this provides ideal conditions for the growth of black coral which can be found much closer to the surface than is common elsewhere in the world. Leave it there, though. It's 100% protected in New Zealand. The Fiordland sounds also have plenty of crayfish and amazing shoals of dolphins who display great interest in the relatively rare appearance of scuba divers.

# Surfing

With its thousands of km of coastline, New Zealand has excellent surfing possibilities. Swells come in from every angle and while any specific beach will have better surfing at some times of year than at others, there's good surfing to be found *somewhere* in New Zealand at any time of the year.

A few spots recommended by surfies are:

**North Island**
Auckland area (within 2 hours drive of the city)
    West coast: Piha, Raglan
    East coast: Whangamata, Matakana Island
Gisborne
    City beaches, Mahia Peninsula
Taranaki
    Stent Rd, Puniho Rd, Greenmeadows Point

**South Island**
Dunedin
    Sandfly Bay, Long Point, Lobsters near Akatore River
Kaikoura
    Meatworks, Mangawhau Point
Westport
    Westport beaches, Tauranga Bay

According to the surfing grapevine, Auckland is the best surfing area in the North Island, and Dunedin the best in the South Island, especially in summer and autumn, but there are hundreds of possibilities. There are guidebooks about surfing in New Zealand. Look for *The New Zealand Surfing*

*Guide* by Mike Bhana (Heinemann Reed, Auckland, 1988).

local NZTP or DOC offices for more information on fishing regulations.

# Fishing

New Zealand is renowned as one of the great sport-fishing countries of the world, thanks largely to the introduction of exotic rainbow trout, brown trout, lake trout, river trout, quinnat salmon, Atlantic salmon, perch, char and a few other fish. The lakes and rivers of central North Island are famous for trout fishing, especially Lakes Taupo and Tarawera and the rivers that feed them. The rivers and lakes of the South Island are also good for trout, notably the Mataura River in Southland.

The rivers of Otago and Southland, in southern South Island, have some of the best salmon fishing in the world.

Saltwater fishing is also a big attraction for Kiwi anglers, especially in the warmer waters around the North Island where surfcasting or fishing from boats can produce big catches of grey mullet, trevally, mao mao, porae, John Dory, gurnard, flounder, mackerel, hapuku, tarakihi, moki and kahawai. The 90 Mile Beach and the beaches of the Hauraki Gulf are good for surfcasting.

The colder waters of South Island, especially around Marlborough Sounds, are good for snapper, hake, trumpeter, ling, butterfish, barracouta and blue cod, and the Kaikoura peninsula is great for surfcasting.

It is not easy to hire fishing gear in New Zealand, so bring your own if you can. Rods and tackle may have to be treated by NZ quarantine officials, especially if they are made with natural materials such as cane or feathers.

If you want to fish on inland waters you will need a fishing permit. They are available for particular regions and can be for a day, a week, a month or a season. If you plan to do a lot of fishing you can also get a special tourist licence that is valid throughout most of New Zealand for 1 month. Contact the

# Whale Watching

Kaikoura, on the north-eastern coast of the South Island, is the centre of whale watching in New Zealand. Two companies operate daily whale-watching tours from there. The main attraction is the sperm whale, which is the largest toothed whale on earth, but there's also a lot of other beautiful wildlife to be seen on the tours: Hector's dolphin (the smallest and rarest of all dolphins), the dusky dolphin (found only in the southern hemisphere, often in huge groups), the NZ fur seal, the orca or killer whale (the largest of all dolphins), common dolphin, pilot whale, blue penguin, the royal albatross, mollymawk and many other sea birds.

Nature being what it is, there's no guarantee of seeing any specific animal on any one tour, but it's fairly certain that something of interest will be out there any time you go. In general, the sperm whales are most likely to be seen from October to August, and orcas from December to March. Most of the other animals are seen all year round.

# Aerial Sightseeing & Skydiving

Planes and helicopters abound in all parts of New Zealand, and there are plenty of pilots willing to take you for sightseeing trips (called flightseeing by the locals).

The incredible contrast in scenery and the spectacular mountain ranges make this one of the best places for aerial sightseeing. Some of the best trips are around the Bay of Islands, the Bay of Plenty, Tongariro National Park and Taranaki in the North Island, and Mt Cook and the West Coast glaciers and fiords in the South Island. You can even arrange to be flown up to the top of the glacial ski fields, from where you have a clear run all the way down to the bottom.

If you get down to the south-western coast of the South Island, try to fit in a flight up the fiords; the scenery is sensational and you can often combine the flight with a trip on the water to see other places of interest.

Most aerial sightseeing companies operate from the local aerodrome. Ask at the local tourist office for information; in some places you can just turn up at the aerodrome during daylight hours and arrange a trip on the spot.

A lot of the aerial sightseeing companies also operate skydiving courses and trips, but you will usually have to book in advance.

# Mazes

For some reason, Kiwis are mad on mazes, and there are some spectacular ones built as tourist attractions around the country. When they tired of ordinary mazes they made three-dimensional ones, most of which are incredibly convoluted – the original three-dimensional maze, at Wanaka in the South Island, can take hours to work through. There's even a waterslide maze at the Olympic swimming pool in Dunedin.

The Fairbank Maze, opposite the airport at Rotorua, is the largest hedge maze in New Zealand, with a 1.6 km pathway. Te Ngae Park, 3 km beyond the Rotorua airport, is a three-dimensional, 1.7 km wooden maze similar to the one at Wanaka.

Admission to the mazes is usually only $3 or $4 for adults and $1 or $2 for children, making them cheap entertainment. There are usually other facilities that make them great fun for families.

Recently New Zealand has even started to export its mazes, a maze craze has developed in Japan where Kiwi consultants advise on the designs.

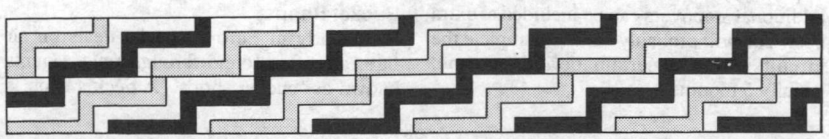

# Getting There

## AIR

The overwhelming majority of visitors to New Zealand fly there. There are three airports that handle international flights – Auckland, Wellington and Christchurch. Most international flights go through Auckland; certainly if you're flying from the USA you're going to arrive in Auckland. Wellington airport has limited runway capacity and international flights are all to and from Australia. Flights to and from Christchurch are also mainly with Australia although there are some connections to other countries.

There are some special ticket types and definitions which may be of interest to visitors to New Zealand:

### Circle Pacific Tickets

These tickets let you circle the Pacific using a combination of airlines. You can start and finish the circle at any point, from the US west coast, via various islands in the Pacific to New Zealand, on to Australia, to Asia and back to the west coast. Typically the fare for a Circle Pacific ticket is around A$2355 or US$2020.

A Circle Pacific route offered by Air New Zealand in conjunction with Singapore Airlines or Cathay Pacific allows you to start from Los Angeles, with Air New Zealand, and fly to Honolulu, then on to Auckland and later continue to Sydney. From Sydney you could switch to Singapore Airlines to fly back to Los Angeles via Singapore, Bangkok, Hong Kong or Taipei. There are countless alternatives.

Circle Pacific tickets usually have some sort of advance purchase requirement and there will probably be restrictions on changing your route once you've bought the ticket. Typically, you're allowed four stopovers but additional stopovers can be included at extra cost. You will probably have to complete the circuit within a certain period of time, usually 6 months.

### Round the World Tickets

Round the World (RTW) tickets can be very useful to visit New Zealand in combination with other destinations. They work particularly well from Europe – having come halfway round the world to New Zealand in one direction you might just as well continue the same way!

RTW tickets usually combine the routes of two airlines. Air New Zealand offers RTW tickets in combination with Singapore Airlines, British Airways, Cathay Pacific, Lufthansa, Thai International and various other airlines. As with Circle Pacific tickets you can join the loop at various places round the world. They typically cost around A$3165, US$2590 or £1600, and you could use a RTW ticket to make stops in Australia, New Zealand, the USA and Europe.

Apart from the official airline RTW tickets there are also RTW combinations put together by travel agents. Out of London, for example, they might put together a combination such as a cheap flight to Asia, hooking up with the popular and heavily discounted UTA trans-Pacific route and then another cheap fare back to London from the USA.

### Advance Purchase Excursion Tickets

Many low fare tickets are Advance Purchase Excursion tickets, which must be booked and paid for in advance (usually 21 days), and once you've entered that advance purchase period you're locked in to your outward and return dates and can only make changes at additional cost. It is possible to insure against some eventualities so that if, for example, you're suddenly taken ill and cannot take your flight you don't lose your fare. Check the small print carefully on Advance Purchase Excursion fares.

### Bucket Shops

Particularly in Europe special deals on air fares are often found through travel agents known as 'bucket shops'. A bucket shop is an agent specialising in discounted tickets. These tickets are usually quite legitimate, as they're tickets which the airline is unable to sell at the full listed fare. Since a normal travel agent cannot sell tickets to some customers at one price and to others at another the airline releases some tickets at a special lower price through selected agents.

The more obscure the airline or the more inconvenient the route the bigger the discount is likely to be. Although it's really only in Europe that ticket discounters are known as bucket shops, similar operations can also be found in the USA, Australia, Hong Kong and in many other places. To find a ticket discounter simply scan the travel ads in the travel pages of newspapers.

## From Australia

The number of air routes between Australia and New Zealand has proliferated in the last few years. The NZ cities with flights to or from Australia are Auckland, Christchurch and Wellington. Australian cities with flights to or from New Zealand are Adelaide, Brisbane, Cairns, Darwin, Hobart, Melbourne, Perth, Sydney and Townsville. Examples of regular one-way economy fares are from Sydney to Auckland, Christchurch or Wellington A$425; from Melbourne to Auckland, Christchurch or Wellington A$491. Fares from Brisbane or Hobart are similar, from Adelaide to Auckland is slightly more.

It's much cheaper to take an advance purchase fare which can get you to New Zealand and back for little more than a regular one-way fare. With these fares you must book and pay for your ticket at least 7 days prior to departure and once the tickets are issued cancellation charges apply should you wish to change your reservation or if you fail to fly. Insurance is available to protect against the advance purchase cancellation fees. You must stay in New Zealand for at least 6 days but at most 120 days.

The fare depends on the day you fly out as well as where you fly to and from. The year is divided up into peak, shoulder and off-peak times. If you fly out during the off-peak

season (June and July) the return fare can be as low as A$572 from Sydney, A$552 from Melbourne. If you want to go out during peak season (mid-December to mid-January) the fare from Sydney will be A$660, from Melbourne A$725. At other times of year the fare falls between these high and low rates.

There's a cheaper Advance Purchase Excursion fare which you must book and pay for a month ahead; tickets cost A$347 one way, A$469 off-peak return and A$499 high season return.

It pays to plan your flight dates carefully – if you were planning to visit New Zealand in the summer, leaving just a few days earlier in December or later in January could save you about A$85.

If you're travelling from Australia to the US west coast via New Zealand, the one-way fare from Melbourne, Sydney or Brisbane can be as low as A$1145. Return fares vary with the season and vary from A$1599 to A$1849 out of Sydney or Melbourne. The Circle Pacific fares ex-Australia are A$2355 and the RTW fares are A$3165.

## From the USA

Regular economy return fares from the US west coast are US$2515 to New Zealand or US$3035 to New Zealand and on to Australia. There are two cheaper excursion fares available, the lower priced of the two has more restrictions and advance purchase requirements. To New Zealand the cheaper excursion fare is US$970 in the low season, US$1400 in the high season. The more expensive excursion fare is US$1170 and US$1550. The same excursion fares to Australia are all US$125 more expensive. Cheaper 'short life' fares are frequently offered, for only limited periods.

You can do better than these straightforward fares with travel agents. The Sunday travel sections of papers like the *New York Times*, the *Los Angeles Times* or the *San Francisco Examiner* always have plenty of ads for cheap airline tickets and there are always good deals on flights across the Pacific. Council Travel and STA, the two student travel specialists, both have good fares on offer. Examples of discounted trans-Pacific fares are west coast-Auckland-west coast for about US$750.

If you're interested in visiting other Pacific destinations on your way to or from New Zealand, compare the stopover possibilities offered by each airline. Air New Zealand flights from the USA to New Zealand offer a maximum of six stopovers, for no extra cost. Other airlines fly to New Zealand for the same price but with more limited stopover options.

## From Europe

There has always been cut-throat competition between London's many 'bucket shops' and London is an important European centre for cheap fares. There are plenty of bucket shops in London and although there are always some untrustworthy operators most of them are fine. You'll find advertisements from agents and examples of their fares in the various London give-away papers like the *Australasian Express*. The weekly 'what's on' magazine *Time Out* has plenty of travel ads and they also give some useful advice on precautions to take when dealing with bucket shops. The magazine *Business Traveller* is another good source of information and advice on discount fares. Two good low-fare specialists are Trailfinders at 42-48 Earls Court Rd, London W8 and STA Travel at 74 and 86 Old Brompton Rd, London SW7 and at 117 Euston Rd, London NW1.

London-Auckland return tickets can be found in London bucket shops for around £700. Some stopovers are permitted on this sort of ticket. Since New Zealand is about as far from Europe as you can get, it's not that much more to fly right on round the world rather than backtracking. The regular airline RTW tickets that go through the South Pacific generally cost around £1575 but agents can organise an RTW route from around £900.

## From Asia

There are far more flights to New Zealand from Asia than there were only a few years ago. From Tokyo, Japan Advance Purchase return fares vary from around 250,000 to 330,000 yen depending on the season. From Kuala Lumpur, Malaysia, you can get return fares for around M$2500 and Malaysia is a very popular place for fare discounting. From Singapore return fares go from around S$2200. Hong Kong is another popular fare discounting centre and discounted return tickets to New Zealand cost around HK$8590 in the high season, HK$7070 in the low season.

## SEA

Cruise ships apart there are no longer any regular passenger ship services to New Zealand and these days arriving on some romantic tramp steamer (something you can still do in various Pacific Island nations) is pretty much a thing of the past. Ditto for the idea of working your passage. But if you're adventurous, flexible and persistent, finding a berth on a yacht is a real possibility.

## Yachts

New Zealand is one of the most enthusiastic yachting nations on earth (look at how they did when they first had a go at the America's

Cup) and it's also a very popular destination for yachts cruising the South Pacific.

There are lots of yachts cruising back and forth in the Pacific and they're very often looking for crew. After all sailing along with just a couple of people soon gets to be boring and hard work, much better to take somebody on in port A, drop them off in port B and recruit somebody else to give a hand from port B to C. Of course yachties would like to have somebody fully skilled in ocean sailing but since those sort of people aren't always waiting round looking for boats quite often the requirements are simply that you're an easy-going, hard working, non-complaining type and that you're willing to chip in money for the food you eat.

To find a yacht you have to go to the appropriate port at the appropriate time. There are lots of favourite islands, ports and harbours where you're likely to find yachts. Examples are Sydney and Cairns in Australia; Bali in Indonesia; various ports in Fiji or Tahiti; Hawaii, San Diego or San Francisco in the USA. In New Zealand, popular yachting harbours are the Bay of Islands and Whangarei (both in Northland), Auckland and Wellington.

Yachts tend to move around the Pacific with the calendar – they sail with the prevailing winds, they stay out of the typhoon areas when it's cyclone season so there are certain times when you're more likely to find yachts. From Fiji October-November is a peak departure season as cyclones are on their way. March-April is the main departure season for yachts heading to Australia. Be prepared for rough seas and storms crossing the Tasman Sea.

To find a yacht looking for crew simply scan notice boards in popular ports, ask at yacht clubs, actually ask around the yachts at their anchorages or check newspaper ads. In Auckland try the *New Zealand Herald* personal columns under 'crew'.

## LEAVING NEW ZEALAND

As from other countries scan the travel small ads for air fare bargains. Typical return fares offered from Auckland (at the height of the summer season) include London $1789, US west coast $1069 to $1299, Singapore $1215, Hong Kong $1285, Honolulu $699, Fiji $549, Sydney $489, Brisbane $555 and Melbourne $535.

### Departure Tax

There's a $15 departure tax at the airport.

# Getting Around

## AIR

Air travel within New Zealand went through quite a revolution in 1987. Once upon a time the government-owned Air New Zealand had more-or-less a monopoly on the major routes around the country. The only competition was Mt Cook Airlines which basically flew between major tourist destinations like Mt Cook, Queenstown and Rotorua. Then Australia's Ansett Airlines, partly owned by expansion-minded media mogul Rupert Murdoch, took a large interest in Newmans Air and created a new airline called Ansett New Zealand. At first it operated a network very similar to Mt Cook but in mid-1987 a batch of Boeing 737s were added to the fleet and Ansett New Zealand started head-on competition with Air New Zealand.

Having things all to themselves had made Air New Zealand rather complacent and the high standards of service passengers enjoy on their international routes certainly didn't apply to domestic passengers. Ansett started up with economy and 1st class service and in reply Air New Zealand quickly added an upper class to their previously all-economy operation. The two airlines continue to compete – one will offer a special fare or service, and the other usually tries to match or better it.

Most of the smaller airlines – Mt Cook Airline, Eagle Air, Air Nelson, Southern Air, Bell Air and Safe Air – are partly owned by Air New Zealand. Combined with Air New Zealand and a host of connecting flights, the network covers the country quite completely, while Ansett's coverage is more limited.

Air New Zealand has regular listed economy fares, but it also has discounts which make it virtually unnecessary to ever have to pay the full fare. The Thrifty Fare gives a 40% discount off the regular fare, while the Super Thrifty Fare provides a whopping 50% discount. These fares are available on a designated number of seats on most flights, the exception being peak flying times such as commuter flights on Monday mornings. The requirements are easy to meet, all you have to do is book and pay for your ticket at least 1 day prior to flight. The best way to get a chance at the Thrifty Fare and Super Thrifty Fare seats is to book a few days in advance, and to have some flexibility on which flights you can take – going a couple of hours or a day earlier or later could save 50% on cost. There's also a 30% Off Peak Saver discount which applies on all flights except those at the busiest times.

The Domestic Air Fares chart shows fares in NZ dollars on some of the main Air New Zealand routes, with prices ranging from the lowest to the highest possible fare. If you purchase your tickets before you arrive in New Zealand you can get further savings, as the government's GST, which is now $12\frac{1}{2}\%$ and may rise to 15%, is charged when you buy the tickets in New Zealand but not if you purchase them overseas.

For overseas visitors Air New Zealand has a special Visit New Zealand fare which can only be purchased prior to arrival and in conjunction with your international flight. The ticket allows four flights for $370 or six flights for $495.

Mt Cook has a Kiwi Air Pass which gives you 30 days almost unlimited travel on Mt Cook Airline services for $799 (children $599). The only restriction is that you can only fly once in each direction on each of their scheduled flights. This pass is available only to overseas visitors, but you can buy it either outside the country or after you arrive in New Zealand.

Although New Zealand is a compact country and ground transport is generally quite good there are still places where flying can make a lot of sense, particularly if you've already done the same journey by land. Travellers have quoted examples of trips between the North and South islands where a long bus trip is followed by the inter-island ferry and

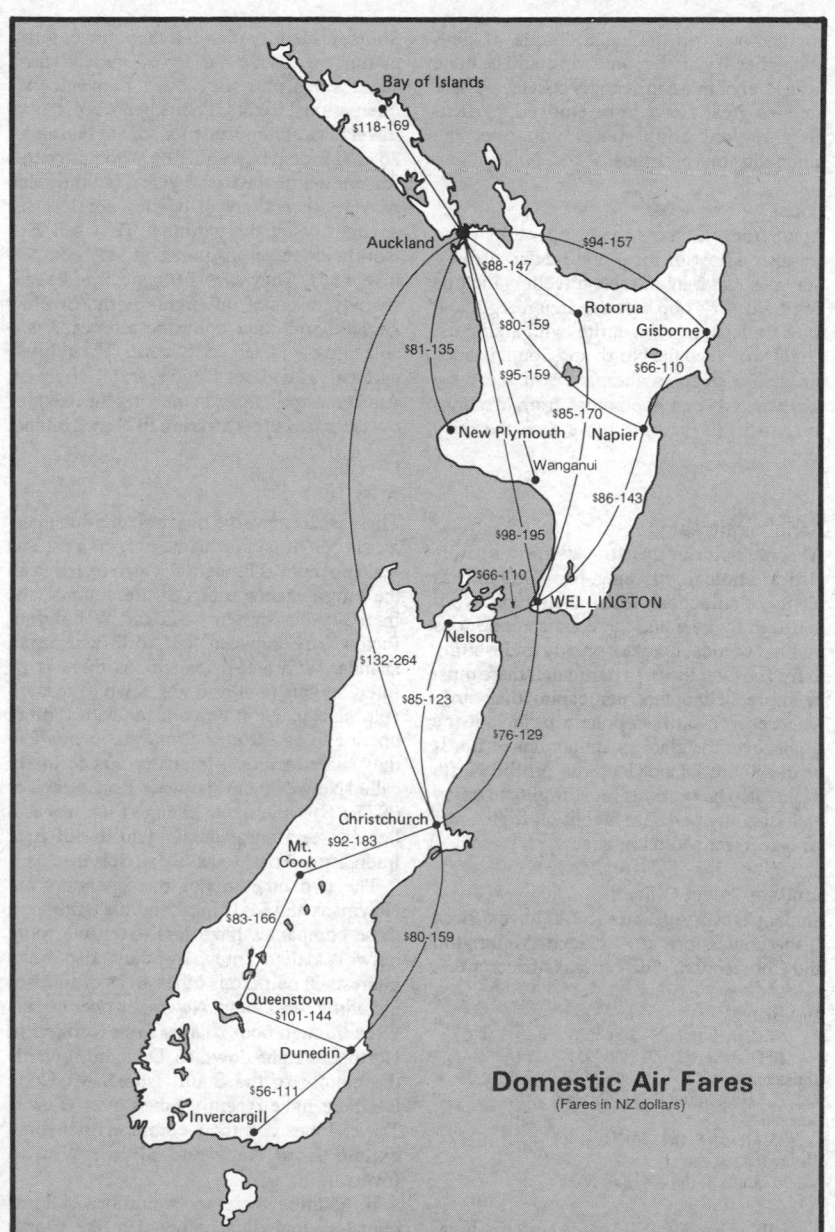

Bay of Islands
$118-169

Auckland
$88-147
$94-157
Rotorua
$80-159
Gisborne
$81-135
$66-110
$95-159
$85-170
New Plymouth    Napier
Wanganui
$86-143
$98-195
$66-110
WELLINGTON
Nelson
$132-264
$85-123
$76-129
Christchurch
$92-183
Mt.
Cook
$83-166
$80-159
Queenstown
$101-144
Dunedin
$56-111
Invercargill

**Domestic Air Fares**
(Fares in NZ dollars)

another bus trip, taking a couple of days altogether. By air the same trip could be done in an hour or two and actually cost less. There are also great views to be enjoyed, particularly if your flight takes you over the mountains or volcanoes.

## Local Air Services

Apart from the three major operators there are also a host of local and feeder airlines. Services that may interest travellers include Southern Air's hop between Invercargill and Stewart Island, a favourite with trampers. Flights between the North and South islands are also a popular alternative to the ferry services, you can hop across from Wellington to Picton for little more than the ferry fare.

## Aerial Sightseeing

At some point in their travels most visitors also do a little flightseeing. New Zealand has plenty of attractions which are simply wonderful to fly over and there are an enormous number of local operators ready and waiting to fly you over them. In particular, there must be more helicopters per capita than anywhere else on earth. Popular trips include the flights over the glaciers, mountains or fiords of the South Island. Rotorua on the North Island also has various local flights to enjoy including my personal favourite, flights in a vintage Tiger Moth biplane.

## Student Travel Offices

Student Travel Agencies (STA) have offices at the universities at Auckland, Wellington and Christchurch. Off-campus offices are:

Auckland
      64 High St (tel (09) 390-458)
      10 High St (tel (09) 399-995)
Christchurch
      223 High St (tel (03) 799-098)
Dunedin
      32 Albany St (tel (24) 740-146)
Wellington
      207 Cuba St (tel (04) 850-561)

As well as issuing ISIC cards (International Student Identity Cards) they have information on a wide variety of student travel concessions plus they book domestic and international flights. Their cheapest discount travel rates are for students, for anyone under 26, and for anyone under 35 who has been a student within the past 5 years, but they also provide general travel agency services for anyone outside these groups. They sell ISIS worldwide travel insurance at very competitive rates. They also offer a 50% student standby discount on flights with Air New Zealand and other domestic airlines, available only with an ISIC card. Their International Travellers Centre at 10 High St, Auckland specialises in meeting the needs of overseas travellers arriving in New Zealand.

## BUS

There is an extensive bus network that operates in conjunction with the rail services. The main operator is InterCity, which operates all the long-distance trains in the country, the InterCity bus system, and the Wellington-Picton ferry between the North and South islands. With a few exceptions there is an InterCity bus to almost any town of reasonable size in New Zealand and they often operate to and from railway stations where they share facilities. InterCity was formerly called New Zealand Railways Road Services (NZRRS) – the name change took place in late '87 and occasionally you'll still hear InterCity referred to as 'Road Services'.

The two other major bus operators are Newmans and Mt Cook Landline. Although these companies have less extensive route networks than InterCity they also have interests in numerous other areas of tourism including local tours. Newmans operate services through both islands from Kerikeri in Northland right down to Dunedin towards the bottom of the South Island. Mt Cook Landline have recently taken over H & H Travel Lines and their combined networks extend from Auckland all the way to Invercargill.

In addition there are a number of local operators including companies like Clarks

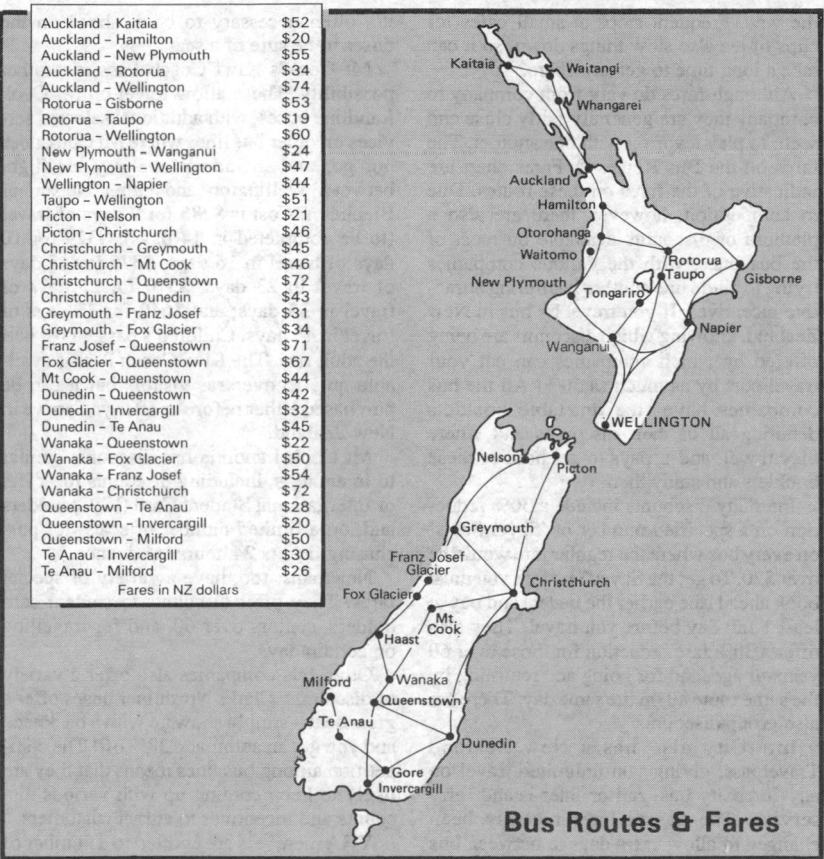

| | |
|---|---|
| Auckland – Kaitaia | $52 |
| Auckland – Hamilton | $20 |
| Auckland – New Plymouth | $55 |
| Auckland – Rotorua | $34 |
| Auckland – Wellington | $74 |
| Rotorua – Gisborne | $53 |
| Rotorua – Taupo | $19 |
| Rotorua – Wellington | $60 |
| New Plymouth – Wanganui | $24 |
| New Plymouth – Wellington | $47 |
| Wellington – Napier | $44 |
| Taupo – Wellington | $51 |
| Picton – Nelson | $21 |
| Picton – Christchurch | $46 |
| Christchurch – Greymouth | $45 |
| Christchurch – Mt Cook | $46 |
| Christchurch – Queenstown | $72 |
| Christchurch – Dunedin | $43 |
| Greymouth – Franz Josef | $31 |
| Greymouth – Fox Glacier | $34 |
| Franz Josef – Queenstown | $71 |
| Fox Glacier – Queenstown | $67 |
| Mt Cook – Queenstown | $44 |
| Dunedin – Queenstown | $42 |
| Dunedin – Invercargill | $32 |
| Dunedin – Te Anau | $45 |
| Wanaka – Queenstown | $22 |
| Wanaka – Fox Glacier | $50 |
| Wanaka – Franz Josef | $54 |
| Wanaka – Christchurch | $72 |
| Queenstown – Te Anau | $28 |
| Queenstown – Invercargill | $20 |
| Queenstown – Milford | $50 |
| Te Anau – Invercargill | $30 |
| Te Anau – Milford | $26 |

Fares in NZ dollars

**Bus Routes & Fares**

Northliner which operate between Auckland and the Bay of Islands; Mainline Coachways which operate from Auckland to the Bay of Plenty, Rotorua and Taupo; or Delta Coachlines which connect Picton and the West Coast on the South Island.

Services on the main routes usually run at least once a day, except on Sundays when some services don't operate at all. Where there is another service operating on the same route as InterCity, the InterCity buses will usually operate more often. The Getting There & Away section of each chapter has more information on buses.

Although bus travel is relatively easy and well organised it can be expensive and time consuming. Bus fares, like everything else in New Zealand, have jumped considerably in recent years and these days it pays to consider the alternatives carefully. Sometimes buying a car can actually work out cheaper than travelling by bus (see the Driving section). Bus trips can also be slow and time consuming. This problem seems particularly prevalent on the once-a-day InterCity services where the bus also operates as a means of local communication, picking up and dropping off mail at every little town along the way. Frequent stops at small cafes for cups of tea also slow things down, so it can take a long time to get anywhere.

Although fares do vary from company to company they are generally fairly close and seem to play leapfrog with one another. The fares on the Bus Routes & Fares chart are indicative of the fares on these routes. Due to competition, however, there are also a plethora of discounts available on most of the bus lines, with the various companies trying to outdo one another in offering attractive incentives. If you travel by bus in New Zealand, knowing which discounts are being offered by which companies can cut your travel cost by as much as 50%! All the bus companies have free timetable booklets detailing all of their discounts and where they travel, and it pays to get hold of these booklets and study them.

InterCity discounts include a 30% reduction on a specified number of 'Saver Seats' on every bus where the regular fare would be over $20. To get the Saver Seat fare you must book ahead (the earlier the better) and pay at least 1 full day before you travel. They also offer a 30% fare reduction for those over 60 years of age, and for going and returning by the same route all on the same day. There are also group discounts.

InterCity also has a New Zealand Travelpass, giving you unlimited travel on any InterCity bus, rail or inter-island ferry service. The passes have recently been changed to allow extra days in between bus trips – for example, you have 14 days in which to use the 8 day Travelpass, rather than having to travel every day for 8 days. Cost for the Travelpass is $299 for 8 days of travel (to be completed in 14 days), $389 for 15 days of travel (completed in 22 days), or $479 for 22 days of travel (completed in 31 days).

As with any unlimited travel pass of this type you have to do lots of travelling to make it pay off – they're best for people whose time is limited and want to see a lot in a short time. If you feel a Travelpass is what you'll need, be prepared to do a lot of pre-planning to work out an itinerary you can stick to. Also it's often necessary to book ahead on the buses to be sure of a seat.

Mt Cook's Kiwi Coach Pass is another possibility. These allow travel on Mt Cook Landline buses, with additional selected services on other bus lines where Mt Cook does not go, and include a one-way air flight between Wellington and either Nelson or Blenheim. Cost is $285 for 7 days of travel (to be completed in 14 days); $329 for 10 days of travel in 16 days; $375 for 15 days of travel in 23 days; $570 for 25 days of travel in 35 days; and $640 for 33 days of travel in 45 days. Children's passes cost half the adult rate. The Kiwi Coach Pass is available only to overseas visitors but it can be purchased either before or after you arrive in New Zealand.

Mt Cook Landline has discounts similar to InterCity's, including discounts for YHA or International Student Card (ISIC) holders and, on a limited number of seats, for purchasing tickets 24 hours in advance.

Newmans, too, have a variety of special fares. They offer discounts to student card holders, seniors over 60, and for travelling on certain days.

Other bus companies also offer a variety of discounts. Clarks Northliner buses offer a great deal – simply show up with a backpack and you get an automatic 30% off! The competition among bus lines means that they are likely to keep coming up with various discounts and incentives to attract customers.

YHA members are entitled to a number of useful discounts on transport, including 30% off on all Newmans bus fares or 25% off on Mt Cook buses. YHA also offers a Travelcard good for a hefty 50% fare reduction for unlimited travel on all InterCity bus, rail and ferry services. The Travelcard costs $75 for 14 days or $99 for 28 days. See YHA Hostels section in the Facts for the Visitor chapter for additional YHA discounts and benefits.

### 'Alternative' Buses

In addition to the regular bus services, several 'alternative' bus companies operate tours lasting several days in various parts of the country. In some places, notably the East Cape of the North Island and the West Coast of the South Island, these can be the best way of seeing the area if you don't have your own wheels, as hitchhiking is difficult and the more conventional bus services simply whiz past many of the most attractive spots. Most of these buses operate only in summer, from approximately October-November until April-May. A notable exception is the West Coast Express, which operates all year round. Other buses could probably begin to run all year round as well if there was sufficient demand.

On all of these trips, the buses are comfortably fitted out, the atmosphere is casual and there are plenty of stops to see the sights along the way, plus stops for walks, picnics, boat cruises, recreational activities and so on. Usually all you need to bring is a sleeping bag, plus the usual travelling gear such as good walking shoes, warm clothes and rain gear, and your own food. Accommodation costs are extra; low-cost overnight accommodation is pre-booked, usually at hostels (cost is about $8 to $12 a night), with an option to camp if you have your own tent ($5 or $6 a night). The exception is the Flying Kiwi bus, a 'rolling travellers home' which comes equipped with 18 bunks.

All of the buses have pamphlets detailing their itineraries, departure times, and costs. Listed here are the buses, where they go, and the contacts for further information and to make bookings. All require advance booking, and usually a deposit. Be sure you understand the deposit refund policy when you make your booking, in case you decide to cancel later on.

Starting from North Island, the Northcape Shuttle departs from Auckland weekly for a 6 day journey through Northland, all the way up to Cape Reinga with stops at the Bay of Islands and many other places. Cost is $150. Contact in Auckland: Ann or John (tel 817-8675), the Parnell Youth Hostel (tel 790-258) or STA Travel (tel 399-995).

The East Cape Fun Etc Bus takes 4 days to go around the East Cape. You can depart from either Rotorua or Gisborne, getting off at the other end ($109) or making a complete return trip back to the starting point ($129). For bookings in Rotorua, contact the NZTP Travel Office (tel 485-179).

The Kiwi Experience bus runs between Auckland and Wellington. South from Auckland it takes 4 days and costs $99; north from Wellington takes 2 days and costs $69; or you can do a complete round trip (the bus takes different routes each way) for $150, a 6 day journey. In early '90 they were planning to expand into the South Island and to more parts of the North Island. For bookings, in Auckland, you could contact the following: Parnell Youth Hostel (tel 790-258), Ivanhoe Lodge (tel 862-800), YHA Travel (tel 794-224) or NZTP (tel 798-180). In Wellington, phone the Youth Hostel (tel 736-271) or NZTP (tel 728-860). In Picton phone Pavlova Backpackers (tel 36-598).

Moving down to the South Island, there's the great grand-daddy of the alternative buses, the West Coast Express, which takes 6 days (5 days in winter) to go between Nelson and Queenstown via (of course) the West Coast route. This was the first such bus in New Zealand, and its great success (it's still the most popular) brought all the others to jump on the bandwagon. Cost is $99 and you can depart from either end of the line. For bookings in Nelson contact the Nelson Youth Hostel (tel 88-817) or Tasman Towers (tel 87-950). In Queenstown contact the Queenstown Youth Hostel (tel 442-8413) or Bumbles Hostel (tel 442-6298).

Also travelling the West Coast route between Nelson and Queenstown, and also taking 6 days to do it, is Magic Bus. Cost is $109, or $99 if you book a week in advance. For bookings in Nelson, contact Bumbles Hostel (tel 442-6298) and in Queenstown, the Information and Track Walking Centre (tel 442-7867).

The Shoestring Travel bus makes a circle of the central part of the South Island. Departing from Christchurch, it takes 5 days to reach Queenstown, heading westwards from Christchurch through Arthur's Pass to Greymouth and then down the West Coast. The fare to Queenstown is $95. The bus then

The West Coast Express

continues from Queenstown back to Christchurch, all in 1 day. The fare to make this leg of the journey separately is $29, or it's $124 for the full round trip. For bookings in Christchurch, contact Trailblazers (tel 666-033) and in Queenstown the FAB (Families and Backpackers) Hostel (tel 442-6095).

Finally there's the Flying Kiwi Bus (tel Picton 38-126), the 'rolling travellers home', taking 18 days to do a rather extended circuit of the South Island, departing from Picton (their schedule tends to vary from year to year). The $580 cost includes accommodation (a bunk on the bus).

All of these alternative buses were operating during the early '90 summer season, at which time there was a boom period, with several in their first year of operation. If they all prove successful, they'll probably stick around and plenty of others will probably pop up too. Some may last for just a season.

## TRAIN

Railways in New Zealand are operated by the InterCity bus, rail and ferry network. In recent years the train service has been streamlined (minor routes and many minor stops discontinued) and now there are just a few main train routes: Auckland to Wellington, Wellington to Napier, Picton to Christchurch, Christchurch to Invercargill, and Christchurch to Greymouth. See the relevant city sections for details. On a map you'll notice quite a number of other branch railways, but don't be deceived – most of them no longer have any passenger trains. The elimination of many of the smaller halts has made train travel a reasonably speedy method of getting from place to place, and the trains are generally modern and comfortable.

Train fares are generally around the same price as bus fares on the same routes, usually just a couple of dollars different if at all. The InterCity Travelpass, described in the section on buses, also provides unlimited use of the country's railway services. The various InterCity Saver discounts also apply to the trains.

## SEA
### Inter-Island Ferries
Between Wellington and Picton there are at

least four services daily in each direction, sometimes more at peak seasons. The ferries are the *Aratika* and the newer *Arahura*. They handle passengers and vehicles and the crossing takes about 3 hours. It can get pretty rough so if you're prone to seasickness come prepared. If it's not too crowded or the sea too rough the crossing can be quite comfortable. It's best to do the trip in daylight, if the weather's good, to see Wellington Harbour and the Marlborough Sounds. Watch out for dolphins during the crossing.

Fares vary with the seasons, see the Wellington chapter for details. You can take a vehicle across but it's important in that case to reserve your space in advance, especially during holiday periods.

A number of travellers have made recommendations about what to do with your baggage and how to make a quick exit after the ferry docks. 'Don't put your pack in the luggage vans if you can avoid it,' wrote one traveller. Because, 'if you are able to hang on to your pack, you can get off the other end without delays – no waiting around for hours until the luggage is unloaded.' Other travellers have reported that the luggage vans are off very quickly, however.

Another traveller warned that cars start driving off almost the second the ferry docks so if you're hitching and have not prearranged a ride all the cars will be on the road out of Picton by the time your feet hit dry land. More seriously there have been reports of backpacks being gone through and valuables stolen during the crossing. Don't leave your camera or other important items in your pack.

The Wellington Ferry Terminal is about 20 minutes walk from Wellington Railway Station or there's a connecting bus service between the bus station and the ferry. In Picton the terminal is right in town.

## DRIVING

Driving around New Zealand is no problem – the roads are good and very well signposted. Traffic is light and distances are short. Petrol (gasoline) is expensive – at around $1 a litre, that's about US$2.50 for a US gallon. Prices vary slightly from station to station, city to countryside, but only by a few cents. Prices in early 1990 were ranging from around 87 cents to 97 cents for Super.

Kiwis drive on the left, as in the UK, Australia, Japan and most of South-East Asia, and there's a 'give way to the right' rule, similar to that in Australia. This is interpreted in a rather strange fashion when you want to turn left and an oncoming vehicle is turning right into the same street. Since the oncoming vehicle is then on your right you have to give way to them. Ask a New Zealander to explain it to you before setting off! This rule is interpreted the same way in some states of Australia, notably Victoria. Some visitors have commented that NZ driving is terrible but I think most people find the driving in other countries terrible in one way or another.

The AA publishes an inexpensive 'Road Code' booklet which explains all of New Zealand's driving laws and rules. It's available for $4 from any AA office. The AA offers many other benefits for drivers; see the Tourist Information section in the Facts for the Visitor chapter for more on the AA.

To drive in New Zealand you need an international driving permit or an ordinary licence from a major country. Drivers licences from Australia, UK, USA, Canada, the Netherlands, Switzerland, Germany, South Africa and Fiji are all honoured in New Zealand. International drivers licences are obtained from the AA. If you want to drive a motorcycle over 50cc in size, you must have a special motorcycle licence.

Speed limits on the open road are generally 100 kph, in built up areas the limit is usually 50 kph although in some smaller towns you may see a sign announcing LSZ. This means Limited Speed Zone and the rule is that although there is no stated limit (except for the overall 100 kph limit) if anything happens you'd better have a good excuse for going as fast as you were!

Excellent road maps are readily available in New Zealand. If you're a member of the AA you can go into any AA office, present your card, and get all the maps you want for free. They also have larger road atlases, which you have to buy. Otherwise the Shell Road Atlas is also excellent. The Department of Land & Survey Information (DOSLI), which publishes topographical and other maps good for trampers (see Tramping in the Outdoor Activities chapter), also publishes various good highway and city maps.

## Car Rental

The major operators – Avis, Budget, Hertz – have extensive fleets of cars in New Zealand with offices in almost every town of any size. Typical costs for unlimited distance rental of a small car (Toyota Corolla, Mitsubishi Mirage) are around $125 to $150 per day with a minimum rental of 3 days. Medium sized cars (Toyota Corona, Ford Telstar) are typically around $150 to $190 per day with unlimited km. In addition there's a daily insurance charge of around $17 a day. All sorts of special deals are available including long weekends, extended hire periods and special discounts if you use certain credit cards.

Apart from the three major international operators there are also a number of other large operators like Thrifty, Dollar or Southern Cross. Plus there are numerous purely local rental operators, found only in certain cities. Their rates often undercut the major operators but there may be more restrictions on use and one-way rentals may not always be possible. Always compare all the costs – one operator's daily charge may be $5 less than another's but their daily insurance might be $5 more. Be careful when comparing daily rates plus a km distance charge with a straight unlimited km charge.

Sometimes you may find special one-way rentals available when the company ends up with too many cars banked up at one place and too few at another. Operators always want cars to be shifted from Wellington to Auckland and from Christchurch to Picton – most renters travel in the opposite directions. Usually you must be at least 21 years old to rent a car in New Zealand and sometimes there will be an insurance excess if you're under 25.

## Campervan Rental

Renting a campervan (also known as mobile homes, motor homes or, in US parlance, RVs) has become an enormously popular way of getting around New Zealand. In some touristically popular, but out-of-the-way areas of the South Island almost every other vehicle seems to be a campervan.

There are numerous companies renting campervans and their costs vary with the type of vehicle and the time of year. Unlike rental cars, which are used for business as well as pleasure, campervans are strictly a pleasure business so demand, and hence costs, depend heavily on the tourist seasons.

Campervans are typically Japanese light commercial vehicles modified locally and equipped with beds, a dining area, cooking facilities, a fridge, a sink with foot operated water system and storage space. Usually the table in the dining area folds down and the seatback cushions rearrange to make a couple of beds at night, one or two more are accommodated in a compartment above the driving cabin. They usually come well-equipped – there'll be towels, bedding, cooking utensils, plates, bowls, knives and forks and so on.

With a campervan you have your transport and accommodation all in one neat package. At night you just find one of New Zealand's excellent camping sites, connect up to the camping site power system, put a bucket under the drain from the sink and you're at home. Of course you don't even have to find a camping site, you can simply find a quiet place off the road in many areas. Apart from transport and accommodation you've also got your own kitchen on wheels – the cooking facilities are sufficient to fix most simple meals so you don't have to worry about finding a restaurant or affording their costs.

Maui Campas are one of the larger campervan operators and their choice of vehicles and rental costs are fairly typical. As with the other operators their costs vary with the season. Costs drop to their lowest level in the mid-May to mid-October winter season, climb up in spring (mid-October to mid-December) or the autumn (mid-January to mid-May). The summer plus school holiday plus Christmas period from mid-December to mid-January is the worst time of the year when costs can be two to three times the winter rate.

Starting at the bottom the typical daily costs for a Maui Hi-Top, going by the seasons, are $90, $133 or $183 with a minimum 6 day hire. This vehicle is a Toyota Hi-ace with a raised roof area. It's really only large enough for two, although you might squeeze a third, small person in. A Maui Mini-Campa is a Mitsubishi L300 which costs $97, $146 or $216. This one is billed as a two plus two but the plus two should be very small children as you'll be cramped with two larger children and four adults would find it impossible. Both these smaller vehicles are powered by petrol engines.

The Maui Campa, a diesel-powered Mitsubishi FB100, costs $107, $155 or $239. This one is fine for a couple with two children or even for four adults. Finally there's the Maui Travel Deluxe which not only can accommodate six people but also has a shower, a chemical toilet, a water heater and a gas oven. The vehicle is a Mitsubishi FE100 and costs are $133, $179 or $234.

While researching the South Island section of the fifth edition of this book I used a Maui Campa and it worked just fine. The four of us, two adults, a 6 year old and 4 year old, had plenty of room, day or night. In fact we had so much room that several times along the West Coast we could pick up all a town's hitchhikers in one go!

Other campervan operators include Newmans, Endeavour, Blue Sky, Adventure Vans, Suntrek, Mt Cook Line and Horizon. There's some variance in vehicle types and costs but each operator has colour brochures explaining all about their campervans and what they have to offer. Although they're good fun and a pleasant way of seeing New Zealand, measured strictly on a cost basis they're not the cheapest way of getting around with a rental vehicle. You could rent a car and spend the night in camping site cabins – even in motels at the high season when campervans are expensive – at comparable or lower costs.

Whether you rent a campervan or not watch out for the colourful and exotic house-trucks you see around New Zealand. These individually built constructions often look like a collision between an elderly truck and a timber cottage, sometimes complete with shingle roof and bay windows! Many of these uniquely Kiwi contraptions look far too fragile for road use but they seem to travel all over the country.

### Buying a Car

If you're planning a longer stay and/or if there are a group of you, buying a car and then selling it again at the end of your travels can be one of the cheapest ways of seeing New Zealand. You're not tied to the often inconvenient and expensive bus schedules nor do you find yourself waiting by the roadside with your thumb out looking for a ride.

You can find cars in the Saturday newspaper small ads just like anywhere else in the world. In Auckland there are a number of car fairs, where private individuals bring their cars to sell, including a Saturday morning car fair at Newmarket on the corner of Khyber Pass Rd and Broadway, another Saturday morning on the North Shore at Takapuna, and a Sunday car fair at Manukau, in South Auckland, in the parking lot of the giant shopping mall near the Manukau motorway offramp. Come early, between 8 and 9.30 am, for the best choice of cheaper cars. Car auctions are also held in Auckland; Turner's Car Auction in Penrose holds them three times a week, with a special day set aside for budget vehicles. The car fairs and auctions have lots of cars available from around $1000 to $4500. These are the real cheapies; a good, late-model used car from a dealer could cost around $8500 (with warranty).

In general, the cheapest prices are found at the car auctions, where car after car is whizzed past a group of bidders, bids are taken, and the car is sold to the highest bidder – all within about 30 seconds. Next cheapest prices will be found at car fairs, where you have more time to browse around. You might try buying at an auction, and selling at a fair, to get the best overall deal. If you do buy at an auction, come early to inspect the vehicles before the hectic bidding starts.

Auckland has a very useful mobile inspection service, Car Inspection Services Ltd (tel 398-084), which will come to wherever you are and perform a very thorough inspection on any car you are considering buying. Cost is \$63 but it's worth it. The AA also does inspections for their members, it's cheaper but also a more limited examination of the car. However, it is available all over New Zealand. The car fairs and auctions have inspection services standing by to provide on-the-spot inspections.

Other travellers buy cars in Christchurch as there are lots of cars, it's a popular arrival and departure point and the dry climate keeps them fairly rust free. Both Auckland and Christchurch have companies which will sell you a car and buy it back again at a specified rate when you're ready to leave; check with the YHA national offices in both cities, or with Wheels in Christchurch.

You'll often see ads at youth hostels from other travellers keen to sell their cars and move on. I even saw two travellers standing in the arrivals lounge at Auckland airport holding a sign saying 'buy our car'! Make sure any car you buy has a WOF or Warrant of Fitness and that the registration lasts for a reasonable period. You have to have the WOF certificate proving that the car is roadworthy in order to register it.

## BICYCLE

With sky-rocketing petrol prices and public transport also becoming increasingly costly, there has been a marked increase in the number of cyclists touring New Zealand. You seem to see touring bicycles almost everywhere, particularly with Canadians aboard! There are lots of hills in New Zealand, so it's hard going at times, but it's a compact country and there's always plenty of variety.

Apart from giving you independence from public transport or hitching, cycling also gives you the ideal means of getting around

once you get to your destination. If you do get fed up with cycling you can easily take your bike by train or, with some packing, by bus. Coming to New Zealand many airlines will carry your bicycle at no additional cost as 'sporting equipment'.

Bicycle rental is becoming increasingly popular in New Zealand, with many companies offering not only daily but weekly rates (about \$70 a week for mountain bikes). Penny Farthing Cycle Shops in Auckland, Wellington and Christchurch offer long-term hire, and there are plenty of other shops in cities and towns all over New Zealand. Of course you can also buy bicycles in New Zealand but prices are high for new bikes. If you want to 'own your own' you're better off bringing one in, or buying a used one. Hostel notice boards frequently have signs offering mountain bikes for sale, or check the newspaper small ads.

Bicycle Tours of New Zealand (tel 591-961), PO Box 11296, Auckland 5 offer long-term bicycle rentals with all the gear you'll need, and they will also draw up an itinerary for the time you want to spend and the distance and level of exertion you want to tackle. Pedaltours (tel 674-605), PO Box 49039, Auckland 4, offer a variety of guided cycle tours but they're not cheap, cost is from \$900 for a 6 day Coromandel Peninsula tour to \$3300 for an 18 day South Island Grand Tour. They also offer long-term rental and a tour planning service if you want to go out on your own.

Special cyclists' guidebooks exist for both islands. Most popular are *Cycle Touring in the South Island, New Zealand* by Helen Crabb (Canterbury Cyclists' Association, PO Box 2547, Christchurch) and *Cycle Touring in the North Island, New Zealand* by J B Ringer (Southern Cyclists Inc, PO Box 5890, Auckland). They give lots of useful information for cyclists, like where the steep hills are!

## HITCHING

Overall, New Zealand is a great place for hitchhiking and although almost anybody who does a fair amount of hitching will get stuck somewhere uncomfortable for an uncomfortably long period of time most travellers rate it highly. It's safe, the roads are not crowded but there are just enough cars to make things fairly easy and the New Zealanders are well disposed towards hitchhikers.

The usual hitching rules apply: If you're standing in one spot, pick your location so that drivers can see you easily and stop safely. Some hitchhikers report they have better luck hitching while walking alongside the road than when standing planted in one spot. In larger towns it usually pays to get out of town before starting to hitch, either by local bus or walking. You may even pick up a lift on the way out, but don't count on it, it's much harder to get a ride in town with a pack. On the other hand on the open road, it's a lot easier to get a lift if you're wearing a pack. Learn which rides not to take – not just crazy drivers but also rides that leave you at inconvenient locations; wait for the right one.

Dress for the occasion – not in your fancy clothes ('they can afford to take the bus') or too shabbily ('don't want them in my car'). One big, brawny traveller from Scotland brought along his full traditional kilt outfit for hitching and never failed to get a ride in short order! If someone else is already hitching on the same stretch of road remember to walk ahead of them so they get the first ride, or leave the road until they get a ride. Most important be cautious and careful – there are some unpleasant people on the road in New Zealand just like anywhere else in the world.

During my last visit two Swedish hitchhikers tossed their backpacks in the back of a car which stopped for them, and the car immediately drove off leaving them standing by the roadside, totally ripped off.

Generally hitching on the main routes on the North Island is good. On the South Island hitching down the east coast from Picton through Christchurch to Invercargill is mostly good. Elsewhere in the South Island there are hundreds of km of main roads with very little traffic. Expect long waits – even days – in some places. It's a good idea to have the InterCity, Newmans and Mt Cook time-tables with you so you can flag a bus down if you're tired of hitching. Make sure you show the driver the colour of your money. Quite a few drivers have been stopped by hitchhikers who have then decided they can't afford the fare so some bus drivers are wary about stopping unless they know you're pre-pared to pay.

It's easier hitching alone if you are male but, unfortunately, even though New Zealand is a safe country for hitching, a woman on her own may experience some tricky – if not dangerous – situations. Better to travel with someone else if possible. Many hostels have local hints for hitching (such as what bus to get out of town, where to hitch from) on their notice boards.

## LOCAL TRANSPORT
### Bus
There are bus services in most larger cities but with a few honourable exceptions they are mainly daytime weekday operations. On weekends and particularly on Sundays buses can be very difficult to find.

### Train
The only city with a good suburban train service is Wellington with regular trains up the main corridors to the north. It's the only electrified railway in New Zealand.

### Taxi
Although there are plenty of taxis in the major towns they rarely 'cruise'. If you want

a taxi you usually either have to phone for one or go to a taxi rank.

## Bicycle

Bicycles can be rented by the hour or day in most major cities and in many smaller locales. Rentals by the week for longer trips are becoming more common – see the Bicycle section in this chapter.

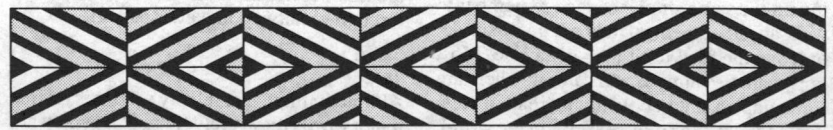

# NORTH
# ISLAND

# Auckland

Population 841,700
On the shores of Waitemata Harbour, Auckland is surrounded by water and volcanic hills. Auckland is the main entry point for visitors to New Zealand. It has many things to see, lots of accommodation, many restaurants and some good places for night-time entertainment. Auckland is also the biggest city in New Zealand and in recent years has become the 'big city' for the Polynesian islands of the South Pacific. So many islanders from New Zealand's Pacific neighbours have moved to Auckland that it now has the largest concentration of Polynesians in the world. This helps to give it a much more cosmopolitan atmosphere than other cities in New Zealand.

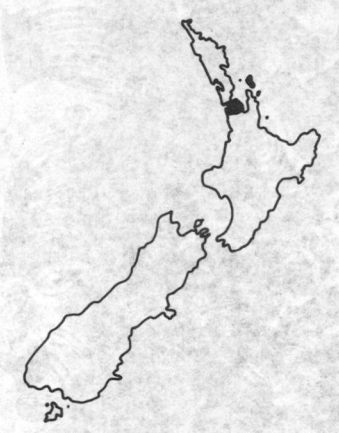

Auckland sprawls between two large harbours and, like Sydney, has a lot of enthusiastic yachties who sail back, forth and around on weekends and make it look very picturesque. Also like Sydney it has a harbour bridge which is every bit as unattractive. It was opened in 1959 with due pomp and ceremony and four traffic lanes. Probably to no one's surprise it was soon discovered that the reason not many people lived on the North Shore was because there wasn't a bridge, and as soon as there was one, so many people moved there to live that the bridge wasn't big enough. Fortunately, the clever Japanese came to the rescue and 'clipped' two more lanes on each side (known locally as the 'Nippon Clippons') to convert it to eight streams of cars.

## Orientation
Auckland's main drag is Queen St, which runs from the waterfront, by the CPO and up (literally) to Karangahape Rd (also called simply 'K Rd' by the locals). The Downtown Airline Terminal is near the waterfront, a block and a half from the CPO.

## Information
**Tourist Information** The NZTP (tel 798-180) is at 99 Queen St. It's open from 8.30 am to 4.45 pm on weekdays, and 9.30 am to noon on Saturdays during summer.

The Auckland Visitors Bureau (tel 366-6888), on Aotea Square, at 299 Queen St near the Town Hall, is more useful for local information. The centre has all sorts of local and regional information and can supply the answers to most visitors' questions. It also has information on many other places throughout New Zealand. It's open from 8.30 am to 5.30 pm on weekdays, 9 am to 4 pm on weekends and public holidays.

The Department of Conservation (DOC) office (tel 379-279) in the Sheraton complex on the corner of Karangahape Rd and Liverpool St has a wealth of information on all of New Zealand's national parks, forests, walkways and tracks, nature reserves, etc.

The AA office (tel 774-640, 774-660) is at 99 Albert St, on the corner of Albert and Victoria streets. If you're a member of an equivalent overseas auto club you can use its services. The AA has free accommodation and camping site directories for both islands and excellent regional maps.

The Auckland YHA office (tel 794-224) is at 36 Customs St East, near the Downtown

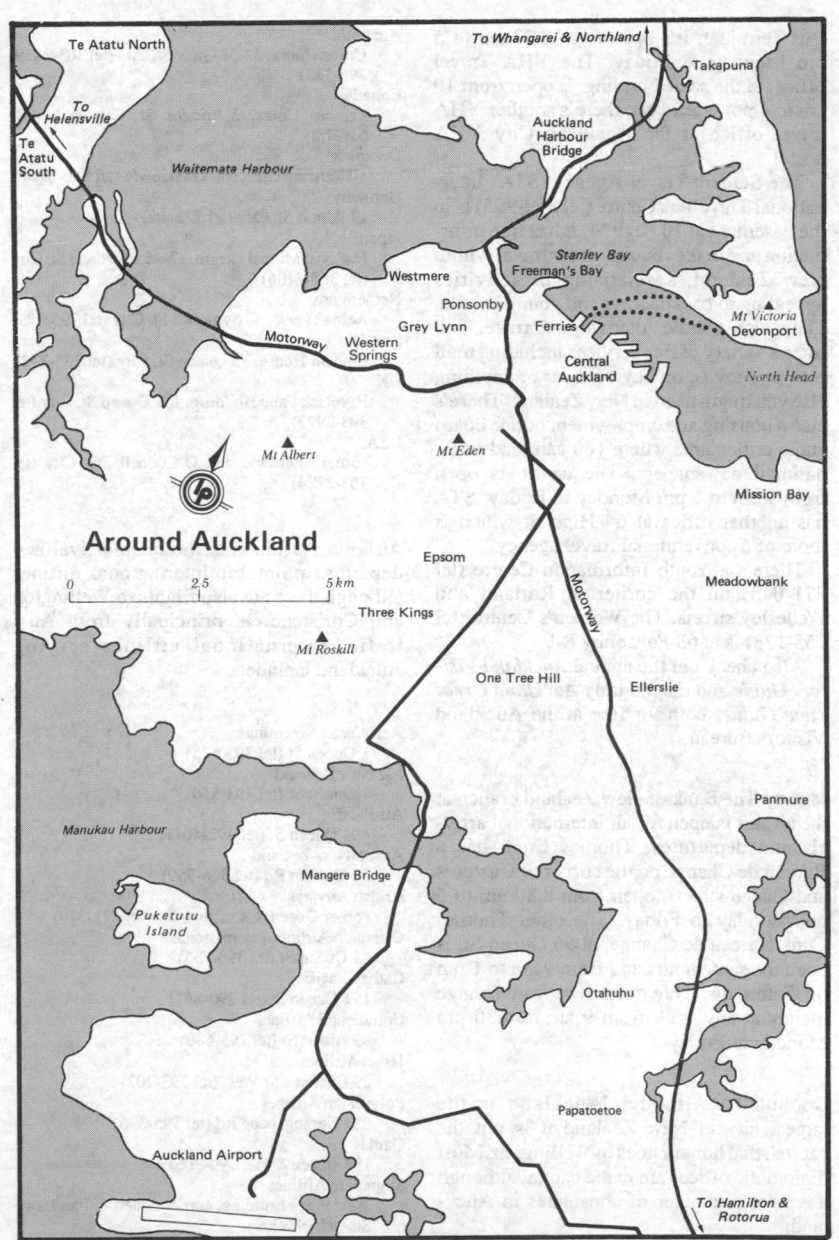

**Around Auckland**

Te Atatu North

To Helensville

Te Atatu South

Waitemata Harbour

To Whangarei & Northland

Takapuna

Auckland Harbour Bridge

Westmere

Stanley Bay
Freeman's Bay

Ponsonby

Grey Lynn

Motorway

Western Springs

Ferries

Central Auckland

Mt Victoria
Devonport

North Head

Mt Albert

Mt Eden

Mission Bay

Epsom

Meadowbank

Three Kings

Mt Roskill

One Tree Hill

Ellerslie

Panmure

Manukau Harbour

Mangere Bridge

Puketutu
Island

Otahuhu

Motorway

Papatoetoe

Auckland Airport

To Hamilton &
Rotorua

0    2.5    5 km

Bus Terminal. It's open from 8.30 am to 5 pm Monday to Friday. The YHA Travel office, in the same building, is open from 10 am to 4 pm weekdays; there's another YHA travel office at the Auckland City YHA hostel.

The Student Travel Agency (STA) International Travellers Centre (tel 399-995) is in the basement at 10 High St. It has free information and makes bookings for travel within New Zealand, specialising in activities appealing to backpackers and young people. They also handle international travel and offer a variety of free services including mail pick-up, advice on buying a car or anything else you might need in New Zealand. There's also a housing and employment notice board and a coffee area where you can read international newspapers. The centre is open from 9 am to 5 pm Monday to Friday. STA has another office at 64 High St which is more of a conventional travel agency.

There's a Youth Information Centre (tel 771-043) on the corner of Rutland and Wellesley streets. The Women's Centre (tel 765-173) is at 63 Ponsonby Rd.

Also check out the annual *Auckland Visitors Guide* and the monthly *Auckland Great Time Guide*, both for free at the Auckland Visitors Bureau.

**Money** The Bank of New Zealand branch at the airport is open for all international arrivals and departures. Thomas Cook has a Bureau de Change on the corner of Customs and Queen streets, open from 8.30 am to 5 pm Monday to Friday. The other Thomas Cook Bureau de Change, at 96 Queen St, is open the same hours and from 9 am to 1 pm on Saturdays. Otherwise you can change money at any bank from 9 am to 4.30 pm Monday to Friday.

**Consulates** Although Auckland is the largest city in New Zealand it is not the capital, that honour goes to Wellington. Most diplomatic offices are in the capital although there are a number of consulates in Auckland:

Australia
  Union House, 32-38 Quay St, City (tel 303-2429, 795-725)
Canada
  Princes Court, 2 Princes St, City (tel 398-516/7/8)
Denmark
  10 Vanessa Crescent, Glendowie (tel 556-025)
Germany
  17 Albert St, City (tel 773-460)
Japan
  National Mutual Centre, 37-45 Shortland St, City (tel 303-4106)
Netherlands
  Aetna House, 57 Symonds St, City (tel 795-399)
Sweden
  Emcom House, 75 Queen St, City (tel 735-332)
UK
  Fay Richwhite Building, 151 Queen St, City (tel 303-2973)
USA
  corner Shortland and O'Connell Sts, City (tel 303-2724)

**Airlines** Auckland is the main arrival and departure point for international airlines although there are also flights to Wellington and Christchurch, principally from Australia. International airlines serving Auckland include:

Aerolineas Argentinas
  1 Queen St (tel 793-675)
Air New Zealand
  1 Queen St (tel 793-510)
Air Pacific
  404 Queen St (tel 792-404)
Ansett New Zealand
  50 Grafton Rd (tel 376-950)
British Airways
  corner Queen & Customs Sts (tel 771-379)
Canadian Airlines International
  45 Queen St (tel 390-735)
Cathay Pacific
  191 Queen St (tel 790-861)
Continental Airlines
  99 Albert St (tel 795-680)
Japan Airlines
  29 Customs St West (tel 793-202)
Polynesian Airlines
  283 Karangahape Rd (tel 395-396)
Qantas
  154 Queen St (tel 790-306)
Singapore Airlines
  West Plaza Building, corner Albert & Fanshawe Sts (tel 793-209)

UTA
    50 Fort St (tel 303-1229)
United Airlines
    7 City Rd (tel 303-3249)

Local airlines operating from Auckland include:

Eagle Air
    (tel Freefone (071) 389-500)
    Auckland Domestic Terminal
Great Barrier Airlines
    Auckland Domestic Terminal
    (tel 275-6612)
Mt Cook Airline
    105 Queen St (tel 395-395)
Waiheke Air Services
    Ardmore Airport (tel 298-7142)

**Books** The Book Corner, upstairs on the Queen St and Victoria St West corner, has lots of books. For second-hand books, try Bloomsbury Books upstairs at 10 O'Connell St, David Thomas' Bookshop at 2 Lorne St near the corner of Victoria St, Jason Second-hand Books on High St beside the Simple Cottage vegetarian restaurant, or the Anah Dunsheath Bookshop, on High St near Shortland St.

Downstairs in the cellar of the Old Customs House, on the corner of Customs St West and Lower Albert Rd, are the New Edition Bookstore, which specialises in travel books and books on everything about New Zealand, and the Pathfinder Bookshop with New Age books. The largest selection of New Age books in Auckland is at Goodey's New Age Bookshop, 20 Chancery St half a block off High St. Scribbles, at 295 Queen St, features Maori and NZ books, and the Polynesian Bookshop at 283 Karangahape Rd has an excellent selection of books on the islands of the South Pacific.

**Newspapers** The *Auckland Tourist Times* is a useful free weekly newspaper of visitor information, events and activities in Auckland. The *New Zealand Herald* is the Auckland morning daily, the *Auckland Star* appears in the evenings.

**Maps** The mini-map series is very handy for finding your way around Auckland – small enough for a pocket, yet detailed enough to show everything. You can get good maps of Auckland from the Auckland Visitors Bureau, DOSLI (tel 771-889) or the AA.

### CENTRAL AUCKLAND

The spine of Central Auckland is Queen St, which starts at the busy waterfront and runs uphill (gently at first and taking a slight kink on the way) to Karangahape Rd which is the centre for Auckland's Maori and Islander population. To the east of Queen St is Albert Park, a popular lunchtime haven for city workers and students and the venue for free rock concerts on Sunday afternoons in summer. Beyond the park is Auckland University, the largest in New Zealand, where visitors are welcome to most activities.

### The Domain

Covering about 80 hectares, the Auckland Domain, near the centre of the city, is a lovely public park that's worth wandering through to take a look at the Winter Gardens and the museum. It's also a pleasant walk down through the Domain and back through the university grounds and Albert Park to Queen St.

### War Memorial Museum

If you're only going to see one thing in Auckland, see the War Memorial Museum on the Domain. The museum has a tremendous display of Maori artefacts and culture: pride of place goes to a magnificent 25 metre long war canoe, but there are many other examples of the Maoris' arts and lifestyle. The museum also houses a fine display of South Pacific items and NZ wildlife, including a giant moa model.

An excellent 1 hour guided tour of the Maori exhibits, followed by a half-hour performance of traditional Maori music and dance, costs $5 (family $10). The tours begin at 10.30 am and 12.45 pm daily. These are a good introduction to Maori culture, and apart from Rotorua this is about the only chance you'll get to see Maori culture so well represented on a regular basis.

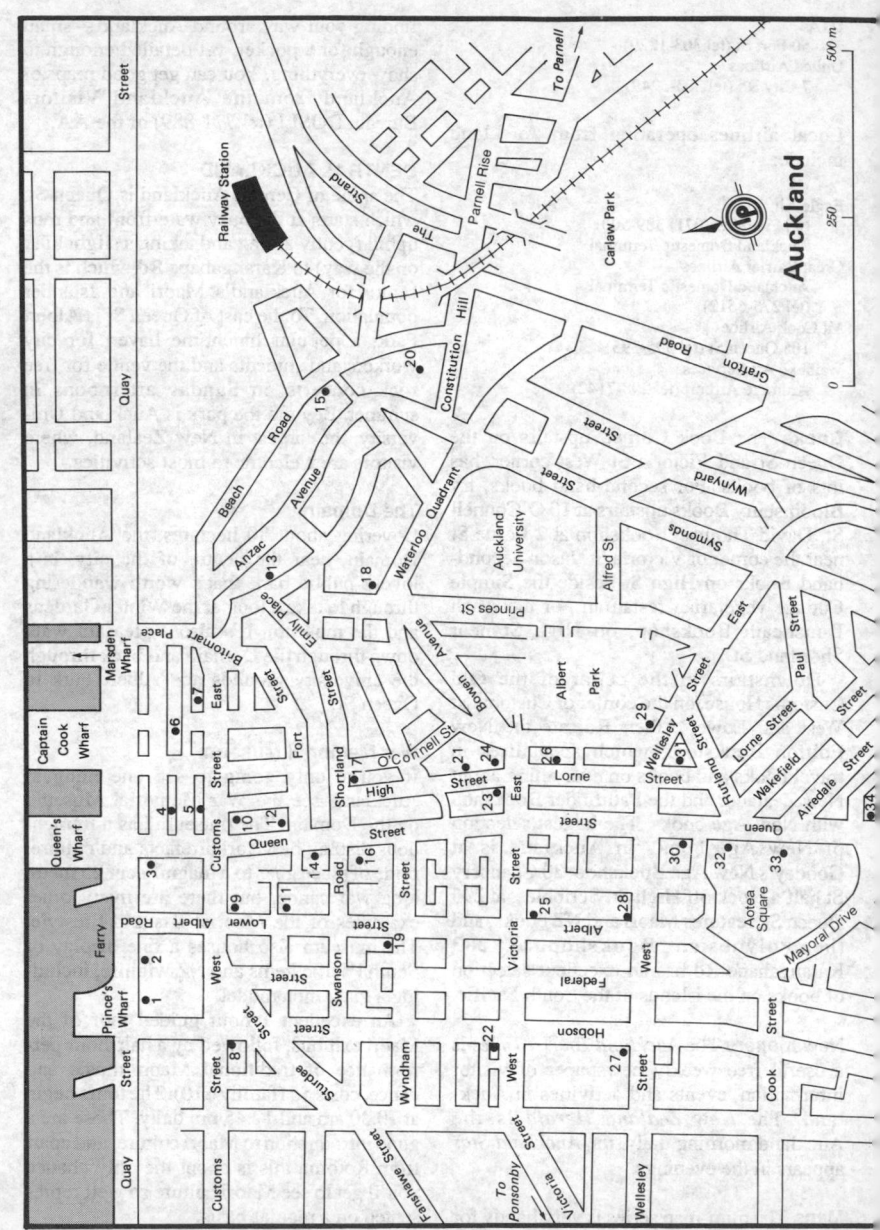

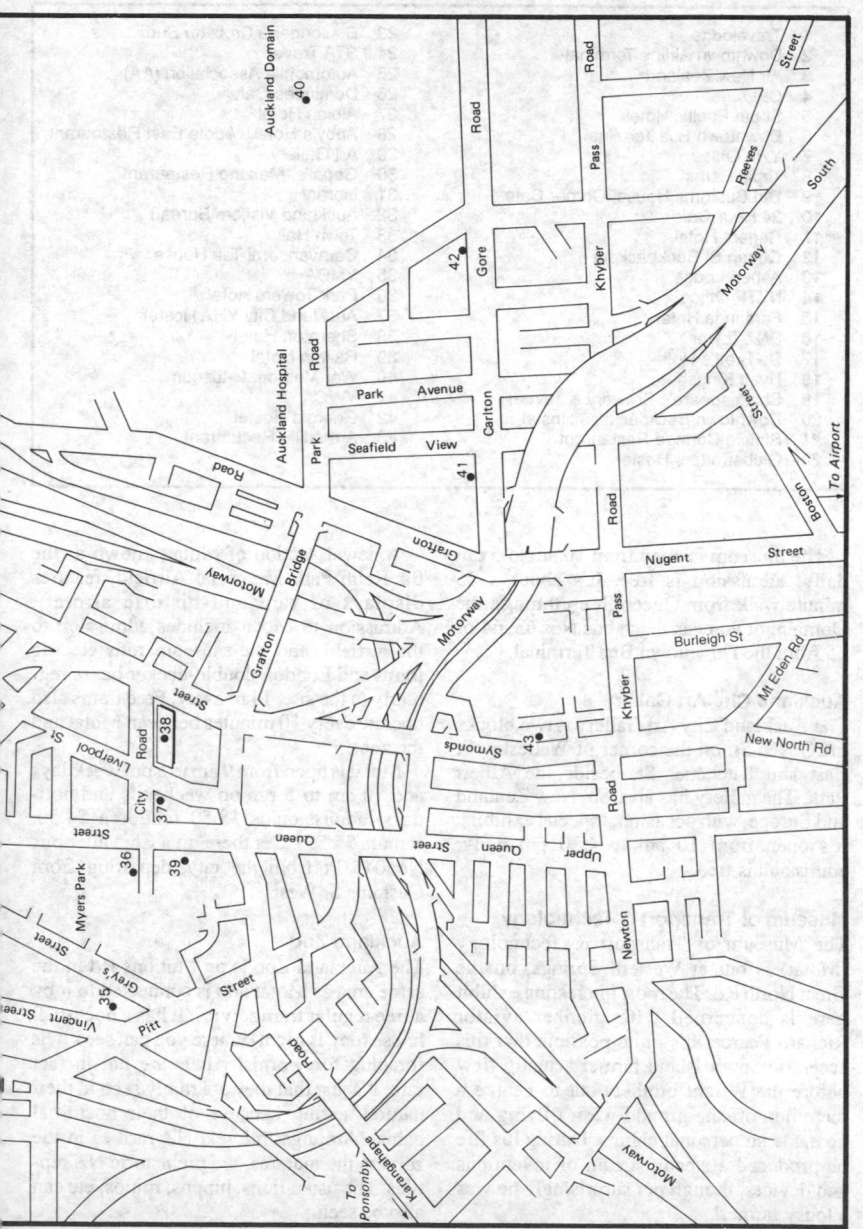

| | | | |
|---|---|---|---|
| 1 | Travelodge | 23 | Boulongerie Croix du Sud |
| 2 | Downtown Airline Terminal | 24 | STA Travel |
| 3 | Air New Zealand | 25 | Automobile Association (AA) |
| 4 | CPO | 26 | Dominoes Cafe |
| 5 | South Pacific Hotel | 27 | Albion Hotel |
| 6 | Downtown Bus Terminal | 28 | Abby's Hotel, Middle East Restaurant |
| 7 | YHA Office | 29 | Art Gallery |
| 8 | Tepid Baths | 30 | Gopal's, Mekong Restaurant |
| 9 | Old Customs House, Corner Cafe | 31 | Library |
| 10 | 24 Hour Cafe | 32 | Auckland Visitors Bureau |
| 11 | Regent Hotel | 33 | Town Hall |
| 12 | Queen St Backpackers | 34 | Caravanserai Tea House |
| 13 | Aspen Lodge | 35 | YMCA |
| 14 | NZTP Office | 36 | Park Towers Hotel |
| 15 | Farthings Hotel | 37 | Auckland City YHA Hostel |
| 16 | BNZ Tower | 38 | Sheraton Hotel |
| 17 | De Brett's Hotel | 39 | Railton Hotel |
| 18 | Hyatt Kingsgate | 40 | War Memorial Museum |
| 19 | Shakespeare's Brewery & Tavern | 41 | YWCA |
| 20 | Downtown Backpacker's Hostel | 42 | Georgia Hostel |
| 21 | Simple Cottage Restaurant | 43 | Armadillo Restaurant |
| 22 | Globetrotters Hostel | | |

The museum is open from 10 am to 5 pm daily; admission is free. It's about a 25 minute walk from Queen St up through the Domain, or you can catch bus Nos 63, 64 or 65 from the Downtown Bus Terminal.

### Auckland City Art Gallery
The Auckland City Art Gallery is two blocks off Queen St, on the corner of Wellesley St East and Kitchener St, beside the Albert Park. The gallery has art from New Zealand and Europe, with occasional special exhibits. It's open from 10 am to 4.30 pm daily; admission is free.

### Museum of Transport & Technology
The Museum of Transport & Technology (Motat) is out at Western Springs, on the Great North Rd. The most interesting exhibit here is concerned with pioneer aviator Richard Pearce. It's quite possible that this eccentric South Island farmer actually flew before the Wright brothers but to Pearce a mere hop off the ground wasn't flying and he made no personal claims. During his life he produced a steady stream of inventions and devices, though not surprisingly he was a lousy farmer!

A newer section of Motat, known as the Sir Keith Park Memorial Airfield, features displays of rare and historic aircraft. Admission to Motat includes admission to the airfield, and the museum runs electric trams and London double-decker buses regularly to the site, 1 km away. Free trams also operate every 10 minutes between Motat and the zoo.

Motat is open from 9 am to 5 pm weekdays and 10 am to 5 pm on weekends and holidays; admission is $8.50 (children $4.50, seniors $6.50). Get there on a Chevalier bus No 045 Pt from the city, departing from Customs St West.

### Auckland Zoo
The Auckland Zoo is on Motions Rd in the same area as Motat and is connected to it by a free regular tram service. It has a nocturnal house (day is night) where you can see kiwis foraging for worms. Kiwis are not in fact rare, it's just that they are rarely seen in their natural setting because of their nocturnal habits. Amongst the real NZ rarities in the zoo are the tuataras, the prehistoric NZ reptiles. The usual lions, hippos, rhinos, etc can also be seen.

Tuatara

The zoo is open from 9.30 am to 5.30 pm daily (last admission is at 4.15 pm); entry is $8 (children $4). The Chevalier bus No 045 Pt from Customs St West will get you to both Motat and the zoo.

## Underwater World

New York may have mythical crocodiles in its sewers but Auckland certainly does have sharks in its stormwater tanks. At Orakei Wharf, on Tamaki Drive, Underwater World is a unique aquarium housed in old storm-water holding tanks. An acrylic tunnel leads through the aquarium and you travel through the tunnel on a moving footpath with the fish swimming all around you. You can step off at any time to take a better look and the whole place is designed to recreate the experience of scuba diving around the coast of New Zealand. The aquarium is divided into two sections, a reef fish area and a sharks and stingrays area. Underwater World was devised and developed by NZ diver Kelly Tarlton who unfortunately died in 1985, only 7 weeks after his aquarium opened.

You can get to Underwater World on bus Nos 72, 73, 74 or 75 from the Downtown Terminal. It's open from 9 am to 9 pm daily (to 8 pm in winter); entry is $9 (children $4.50).

## Parnell

Parnell is an old inner suburb, only 1 or 2 km from the centre, where there was a concerted effort to stave off the office developers and restore the old houses and shops, many of them with a decidedly eccentric touch. Parnell now has one of the most appealing streets in New Zealand with lots of arty-crafty shops, good (and expensive) restaurants, galleries and trendy Kiwis. It's a good place to have a snack in one of the open-air cafes and people-watch. Everything here is open 7 days a week. You can walk to Parnell from Queen St in about 25 minutes (it's a pleasant walk through the Domain) or take bus Nos 63, 64 or 65 from the Downtown Bus Terminal.

## Historic Buildings

There are a number of restored and preserved colonial-era historic buildings around the city. Highwic, at 40 Gillies Ave, Epsom, and Alberton, at 1 Kerr-Taylor Ave, Mt Albert, on the corner of Kerr-Taylor Ave and Mt Albert Rd, are both large houses of rich mid-Victorian New Zealanders, originally built in the 1860s, added on to with time, and ultimately bequeathed to the Historic Places Trust. Ewelme Cottage, at 14 Ayr St, Parnell, off Parnell Rd, was built in the 1860s of the fine native kauri wood by an early clergy-man. All are open daily from 10.30 am to noon and from 1 to 4.30 pm. Admission to Ewelme Cottage is $2 (children 50 cents); $3 (children $1) for the others.

Very near to Ewelme Cottage, Kinder House, 2 Ayr St on the corner of Parnell Rd, is a fine example of early (1857) architecture and contains two galleries of artwork and memorabilia of the Rev Dr John Kinder. His original watercolours are found in the Auckland and Waikato art galleries, with photographic reproductions here. The restored home is open daily from 10.30 am to 4 pm; admission is $1.

Renall St, coming off Ponsonby Rd, has

been declared a conservation area by the Auckland city council, and is a registered place of historic interest for its 19th century atmosphere. The houses along this block are still used as private homes and are not open to the public, but you can stroll along and see the 20 or so early artisans' houses and the larger Foresters' Hall at No 5. The Auckland Visitors Bureau has an interesting pamphlet prepared by the city council which details the history of the street and the people who lived on it from 1844 onwards.

Mt Wellington Stone Cottage is at the Shopping Centre in Panmure. There are several of the early 'Fencible Cottages', including one from the 1840s, at Jellicoe Park, Quadrant Rd, Onehunga. It's open from 1.30 to 4.30 pm on weekends.

In south Auckland, Howick Colonial Village in Lloyd Elsmore Park, Bells Rd, Pakuranga is a restored village of the 1840-1880 period, on the old military settlement of Howick. It has over 20 restored colonial buildings including a thatched sod cottage, forge, schoolhouse, village store, church and settlers' houses. It's open from 10 am to 4 pm daily; entry is $6 (children $1, family $14).

### Swimming & Thermal Pools

There are swimming pools in the city and various swimming centres outside. The Tepid Baths, locally known as 'the Teps', is in the heart of the city on the corner of Customs St West and Hobson St, two blocks from Queen St. It has a large indoor swimming pool, a spa pool, saunas and steam room. Admission to all of these is $5.50 (children and seniors $3), or $3.50 ($1) for the swimming pool only. The Teps is open from 6 am to 10 pm weekdays, 8 am to 7 pm on weekends and holidays.

Other pools in the city include the heated Point Erin pool, the Parnell Baths with a saltwater pool right on the waterfront (closed in winter), and the Takapuna Pools.

The Aquatic Park at Parakai, 45 km northwest of Auckland (bus No 069 from the Downtown Bus Terminal), has indoor and outdoor hot mineral pools and various waterslides. The centre is open from 10 am to 10 pm daily. You can stay there at the camping ground or at *Craigwell House* where there are rooms and dorm beds.

The Waiwera Thermal Pools, another big complex of hot pools, are at Waiwera, 48 km north of Auckland (bus No 895 from the Downtown Bus Terminal). They are open daily from 9.30 am to 10 pm. Within walking distance of Waiwera is the Wenderholm Regional Park with a good beach, estuary, lawns, trees and bushwalks.

The Miranda Hot Springs on the Miranda coast road off the Thames/Pokeno Rd has open and covered hot pools, private spas, children's play areas, and powered camping sites. It's open from 10 am to 9 pm daily; admission is $4 (children $2).

### Beaches

Auckland is known for its fine and varied beaches dotted all around the harbours and up and down both coasts. You can run around them with 80,000 fit New Zealanders in the 'Round the Bays' run which is held in March every year. It is one of the largest fun runs in the world.

East coast beaches include Judges Bay, Kohimarama, Mission Bay, Okahu Bay and St Heliers Bay, all accessible from Tamaki Drive. With most east coast and harbour beaches, swimming is better at high tide. Popular north shore beaches include Takapuna and Milford.

There's good surf on west coast beaches within an hour's drive from the city. Try Bethells where the water is often very rough, Karekare, Muriwai, and Whatipu with good day walks in the area. These beaches are all less than 50 km from the city centre, and most have surf clubs near the shore. Serious surfers in the Auckland area recommend Piha and Raglan on the west coast and Whangamata on the east coast. See the Around Auckland section for more on Piha.

### Auckland Observatory

The Auckland Observatory, in the One Tree Hill Domain, off Manukau Rd, is open to the public from 8 to 10 pm every Tuesday evening with an illustrated talk on some aspect of astronomy and, on clear nights, telescope viewing and help in finding the southern hemisphere constellations. Admission is $5 (children $2, family $13). To get there, take bus Nos 302, 304, 305 or 312 from Victoria St East.

### One Tree Hill & Mt Eden

One Tree Hill is a small (183 metres) extinct volcano cone which, like the other extinct volcano cones all around the Auckland area, was used by the Maoris as a fortified pa. This was the largest and most populous of the Maori pa settlements, and you can still see the terracing and dugout storage pits they made, and look down into the crater. One Tree Hill was named for a sacred totara tree which stood on the hilltop until 1876, now replaced by a huge pine tree. Get there on bus Nos 302, 304, 305 or 312 from Victoria St East.

You get a good view of the city from One Tree Hill but the view from Mt Eden, the highest volcanic cone in the area at 196 metres, is the best in Auckland. From Mt Eden you can see the entire Auckland area, all the bays, both sides of the isthmus, and scope out the coast-to-coast walkway. You can also see the old Maori pa terracing and storage pits and look 50 metres down into the volcano's crater. It's worth the trouble to get up there. You can drive to the top or take bus Nos 274 or 275 from Customs St East.

### Markets & Flea Markets

Victoria Park Market on Victoria St West opposite Victoria Park is a big outdoor market, operating every day of the week from 9 am to 7 pm. There's a lively atmosphere, with outdoor cafes and entertainment on weekends. It's about a 20 minute walk from the centre, heading west on Victoria St from Queen St, or you can take a bus No 005 from Customs St West (this bus does not run on weekends).

The Oriental Market on Quay St, a few blocks east of the centre, is another interesting market, housed in a huge brightly-coloured warehouse with lots of import shops, international food concessions, unusual merchandise and some good deals.

There are also a number of weekend flea markets in the city and surrounding suburbs. Sunday mornings are the most popular time, with flea markets in Avondale at the Avondale Racecourse from 8 am to noon, in Waitemata at the Waitemata City Council Car Park from 7 am to noon, and in Takapuna at the Shore City Car Park, again from 7 am to noon. There's also a Saturday morning flea market in Otara off Otara Rd on the corner of Newbury St and Bayrds Rd.

### Parks

Pick up a copy of the Auckland Regional Authority's pamphlet guide to the Regional Parks of Auckland from the Regional Parks Central Office on the corner of Wellesley and Nelson streets in the centre or from the Auckland Visitors Bureau. The colour pamphlet has photos, details of facilities and activities, and maps for over 20 parks in the Auckland area. Some have camping, others are interesting day parks.

### Amusement Parks

The Something Different Fun Park has been combined with the former Auckland Lion Safari park, and now includes over 20 rides and attractions, a zoo, slot cars, trains, and so on. It's on Te Atatu Rd, just off the North West motorway, a 10 minute ride from the centre on the Te Atatu North bus, leaving from the bottom of Albert St. It's open from 10 am to 6 pm daily, later in summer. An all-day pass allowing you to go on all the rides as many times as you want costs $20 (children $16, family $15 each). Otherwise, admission to the park is $4 for adults or children, and you pay for each ride you go on.

Rainbow's End Adventure Park on the Great South Road (corner of Wiri Station Rd) at Manukau is a similar place with lots of rides. Take bus Nos 447, 457, 467, 487 or 497 from the Downtown Bus Terminal or take the Manukau exit off the Southern Motorway and drive 400 metres to the park.

## Other City Attractions

The Museum of Puppets at 305 Queen St has displays of Burmese marionettes, Indonesian shadow puppets, a rare Vanuatuan puppet and more. It is open from 1 to 5 pm Monday to Friday. The Parnell Rose Gardens on Gladstone Rd, Parnell, has harbour views and is in bloom from November to March. The Bungy Bats (tel 393-389) do bungy jumping off the Mt Smart Stadium both day and night for $50, followed by a party.

## Tours

You can do your own tour of several major attractions around Auckland by getting a United Airlines Explorer All Day Bus Pass for $7 (children $4). The double-decker bus departs from the Downtown Airline Terminal at hourly intervals from 10 am to 4 pm, 7 days a week, and stops at Victoria Market, the Oriental Market, Mission Bay, Kelly Tarlton's Underwater World, the Rose Park Gardens, Auckland Museum, and Parnell village. You can get off wherever you wish and get on the bus when it comes around the next hour. You can join the tour at any point along the way, getting your ticket from the bus driver.

A Gray Line (tel 395-395) morning tour of Auckland costs $30, and there's another afternoon tour covering different attractions for $28. A lunchtime harbour cruise costs $20. You can combine all three and 'do' all of Auckland in a day for $74, or combine any two (children half price).

Various other operators also have bus tours of the city and further afield. Scenic Tours (tel 640-189) has a 3 hour City Highlights tour twice daily for $24, an Afternoon Country tour for $39, or a full-day Town & Country tour combining both for $59 including lunch; they also have tours to Rotorua and Waitomo. That Other Tour (tel 366-3523) is a smaller company doing more personal 'off the beaten track' tours in the morning ($35), afternoon ($55), or all day ($90).

Bush & Beach (tel 378-209) offers half-day, small-group natural history tours to the Waitakere Rainforest & West Coast Beaches ($55) and to the Muriwai Gannet Colony ($45) during the gannets' breeding season from September to May.

The Old Devonport Ferry & Coach tour (tel 733-776, 450-122) makes an enjoyable way to visit Devonport, on the North Shore just across the harbour. You ferry to Devonport and when you get there, a van is waiting to take you around to Devonport's many sights, including trips to the summits of North Head and Mt Victoria, two volcanic cones with excellent views which are quite a climb otherwise. The whole tour takes about 2 hours, but you can stay around Devonport as long as you like before catching the ferry back to Auckland. The tour departs from the Auckland Ferry Building hourly on the hour from 10 am to 3 pm; cost is $19 (children $9.50).

Great Sights (tel 303-1170, 793-591) offers a 'Backpackers Special' tour to Waitomo and Rotorua, leaving Auckland daily at 8 am. For $35 it takes you from Auckland to the Waitomo Caves (there's a $10 admission fee to enter the caves) and on to Rotorua, arriving in Rotorua about 4.30 pm. The round-trip fare to return to Auckland on another day and by a different route than the way you went is $55. Be sure you went ask for the 'Backpackers' Special', as the regular fare is $71. Great Sights also has morning and afternoon tours of Auckland similar to the Gray Line tours.

Many other tours depart from Auckland to visit places all over New Zealand. One of the more economical is Thrifty Tours (tel 410-3191 or any InterCity office or travel agent), offering a wide range of tours incorporating travel on public transport with accommodation and guided tours in a number of stopoff points. There are other tour companies; ask at NZTP or the Auckland Visitors Bureau.

## Harbour Cruises

A ferry across the harbour to Devonport makes an interesting trip. There are hourly departures from each side (more frequent during commuter hours) and the fare is $5 return ($2.50 one way), half price for chil-

Top: Northland tree ferns (NZTP)
Left: Kiwi (NZTP)
Right: Tuatara (NZTP)

Top: City Centre, Auckland (TW)
Bottom: The marina, Auckland (MC)

dren, for the 15 minute trip. The ferry leaves from the wharf on Quay St. See the Devonport section for details on this little town across the water.

Ferries go between Auckland and Birkenhead during the morning and afternoon rush hours, making a stop at Northcote along the way. They leave from opposite the Downtown Airline Terminal and take 15 minutes each way; the fare is $4 return, $2 one way (half price for children).

The Auckland Harbour Cruise Co (tel 734-557) has five large sailing yachts (you can't miss them on the water with their distinctive blue-and-white-striped sails) making 3 hour Coffee, Luncheon and Dinner sailing cruises around the harbour.

Fuller's Captain Cook Cruises (tel 774-074) has absorbed several other harbour boat companies and now has the largest selection of cruises available. They do inner harbour cruises including an Early Bird Breakfast Cruise, a Luncheon Cruise, an Afternoon Coffee Cruise, a Nightlife Cruise, a Jazz Cruise to Devonport, plus longer journeys including a 3½ hour Gulf Explorer Cruise and day trip cruises to various islands including Rangitoto, Waiheke, Pakatoa, Great Barrier Island and Kawau. On most of the outer island cruises you can make it a day trip or get off on the island and return whenever you want.

*Quick Cat*, the catamaran serving Waiheke and Pakatoa islands, does Hauraki Gulf cruises on its normal island services. See the Islands Around Auckland section for details. Departures are frequent from the Ferry Building. *Sea Flight* is another large catamaran, doing day cruises to Kawau Island ($38) and Great Barrier Island ($52), plus a Coromandel Islands cruise and a Night Flight dinner cruise.

In summer, a host of other boats ply the harbour (they don't call this the City of Sails for nothing!) and you can even take a trip around the harbour on the tug *William C Daldy* on summer Sundays.

Auckland makes particularly good use of its fine harbour on the annual Anniversary Regatta in late January every year. The waters are dotted with more boats than you'd believe possible and if it's a good windy day, there'll be a fair number of dunkings!

### Te Aroha Cruises

The historic (1909) auxiliary schooner *Te Aroha* sails from the Captain Cook Wharf in central Auckland every few days from November to April on a 4 day Hauraki Gulf cruise that stops at Tiritiri Matangi, Kawau, Little Barrier and Great Barrier islands, with possible additional stops at Waiheke, Ponue or Pakatoa Islands. You can sleep on bunks in the hold or on the deck. There's plenty of time to explore around on the various islands, lots of good food and drink, diving, snorkelling and fishing and if you like you can even help out on deck with the sails. All in all this is a great trip. All-inclusive cost is $388.

They also have a 5 day 'Bird Islands of the Gulf' cruise for nature and natural history buffs, stopping at Tiritiri Matangi, Kawau, and Great Barrier islands in addition to Little Barrier and Mokohinau islands, both of which are national bird sanctuaries for which special landing permits have been arranged. The $790 fare includes a resident lecturer/guide and many other amenities. There's also a 3 day 'Bird Islands' tour for $304, stopping at Tiritiri Matangi, Kawau and Little Barrier islands. Other *Te Aroha* cruises include a weekend cruise to the Coromandel Islands ($198) and a Northland pilgrimage to Totara North, the place of the schooner's 1909 launching ($675). Check with the NZ Adventure Centre (tel 399-192/4) in the Victoria Park Market for bookings and schedules.

### Aerial Sightseeing

There are scenic flights over Auckland and the islands of the Hauraki Gulf. Check with Sea Bee Air (tel 774-405/6) about their amphibious aircraft flights. Sea Bee also have helicopter flights and charters on The Helicopter Line. Flightline (tel 298-7142) also has scenic flights and charters. Other flightseeing operators include Ardmore Air,

Air North Shore, Capt Al's Fantasy Flights and others.

## Places to Stay

**Hostels – City Centre** Just off Queen St and right behind the Sheraton Hotel, the *Auckland City YHA Hostel* (tel 392-802) on the corner of City Rd and Liverpool St is clean and new and has 75 rooms with 130 beds. Many of the rooms – mostly twins, with some singles and triples – have great views of the city and harbour. Nightly cost is $17 and the hostel is open 24 hours. The cafe on the ground floor has very economical meals and snacks, and there's a YHA travel agency in the lobby.

The *Queen St Backpackers* (tel 604-386), on the corner of Queen and Fort streets, opened in late '89. It is one of Auckland's most centrally located hostels. Rates per person are $15 in four-bed dorms, $17.50 in double or twin rooms and $20 in single rooms; linen is provided.

*Globetrotters* (tel 733-737) at 51 Hobson St, on the corner of Victoria St West, is another large, central hostel but it's a bit more run-down. Rates per person for dorm rooms are $13 and for double rooms $15.

The International Travellers Network has three hostels around Auckland – in Parnell, Ponsonby and Constitution Hill. All of them get together for a weekly barbecue. Their *Downtown Backpacker's Hostel* (tel 303-4768) is conveniently located at 6 Constitution Hill, near Auckland University. Rooms cost $15 per person.

The *YMCA* (tel 303-2068) is in a tall, modern building on the corner of Pitt St and Grays Ave. Men and women are segregated by floors in 126 single rooms which cost $30 on the first day, $22.50 thereafter, including breakfast and dinner. On weekends it's brunch and dinner, and on weekdays you can fix yourself lunch in the mornings to take with you. Although it is aimed more at long-term residents, rooms are usually available.

The *YWCA* (tel 778-763), at 10 Carlton Gore Rd, Grafton, an easy stroll from the Queen St and Karangahape Rd intersection, is a small but pleasant little hostel with

accommodation for men and women. The bunkroom out the back has a six-bed dorm and two twin rooms and costs $12 a night plus a $10 key bond. The main building is for females only, with single/twin rooms at $17/15 per person. Sheets and blankets can be hired. Take a Hospital bus No 283 from the city terminal, or bus Nos 274 or 275 from Customs St.

The *Georgia Hostel* (tel 399-560), 2 km from the city, is a little further up Carlton Gore Rd, on the corner at 189 Park Rd. This is another of Auckland's more run-down hostels. Dorm beds cost from $13 and there are also double rooms from $15 per person. To get there, take bus No 31 from Victoria St East.

**Hostels – Mt Eden** The Mt Eden district, about 20 minute walk or 5 minute bus ride from the city centre, has two excellent hostels. You could take bus Nos 274 and 275 from the bus terminal or take bus Nos 255 to 258, 265 or 267 from the St James Theatre on Queen St.

The *Eden Lodge Tourist Hostel* (tel 600-174) at 22 View Rd, Mt Eden is a very 'up-market' hostel. Billed as a 'jetsetters 5-star hostel' it's in a huge colonial-era home, surrounded by gardens and filled with antique furnishings, leather couches, original art, and many large pleasant spaces. Four-bed dorms cost $14, singles or doubles cost $16 per person and it's $12 in the bunkroom behind the house. Communal dinners, cooked several times weekly, cost about $2. Buses stop at View Rd.

The *Auckland Backpackers* (tel 604-386) at 10 Akiraho St is another fine hostel highly recommended by travellers. The four or six-bed dorms cost $14 and the double rooms cost $15 per person.

**Hostels – Parnell** There are also three good hostels in Parnell, one of Auckland's more stylish districts. From the city centre, you could either walk there (a 20 minute walk) or take bus Nos 635, 645 or 655.

The *Parnell Youth Hostel* (tel 790-258, 793-731) at Churton St is on the corner of

Earle St, three short blocks east of Parnell Rd. The 75 dorm beds cost $15 per night.

The *Parnell Garden Lodge* (tel 302-0570) at 25 St George's Bay Rd just off Parnell Rd is one of the International Travellers Network hostels, a fine place in a large, elegant old home originally built for the Queen of Tonga. Rates are $15 in dorm rooms or $25/35 for single/double rooms.

About 50 metres down the hill, at 60 St George's Bay Rd, *Lantana Lodge* (tel 734-546) has dorm bunks at $15, single rooms at $25 and double rooms at $35 and $40 per day. If you stay 7 nights, you get 1 night free.

**Hostels – Other Areas** The *Franklin International Network Hostel* (tel 780-168), at 2 Franklin Rd just off Ponsonby Rd, is in Ponsonby, another of Auckland's trendy districts (though not so 'up-market' as Parnell), with lots of inexpensive restaurants and music venues. This hostel, another of the International Network hostels, is the scene of the big weekly barbecue party and it's mostly a young peoples' party house, with a beer bar and 35 beds, all in dorm rooms. It costs $15 per night. To get there, take bus Nos 015 or 016 from the city centre.

The *Picton St Backpackers* (tel 780-966), at 34 Picton St, Freemans Bay, is about a 15 minute walk from the city centre. It's in a big old three-storey kauri house with great views looking out to the sea, clean and peaceful with the occasional party or barbecue. Per-person costs are $14 in dorm rooms or $17.50 in double rooms. They provide free pick-up from the city centre or you can take bus Nos 15, 16 or 28.

The *Ivanhoe Traveller's Lodge* (tel 862-800) is a large 80-bed hostel at 14 Shirley Rd, Western Springs, near Motat and the zoo. It's a popular hostel with a sauna, pool table and other amenities. Costs are $12 in dorms, $15 per person in double, twin or triple rooms, or $40 in self-contained tourist flats. Stay a week and you get 1 day free. To get there, take bus No 045 to Grey Lynn shops, then walk down Turangi Rd to No 54, following the signs. They operate a courtesy bus from the airport.

The *Plumley House* (tel 520-4044) at 515 Remuera Rd on the corner of Ladies Mile is another large hostel in a converted former home. Rates per person are $14 in dorm rooms, $16 in double rooms or $18 in single rooms, with a 10% discount for weekly stays. Bus Nos 635, 643, 644, 645, 653 or 655 all come from the city centre and they also provide free pick-up.

Near the airport, *Willow Lodge* (tel 275-5625) at 6 Jordan Rd, Mangere, is only a 5 minute ride from the airport but about a 30 minute ride from central Auckland. Cost per person is $14.50 in dorm rooms, $18 in twin rooms or $20 in single rooms. To get there, take the Mangere bus to Jordan Rd.

During university vacations you may find some student accommodation available to visitors. Try phoning *Student Accommodation* on 737-691 or 737-686.

**Guest Houses** In Parnell, the *Ascot Parnell* (tel 399-012) at 36 St Stephens Ave, off Parnell Rd, has nine guest rooms in a restored historic home. Rooms with attached bathroom cost $65/89 for singles/doubles; an ample breakfast is included. It's a lovely, peaceful place to stay.

Close to the city centre, at 62 Emily Place, the *Aspen Lodge* (tel 796-698) is a straightforward place but clean, tidy and well organised, in an older building with character. Rooms, all with shared bathrooms, are $41/56 including breakfast.

The *Heathmaur Lodge* (tel 763-527) at 75 Argyle St, Herne Bay, is in a big three-storey old home which is a 2 minute walk to the sandy beach, also an easy walk to restaurants and a 10 minute ride to the city centre. With the water nearby, the open view, the quiet neighbourhood, the spacious accommodation and the homy atmosphere, it seems far removed from the big city even though it's so close. Basic room rates are $35/50 for share-facility rooms, add $10 for private bathrooms. There are lower weekly rates. It's an extra $5 for a continental breakfast or $10 for cooked breakfast, and $15 for a three-course dinner.

The *Rosana Travel Hotel* (tel 766-603) at

217 Ponsonby Rd, Ponsonby, is in a rather loud but convenient location, near to Victoria Market and all the restaurants and shops on Ponsonby Rd. The 14 rooms here are $40/60 for share-facility rooms, $70 for private-facility rooms, including a 'homestyle' breakfast.

The *Freeman's Travellers' Hotel* (tel 765-046) at 65 Wellington St, Freeman's Bay, is a simple place, also a bit loud, but the rooms stretch back from the road in a garden with a small swimming pool. The rates of $35/50 include a continental breakfast. *Aachen House* (tel 520-2329) at 39 Market Rd, Remuera is another guest house in a fine old home, with seven rooms, including English breakfast, at $41/63.

Two guest houses run by the same fellow provide budget accommodation in converted private homes, with nightly rates at $25/44 or weekly rates at $140/280. No meals are served, but there's free use of the kitchen, laundry rooms, and other facilities. The *Budget Inn*, with 13 single rooms, is at 36 Cardigan St, Grey Lynn, and the *Rosalee Lodge* is at 108 Grange Rd, Mt Eden, with seven large twin rooms. Phone 688-887 for bookings at either place.

**Hotels** The *Park Towers Hotel* (tel 392-800) at 3 Scotia Place, just off Queen St, is new and clean, with a simple, student-like decor and 108 rooms, about half with private facilities and the other half without. Rates are $75 for the plain rooms, or $130 with private bathrooms.

Nearby, the *Railton Travel Hotel* (tel 796-487) at 411 Queen St is a well-kept long runner with 130 rooms. Regular rooms, with attached bathrooms, colour TV and telephone, are $58/82 for singles/doubles, including an English cooked breakfast and a newspaper at your door in the morning. Budget rooms, with a sink, shared bathrooms and no breakfast, are $44/63. A smorgasbord dinner for $15 is served in the restaurant.

The *Albion Hotel* (tel 794-900), on the corner of Wellesley and Hobson streets, has 20 rooms in an older building done up with a bit of style. Rates are $73/84.

Very centrally located, *Abby's Hotel* (tel 303-4799) is on the corner of Wellesley and Albert streets and has rooms, all with attached bathrooms, at $69/83 including breakfast. There's a good selection of bars and restaurants here and the only real drawback is that some of the singles are extremely compact, postage-stamp size. Opposite the railway station at 131 Beach Rd, *Farthings Hotel* (tel 390-629) has rooms at $30/55 without private facilities or $55/75 with attached bathrooms.

If you want Auckland's best you can move right up into the *Hyatt, Regent, Sheraton* bracket. At the Regent a single is over $200 and you can pay $1000 a night for their best suite!

**Motels** Auckland has over 100 motels, so it's hard to make any particular recommendations. Generally costs start from around $50 for singles, $60 for doubles or twins. Some of the camping grounds (see Camping & Cabins) have tourist flats or motel units. Try the *Remuera Motor Lodge*, the *Tui Glen* or *Avondale* camps for example.

There are several areas reasonably close to the city with a selection of motels. On the corner of St Stephens Ave and Parnell Rd the *Casa Nova Motor Lodge* (tel 771-463) has 17 units in an older building and in a newer extension, with studio units at $77/84, or $88/94 for one-bedroom units. Some of them are quite spacious – sizes range from single to one big family unit sleeping seven – and all are self-contained and very well-equipped.

Going down Parnell Rd towards the city the *Parnell Budget Motor Lodge* (tel 303-3462) at No 320 is another reasonably priced motel with 15 rooms at $56 to $62 single, $68 to $73 double, with a 20% discount for stays of a week or more. You can bargain for a discount here.

Another alternative is Jervois Rd in Herne Bay from the junction with Ponsonby Rd. There are a number of places along here or off Jervois Rd along Shelly Beach Rd. This is close to the southern end of the Harbour Bridge. At 6 Tweed St, which in turn is off

Shelly Beach Rd, the *Harbour Bridge Motel* (tel 763-489) has singles from $50, doubles and family units from $65. It's an older (1886) building full of character and style with a new extension. There's an outdoor barbecue, an attractive garden, and it's a convenient location. You can bargain for a rate here and probably get it.

Continue across the bridge and there are more reasonably priced motels in Takapuna or Birkenhead. If you have an early flight to catch and want to stay out near the airport there are lots of motels in Mangere, particularly along Kirkbride Rd and McKenzie Rd. Almost every one of them manages to get the word 'airport' into their names and most of them are from around $70 a night. The *Auckland Airport Skyway Lodge* (tel 275-4443) at 28-30 Kirkbride Rd has a share-facility lodge with rooms at $39/49 and a bunkroom with beds at $26 per person. There are also two-bedroom family units starting at $74 double. There's a swimming pool, spa pool, sauna, TV lounge and billiard table, and courtesy airport transport.

**Camping & Cabins** The *Takapuna Tourist Court* (tel 497-909) is at 22 The Promenade, Takapuna, 8 km from the CPO, right on the beach on the North Shore with a view of Rangitoto Island. It's an easy walk to the shops and centre of Takapuna, and a 10 minute drive or bus ride into Auckland centre. Camping sites are $11/17 for one/two people, $22.50 with power, plus there are cabins at $32 and on-site caravans at $40. It's the usual story – supply your own bedding, cutlery, etc.

The *North Shore Caravan Park* (tel 419-1320) at 52 Northcote Rd is also in Takapuna, 4 km north of the Harbour Bridge. Camping sites are $14/20 for one/two people, and there are cabins at $20 per person, or bunkrooms at $15 per person. The *Tui Glen Camping Park* (tel Henderson 838-8978) is at Henderson, in the wine country 13 km north-west of Auckland. Sites are $6 per person, $9 with power. Cabins are $28 to $33 for two, and they also have tourist flats at $46.

The *Avondale Motor Park* (tel 887-228) at 46 Bollard Ave, off New North Rd, is 9 km from the CPO but fairly close to Motat and the zoo. Sites are $8 per person, $9 with power, and they also have on-site caravans at $26/33 for one/two people, cabins at $29/39 and tourist flats at $39/49.

South of the city centre you could check out *Remuera Motor Lodge* (tel 545-126) at 16A Minto Rd, off Remuera Rd, 8 km from the CPO, which in addition to the usual comforts also has a swimming pool. There's a variety of accommodation here, with motel rooms at $68, tourist flats at $49, cabins at $33, caravan sites at $17, and tent sites at $7.50; all prices are for two people.

The *Manukau Central Caravan Park* (tel 266-8016) at 902 Great South Rd, Manukau, is a quiet place, away from the motorway. Sites are $6 per person, on-site caravans sleeping four to six people cost $30 to $36 for two, depending on equipment provided, and there's also a tourist flat. The *Meadow Court Motor Camp* (tel 278-5612) is also in Manukau at 630 Great South Rd, not far from the airport. There's a swimming pool, a children's play area, and it's handy to Rainbow's End amusement park. Sites here cost $7 per person; $8 with power.

Finally *South Auckland Caravan & Camping Park* (tel 294-8903) is on the Great South Rd at Ramarama. It's a large park, on a 48 hectare dairy farm 500 metres from the Ramarama motorway offramp. You can walk around on the farm, see the dairy operations, enjoy the private lake, and it also has a colour TV room, fish & chips, shops and a laundry. Powered caravan sites are $11/16 for one/two people, tent sites without power are $9/13. Cabins and on-site caravans cost $25 for two.

## Places to Eat

Auckland, once the home of overwhelming blandness, has undergone something of a culinary revolution in the last decade. There are now all sorts of dining possibilities but, unlike some cities, there are no distinct ethnic areas. You can find almost anything almost anywhere.

**Cheap Eats** There are numerous places in the city ready to turn out a good sandwich for you. Try *Matthew Mulvaney* at 18 Lorne St, where $3 will get you a bowl of soup or a hot roast beef sandwich to take away or eat there. Nearby on High St, almost on the corner with Victoria St East, *Sarnie's Takeaways* has a good local reputation. Actually on the High St/Victoria St East corner is *Boulangerie Croix du Sud* with a good selection of croissants, French-style bread, baguette sandwiches and lunchtime snacks.

In the old Customs House on the corner of Customs St West and Albert St is the pleasant little *Corner Cafe*, bright and sunny, with burgers in a bun or pita, sandwiches, soups, cappuccino, and bottomless cups of coffee and tea, all at great prices. It's open from 7.30 am to 4 pm weekdays, 7.30 am to 5.30 pm on weekends. Downstairs in the cellar is the *Cellar Cafe*, open from 9.30 am to 4.30 pm every day. In the small shopping centre by the Downtown Bus Terminal *Peppercorns Deli* has ready-to-go sandwiches and rolls.

The *Bytes Cafe* at the Auckland City YHA Hostel, just off Queen St on the corner of City Rd and Liverpool St, is a good place to get a cheap meal or snack and swap travellers' tales. Don't forget the *University Cafeteria* as another city cheap eats possibility.

The cheap eats and late nights quandary can be solved by the *The White Lady* mobile hamburger stand on Shortland St off Queen St. It's open 6 pm to 2.30 am Monday to Wednesday, until 4 am on Thursdays, and 24 hours on weekends and holidays. A variety of burgers start at $3.50, there are plenty of toasted sandwiches, or you can splurge all the way up to $9 for a big steak.

The *24 Hour Cafe* on Customs St East just off Queen St is just what the name says – a very simple place to get breakfast or basic meals and snacks any time of the day or night. There's another 24 hour restaurant, *Mickey Finn's*, at 26 Lorne St.

**Fast Food & Pubs** Yes, Auckland has *McDonald's*, quite a number of them in fact. You'll find one of them about halfway up Queen St and another just around the corner on Karangahape Rd. There's also a *Wendy's* more or less opposite the Queen St McDonald's and upstairs. In the same vicinity is a *Pizza Hut*, downstairs in the Strand Arcade.

Also downstairs is *Ziggies*, a clean and glossy up-a-notch cafeteria-style fast food outlet, licensed, with a bar to one side. Main courses are around $8.50 to $12. There's another *Ziggies* upstairs in the Mid-City Centre, also on Queen St.

Two places have come up with the idea of putting several varied low-cost, fast-food ethnic counters all together in one spot, tables in the centre, and letting customers pick and choose from the international offering. The lower ground floor of the *BNZ Tower* on Queen St is an open hall with many different counters including Turkish, Chinese, Italian, a coffee shop and salad bar, seafood, fish & chips, a delicatessen, and one counter specialising in NZ lamb, beef and pork. A similar place, only smaller, is in *The Plaza*, an assortment of shops hidden off Vulcan Lane, a tiny walking lane between Victoria and Shortland streets, connecting Queen and High streets. You can lunch here for around $5, choosing from Mexican, Middle Eastern, Chinese, fish & chips and other stalls.

The various city pubs are another economical possibility, particularly at lunchtime. The three pleasant pubs at the *Shakespeare Brewery*, on the corner of Albert and Wyndham streets, all serve food, as does the Malaysian bistro of the *London Bar* up on the 1st floor at Wellesley St West near the corner of Queen St. In the Downtown Airline Terminal on Lower Albert St the *Akarana Tavern* has a big selection of meals from $6 to $8 at lunch time.

**Restaurants** The *Caravanserai Tea House* at 430 Queen St is run by two Kiwi sisters who have backpacked in many parts of the world. They returned with a love of the Middle East and opened this tiny restaurant as a sort of caravanserai or way-station for relaxation and revitalisation of weary travellers. There's a casual atmosphere and lots of Turkey, Egypt, etc in the decor. Arabic, Turkish and Greek food is served, mostly vegetarian but with a few meat dishes too, and you can get a good *meze* combination platter for $6.50 or order à la carte. It's open from 11 am to 8 pm Sunday to Wednesday and 11 am to 11 pm Thursday to Saturday.

The *Middle East* at 23A Wellesley St West is a tiny place and is usually pretty crowded. Deservedly so since the food is excellent and economical – the usual Lebanese specialities (schwarma, kebabs, felafel) at around $4 to $6 for snacks or $10 to $12 as full meals with salad and pita bread. Check out their great collection of camel art. It's open for dinner every night but for lunch only from Monday to Friday. Also on Wellesley St West at No 58 the *Baalbeck Lebanese Restaurant* has traditional Lebanese food and belly dancing on Friday nights. Lunch and dinner is served every day, with main dishes $11 to $13, soups and starters $4.75, and lunchtime takeaways at $4.

*Tony's* at 27 Wellesley St West must be doing something right because they've been carrying on unchanged while plenty of other places have come and gone. They have a basic steakhouse menu which also features NZ lamb dishes and pastas. A good steak dinner, with starter and dessert, may cost around $30, or about $12 for lunch. There's another *Tony's* at 32 Lorne St and the very similar *Lord Nelson Steak House* at 39 Victoria St West.

The *Mekong* at 295 Queen St has been consistently voted the 'best ethnic restaurant in Auckland' by all and sundry. It's got a varied collection of Vietnamese specialities with main courses around $15. There's a lunchtime buffet for $14 and a special Sunday 10-course buffet dinner for $17 served from 6 to 8.30 pm.

A number of places in the city provide Italian food including *A Little Italy* at 43 Victoria St West where you can get good pizzas or pasta.

For Mexican food, the *Hard to Find Cafe* at 47 High St is a small place with a bright Mexican decor and healthy food. It is indeed hard to find, tucked away back from the street in an arcade. Main courses are around $14. It's open for dinner every night, for lunch Monday to Friday.

You can go Chinese at anything from cheap takeaways to flashy restaurants. The *New Orient Chinese Restaurant* in the Strand Arcade on Queen St has a buffet lunch from noon to 2.30 pm Monday to Friday for $14, dinner nightly with dancing every night except Sundays.

There are several Indian restaurants around town, including the *Poppadom* downstairs at 55 Customs St, open for dinner Monday to Saturday, and the *Maharajah* at 19 Khyber Pass Rd, serving dinner every night but Mondays. Both have won awards for the 'best Indian restaurant in Auckland'. There's also the tiny *New Delhi Indian Cafe* at 38 Wellesley St West or *The Curry Cafe* at 47 High St with excellent food, a generous vegetarian dinner for $14 and many selections of vegetarian and meat starters and main dishes.

Several glossy places provide drinks and meals with a stylish air. Try the Wine Bar in the *Hotel De Brett* on the corner of High and Shortland streets or *Cheers Cafe & Bar* at 12 Wyndham St, just off Queen St, open every day of the year from 11 am to 1 am. The *Cin Cin Brasserie & Bar* in the Auckland Ferry Building at 99 Quay St has a fine view of the ferries and harbour; it's open from 10 am to 2 am.

Surprisingly, despite the big Polynesian population there's no Polynesian restaurant as yet.

**Restaurants – Symonds St** There's a string of restaurants up Symonds St from the university – not too far from the centre. The extremely popular *Armadillo* at 178 Symonds St is a greatly enlarged version of the restaurant of the same name in Wellington. It's a cavernous and noisy place done up in John-Wayne-Western style. 'Born to grill' the sign over the kitchen announces and the menu features burgers and similar straightforward 'Western' food at $17 for main courses. Desserts are all $7. It's not cheap but you won't leave hungry. It's licensed and BYO, open from 6 pm daily.

The *Ali Baba* at 181 Symonds St is a small, informal but good Middle Eastern place with take away or eat there facilities and lunchtime or takeaway prices are around $5. Sit-down dinners are more expensive, with meat or vegetarian main courses from $14 to $18, starters and salads $4.50 to $6, desserts $3.50. It's open for lunch and dinner Monday to Friday but on Saturdays for dinner only.

Other places in the same area include the *Front Page Cafe* at No 163 with a newspaper decor and straightforward but well prepared food with main courses from $8.50 to $16. It's open from 6 pm to 1 am Wednesday to Sunday. There are a number of other restaurants and cafes in the vicinity, although a few old favourite spots have fallen to the bulldozer in an area redevelopment programme.

**Restaurants – Parnell** There are all sorts of restaurants along Parnell Rd in Parnell. They range from pizzerias to pub food specialists to Chinese takeaways to espresso coffee shops and a number of Italian restaurants. Lots of places have tables outside so you can enjoy the fresh air.

The Parnell Village conglomeration of shops has some good medium-priced restaurants hidden away including *Papagayo* for Mexican food, *Valerio's* for Italian food, and the bright and pleasant *Bouquet d'Or* coffee shop with an accent on French pastries, coffees and light meals. Other good coffee shops along Parnell Rd are *Oliver's Cafe* and the *Colonial Coffee Shoppe*.

Tucked away behind some other shops at No 237, the *Elephant House Crafts Centre and Vegetarian Cafe* is worth looking for. Delicious food and strong coffees, all at low prices, are served in a greenhouse-like cafe area loaded with plants, while soft jazz plays in the background. It's open from 8 am to 3 pm daily.

The *Alexandra Tavern* at No 269 was once a straightforward pub but has now been upgraded to a large, popular restaurant with an interesting menu of snacks and meals

from around $13 to $17; also check out the wine list, and the live jazz on Saturday and Sunday afternoons from 1 to 4 pm. Next door, *La Trattoria Cafe* is a fancy Italian restaurant with pasta dishes from $8, meals from $14 to $20. Other Italian places include *La Visola* and the *Italian Cafe* plus a number of pizzerias. The trendy *Veranda Bar & Grill* is another good spot.

The *Kebab Kid* opposite the library near the top of the hill at No 363 Parnell Rd is small and nothing much to look at, but it's been voted one of the top spots of its kind in Auckland, with tasty Middle Eastern food to take away or eat there and prices lower than most places in town, even though it's in fancy Parnell. You can get a full dinner with a felafel or meat main course, Turkish rice and a selection of salads for $9.50 to $11, a *meze* selection of five salads for two people for $11, or a simple salad, felafel or meat-filled pita for around $5. The Kebab Kid opens at 5 pm every evening.

**Restaurants – Ponsonby** Numerous restaurants are strung along Ponsonby Rd, again offering all sorts of cuisines. Don't miss *Fed Up* at No 244, open in the evenings only. It's kind of shabbily kitsch but there's real art on the walls and real food at reasonable prices as well. The dishes are imaginative, well prepared and great value. Anyway, a restaurant playing Derek and the Dominoes' *Layla* as you step through the door can't be bad! Next door, the *Bake Haus* has wonderful baked goods of every description.

The *Cafe Cezanne* at 296 Ponsonby Rd is another small, casual place with excellent atmosphere and food at good prices. Breakfasts, light meals, gourmet burgers and unusual pies are served all day, all at around $5, and someone will come around to your table and serve you bottomless cups of coffee. It's open from 8 am to 6 pm Monday to Friday and 9 am to 5 pm on weekends. Next door the *Cafe Mediterranean* has Middle Eastern takeaways at about $4.50 but it's lots more expensive if you sit down to eat in the restaurant. The *Expresso Love* coffee shop is just across the road.

The *Open Late Cafe* at 134A Ponsonby Rd has straightforward food, good desserts and coffee and it is indeed open late. Also open late is *Hamburger Heaven*, on the corner of Ponsonby Rd and Tole St, with 20 different burgers from $3.50 to $6.50.

The *Star Horse* at 185 Ponsonby Rd near the corner of Franklin Rd offers a Chinese all-you-can-eat buffet for only $8.50 from 6 to 10 pm every evening and, naturally, it's always busy. Just about every dish contains meat. Another place where you can get cheap Chinese food is the *Golden Bowl Takeaways* at No 268. A four-course Chinese meal costs $5.30; it's open every day except Tuesdays.

Other ethnic possibilities are the acclaimed *Spanish 260 Restaurant* at No 260, with seafood or vegetarian paella for $17, open from Tuesday to Saturday in the evenings; the *Treble Clef Cafe* at No 181, serving hearty, authentic German food for lunch and dinner except on Sundays; and the *Binto Egyptian Cafe* at No 107, with $12 vegetarian or $15 meat Egyptian dinners from 6 to 10 pm every evening except Mondays .

The *Cafe Niche* round the corner from Ponsonby Rd on College Hill is a very small cafe with an artsy atmosphere serving a wholefood cuisine of vegetarian and seafood dishes including paella, curry, vegetarian lasagne, and Shiitake mushrooms. All main dishes cost $13.50, salads $3 to $5, soups $5.50, and there's quite a selection of special coffees, teas, and other drinks. It's open from 6 pm until late every day.

Nearby, right on the Ponsonby/Jervois Rd corner, the *Ponsonby Hotel* has reasonable pub food in their pleasant *Corner Bar*.

The *Java Jive* on Pompelier Terrace just off Ponsonby Rd has a reasonably priced menu with a wide selection of international meat and vegetarian dishes, plus strong coffees and good desserts. The owner, a jazz & blues buff who used to own a record shop, has a great collection of music playing on tape and also on the jukebox. One whole wall is taken up by a colourful jazz/blues mural,

and there are photos and art of many of the jazz/blues pioneers. It's a very enjoyable spot, open from 6 pm every day and for brunch from 11.30 am to 2.30 pm on Sundays.

**Vegetarian** The High St/Lorne St area is a great place for vegetarians who are fairly well catered for in Auckland. The very popular *Dominoes' Cafe* at 2 Lorne St has a wide assortment of meals from around $5 to $7 plus good fruit juices, lassis, espresso and a mouth-watering selection of cakes from around $2. There's a pleasant courtyard out the back and best of all it's open long hours – 8 am to 9 pm Monday to Friday, 9 am to 9 pm on Saturdays and 4 to 9 pm Sundays.

The *Simple Cottage* at 50 High St is another popular vegetarian place with good meals from around $6 and more fine desserts. Vegetarian places really seem to turn out great desserts! This, too, is open long hours, 9 am to 9 pm Monday to Saturday and 9 am to 3 pm on Sundays. Across the road is *Badgers* at No 47, a tiny place with a good variety of wholesome vegetarian food to take away or eat there. Hot lunches are about $3 to $5.50, salads an extra $4. It's open Monday to Thursday from 10 am to 8 pm, Friday until 9 pm.

*Gopals* at 291 Queen St, upstairs on the 1st floor, is run by the Hare Krishnas. At this relaxed, comfortable place Indian vegetarian food is served and you can get snacks, à la carte meals, or an all-you-can-eat combination plate for $6.65. It's open from noon to 2.30 pm Monday to Friday, and 5 to 8.30 pm Thursday to Saturday. There's a special festival programme from 5 to 7.30 pm on Sundays, with a feast for only $2.

**Entertainment**
Auckland has a pretty good variety of places to go after the sun sets, many of them with music. Whatever you're doing late at night in Auckland keep your eye on the time if you're dependent on public transport – there isn't any. You can make it home from the pictures or a pub but you'll hit trouble if you're out later than that.

**Pubs** The *Hotel de Brett* on the corner of Shortland and High streets in the city has a variety of pubs and bars, including a *Wine Bar* that's a popular meeting place with good food and the downstairs *Shortland Bar* that's more of a punk hangout. There's music in the upstairs lounge. The *Four Seasons Pub* is also nearby.

The *Shakespeare Brewery* on the corner of Albert and Wyndham streets has several pubs and bars, with live music in the upstairs one. They make several different beers right on the premises and it's got great atmosphere. The *London Bar* and the *London Underground Pub* on Wellesley St West near the corner of Queen St are another enjoyable combination, with a beer bar sporting 150 beers from around the world in the underground section, while the upstairs is a more classier bar where there's a pianist at the beginning of the week, and a jazz combo Wednesday to Saturday, playing from around 7 to 10 pm. *Abby's Hotel* on the corner of Wellesley St East and Albert St has several bars featuring live entertainment. *Alfie's* in the Century Arcade on High St is a gay bar with a DJ, live entertainment and meals.

In Ponsonby, the *Corner Bar* on the corner of Ponsonby and Jervois roads, is another pub with good atmosphere, live jazz and rhythm & blues music in the evenings and on Sunday afternoons, and big screen videos.

On Parnell Rd in Parnell try the *Alexandra Tavern*, with live jazz on Saturday and Sunday afternoons, or *Frame's* with pool tables and a big video screen. Also in Parnell the *Nag's Head Tavern* down at the bottom of St George's Bay Rd is a popular English-style pub where it's a challenge to squeeze through the door on Friday nights.

**Jazz** In addition to the pubs mentioned here, many with live jazz music, probably the most popular jazz hangout in town is *The Bird Cage* on the corner of Victoria St and Franklin Rd, with live jazz, blues, and rhythm & blues in the evenings and on Sunday afternoons. If you're a jazz and blues buff, check out the *Java Jive* cafe (see Restaurants —

Ponsonby) for good sounds and jazzy artwork.

The 'Jazz Ferry' Friday nights on the Devonport ferry, with a jazz band playing on the ferry as it goes back and forth, is a good time; for $9 you can stay on the ferry all evening if you want, getting on and off again whenever you like. The *Masonic Tavern* in Devonport has live jazz on Thursday evenings.

**Rock** *Candyo's* in the Chase Plaza Building, 92-96 Albert St, is about the biggest nightclub in town, with rock music attracting a young following. The *Club Roma* in the Civic Theatre on Queen St is another one, with a trendy mid-20s crowd, or try the *Grapes* nightclub at 184 Victoria St West. *Le Bom* at 51 Nelson St and *The Venue* also have rock, and the *Akarana Tavern* in the Downtown Air Terminal has live rock music on weekends. The *Shakespeare Brewery* and *Abby's Hotel* also have rock music (see Pubs). Over in Ponsonby, on Ponsonby Rd near the corner of Jervois Rd, *The Gluepot* has rock and alternative music Wednesday to Saturday nights. Larger rock concerts are held at *The Power Station*.

**Other Entertainment** *Auckland University* has a restaurant, pub, live music, plays, film series, lectures, and more. Art films can be seen at the University or at the *Vogue*, *Academy*, *Charley Grey's* or *Bridgeway* theatres, the last being in Northcote. Many of the harbour boats offer evening entertainment, with dinner cruises, dancing, etc in addition to the Friday night 'Jazz Ferry'.

**Getting There & Away**
**Air** Auckland is the major international arrival point for flights to New Zealand. See the Information section for airline office locations and the Getting There chapter for information on international flights.

Air New Zealand connects Auckland with the other major centres in New Zealand. See the introductory Getting Around chapter for fare details. Ansett New Zealand also has a variety of flights in and out of Auckland and there are Mt Cook flights to Rotorua and other destinations in the South Island. A number of local operators like Eagle Air also have flights in and out of Auckland.

**Bus** InterCity buses have services from Auckland to just about everywhere in New Zealand. See the relevant sections for details. InterCity buses (tel 792-500) operate from beside the railway station. Other companies with services to and from Auckland include:

Clarks Northliner
    Downtown Airline Terminal (tel 796-056) – services north to Whangarei and the Bay of Islands, south to Mt Maunganui and Tauranga
Mt Cook Landline
    105 Queen St (tel 395-395) – services south through Hamilton, Rotorua and Taupo to Napier or Wellington. Departures are from the corner of Quay and Albert streets, by the Downtown Airline Terminal
Newmans
    69 St George's Bay Rd, Parnell (tel 399-738) – services to Whangarei in Northland and south through Hamilton to New Plymouth, Tauranga, Rotorua, Taupo, Palmerston North, Napier, Mt Maunganui, Wanganui and Wellington. Buses leave from the Downtown Airline Terminal

The Northcape Shuttle and Kiwi Experience buses also depart from Auckland, see the Getting Around section for details.

**Train** Trains run twice daily between Auckland and Wellington, operating from the railway station (tel 792-500) on Beach Rd. The Silver Fern train departs from both ends of the line at around 8.30 am and arrives around 6.30 pm, Monday to Saturday. The Northerner is an overnight train, departing both Auckland and Wellington Sunday to Friday nights around 9 pm and arriving around 8.30 am.

**Hitching** As usual, it's easier hitching if you get out of town before starting to hitch, but if you want to hitchhike from town use the Beaumont St motorway ramp near Victoria Park to go north, the Grafton Bridge ramp behind the hospital to go south. Otherwise, to get out of the urban sprawl and start hitch-

ing northwards take a bus from the Downtown Bus Terminal to Waiwera (bus No 895), Hatfields Beach (bus No 894), Orewa (bus No 893) or Silverdale (bus No 899). All leave about six times a day and cost about $5. Alternatively, you can take an hourly bus to Albany for about $2.50 and start hitching from there. Going south, take the Hamilton-bound bus and get off at the Bombay Hills crossroads. This bus leaves six times a day on weekdays, three or four times a day on weekends, and costs around $9.

### Getting Around
**Airport Transport** The Auckland Airport is a fair way out (21 km) from the centre. Super Shuttle (tel 375-210) and Airporter Express (tel 275-1234) provide door-to-door airport transport; the cost is $12 per person or $18 for two.

There's also an airport shuttle bus which runs every half hour between the airport and the Downtown Airline Terminal, beginning at 6 am and finishing at 9 pm, with stops at the Sheraton Hotel and the railway station. Fares are $8 one way, $14 return.

Between the terminals at the airports the shuttle bus costs $2 or a taxi will set you back about $4. There's a signposted footpath between the International and Domestic terminals, the distance is about 900 metres, good practice for tramping the park trails!

The airport has a tourist information counter, a bank, a couple of rent-a-car desks and a dial-it-yourself hotel booking counter. There's a left luggage facility at the Airporter Shuttle Bus ticket booth in the Domestic Terminal (open 6.45 am to 10 pm daily) and another at the Downtown Airline Terminal (open 6 am to 9 pm Monday to Friday, 6 am to 7 pm on Saturdays, 8 am to 9 pm on Sundays).

**Bus** The Downtown Bus Terminal is on Commerce St, behind the CPO, but not all buses leave from here. Local bus route time-tables are available from the bus terminal or from newsagents or you can phone Buz-a-Bus (tel 797-119) for information and schedules. It operates from 7.30 am to 5 pm daily although on weekends you may have trouble getting an answer as there aren't enough people to answer the phone. There's a bus info kiosk at the Downtown Bus Terminal open 7 am to 9.30 pm Monday to Saturday, 9 am to 5 pm on Sundays. The Bus Place at 93 Victoria St near the corner of Hobson St is another source of information, open from 8.15 am to 4.30 pm Monday to Friday.

Inner city fares cost 40 cents, further distances cost $1, then $2 and so on. Busabout passes are available for unlimited bus use from 9 am (anytime on weekends) for $6 (children $3). The passes can be bought on board the bus. Weekly passes are also available or there are family passes for $7.

An inner city shuttle bus (yellow with red destination band) runs from the railway station along Customs St and up Queen St to Karangahape Rd, returning to the station via Mayoral Drive and Queen St. It costs 40 cents for any distance.

**Taxi** There are plenty of taxis in Auckland but, as elsewhere in New Zealand, they rarely cruise. You usually have to phone for them or find them on taxi ranks.

**Ferry** For harbour ferry information phone 303-3319 for the Devonport ferry, 774-074 for the Birkenhead ferry. See also the Harbour Cruises section.

**Car Rental** The major rental operators plus a host of smaller ones have offices in Auckland, many of them at Mangere, near the airport. They include:

Ace Rent-A-Car
    465 Great North Rd (tel 767-353)
*Adventure Rental Vehicles
    142 Robertson Rd, Mangere (tel 275-8994)
Avis
    22 Wakefield St (tel 792-545, 792-650)
    Auckland Airport (tel 275-7239)
*Backpacker's Car Rentals
    free delivery (tel Piha 933-046, 267-7328)
*Blue Sky Motorhomes
    41 Veronica St, New Lynn (tel 876-399)

*Budget Rent-A-Car
    83 Beach Rd, Auckland (tel 796-768)
    Auckland Airport (tel 275-7097)
    Campervans
    5 Aintree Ave, Mangere (tel 275-7139)
Econocar
    100 New North Rd (tel 793-277)
Economy Rental Cars
    corner Favona and Tui Sts, Mangere East (tel 276-4250)
*Endeavour Motor Homes
    B/39 Rennie Drive, Mangere (tel 275-3034)
    72 Barrys Point Rd, Takapuna (tel 495-860)
*Henderson Rentals
    9 Dora St (tel 836-8089, 832-4953)
Hertz Rent-A-Car
    154 Victoria St West (tel 390-989, reservations 303-4924)
    Auckland Airport (tel 275-9953)
*Horizon Motor Homes
    154 Mackenzie Rd, Mangere (tel 378-226, Campas 275-1159)
*Johnston's Blue Motors
    corner Richard Pearse Drive & Brigade Rd, Mangere (tel 275-9396)
Letz Rent-A-Car
    51-53 Shortland St (tel 390-145)
*Maui Campavans
    100 New North Rd, Eden Terrace (tel 793-277)
*Mt Cook Line Motor Homes
    Ascot Rd, Mangere (tel 275-8674)
*Newman's Rentals
    Richard Pearse Drive, Mangere (tel 275-3409)
Percy Rent-A-Car
    219 Hobson St (tel 303-1122, 303-1129)
Travellers International Motor Inn
    190 Kirkbride Rd, Mangere (tel 275-7674)
*Scottie's Cheap Rental Cars (tel 602-625)
Southern Cross Rental Cars
    28 Rennie Dr, Mangere (tel 275-3099)
*Suntrek Campavans
    120 Great South Rd, Newmarket (tel 501-404)
Thrifty Car Rental
    154 McKenzie Rd, Mangere (tel 275-0473, 275-6728)
    10-12 Gladstone Rd, Parnell (tel 376-591)

*All the ones with an asterisk have campervans; many of these also have rental cars.

**Bicycle Rental** The Penny Farthing Cycle Shop (tel 792-524) on the corner of Symonds St and Khyber Pass Rd hires 10-speed bicycles for $15 a day or $60 a week plus a $30 deposit. They also have mountain or touring bikes with racks for $20 a day or $120 a week plus a $100 deposit. Panniers are $3 a day, $20 a week, with a $50 deposit.

Bicycle Tour Services (tel 591-961) also rents bicycles and touring gear, and if you like they can help you make a touring itinerary. Pedaltours (tel 674-605) offers guided group cycling tours of both the North and South islands, and you can hire a bike from them even if you don't join one of their tours. Over in Takapuna, Pack 'n' Pedal (tel 496-907) hires cycles and gear plus camping and outdoor equipment.

# Around Auckland

## Walks around Auckland

The Auckland City Council has a series of guided introductory walks, taking various routes around Auckland. Most walks take about 2 hours. They're free but you do need a reservation, phone 377-607 Monday to Friday, 9 am to 4 pm. The City Council and the Auckland Visitors Bureau also have printed pamphlets detailing a number of interesting walks within the city.

For those footing it a coast-to-coast walkway has been marked out between the Waitemata Harbour on the east coast and the Manukau Harbour on the west. The walkway encompasses Albert Park, the university, Auckland Domain, Mt Eden, One Tree Hill, and other points of interest, keeping as much as possible to reserves rather than city streets. Total walking time for the 13 km route, at an easy pace, is 4 hours and it's near bus routes all the way. An information pamphlet is available from the Auckland Visitors Bureau.

The Auckland Regional Authority Parks Division (tel 794-420) at 121 Hobson St has info on similar walkways in the greater Auckland region, including the many outlying parks they administer.

**New Zealand Walkway** Sections of the New Zealand Walkway have been opened in the Auckland area, the closest and most accessible being the Motutapu Farm Walk on Motutapu Island which is connected by causeway to Rangitoto and has a camping site at Home Bay. Check with the DOC for other NZ Walkways around Auckland. Some of these walks can take up to 5 hours but others are short and can be done in an hour.

**Other Walks** There is bush on the western fringe of Auckland at the Waikakere Ranges where there's a scenic drive, miles of bushwalks and tracks (some not recommended for the inexperienced) and wild, open beaches. The Auckland Visitors Bureau and DOSLI on the 6th floor of the AA Building have good maps. Apart from tour buses on the scenic drive, bus services are almost nonexistent so it is best to catch a bus to the fringing suburbs of Titirangi, Glen Eden, Henderson or Ranui, then walk or hitch.

## Vineyards

New Zealand's wines have suddenly earned themselves an excellent worldwide reputation and there are numerous vineyards in the west Auckland area. A leaflet available from the Auckland Visitors Bureau details the vineyards, their addresses, opening hours and shows their locations on a map. A number of the vineyards are within walking distance of Henderson which you can reach by public transport.

## DEVONPORT

Devonport is an attractive suburb on the tip of Auckland's North Shore peninsula. It was one of the earliest areas of European settlement and with its many well-preserved Victorian buildings it retains a 19th century atmosphere. Nowadays it also has a tourist atmosphere – it's the most popular excursion from Auckland centre, only 15 minutes away on the hourly ferry – and has lots of small shops, arts and crafts galleries, cafes and takeaways in the area surrounding the ferry dock.

Devonport also has several points of interest. Two volcanic cones, Mt Victoria and North Head, were once Maori pa settlements – you can see the terracing they made on the sides of the cones. Mt Victoria is the higher of the two, with a great 360° view and a map at the top pointing out all the landmarks and telling the names of the many islands you can see from up here. You can walk or drive to the summit of Mt Victoria, the road is open all the time except from 6 pm to 7 am Thursdays, Fridays and Saturdays.

North Head on the other cone is a historic reserve riddled with old tunnels built at the end of the last century due to fears of a Russian invasion. The fortifications were extended and enlarged during WW I and WW II but dismantled after the last war. Some of the old guns are still up here and a ranger is on hand with historical info. The reserve is open to vehicles every day from 6 am to 6 pm, to pedestrians until 10 pm.

The waterfront promenade of Devonport, with a view back towards the city, makes a lovely stroll. Around the ferry docks is a big lawn area where families picnic on sunny days. Walk west from the dock along the promenade and you come to the small Naval Museum, open from 10 am to 3.30 pm daily; admission is free.

### Places to Stay

Devonport is an enjoyable place to stay, outside of the city but within easy reach of it. The *Esplanade Hotel* (tel 451-291), directly opposite the ferry dock on the corner of Victoria Rd and Queen's Parade, has basic single/twin rooms at $35/50, double suites with private facilities at $80. The hotel's former Victorian grandeur is still evident. The *Devonport Manor* at 7 Cambridge Terrace (tel 452-529), a large Victorian home now housing a California-style B&B inn, has five rooms from $70 to $90 single, $92 to $112 double, including breakfast.

### Places to Eat

The *Devonport Cafe* near the dock at 18 Victoria St is a casual cafe with good food, serving everything from toasted sandwiches to fancy steak dinners and a selection of tempting cakes and pies, all at average prices. It's open from 10 am to 11 pm daily.

In this area, there are many other restaurants, cafes and takeaways.

The *Masonic Tavern*, on the corner of Church St and the waterfront parade, a few blocks east of the docks, has pub food, with lunch from noon to 2 pm, dinner from 5.30 pm Monday to Saturday. It has a relaxed local atmosphere and good views of the harbour.

### Entertainment

The *Masonic Tavern* has live entertainment on Thursday, Friday and Saturday evenings, with jazz nights on Thursdays and poetry readings on the first Wednesday of the month. The *Esplanade Hotel* also has live music Thursday to Saturday.

'Jazz Ferry' nights every Friday are also a good time. The ferry goes back and forth between Devonport and Auckland with live jazz music playing, and you can ride back and forth as many times as you want with a $9 open ticket.

### Getting There & Away

Buses run regularly from the Auckland Downtown Bus Terminal. The Devonport ferry departs from the Auckland Ferry Building every hour on the hour, from the Devonport dock back to Auckland every hour on the half hour. Return fare is $5 (children $2.50, family $14). There are extra sailings during commuter hours. The *Kestrel* ferry has 'Jazz Ferry' evenings Friday from 7 pm, and sometimes on Saturday too, see Entertainment.

You can also visit Devonport on a guided tour from Auckland, see Tours. If you're already in Devonport and want to take the tour you can show up to meet the van at the dock about 15 minutes past the hour, every hour from 10 am to 3 pm.

### PIHA & WHATIPU

Piha, about 40 km west of Auckland, is a seaside village of maybe 500 to 1000 souls (many artists, craftspeople and alternative types) that comes alive in summer with hundreds of beachgoers, holidaymakers and

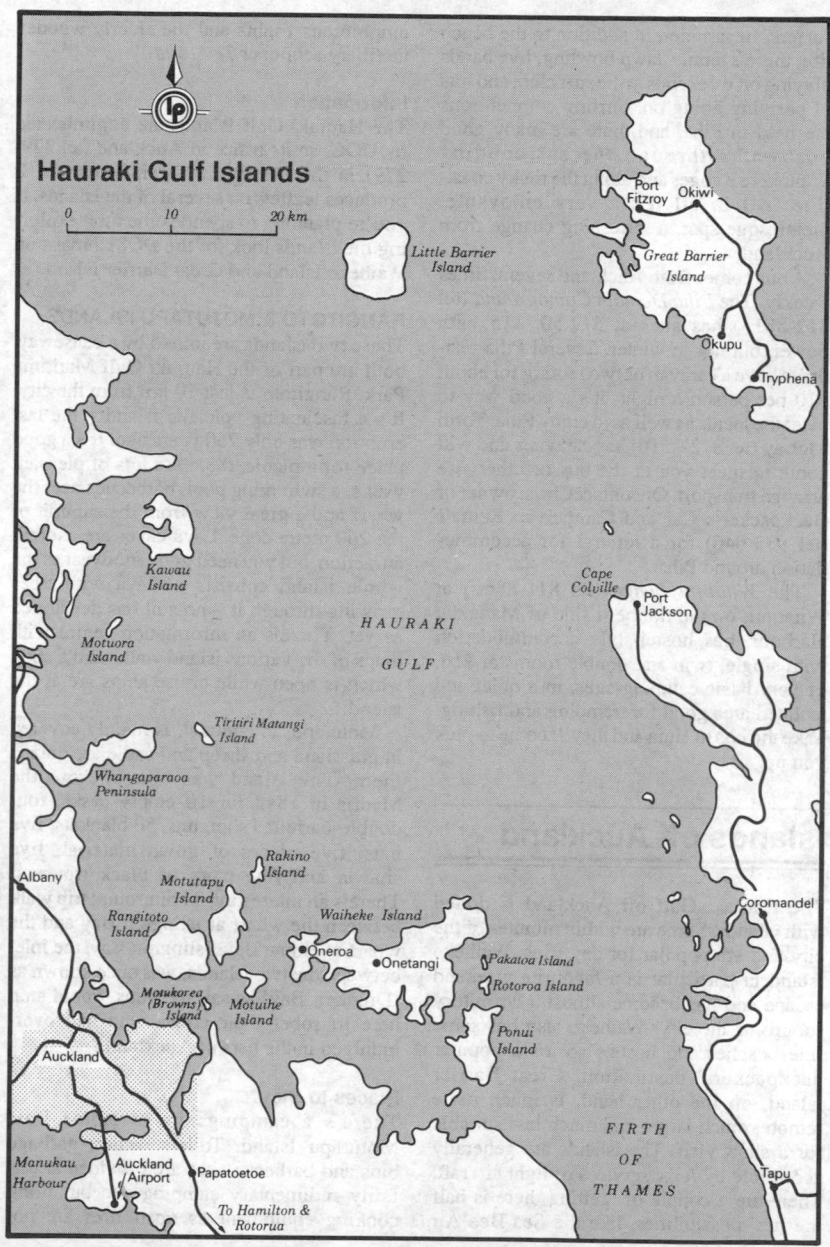

Hauraki Gulf Islands

0    10    20 km

Little Barrier Island

Port Fitzroy    Okiwi

Great Barrier Island

Okupu

Tryphena

Kawau Island

Cape Colville

Port Jackson

Motuora Island

HAURAKI

GULF

Tiritiri Matangi Island

Whangaparaoa Peninsula

Albany

Rakino Island

Motutapu Island

Rangitoto Island

Waiheke Island

Coromandel

Oneroa    Onetangi

Pakatoa Island

Rotoroa Island

Motukorea (Browns) Island

Motuihe Island

Auckland

Ponui Island

Manukau Harbour

Auckland Airport    Papatoetoe

FIRTH
OF
THAMES

Tapu

To Hamilton & Rotorua

surfers. In summer, in addition to the beach life, there's tennis, lawn bowling, live bands playing on weekends at the surf club, and lots of partying going on. Surfing competitions are held in Piha, and there are many good bushwalks through the surrounding Waitakere Ranges and along the rocky coastline. All in all it's a very enjoyable, picturesque spot, a refreshing change from Auckland.

A bus comes from Auckland several times weekly. The *Piha Domain Campground* (tel 812-8815) has sites at $12.50, $15 with power, but not in winter. Several Piha residents have a caravan or two renting for about $10 per person a night, it's a good way to meet the locals as well as to enjoy Piha. Tordi McLay (tel 812-8516) has caravans and will come to meet you at the bus or otherwise arrange transport. Or contact Chris, owner of Backpacker's Car and Campervan Rentals (tel 933-046) for a referral for accommodation around Piha.

The *Whatipu Lodge* (tel 811-8860) at Whatipu, on the northern side of Manukau Harbour, has hostel-style accommodation with single, twin and double rooms at $16, or very basic camping sites, in a quiet and isolated area good for tramping and fishing. Take the bus to Huia and they'll come to pick you up.

# Islands off Auckland

The Hauraki Gulf off Auckland is dotted with islands. Some are within minutes of the city and are popular for day trips. Waiheke Island in particular is a favourite weekend escape and has become almost a dormitory suburb of the city. Waiheke also has some fine beaches and hostels so it's a popular backpackers' destination. Great Barrier Island, on the other hand, is much more remote, much larger and much less suitable for a short visit. The islands are generally accessible by ferry services or light aircraft. There are a couple of 'getting there is half the fun' possibilities, like the Sea Bee Air amphibious flights and the elderly wooden auxiliary schooner *Te Aroha*.

## Information

The Hauraki Gulf Islands are administered by DOC, so its office in Auckland (tel 379-279) is the best place for information. It produces leaflets on several of the islands. If you're planning to spend some time exploring the islands look for the DOSLI maps on Waiheke Island and Great Barrier Island.

## RANGITOTO & MOTUTAPU ISLANDS

These two islands are joined by a causeway, both are part of the Hauraki Gulf Maritime Park. Rangitoto is just 10 km from the city. It's a fascinating volcanic island – the last eruption was only 250 years ago. It's a good place for a picnic, there are lots of pleasant walks, a swimming pool, barbecues near the wharf and a great view from the summit of the 260 metre cone. Lava caves are another attraction, but you need good footwear as the whole island consists of lava with trees growing through it – no soil has developed as yet. There's an information centre with maps of the various island walks and a shop which is open while cruise ships are at the island.

Motutapu, in contrast, is mainly covered in grassland and sheep and cattle are grazed there. The island was bought from the Maoris in 1842 for 10 empty casks, four double-barrelled shotguns, 50 blankets, five hats, five pieces of gown material, five shawls and five pairs of black trousers! There's an interesting 3 hour round trip walk between the wharf at Islington Bay and the wharf at Home Bay. Islington Bay, the inlet between the two islands, was once known as 'Drunken Bay' as sailing ships would stop here to sober their crews who had overindulged in the bars of Auckland.

## Places to Stay

There's a camping site at Home Bay, Motutapu Island. Toilets, water, garbage bins and barbecue sites are provided at this fairly rudimentary camping site but bring cooking equipment as open fires are not

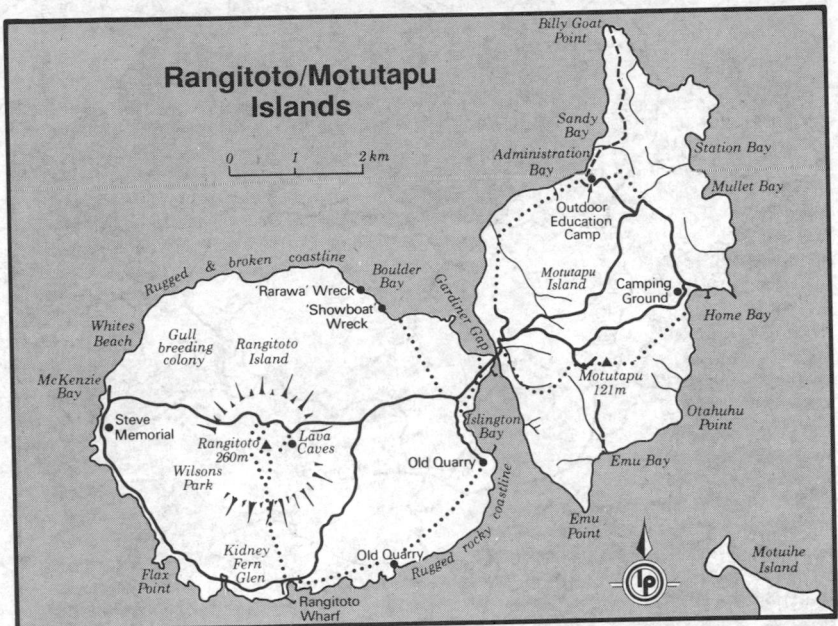

permitted. Camping fees are $6 per night. For further info contact the island's Senior Ranger (tel 727-348, 727-677) or the DOC in Auckland.

### Getting There & Away

Rangitoto, Motutapu, Motuihe and Rakino are served by Fuller's Captain Cook Cruises ferries (tel 774-074). The ferry departs from opposite the Downtown Air Terminal in Auckland at 9.30 am daily, plus at 12.30 pm on weekends and holidays, and there's an evening ferry departing at 6 pm on Fridays only.

## WAIHEKE

Waiheke is the most visited of the gulf islands and at 93 sq km it's one of the largest. It's reputed to be sunnier and warmer than Auckland and there are plenty of beaches so it's a popular day trip from the city. There's also plenty of accommodation should you want to stay longer.

The main settlement is Oneroa, at the western end of the island. From there it's fairly built up through Palm Beach to Onetangi in the middle. Beyond this the eastern end of the island is lightly inhabited although a rough road runs right round it. The island is very hilly so riding right around on a bicycle is hard work.

Waiheke was originally discovered and settled by the Maoris. Legends relate that one of the pioneering canoes came to the island and traces of an old fortified pa can still be seen on the headland overlooking Putiki Bay. The Europeans arrived with missionary Samuel Marsden in the early 1800s and the island was soon stripped of its kauri forests. It's still a good place for bushwalking, however.

### Information

The ferry operators have information on the island. The *Gulf News* is a weekly news-magazine of island events. *Waiheke Island –*

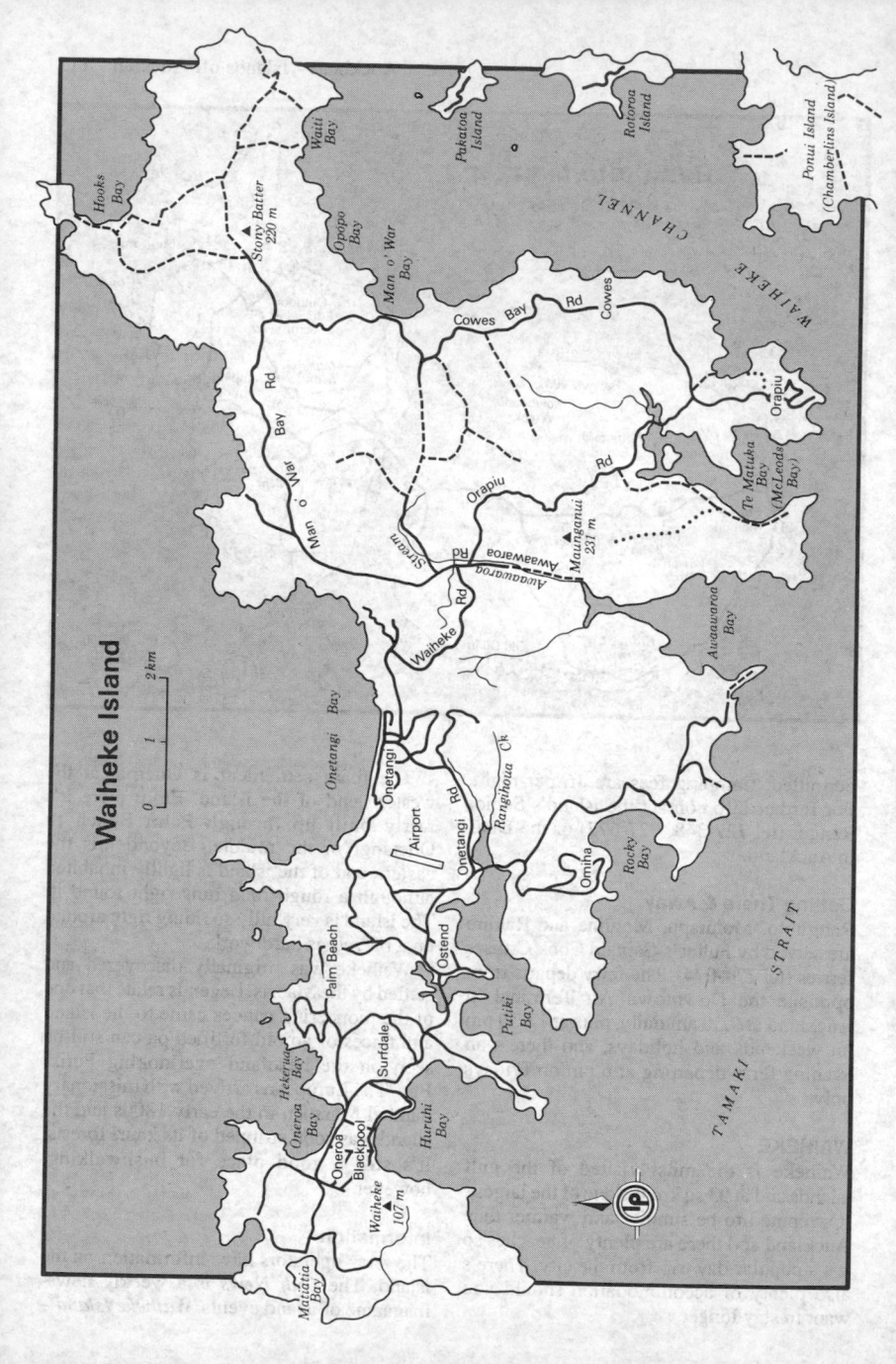

*A Tour* is an interesting little booklet produced by the Waiheke Historical Society.

Waiheke is a local telephone call from Auckland but you have to dial 72 before the Waiheke number. There's a bank open on Mondays, Tuesdays, Thursdays and Fridays in Oneroa.

### Historical Society Museum
There's a small historical museum at Ostend, midway between Oneroa and Onetangi. It's open from 10 am to 1 pm daily except Mondays during the summer and on Saturdays and Sundays only during the winter. The society is planning to restore the old woolshed near Onetangi, one of the few remaining buildings built by the early settlers.

### Stony Batter Walk
At the eastern end of the island the farmland derives its name from the boulder-strewn fields. There's an interesting walk leading to the old WW II gun emplacements with their connecting underground tunnels. The site is reached along the private road to the Man 'o War Station but vehicles are not permitted to go beyond the car park. From the gun emplacements you can continue walking north to Hooks Bay or south to Opopo Bay. From the entrance the walk to the WW II site takes 1½ hours return. From the site it's an additional 1½ hours return to either of the bays.

### Beaches
Popular beaches with good sand and good swimming include Oneroa Beach and the adjacent Little Oneroa Beach, Palm Beach and the long stretch of sand at Onetangi Bay. You can even find nudist beaches at Palm Beach and on the western end of Onetangi Beach. There's snorkelling at Hekerua Bay and Enclosure. A number of the beaches have shady pohutukawa trees growing in the sand.

### Activities
The atmosphere on Waiheke is very relaxed, the beaches are lovely as can be, and it's an excellent place for taking it easy. Fishing,

horse-riding, bushwalking, scuba diving, kayaking and generally lazing around are all popular activities on Waiheke.

You can hire horses from the Shepherds Point Riding Centre (tel 8104) on Ostend Rd in Ostend, it's $24 for a 2 hour beach ride and lessons are also available. Hauraki Tours (tel 7262) rents kayaks when there's a minimum of four people interested, prices are $15 per day for experienced kayakers who can take the boats out on their own, $22 for a half-day tour with an instructor, and they'll come to pick you up. Films are shown at the Surfdale Hall. There are a number of craftspeople on Waiheke and their work is displayed in the local craft shops. There's a weekly market at Ostend Hall on the main road in Ostend from 7 am to noon Saturday mornings, it's best to get there early. There's also a good winery on the island, the Goldwater Estate.

### Tours
Tour Waiheke (tel 7151), offers half-day minibus tours of Waiheke for $20. They meet the 10 am ferry coming from Auckland and they can make arrangements to pick you up and drop you off anywhere on the island.

Bellbird

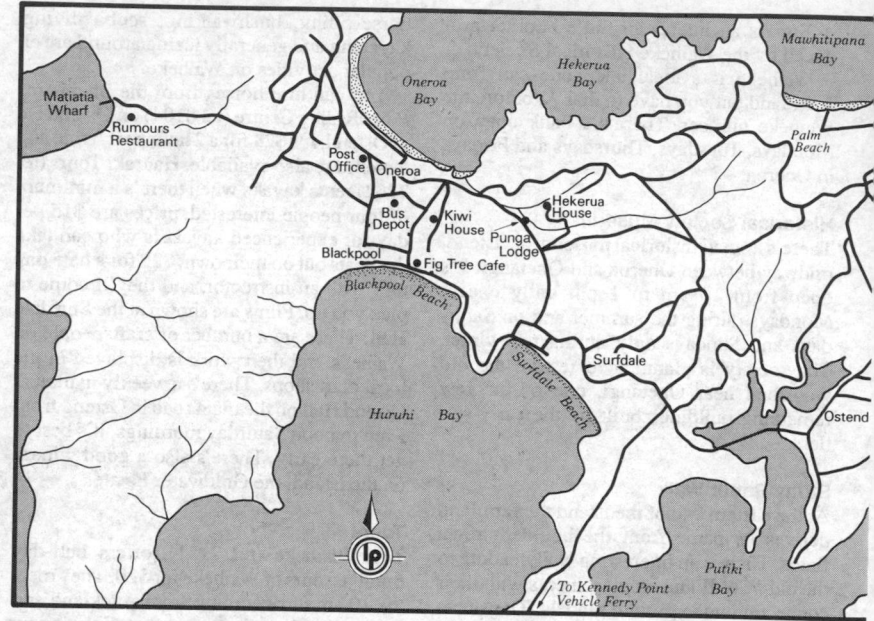

They also do tours of the Stony Batter tunnels on request.

The mailman, Peter Ward (tel 7802) takes up to three people out with him on the Monday to Friday mail run. It's an excellent tour – he stops at many scenic spots to give you a look, stops to chat with the locals, and tells stories about the island as you go around it. The trip takes from about 8.30 am to noon and costs $10. Arrange in advance for him to pick you up. On the water, several of the Fullers cruises around the Hauraki Gulf can be taken from Waiheke.

### Places to Stay

**Hostels** The two hostels on Waiheke are fiercely competitive. The *Waiheke Island Youth Hostel* (tel 8971) is at Onetangi. To get there just take the bus from the ferry right to the end of the line. Nightly cost is $13 in this pleasantly situated hostel, up the hill overlooking the bay, and every room has just two bunks. It's a bit of a hike to the shop so take your food with you when you go there. The YHA offers two and three-night discount packages including the return ferry fare and the return bus fare on the island.

*Hekerua House* (tel 8371) is just beyond Oneroa at 11 Hekerua Rd. From the ferry terminal take the Palm Beach bus and get off at Hekerua Rd, just up the hill from Oneroa. The hostel is nestled in one of the island's few patches of native bush, with a big swimming pool and deck, and it's not far from shops and beaches. Dorm beds are $12, double rooms $13 per person, or there are 'canvas twins' (tents) at $10 per person. In summer there's a nightly $5 barbecue. Phone ahead from Auckland to make sure there's room. And bring your guitar!

**Cabins & Guest Houses** There's no camping site on the island but there are cabins at the *Midway Motel & Cabins* (tel 8023) at 1 Whakarite Rd, Ostend. The more basic ones cost $20/25 for one/two people,

Oneroa – Onetangi
(Waiheke Island)

0    1    2 km

Onetangi    Bay

Uncle McGinty's Lodge

Post Office    Onetangi Hotel

Waiheke Island Youth Hostel

Midway Motel & Cabins

Historical Society Museum

Airstrip

To Stony Batter

Old Woolshed

more luxurious ones cost a bit more; all share communal showers, toilets and kitchens. They also have '4-star' motel units from $60 for doubles. In January prices are higher.

The *Kiwi House* (tel 8626) at 23 Kiwi St, Blackpool, has B&B at $23/40 most of the year, in summer the rates are $28 single, $50 and $60 double. There's also the popular *Hauraki House* (tel 7598) at 50 Hauraki Rd, Oneroa, a B&B guest house which has good views and charges $30 per person all year round.

Just up the hill from Hekerua House, *Punga Lodge* (tel 6675) at 227 Ocean View Rd is a very small guest house, just a timber chalet sleeping four people and an apartment out the back sleeping two. Rates in the chalet are $15 per person for a basic bed if you bring your own sleeping bag, $25 per person if you use the lodge's linen and other amenities, or if you take the double apartment, which is very well appointed. The two can be linked together for groups.

**Hotels & Motels** The *Onetangi Hotel* (tel 8028) on the beachfront at Onetangi has rooms at $25/50 for singles/doubles. Also on the beachfront *Uncle McGinty's Lodge* (tel 8118) is rather more luxurious, the rooms all have attached bathrooms and cost $40/60, rising to $50/75 in summer.

The *Midway Motel* (see Cabins & Guest Houses) is a good motel, and there's also the *Roanna-Maree Motel* (tel 7051) at Onetangi, with a swimming and spa pool and well-equipped double and family units. Rates are $50 for singles, $72 to $77 for doubles; cheaper in winter.

### Places to Eat

**Oneroa** There are plenty of places to eat at Oneroa including a string of snack bars and takeaways. Try *Aoreno's Pizza, Poppy's*, the *Pickle Palace Deli*, the *Breeze Inn* or the *Schooner Cafe*, all along Ocean View Rd. Back close to the wharf at Matiatia Bay is the more expensive *Rumours Restaurant*.

The *Fig Tree Cafe* is near the waterfront on the corner of the Esplanade and Moa Ave in Blackpool, between Surfdale and Oneroa. It's open every day for breakfast, lunch and dinner in summer, closing on Wednesdays in winter. There's a pleasant courtyard, the food is good with a blend of steak, seafood and vegetarian and main courses are about $10 for lunch, $15 for dinner.

**Onetangi** The *Onetangi Hotel* has good bistro meals, a pleasant beer garden and the more exclusive *Country Kitchen Restaurant* where you're advised that booking is essential. There's also a restaurant at *Uncle McGinty's Lodge* or you can get sandwiches and snacks in the somewhat scruffy Post Office Store.

### Getting There & Away
**Air** Waiheke Air Services (tel 298-7142) flies to Waiheke from Auckland's Ardmore Airport three times daily. The flight takes only about 10 minutes and costs $27 (children $23) one way or $46 ($39) return. Other air services fly to Waiheke, but only by charter. The Waiheke landing strip is between Ostend and Onetangi.

**Boat** The *Quick Cat* is a high-speed, 500-seat catamaran service out to the island. It zips you out in about half an hour at a return cost of $18 (children $9). You can get a combination ferry/bus ticket for $23 return, which includes the bus trip to and from the ferry. From Auckland the boat departs from opposite the Downtown Airport Terminal several times daily, phone 774-074 for schedule information. On Waiheke the ferries arrive and depart from Matiatia Bay at the western end of the island. Some of them continue on from Waiheke to Pakatoa Island.

If you've got your own car the Subritzsky Shipping Company (tel 534-5663) operates a vehicle ferry two or three times a day during the week and once on Saturdays and Sundays. The cost depends on the size of the car – for a small car it's $52 each way ($104 return), for a motorcycle it's $27 each way

($54 return). Prices include the driver but each additional passenger is $10 extra. The ferry goes from Half Moon Bay on the mainland and from Kennedy Point on Putiki Bay on Waiheke.

Another option for vehicles is the Gulf Trans Ltd ferry (tel 734-036) departing from the Western Viaduct on the corner of Jellicoe and Brigham streets at 10 am on Mondays and Fridays.

### Getting Around
**Bus** There's a bus service which connects with all the ferry arrivals and departures and operates from the ferry wharf through Oneroa to Onetangi. The fare is $3.10 right to the end of the line.

**Taxi** There are a number of taxis on the island, phone 8038 to get one. If you have a group of four together, taking a taxi costs about the same as the bus.

**Rental Vehicles** Waiheke Rental Cars (tel 8635, 8386 after hours) rents cars from $50 per day, motorcycles from $35 per day and bicycles from $15 per day. They're at 13 Tahi Rd, Ostend and they have an office by the ferry wharf at Matiatia Bay. They will meet you on arrival by arrangement. Petrol is included with motorcycle or car hire.

**Hitching** Hitching around the island is very easy, many people find it the best way to get around.

### PAKATOA ISLAND
Pakatoa Island is a small tourist resort 36 km out from Auckland and just beyond Waiheke. The resort has a restaurant, bar, coffee shop, swimming pool and various sporting facilities. There are great views of the gulf and across to the Coromandel Peninsula from the island's high point.

### Places to Stay
Phone 796-780 or 734-084 in Auckland about accommodation at the island's resort.

## Getting There & Away

**Air** There are no regular air services to Pakatoa, but you can arrange a flight through Sea Bee Air (tel 774-405).

**Boat** The *Quick Cat*, the high-speed catamaran which serves Waiheke, also continues to Pakatoa once a day except Saturdays. The return fare to Pakatoa is $25 (children $12.50). You must reserve in advance for the boat trip to Pakatoa, phone 774-074.

## KAWAU ISLAND

Kawau is close to the coast, unlike Great Barrier Island, but well to the north of the islands off Auckland. It's reached by turning off the main road north at Warkworth and travelling a few km east to Sandspit, 45 km from Auckland, from where the ferry departs.

On Kawau Sir George Grey's old home, Mansion House, which was used as a hotel for many years has now been restored to its original state and is open to the public. Sir George, an early governor of New Zealand, built Mansion House 150 years ago. There are many beautiful walks on Kawau, starting from Mansion House and leading to beaches, an old copper mine, and a lookout. You'll see numerous wallabies around here – they're not native to New Zealand so they're an unusual sight in this part of the world.

### Places to Stay

There's camping at *Heavens Camping Ground* (tel 822) at Moores Bay, Bon Accord harbour, cost is $9 per person. You have to book ahead to arrange boat pick-up from Bon Accord Harbour. Many good bushwalks lead from the site to various places on the island.

### Getting There & Away

**Air** Although there are no scheduled services Sea Bee Air can arrange flights from Auckland to Kawau.

**Boat** Mansion House Ferries (tel Sandspit 8006) depart from Sandspit, just outside of Warkworth, about an hour's drive north of Auckland on SH 1. The ferries take about 45 minutes to reach the island and the fare is $10 return. Departures are daily at 7.45 am, 10.30 am (mail run) and 2 pm, weekends at noon, with more frequent sailings in summer. Be sure to check your connections when getting to Sandspit from Auckland if you're using public transport as it is not always easy.

Sea Flight Cruises (tel 366-1421) has day trips to Kawau on Wednesdays, Fridays and Sundays, leaving Auckland at 10 am and arriving back at 4 pm. Bookings are made at the Ferry Building. It's a 1½ hour boat trip, with about 3 hours for visiting the Mansion House and exploring the island. Cost is $38 (children $19, family $88). An optional lunch on the island is $15. The schooner *Te Aroha* also stops at Kawau on some of its cruises.

## GREAT BARRIER ISLAND

Great Barrier Island, 88 km from the mainland, is the largest island in Hauraki Gulf. Tramping, swimming, fishing, boating and just relaxing are the popular activities on the island. With a population of only about 1000 souls living on the 110 sq km island, there's plenty of open space. Great Barrier has hot springs, historic kauri dams, a State Forest and Forest Sanctuary, and a network of tramping tracks. There are three huts along the trails in the State Forest and free camping grounds at Harataonga Bay, Medlands Beach and Awana Bay. The west coast has safe sandy beaches; the east coast beaches are good for surfing.

The island was originally sighted and named by Captain Cook. Later it became a whaling centre, a number of ships were built there and the island has also been the site for some spectacular shipwrecks including the *SS Wairarapa* in 1894 and the *Wiltshire* in 1922. There's a cemetery at Katherine Bay where many of the victims of the *Wairarapa* wreck were buried.

Great Barrier Island is decidedly isolated, there are periodic complaints in the Auckland papers about how lousy the roads are and how the government on the mainland forgets about the islanders' existence. The

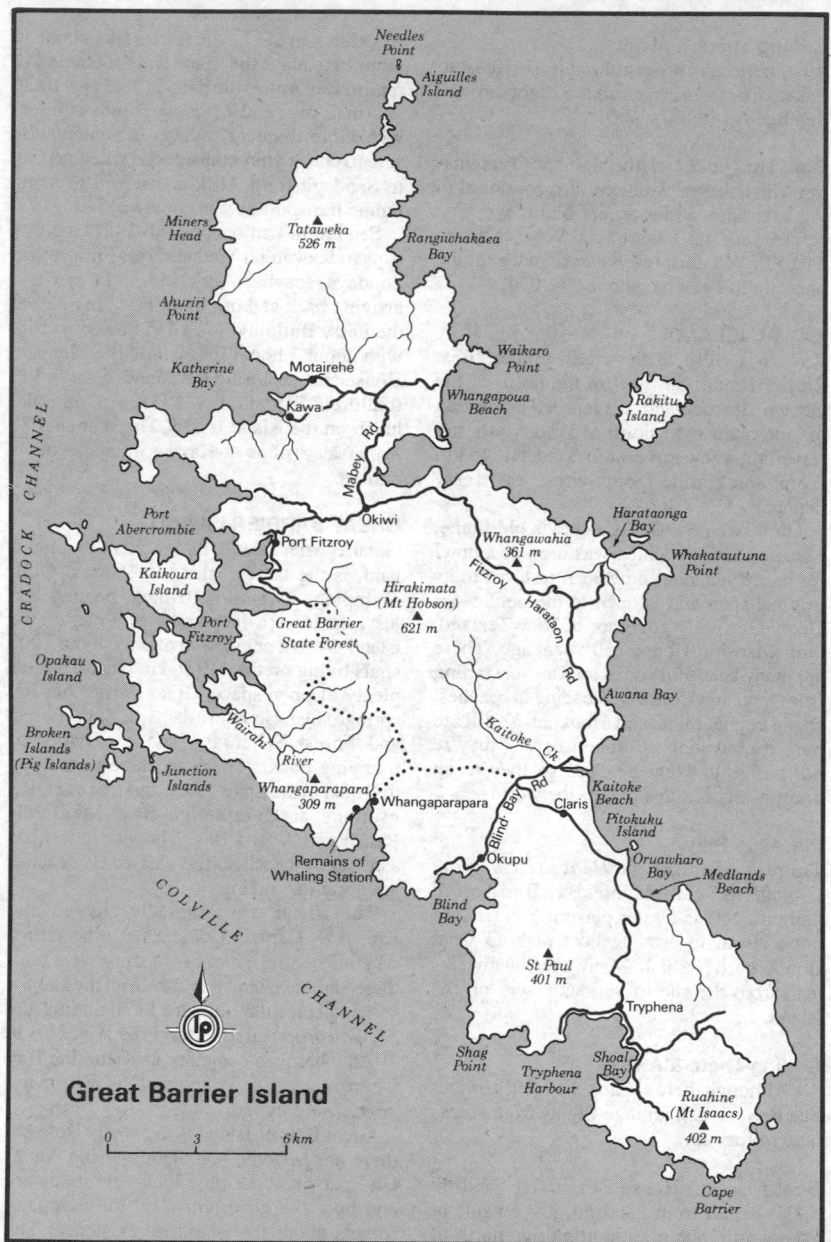

**Great Barrier Island**

0        3        6 km

island doesn't even have a pub. Tryphena is the main town and arrival and departure port. Whangaparapara is an old timber town and the site of the island's whaling activities. The Great Barrier State Forest between Whangaparapara and Port Fitzroy is being developed for tramping although almost all the kauri trees were cut down by early this century. There are hot springs off the Claris-Whangaparapara track.

### Information

The NZ Adventure Centre (tel 399-192/4) at Victoria Park Market, Auckland specialises in Great Barrier Island and can supply information on the island as well as make bookings. There's also a Great Barrier Island office in the Auckland Ferry Building (tel 366-1421). The DOC offices in Port Fitzroy (tel Port Fitzroy 4K) and Auckland (tel 379-279) have information about the island's walking tracks, camping grounds and huts. The island's manual telephone exchange officially operates weekdays from 8.30 am to 8.30 pm, although actual times may be a bit erratic.

### Places to Stay & Eat

The DOC operates camping grounds at Port Fitzroy, Harataonga, Medlands Beach, Awana and Whangaparapara, plus a hut at Port Fitzroy, two tramping huts and a number of lodges.

Until recently, there were no restaurants or takeaways on the island, you either had to fix your own food or eat at the place you stayed. Nowadays a few eateries do exist, but some guest houses still quote prices inclusive of all meals. Be sure to ask about this when booking. Several of the hotels have in-house restaurants.

**Tryphena** The *Pohutukawa Lodge* (tel Tryphena 20) on the Tryphena Harbour beachfront is an associate YHA hostel with bunks at $13 ($16 for non-YHA members) plus a guest house with double and twin rooms at around $60. You can fix your own food and there's a shop at the lodge, plus restaurants nearby.

The *Mulberry Grove Motel* (tel Tryphena 16) has motel rooms and is right behind the Tryphena General Store which has a reasonable food selection.

The *Pigeons Guest House* (tel Tryphena 8A) is at Shoal Bay on the beachfront and costs $45 per person in the off season, more in summer. Shoal Bay is south of the other Tryphena accommodation and it's also somewhat more expensive. The setting is pleasant, however, and the guest house has a private beach access, free dinghies and fishing equipment, and some good bushwalks nearby, plus excellent meals available. The *Tipi & Bob's Holiday Lodge* (tel Tryphena 5A) and the nearby *Valley View Lodge* (tel Tryphena 6D) are two more central guest houses.

**Medlands Beach** Across the island, about 5 km from Tryphena, Medlands Beach is on the way to Claris. You can stay here at the *Rangimarie Farmlet* (tel Claris 6M), a lovely old homestead-cum-guest house which has vegetarian food and reasonably priced accommodation. Nearby on Mason Rd is *Golden Goose Farmhouse* (tel Claris 6U), a more modern place, with three double rooms in a farm guest house and rates of $50 per person including all meals. There's also the *Oriana Cottage* at about $80 per night, and a DOC camping ground.

There's a free camping site at Medlands Beach and another on the other side of Claris at Awana Bay. A third free camping site is up north at Harataonga Bay. You need portable cooking equipment and fuel for all these sites.

**Whangaparapara** The *Great Barrier Lodge* (tel (025) 930-504) is at Water's Edge, Whangaparapara Harbour and has rooms at $85, self-contained cabins at $55/65. The town also has a free DOC hut, useful for those walking across the island.

**Port Fitzroy** Near the DOC office (tel Port Fitzroy 4K) are a DOC camping ground and a hut. They're both some distance from the store, which doesn't really matter because the store doesn't have much anyway. Port Fitzroy also has *Fitzroy House* (tel Port Fitzroy 2), a guest house with double rooms and self-contained cottages, and *The Jetty* (tel Port Fitzroy 1K), which is rather more expensive but a great spot for relaxation.

Kaikoura Island, offshore from Port Fitzroy, has the *Lost Resort* (tel Port Fitzroy 8) with cabins.

### Getting There & Away

**Air** Great Barrier Airlines (tel 275-9120, 275-6612 in Auckland) fly twice daily to Claris, and in summer to Okiwi as well. The flight from Auckland takes half an hour and costs $152 return. The airline operates a free transfer bus from Claris to Tryphena and from Okiwi to Port Fitzroy. Other flights to the island are operated by Air North Shore and Ardmore Air Charters.

**Boat** Sea Flight Cruises (tel 366-1421) have direct service to Tryphena leaving Auckland at 5.30 pm on Fridays (departing Tryphena at 7.30 pm) and Sundays at 5 pm (departing Tryphena at 7 pm). Return fare is $104 (children $52). They also offer day trips stopping at several places around the island, departing from Auckland on Tuesdays, Thursdays and Saturdays at 9.30 am, arriving back at 4.30 pm. Day trip fares are $52 (children $26), with an optional lunch and bus trip on the island. Bookings are made at the Auckland Ferry Building office.

Fuller's Captain Cook Cruises (tel 774-074) goes to the island on the *Supercat* catamaran every Friday, departing from Auckland at 5.30 pm and from Tryphena at 8 pm to return. On Sundays it departs Auckland at 10 am and makes stops at Port Fitzroy and Tryphena, arriving back in Auckland at 6.15 pm. Passage to the island takes about 2¼ hours, return cost is $89 (children $45). On Sundays you can do it as a day trip, in which case the fare is $52 (children $26), with an optional lunch and bus tour.

One of the most enjoyable ways to visit the island is on the 1909 schooner *Te Aroha* – its 4 and 5 day cruises stop here and allow time to explore around. See *Te Aroha* Cruises in the Auckland section.

You can take a car to the island on the Gulf Trans car ferry (tel 734-036). One-way trips take about 6 hours and cost $49.50 ($99 return), half price for children, $421 return for the car. Subritzsky Shipping (tel 390-161) also operates a car/passenger ferry, leaving Auckland on Wednesdays and Thursdays and arriving on the island the following day.

### Getting Around

Roads on the island are rough and ready. From Tryphena in the south to Port Fitzroy in the north is about 40 km via Whangaparapara using the walking tracks. The roads are bad enough that you may decide walking is a good idea!

There are a handful of taxis on the island but they aren't cheap. You can hire motorcycles from Safari Tours (tel Tryphena 22H) for $40 per day or part thereof; other motorcycle rentals are in Tryphena and Port Fitzroy. Campervans are also available on the island, you can book them in advance through the NZ Adventure Centre.

### OTHER ISLANDS

Dotted around Rangitoto-Motutapu and Waiheke or further north are many smaller islands. They include:

### Motukorea Island

The small island of Motukorea, or 'Island of the Oystercatcher', is also known as Browns Island. It was settled by Polynesians by about 1300 AD, who had developed three fortified pa settlements on the volcanic cones by 1820. It was purchased from the Maoris by John Logan Campbell and William Brown in 1839, before the founding of Auckland City, and used as a pig farm. It's now part of the Hauraki Gulf Maritime Park. The old wharf collapsed long ago and along the west coast lie the rotting wrecks of five old ferries that were ran aground and abandoned.

### Motuihe Island

Halfway between Auckland and Waiheke

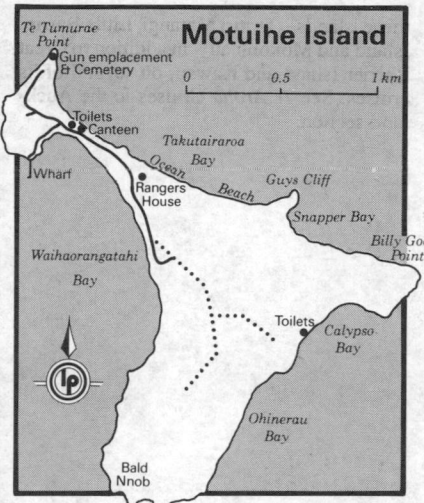

this small 2 sq km island with its fine beaches is a popular day trip from the city. At one time the island was used as a quarantine station and the cemetery at the north-western tip has graves of victims of the 1918 influenza epidemic. In WW I it was used as a prisoner-of-war camp and it was from here that the German captain Count Felix von Luckner made a daring, but ultimately unsuccessful, escape.

The peninsula pointing out north-west has fine sandy beaches on both sides so one side is always sheltered from the wind. On a sunny weekend there may be over 500 boats anchored in the bay! There are some walking tracks on the island, it takes about 3 hours to walk all the way around.

### Rotoroa Island
Another small island, just south of Pakatoa Island.

### Ponui Island
Also known as Chamberlins Island this larger island is just south of Rotoroa and has been farmed by the Chamberlin family ever since they purchased it from the Maoris in 1854. South again from Ponui is Pakihi or Sandspit Island and tiny Karamuramu Island.

### Rakino Island
This small island is just to the north of Motutapu Island. Beyond Rakino there is a cluster of tiny islands collectively known as The Noises.

### Tiritiri Matangi
Part of the Hauraki Gulf Maritime Park, this island is further north, about halfway between the islands close to Auckland and Kawau Island. The island is an 'open sanctuary' where native wildlife is protected but visitors are permitted. Attempts are being made to re-vegetate the island with native species and re-establish native birds.

### Little Barrier Island
Little Barrier Island, 25 km from Kawau Island, is one of New Zealand's prime nature reserves, being the last area of NZ rainforest that remains unaffected by humans, deer or possums. Several rare species, particularly birds, reptiles and plants, live in the varied habitats on the volcanic island. Access to the rugged coastline is difficult, and a permit is required before any landing is made on this closely guarded sanctuary.

### Motuora Island
Motuora Island is halfway from Tiritiri Matangi to Kawau. There is a wharf and a camping ground on the west coast of the island but there is no regular ferry service to Motuora. A camping permit can be obtained from the ranger on Kawau (tel Kawau Island 882), or you can just show up on the island and get your permit from the caretaker there. Camping cost is $3 per person.

### Mokohinau Islands
These are the most remote islands of the Hauraki Gulf Maritime Park, 23 km north-west of Great Barrier Island. They are small, low-lying islands receiving little rain. They are all protected nature reserves, requiring a permit for landing.

### Getting There & Away

The Fuller's Captain Cook ferry service to Rangitoto also goes to Rakino and Motuihe, but not on every sailing. Phone 774-074 for details.

The *Te Aroha* schooner stops at several of these islands – Tiritiri Matangi, Little Barrier Island and Mokohinau – in addition to Great Barrier Island and Kawau, on several of its cruises. See *Te Aroha* Cruises in the Auckland section.

# Northland

The region known as Northland is like a finger pointing north from Auckland. Often referred to as the 'winterless north', its climate tends to be mild compared to the rest of New Zealand. It's a popular holiday resort area with beaches and water sport activities and close enough to the big city for weekend trips. Northland is also modern New Zealand's cradle – it was here that Europeans first made permanent contact with the Maoris, here the first squalid sealers' and whalers' settlements were formed, and here the treaty of Waitangi was signed between the settlers and the Maoris. To this day there is a greater proportion of Maoris in the population than elsewhere in New Zealand.

Many travellers to the region only visit the rather touristy Bay of Islands, which is a shame since there are so many other beautiful and interesting places around Northland.

### Getting Around

In addition to the regular bus services there are two other services catering specifically for the backpacking visitor.

The Northland Backpackers Express (tel Auckland 535-9352, Kaitaia 82-826) is an alternative transport bus which makes a circle of Northland, departing from Auckland once a week from July to September, three times a week from October to June, stopping at Whangarei, Paihia, Kerikeri, Whangaroa, Mangonui, Kaitaia, Opononi and Dargaville. Cost is $109 for the full circle, and you can get on and off whenever and wherever you like, stay as long as you like and get back aboard to continue on, or you can also go only part way. Bookings are essential to assure your space.

The Northcape Shuttle, departing weekly from Auckland, is a 6 day Northland tour which includes many of the region's most interesting sights and activities. See Alternative Buses in the Getting Around chapter for details.

## Western Route

From Auckland there are two main routes through Northland to the Bay of Islands – the major attraction of the area. The simplest and fastest route is to head straight up through Whangarei on the eastern side of the peninsula. The west coast route is slower – the road is unsealed for a stretch – and longer, but it takes you through Dargaville, the Waipoua Forest and the Hokianga Harbour. To reach Northland you can go through Helensville or Warkworth to Wellsford and then on to Brynderwyn, 112 km north of Auckland, from where you take the east or west coast route.

### AUCKLAND TO DARGAVILLE
#### Waiwera & Orewa

The Waiwera Hot Pools are in the coastal village of Waiwera, 48 km north of Auckland on SH 1. It's a big holiday complex of thermal pools, open daily from 9.30 am to 10 pm. Nearby are camping grounds and, in the neighbouring town of Orewa, there are many hotels and a good hostel, the *Marco Polo Backpackers Inn* (tel Orewa 68-455), on

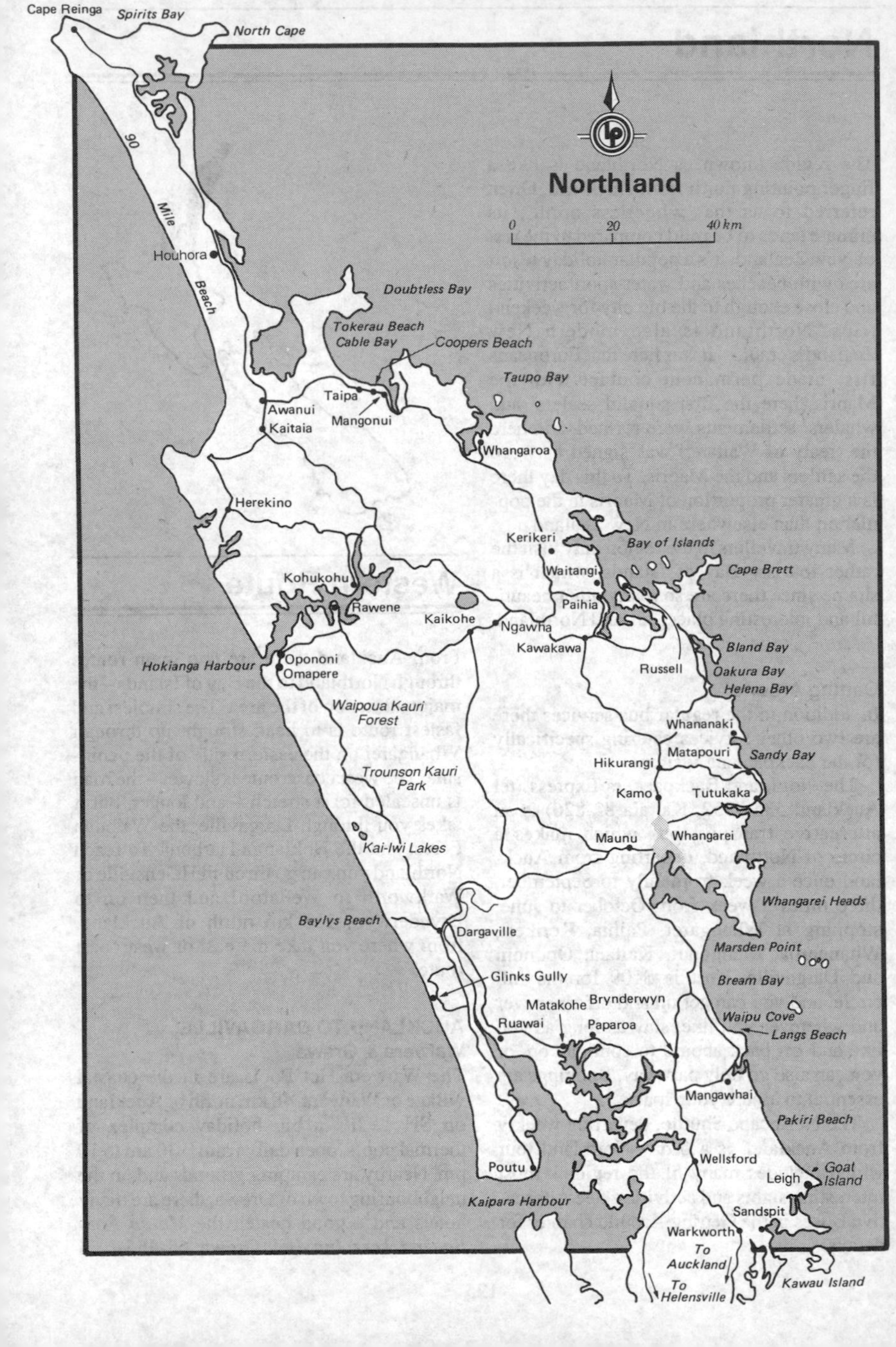

**Northland**

0      20      40 km

Cape Reinga
Spirits Bay
North Cape
90 Mile Beach
Houhora
Doubtless Bay
Tokerau Beach
Cable Bay
Coopers Beach
Taupo Bay
Taipa
Awanui
Mangonui
Kaitaia
Whangaroa
Herekino
Kerikeri
Bay of Islands
Cape Brett
Kohukohu
Waitangi
Rawene
Paihia
Kaikohe
Ngawha
Bland Bay
Kawakawa
Oakura Bay
Opononi
Russell
Helena Bay
Omapere
Hokianga Harbour
Waipoua Kauri
Forest
Whananaki
Trounson Kauri
Park
Hikurangi
Matapouri
Sandy Bay
Kamo
Tutukaka
Kai-Iwi Lakes
Maunu
Whangarei
Whangarei Heads
Baylys Beach
Marsden Point
Dargaville
Bream Bay
Glinks Gully
Brynderwyn
Matakohe
Waipu Cove
Ruawai
Paparoa
Langs Beach
Mangawhai
Pakiri Beach
Poutu
Wellsford
Goat
Island
Kaipara Harbour
Leigh
Sandspit
Warkworth
To
Auckland
To
Helensville
Kawau Island

Hammond Ave at Hatfields Beach, Orewa. It is clearly signposted from the highway. Take Auckland city bus Nos 894, 895 or 899.

Wenderholm Regional Park, 8 km north of Orewa, has splendid views, bushwalks, beach swimming, and picnic spots. The Waiwera Scenic Reserve is another scenic spot along the highway, good for a stop.

### Moir Hill Walkway
A few km before you reach Warkworth there is a waterfall, lookout and views of the Hauraki Gulf from the Moir Hill Walkway. The track is directly off the main road so the bus services can drop you there. The return trip takes 3 to 4 hours and walking boots are only necessary in winter. Just north of the walkway is New Zealand's satellite tracking station.

### Warkworth
Just north of Warkworth is a track to The Dome. It leaves from the main road and is easily accessible. There are some beautiful beaches between Warkworth and Whangarei, especially Pakiri, Mangawhai Heads and Waipu Cove. Access is not very easy for the traveller without wheels, but you can often hitch a ride with surfies.

Four km north of Warkworth, Sheep World is an unabashedly tourist attraction demonstrating many aspects of NZ sheep farming including sheepdog manoeuvres, shearing, and things you can try for yourself such as carding, spinning, weaving, feeding tame sheep and lambs. There's even a video of a year in the life of a sheep, starring 'Gladys'. It's open daily from 9 am to 5 pm, with show times at 11 am, 1 and 3 pm; admission is $6 (children $4).

### Dome State Forest
The Dome State Forest is 10 km north of Warkworth, 12 km south of Wellsford, on SH 1. The 401 hectare forest was logged about 90 years ago and is now protected and regenerating. There's a walking track to the Dome summit (336 metres) departing from the car park opposite Kraacks Rd on SH 1. It takes about an hour's steady walking to reach the summit, with great views of the Hauraki Gulf and beyond. Another 800 metres further on past the summit is the Waiwhiu Kauri Grove, a stand of 20 mature kauri trees which the loggers didn't take.

As you continue north on SH 1 you'll pass the Sunnybrook Scenic Reserve, another lovely spot.

### Sandspit
East of Warkworth, a few km from the main road, is Sandspit, where a ferry service departs for Kawau Island. See Kawau Island in the Islands off Auckland section in the Auckland chapter for more details. The Sandspit turn-off also leads up to Goat Island, a scenic reserve of the Hauraki Gulf Maritime Park.

### Mangawhai Cliffs Walkway
The Mangawhai Cliffs Walkway leads from Mangawhai Heads to Bream Tail (1½ to 2 hours one way), giving extensive views both inland and of the Hauraki Gulf islands. The return trip can be made around the foreshore at low tide when the sea is not rough.

### Brynderwyn Hills Walkway
Also in the same area is the Brynderwyn Hills Walkway (eastern section), starting from the Mangawhai-Waipu Cove road. It's an easy 2 hour return climb affording panoramic views of Northland and the Hauraki Gulf from the highest point. The road continues to Langs Beach, where it's possible to camp, before it rejoins the main highway at Waipu.

### Kauris
As you travel through the Northland region you'll hear and see a lot about kauris. Kauris are gigantic native NZ trees, a competitor in size to the Californian redwood but entirely different in type. They only grow in the northern part of the North Island. They were once ruthlessly cut down for their excellent timber and Northland is covered with evidence of the kauri days. Kauri gum was found to be an important ingredient for making varnish and at one time there were

Kauri

many 'gumdiggers' who roamed the forests, poking in the ground for hard lumps of kauri gum.

## Matakohe

Turning off at Brynderwyn for Dargaville you pass through Matakohe, where the Otamatea Kauri & Pioneer Museum has a strange and wonderful collection of kauri gum in the basement. It also has magnificent lifelike displays of various aspects of the life of the kauri bushpeople and a very extensive photographic collection. It's a superb museum, well worth the short detour off the road to see it.

The museum shop has some excellent bowls and other items crafted from kauri wood. They're expensive but very well made. Look for the items made of 'swamp kauri', ancient kauris which lay in swamps for thousands of years, their gum-saturated wood still remaining in good condition. The museum is open daily from 9 am to 5 pm; admission is $3.50 (children $1).

Facing the museum is the Matakohe Pioneer Church, built in 1866-67 of local kauri wood. When the tiny church was built it served as the interdenominational church for both Methodists and Anglicans, as well as the town hall and schoolhouse for the pioneer community. Later on a schoolhouse was built and you can see it on the far side behind the museum. The Pioneer Church was renovated in 1978 and is once again in use. The large brick Coates Memorial Church nearby was built in 1950.

## DARGAVILLE

Population 4900

Dargaville, 185 km north of Auckland, is named after its founder, Joseph McMullen Dargaville (1837-96), who was born in Ireland and came to New Zealand in the 1860s when the kauri timber trade was at its height. Seeing potential in this site at the confluence of the northern Wairoa River and Kaihu Creek, he bought 171 acres in 1872 for £1 an acre and laid out a private town. The river town at the heart of the kauri district became an important centre for the seagoing exports of kauri timber and gum, and at one time it was the busiest port in New Zealand.

As the kauri forests were decimated, Dargaville continued its central role and today is the principal service centre of the predominantly farming Northern Wairoa area. It has an active community of Yugoslavs descended from the original Dalmatian kauri gumdiggers.

### Information

There's a handy little Information Centre (tel

Top:  Duke of Marlborough Hotel, Russell (TW)
Left:  Signpost at lighthouse, Cape Reinga (MC)
Right:  Large kauri tree in the Waipoua Forest, Northland (NZTP)

Top: Bay of Islands (MC)
Bottom: Stone Store, Kerikeri (TW)

7056) on Normanby St in the town centre. It's open all year from 8.30 am to 5 pm Monday to Friday, with additional summer hours of 9 am to 3 pm on weekends and public holidays. This office also houses the AA, making it convenient for picking up AA maps and publications.

### Northern Wairoa Museum

Dargaville's eccentric little museum is not of the same standard as Matakohe but it's still worth visiting. Maori exhibits include a gigantic 18th century war canoe found buried in sand dunes, the only surviving one made in pre-European times from stone tools. There are also early settlers' items, kauri gum samples and historical photographs. The highlight of the museum is the maritime section. Hundreds of ships were built and worked on in the Kaipara Harbour which was also notorious for shipwrecks.

The museum is at the top of a small hill in Harding Park on the outskirts of town, about 3 km from the centre. In front of the museum are the masts from *Rainbow Warrior*, the Greenpeace boat sunk by French government terrorists in Auckland in 1985. An exhibit tells the day-by-day story of the attack on the flagship and the subsequent investigation which revealed the first case of international terrorism to occur in New Zealand. The museum is open daily from 9 am to 4 pm; admission is $2.50 (children 50 cents).

### Harding Park

Harding Park is an interesting area as it is the site of an old Maori pa, Po-tu-Oterangi. Tucked into the bottom of the hill is an early European cemetery. There are great views over Dargaville and the surrounding countryside from the park, and picnic areas have been set up near the museum. The Lighthouse Restaurant adjoining the museum takes maximum advantage of the view.

### Cattle Sale

Every Monday from 11 am to 1 pm there's a roundup and cattle sale at the Mangawhare cattle yards. You're welcome to attend, just don't make any sudden movements!

### Tours

Check with the Information Centre for a couple of excellent tours of the area. One tour visits the Waipoua Forest, the Trounson Kauri Park, and the Kai-Iwi Lakes; the other is a beach tour which goes to the Kaipara Lighthouse and returns to Dargaville driving along the beach. They're run by a local fellow who is an excellent guide, and the $40 price includes both the morning and afternoon meals. Book through the Information Centre.

### Places to Stay

The Information Centre has a leaflet on accommodation in Dargaville and can also arrange accommodation in homes and farms in the area.

**Hostels** The *Green House Youth Hostel* (tel 6342) is at 13 Portland St on the corner of Gordon St, near the centre of town. Nightly cost is $13 in this pleasant hostel. They have surfboards and bicycles for hire, and hostellers get a 10% discount on Baylys Beach horse rides.

**Hotels & Motels** There are several hotels in and near Dargaville. The *Northern Wairoa Hotel* (tel 8923) on Hokianga Rd has single rooms at $20, $25 with private facilities, and twin rooms at $40. At the *Commercial* (tel 8018) on River Rd, Mangawhare, rates are $22/44, or $32/64 with breakfast. The *Central Hotel* (tel 8034) at 18-22 Victoria St has single/double rooms at $40/70, breakfast included.

The *Kauri House Lodge* (tel 8082) on Bowen St is a more expensive place with rooms at $68/85, all with bathroom. The rooms in this old colonial homestead are all furnished with antiques and there's a swimming pool.

The *Dargaville Motel* (tel 7734) at 217 Victoria St has rooms at $44/55. At the *Best Western Parkview Motel* (tel 8339) at 36 Carrington St, rooms are $61/73. There's a restaurant and swimming and spa pools. Also in town are the *Glendene Motel* (tel 7424) with units at $35/49 and *Hobson's Choice* (tel 8551) with a swimming pool and a variety of studio, one and two-bedroom units.

**Camping & Cabins** Both are available at *Selwyn Park* (tel 8296), 1½ km from the town centre. Camping sites are $7 per person, $9 with power. They also have simple cabins at $7 to $10 per person and fully equipped tourist cabins at $22 per person. See Around Dargaville for other camping possibilities.

### Places to Eat

There are a number of takeaway places and cafes including the *Chicken Inn* on Kapia St opposite the bus station or the *Bella Vista* on Victoria St. *Mangawhare Fast Foods, Ocean Beach Fisheries & Takeaways*, and *River Road Takeaways* are all on the main road. The *Golden Lion* has Chinese food to eat there or take away.

The *Northern Wairoa Hotel* has pub food and a Friday night smorgasbord. The *Lorna Doone* on the corner of Victoria and Gladstone streets, and the *Lighthouse* up on the hill in Harding Park beside the museum, both won the 'Taste NZ' award in 1989. The *Lighthouse* is licensed, has a fine view, and a Sunday family smorgasbord dinner for $18. It's open every day and evening in summer, from Wednesday to Sunday the rest of the year.

### Getting There & Away

**Bus** The InterCity bus station (tel 8134) is on Kapia St. There's a bus route from Auckland via Dargaville to Paihia Monday to Friday, with an additional Sunday bus to Auckland. There are also weekday buses to Whangarei which continue on to Auckland. From Dargaville it's 3¼ hours to Auckland, 4 hours to Paihia, 1 hour to Whangarei.

You can also get to Dargaville on the Northland Backpackers Express bus (see the end of this chapter).

## AROUND DARGAVILLE
### Kaipara Lighthouse

A worthwhile trip from Dargaville, if you can find a way to get there, is the 71 km run south-east to Kaipara Lighthouse; the last 6½ km is on foot along the foreshore. If you don't have wheels check with the Information Centre about tours that go there. Built in 1884, the lighthouse has now been restored to its original condition.

### Ocean Beach

Only 15 minutes from Dargaville is Ocean Beach, site of many shipwrecks. It's said that the hulks of a French man o' war and an ancient Spanish or Portuguese ship can occasionally be seen. A French boat sank off Baylys Beach in 1851; you can read about it at the Dargaville museum.

Ocean Beach is over 100 km long and is the longest stretch of beach in the country that you could drive a vehicle on, although this is not the best idea for your car since the salt water is corrosive and the soft sand can trap the car in the incoming tide. But it is a very long, smooth stretch of beach. There is access at Baylys Beach (14 km west of Dargaville), Glinks Gully, Mahuta Gorge and Omamari – the main road does not touch the beach.

Horse rides on Baylys Beach are a popular activity from Dargaville. For $25 you get half a day of riding plus transport to and from Baylys Beach. You can book at the Green House Hostel – there's a 10% discount for hostellers – or phone 6730.

**Places to Stay** The *Baylys Beach Motor Camp* (tel 4453) at Baylys Beach, 14 km from Dargaville, has tent sites at $7.50 per person and cabins at $25 for two.

### Kai-Iwi Lakes

Only 34 km north of Dargaville are three superb freshwater lakes called the Kai-Iwi Lakes (Taharoa Domain) and, although they've been developed as a resort for swimming, trout fishing and so on, the area is still relatively unspoilt. The largest of the lakes,

Taharoa, is fringed with pines and dotted with gleaming white sand beaches.

A walking track leaves from the Kai-Iwi Lakes out to the coast, then north along the beach to Maunganui Bluff where it climbs to the summit and drops down to the beach again. The track continues past the Waikara Beach camping site to the Kawerua camping site and on to Hokianga South Head near Omapere. Allow 3 days for this walk if you plan to do it all (it can also be done in shorter sections) and make sure you organise to cross the Waipoua and Waimamaku rivers at low tide. You can get more information from the Dargaville Information Centre or the rangers at Trounson Kauri Park or Waipoua Forest. Look for the pamphlet on 'New Zealand Walkways – Dargaville District.'

**Places to Stay** There are two rustic camping grounds at the Kai-Iwi Lakes, one at Pine Beach right on the main lake, and another at Promenade Point (tel Dargaville 7056). They have toilets, cold showers, fireplaces, and no power points, and cost $5 per person.

Also at the Kai-Iwi Lakes, *Waterlea Farms* (tel 727) has a two-bedroom chalet at $70 a double and another at $60 a double. They provide many amenities such as a canoe and dinghy, colour TV, farm activities and more.

### Trounson Kauri Park

Heading north from Dargaville you can take a route passing by the 573 hectare Trounson Kauri Park, 40 km north of Dargaville. There's an easy half-hour walk leading from the parking and picnic area by the road, passing through beautiful forest with streams and some fine kauri stands, a couple of fallen kauri trees and the 'four sisters' – two trees each with two trunks. There's a ranger station and camping in the park.

**Places to Stay** The turn-off for the Trounson Kauri Park is 32 km north of Dargaville. Just after the turn-off, the *Kauri Coast Motor Camp* (tel Dargaville 36-521) is in a lovely riverside spot which is central to the lakes, the kauri forest, and generally everything of

interest around the area. They do bushwalks, pony rides, river, lake and sea fishing. Per-person rates are $7 in tent or power sites, $10 in basic cabins, or $12 in self-contained cabins.

There's also a DOC camping ground at the Trounson Kauri Park (tel Mamaranui 36-615). It's a beautiful place, ringed by superb kauris. Sites are $5 per person, with or without power. They will also be putting in cabins. Night walks are organised by the resident forest ranger, and in addition to kiwis you'll see glow-worms on a fallen log.

### WAIPOUA TO HOKIANGA
### Waipoua Kauri Forest

The road north enters the Waipoua Kauri Forest 50 km out of Dargaville. The Waipoua Forest Sanctuary, proclaimed in 1952 after much public pressure and antagonism at continued milling, is the largest remnant of the once extensive kauri forests of northern New Zealand. There is no milling of mature kauri trees now, except under extraordinary circumstances such as the carving of a Maori canoe. The kauri management programme which allowed for some thinning of adolescent trees to make room for others is under review. Milling in the Puketi State Forest was stopped some years back not only to protect the kauri but also because this area was the home of the rare native bird, the kokako.

The road through the forest passes by some huge and splendid kauris. Turn off to the forest lookout just after you enter the park – it was once a fire lookout and offers a spectacular view. A little further north another turn-off leads to the park Information Centre (tel Mamaranui 36-605), which in addition to plenty of information also has excellent exhibits on kauri trees, the history of the kauri in New Zealand and on native birds and wildlife. Nearby is Maxwell Cottage, a tiny hut used by the first ranger, now set up as an interesting little museum. Here you can pick up a brochure on the park which tells the full story of the trees. A fully grown kauri can reach 60 metres high and have a trunk 5 metres or more in diameter.

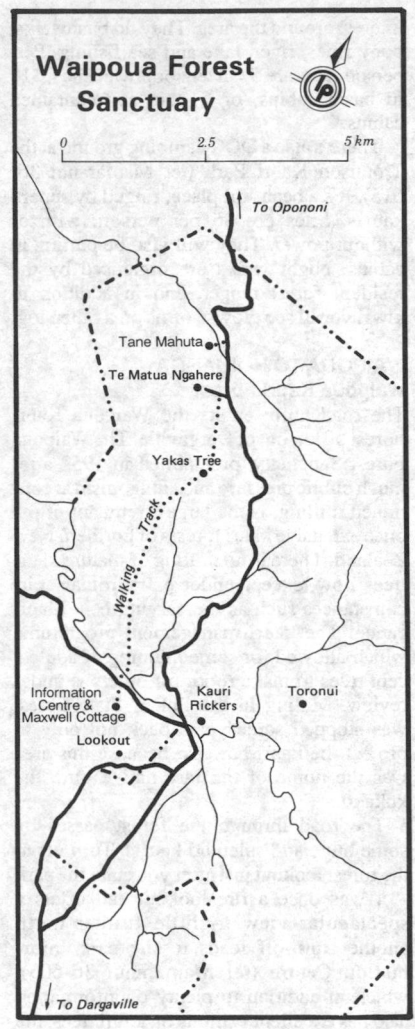

**Waipoua Forest Sanctuary**

To Opononi
Tane Mahuta
Te Matua Ngahere
Yakas Tree
Walking Track
Information Centre & Maxwell Cottage
Lookout
Kauri Rickers
Toronui
To Dargaville

tree in New Zealand. This massive tree is a short drive then a 10 minute walk from the main road. From the same access road you can follow a half-hour walking track to the Yakas Tree, the seventh largest kauri in New Zealand, and continue on if you like for the whole 2 to 3 hour trek to the park Information Centre. Do the walk in that direction as it's downhill.

Further up the road is Tane Mahuta, 'lord of the forest', the largest kauri tree in New Zealand, which stands much closer to the road and is estimated to be 1200 years old. At 52 metres, it's much higher than Te Matua Ngahere but doesn't have the same impressive bulk – although its cubic volume is said to be even greater. The park contained an even larger tree called Toronui but it fell, apparently from old age, in the '70s.

**Places to Stay** Just across the bridge from the Kauri Rickers there's a picnic area where you used to be able to camp but not anymore. Ask at the park Information Centre to see if the park has developed other camping sites, as they were considering doing so. Meanwhile, they have a few three bedroom houses near Maxwell Cottage, each sleeping up to six people, which can be hired for $45 a night for the whole house.

Near Waimamaku, just north of the Waipoua Forest, the *Solitaire Guest House* (tel Waimamaku 891) has B&B in a beautifully restored old kauri house for $34/45 a single/double, or $45/72 with dinner. It's a pleasant, friendly place with plenty of good walks, horse-riding and surfcasting off the beach.

### HOKIANGA HARBOUR

Further north the road winds down to the Hokianga Harbour and the tiny twin townships of Omapere and Opononi. The Hokianga is a popular area for city slickers wishing to escape to an alternative lifestyle, but it's still fairly unspoilt – much less commercial than the Bay of Islands – and a good place for travellers who want to take time out and drift for a while.

As you come up over the hill from the

They are slow growing and some kauris are over 1500 years old.

Several huge trees are easily reached from the road. Te Matua Ngahere, the 'father of the forest', has a trunk over 5 metres in diameter, by far the widest girth of any kauri

south there's a rest stop on Pakia Hill with a great view of the harbour; it's worth a stop.

Further on down the hill, 2 km west of Omapere, Signal Station Rd leads out to the Arai-Te-Uru Recreation Reserve and Lookout, on the South Head of the Hokianga Harbour. It's about a 30 minute walk from Omapere, or if you're driving, a 5 minute walk from the car park to the Signal Station Point which overlooks the harbour entrance, the massive sand dunes of the North Head, and the turbulent confluence of the harbour and the open sea. There's a swimming beach here, people fish off the rocks, and it's also the northern beginning/ending point of the Hokianga Track.

There's a tiny museum at Omapere, on the main road through town, which also houses the Hokianga Visitors Information Centre. Opening hours are very limited in winter, longer in summer.

## OPONONI

Only 3½ km past Omapere the road passes through the tiny settlement of Opononi. The stone walls along Opononi's seafront were constructed from rock ballast used in timber ships which were sailed out from Sydney by convicts.

Back in 1955 a dolphin paid so many regular, friendly visits to the town that it became a national attraction. Opo, as the dolphin was dubbed, played with children and learned to perform numerous tricks with beach balls. Unfortunately, Opo was killed, some say accidentally, by illegal dynamite fishers. A sculpture of Opo marks the dolphin's grave outside Opononi's pub. You can see a video of Opo at the Hokianga Visitors Information Centre/Museum in Omapere.

### Cruises & Fishing

Both of the Opononi hostels have boats and they frequently take hostellers out for fishing and shellfish excursions and on trips across to the North Head sand dunes. A water taxi operated by the owner of the Taha Moana Motel (tel Opononi 824) is available for

harbour cruising, water-skiing, parasailing and trips across to the dunes.

The MV *Sierra* is an historic 12 metre boat built of local Hokianga kauri wood in 1912, at the end of the logging boom. The boat plied the Hokianga Harbour for 42 years, carrying passengers and freight and, after a varied history including a sojourn in Auckland, is now once again operating in the harbour. It is licensed to carry 39 passengers and does several enjoyable cruises including an historic 'mail run', departing from Opononi and stopping at wharves in Te Karaka, Rawene, Kohukohu and Horeke. It costs about $20 to make the full return cruise, less if you just want to stop off somewhere. The boat also does twilight cruises, sandhill excursions, fishing, a tavern run (there are five on the harbour), and private charters. Phone Opononi 702 or 859 to check details, which vary with the season.

Fishing and shellfishing are excellent around the Hokianga Harbour. Fishing trips are easily arranged; even fishing off the wharf or the rocks near the harbour entrance is not bad.

### Walks

**Hokianga Track** The Hokianga track begins/ends at the South Head of the Hokianga Harbour and extends southwards along the coast – it's 4 hours to the Waimamaku Beach exit, 6 hours to the Kawerua exit which also has a camping site and hut, 12 hours to the Kerr Rd exit where there's a camping site at Waikara Beach, or you could continue the entire 16 hours (allow about 3 days) to the Kai-Iwi Lakes. Pick up a 'New Zealand Walkways – Dargaville District' pamphlet from any DOC office.

**Walks** In addition to the Hokianga Track there are several shorter local walks.

Cemetery Rd is on the eastern outskirts of Opononi. From this road you can make a half-hour climb up Mt Whiria, one of the oldest unexcavated pa sites, with a splendid view of the harbour. Simply walking down Cemetery Rd to the end is another pleasant stroll – it's a private road but you can walk through, just be sure to close the gate behind you.

Two km east of Opononi the Waiotemarama Gorge road turns south for 6 km to the Waiotemarama bush track. This track climbs to Mt Hautura, 680 metres high. It's a 4 hour walk to the summit (8 hours return), but there's a shorter loop walk starting from the same place which takes only about 2 hours and passes a picturesque waterfall and kauri trees. The highest point in Northland, 774 metres, is nearby but there is no regular track.

Just when you turn off the highway onto Waiotemarama Gorge Rd, you'll see a big hill on your left, and that one, too, makes for a good climb.

Between Waima and Taheke is the old Waoku coach road, once the sole route to Dargaville and, because of the rainfall, only open during summer. The track at the end of the road leads to some old, handmade culverts and excellent views of the valley. It takes about 3 hours there and back. If you continue to follow it, it winds south to Tutamoe and then west to Wekaweka Valley. You can enter the track from Waoku Rd or from Wekaweka Rd, and it can take a full or a half-day to do the trek depending where you start and finish; there's another branch of the track that winds down through the Mataraua State Forest. Get information from DOC before starting out, it's part of the New Zealand Walkway system.

## Other Activities

The postal worker from Kohukohu takes visitors to see the west coast, north of the harbour entrance, for $6 one way, $12 return. Catch the 9.30 am ferry from Rawene and he'll meet you at the Narrows (you take the 4 pm ferry back), or travel down to Te Karaha on the *Sierra* and meet him there. Phone Dick Reeves (tel Kohukohu 871) to make arrangements.

The King family (tel Opononi 815) does pony trekking in the Hokianga area.

The Heritage Restaurant & Art Gallery at the Opononi Best Western Hotel has a display of artwork done by locals.

## Places to Stay

**Hostels** The *Opononi Youth Hostel* (tel 792) is 2 km east of Opononi at Pakanae, it's the second driveway from the highway on Waiotemarama Gorge Rd. It's a good, rustic hostel, in the former old Pakanae schoolhouse, but a little far from the town. It costs $9 per night, or $8 if you're staying three nights or more.

The *Te Ranginarie – Harmony House* (tel Opononi 778) is more convenient than the YHA hostel but can be a little crowded and cramped. Cost is $10 a night in dorm or double rooms. There's plenty of action, with boat trips to the dunes and the mangrove forest, fishing and oyster hunts, and frequent parties. It's up the steep driveway beside the South Hokianga War Memorial Hall in the centre of Opononi.

**Hotels & Motels** Smack on the bay is the *Omapere Tourist Hotel & Motel* (tel 737) which has such a great setting it's almost worth staying for that alone. Rooms sleeping five are $74 per night, larger ones sleeping six are $80.

Also at Omapere is the *Motel Hokianga* (tel 847), with six two bedroom units and a spa pool. Prices are $68 a double, $72 for four during the high season, but drop down to $55 per night, or $170 per week, in the off season from June to August. The rest of the time they'll be somewhere in between; a little bargaining may go a long way.

In central Opononi, the *Opononi Hotel/Motel* (tel 858) is part of the Best Western chain. One bedroom motel units are $65, with two bedrooms they're $75, less in winter. Most of the hotel rooms share facilities and cost $25/35, or $45 a double with private bath. They also have a backpackers' section, where beds are just $12 a night.

Also in Opononi the *Taha Moana Motel* (tel 824) has one-bedroom units at $58 a double, two-bedroom units at $79 for four, remaining the same all year.

**Camping & Cabins** The *Opononi Beach Motor Camp* (tel Opononi 791) has camping sites at $6 per person, $7 with power, and a handful of on-site caravans at $10 per person. There are also a couple of chalets sleeping four at $30 per unit. The *Omapere Tourist Hotel & Motel* also has camping sites at $6.50 per person, $7.50 with power, and some very basic cabins at $20 per person.

## Places to Eat

On the main road in Opononi the *Blue Dolphin Restaurant* has burgers, sandwiches and other light meals plus a separate dinner menu. You can eat indoors or out on the deck overlooking the harbour. The *Heritage Restaurant & Art Gallery* at the Opononi Hotel has basic food at moderate prices. For a splurge there's the fancier *Harbourmaster's Restaurant* at the Omapere Tourist Hotel & Motel where you can eat indoors or outside, watching the boats and all the activity in the bay.

In Omapere the Village Shopping Centre has takeaways, a bakery and store. About 2 km outside of Omapere heading south the *Panorama Tea Rooms* has, yes, a panoramic view of the harbour, whether from inside or out on the deck. It serves light meals and takeaways plus home-baked goods and a separate dinner menu.

Not surprisingly, most of the restaurants here specialise in seafood, and it's excellent.

## Getting There & Away

**Bus** InterCity buses stop at Omapere and Opononi on their Monday to Friday run between Dargaville and Paihia, each about 2 hours distant. The bus driver heading south through the Waipoua Forest will pick you up in the morning, drop you off in the forest, and arrange to pick you up for the return trip in the afternoon. Another route goes to Whangarei Monday to Saturday, a 3 hour trip. A minibus (tel Rawene 795) goes daily from Waimamaku to Kaikohe, stopping at Omapere, Rawene and Waima.

## ROUTES TO KAITAIA

From the Hokianga you can head north to Kaitaia and the 90 Mile Beach or east to the Bay of Islands. There are two routes north to Kaitaia. The longer and busier route goes via Kaikohe and is easier for hitchhikers. The alternative route is 70 km shorter and takes you on the Rawene-Kohukohu ferry.

The ferry departs Rawene every hour on the half-hour between 7.30 am and 5.45 pm and goes from the Narrows on the Kohukohu side at 7.45 and 8.30 am and then every hour from 9 am to 6 pm. Starting time may be an hour later and finishing time an hour earlier in winter; the crossing takes 20 minutes. Fares are $8 for cars, $2 for motorcycles, $1 for people.

## Rawene & Kohukohu

While you wait for the ferry at Rawene you can visit historic Clendon House, open from 10 am to 4 pm daily. Admission is $2 (children $1). Outside the Westpac Bank is Te Hawera, an old Maori dugout canoe.

Rawene is quite a pleasant little settlement, you might decide to stay longer than just the wait for the ferry. Tiny though it is, Rawene is full of history. It's the third oldest European settlement in New Zealand, and in addition to Clendon House there are plenty of other historic buildings. The Wharf House, now housing a restaurant, is the oldest building in Rawene and has been a hospital, a private home, and many other things during its long lifetime. The hotel, too, is an historic place, built in the 1870s.

Kohukohu, across the river, is a minor arty-crafty-trendy centre.

**Places to Stay** Rawene has a motor camp (tel 720) in Mamon St just off Manning St, with tent sites at $7 per person ($8 with power), cabins at $14 per person, and two self-contained units at $20 per person. The *Masonic Hotel* (tel 822), just a few steps up from the ferry landing, has rooms from $26/37.

## Ngawha Springs

Near Kaikohe is Ngawha Springs which has a series of hot springs of varying temperatures at the Domain Pool – pick one to suit your mood. It's very basic but it's a great way to spend a bleak day and only about 3 km off the main road. Admission is $2.

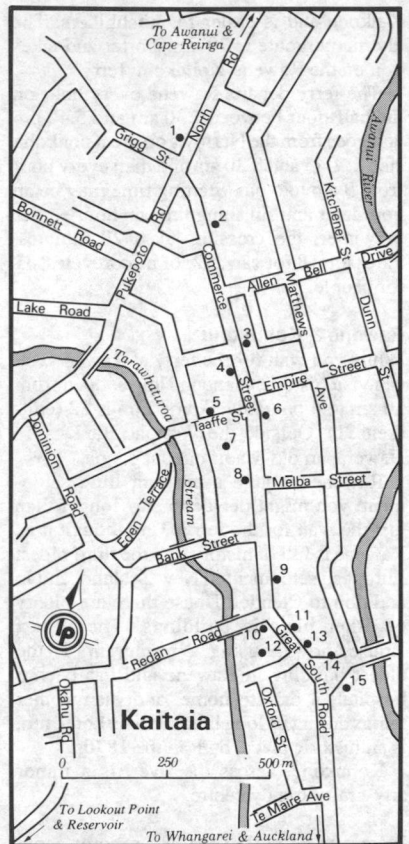

1  Capri Motel
2  Main Street Hostel
3  Mt Cook
4  Kaitaia Youth Hostel
5  InterCity Depot
6  Steve's Snapper Bar
7  Pac'N Save Supermarket
8  Kaitaia Post Office
9  Kaitaia Hotel
10  Yugoslav Cultural Club
11  Far North Regional Museum
12  Fuller's
13  Far North Community Public
    Relations Office
14  Far North Arts & Crafts Gallery
15  Far North Community Centre

### Mangamuka Gorge Route

Near Takahue the Mangamuka Gorge route begins from Takahue Valley Rd and heads off through the Raetea State Forest to the summit of Mt Raetea (751 metres) where there's a sweeping view over all the region's forests to Hokianga Harbour, the Bay of Islands, Doubtless Bay, the Karikari peninsula and North Cape. It's a full-day walk for experienced trampers and since there's no water along the way you have to carry your own.

The route emerges on SH 1 and from here another track goes up to a radio tower (581

metres), again with great views. It's a 3 to 4 hour walk which can be done as a loop.

### KAITAIA

Kaitaia is a small but pleasant town of no great interest in itself; it's primarily a jumping-off point for trips up 90 Mile Beach to Cape Reinga. Buses leave every morning on this trip – see the following section on 90 Mile Beach.

Entering Kaitaia you'll see a welcome sign in three languages – Welcome, Haere Mai (Maori) and Dobro Dosli (Yugoslav). Many Maoris and Yugoslavs live in the area and, as in many other parts of the Far North, the Slavs are descendants of the immigrant Dalmatian gumdiggers. Both groups are culturally active, with a Maori marae and a Yugoslav Cultural Club being the focus of activities.

### Information

The Far North Community Public Relations Office (tel 80-879) is on Commerce St. They have information on Kaitaia and the entire Far North region. They also book accommodation, tours and activities for the Far North. The office is open from 9 am to 4.30 pm Monday to Friday.

### Far North Regional Museum

The Far North Regional Museum houses an interesting collection including a giant moa skeleton, various bits and pieces from ship-wrecks, and the Northwood Collection – hundreds of photographs taken around 1900 by a professional photographer. The giant 1769 de Surville anchor, one of three the explorer lost in Doubtless Bay, is one of the museum's prize pieces. It's open from 10 am to 5 pm weekdays, 1 to 5 pm on weekends, with extended summer hours. Admission is $2 (children 50 cents).

### Community Centre Mural
The unusual three-dimensional mural at the Far North Community Centre is an excep-tional combination of painting, sculpture, backlighting and other innovative tech-niques, paying tribute to the Far North region. Three-dimensional scenes include a Maori canoe on a turbulent sea, whalers, kauri forestry, and others. The Community Centre is open from about 8 am to 4.30 pm Monday to Friday, but is also open on many evenings and weekends for various func-tions. It's just a short walk around the corner from the PR office and the museum.

### Sullivan's Nocturnal Park
In Fairburn, about a 20 minute drive from Kaitaia, Sullivan's Nocturnal Park (tel 84-100) is open every day from noon to midnight. The main attraction is a glow-worm grotto beside a waterfall; in the dark of night you're taken on a guided nature walk for a close-up view of the glow-worms in their natural habitat. There's also a nocturnal kiwi room and areas for picnics in the daytime. Entry is $5 for adults in the evening, $3 during the day (children always $3).

To reach the park from Kaitaia, go 8 km south-east on SH 1, turn left at the Fairburn signpost and continue for another 9 km. Coming from Taipa it's about a half-hour drive.

### New Zealand Walkway
The Kaitaia section of the New Zealand Walkway, also known as the Kiwanis Bush Walk, makes a good day trip and has excel-lent views. Originally planned as a road, the track has a gentle gradient along its 9 km, for which you should allow 5 hours. To get to it head south from Kaitaia on SH 1 for 3 km, then turn right into Larmer Rd and follow it to the end at the Kiwanis Club Bush Camp Hut where you can overnight if you've made prior arrangements.

The track finishes at Veza Rd, off Diggers Valley Rd, which can be an awkward place to get out of as there is no transport and it is quite a long way from the main road. Going back the way you came is one option or you could try your luck hitching. Keen bush-walkers can get permission from the farmer on Diggers Valley Rd to cross the few km to Takahue Valley where the Mangamuka Gorge Walkway is a good full day's tramp to SH 1.

### Tours
Kaitaia is a small town but it's quite a centre for tours to surrounding areas, notably Cape Reinga. See the section on 90 Mile Beach for info on tours to that region.

Other popular tours from Kaitaia are oper-ated by Tipihaere Tours, based at the Main Street Hostel (tel 81-275). Full-day tours to Matai Bay for fishing and snorkelling cost $20, and they also do tours to Sullivan's Nocturnal Park which for $12 include the park entrance fees.

### Other Activities
It's easy hitching a ride out to the beach at Ahipara, 14 km west of Kaitaia. Ahipara is the southernmost section of 90 Mile Beach and is popular with locals and visitors. There's fishing, surfing, horseback riding, a motor camp and lots of picnicking and playing around on fine days.

The Aero Club (tel 77-320, 77-425) will take you for a 1 hour flight up to Cape Reinga and back, or for any other scenic or charter flight. It's quite economical if you can get a group of three together.

The Kaitaia Scottish Country Dance Club meets at 7.30 pm every Monday at the Men's Bowling Club Pavilion in Matthews Ave, visitors are welcome. The biggest dance of the year is the Yugoslav Ball, held annually on the last weekend in June, which includes performances of the Yugoslav national dances in gay traditional costume.

There's a park and children's playground on Commerce St between the museum and the PR office. Further down in the park, opposite the Far North Community Centre, the Far North Arts & Crafts Gallery has many unusual items.

## Places to Stay

**Hostels** Kaitaia has two excellent hostels. The *Kaitaia Youth Hostel* (tel 81-840) is very central at 160 Commerce St (the main drag). It sleeps 39 and since there are plenty of twin rooms and family rooms you have a pretty good chance of getting a room to yourself. Cost is $12 a night.

In the next block at 235 Commerce St, is the privately run *Main Street Hostel* (tel 81-275). The hospitable live-in owners, Peter and Kerry, organise many activities including Maori hangis, lamb on the spit parties, diving, fishing and pig-hunting expeditions, surfing and windsurfing, bushwalks, and various others. Peter is active in the Maori community and takes visitors to see the local marae. It's a great place to stay and rates are $12 the first night, $11 the second night and $10 after that.

**Hotels & Motels** The *Kaitaia Hotel* (tel 80-360) on Commerce St is a venerable hotel with 30 rooms at $44/50, all with bathroom. Right at the centre of town, the hotel is a Kaitaia institution and has a good licensed restaurant plus a house bar, a lounge bar and a popular pub.

Kaitaia has a surprising number of motels, presumably in part because the town is so popular as a 90 Mile Beach jumping-off point. At last count there were nine of them along the stretch from South Rd to North Rd. They have various amenities such as swimming pools, saunas, spas, gyms, etc, and rates from $40 to $80 a double. Your best bet is to book through the PR office (tel 80-879) to get the prices and features closest to what you're looking for. Otherwise you can ring the motels directly:

| Motel | Tel |
| --- | --- |
| Arondale Motel | 83-300 |
| Capri Motel | 80-224 |
| Kaitaia Motor Lodge | 81-910 |
| Kauri Lodge | 81-190 |
| Loredo Motel | 83-200 |
| Sierra Court | 81-461 |
| Wayfarer Motel | 82-600 |
| Northerner Motor Inn | 82-800 |
| Orana Motor Inn | 81-510 |

There are a few B&B inns around the Far North region, and these, too, can be booked through the PR office.

**Camping & Cabins** The *Dyer's Motor Camp* (tel 80-333) at 67 South Rd on the southern end of town, and the *Pine Tree Lodge Motor Camp* (tel 74-864), 18 km west on the coast at Ahipara, each have tent and power sites at $7.50 per person.

The *90 Mile Beach Holiday Park* (tel 77-298) is 18 km north on the Cape Reinga road and has tent and power sites at $8 per person, basic cabins at $25 for two and fully equipped tourist cabins at $35 for two. There's a licensed restaurant on the premises; lamb on the spit is the speciality.

## Places to Eat

The *Steve's Snapper Bar* at 123 Commerce St is good and economical, with a big serving of fish & chips for just $2.50. It's across the road and a little down from the YHA and although it's essentially a takeaway place you can eat your 'takeaways' there. They also do fried chicken and pizzas and they sell fresh fish. Across the road the *Sea Dragon* has Chinese takeaways. *VIP Takeaways* is another good spot for fish & chips and there are several other takeaways around town.

There are also a few good cafes including the *Time Out Cafe* right in the centre of town with an excellent selection of inexpensive food and a comfortable atmosphere. The *Kauri Arms Tavern*, the *Collard Tavern* and the *Kaitaia Hotel Pub* all serve pub food. For a late-night bite the *White Lady Pie Cart*, just off Commerce St, is open some nights until 3 am and also serves drinks.

For a fancier meal try the *Beachcomber* or

the *Kaitaia Hotel* where the bar looks like it was time-warped from the '50s and the restaurant from an even earlier era.

Pac'N Save is a gigantic supermarket on the main drag, an anomaly in this small town. Prices are lower here than anywhere else and it attracts customers from far and wide. Also look for the large bakery on Commerce St; it has a good selection of baked goodies. It's open from about 6 am.

### Entertainment

For years Kaitaia had only one bar and pub, at the *Kaitaia Hotel*, but the town now has three pubs including the *Kauri Arms Tavern* on Commerce St and the *Collard Tavern* on the western side of town. With the competition they all have to try harder and now they all bring in live bands on the weekends.

### Getting There & Away

**Air** Eagle Air (tel 77-411) has two daily flights between Kaitaia and Auckland, with connections to other centres, and weekday flights to Whangarei.

**Bus** The InterCity bus station (tel 81-333) is on Taaffe St. Several daily buses go between Kaitaia and Auckland via Doubtless Bay, the Bay of Islands and Whangarei. Travel time is 30 minutes to Doubtless Bay, 2½ hours to Paihia, 3½ hours to Whangarei or 7 hours all the way to Auckland.

### Getting Around

The major rental car companies have agents in Kaitaia: Budget is at Star Garage (tel 82-510), Avis is at Fuller's (tel 81-500) and Hertz is at Kaitaia Toyota (tel 80-440). Haines Haulage (tel 80-116) provides airport transport for $3 per person.

### 90 MILE BEACH

The tip of Northland – ending in Cape Reinga – is known as 90 Mile Beach. When they metricate it to 90 Km Beach the name will be a lot more accurate as it's a good bit short of 90 miles! Trips up the beach are very popular. The buses travel up the beach and down the road, or vice versa, depending on the tides.

The bus trips start from Kaitaia, Doubtless Bay and the Bay of Islands. It's preferable to start from Kaitaia or Doubtless Bay – two of the small, local operators start out from both places, one from Kaitaia only, and you're that much closer to Cape Reinga. Going from the Bay of Islands you have a couple of hours extra travel at each end of the day to contend with, and you're limited to going with a larger, more commercial tour company.

If you're staying awhile in the Cape Reinga-90 Mile Beach area, a network of tracks has been opened up connecting the various beaches, and there are a couple of camping sites with road access. The New Zealand Walkway goes down the 90 Mile Beach but you'll need to be well prepared as there are no huts and although it may not be as long as 90 miles it certainly seems like it to walk! The main attraction of the Far North is the coastline, which is scattered with beautiful beaches – far too many to mention here.

The Aupouri State Forest, about 75 km long and 5 km wide, covers two-thirds of the western side of the peninsula. It's an artificial forest, mostly pine, planted for timber. Kauri forest used to cover the area, in fact traces have been found of three separate growths of kauri which were buried and then grew up again. This was a fruitful area for gum-diggers, as was most of the northern region. On the northern edge of the Aupouri Forest a volcanic rock formation called The Bluff is part of a 36 hectare private reserve used for fishing by the Maori tribe living in nearby Te Kao.

North of The Bluff, the 17.2 sq km Te Paki Farm Park is public land and you can go where you wish on it, just leave the gates as you found them and don't disturb the animals. There are about 7 sq km of giant sand dunes on either side of where the Te Paki stream meets the sea; a stop to take flying leaps off the dunes is one of the highlights of the locally operated tours.

## Wagener Museum

The Wagener Museum at Houhora is an astonishing place, with over 50,000 items on display, spanning almost 9 centuries. Worldwide nature exhibits include a 5 cm mouse deer and 30 cm insects; an 1878 Symphonion is among a collection of antique gramophones, player pianos and other musical instruments that the attendant will play for you. Other operational antiques include various inventive washing machines, telephones, clocks and carriages. Top quality Maori carvings are found both inside and outside, and the prehistory and old photographs section is equally interesting. This is one of the most fascinating museums in New Zealand. It's open daily from 9 am to 5 pm; admission is $4 (children $2.50).

## Tours

Several small, locally owned tour operators run from Kaitaia and Doubtless Bay up to Cape Reinga. Mike's Tours (tel Kaitaia 82-826) and Sand Safaris (tel Kaitaia 81-778) go in small 4WD buggies which carry about a dozen people. Both are very popular and enjoyable. The main difference between them is that Mike's stops at the Wagener Museum, and departs from both Kaitaia and Doubtless Bay; Sand Safaris leaves from Kaitaia only and skips the museum, but this allows for more time to enjoy the peninsula's many natural attractions, and they give a 10% backpackers' discount. Northway Tours (tel Kaitaia 77-425) is another good local company, much the same as the other two except that it may go in a larger bus, but it still retains the informal local character. Northway departs from Kaitaia or Doubtless Bay and it, too, stops at the Wagener Museum. All three of these companies charge the same price, $30 (children $15), including a picnic lunch.

Other small-group local tours to the Cape Reinga area are operated by Tipihaere Tours, based at Kaitaia's Main Street Hostel (tel 81-275). They include various options such as stops for fishing, snorkelling or scuba diving, visits to the Wagener Museum, and visits to a marae.

Fuller's (tel Kaitaia 81-500) also does cape tours, leaving from Kaitaia or Doubtless Bay ($35) and the Bay of Islands ($45). King's Adventure Tours come from the Bay of Islands only. In addition to being a bit more costly these tours are also more formal, done in big buses with a time schedule to adhere to. You'll have a better time on one of the small local tours.

Of course you could go up to Cape Reinga on your own, there's no bus but there are rental car companies in Kaitaia if you didn't bring your own and even hitching is not too difficult. The main advantage with a tour is that you'll see the best parts of the region, learn something about it, and especially in the 4WD vehicles you can go to places you'd never reach by car. Driving on the beach is something you wouldn't want to inflict on your own car (it causes rust) and car rental companies strictly disapprove: in a car you have to stick to the roads. Motorcycling on the beach would be OK but if you try this take it slow and be extra careful, a few bikers have been killed when they suddenly rode into washouts or soft sand. If you want to spend more time than the 1 day tour allows, you can make arrangements with one of the smaller tour operators to get off the tour and be picked up on another day.

## Places to Stay

If you do plan to stay on the cape there are several DOC camping sites in the Cape Reinga area. There's a site at *Spirits Bay*, with water and limited toilet facilities, and another at *Tapotupotu Bay*, with toilets and showers; neither has electricity and you should bring a cooker with you as fires are not allowed. Spirits Bay is a sacred area to the Maoris – in Maori folklore, the spirits departing from the dead come here and leap off the cliffs into the sea, leaving New Zealand to return to the legendary homeland Hawaiki. Both bays are infested with mosquitoes and biting sandflies, so come prepared with coils and insect repellent.

There's another DOC camping site at *Rarawa Beach*, 3 km north of Ngataki, with water and toilet facilities only. No prior bookings can be made and fires are only allowed in the fireplaces provided.

The *Pukenui Lodge Motel & Hostel* (tel 58-837), the northernmost accommodation in New Zealand, is in a lovely setting overlooking Pukenui Harbour. The motel has one-bedroom flats sleeping four at $57. The hostel is in a separate house behind the motel. It's pleasant, comfortable and homely, with twin and double rooms at $12.50 per person. If you telephone collect from Kaitaia they will come to pick you up free of charge. No buses pass here but it's an easy hitch.

Follow Lamb Rd west about 500 metres and there's the *Pukenui Motor Camp* (tel 58-803) with tent and power sites at $6 per person, on-site caravans at $10 per person and a tourist flat at $30 for two.

The *Houhora Camping Ground* is opposite the Wagener Museum. It's an attractive location but with minimal facilities – no power and cold showers only. Nonetheless rates are low and if you happen to be towing a boat there's a boat ramp here. At the turn-off to the museum from the highway the *Houhora Chalets Motel* (tel Houhora 860) has A-frame chalets. This and other Far North motels (there are more) can be booked through the PR office in Kaitaia (tel 80-879).

### Places to Eat

Opposite the Pukenui Lodge, at the corner of Lamb Rd and the main highway, is *Norm of the North's* restaurant, tearoom, takeaway and shop.

## DOUBTLESS BAY

From Kaitaia it's about 40 km to Doubtless Bay, heading north a few km to Awanui and then turning east on SH 10. The bay gets its unusual name from an entry in Captain Cook's logbook, where he wrote that the body of water was 'doubtless a bay'. The area is much less touristed than the Bay of Islands, it has plenty of unspoiled scenic beauty and a few good activities and places to stay. Tours to Cape Reinga depart from here and take only about half an hour longer in travel time than if you go from Kaitaia.

The area is full of tiny picturesque bays

and coves. On the northern and western sides the bay is bounded by the Karikari Peninsula, with beautiful beaches and several camping spots. Matai Bay on the peninsula is especially lovely, with its tiny 'twin coves'; you can climb a small hill and look down between them, and there's a DOC camping site. Other beaches circle the bay and include the popular beach resorts of Taipa, Cable Bay and Cooper's Beach. Mangonui, the principal town, is a charming historic village. The whole area is great for fishing and shellfishing, boating, swimming and other watersports.

### Taipa

According to Maori legend, Taipa is the place where Kupe, the original Polynesian discoverer of New Zealand, first set foot on the new land in about 900 AD. Today it has a fine beach, a harbour where the Taipa River meets the sea, and several motels and motor camps. You can get a good view overlooking Taipa by turning off the main road onto Bush Point Rd.

East of Taipa is Cable Bay, once the home of the longest cable in the world: from 1902 to 1912 a cable stretched 3500 nautical miles from here to Queensland, Australia. The cable station was closed down in 1912 when another cable was laid between Sydney and Auckland. Today Cable Bay and Cooper's Beach are popular beach resorts, especially during the summer.

It's about a 30 minute drive from Taipa to Sullivan's Nocturnal Park in Fairburn (see Kaitaia), turning from SH 10 onto Peria Rd and continuing for about 24 km.

### Rangikapiti Pa

Between Cooper's Bay and Mangonui is the Rangikapiti Pa Scenic Reserve, with ancient Maori terracing and a spectacular sweeping view of Doubtless Bay.

### Mangonui

Mangonui, the principal town of Doubtless Bay, is a tiny, picturesque historic village. It has all the basic services and a few interesting spots to visit. The Mangonui wharf has a small saltwater aquarium and there's good fishing off the wharf. The Mangonui Courthouse is a historic reserve and the nearby Wharf Store has a variety of arts and crafts. Dances are held on Saturday nights at the Mangonui War Memorial Hall, beginning at 8 pm.

Also at Mangonui is the attractive little Mill Bay, dotted with tiny boats; you can take Silver Egg Rd out to Mill Bay's Mangonui Cruising Club and an assortment of historical markers. This was the spot where Mangonui's first European settler made his base, and the whaling boats stocked their water from this stream.

## Places to Stay

**Hostels** The *Old Oak Inn* (tel 60-665) in Mangonui is an 1861 kauri house with hostel accommodation from $12.50. It's a pleasant small lodge with twin and double rooms, a seafood restaurant and an arts & crafts shop. Many inexpensive activities are organised from the hostel including canoe and kayak trips around the inner harbour and mangrove swamps, fishing trips, and excursions to Sullivan's Nocturnal Park in nearby Fairburn. They hire mountain bikes for $5 a day. It takes just a couple of hours to bike to the Karikari Peninsula and the area has many other interesting spots to visit.

**Hotels & Motels** In Mangonui the historic *Mangonui Hotel* (tel 60-003) is comfortable and refurbished, with regular rooms at $35/53 and two twin backpackers rooms at $20 per person.

There are many motels in the area including the Mangonui Motel (tel 60-346) in Mangonui, the *Blue Pacific Motel* (tel 60-010) and the *Taipa Sands Motel* (tel 60-446) in Taipa and the *Driftwood Lodge* (tel 60-418) in Cable Bay. The *Cooper's Beach Motel* (tel 60-271) is popular and has typical rates at about $60 a double.

Bookings for all accommodation in the area can be made through the Far North Community Public Relations Office (tel 80-879) in Kaitaia.

**Camping & Cabins** There's a DOC camping site at Matai Bay on the Karikari Peninsula. Services are basic (cold water showers and fireplaces) but it's a beautiful spot, costing about $2 per site. Across the peninsula the *Karikari Bay Motor Camp* (tel 87-051) has camping at $9 per site, on-site caravans, cabins, tent and boat hire, and there's also the *Tokerau Beach Motor Camp* (tel 87-510).

At Cooper's Beach the *Cooper's Beach Holiday Park* (tel 60-597) is one of the largest and most popular camping spots in the area, with a 1 km private beach. In low season camping sites are $6 per person, $7 with power; on-site caravans are $25 for two people, and two bedroom self-contained units sleeping four are $30. Summer rates are a few dollars higher.

Similar holiday camping grounds are dotted around the bay. In Taipa are the *Blue Pacific Caravan Park* (tel 60-010) and the *De Surville Holiday Park* (tel 60-656, 60-657). On Hihi Beach, 11½ km from Mangonui, is the *Hihi Beach Motor Park* (tel 60-307).

## Places to Eat

In Mangonui the *Nina Cafe* is a cosy little cafe with good food at low prices, the kind of place you can sit around and listen to good music, drink cappuccino and have a game of chess or backgammon.

Also in Mangonui, *Harbour View Takeaways* has tables indoors or out on the deck overlooking the harbour. The *Mangonui Fish Shop* hangs out over the water near the wharf and in addition to fresh shellfish and smoked fish it serves award-winning fish & chips and seafood salads.

For a step up the *Mangonui Hotel* has a restaurant with an outdoor barbecue area to one side, and the *Old Oak Inn* has a seafood restaurant. At Cooper's Beach the Cooper's Beach Motel has the *Pamir Restaurant* with steak and seafood.

## Entertainment

This is not exactly Auckland for entertainment but there is a pub at the *Mangonui Hotel* and a Saturday night dance at the *Mangonui*

*War Memorial Hall*. In Taipa the singer Ray
Woolf has a nightclub called *Woolfie's*.

## Getting There & Away
**Bus** InterCity buses pass through Mangonui
twice a day on the Bay of Islands-Kaitaia
route. Travel time is 30 minutes to Kaitaia, 2
hours to Paihia.

## WHANGAROA
The main road to the Bay of Islands passes
close to Whangaroa, where in 1809 the ship
*Boyd* was attacked and burnt by Maoris, who
killed all the crew and passengers except a
woman, two children and a young cabin boy.
Whangaroa is 6 km off the main road and is
a popular game fishing centre. The outer
harbour is surrounded by high, rugged cliffs
and curious hills. The domed summit of St
Paul's, above the town to the south, offers
fine views.

## Information
The Boyd Gallery (tel 50-230) is a gallery,
dairy and general store which also houses the
town's informal tourist information office.
They make bookings for harbour cruises,
fishing trips and other activities and can also
book accommodation around Whangaroa.
It's open every day, from 8 am to 5 pm in
winter, from 7.30 am to 7 pm in summer.

## Cruises & Fishing
Fishing trips and harbour cruises on the MV
*Friendship* go twice daily in summer and
cost $22 per person or $55 per family.
Several other boats are available for line
fishing and deep sea fishing, water-skiing
and diving. Diving expeditions to the sunken
*Rainbow Warrior* at the Cavalli Islands just
off the coast are especially popular. You can
book boats through the Marlin Hotel or the
Boyd Gallery. Much of the harbour is completely unspoilt since there is no road access
to it.

In the holiday season a lunch cruise goes
out to the famous Kingfish Lodge, a licensed
fishing lodge accessible only by boat, with a
lovely private beach, a seafood restaurant
and a 2 hour walking track to Tauranga Bay

(4 hours return). You can also go there on the
MV *Friendship*, taking the morning harbour
cruise out and being picked up again on the
return of the afternoon harbour cruise.

## Walks
The St Paul's Walk begins from Whangaroa
Harbour and takes about half an hour, climbing to the St Paul's Scenic Reserve for a
splendid view of the bay.

On the northern side of the harbour the
Wairakau track goes from Totara North to the
Lane Cove Cottage – 5 hours return at a
sedate pace. The marked track begins from
the signpost near the church hall on Campbell Rd in Totara North and passes through
farmland, hills, flats, shoreline, the Wairakau
Stream, and Bride's Veil Falls before arriving at Lane Cottage, built in 1922.

There's a long walk on Mahinepua Bay,
heading out onto Hororoa Point. From the
Kingfish Lodge a 2 hour track comes out at
Tauranga Bay. There are also many enjoyable walks in the Puketi and Omahuta state
forests, about 20 km south-west of
Whangaroa.

## Other Activities
For a scenic drive passing by many of the
area's most beautiful spots, depart from
Whangaroa, stopping first at Tauranga Bay,
then Mahinepua Bay, then Te Ngahere, and
perhaps a short detour to Matauri Bay,
emerging on SH 10 just south of Kaeo. All
of these bays have fine beaches.

Guided pony trekking expeditions (tel
143U or 143S) go through native and pine
forest and up to scenic lookout points.

Lane's Mill at Totara North is an old mill
which opens in the summer to show visitors
how the mill used to work.

## Places to Stay
**Hostels** The *Sunseeker Lodge* (tel 50-496)
is a YHA associate hostel, up on a hill about
500 metres beyond the wharf, with a great
view of the harbour and an outdoor barbecue
and lawn area to enjoy it from. Cost is $10
in dorms, $15 per person in double rooms.

At Totara North the *Historic Gumstore*

*Hostel* (tel 75-703, 75-838) dates from 1890 and has hostel accommodation from $10, with dorms and two private rooms. You can rent dinghies here and they also do fishing trips.

The *Lane Cove Cottage* on the western arm of the harbour is operated by the DOC. Cost is $5 a night and it can only be reached by the 2 hour Wairakau Track from Totara North, or by boat – the MV *Friendship* will drop you off there on its harbour cruises. There are showers and flush toilets, but you have to bring your own cooker. Make arrangements first at the DOC office in Kerikeri, or at other DOC offices.

**Hotels & Motels** Right by the wharf the *Marlin Hotel* (tel 50-347) has share-facility rooms at $28/40 for singles/doubles, plus one twin room with private facilities at $45. The hotel has the town's only restaurant and pub, and it also has diesel for boats, petrol for cars, and dive tank filling. The *Motel Whangaroa* (tel Kaeo 33) and the *Truant Lodge Motel* (tel Kaeo 50-133) have motel rooms at about $40/55. At the *Kingfish Lodge* (tel 777), reached by boat, double rooms are $68, with lower off-season rates.

**Camping & Cabins** The *Whangaroa Motor Camp* (tel Kaeo 36) costs $6 per person for tent sites, $8 for caravan sites, and has cabins at $16 for one, $21 to $25 for two. The camp is about 2½ km before the wharf. Other motor camps are at Matauri Bay, Taupo Bay and Tauranga Bay.

**Places to Eat**
The *Marlin Hotel* has a 'Sunday Special' three-course family dinner for $14, bookings encouraged. Other days most dinner main courses are about $14 and it serves breakfast and lunch too.

**Around Whangaroa**
**Puketi & Omahuta State Forests** The Puketi State Forest and the Omahuta State Forest comprise one large forest area about 20 km south-west of Whangaroa, with kauri sanctuaries and other exotic trees and foliage, camping and picnic areas, streams and pools, and the Mangahorehore Viewpoint.

The two forests are reached by several entrances and contain a network of 17 walking tracks varying in length from 10 minutes to 2 days. A pamphlet detailing the tracks and features of the forests is available from any DOC office; the Puketi Forest Headquarters is on Waiare Rd about halfway between Pungaere Rd and Puketotara Rd.

# Bay of Islands

The Bay of Islands was the site of New Zealand's first permanent European settlement and today it has become one of the country's major tourist attractions. The two routes north through Kaitaia and Whangarei, together with the direct route east from the Hokianga, all meet at the Bay of Islands.

## Orientation
The townships around the Bay of Islands are all on the mainland, there are no island resorts. To the north is Kerikeri – 'so nice they named it twice', claim the tourist brochures. Paihia, the main centre on the bay, is virtually continuous with Waitangi. A little south again is Opua from where a car ferry shuttles across the Waikare Inlet to take you to Russell. You can also reach Russell from Paihia by road but it's a long and roundabout route.

## Cruises
The Bay of Islands is a very popular holiday area, so there's quite a bit to see and do although it's the bay itself which is the main attraction. Nearly 150 islands dot the waters of the bay – it's aptly named.

The best way to introduce yourself to the area is to spend the money and take a cruise. Fuller's (tel 27-421) operate very popular regular cruises and they're supplemented by a host of other cruises from smaller operators including two of the hostels.

Best known of the cruises is Fuller's

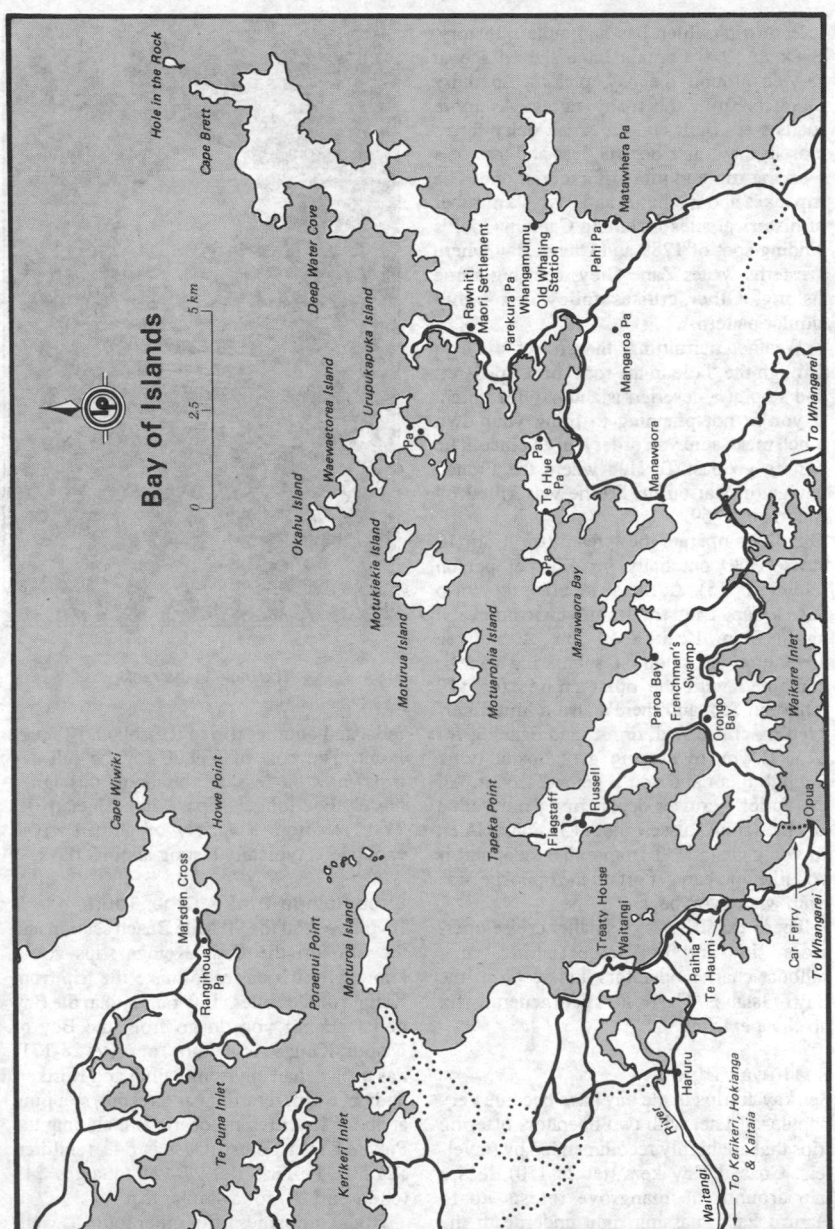

'cream trip' which has had quite a history. Back in 1920 Captain Lane started a boat service around the bay, picking up dairy products from the many farms. As more roads were built and the small dairy farms closed, the cruise became less and less of a working trip and more of a tourist one. The trip takes about 5 hours and passes a number of historical sites including Captain Cook's landing spot of 1789 and Otehei Bay where Westerns writer Zane Grey went big game fishing. Other cruises follow a roughly similar pattern.

Weather permitting, the cruises may go through the 'hole in the rock' off Cape Brett and stop at a deserted island bay for lunch. If you're not planning to bring your own lunch make sure you order it in advance. The cruises go past Te Hue where the French navigator Marion du Fresne was killed by Maoris in 1769.

Fuller's operate the 'cream trip' from 10 am to 3.30 pm daily for $39 per person (children $15). At the same price they also have a Cape Brett trip from 9 am to noon and again from 12.30 to 4 pm. A 'subsea adventure' in a tourist submarine can be combined with the other cruises for $10 (children $5), and there's also a 'nite-tiger' evening cruise with drinks and dancing for $25. If you're staying at a hostel book through them and you'll get a discount. All the Fuller's cruises depart first from Paihia and then from Russell about 15 minutes later, so you can start off from either side, and if you like you can get off on the opposite side from where you began.

There are all sorts of smaller cruise operators, line and big game fishing trips, sailboat charter operators and so on in the Bay of Islands. The hostels here generally fix up cheaper trips.

### Sea Kayak Trips
Sea kayak trips in the bay have become very popular of late, with two operators offering trips that are highly recommended by travellers. Coastal Kayakers (tel 28-110) does a trip around the mangrove forests up to Haruru Falls, passing right underneath the

The 'hole in the rock'

falls, and another trip to Russell and Tapeka Point. The cost of $39.50 for the full-day trips may be less if you book through a hostel. For longer trips, Mark Hutson (tel 27-151) offers a variety of guided kayak excursions typically lasting about 3 days.

### Cape Reinga Trips & Other Tours
If you've read the 90 Mile Beach section and the info on the Cape Reinga trips you'll know why it's easier to make the trip from Kaitaia or Doubtless Bay rather than the Bay of Islands. If you do go from the Bay of Islands, King's Adventure Tours (tel 28-171) has trips departing from Paihia and Kerikeri daily at 8 am, returning at 6.45 pm, stopping at about 15 different locations including the Puketi Kauri Forest. Cost is $43 (children $21.50). Fuller's (tel 27-421) charges $45 (children $20) for a similar trip.

Both companies offer other tours as well.

King's has a half-day 'Bay Wonder' tour for $25 (children $12.50) visiting many attractive spots around the region, and a 'Northland Wonder' tour for $58 (children $44) which goes farther afield, all the way up to 90 Mile Beach, and includes a spit roast lamb dinner. Fuller's has a 'Tu-Tu' tour which features dune riding in the massive west coast dunes and visits to the historic kauri gumfields for $45 (children $20), including lunch.

Flying over the Bay of Islands is magnificent and surprisingly inexpensive: you can take a short aerial tour (about 20 minutes) for $15. Book flights through the hostels, the Information Centre, Fuller's or phone 27-456.

### Places to Stay
Camping is permitted at *Urupukapuka Bay* on Urupukapuka Island but you must make your own transport arrangements and be completely self-sufficient. You need food, stove and fuel and a shovel for digging a toilet. Contact the Bay of Islands Maritime Park offices in Russell or Kerikeri.

### Getting There & Away
**Air** Mt Cook Airlines (tel 27-421) has daily flights to Kerikeri from Auckland and Rotorua, but the closest that Air New Zealand can get you is Whangarei. Great Barrier Airlines costs less than Mt Cook and it comes up from Auckland to Paihia daily during the summer, by charter only the rest of the year.

**Bus** All the buses serving Paihia arrive and depart from the Maritime Building by the wharf, and all bookings and tickets can be arranged from the Information Centre there.

InterCity has buses several times daily from Auckland to the Bay of Islands, via Whangarei and Opua. The trip takes about 4 hours to Paihia (5½ hours on the slower bus with more stops) and about 30 minutes later it stops in Kerikeri before continuing north to Kaitaia, 2 hours further on. Another Inter-City route goes from Paihia to Dargaville via the Waipoua Forest, a 4 hour trip.

Clarks Northliner has an Auckland-Whangarei-Bay of Islands video bus service. It departs from the Downtown Airline Terminal in Auckland and stops at the Paihia Maritime Building, Haruru Falls, Puketone Junction and Kerikeri. There's a connecting service to Russell and also a direct Whangarei-Russell service. Clarks' service is more direct than InterCity (not so many stops) but it goes only once a day, except for Saturday when it doesn't go at all.

Newmans buses coming from Auckland connect with the Clarks Northliner buses at Kawakawa to reach the Bay of Islands.

### Getting Around
A passenger ferry connects Paihia with Russell. It departs Paihia from 7.20 am to 6.45 pm (to 10 pm in summer); from Russell from 7 am to 6.10 pm. The fare is $4.40 return (children $2.20).

Or you can drive a few km south to Opua where the car ferry runs a continuous shuttle service during the day to Okiato Point, still some distance from Russell. This ferry operates from 6.30 am to 8.50 pm (9.50 pm on Fridays). The one-way fare is $6 for a car and driver, $9 for a campervan and driver, $2.50 for a motorcycle and rider, plus $1 for each additional adult passenger.

There's also a water taxi (tel 37-123, 37-378) for getting around the bay.

### BAY OF ISLANDS MARITIME & HISTORIC PARK
The Bay of Islands Maritime & Historic Park is comprised of 38 different sites extending all the way from Mimiwhangata Bay in the south to Whangaroa Harbour in the north. Marked walks of varying levels of difficulty (many very easy) take anywhere from 10 minutes to 10 hours and include tramps around islands, Maori pas and other historical sites, scenic, historic and recreational reserves and the Mimiwhangata Marine Park.

The Park Headquarters is at Russell (tel 37-685), and the Kerikeri Ranger Station (tel 78-474) can also supply you with information. If you're coming directly up from

Auckland you might check with the DOC office there, on Karangahape Rd.

## PAIHIA & WAITANGI

The main town in the area, Paihia, was settled by Europeans as a mission station in 1823 when the first raupo hut was built for the Reverend Henry Williams. Paihia still has a pretty setting but the missionary zeal has been replaced with an equally fervent 'grab the tourists and show em a good time' attitude, and as a result, it positively reverberates with the sound of the cash registers. Nevertheless it's basically an accommodation, eating and tours centre and a good starting point to see the rest of the Bay of Islands.

Adjoining Paihia to the north is Waitangi, site of the historic signing of the 6 February 1840 treaty between the Maoris and the representatives of Queen Victoria's government. Since this is where modern NZ history commenced, Waitangi is a particularly interesting place to be on New Zealand Day, 6 February.

### Information

Most of the information places are conveniently grouped together in the Maritime Building right by the wharf in Paihia. Here you'll find the helpful Bay of Islands Information Centre (tel 27-426), which can give information, advice, and make bookings for everything in the region. Also in the Maritime Building are the Fuller's office for cruises and tours, a fishing centre for fishing boat bookings, the bus station, and the terminal for the ferry to Russell. The offices are open every day from 8 am to 5 pm.

### Waitangi National Reserve

The Treaty House in Waitangi has special significance as the starting point for the European history of New Zealand. Built in 1832 as the home of British Resident James Busby, 8 years later it was the setting for the signing of the historic Treaty of Waitangi. It was here that many Maori chiefs accepted British 'sovereignty' and 'protection'. The

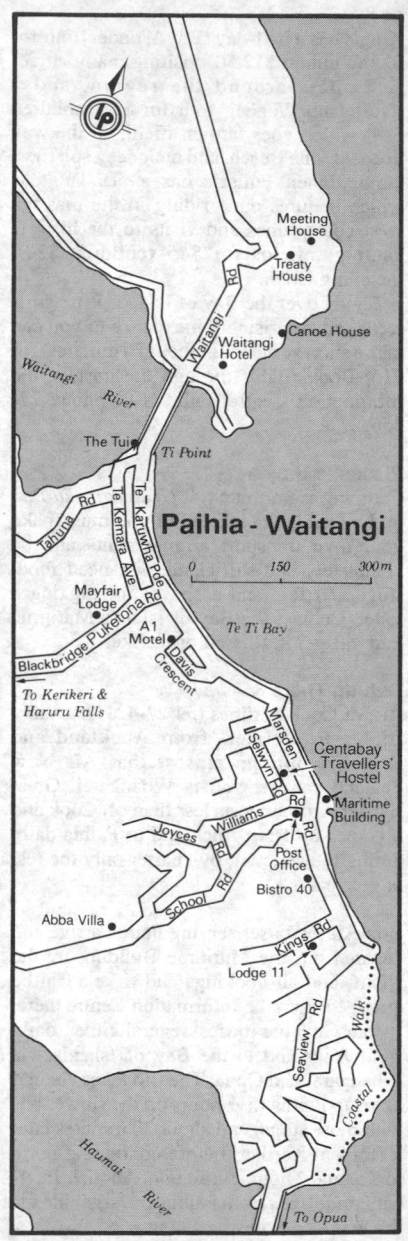

house, with its beautiful sweep of lawn running down to the bay, is preserved as a memorial and museum.

A few metres across the lawn, the magnificently detailed Maori Whare Runanga (meeting house) was completed in 1940 to mark the centenary of the treaty. The carvings represent the major Maori tribes.

Down by the cove is the largest war canoe in the world, the Maori war canoe Ngatokimatawhaorua, named after the canoe in which the Maori ancestor Kupe discovered New Zealand. It too was built for the centenary, and a photographic exhibit details how the canoe was made from two gigantic kauri trees. The canoe is launched every year on 6 February (New Zealand Day) for the annual treaty-signing commemoration ceremonies.

Beyond the Treaty House a road climbs Mt Bledisloe, from where there are commanding views of the area. Beginning from the visitors' centre, a walking track takes off through the reserve, passing through the mangrove forest around Hutia Creek and on to Haruru Falls. The walkway has a boardwalk among the mangroves so you can explore them without getting your feet wet. The walk to the falls takes about 1½ hours one way.

Admission to Waitangi Reserve is $3.50 (children free) and it's open from 9 am to 5 pm daily. At the visitors' centre where you enter the reserve an audiovisual presentation relating the story of the developments surrounding the signing of the treaty begins every half-hour.

### The Tui

Beached beside the bridge over the Waitangi River is the barque *Tui*, an old sailing ship, imaginatively fitted out as a museum of shipwrecks. It's open from 9 am to 5.30 pm daily, with extended hours during holiday periods; admission is $4 (children $2). Recorded sea chants, creaking timbers and swaying lights add to the eerie mood as you look at the collection of over 1000 bits and pieces diver Kelly Tarlton dragged up from wrecks around the coast.

### Haruru Falls

A few km upstream from the *Tui* are the very attractive Haruru Falls which are also accessible via the walkway through the Waitangi National Reserve. At the foot of the falls there's good swimming, several motor camps, a licensed restaurant and a tavern.

### Opua Forest

Just behind Paihia is the Opua Forest, a regenerating forest with a small stand of kauris and a number of walking tracks ranging from 10 minutes to 3 hours in length. Walking up from School Rd there are a couple of good lookout points about a 20 minutes walk up, and beyond this the trail splits into two alternate trails scaling up through the forest to yet another lookout point. DOC publishes pamphlets with details on all the Opua Forest walks. You can also drive into the forest by taking the Oromahoe Rd west from Opua.

### Boats & Diving

There are small boats for hire at both ends of the Paihia beach. At the Waitangi end 3 metre catamarans cost $17 an hour, larger ones are $22 an hour. Or you can hire powerboats for $30 an hour or $100 for 4 hours – plus fuel. Sportskis, those noisy motorcycle-on-water creations, cost $20 for 20 minutes. Or more mundanely you can paddle yourself around on an aquabike at $8 for 30 minutes – half an hour on one of those things is about all the average human can stand. Smith's Camp also have small dinghies for hire. All of these prices will vary tremendously with the seasons – summer is definitely the high season around here for both attractions and prices.

At the more serious end of the boating scale there are a number of sailboat and yacht charter operators on the bay. Of course you have to be able to prove you can handle a boat competently but assuming you can then Great Escape Budget Yacht Rentals (tel Kerikeri 78-920) are the people to talk to, with prices starting at $66 per day, $350 per week for a 5 metre trailer sailer sleeping two. They also have larger yachts which sleep up to six people and all you need to bring is a sleeping bag and food. Other operators are Rainbow Yacht Charters (tel Paihia 27-821), Freedom Yacht Charters (tel Russell 37-781) and Bay of Islands Yacht Charters (tel Kerikeri 77-384).

Moving from above the water to under it Paihia Dive Hire (tel 27-551) on Williams Rd hires full sets of scuba gear to qualified divers. They also offer scuba and snorkelling courses, tank filling and scuba gear servicing, a dive shop, and diving trips, including expeditions to the sunken *Rainbow Warrior*.

## Walks & Other Activities

There are a variety of good short and long walks around the Bay of Islands and on the islands themselves. The Park Information Centre in Russell and the Kerikeri Ranger Station have lots of walk information. You could start with the 2 minute stroll to the top of the headland on the southern end of Paihia or take the mangrove walk near the *Tui* barque or the coastal walk from Paihia to Opua.

The hostels or the Information Centre can fix you up with horse-riding; there are various possibilities in the area. In addition to diving equipment, you can rent fishing tackle and bicycles from Paihia Dive Hire. The hostels also hire bicycles.

## Places to Stay

The Bay of Islands Information Centre will tell you what is available and make bookings. They're particularly good for B&B bookings which can be a worthwhile deal in Paihia, where accommodation is often quite expensive.

**Hostels** There is no YHA hostel in Paihia (it's out at Kerikeri) but there are three good private hostels. All of them make bookings for local activities at significantly discounted prices, and they all have bicycles for hire.

The *Centabay Travellers' Hostel* (tel 27-466) on Selwyn Rd, just behind the shops and a short stroll from the Maritime Centre, is a former motel that's been converted into a hostel with four self-contained flats, each

with two bedrooms, a fully equipped kitchen and a TV lounge. Nightly cost is $12 in bunkrooms, $14 per person in double and twin rooms.

The *Lodge Eleven* (tel 27-487) on the corner of Kings and MacMurray roads is another former motel, charging $12 a night in double, twin, triple and dorm rooms. Each room has its own toilet and shower and there are communal kitchen, barbecue and lounge facilities. They have their own boat for fishing and sightseeing trips, a courtesy car and a friendly atmosphere and staff.

Down at the Waitangi end of Paihia the *Mayfair Lodge* (tel 27-471) at 7 Puketona Rd has bunkrooms at $12, twins and doubles at $13 per person. It's well equipped with the usual kitchen and lounge facilities, billiards and table tennis, a barbecue and also a spa pool.

**Guest Houses** Several B&B guest houses are found around Paihia and the Bay of Islands; the Information Centre makes referrals and bookings. *Abba Villa* (tel 28-066) at 21 School Rd is one of the Paihia B&B places, rates are $36/58 for singles/doubles.

**Hotels** If you really want to spend, here's plenty of opportunity but the *THC Waitangi Hotel* (tel 27-411) with its fine setting, excellent restaurant, Zane Grey bar, heated pool and room prices from around $85 to $225 shouldn't be forgotten. Suites are much more!

**Motels** With about 40 motels to choose from you'd think the competition would keep prices down but they're as expensive as anywhere. Motels stand shoulder to shoulder along the waterfront and minimum double rates are around $70 to $90 during the peak summer season, dropping to $40 or $50 during the off season. Rates tend to vary with the room, the season, current demand and probably a few other secret factors as well.

With so many to choose from the best advice is probably to ask the Information Centre, cruise the motel strip looking for a likely vacancy sign or simply take pot luck.

On the plus side most of the Paihia motels offer pretty good standards and most have good kitchen facilities. A few likely places to try, listed with their high season rates (winter rates will be lower) are:

*Al Motel* (or Aywon) (tel 27-684), Davis Crescent; $67 for doubles

*Aloha Motel* (tel 27-540), Seaview Rd; swimming pool, spa, games room and video, $55 singles, $66 to $88 doubles, with units up to three bedrooms and sleeping up to nine people for $110 to $165

*Ala-Moana Motel* (tel 27-745), Marsden Rd on the waterfront; $85 doubles for side units, $95 double for seaview units

*Ash Grove Motel* (tel 27-934), Blackbridge Rd, Haruru Falls; swimming pool, spa pool and 3 hectares of land, $85 doubles

**Camping & Cabins** There are a number of camping sites around Paihia and Waitangi, most of them a few km back from the coast near the Haruru Falls. The *Panorama Motor Lodge & Caravan Park* (tel 27-525), beside the river and facing the falls, has tent and power sites at $9 per person in peak summer season, $6.50 the rest of the year, and motel units at $65/77 at peak season but $40/50 at other times. The camp is well equipped with a large swimming pool, a bar and restaurant, and their own charter boat which does full-day cruises.

The *Twin Pines Motor Camp* (tel 27-322) on Puketona Rd at the falls has tent and power sites at $8 per person, cabins and on-site caravans at $13.50 per person, and more expensive tourist flats. Next door the *Falls Caravan Park* (tel 27-816) has tent and power sites at about the same rates plus on-site caravans sleeping five which cost $34 most of the year, $56 during the summer rush. At Puketona Junction there's another camping ground, *Puketona Park*.

The *Lily Pond Holiday Park* (tel 27-646) is 3 km from the falls, 6½ km from Paihia, on Puketona Rd and has tent and power sites at $7 per person, cabins at $10 per person.

The *Smiths Holiday Camp* (tel 27-678) is at a lovely spot right on the waterside, 2½ km south of Paihia towards Opua. Tent and power sites are $8 per person, cabins are $30

for two, motel units are $55 a double and there are also tourist cabins and tourist flats. It has its own beach, dinghies for hire, a camp store and a courtesy car.

**Places to Eat**
**Takeaways & Cheap Eats** There are a number of takeaway places scattered around, particularly in the shopping centre opposite the Maritime Centre and the post office. On the Selwyn Rd side of the centre *Maree's Backpackers & Family Licensed Restaurant* is open all day until midnight, with a buffet set out from 11.30 am until 8 pm daily where you can load up your plate with as much as you can for $10 (but no refills!). It also has $5 'mini-meals', takeaways, and the bar is open 7 days a week.

The *Cafe Over the Bay* upstairs opposite the Maritime Building has a good view of the bay and good food too, with lots of European dishes (mostly French and Italian). Lunches are about $6 to $10, dinners $15 or you can dine on pasta and salad for $12.50, or just have a pastry and cappuccino. Also upstairs here is the *Lighthouse Tavern Bars & Restaurant*.

On Williams Rd *Esmae's* is open for dinner and tends to be more expensive but they do have 'budget meals' served with salad and chips for about $12, other dinners are about $20.

**Restaurants** There are quite a number of restaurants where the prices are somewhat higher, with main courses averaging around the $20 mark. *Tides*, on Williams Rd, is one of the better places. *Bistro 40* on Marsden Rd has an attractive decor, it's in a converted old home with sections indoors and out on the brick patio overlooking the sea. The food here has won awards. The *La Scala* licensed restaurant on Selwyn Rd is about the priciest place in town, with a mixed seafood platter for two at about $75.

The two fancy restaurants out at the *THC Waitangi Hotel* are expensive (main courses around $16 to $25) but actually not so much more than some of the places in town.

## Entertainment

The *Lighthouse Tavern* upstairs on Marsden Rd has various sections including a restaurant, bars and a pub and features live bands. At Haruru Falls the *Twin Pines* also has entertainment and a tavern. The *Terrace Nightclub* at the Bay Holiday Inn Resort on the Opua-Kawakawa Rd is open from 10 pm until late every night; they also have a licensed steakhouse restaurant and they advertise 'don't drink and drive – catch our shuttle bus, phone 27-911'. The *Roadrunner* is about a 5 minute drive south of Paihia en route to Opua.

The *Waitangi Hotel* has a couple of public bars in a separate building and the expensive 'Zane Grey' piano bar in the hotel itself. Fuller's has evening cruises with entertainment and dancing on the *Tiger Lily III* from December to March.

## Getting There & Away

For information on travel to/from Paihia, see the Getting There & Away entry under the Bay of Islands heading.

## RUSSELL

A short ferry ride across the bay is Russell, originally a fortified Maori settlement which spread over the entire valley then known as Kororareka. Russell's early European history was turbulent. In 1830 it was the scene of the 'war of the girls' which occurred when two Maori girls from different tribes each thought they were the favourite of a whaling captain. This resulted in conflict between the tribes, which the Maori leader, Titore, who was recognised as the chief of chiefs in the area, attempted to resolve by separating the two tribes and making the border at the base of the Tapeka Peninsula. A European settlement quickly sprang up in place of the abandoned Maori village.

In 1845 the government sent in soldiers and marines to garrison the town when the Maori leader, Hone Heke, threatened to chop down the flagstaff – symbol of Pakeha authority – for the fourth time. On 11 March 1845 the Maoris staged a diversionary siege on Russell. It was a great tactical success with Chief Kawiti attacking from the south and another Maori war party attacking from Long Beach. While the troops rushed off to protect the township, Hone Heke felled the hated symbol of European authority on Maiki Hill for the final time. The Pakehas were forced to evacuate to ships lying at anchor off the settlement. The captain of HMS *Hazard* was wounded severely in the battle and the first lieutenant ordered the ships' cannons to be fired on the town, during the course of which most of the buildings were razed.

Russell today is a relaxed, peaceful and pretty little place. It's a marked contrast to the neon hustle of Paihia across the bay.

## Information

The Tourist Information office is out at the end of the pier. There's a Fuller's office at the land end of the pier. The excellent Bay of Islands Park Information Centre (tel 37-685) is next to the Captain Cook Museum and has displays about the area and lots of information on nature, camping, walks, snorkelling, diving and many other activities throughout the 38 or so separate far-flung regions of the park. The centre is open every day from 9 am to 5 pm (May to August until 4.30 pm) and has an audiovisual show beginning every half-hour.

## Captain Cook Memorial Museum

The Captain Cook Memorial Museum was built for the bicentenary of his Bay of Islands visit in 1769. It's small but it houses maritime exhibits, exhibits relating to Cook and his voyages, and a fine 1:5 scale model of his barque *Endeavour* – a real working model – in addition to a collection of early settlers' relics. The museum is open from 10 am to 4 pm every day; admission is $1.50 (children 25 cents).

## Pompallier House

Close by, on a lovely waterfront site, is Pompallier House, built to house the printing works for the Roman Catholic mission founded by the French missionary Bishop Pompallier in 1841. It also served as a

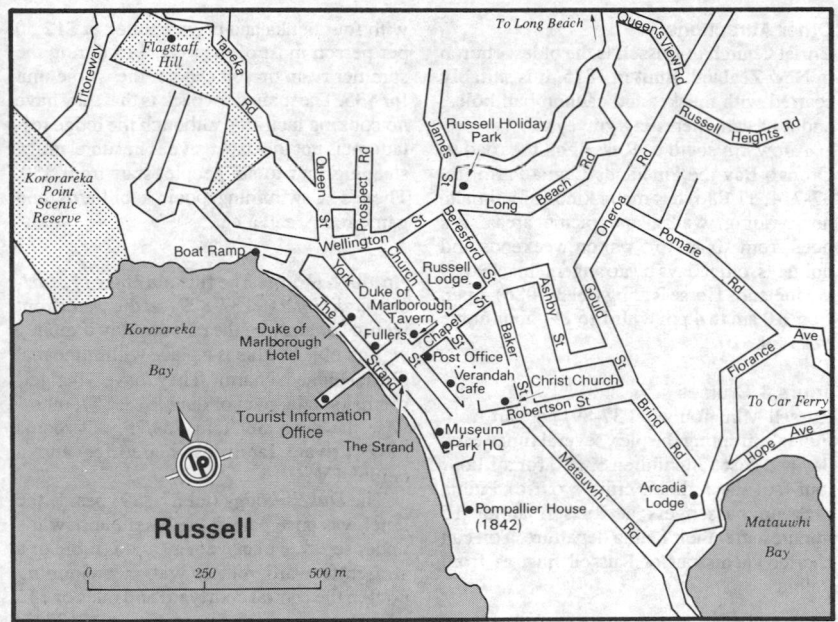

**Russell**

tannery and only in the 1870s was converted to a private home. It is one of the oldest houses in New Zealand and has a small museum. It's open daily from 10 am to 12.30 pm and 1.30 to 4.30 pm; admission is $3 (children $1).

### Flagstaff Hill

Overlooking Russell is Maiki (Flagstaff) Hill, where Hone Heke made his attacks – this, the fifth flagpole, has stood for a lot longer than the first four. The view is well worth the trouble to get up there, and there are several routes to the top. If you're walking, you can take the track west from the boat ramp along the beach at low tide, or up Wellington St at high tide. The track passes through the Kororareka Point Scenic Reserve. Alternatively you can simply walk to the end of Wellington St and take the short track up the hill from there, about a 5 minute climb. If you want to drive up to the summit, drive up Tapeka Rd.

### Waitata Bay

About 1 km behind Russell to the east is Waitata Bay, with a beautiful beach known variously as Waitata Bay Beach, Donkey Beach or Long Beach. It's about a 15 minute walk from the Russell wharf, heading over the hill on Long Beach Rd. When you reach the summit of the hill, at the intersection with Queen's View Rd, there's a tiny old graveyard with benches and a good view of Waitata Bay. Take a turn here and go about a block up Queen's View Rd to where it meets Oneroa Rd and the view is even better – a sweeping vista of both sides of the peninsula. There's an unofficial nudist beach past the rock outcrops on the northern end of the main beach.

### Mt Tikitikioure

Mt Tikitikioure, behind the Orongo Bay Holiday Park, also offers fine views. It's about a 15 to 30 minute climb to the top.

## Other Attractions

Christ Church in Russell is the oldest church in New Zealand. Built in 1835, it is suitably scarred with musket and cannon ball holes, and it has an interesting graveyard.

A few km south of Russell on the road to Orongo Bay the Pinelands Llama Farm (tel 37-714, 37-086) has many kinds of animals, horse-riding, walks, and picnic areas. It's open from 10 am to 5 pm on weekends and holidays, other days by arrangement. Nearby is Pinelands Horse Riding (tel 37-086), open from 10 am to 4 pm with 1 to 1½ hour horse treks for $20.

## Tours & Cruises

Russell Mini Tours (tel 37-891) depart from Fuller's, fronting the pier, several times each day and cost $7 (children $3.50) for a 1 hour tour. All the Fuller's cruises out of Paihia pick up passengers at Russell about 15 minutes after their Paihia departure. You can charter yachts out of Russell, just as from Paihia.

## Places to Stay

**Hostels** Three places around Russell offer hostel-style accommodation. *Orongo Bay Holiday Park* (tel 37-704) is 3 km south of Russell on the road to the Opua car ferry – it's an easy hitch if you don't have a car but they also provide a free pick-up service if you arrive in Russell by ferry. Orongo Bay is an associate YHA hostel, nightly cost is $11 in one to four-bed rooms whether or not you're a YHA member. They also have camping in tent or power sites at $6.50 per person. There's a swimming pool, a TV/games room, and bicycles for hire at $2 per day.

The *Arcadia Lodge* (tel 37-756) is on Florance Ave, about a 10 minute walk from the wharf. It's a splendid place up on a hill, with a magnificent view and several decks to enjoy it from. Cost is $15 per person in four units sleeping two to six people. Each unit has its own kitchen; toilets and showers are shared.

Two blocks behind the wharf, *Russell Lodge* (tel 37-640) has budget units, each with four bunks and private toilet, at $12.50 per person most of the year, $15 during the summer rush, or you can get the whole unit for $35. The main drawback is that they have no cooking facilities, although the lodge restaurant is not too expensive. The motel units, sleeping four to six people, start from $50. There's a swimming pool, a billiards and game room, and a bar.

**Hotels & Motels** The fine old *Duke of Marlborough Hotel* (tel 37-829) on the waterfront would certainly be the place to stay if money was no object. This is a place with some real old-fashioned charm. They have 'budget' rooms (single, twin or double) at $57, otherwise the rates are from $68/79. All rooms have private facilities, tea/coffee and a colour TV.

The *Duke's Lodge* (tel 37-899) beside the hotel was once part of the hotel but now it's under separate management and is more of a straightforward motel, with a swimming pool in the central courtyard and rates of $55 to $75 most of the year, $95 to $120 in summer.

Motels in Russell generally cost from around $50 a night, particularly during the summer season when minimum rates often apply. There are a host of motels and the same general advice applies as for the Paihia motels. You can book through the Bay of Islands Information Centre in Paihia.

**Camping & Cabins** The *Russell Holiday Park* (tel 37-826) on Long Beach Rd is centrally located, with tent and power sites at $7 per person, on-site caravans at $22 to $32 for two, and cabins with kitchen sleeping four to six people at $12 per person. Prices increase by a couple of dollars during the summer rush.

The *Jack 'n Jill Beach Camp* (tel 37-325) is 17½ km east of Russell, in a lovely setting right on the coast. Sites are $8 or $11 with power; cabins are $34 for two; motel units $60 for two. It has free dinghies and a scuba air filling station, but it's open only during the summer from October to March. The

*Orongo Bay Holiday Park* (see Hostels) also has camping sites.

### Places to Eat
There's a selection of cafes and takeaways in Russell including the waterfront *Strand* with sandwiches, snacks, a courtyard at the back and a verandah in front. Back a block are the pleasant *Verandah Cafe* and the *Traders Cafe* with indoor and patio sections. Near the Traders is *Simply Good*, a health food store and delicatessen with a small dining counter.

The *Duke of Marlborough Tavern* has typical pub food in its family pub section, with main dishes around $10. There's more 'refined' dining in *Somerset's Restaurant* at the Duke of Marlborough Hotel on the waterfront. Also on the waterfront are the *Quarter Deck Restaurant* with main courses from $15 to $23 and the expensive and licensed *Gables*, with main courses up around $22 to $30.

### Entertainment
The 'new' *Duke of Marlborough Tavern* was the first pub in New Zealand to get a licence, back on 14 July 1840. Its three predecessors all burnt down. The tavern, in the block behind the hotel, has both a family pub and a more serious bar. There's also a lounge bar in the *Russell Lodge*, one block further back from the wharf.

### Getting There & Away
Basically your choices are to come on the ferry from Paihia, to drive or hitch in via the Opua car ferry, or to take the Clarks Northliner bus. There's a much longer dirt road which avoids the Opua ferry, but it's a long haul to Russell via this route.

### OPUA
As well as being the car ferry terminus, Opua is a busy, deep sea port from which primary produce – meat, wool and butter – is exported. The town was established as a coaling port in the 1870s when the railway line was constructed. Before the wharf was built, after WW I, the coal was transported out to ships on lighters (flat bottomed

barges). Today, the occasional cruise ship may be seen alongside the wharf, as well as many local and overseas yachts during the summer. If you're trying to hitch a ride to faraway places this could be a good spot to look. Yachties are often willing to take more crew.

The Opua Forest, for the most part a regenerating forest, is open to the public. There are lookouts up graded tracks from the access roads and a few large trees have escaped axe and fire, including some fairly big kauri. You can enter the forest by walking in from Paihia on School Rd (see Paihia), driving in from Opua on the Oromahoe Rd, or a couple of other access roads. Get a leaflet from the Park Information offices in Russell or Kerikeri, or from the Bay of Islands Information Centre in the Maritime Building in Paihia.

There's a historic steam train service which operates from Opua to Kawakawa.

### Places to Eat
At Opua there's the *Ferryman's Restaurant & Bistro* by the car ferry dock. The restaurant section is expensive but the bistro is a great place to sit out on the waterside and enjoy a light meal, sandwich or burger.

### KERIKERI
Nestled into the northern end of the bay, Kerikeri is an attractive town with a sleepy, laid-back atmosphere. The word *kerikeri* means 'to dig' and it was right here, in 1820, that the first agricultural plough was introduced to New Zealand, and here that the Maoris grew large crops of kumaras (sweet potatoes) before the Pakeha arrived.

Today it is primarily an agricultural region, with kiwi fruit, citrus and other orchards. Large numbers of itinerant farmworkers congregate in Kerikeri for the 6 week kiwi fruit harvest beginning the first week in May, but orchard work of one kind or another is usually available all year round except perhaps during February. It is also a centre for a wide variety of arts and crafts.

Kerikeri is significant in NZ history. It became the site of the country's second

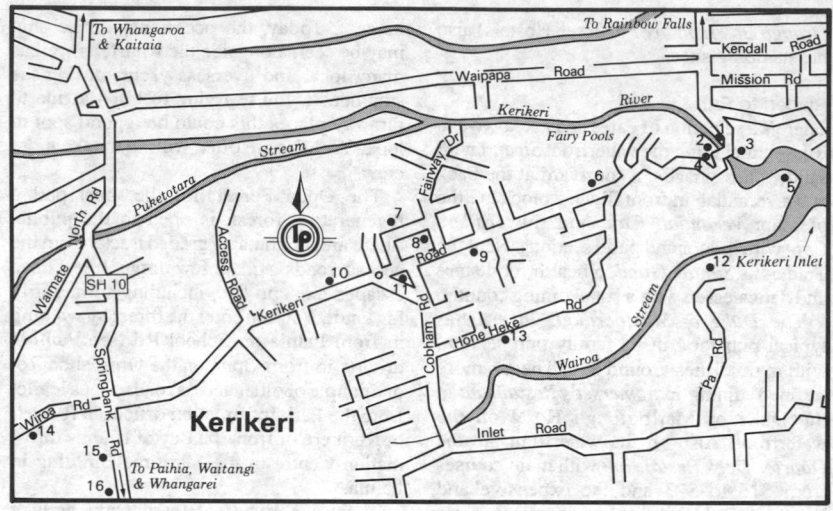

1 Scenic Reserve
2 Kemp House
3 Rewa's Maori Village
4 Stone Store & Museum
5 Kororipo Pa
6 Youth Hostel
7 Homestead Lodge & Restaurant
8 New World Supermarket
9 Cottle Court Motel
10 Aranga Holiday Park
11 Post Office, Bus Station
12 Pagoda Lodge Caravan Park
13 Hone Heke Lodge
14 Hideaway Lodge, Adventure Park
15 The Orange Centre
16 Puriri Park

mission station when the Reverend Samuel Marsden chose the site at the head of the Kerikeri inlet under the protection of the Maori chief, Hongi Hika. In November 1819 the Reverend John Butler arrived at the site and set up the mission headquarters. New Zealand's oldest wooden building, Kemp House, and its oldest stone building, the Stone Store, were part of the mission station and are still in superb condition.

Kerikeri is occasionally subject to flood-ing and in March 1981 it was inundated when the river burst its banks.

### Information
There's no tourist information centre in Kerikeri – the whole Bay of Islands is served by the one in Paihia – but the Kerikeri Ranger Station (tel 78-474), in the Kerikeri Scenic Reserve across the river from the Stone Store, has pamphlets and information on the entire region's parks, walks, and so on. It's open from 8 am to 12.30 pm and 1.30 to 5 pm Monday to Friday, but you can pick up pamphlets anytime from the display outside the door.

### Stone Store & Museum
The Stone Store & Museum is the oldest stone building in New Zealand; construction began in 1833 and was completed in 1836. It still operates as a general store selling refreshments, souvenirs and antiques. There's a museum upstairs with excellent exhibits and commentary telling the history of the Kerikeri Basin, which has had a sur-prisingly eventful history. The museum is open from 9 am to 5.30 pm; admission is $1.50 (children 50 cents).

## Kemp House
Near the Stone Store is Kemp House, a wooden building erected in 1821 by John Butler. It's open daily from 10 am to 12.30 pm and 1.30 to 4.30 pm; admission is $3 (children $1).

## Rewa's Maori Village
Just across the river from the Stone Store, Rewa's Maori Village is built on a site thought to have been occupied at one time by Chief Rewa. The various buildings are an authentic reproduction of a *kainga*, a pre-European unfortified Maori village, with various habitations, kitchen buildings, storerooms and so on, and exhibits of the many plants the Maoris used. It's always open, admission is $1 (children 20 cents) and there are fine views across the inlet.

## Walks
Just up the hill behind the Stone Store Tearooms is a marked Historical Walk which takes about 20 minutes and leads to Kororipo Pa, the fortress of Maori chief Hongi Hika, from which huge warfaring parties of Maoris once departed on raids terrorising most of the North Island. The walk emerges near the St James Anglican church, built in 1878.

Across the bridge from the Stone Store is a verdant scenic reserve with several marked tracks. There's a 4 km Kerikeri River track leading to Rainbow Falls, passing by the Fairy Pools along the way. Alternatively you can reach the Rainbow Falls from Waipapa Rd, in which case it's only a 10 minute walk to the falls. The Fairy Pools are great for swimming and picnics and can be reached from the dirt road beside the Youth Hostel if you aren't up for the hike along the river.

The 4 km river trek is part of the New Zealand Walkway system. Another part is called the Kerikeri Walk and departs from SH 10 near the crossing of the highway and the river. The walk takes about 3½ hours return, following the Maungaparerua Stream up to the 241 metre Maungaparerua trig, attaining a panoramic view of the area.

## Arts & Crafts
The Kerikeri area is home to many artists and artisans. Several shops display their work, and in most you can see work in progress, especially pottery. On Kerikeri Rd at the northern end of town there's Red Barn Pottery; on Kerikeri Rd just out of town to the south The Black Sheep shows pottery, sheepskins, artwork and woodcraft. North of Kerikeri, Te Awa Pottery on Waipapa Rd and Cherry House at Waipapa Landing have pottery in progress. On SH 10 there are several good shops including the Origin Art and Craft Co-Operative with many kinds of crafts; Blue Gum Pottery; the Orange Centre shop; and the Potting Shed with pottery and weaving.

## Other Attractions
At the Orange Centre (tel 79-397) you can learn all about citrus fruits and take a $3 tour of the orange, kiwi fruit and other orchards in the 'orange-mobile'. The tour also includes a visit to the shed where fruits are graded and sized. The Orange Centre is by the Kerikeri crossroads on SH 10, open daily from 9 am to 5 pm.

For children the Adventure Park on Wiroa Rd has 2½ hectares of good old-fashioned amusements. It's open daily from 10 am to 5 pm; admission is $2.75. Kids will also like the Kerikeri Orchard Railway on SH 10.

The Aero Club at the Kerikeri Airport, on Wiroa Rd 6 km west of town, does scenic flights and charters. Kerikeri Tours (tel Paihia 28-511 or Kerikeri 78-606) does half-day tours of Kerikeri. You can hire a row boat and explore the Kerikeri Inlet in front of the Stone Store.

The King family of Okaihau (tel Okaihau 64-303) does horse trekking, and will come to pick you up in Kerikeri.

## Places to Stay
**Hostels** Since Kerikeri is a centre both for tourists to the Bay of Islands and for itinerant agricultural workers, its hostels attract both kinds of people. In general, the YHA and Puriri Park are more oriented towards travellers and tourists passing through, while the

Hone Heke Lodge and the Hideaway Lodge, both run by the same family, usually have a number of long-term orchard workers, though of course travellers are also welcome. If you're looking for orchard work, these two may be able to help you find it.

The *Kerikeri Youth Hostel* (tel 79-391) is on the main road. Nightly cost is $13 and various trips are organised from the hostel including full-day Bay of Islands sailing trips, horse-riding, and a 4 hour tour through the Northern District with the local postal worker.

The *Hone Heke Lodge* (tel 78-170) is on Hone Heke Rd in a quiet residential area about 10 minutes walk from the town centre. Cost per person is $9 in bunkrooms, $11 in twin rooms or $12 in double rooms.

The *Hideaway Lodge* (tel 79-773) is on a 3½ hectare orchard on Wiroa Rd, out beyond the SH 10 junction. It's several km from town but they offer free rides to town twice daily and they also hire bicycles. Per-person cost is $10.50 in dorm rooms, $12.50 in twin or double rooms, and there's a big field where camping sites are $7 per person. There's a swimming pool, barbecue, games room and so on, plus sports gear and activities. This is a big place which may hold 200 people during picking season, it's the main accommodation for itinerant orchard workers.

A number of travellers have reported being promised to be given agricultural work contacts only after they'd been paying guests at the Hideaway Lodge for a week. Sometimes the work was still not forthcoming, so beware of making deals.

The *Puriri Park* (tel 79-818) is a different kind of place, also in an orchard, but all on a very small scale, with a comfortable cottage behind the family home offering bunks in triple rooms at $12 per person, or $15 per person for a couple to have the room to themselves. The cottage is pleasant, with kitchen and sitting areas, and you're welcome to use the swimming pool, walk through the orchard and go on some nearby bushwalks. Puriri Park is just past the Orange Centre on SH 10 heading towards Paihia.

**Guest Houses** The *Puriri Park* (see Hostels) also has 'homestay' rooms in the family home at $28/40 for singles/doubles, or $40/60 with breakfast. Check with the Information Centre in Paihia for other B&B homestays in the area.

**Motels** Several motels are found along Kerikeri Rd. Near the youth hostel, *Kemp Lodge* (tel 78-295) is small, with a swimming pool and three chalets costing $58 for singles, $65 to $78 for doubles during the high season; off-season rates will be lower. Next door the *Abilene Motel* (tel 79-203) has a swimming pool and 10 units, two with private spa pools, at $59/68. The *Cottle Court Motel* (tel 78-867) has units at $59/69.

The *Central Motel* (tel 78-921) has 14 units with features like a waterbed suite, swimming and spa pools, colour TVs and so on. Summer rates start at $74, dropping to $45/56 in winter. There are plenty of other motels.

**Camping & Cabins** There are several camping sites at Kerikeri. The *Pagoda Lodge Caravan Park* (tel 78-617) is on Pa Rd at the inlet near the Stone Store. Camping sites are $8.50 per person, tourist flats $35 for two, and they have free dinghies and canoes that you can use to explore the inlet.

The *Aranga Holiday Park* (tel 79-326) is on Kerikeri Rd in a lovely setting beside the Puketotara River, only 5 minutes walk from town. Tent or power sites are $7 per person, cabins are $15/24 for one/two people, or $9 per person in bunkrooms. There's a 20% discount for stays of a week or more, bringing the price down to $12 a night for your own single cabin or $10 per person for two. Cabins with private facilities are $30 for two.

**Places to Eat**

Kerikeri has several fast food places and cafes. On the main road *Barque & Bight* is an ice-cream parlour with takeaways, and the *Calypso* has good fish & chips and other takeaways. Cafes include *Goodies Cafe* with sandwiches, snacks and cakes, *Food Affair* and the *Adam & Eve Cafe*. As You Like It is an attractive little mainly vegetarian restaurant off the main road with tables indoors or out on the brick courtyard.

Across from the Stone Store the *Stone Store Tearooms & Restaurant* is open daily from 9 am to 4 pm. It's a lovely spot to eat indoors or out on the verandah overlooking the lawn and the boats moored in the inlet.

More expensive places include the licensed *Spokes* and, out of Kerikeri on the Paihia road, *Jane's Restaurant* which has traditional food of the steak, chicken and seafood variety.

### Getting There & Away

**Bus** InterCity and Clarks Northliner buses come and go from Travel Lee's (tel 78-013) on Cobham Rd, just off Kerikeri Rd in the town centre, stopping at Kerikeri half an hour after Paihia. InterCity buses heading north and south stop through several times daily. Kerikeri is the northern end of the line for Clarks Northliner buses, which come once a day (except Saturday). See Getting There & Away under the Bay of Islands heading for more details on long-distance buses.

Both companies have buses departing Kerikeri in the morning for the half-hour trip to Paihia, returning in the late afternoon, every day except Sunday.

# Eastern Route

If you head directly south from Russell there's a long stretch of dirt road before you get back on the main road, but it is quite a beautiful route. There's access to the Russell State Forest and walkway along this route. You can camp at Papakauri Rd or Punaruku Rd or at Whangaruru North Head. It's also possible to walk out to Cape Brett lighthouse and stay there, but you must get permission and book accommodation with the ranger at the Park HQ in Russell.

The main road south to Whangarei meets SH 1 at Kawakawa, where the railway line runs down the middle of the main street. Just

south of Kawakawa, a km off the main road, are the Waiomio Caves. Like Waitomo they have glow-worms, but they're not as impressive.

## WHANGAREI

Population 43,800

Back on the main road you soon reach Whangarei, the major town of Northland and a haven for yachts. Boats from around the world are moored in Town Basin, an attractive area right on the edge of the town centre. The beaches at Whangarei Heads about 65 km east of town are incredibly beautiful, with many tiny bays and inlets, although they are somewhat difficult to reach if you don't have your own transport.

The Poor Knights Islands Marine Reserve 22 km off the coast is acclaimed for the best diving in New Zealand, in fact some of the best in the world. Diving trips are organised from Whangarei. Whangarei Falls just 5 km from the town centre is worth a visit too, and there's also a kauri park. Many people view Whangarei as only a place to pass through but if you have transport and want to stick around for a couple of days you'll find plenty to do.

### Information

The PR office (tel 481-079) is at Tarewa Park on SH 1 at the southern entrance to town. It's open every day from 8.30 am to 5 pm and the staff are very helpful and friendly, with good maps and suggestions on things to do in the area. The AA office on James St near the mall also has good maps of town and of the surrounding region. The DOC office (tel 480-299) at 154 Bank St has info on scenic areas, camping, parks, and the Poor Knights Islands Marine Reserve.

### Cafler Park

Cafler Park spans a little stream in the centre of town. It has many well tended flowerbeds, a conservatory and fernery, both open daily from 10 am to 4 pm; admission is free.

### Clock Museum

If you're interested in time and timepieces

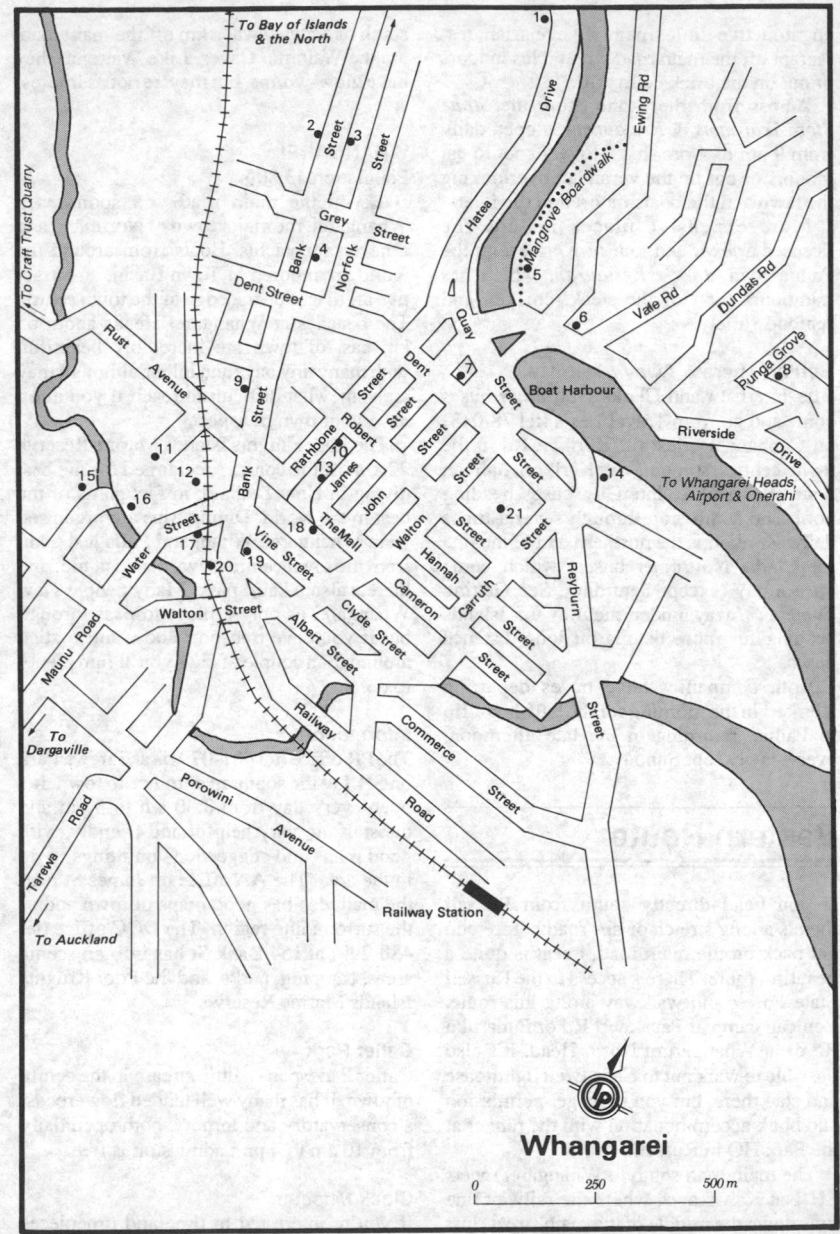

**Whangarei**

To Bay of Islands & the North

To Craft Trust Quarry

Rust Avenue

Dent Street

Grey Street

Bank Street

Norfolk Street

Rathbone Street

Robert Street

James Street

John Street

Dent Street

Quay Street

Hatea Drive

Ewing Rd

Mangrove Boardwalk

Vale Rd

Dundas Rd

Punga Grove

Riverside Drive

Boat Harbour

To Whangarei Heads, Airport & Onerahi

The Mall

Vine Street

Water Street

Bank Street

Walton

Cameron

Hannah

Carruth

Walton Street

Clyde Street

Albert Street

Maunu Road

To Dargaville

Tarewa Road

To Auckland

Porowini Avenue

Railway

Commerce Road

Reyburn Street

Street

Railway Station

0    250    500 m

1   Hatea House Hostel
2   McDonald's
3   Department of Conservation (DOC)
4   Pizza Hut
5   Olympic Swimming Pool
6   Maureen's Restaurant
7   Reva's Pizza Parlour
8   Youth Hostel
9   Plumes Restaurant
10  Post Office
11  Forum North Centre
12  Civic Arcade
13  Air New Zealand, Eagle Air,
     Automobile Association (AA)
14  Reyburn House Art Gallery
15  Fernery & Conservatory
16  Clapham Clock Museum
17  Taste Spud
18  Whangarei Hotel
19  The Grand Establishment Hotel
20  City Bus & InterCity Station
21  Pac'N Save Supermarket

don't miss one of Whangarei's claims to fame, the Clapham Clock Museum in Cafler Park. It has an awesome variety of clocks – big, small, musical, mechanical or just plain weird, all ticking away furiously. Altogether there are over 1300 timepieces, with about 900 clocks and 400 watches. The museum custodian will show you around and demonstrate various oddities. The museum is open from 10 am to 4 pm on weekdays, 10.15 am to 3 pm on weekends and holidays; admission is $3 (children $1).

### 'The Quarry'

The Northland Craft Trust, informally known as 'The Quarry' (tel 481-215), is about 500 metres west of the town centre in an old converted quarry. It's a cooperative of artists and artisans of every description, with many studios where work is in progress and a showroom where the wares are exhibited and sold. Each summer their summer school attracts both NZ and international artists and artisans. From the town centre head west on Rust Ave, which becomes Selwyn Ave, and the Quarry is a couple of blocks further on. It is open daily from 10 am to 4 pm.

### Whangarei Falls

The Whangarei Falls are rated one of the most photogenic in New Zealand. Adjacent to the Ngunguru Rd, in the suburb of Tikipunga about 5 km north of the town centre, the falls may be reached by catching a Tikipunga bus and walking the last bit (but there's no bus on Sundays). There are three natural swimming pools in the river, and a small amusement park and numerous picnic spots within the domain.

### Reed Memorial Kauri Park

The A H Reed Memorial Kauri Park spans a pretty stream and has a waterfall, several easy walkways and over 50 kinds of native trees including punga, totara and a few large kauris. It's about 5 km from the town centre, going out Whareora Rd.

### Scenic Reserves & Walks

There are two scenic reserves handy to the centre of town, on the hills on either side of the valley. Coronation Scenic Reserve, on the west, has a lookout, an old pa site, Maori pits and an old gold mine, as well as lots of bush. It is accessible from Kauika Rd. On the eastern side is the Parahaki Scenic Reserve. There is a road to the summit of Parahaki, turning off Riverside Drive (the road towards Onerahi and the airport). Three tracks lead down from the summit, two finishing at Mair Park and one at Dundas Rd.

The 2 hour Onerahi Mangrove Walk in Onerahi is an easy, level walk along an old (1880) railway embankment, passing through mangrove swamps and over a harbour bridge. The pathway can be entered from the end of Cockburn St on one side, or from the end of Waimahanga Rd on the other side. If you're coming from town on the bus, take the Onerahi bus and get off at Handforth St, then turn into Cockburn St off Handforth.

There's a shorter, 15 minute mangrove walk over boardwalks in the centre of town, just behind the Olympic swimming pool.

Ten minutes up from Dundas Rd are some falls, with lots of glow-worms on the cliffs nearby, making a good evening walk. As a round trip from the bottom it takes about 20 minutes to reach the falls. Avoid going up Drummond Track as it is quite steep. Information on these and other walks is available from the PR office and DOC.

## Other Attractions

A flea market takes place every Saturday from 6 to 10 am at the Blue Light Centre on John St. The Blue Light Centre has a skating rink and there are several other sports complexes including the Ted Eliott Memorial Pool Complex with Olympic-size indoor and outdoor pools, saunas and spas, bowling, netball, squash, square dancing and other activities.

The Whangarei Tramping Club (tel 52-406, 61-437) and YWCA Tramping Club (tel 487-535) both welcome visitors. If you prefer to take a horse try the Whau Valley Riding and Trekking Centre (tel 71-729) or Whananaki Trail Rides (tel 25-299, 50-558).

Scenic flights taking up to three people are about $20 to $30 per person for flights of 45 minutes to 1 hour; phone 51-381 after 5 pm for details.

There's an Art Gallery at Forum North, and another at the historic Reyburn House. Other Whangarei attractions include the 1885 Clarke Homestead and Northland Regional Museum in nearby Maunu. The best scuba diving in New Zealand is at the Poor Knights Islands off the coast, see the Around Whangarei section.

## Places to Stay

**Hostels** The Whangarei Youth Hostel (tel 488-954) is across the river at 52 Punga Grove Ave, with 20 beds at $13 per night. The manager hires bicycles at $6 per day, takes the hostellers on free night-time glowworm walks, arranges farmstays, and provides YHA discounts for the swimming pool, diving and other activities.

The Hatea House Hostel (tel 482-173) at 67 Hatea Drive is a small, friendly hostel with only 10 beds (two bunkrooms and one single room) in a converted family home by the Hatea River, 1 km from the centre. Rates are $13 per person and they do canoeing and

boating on the river. Phone ahead for free pick-up.

The Langstrath (tel 31-822) is a farm hostel about 35 km out of Whangarei towards Kaikohe. Rates are about $30, including all meals; you must book ahead.

**Hotels & Motels** Whangarei has a surprisingly large number of hotels and motels. The Grand Hotel (tel 484-279) on the corner of Bank and Rose streets really is a grand place in the old style, with high gilt carved ceilings, red plush carpet, statues and so on – various governors have stayed here and the Queen even stayed here on her first visit to New Zealand in 1954 (see the photo in the lobby). There's a fancy restaurant and several bars. Rooms cost $50/65, with some budget rooms at $13.50, less for longer stays, when they're available.

The Whangarei Hotel (tel 483-379) on Cameron St has rooms from $15.50 to $21 for singles, $31 to $41.50 for doubles and twins. The more expensive ones have private bathrooms. Budget single rooms, with skylights instead of windows, are $10.50, you may have to ask for them. They also have a restaurant, several bars and a cabaret.

Whangarei's motels generally cost from around $50/60. The Kauri Lodge (tel 483-526) at 15 Lupton Ave and the Hibiscus Motel (tel 488-312) at 2 Deveron St are marginally cheaper.

**Camping & Cabins** The Alpha Caravan Park (tel 489-867) at 34 Tarewa Rd is the most centrally located camp, less than a km from the town centre. Camping is $6 per person, $7 with power, cabins are $30 to $35 for two, and self-contained units are $45 for two. The William Jones Camp (tel 487-846) on Mair St, 2.5 km from the town centre by Mair Park, has tent or power sites at $6 per person, cabins at $22 for one or two people.

The Otaika Caravan Park (tel 481-459) at 136 Otaika Rd is at the southern entrance to Whangarei, with tent and power sites at $7.50 per person, well equipped tourist flats at $33/40 for one/two people and motel units at $48/60.

The *Whangarei Falls Motor Camp* (tel 70-609) near the falls, 5 km from the town centre, has tent and caravan sites at $7 per person, a hostel-style bunkroom at $12, and cabins at $22/30 for one/two people, sleeping up to four. They have swimming and spa pools, and in summer a big barbecue twice a week for just $5. Diving and fishing trips, horses, etc are arranged. Phone for free pick-up if you don't have wheels; they're rather removed from town. It's a very friendly place.

The *Nook Beach Resort* (tel 21-746) is on Nook Bay, a small, sheltered private bay 24 km east of Whangarei. Water-skiing, parasailing, swimming, fishing and boating are popular activities. It's a good family camp with tent and power sites at $8.50 per person, on-site caravans at $37 for two, tourist flats at $44/48 and motel units at $56/60. From the town centre, go out Riverside Drive.

Other sites include *Kamo Springs* (tel 51-208) at 55 Great North Rd, Kamo, and *Tropicana Holiday Park* (tel 60-687) on Whangarei Heads Rd by the beach, 10 km from Whangarei.

## Places to Eat

**Takeaways & Fast Food** You can have a pleasant and economical lunch on a sunny day in Whangarei's Mall, tables and chairs provided – the *Sidewalk Cafe* is popular. *Taste Spud* on Water St has about 20 different kinds of baked potatoes, a few Mexican and Indian snacks and a sit-down counter. *Something Else* in the Civic Arcade is another pleasant place, with healthy food (good soups, salads and cakes) to take away or eat there. Locals say *Maureen's* on Riverside Drive, with a restaurant and takeaway section, has the best fish & chips in Whangarei.

Fast food fans can find a *McDonald's*, a *Kentucky Fried* and a *Pizza Hut*, all a km or so from the town centre on the main road heading north.

A huge Pac'N Save supermarket between Walton and Carruth streets has the lowest prices in town.

**Pub Food** The *Forum Bistro* in the Forum North civic centre has typical pub meals. The *Carvery* in the Whangarei Hotel on Cameron St is good value. There's a *Cobb & Co* restaurant at the Kamo Hotel, 567 Kamo Rd, about 2 km north of the town centre, with the usual Cobb & Co menu.

**Restaurants** The *Reva's Pizza Parlour* on Dent St near the yacht basin has an art gallery, spontaneous musicianship and an international clientele of boaties, yachties and other travellers and artistic folk. *Maureen's Restaurant* on Riverside Drive just across the harbour has good seafood meals.

For ethnic food try the *Shaolin Vietnamese Restaurant* at 2 Clyde St, with about 30 different specialities including Indian curries, or the *Maxim Chinese & Vietnamese Restaurant* at 74 Cameron St, with a weekday smorgasbord lunch for around $10 and also a Sunday night smorgasbord.

For a fancy night out Whangarei has several possibilities including *Cafe Monet* at 144 Bank St and the *Classic Cafe* at 1D Grant St in the Kamo suburb on Whangarei's northern side. At 2 Bank St the *Ivory Room Restaurant* in the Grand Hotel serves breakfast, lunch and dinner daily, with a $10 Sunday night smorgasbord.

## Entertainment

The best music places are out of town. The *Tutukaka Hotel*, north-east of town, and the *Parua Bay Hotel*, south-east at Whangarei Heads, are popular on weekends. Closer in, the *Onerahi Hotel* and the suburban *Tikipunga Tavern* on Derby Crescent have entertainment.

The Grand Hotel has a disco in *Oscar's Bar* and a duo singing in *Charlie's Bar*; the Whangarei Hotel has several bars including *Pip's Cabaret* where there's live music; and the *Forum North Bar* in the Forum North Centre also has live music, all from Wednesday to Saturday nights. The *Settlers Motor Inn* and the *Kamo Hotel* also have music from time to time.

## Getting There & Away

**Air** Eagle Air has six flights daily between Auckland and Whangarei, with connections to other centres. Roseman & Warren Travel (tel 484-939) in the James St Arcade is the agent for Eagle Air and Air New Zealand.

**Bus** The InterCity bus depot (tel 482-659) is on Railway Rd. InterCity has frequent buses between Auckland and Whangarei, continuing north to the Bay of Islands, Hokianga Harbour and Kaitaia, with another route to Dargaville. From Whangarei it's 3 hours to Auckland, 1½ hours to Paihia, 3½ hours to Kaitaia or an hour to Dargaville.

Clarks Northliner have a Monday to Friday Auckland-Whangarei-Bay of Islands bus service, with a route to Kerikeri via Paihia or directly to Russell on the Opua ferry. The bus operates from the Clarks Terminal (tel 483-206) at 3 Albert St. Newmans (tel 488-291) also has a weekday Auckland-Whangarei service.

**Hitching** Being the only big town between Auckland and the Bay of Islands, and the principal town of the region, Whangarei is a very busy spot for hitchhikers going north and south.

Heading north, the best hitching spot is on SH 1 just after the Three Mile Bush Rd intersection, in the Kamo suburb about 5 km north of the town centre. Any Kamo bus from the town centre will drop you there. Heading south, the best hitching spot is on SH 1 opposite Tarewa Park or, second best, about 500 metres further south, by the New World supermarket.

## Getting Around

Whangarei Bus Services (tel 483-104) operates local buses from around 6.30 am until 5 or 6 pm on weekdays, with Friday buses operating a bit later, until around 8 or 9 pm. Bus service is very limited on Saturdays and there are no buses at all on Sundays. The Onerahi bus route serves the airport on this same schedule. Rental cars are available from Avis (tel 482-929) and Budget (tel 487-292).

## AROUND WHANGAREI

### Maunu

A few km west of Whangarei, on the Dargaville road, is Maunu. The main attraction is the Northland Regional Museum, open from 10 am to 4 pm Tuesday to Sunday. The museum is set in a large park which includes the 1885 Clarke Homestead, where the attendant gives you a guided tour explaining how the homesteaders lived and settled the area 100 years ago. The museum domain also includes a kiwi house, an old locomotive which runs through the park during the summer, an abandoned mercury mine and more. Admission is $2.

### Whangarei Heads

There is magnificent scenery at Whangarei Heads, though it's hard to get to without a car as there is no bus and not much traffic for hitching a ride. On the way is the Waikaraka Scenic Reserve on Mt Tiger, with excellent views (turn-off at Parua Bay). The coast is beautiful at Matapouri, Tutukaka and Ocean Beach. Whale Bay is another fine spot, more secluded since it can only be reached by taking about a 10 minute bushwalk down from the car park, but it's a lovely walk with good views all the way.

There are great views from the top of 419 metre Mt Manaia. The trail to the top starts from the main road beneath the mountain (but it's easy to miss), and you climb up through forest. Close to the top are cables to help you scale a steep rock. Two hours of hard work will get you to the summit where there are incredible views of the sea, the mountains, the surrounding dairyland and, just as a contrast, the oil refinery at Marsden Point.

### Marsden Point

New Zealand's oil refinery is at Marsden Point, across the harbour from Whangarei Heads. They have an information centre you can visit to learn about oil refining.

### Poor Knights Islands Marine Reserve

The Poor Knights Islands Marine Reserve, off the coast of Whangarei, is reputed to have the best scuba diving in all New Zealand. Diving trips depart from Whangarei, Tutukaka and other places. Contact the Whangarei DOC office for information on the islands and the trips.

### New Zealand Walkway

Continue past Maunu on the Dargaville road and 16 km south-west of Whangarei you reach the Maungatapere section of the New Zealand Walkway. A round trip takes 1½ hours through farmland and regenerated scrub with extensive views inland and out to sea. The track starts at the end of Pukeatau Rd, on the daily Whangarei-Dargaville bus route; it's also an easy hitch there.

### Other Attractions

Heading south towards Brynderwyn and Auckland the Otaika Valley Walkway is off to the right just beyond the town limits. After passing through Waipu from Whangarei it is 9 km to Waipu Cove, a popular surfing beach. The main road turns inland from Waipu, climbing over the hills back to the Dargaville turn-off. Remember to look over your shoulder at the magnificent view of Whangarei Heads and the entire area. On the top of the hill is the entrance to Brynderwyn Hills Walkway (western section) and if you walk just a little way down the track you'll get great views – worth the time if you have it. This walkway eventually links up with the eastern section near Mangawhai Heads.

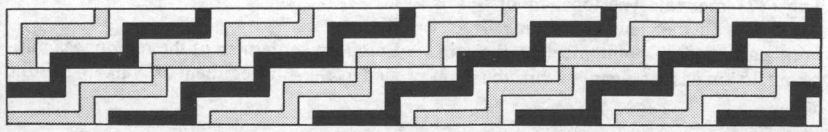

# South of Auckland

The trip to Hamilton by road from Auckland takes about 2 hours and there are a few points of interest along the way. If you're a steam train enthusiast and heading towards Hamilton on a Sunday or public holiday (except Christmas Day) then pause at the Glenbrook Vintage Railway (tel Patumahoe 669-361 on operating days only) where between 11 am and 4 pm you can take a 12 km steam train ride. From 26 December to 4 January the line operates every day. To get there follow the yellow signs after leaving the southern motorway at Drury, 31 km south of Auckland, and head for Waiuku. There is also a farm and deer park at Glenbrook.

Te Kauwhata, 67 km south of Auckland and just off the main road, is a good place for a bit of wine tasting. From here the road follows New Zealand's longest river, the Waikato, all the way to Hamilton. Along the way is Huntly, a coal-mining town with a large power station (tel Huntly 89-590), which can be visited by appointment, and a Mining & Cultural Museum on Harlock Place, open from 10 am to 4 pm daily. South of Huntly the road enters Taupiri Gorge, a gap through the ranges. On your left, as you emerge from the gorge, is a Maori cemetery on the hillside.

If you're fit there is an excellent view from Taupiri Mountain, and on the opposite side of the river the Hakarimata Track also gives good views. To walk the length of the track takes 7 hours. The northern end leads off Parker Rd, which can be reached by crossing the river at Huntly and following the Ngaruawahia-Huntly West Rd. The southern end meets the Ngaruawahia-Waingaro Rd just out of Ngaruawahia.

A shorter walk, and easier if you have no transport, is a 3 hour return trek from Brownlee Ave, Ngaruawahia, to Hakarimata Trig (371 metres). The top part of this is fairly steep but the view is rewarding. Tracks from each access point meet at the trig. About 25 km east of Ngaruawahia, the main

centre for the Waikato Maori people, are the popular Waingara Hot Springs. A few hundred metres off the main road, on River Rd, is Turangawaewae Marae.

# Hamilton

Population 103,500
New Zealand's largest inland city and fifth largest overall, Hamilton is 129 km south of Auckland. It is the centre of a rich farming area, the Waikato, and in the past few decades the city, which looks new and glossy, has undergone spectacular growth. The Waikato River was once Hamilton's only transport and communication link, but it was superseded by the railway 100 years ago and since then by roads. Frankton Junction is New Zealand's largest and busiest railway junction. Hamilton Station is on a branch line; the main trunk railway does not pass through the centre of the city.

### History
European settlement of the region was initiated by the 4th Regiment of Waikato Militia,

who were persuaded to enlist with promises of 1 acre (less than half a hectare) in town and another 50 acres in the country. The advance party, led by Captain William Steele, travelled up the Waikato River on a barge drawn by a gunboat, and on 24 August 1864 went ashore at the deserted Maori village of Kirikirioa. The township built on that site was named after Captain John Hamilton, the popular commander of HMS *Esk*, who had been killed in battle at Gate Pa 4 months earlier on 30 April.

## Information

The Waikato Visitors Centre (tel 393-360) is on Ward St, between Victoria and Anglesea streets. It's open from 9 am to 4.30 pm on weekdays and from 9 am to noon on Saturdays, except during January when it's open from 9 am to 4.30 pm every day. If you don't find it at this address, ask around – it may be moving to another location. The AA office is on Anglesea St, and DOC (tel 383-363) has an office nearby in the RDO House on Little London St.

## Waikato Museum

The Waikato Museum of Art & History, on the corner of Victoria and Grantham streets near the Waikato River, combines the old Waikato Museum and the Waikato Art Gallery in an attractive, modernistic new building. The museum has a good Maori collection with lots of carvings and the large Te Winika Canoe, dating from 1836. The canoe has had an eventful history and has now been beautifully and lovingly restored, a project completed in 1986 and detailed in photos along the wall. The art collection includes many interesting paintings and the museum also sponsors numerous events. It's open from 10 am to 4.30 pm every day; admission is free.

A few doors away on Victoria St, the Hamilton Arts Centre Gallery has regular exhibitions by NZ artists.

## Gardens & Parks

The huge Hamilton Gardens complex contains about 100 different gardens, each with its own theme. There are rose gardens, a riverside magnolia garden, a perfume garden, cacti and succulents, vegetable gardens, carnivorous plants, glasshouse gardens and many more, with new ones still under construction. The complex is on Cobham Drive just east of the Cobham Bridge, and can be reached by walking eastwards along the river walkways from the centre. The gardens are always open, and admission is free.

Other relaxing spots are Hamilton Lake (Rotoroa) and the green domains along the Waikato River. Walkways pass through verdant parks and bushy areas on both sides of the river all the way from Cobham Bridge to Whitiora Bridge (both beyond the limits of our map) and there are a couple of sandy riverside beaches right in town. The area below the traffic bridge (Bridge St) is particularly attractive.

## Hilldale Zoo Park

Hilldale Zoo Park, with 40 species of animals, is quite good, though really more fun for the kids. The zoo is 8 km from the CPO – take SH 23 west towards Raglan, turn right at Newcastle Rd and then onto Brymer Rd. The zoo is open from 9 am to 5 pm every day, except during the Christmas holidays; admission is $4 (children $2).

## Farmworld

The interesting Clydesdale Agricultural Museum, also called Farmworld, is on Mystery Creek Rd, Mystery Creek, 16 km south of Hamilton and 1½ km south-east of Hamilton airport. Its aim is to 'obtain, preserve and restore agricultural equipment and articles relating to New Zealand's pioneering and rural development and to breed, work and display the associated animals'. There are stage shows at 10.30 am and 2.30 pm – and if you ever wanted to have a go at milking a cow, this is your chance.

It's a little difficult to get there by public transport. Buses run via the airport turn-off but that still leaves you 4 km from Farmworld. It's open from 9 am to 5 pm

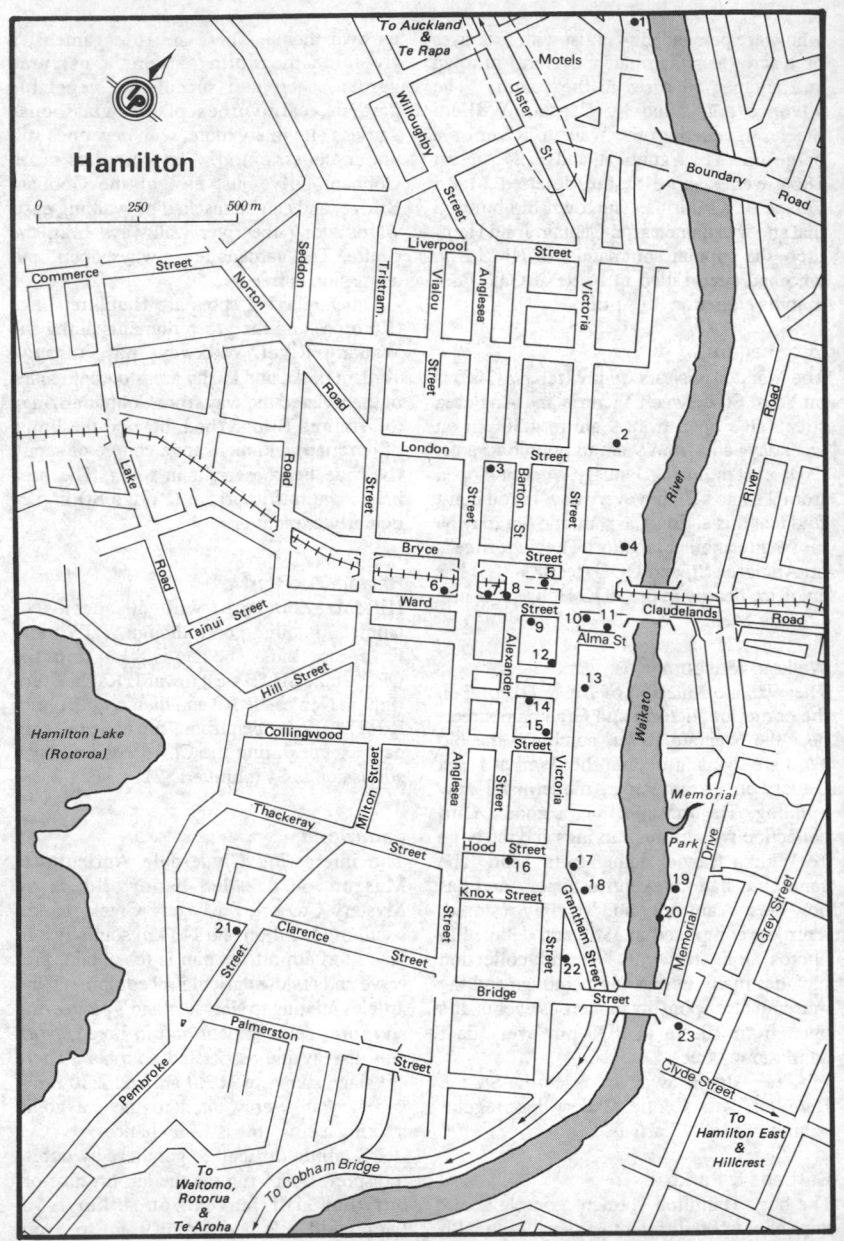

| | |
|---|---|
| 1 | Youth Hostel |
| 2 | Department of Conservation (DOC) |
| 3 | Automobile Association (AA) |
| 4 | Governor's Tavern |
| 5 | Centreplace |
| 6 | InterCity Travel Centre |
| 7 | Waikato Visitors Centre |
| 8 | French Bakery |
| 9 | Air New Zealand |
| 10 | McDonald's |
| 11 | Eldorado & No 8 Restaurants |
| 12 | Singapore Restaurant |
| 13 | CPO |
| 14 | Italian Pizza |
| 15 | Cobb & Co |
| 16 | Grand Central Guest House |
| 17 | Hamilton Arts Centre Gallery |
| 18 | Waikato Museum of Art & History |
| 19 | SS Rangiriri |
| 20 | Cruiseboats |
| 21 | YMCA & YWCA |
| 22 | Riverview Private Hotel |
| 23 | Parklands Travel Hotel |

every day, except during the Christmas holidays; admission is $5.50 (children $2.50).

## Temple View

People interested in comparative religious studies might want to take a trip to Temple View, 8 km south-west of Hamilton, site of a Mormon Temple and college. Only Mormons are allowed inside, but there is a Visitors Centre, open from 9 am to 9 pm daily. It has large pictures of the temple's interior, as well as videos, tours and brochures. The staff is gracious and friendly. To get there, catch the Temple View bus from the town centre.

## Walks

The Visitors Centre has a map for a 1 day scenic walk that makes a big circle from the city centre, along the river, over to Lake Hamilton and back to the river again. The Visitors Centre and the DOC office have info on many other walks in and around Hamilton.

## Cruises

River cruises on the Waikato River are a popular attraction. The boats depart from Memorial Park, on the riverbank opposite the town centre. The MV *Spirit of Waikato* does 1 hour cruises twice daily for $10 (children $5).

Fanciest of the Waikato cruisers is the paddleboat MV *Waipa Delta*, who made her maiden voyage on the Waikato River in March 1877. There are morning and afternoon tea cruises for $18, a luncheon cruise for $30, and a moonlight dinner cruise for $67 (children half price). The morning cruises go only in summer but the others go daily all year round. Reservations are recommended (tel 394-419, 394-415).

Embedded in the riverbank walkway are the remains of the gunboat SS *Rangiriri* which played a part in the Maori Wars in 1864.

## Other Activities

The Visitors Centre can supply details on many things to do around Hamilton if you have the time including river and lake amusements, horse-riding, hot-air balloon safaris and even bungy jumping. Centennial Pools, on Garnett Ave, Te Rapa, is a large complex in pleasant surroundings with several indoor and outdoor pools and waterslides. Day tours operate to the Waitomo Caves.

## Places to Stay

**Hostels** The *Hamilton Youth Hostel* (tel 380-009) at 1190 Victoria St, beside the river north of the town centre, is a modern hostel where the nightly cost is $13 in dorm, family and twin rooms.

The *YWCA* (tel 382-218), on the corner of Pembroke and Clarence streets (about 1 km from the town centre), takes both men and women casuals when there is room. Rates are $10.50 a night with your own sleeping bag, $21 a night with linen provided, or $77 weekly, all in single or double rooms with shared kitchenettes.

**Guest Houses** The wonderfully old-fashioned *Grand Central* (tel 381-619), at 27 Hood St, has B&B at $25/40 for singles/doubles. It is indeed quite central. Around the corner near the Waikato Museum, the *Riverview* (tel 393-986), 60 Victoria St, has small, simple rooms for $24 to $27 per person including breakfast.

The *Parklands Travel Hotel* (tel 382-461), across the river at 24 Bridge St, has rooms from $27.50 to $30.50 for singles, $55 to $70 for doubles or twin rooms, including breakfast. There are also motel-style single rooms at $40 to $44 and twin or double rooms at $55 to $61.

**Hotels** Right in the city centre on Victoria St, the *Commercial Establishment* (tel 391-226) has single, double or twin rooms for $44 ($79 with a private bathroom) plus family rooms for $90.

**Motels** Hamilton has plenty of motels, particularly along Ulster St, the main road into the city from the Auckland side. In fact Hamilton has one of the biggest concentrations of motels in New Zealand. The Parklands Travel Hotel (see Guest Houses) is OK but some of the other moderately priced places include:

*Abbotsford Court Motel* (tel 390-661), 18 Abbotsford St, just off Ulster St, $55/64 for singles/doubles
*Bavaria Motel* (tel 392-520), 203-207 Ulster St, $56/68
*Classic Motel* (tel 496-588), 451 Ulster St, swimming and spa pools, $50/61
*Motel Whitiora* (tel 381-695), 157 Ulster St, swimming and spa pools, $52/60 with some cheaper units for $45/52

**Camping & Cabins** At the *Municipal Camp* (tel 558-255) on Ruakura Rd, Hamilton East, tent sites cost $9/12 for one/two people; sites with power cost $12/15.

The *Hamilton East Tourist Court* (tel 566-220) on Cameron Rd, Hamilton East, has tent or power sites at $14 for two, cabins from $15 per person, and tourist flats at $42 for two.

**Places to Eat**
**Snacks & Fast Food** There are plenty of

restaurants in Hamilton including a full complement of international fast food outlets.

At the Auckland end of Victoria St are a *Pizza Hut* and a *Kentucky Fried Chicken*. Continue into town on that same road and you come to a large *McDonald's* on the corner of Claudelands Rd. Keep going out the other side of town and you'll find a much smaller *Wimpy Bar* – an example of the British attempt at the international burger market.

The modern Centreplace shopping centre is a good place to go for a quick and cheap breakfast. On the mezzanine level is the pleasant *Chequers*, or try the *Presto Coffee Lounge* for good sandwiches. The *Whole Food Cafe* downstairs has pies, samosas and the like to take away or eat there. Just outside the centre at 68 Ward St there's a *French Bakery*. That selection should provide an economical breakfast or lunch, but if you want more you can walk a block or two to the *Italian Pizza/Gelato Arlecchio* for pizza and ice cream.

**Pub Food** Moving on to pub food, there's a very popular *Cobb & Co* in the Commercial Establishment on the corner of Victoria and Collingwood streets, open from 7 am to 10 pm daily. It has the usual Cobb & Co menu, with main courses around $12 to $17. Or there's the *Governor's Tavern* on Bryce St, by the river.

Other pub food possibilities include the *Jolly Poacher* at the Chartwell Tavern and the *Bloody Steak* at the Tavern Hillcrest on the corner of Clyde and York streets (see Entertainment in this section). *Ward Lane* on Ward St has good lunches. The *Riverina Hotel* on the corner of Clyde and Grey streets has a bar with food and it's a good place to meet young people and university students. The *Roundabout Cafe* on Grey St is open late.

**Restaurants** You can spend plenty of money in restaurants if you want but try the excellent *Eldorado* at 10 Alma St, where you can get good Mexican food. Main courses cost between $12 and $20. They're also open for lunch when a taco ($5.50 to $9.50), enchilada or tostada with salad can make an interesting escape from the usual NZ fare.

Next door is the pleasant-looking *No 8* which has Italian food with starters for $6.50, pastas for $13, and main courses for $17. The next building along is the *Casablanca Middle Eastern Cafe* with meals for $12, or single dishes from $4 to $6.

Across Victoria St is the *Singapore Restaurant* on Garden Place. It's one of many Chinese restaurants in Hamilton but since the food features that spicy Malaysian flavour it's a good change from the usual Chinese dishes. The *Chinoserie* on Anglesea St has Chinese food, and *Boonjo* on Grey St has Malaysian food. Both are economical and serve good food. *Rivers Bar & Carvery* on Ward St is another good spot (see Entertainment in this section).

The *Mikado Drive-In Japanese Restaurant* on SH 1 in Te Rapa attracts lots of Japanese tourists.

Other possibilities include the *Left Bank Cafe* and *The Hungry Horse Restaurant & Bar* down Victoria St at the Hamilton Arts Centre Gallery. Or break out your fancy clothes, grab the plastic money, and head for one of Hamilton's many up-market restaurants – try *Harwood's, Seddon House* or *Montana*. Finally don't forget the floating meals served on the MV *Waipa Delta* several times daily (see Cruises in this section).

### Entertainment

**Pubs** The *Tavern Hillcrest* on the corner of Clyde and York streets attracts lots of university students, as does the *Riverina Hotel* bar on the corner of Clyde and Grey streets. *Rivers* on Ward St has a piano bar at dinner time. The *Eastside, Governors, Victorian* and *Chartwell* taverns all have live music on Friday and Saturday nights. Chartwell has a good restaurant, the Jolly Roger, to one side. The *Cobb & Co* in the Commercial Establishment on Victoria St has light entertainment on Thursday, Friday and Saturday evenings.

**Nightclubs & Other Entertainment** As usual nightclubs come and go but you can try *Shakes* at 30 Alexandra St or *Zaks* in Te Rapa. Other nightclubs in town are *Candyo's, Rocksoft* and the *Exchange*. *Rivers* on Ward St, just off Victoria St was once somewhat wilder, but now it has a piano bar. Try *Founders Theatre* for various performances.

### Getting There & Away

**Air** Air New Zealand (tel 399-800) has direct flights to and from Auckland, Wellington and Rotorua, with connections to other centres. Eagle Air (tel 389-500) has direct flights to Auckland, Palmerston North and Tauranga, again with further connections.

**Bus** InterCity, Newmans and Mt Cook all have bus services that pass through Hamilton. InterCity (tel 381-979) and Newmans (tel 476-119) are on Ward St. Mt Cook (tel 380-929) operates from Focus Travel at 630 Victoria St.

Services to and from Auckland are very frequent – among all three companies there are over 16 buses running every day in each direction for the 2½ hour trip. Buses are also frequent to and from Rotorua (2 hours), Taupo (2½ hours) and Wellington (10 hours).

There are a number of local bus operators, such as Buses Ltd and Hodgsons, with regular services to Te Awamutu, Raglan, Te Aroha and Paeroa (for the Coromandel Peninsula). Any bus to Tauranga, Rotorua or Taupo passes the Karapiro turn-off.

**Train** The day and evening trains between Auckland and Wellington stop at the railway station outside the city – the main railway line does not go via the branch station in the centre of town. Tickets are sold at the InterCity bus depot in town.

**Hitching** There's lots of traffic for hitching but getting out of Auckland can be a hassle because pedestrians are not allowed on the motorway – a law which is enforced. Hamilton itself can be a tricky place to hitch through with a pack. It may be best to take a local bus to the edge of town and hitch from there.

Heading south to Waitomo or New Plymouth, catch a Melville bus to the outskirts. Heading to Paeroa, take a Paeroa bus, which will stop at Te Aroha. For hitching to Rotorua, Taupo, Tauranga or Wellington, catch a Hillcrest bus and get off by the Hillcrest School. Hitching north to Auckland is easiest if you take a Huntly bus to the outskirts or to Huntly.

In Hamilton, SH 3 leads off towards Otorohanga, Waitomo and New Plymouth, while SH 1 continues towards Taupo and Wellington (take the road for Rotorua).

### Getting Around
**Airport Transport** A minibus from the city minibus terminal, opposite the InterCity bus terminal, serves all incoming and outgoing Air New Zealand flights.

**Bus** Keep in mind that Hamilton's local bus service does not run on weekends.

**Car Rental** There are many car rental agencies, including Rent-a-Dent (tel 555-886).

**Motorcycle Rental** Mopeds (for which a motorcycle licence is not required) or motorcycles can be hired from Road & Sport (tel 394-445) at 56 Rostrevor St, Hamilton North.

### AROUND HAMILTON
### Waingaro
The Waingaro Hot Springs are a popular day trip from Hamilton, with three thermal mineral pools of varying temperatures ranging from 32°C to 42°C, private spa pools, saunas, giant waterslides, children's play areas, bumper boats, barbecues, animals and a deer park. The complex is open from 9 am to 10 pm daily; admission is $5 (children $2.25).

You can stay at the springs in the *Waingaro Hot Springs Caravan Park* (tel 254-761). Camping sites cost $12/16 for one/two people, on-site caravans cost $32/36

and motel units cost $55/60. To get there, head out on SH 23 from Hamilton towards Raglan for about 35 km, then turn north on SH 22.

### Raglan
The nearest beach is Raglan, 48 km west of Hamilton. A popular place in summer, it has one of New Zealand's most famous surfing beaches and a sheltered inner harbour good for swimming and windsurfing. The Bryant Memorial Scenic Reserve is 9 km south-west of Raglan on Whaanga Rd, past the ocean beach. From there a track leads down to the beach. An easy bushwalk to the Bridal Veil Falls starts off the Kawhia road, 20 km south of Raglan.

**Places to Stay** There are several places to stay at Raglan. The *Hartstone House* (tel 258-601, 258-149), 15 John St, is a hostel, with the luxury of a spa pool for resting those tired muscles after a long day at the beach. Rates are $11 per night.

Camping sites at the *Kopua Motor Camp* (tel 258-283) cost $9 for two ($10.25 with power); cabins cost $26 for two, and tourist flats cost $32. The *Harbour View Hotel* (tel 258-010) has single/double rooms at $35/45. On the water's edge at 14 Wainui Rd, Raglan West, the *Raglan Motel* (tel 258-153) has single/double units at $35/50.

### Kawhia
The west coast port of Kawhia, with harbour and ocean beaches, is 98 km south-west of Hamilton via Temple View and 57 km west of Otorohanga. About 2 hours on each side of low tide you can find the Puia Hot Springs in the sands – just dig a hole and you have your own little natural spa. The coast is reputed to be dangerous for swimming. There's a driveable track over the dunes. A round trip from Hamilton can include Bridal Veil Falls and Raglan.

Between the Raglan and Kawhia roads is the Pirongia Forest Park, with its focal point the 961 metre Pirongia Mountain. The mountain is usually climbed from Corcoran Rd on the Hamilton side (ask the DOC for tramping information). The township of Pirongia is 32 km from Hamilton.

## Te Awamutu

Midway between Hamilton and Otorohanga on SH 3, Te Awamutu is noted for its rose gardens. November to April is the time to see the roses at their best.

On the third Sunday of each month, from 10 am to 4 pm, the Waikato Railway Museum has the biggest static display of large steam locomotives in New Zealand. Railway enthusiasts can ring Te Awamutu 7950 or 4887 to inquire about the possibility of other opening times.

The Te Awamutu District Museum houses a fine collection of Maori *taonga* (treasures), the centrepiece of which is the Uenuku:

Uenuku is one of the traditional Maori gods or spirits and it is said to manifest as a rainbow. The spirit of Uenuku is said to have been brought to New Zealand on the Tainui Canoe. This Maori totara carving, probably the oldest in New Zealand, was made to contain this spirit. The carving was made using only stone tools.

**Jennifer Evans, Te Awamutu District Museum**

## Morrinsville

About 33 km north-east of Hamilton on SH 26, Morrinsville is a small centre for the Waikato dairying industry. In fact its tourist literature boasts that 'there are more cows within a 25 km radius of Morrinsville than in any other part of the world'! To reassure city folk it also states, 'Our retailers are *not* country bumpkins.' It's a very friendly town, with gardens dotted around, a Pioneer Museum & Cottage open on Sunday afternoons, and a home and farmstay programme enabling visitors to experience Kiwi farming and small-town life first-hand. There's also a camping ground (tel 7440, 7032).

The town's clothing, ceramics and mushroom factories offer tours on specified days of the week, and a couple of scenic reserves are nearby. Ask at the friendly Public Relations Office (tel 5575) on the eastern end of the main street for anything you want to know about Morrinsville.

## Te Aroha

Te Aroha, 55 km north-east of Hamilton on SH 26, is at the foot of the mountain (952 metres) of the same name. From the top you can see as far as Tongariro and Mt Egmont so it's well worth the climb. Te Aroha also has many other good bushwalks, some hot mineral soda pools in the domain to relax in afterwards, and a pioneer museum. There's a DOC office for tramping information.

If you want to spend a longer time at Te Aroha there's a *Youth Hostel* (tel 48-739) on Miro St. It's a pleasant small hostel (just 12 beds) and costs $10 a night. Family rooms and bicycles are available.

## Karapiro & Arapuni

Karapiro, furthest downstream of a chain of hydroelectric power stations and dams on the Waikato River, is 28 km south-east of Hamilton, just off SH 1. You can arrange to visit the power house if you're interested. The road passes over the dam and the lake is popular for aquatic sports.

Arapuni, the first government-built hydroelectric station on the river, is 66 km from Hamilton via Te Awamutu. Take SH 3 to just south of Te Awamutu, and turn left (east) at Kihikihi. It is also accessible from Karapiro or Tirau on SH 1. The dam was built across the Arapuni Gorge and is worth a look. Visitors are allowed access to most of the works.

## Maungakawa Scenic Reserve

From SH 1 take the turn-off at Cambridge, 20 km south-east of Hamilton, and you'll reach Maungakawa Scenic Reserve, a regenerating forest with some exotic timber species. There's a fairly easy short bushwalk here. From the eastern side of Mt Maungakawa, a track suitable for experienced trampers ascends from Tapui Rd; it takes half a day to walk there and back.

# Otorohanga

Otorohanga, in the upper Waipa basin, is just

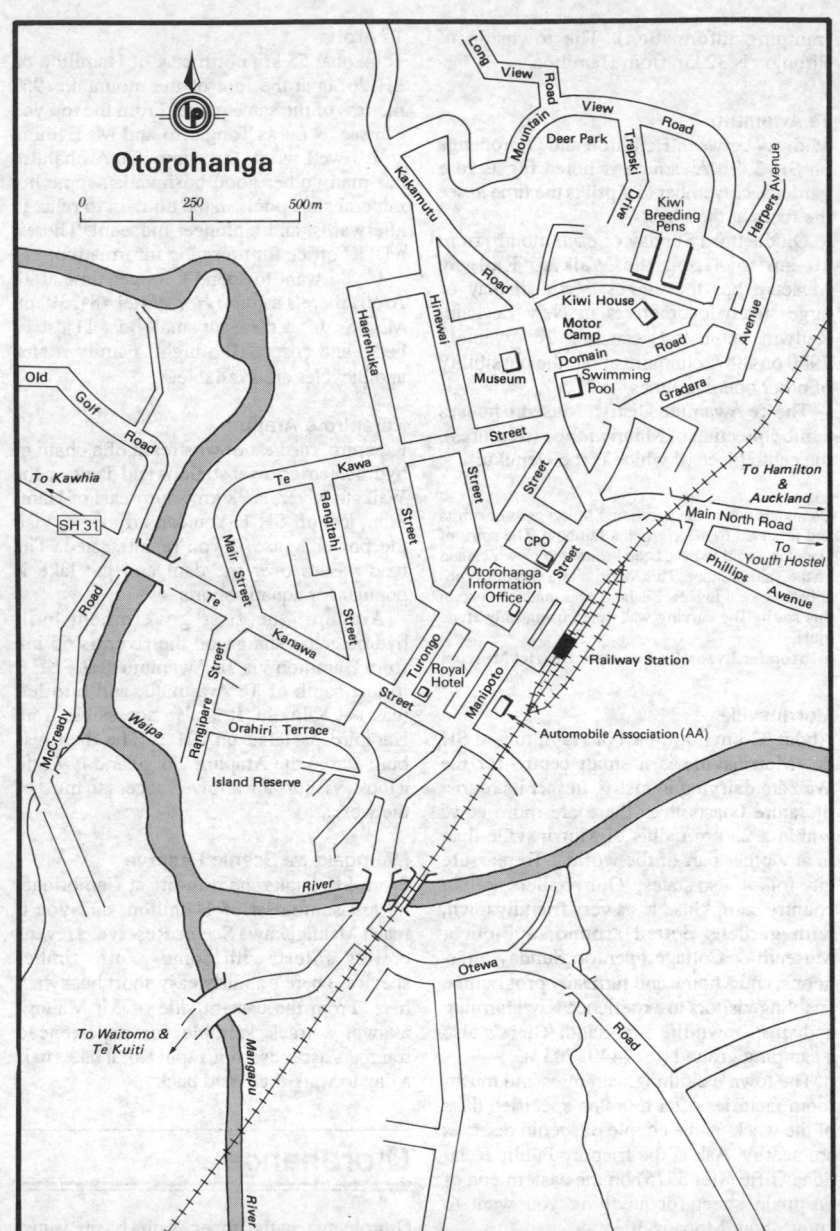

**Otorohanga**

0    250    500 m

under 60 km south of Hamilton on SH 3, only a short distance before the Waitomo turn-off. Principally a dairying community, it is the first township you come to at the northern end of the King Country, the stronghold of the Maori chiefs who held out there against the Europeans longer than anywhere else in New Zealand. This area was forbidden to the Pakehas by Maori law until the 1880s.

Most people go through Otorohanga or stay overnight there on the way to the Waitomo Caves, 16 km away. It's a convenient base for visits to Waitomo, Kawhia and Pirongia.

### History
The earliest Europeans to settle in Otorohanga were timber millers, the first of them arriving in 1890. From 1884, when the Pakehas were allowed into the district, until 1955 the King Country was 'dry'. This condition was apparently imposed by Maori chiefs when they agreed to the Europeans building the Main Trunk Railway Line through their country, opening it up even more to the outside world. Needless to say there are now numerous hotels everywhere, so you won't go thirsty.

### Information
The Otorohanga Public Relations Office (tel 8951) is on Manipoto St, the main road through town beside the town hall. It's open from 10 am to 4 pm on weekdays and 11 am to 2 pm on weekends. There's also an AA office on Manipoto St.

### Kiwi House
The well-signposted Otorohanga Kiwi House is the town's main attraction and worth a visit. In a kiwi house night and day are reversed, so you can watch the kiwis in daytime under artificial moonlight. There are also various other native birds including some keas, which more than live up to their reputation for being inquisitive. The walk-in aviary is the largest in New Zealand. Other birds you can see include morepork owls, hawks, wekas and reptiles, including tuataras.

Kea

The Kiwi House is open from 10 am to 5 pm daily, except from June to August when it closes at 4 pm. The last admission is half an hour before closing time. Admission is $5 (children $1.50).

### Historical Society Museum
In the same area as the Kiwi House is the Otorohanga Historical Society Museum (tel 8462, 8758) in the old Courthouse. It's open from 2 to 4 pm on Sunday, but at other times call up and the friendly old guy who maintains it will wander over and open it up for you. Make a donation; it's a nice little local museum.

### Other Attractions
There is a deer park near the kiwi house. It's basically a high-fenced paddock where you can look at the deer from a distance, and there's also an enclosure with peacocks and ducks. There's no entry charge but there is a donation box. Between the deer park and the kiwi house are kiwi breeding pens and the Rhododendron Gardens.

Nearby there's an Olympic-size swimming pool open daily in summer, and a heated pool open all year round, except on Fridays in winter. Admission is $2 (children $1, family $4).

## Places to Stay

**Hostels** Otorohanga has an *Associate Youth Hostel* (tel 8908, 8951) in a private home at 70 Main North Rd, about 2 km north of the CPO on SH 3. It sleeps nine and the cost is $10 per night. Try to arrive before 8.30 pm. Since this is an associate youth hostel, you can stay here with or without a YHA card.

**Hotels & Motels** The *Royal Hotel* (tel 8129) on Te Kanawa St has single/double rooms for $33/55, with meals available at reasonable prices. The *Otorohanga Colonial Motel* (tel 8289) on the Main North Rd has single/double units for $59/68.

**Camping** The *Otorohanga Motor Camp* (tel 8214) is on Domain Rd, adjacent to the Kiwi House. Camping costs $10.50 for one or two people, $12 with power, and there are some on-site caravans for $12 plus the camp charges. You may hear kiwis calling between 7 and 9 pm.

## Places to Eat

Along the main street there are several takeaways and coffee shops, many open every day. The *Regent Tea Rooms* is open every day for breakfast and lunch, on Friday evenings for a set dinner meal ($8.50 small, $11 large) and on Sunday evening for a family smorgasbord ($13.50). The *La Kiwi* licensed restaurant and takeaway is open every day for dinner from 4 pm, with à la carte dinners around $15, and there's a fancy Sunday night smorgasbord for $16. The *Royal Hotel* on Te Kanawa St has bistro meals, smorgasbord lunches, a licensed restaurant, a pub, and a lounge bar which sometimes has live music on weekends.

## Getting There & Away

Otorohanga is serviced by InterCity and Newmans buses, with several buses daily in each direction. By bus, Otorohanga is about 3½ hours from Auckland, 1 hour from Ham-

ilton, 3 hours from New Plymouth, and 30 minutes from Waitomo.

The daily InterCity excursion bus to the Waitomo Caves from Auckland goes through Otorohanga at about 12.30 pm, leaving Waitomo for the return trip at 2.30 pm. It costs about $5 each way between Otorohanga and the caves; you can take it for the round trip or just one way, and you can transfer at Waitomo to the Rotorua excursion bus to continue on to Rotorua. A taxi (tel 8214) could be competitive and more convenient for a group of people going to Waitomo. It's also easy to hitch.

# Waitomo

Waitomo is famous for its limestone caves. The Waitomo, Ruakuri and Aranui caves are the feature attraction but the whole region is riddled with caves and strange limestone formations. There are also some good bushwalks so it's an interesting area to visit for a day or two.

In English Waitomo means water *(wai)* hole *(tomo)* – the river flows into a hole.

Rivers going underground, great springs emerging from the ground, independent hollows and basins instead of connecting valleys, deep potholes and vast caves, isolated tower-like hills...these are some of the distinctive features of karst, the name given to the kinds of country that owe their special characteristics to the unusual degree of solubility of their component rocks in natural waters.

(*Karst* by J N Jennings, **Australian National University Press, Canberra, 1971**)

## Information

Waitomo is 8 km off the main highway, SH 3. The Information Centre is at the Caves Museum (tel Te Kuiti 87-640) in the centre of the tiny town, a km or so before the caves themselves. A lot of caving information is available at the Waitomo Caves – Tomo Group Hut (see Hostels under Places to Stay in this section).

Groceries are available at the general store beside the museum, but the choice is wider at nearby towns like Otorohanga or Te Kuiti. If you're planning to camp or stay at the hostel and prepare your own food it's worth bringing supplies with you.

### The Caves

There are three major caves in Waitomo – the Waitomo (Glow-worm), the Aranui, and the Ruakuri.

The Waitomo Glow-worm Cave is just a big cave with the usual assortment of stalactites and stalagmites until you board a boat and swing off onto the river. As your eyes grow accustomed to the dark you'll see a Milky Way of little lights surrounding you – these are the glow-worms. They are the larvae of a type of gnat which looks much like a large mosquito except without mouth parts. The larvae have luminescent organs which produce a soft, greenish light, and they weave sticky threads to hang down and catch unwary insects attracted by their 'lights'.

The adult of the species is often caught and eaten by the larval glow-worm. Even if it avoids that fate, the adult insect does not live very long because it does not have a mouth; after spending about 2 weeks in a cocoon state, the adult emerges, mates, lays eggs and dies, all within about 3 or 4 days.

The Aranui and Ruakuri caves are 3 km further up the road from the glow-worm cave. Transport to the Aranui Cave is not included with the tour ticket. You may be able to catch a ride with the tour guide or other visitors, but if not you'll have to hitch or walk. The Aranui Cave is different from the other caves; its beauty is more delicate, with thousands of tiny, hollow 'straw' stalactites hanging from the ceiling, and there's no river running through. The Ruakuri Cave has been closed to the public due to a dispute involving Maori land rights and now can only be visited on a Black Water Rafting trip (read on).

All three caves have their own distinct characteristics and beauty, and all are worth a visit – although visits to the Waitomo and Aranui caves seem awfully tame if you've been Black Water Rafting. The glow-worm cave tours, in particular, with their large crowds of tourists, may seem like a bit of a tourist rush-through and it's a shame that this is all that many people ever see of the Waitomo area – arriving in a big tour bus around lunch time, being shuttled through the one cave and off again. If you do visit the Waitomo Glow-worm Cave, try to go on the first tour of the day – you'll get to visit some smaller caverns that the big groups later in the day can't enter for fear of depleting the oxygen supply.

The Waitomo and Aranui caves can be visited independently or you can get a combined ticket for both. Tickets are sold at the Glow-worm Cave & Grotto. Entry to just one cave costs $9.60 (children $4.80), the combined two-cave ticket is $15 (children $7.50, family $40). There's also a combination ticket for the Glow-worm Cave and museum for $11.60 (children $4.80) and a 'lunch-cave special' offering a smorgasbord lunch and one cave tour for $24.35 (children $12.20).

The 45 minute tours of the Glow-worm Cave depart on the hour from 9 am to 4 pm, and there are additional tours at 4.30 pm and 5.30 pm from late October to Easter. There may be other additional tours at the height of the summer season. Aranui Cave tours begin at 10 and 11 am, and at 1, 2 and 3 pm, and take about 40 minutes.

Without a doubt, though, the most exciting way to see the caves is Black Water Rafting.

**Black Water Rafting** Black Water Rafting started in Waitomo in 1987 and quickly became one of New Zealand's most popular adventures. It's a 3 hour trip through the Ruakuri Cave, expertly guided and organised in groups of no more than 12 at a time.

First you get into a wetsuit and caver's helmet with a light on the front, grab a black inner tube, and you're off on a trek through the cave which involves leaping over a small waterfall, floating through a long glow-worm passageway, and plenty of Kiwi-style joking and laughs. At the end of the journey

there's a hot shower and soup to warm up your innards, but in the wetsuit you probably won't get too cold. The $40 fee includes admission to the Caves Museum for more education on glow-worms and caves, and altogether it's well worth the outlay. Trips leave from the museum several times daily; phone in advance (tel Te Kuiti 87-640) for a reservation.

This tour is raved about by just about everyone who goes on it. Highly recommended.

### Caves Museum

If you want to find out more about caves, visit the excellent Waitomo Caves Speleological Museum. You'll learn about how caves are formed, the fauna and flora that live in caves, the history of caves and cave exploration. Exhibits include a working cave model, fossils of extinct birds and animals that have been discovered in caves, and a cave crawl for the adventurous. There's also a 27 minute, 9 projector audiovisual presentation about caving, and 10 minute videos about glow-worms and the many other natural attractions found in the Waitomo area.

Be sure to look at the large Tane Mahuta carving outside the caves ticket office. It was commissioned for the centennial of the first recorded exploration of the Waitomo Cave and has many interesting figures relating to the area and the caves. The museum has a leaflet explaining the various details of the carving.

The museum is open from 9 am to 5 pm daily; admission is $3 (children free). You can get a combined ticket to the museum and the Glow-worm Cave for $11.60 (children $4.80); admission is included with Black Water Rafting.

### Ohaki Maori Village

The Ohaki Maori Village is a replica of a pre-European Maori pa. Visitors can see demonstrations and displays of Maori weaving, and there's an excellent shop selling authentic Maori arts and crafts. The village is open from 10 am to 5 pm daily; admission is $3.50 (children $1). The village is on the road in from the main highway to the caves.

### Mountain View Stud Farm

Along the same road, 10 km past the caves, the Mountain View Angora Rabbit Stud Farm runs daily tours showing the life cycle of Angora rabbits, wool handling, shearing and breeding. Cost is $3.30 (children free), and they also sell raw Angora fibre, yarn, and crafts.

### Bushwalks

The Caves Museum has leaflets on various walks in the area, and there are some good ones. From the caves ticket office the 5 km Waitomo Walkway takes off through farmland, terminating in the Ruakuri Caves & Bush Scenic Reserve, where a half-hour return walk passes by the river and caves and a natural limestone bridge.

Ask at the museum about guided night walks through the Ruakuri Reserve, and if one is going, take it – you'll see many glow-worms and the bush and caves take on a different aspect at night. You can also do this by yourself but you wouldn't see as much as the guide will show you and the tours aren't expensive (maybe around $5). These night walks became famous a couple of years ago as the 'Dead Sheep Tours'.

A 45 minute return walk to Opapaka Pa begins at the Ohaki Maori Village. There's also a short forest walk near the Glow-worm Cave and a variety of other short walks in the area.

### Other Activities

Waitomo Horse-Trekking (tel Te Kuiti 87-649, 88-393) offers treks of 2 to 5 days through the Waitomo wilderness with optional hunting. The price of $60 per day includes food and accommodation. They also have 2 hour, half-day and full-day horse treks.

There's golf, squash and bridge at the Waitomo Golf Course on SH 3 heading north towards Otorohanga.

### Places to Stay

Hostels To get to the hostel, go via the town centre and about 2 km past the caves to the *Waitomo Caves – Tomo Group Hut* (tel Te Kuiti 87-442). Accommodation is rustic hostel style and there's room for 30 people in bunks (lots more with a squeeze). Cost is $8 the first night and $5 a night after that. You can pitch a tent on the lawn for the same rates. Bring your own sleeping bag. If you're walking up to the hostel from the town centre, buy some goods at the store or you'll have a 2 km walk back from the hostel.

The hostel is also the clubroom of the Hamilton Tomo Group, the largest caving club in New Zealand. If you're lucky you may be invited on a caving trip to one of the many non-tourist caves in the area, particularly on weekends when the hostel fills up with cavers. The hut has detailed maps on many caves but it's not advisable you go off caving alone in the area, unless you are an experienced caver. Caves can be dangerous: some have networks spanning several km and people have been lost underground. Altogether there are over 100 km of caves in the Waitomo region, many still unexplored, so there's ample field for caving adventure.

*Juno's Budget Accommodation* (tel Te Kuiti 87-649) has hostel-style accommodation in a large private home for $11 per night. It's on the main road in from the highway to the caves, 1 km before the museum and opposite the Merrovale Tea-rooms. Juno's also has horse treks (see Other Activities) and can organise farmstays and hunting expeditions.

The Waitomo Caves Motor Camp also has cheap cabins (see Camping & Cabins in this section).

Hotels The *THC Waitomo Hotel* (tel Te Kuiti 88-227/228) has standard rooms at $38/45 for singles/doubles, and premium rooms for $95/101. There are also family rooms, and children can stay free of charge. Most THC hotels are definitely at the top end of expensive, but here the cheaper rooms are very reasonably priced. If it's not expensive enough, there are suites at over $280! It is very convenient for the caves, and the THC tavern and restaurant are the best in town.

Motels Other accommodation is some distance from the caves. The *Glow Worm Motel* (tel Otorohanga 8882) is at the SH 3 turn-off and rooms cost from $50/60. Also near the turn-off, the *Waitomo Country Lodge* (tel Otorohanga 8109) has rooms for $50/64. The *Waitomo Colonial Motel* (tel Otorohanga 8289) is 8 km north of the turn-off, so it's 16 km from the caves. Rooms there cost $59/68.

Camping & Cabins The *Waitomo Caves Motor Camp* (tel Te Kuiti 87-639) is opposite the general store – you can book into the camp there. Camping sites cost $5 per person, or $6 with power. It also has cabins at $10 or $11 for one person and $18 or $20 for two, or you can get the backpackers' share rate of $7 per person.

Homestays, Farmstays & B&Bs Several homes and farms in the area offer lodging and B&B arrangements. Check with the Caves Museum, where many are listed. B&B costs $32/52 for singles/doubles (dinner $10 extra) on a sheep and cattle station 14 km from the caves towards Te Kuiti (tel Te Kuiti 88-372). B&B at the *Mountain View Angora Rabbit Stud Farm* (tel Te Kuiti 88-593, 88-371), 10 km west of the caves, costs $40 for two, and there are a number of others.

### Places to Eat
**Snacks & Fast Food** The general store beside the Caves Museum is open from 8.30 am to 6 pm every day, with a tearoom off to one side where you can get inexpensive meals. *Merrovale Tearooms*, 2 km from the caves out towards the main highway, has both indoor and patio seating and is open from 9 am to 3 pm daily, as well as 5 to 8 pm from Wednesday to Saturday.

**Restaurants** For more elegant dining the *THC Waitomo Hotel* is the fancy restaurant in town, with à la carte breakfast and dinner every day and a $16 smorgasbord at lunch time. They also do a barbecue lunch for the tour buses for the same price and it's sometimes open to individual diners. At dinner time main courses cost $14 to $17, with both vegetarian and meat dishes.

*Roselands Restaurant* (tel Te Kuiti 87-611), 4 km from the caves and 3 km off the road leading towards the main highway, is another good place for a meal at lunch time. They primarily cater to Japanese bus tours but they do offer a very ample barbecue lunch for $20 in an attractive setting with garden, verandah or indoor seating. They're open from noon to 2 pm every day, and if you telephone first you can arrange to avoid the tour bus crowd.

You can also get a 'lunch-cave special' where you get lunch and a cave tour for $24.35 (children $12.20). Tickets are available from the Glow-worm Cave & Grotto.

### Getting There & Away
**Bus** On weekdays a bus runs the 8 km out from Waitomo to the main road (SH 3) and on to Te Kuiti, passing by the Tomo Hut at about 8.40 am. The same bus returns via Waitomo and continues to Te Anga and some of the way towards Kawhia, before heading

off for Taharoa. Iron sands are being mined at Taharoa but it is not really worth the trip out.

InterCity has day-trip bus services to the caves from Auckland and Rotorua. You only get to spend an hour at the caves so it's a very rushed trip. Fares from Auckland (via Otorohanga) cost about $35, and from Rotorua about $30. If you are already in Otorohanga you can catch the InterCity bus to the caves as it passes through at about 12.30 pm ($5 each way). There are also return excursion fares that include admission to the caves.

Since the Auckland and Rotorua excursion buses arrive and depart from the caves at the same times, you could arrive on the bus from Auckland and leave an hour later on the bus to Rotorua, or vice versa. You can also take these buses just one way to or from Waitomo, to spend a longer time in the area. Leaving Waitomo, both buses depart from the caves at 2.30 pm every day.

Frequent bus services along SH 3 will drop you at the Waitomo turn-off, 10 minutes south of Otorohanga and 15 minutes north of Te Kuiti.

**Hitching** Hitching to the caves from the Waitomo turn-off is usually pretty easy.

### Getting Around
**Cycling** You can hire bicycles around Waitomo; ask at the museum or the motor camp. Since the region is hilly this may be only for the stout of heart and leg.

**Hitching** If you don't have your own transport the alternatives are hitching, which fortunately is usually easy, and walking.

### AROUND WAITOMO
There are many scenic reserves around the Waitomo area and the Waitomo Caves Museum has plenty of printed information about them.

### Kiritehere Road
Heading west from Waitomo, the road follows a rewarding and scenic route with a

couple of natural beauties worth visiting. Ask at the museum for the booklet *A Trip Through Time* by Peter Chandler, founder of Black Water Rafting, with suggestions for a 4 to 6 hour exploration of the 53 km road from Waitomo to Kiritehere on the coast. Of course you can also visit just one place but it's a great little booklet if you want to do more.

### Natural Bridge
The Mangapohue Natural Bridge Scenic Reserve, 26 km west of Waitomo, is a 5.5 hectare reserve with a giant natural limestone bridge formation, which is a 20 minute walk from the road. At times you may see cavers practising their manoeuvres by dangling from the summit on ropes. You can easily walk to the summit. On the far side, big rocks full of oyster fossils jut up from the grass. At night you'll see glow-worms.

### Piripiri Caves
About 4 km further west is the Piripiri Caves Scenic Reserve, where a 30 minute track leads to a large cave containing fossils of giant oysters. Bring a torch (flashlight) if you want to explore the cave.

### Marakopa Falls
The impressive 36 metre Marakopa Falls are 32 km west of Waitomo. You can view them from the road above, or walk to the bottom on a track starting just downhill from the roadside vantage point.

### Marakopa & Te Anga
To get to Marakopa village, on the coast 48 km from Waitomo, turn left (south-west) at Te Anga. The pleasant Te Anga Tavern is worth a stop if you've worked up a thirst. The whole Te Anga-Marakopa area is riddled with caves. The bitumen road ends just out of Marakopa, but it is possible to continue, on a difficult but scenic road, 60 km further south until you meet SH 3 at Awakino. From

Te Anga you can also get to Kawhia, 53 km to the north on a sealed country road (see the Around Hamilton section in this chapter).

### District Museum
The District Museum at Ohura, south of Waitomo, has an interesting King Country exhibit.

### Te Kuiti
The town of Te Kuiti is 19 km south of Otorohanga on SH 3 and 19 km from the Waitomo caves. It's a larger town than Otorohanga. While Te Kuiti has nothing of particular attraction for visitors, it does have basic services and makes another base for visiting Waitomo.

**Information** The Te Kuiti Information Centre (tel 88-077), on the main street in the centre of town, is open from 8.30 am to 5.30 pm on weekdays, 8.30 am to 1 pm on Saturdays, and sometimes from around 10 am to 1 pm on Sundays. It has information on Waitomo, bushwalks and homestays in the area. There's an AA office (tel 88-294) on the main street.

DOC (tel 87-299) has an office at 78 Taupiri St, one block off the main street, which is open from 8 am to noon and 1 to 4.30 pm on weekdays. It has plenty of information on the area's tracks and forests, including the large Pureora Forest Park. If you're in the area in summer, ask about the summer programme of nature activities.

### Pureora Forest Park
The large Pureora Forest Park, east of Te Kuiti, has camping and hut facilities, swimming, fishing, and long and short forest treks, including tracks to the summits of Mt Pureora (1165 metres) and Mt Titiraupenga (1042 metres). Hunting is permitted in the northern section of the park, designated as a recreational hunting area, but you must obtain a permit from the park headquarters.

# Taranaki

The Taranaki region lies between the Wanganui River in the east and the Tasman Sea in the west, and is dominated by the massive cone of Mt Egmont. The volcano was known as Taranaki to the Maoris and there is some talk of returning to the historical name, which the region as a whole has always kept.

## New Plymouth

Population 47,800

New Plymouth is about midway between Auckland (373 km) and Wellington (357 km), on the west coast. From Waitomo it's 180 km on SH 3, which has two scenic but winding sections: the Awakino Gorge and Mt Messenger. Between these two parts of the road is a strip of exposed west coast beaches, broken now and again by river estuaries.

### History

Back in the 1820s the Taranaki Maoris took off to the Cook Strait region in droves to avoid a threatened attack by the Waikato tribes, but it was not until 1832 that the Waikatos attacked and subdued the remaining Ngati-awa Maoris, except at Okuku Pa (New Plymouth) where the whalers had joined in the battle. So when the first European settlers arrived in the district in 1841 the coastlands of Taranaki were almost deserted. Initially it seemed there would be no opposition to land claims, so the New Zealand Company was able to buy extensive tracts from the Ngati-awa who had stayed.

When the others returned after years of exile and slavery they objected strongly to the sale of their land. Their claims were substantially upheld when Governor Fitzroy ruled that the New Zealand Company was only allowed to retain just over 10 sq km around New Plymouth – of the 250 it had claimed. The Crown slowly acquired more

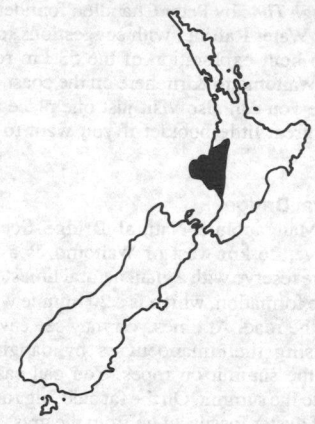

land from the Maoris, but the Maoris became increasingly reluctant to sell and the European settlers increasingly greedy for the fertile land around Waitara, just north of New Plymouth.

The settlers' determination finally forced the government to abandon its policy of negotiation, and in 1860 war broke out. For 10 years the Maoris kept the military engaged in guerrilla warfare. During this time the settlers had moved in on Waitara and were in control there, but the Maoris came and went as they pleased throughout the rest of the province. The Taranaki chiefs had not signed the Treaty of Waitangi and did not recognise the sovereignty of the Queen, so they were treated as rebels. By 1870 over 500 hectares of their land was confiscated and much of the remainder was acquired through extremely dubious transactions.

Today, the district of Taranaki is undergoing an economic boom, due to the discovery of natural gas and oil at Kapuni in 1959 and more recently at Maui off the coast of South Taranaki.

### Information

Devon St (East and West) is the main street;

its central section is a mall. The PR office (tel 86-086) at 81 Liardet St, open from 8.30 am to 5 pm Monday to Friday, is very helpful and has lots of printed information including a good city map.

The DOC (tel 80-433) is in the Atkinson Building on Devon St West on the corner of Robe St. It's open from 8 am to 4.30 pm Monday to Friday. There's an AA office at 49-55 Powderham St.

## Historic Buildings

New Plymouth has numerous historic buildings, described in a leaflet available from the PR office. The 1853 Richmond Cottage on Brougham St is open from 2 to 4 pm on Mondays, Wednesdays and Fridays and from 1 to 4 pm on weekends, but it's closed on Monday and Wednesday from June to October. Admission is $1 (children 50 cents). Unlike most early cottages, which were timber, Richmond Cottage was sturdily built of stone.

St Mary's Church, on Vivian St, dates from 1846 and its graveyard has numerous interesting gravestones of early settlers and of soldiers who died during the Taranaki wars. Impressed by their bravery, the British also buried several of the Maori chiefs here. Brooklands Park was once the land around an important early settler's home; the fireplace and chimney are all that remain of the house after the Maoris burnt it down.

The Gables, on Brooklands Park Drive, is an early hospital built in the late 1840s. In 1854 a notable Maori chief died here from wounds received in a tribal feud. The hospital consequently became tapu, which saved it during the Taranaki wars as its forbidden status prevented the Maoris from burning it down! On Devon St at the eastern end of town is the Fitzroy Pole, erected by Maoris in 1844 to mark the point beyond which Governor Fitzroy had forbidden settlers to acquire land. The carving on the bottom of the pole depicts a sorrowful Pakeha topped by a cheerfully triumphant Maori.

If you're wandering around the city, have a look at the curious transparent clocktower on the corner of Devon St West and Queen St. It was erected in 1985 to replace the old post office tower which was demolished 16 years earlier. There is an observatory and planetarium on Marsland Hill off Robe St which opens at varying hours depending on the weather; check with the PR office to confirm opening times. There's also a carillon here and fine views over the central city. St Mary's Church is directly below the hill.

## Parks

New Plymouth is an attractive city renowned for its superb parks. A visit to Pukekura Park, 10 minutes walk from the city centre, is a must. Numerous magnificent display houses are open (Easter to Christmas) from 9 am to noon and 1 to 4.30 pm on weekdays and from 2 to 4.30 pm on Sundays. They are closed on Saturdays, except on long weekends when they're open daily for the same hours as on weekdays. From Christmas to Easter they're open from 9 am to noon and 1 to 4.30 pm every day.

Adjoining it is Brooklands Park, another lovely park, and between the two, the Bowl of Brooklands, an outdoor soundshell in a bush and lake setting. On Tisch Ave on the waterfront is Kawaroa Park, with a pool, squash and tennis courts. The pool is only open in summer.

## Power Station

At the western end of town is the New Plymouth Power Station, designed to run on oil or gas. The original intention was to burn coal, but the discovery of natural gas in Taranaki changed this. The station is dominated by its towering 200 metre chimney. Tours are conducted at 10 am on Wednesdays and at 2 pm on Sundays. You can get to it on the port bus service on Wednesdays but there is no bus on Sundays.

## Paritutu

Above the power station is Paritutu, a steep hill with a magnificent view from the top. The name means 'rising precipice' and it's worth the tiring but quick scramble to the summit. Not only do you look down on the

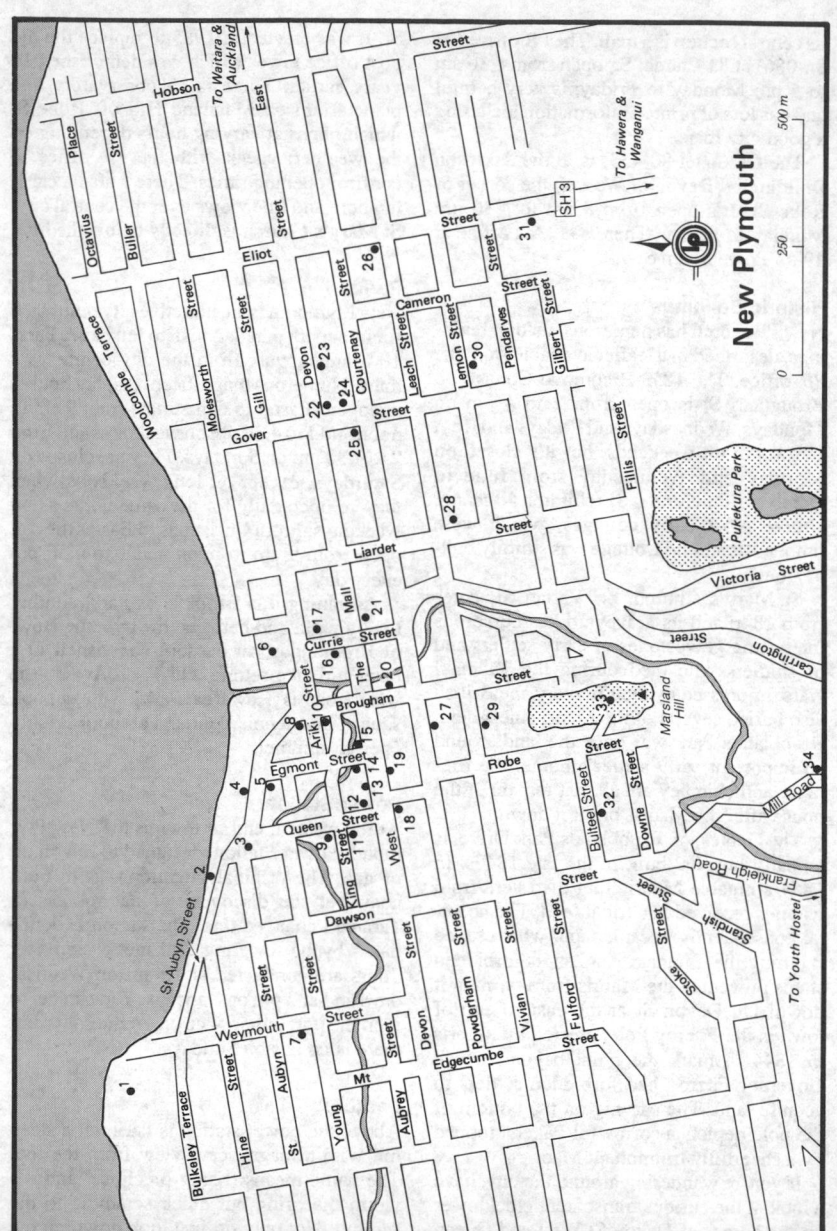

| | |
|---|---|
| 1 | Kawaroa Baths & Waterslides |
| 2 | Tasman Hotel |
| 3 | Monument |
| 4 | InterCity Bus & Railway Station |
| 5 | City Council & Bus Depot |
| 6 | City Centre Mall |
| 7 | Aotea Private Hotel |
| 8 | Richmond Cottage |
| 9 | Newmans Coachlines |
| 10 | Taranaki Museum & Library |
| 11 | Govett-Brewster Art Gallery |
| 12 | White Hart Hotel |
| 13 | Opera House |
| 14 | Black Olive Restaurant |
| 15 | Dancing Bear Restaurant |
| 16 | Bellissimo Restaurant |
| 17 | Post Office |
| 18 | Clocktower, Department of Conservation (DOC) |
| 19 | Taj Indian Cafe |
| 20 | L'Escargot Restaurant |
| 21 | Air New Zealand |
| 22 | State Establishment, Cobb & Co |
| 23 | Gareth's Restaurant |
| 24 | The Steps Restaurant |
| 25 | Kentucky Fried Chicken |
| 26 | McDonald's |
| 27 | Automobile Association (AA) |
| 28 | Information Office |
| 29 | St Mary's Church |
| 30 | Inverness Hotel |
| 31 | Central Motel |
| 32 | YWCA Hostel |
| 33 | Observatory |
| 34 | Hostel 69 |

station but out over the town and the rocky islets rising just offshore.

### Arts & Crafts Centre

Just below the Paritutu car park is the Rangimarie Arts & Craft Centre on Centennial Drive. It features a display of traditional Maori arts and crafts and you can watch the members working on their carving, weaving and other skills. It's open from 8.30 am to 4 pm on weekdays, and by appointment on weekends.

### Museums & Galleries

The Taranaki Museum, on the corner of Brougham and King streets, has a collection of Maori artefacts and an early colonists'

exhibition. The Govett-Brewster Art Gallery, a modern gallery on Queen St, has a good reputation for its adventurous shows. Both are open from 10.30 am to 5 pm Tuesday to Friday and from 1 to 5 pm on weekends.

### Beaches

Fitzroy and East End beaches are at – you guessed it! – the eastern end of town. Fitzroy is a surf beach. There's also good surf at Back Beach, by the Paritutu Centennial Park at the western end of town, and at Oakura, west of New Plymouth.

### Walks

The PR office has a leaflet on walks around New Plymouth including coastal walks and others through local reserves and parks.

### Tours

The local bus and tour company Neuman's (tel 84-622) at 76 Devon St East – not the national Newmans line – has a variety of local sightseeing tours, ranging from a $17 scenic city tour to an all-day tour around Mt Egmont for $50.

### Aerial Sightseeing

Air New Plymouth (tel 70-500) offers scenic flights around the area including a flight over the snow-capped summit of Mt Egmont – superb if the weather's clear.

### Places to Stay

**Hostels** The *New Plymouth Youth Hostel* (tel 35-720) at 12 Clawton St is fairly new, well equipped and comfortable, but a bit of a walk (1.5 km) from the town centre. Get there on a Frankleigh Park bus (No 4 or 10) departing from Liardet St in the town centre. The nightly cost is $13 and since it's an associate youth hostel you can stay with or without a YHA card.

The *Hostel 69* (tel 87-153) at 69 Mill Rd is a pleasant private hostel with dorm beds for $13 per person ($14 in double rooms). It offers many convenient services including daily shuttles to Mt Egmont, free pick-up when you arrive and free rides to good hitching spots when you leave. It's a friendly place with a large well-kept garden, and if it's not raining there is a fine view of Mt Egmont.

The *YWCA* (tel 86-014) at 15 Bulteel St has accommodation for both women and men when it's not full. Cost is $10 a night with your own bedding, $12 if you use theirs, or $45 a week. The Y is cheap and central but phone ahead to see if it has any vacancies. There is no sign outside it either, so don't think you're at the wrong place when you arrive. The local YMCA has no hostel.

**Guest Houses** The *Aotea Private Hotel* (tel 82-438) on the corner of Young and Weymouth streets has single and twin rooms from $24 per person, B&B from $30 per person. A family-style dinner is available for $10 if you book by lunch time. There's also the *Inverness Inner City Budget Hotel* (tel 80-404) at 48 Lemon St. Both are only about a 5 minute walk from town.

**Hotels** There are several old-style hotels around central New Plymouth, with simple rooms and no private bathrooms. The *White Hart Hotel* (tel 75-442) on the corner of Queen and Devon streets has singles/doubles for $18/30. The *Royal* (tel 80-892) on Brougham St has single rooms for $21 or $31 and double rooms for $36.

The *Tasman Hotel* (tel 86-129) on St Aubyn St is in the same price range. This modern-looking six-storey hotel is beside the sea. The upper and seaside rooms have a great view and it looks like it should be more expensive, but it was actually built just before private bathrooms became the norm and this oversight has forced it to price its rooms at a lower level. Singles/doubles cost $25/39 for one night; if you stay two nights or more it's just $20/31. It has several bars where bistro meals are served, a seaview restaurant, and a band on Friday nights.

On the corner of Devon and Gover streets the *State Establishment* (tel 85-373) has rooms with private bathrooms for $55/60 and it has a Cobb & Co restaurant.

**Motels** New Plymouth has plenty of motels, most of them starting from around $50/60 and up. Some good value places are listed here.

The *Aaron Court Motel* (tel 34-012), 57 Junction Rd, is on the main south highway 3 km from town. It's part of the Aaron Court Caravan Park and has a swimming pool. The *Mid City Motel* (tel 86-109), on the corner of St Aubyn and Weymouth streets, has a spa pool. *Central Motel* (tel 86-444), 86 Eliot St, east of the town centre, is small but fairly convenient.

The *Oakura Beach Motel* (tel Oakura 680), Wairau Rd, Oakura, is 13 km out of town but a bit cheaper than the ones in town. *Timandra Unity Motel* (tel 86-006), 31 Timandra St off Coronation Ave, is within walking distance of town.

**Camping & Cabins** There are several camping sites within easy reach of the centre. The *Belt Rd Camp* (tel 80-228) at 2 Belt Rd is 1.5 km from town, with a sea view overlooking Port Taranaki. Tent sites cost $12 a night for one or two people ($14 with power), or there are on-site caravans for $31 for two.

In Fitzroy, 3.5 km east of the town centre, is the *Fitzroy Camp* (tel 82-870) beside the beach on Beach St. Tent sites cost $6.60 per person, caravan sites cost $14 for two and on-site caravans cost $31 for two. *Princes Tourist Court* (tel 82-566) at 29 Princes St, Fitzroy has sites at $6/11 for one/two people; sites with power cost $13 for one or two people. They also have cabins starting at $23, tourist flats from $35 and motel units from $42 (all two-person rates).

The *Aaron Court Caravan Park* (tel 34-012) is 3 km from the town centre. Rates for one or two people cost $12 for camping sites, $14 with power, $26 for cabins or $44 for tourist flats.

**Home Hosting** New Plymouth has a home hosting scheme which provides local guides to show you the sights and a host panel who welcome you into their homes. Contact the PR office.

## Places to Eat

**Snacks & Fast Food** New Zealand is a small country and New Plymouth is a small town but the *McDonald's* on the corner of Leach and Eliot streets is absolutely huge. There's an equally huge *Kentucky Fried Chicken* on the corner of Courtenay and Gover streets and a *Pizza Hut* east of the town centre on the corner of Sackville St and Clemow Rd, Fitzroy. *California Takeaways* at 201a Coronation Ave and *Lotus Chinese Takeaways* at 63 Devon St East are both open every day for lunch and dinner.

*The Steps Restaurant* at 37 Gover St is a pleasant and popular place for breakfast or lunch to take away or eat there, and there's an outdoor patio. Health food is the speciality and it's inexpensive. Most main courses, served with a choice of salads, cost just $3 to $5 and desserts start around $2.50. The Steps is open from 7.30 am to 4 pm Monday to Thursday and 7.30 am to 9 pm on Friday.

Up in Pukekura Park, the *Park Kiosk* has good snacks in beautiful surroundings.

For more variety right in the City Centre shopping mall there's a dining area surrounded by a number of takeaways including Chinese, Italian, seafood, wholefood, sandwich and dessert counters.

**Pub Food** There's a *Cobb & Co* in the State Establishment on the corner of Devon St East and Gover St, with the usual Cobb & Co menu and the usual excellent hours of 7 am to 10 pm daily. Other places with pub food include the *Tasman Hotel* on St Aubyn St and the *Westown Motor Hotel* on Maratahu St, near the youth hostel. Old-style hotels in the town centre that have restaurants include the *Royal Hotel* on Brougham St and the old-fashioned *White Hart Hotel* on the corner of Devon St West and Queen St.

**Restaurants** The *Black Olive Restaurant*, on Egmont St near the Devon St West corner, has a curious menu, half of which is of absolutely straightforward pub-style dishes like schnitzel, steak and ham steak, and half of which is Indonesian dishes. Main courses cost $14 to $19 and it's BYO, as is

*Bellissimo*, upstairs at 38 Currie St. Here the flavour is Italian, with starters for $7, main dishes for $15 and desserts for $5, plus many lighter meals and snacks. It's a surprisingly large and locally popular restaurant, open every night from 5 to 11 pm, except Sundays and Mondays. The blackboard at the top of the stairs announces 'bonjorno' – I think it's Italo-Australian for a good journalist.

The *Taj Indian Cafe* opposite the Opera House on Devon St West is small, relaxed and has excellent food. For dinner, starters cost from $2 to $4.50, main courses from $7 to $9, and side dishes $3. There's a lunch time special of one meat dish, two salads and rice for $4.75, as well as regular NZ-style lunches and takeaways.

There are many Chinese places including the *Tong*, 39 Devon St West, which also does takeaways. *Gareth's*, 182 Devon St East, is good but more pricey. The *Dancing Bear* on the corner of Devon St West and Egmont St is good for a night out, with steaks, seafood and a big salad bar; it's open every night. Right up, price-wise, towards the New Plymouth stratosphere is *L'Escargot* at 37-39 Brougham St, which is *the* licensed place for a fancy night out.

## Entertainment

The Brooklands Bowl at the entrance to Brooklands Park is a large, fine outdoor theatre. All kinds of concerts are held here; the PR office will have current schedules and ticket prices. At the Opera House on Devon St West you can see not only operas but every other kind of performance as well.

Many of the local pubs and hotels have live entertainment several nights a week. The *Westown Motor Hotel* on Maratahu St has a band, lots of people and a moderate cover charge on weekends. It's fairly close to the youth hostel. The *Tasman Hotel* on the seafront has a live band for dancing on Friday nights.

Other central spots with entertainment include the *White Hart Hotel*, *Ziggy's Nightclub*, the *Duke of Devon* and the *DB Tasman*. The *Bell Block Hotel* just east of town also has bands at weekends.

## Getting There & Away
**Air** Air New Zealand (tel 87-674) has direct flights several times daily to Auckland and Wellington, with connections to other centres. Its office is at 12-14 Devon St East.

**Bus** The InterCity bus depot (tel 87-729) is on St Aubyn St, near Egmont St. Newmans Coachlines (tel 75-482) is at 32 Queen St. Both companies have frequent buses heading north to Hamilton or Auckland and south-east to Wanganui or Wellington, with a transfer at Bulls for buses to Palmerston North and on to Napier. To or from Auckland or Wellington takes between 6½ and 7½ hours; to or from Wanganui takes about 3 hours.

Don't confuse the national Newmans bus line that operates long distance services with the local Neuman's bus line that does sightseeing tours.

**Hitching** Hitching is reasonable from Wanganui and Wellington in the south. From Auckland, you might have to wait a long time around Awakino Gorge. It's all a matter of luck.

## Getting Around
**Airport Transport** Withatruck (tel 511-777, 512-328 after hours) operates an airport bus service every day except Saturdays; the fare is $7.

**Bus** There are local buses in New Plymouth but they don't run particularly often, and not at all on Sundays.

## AROUND NEW PLYMOUTH
Mt Egmont, of course, is the primary attraction of the New Plymouth area, but there are several other places of interest.

### Waitara
Waitara is 13 km east of New Plymouth on SH 3. If you turn off SH 3 at Brixton, just before Waitara, and head 7 km south, you'll reach the site of the Pukarangiora pa. It's beautifully sited on a high cliff by the Waitara River, but historically it was a particularly bloody site.

Rafting and canoeing on the Waiwhakaiho and the Waitara rivers is a local activity. Check with Waiawaka Rafting/Canoeing (tel 72-068) at Inglewood.

Just beyond Waitara on SH 3 east of New Plymouth is a conversion plant which converts natural gas to petrol.

### Tupare
Tupare, 7 km south of New Plymouth, is a fine three-storey Tudor style house surrounded by 3.6 hectares of lush English garden. It's part of the Queen Elizabeth II National Trust; look for it at 487 Mangorei Rd on the Waiwhakaiho River. Admission is $4 (children free).

### Hurworth
This early homestead, on Carrington Rd, about 8 km from New Plymouth en route to Pukeiti, dates from 1856. Its builder and first occupant, Harry Atkinson, later became premier of New Zealand four times. The house was the only one at this site to survive the Taranaki wars and is today owned by the New Zealand Historic Places Trust. Further on towards Pukeiti is the Pouakai Wildlife Reserve with deer, donkeys and other animals.

### Pukeiti Rhododendron Trust
The Pukeiti Rhododendron Trust is a private garden surrounded by native bush, 29 km from New Plymouth. To get there, just keep following Carrington St all the way from town. The road passes between the Pouakai and Kaitake ranges, both part of Egmont National Park, but separated by the Trust. Peak flowering of rhododendrons generally takes place in September, October and November, though it's worth going up any time of the year. Admission is $5.

# Mt Egmont – Taranaki

The coastal city of New Plymouth is backed

by the cone of 2518 metre Mt Egmont – a dormant volcano that looks remarkably like Japan's Mt Fuji or the Philippines' Mayon. There's an ongoing dispute about whether the mountain's official name should remain Mt Egmont or revert to its pre-Pakeha name of Taranaki.

Geologically, Mt Egmont is the youngest of a series of three large volcanoes on one fault line: the others being Kaitake and Pouakai. Egmont last erupted 350 years ago, but it is regarded as being dormant rather than extinct. An interesting feature of Egmont is the small subsidiary cone on the flank of the main cone and 2 km south of the main crater, called Fantham Peak (1962 metres). The top 1400 metres of Egmont is covered in lava flows and there are a few that descend to 800 metres.

There's a saying in Taranaki – Taranaki also refers to the region surrounding Egmont – that if you can see Egmont it's going to rain, and if you can't see Egmont it's already raining! There is some truth in this. The mountain is one of the wettest spots in New Zealand with about 7000 mm of rain recorded annually at North Egmont (compared with 1584 mm in nearby New Plymouth), as the mountain catches the moisture-laden winds coming in from the Tasman Sea and sweeps them up to freezing heights.

Naturally it tends to be quite windy up there too. Nonetheless it doesn't rain *every* day and Egmont really is a spectacular sight on a clear day, even if it does try to cover itself in protective cloud.

## History

The mountain was supremely sacred to the Maoris, both as a burial site for chiefs and as a hideout in times of danger. According to legend, Taranaki – Mt Egmont's Maori name – was once a part of the group of volcanoes at Tongariro. He was forced to leave rather hurriedly when Tongariro caught him with Pihanga, Tongariro's lover – the volcano near Lake Taupo.

So angry was Tongariro at this betrayal that he blew his top (as only volcanoes can

when upset) and Taranaki took off for the coast. Heading south he gouged out the Wanganui River on the way and then strolled across to his current location where he's remained ever since.

The Maoris did not settle the area between Taranaki and Pihanga very heavily, perhaps because they feared the lovers might be reunited with dire consequences. Most of the Maori settlements in this district were clustered along the coast between Mokau and Patea, concentrated particularly around Urenui and Waitara.

The Egmont National Park was created in 1900 and is the second-oldest national park in New Zealand.

## Information

If you plan to tramp in Egmont National Park, get a map from the DOC office in New Plymouth. There is a National Park Interpretation Centre open daily at Dawson Falls (tel Stratford 5457), a Visitors Centre at North Egmont (tel Inglewood 68-710) also open daily, and a ranger station on the road to Stratford Mountain House. There are also information centres around the mountain in Stratford (tel 5399), Hawera (tel 86-599, 88-599) and Manaia (tel 8189, ext. 76).

## Trekking & Skiing

The mountain is a popular winter skiing centre and in the summer you can climb it in a day. The Taranaki Alpine Club, the PR office or DOC can provide more information and will be able to put you in touch with a licensed guide. Wilderness Treks (tel Hawera 87-400) at Hawera also organise guided bushwalks and mountain climbs including summit climbs on Mt Egmont.

Egmont should not be climbed by the inexperienced without a guide. In good conditions the climb can be reasonably easy, but there are precipitous bluffs and steep icy slopes, and Egmont is subject to very rapid weather changes. It is said to have claimed over 50 lives. Don't be put off, but don't be deceived.

If you intend tramping, get a map and consult a Park Ranger, as some tracks have

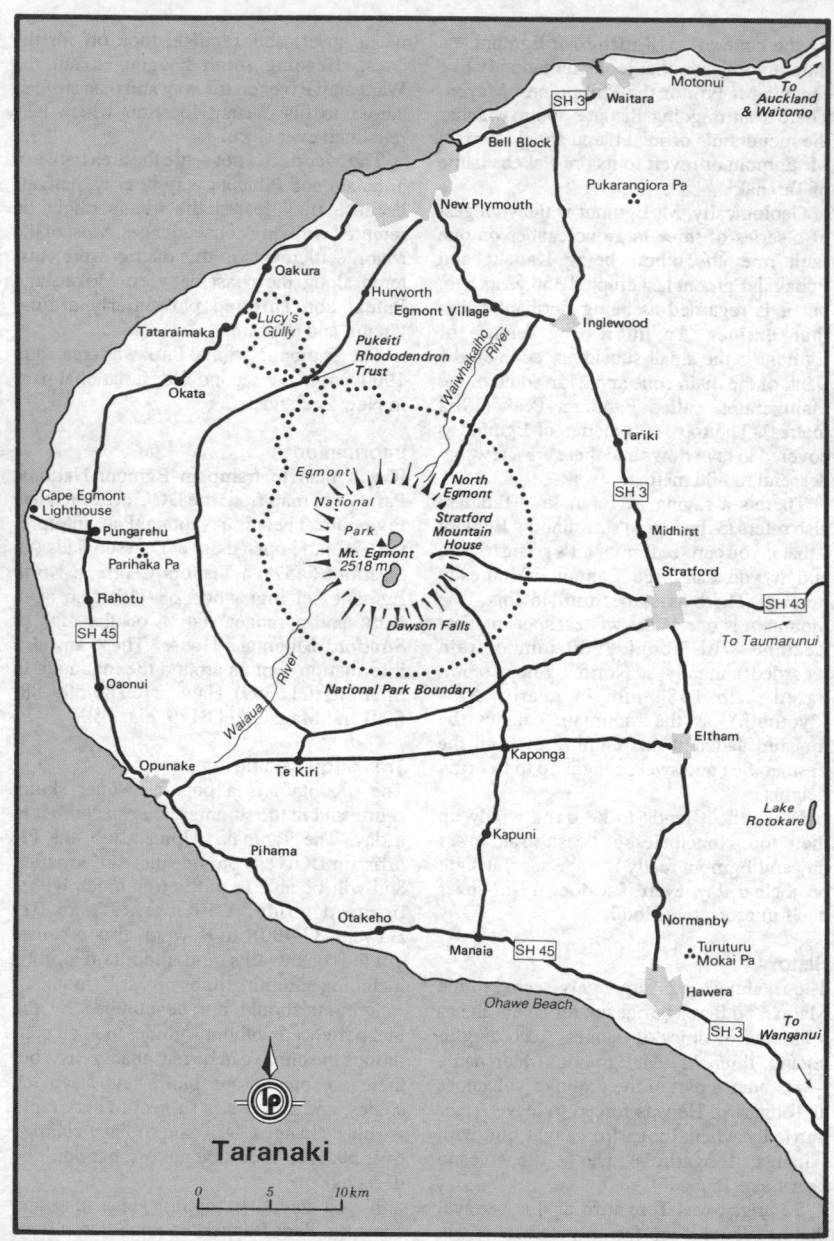

Taranaki

been closed and other planned ones may have opened. The North Egmont Chalet, marked on many maps, no longer exists.

A trip to the end of Egmont Rd is worthwhile for the view, but there are numerous long and short tracks and bushwalks as well. The Visitors Centre at North Egmont has lots of interesting displays on the park and the mountain, an audiovisual feature, and a cafe.

The roads to the Stratford Mountain House and Dawson Falls also have many worthwhile tracks and bushwalks. From the Mountain House, Pembroke Rd continues 3 km to the Plateau and from there a 1.5 km walk takes you to the main ski field (not much by comparison with Ruapehu, the main skiing area of North Island) on Egmont. You can hire skiing equipment at the Mountain House (see Places to Stay).

### Places to Stay

**Hostels** *The Camphouse*, a bunkhouse beside the North Egmont Visitors Centre, has bunks at $8, with hot plates for cooking and hot showers; bring your own sleeping bag and cooking utensils. *Rahiri Lodge*, at the North Egmont entrance to the park, has just three double rooms. Both are administered by the North Egmont Visitors Centre (tel Inglewood 68-710).

At Dawson Falls, by the Park Information Centre, there is bunkhouse accommodation for trampers at *Konini Lodge* for $12 per person. Bring your own sleeping bag, food supplies and eating utensils.

**Guest Houses** The *Dawson Falls Tourist Lodge* (tel Stratford 5457) has accommodation for $75/98 for singles/doubles, including breakfast. A courtesy car will meet public transport in Stratford. Bookings for Konini Lodge are made through Dawson Falls Tourist Lodge.

On the eastern side of Mt Egmont, the *Mountain House* (tel Stratford 6100) on Pembroke Rd, Stratford, has serviced units for $69/77 for singles/doubles or chalet motel-type units with kitchen facilities at $60/70. It's about 15 km off the main road.

**Camping & Cabins** There are also a number of tramping huts scattered about the mountain, administered by DOC and reachable only by trails. Most cost $8 a night, but some cost only $4. You provide your own cooking, eating and sleeping gear, they provide bunks and mattresses, and no bookings are necessary, it's all on a first come, first served basis.

There are motor camps in Stratford and Eltham, handy to the eastern and south-eastern sides of Egmont, but camping is not allowed within the park itself, you're supposed to use the tramping huts.

### Getting There & Away

There are quite a few points of access to the park, but three roads lead almost right up to where the heavy bush ends. The closest to New Plymouth is Egmont Rd, turning off SH 3 and leading to North Egmont (24 km). The other two roads lead from the east to Stratford Mountain House and from the southeast to Dawson Falls.

Public buses don't go to the Egmont National Park but there's a private shuttle service from New Plymouth (tel 72-569) which costs $10 for a round-trip sightseeing tour, or $15 if you want to be dropped off in the park and picked up at another time, either later in the same day or on another day. Mountain Excursions in New Plymouth (tel 82-315) provides a similar service.

### AROUND MT EGMONT-TARANAKI

The mountain route follows SH 45 from New Plymouth anticlockwise around the coast, meeting SH 3 again at Hawera. The round trip (SH 45, returning via SH 3) is 186 km, although short cuts can be taken. There are numerous attractions en route or nearby.

### Lucy's Gully

Lucy's Gully, 23 km from New Plymouth on SH 45, is one of the few places where exotic trees are being maintained in a national park. A pleasant picnic area, it is also the start of a couple of tracks into the Kaitake Ranges. Further along SH 45, turn west at Pungarehu onto Cape Rd to reach Cape Egmont Light-

Mt Egmont

house, an interesting sight but not open to visitors.

### Parihaka

Inland 1 or 2 km from Pungarehu is the Maori village of Parihaka, formerly the stronghold of the Maori prophet and chief Te Whiti and once one of the largest native villages in New Zealand. Te Whiti led a passive resistance campaign against the ruthless land confiscation that was taking place with the expansion of White settlement. In the last military campaign in Taranaki, Te Whiti was defeated and jailed, and in 1881 Parihaka was razed. The heavily armed troops found themselves opposed only by dancing children.

The spirit of Te Whiti still lives on, and descendants and followers meet at Parihaka annually. Many other places in Taranaki are steeped in their Maori past.

### Oaonui

Further south along the coast is Oaonui, the landfall of the gas pipeline from the Maui platform and the site of the onshore processing plant. The Information Centre at Oaonui houses scale models of the platform and processing plant. You can't visit the plant itself.

### Kaponga

In Kaponga, on the road between Opunake and Eltham about 8 km south of the national park, are the large Hollard Gardens, administered by the Queen Elizabeth II National Trust. It's most colourful from September to November when the rhododendrons are blooming but many other plantings provide colour all year round. The vast number of rare plants make it a horticulturalist's delight, with posted half hour and 1 hour walks through various gardens. Admission is $4 (children free).

### Kapuni

Just over 70 km from New Plymouth, off the main road to the south of Egmont, is Kapuni. Natural gas discovered at Kapuni was the first petroleum find of any size in New Zealand. It is now piped to Auckland and Wellington. The oil condensate is also piped out of Kapuni to New Plymouth, from where it is shipped to New Zealand's oil refinery at

Top:  Tudor Towers, Rotorua (TW)
Left:  Mt Tarawera, Rotorua (TW)
Right:  Geyser at Whakarewarewa Thermal Reserve, Rotorua (MC)

Top: New Plymouth Power Station (TW)
Left: Wairakei Geothermal Power Station (TW)
Right: Black Water Rafting, Waitomo (BWR)

Marsden Point near Whangarei, north of Auckland.

## Hawera

At Hawera the SH 45 coast road meets SH 3, which runs inland around the mountain. Elvis fans might be interested in visiting the Kevin Wasley Elvis Presley Record Room (tel 87-624) on Argyle St. Hawera also has the private Tawhiti Museum on Ohangai Rd, with dioramas and life-size models depicting aspects of Maori and colonial life. It's open from 10 am to 4 pm Friday to Monday, except from June to August when it's open on Sundays only.

Two km north of Hawera on the Turuturu road are the remains of the pre-European Turuturu Mokai Pa.

## Eltham & the Lakes

About 20 km north of Hawera is Eltham, well known for its cheeses. You can head south-east for 11 km down the Rawhitiroa Rd to Lake Rotokare, the largest stretch of inland water in Taranaki. Here there is a 1½ to 2 hour walk around the lake through native bush. The artificial Lake Rotorangi, popular for boating and fishing, is also near by, with cruises operating on the lake.

## Stratford

North of Eltham is Stratford, named after Stratford-on-Avon in England and with all the streets named after Shakespearian characters. There is a Pioneer Village in the town.

## Taumarunui

From Stratford, the Whangamomona-Tangarakau Gorge route (SH 43) heads off towards Taumarunui in central North Island. It's a good trip if you can put up with the road; the worst part is unsealed and it's hilly bush country.

# Wanganui

Population 41,000

The coastal city of Wanganui is midway between Wellington and New Plymouth. Its tourist brochure proclaims it as 'The Friendly City' and the people really do seem very friendly and helpful. The city has a number of attractions and it's the jumping-off point for jet-boat and canoeing trips on the Wanganui River.

The river, which enters the sea at Wanganui, is the longest navigable and the second-longest river in New Zealand. It starts off on Mt Tongariro and travels 315 km to its mouth in the Wanganui basin. The estuary, over 30 km long, is the area known to the early Maoris as Wanganui or big inlet.

## History

Kupe, the great Maori explorer and navigator, is believed to have travelled up the Wanganui River for about 20 km around 900 AD. The Maoris established themselves in the area soon after the great migration from Hawaiki (after 1350), and by the time the first White settlers moved in around the late 1830s there were numerous Maori settlements scattered up and down the river.

White settlement at Wanganui was hastened along when the New Zealand Company was unable to keep up with the supply and demand for land around Wellington. In 1840 many Wellington settlers moved to Wanganui and founded a permanent settlement there, the signing of the deed being conducted on the site now known as Moutoa Gardens.

The settlement was initially called Petre after one of the directors of the New Zealand Company, but his name wasn't destined to last on the maps for long. In 1854 it was changed to Wanganui, the name Kupe had given the river, which means large bay or stretch of water. When the Maoris understood that the gifts the Pakehas had presented them were in exchange for the permanent acquisition of their land, 7 years of bitter opposition followed. The Whites brought in thousands of troops to occupy Queen's Park, and the Rutland Stockade dominated the hill. Ultimately, the struggle was settled by arbitration and when the Maori wars were waged

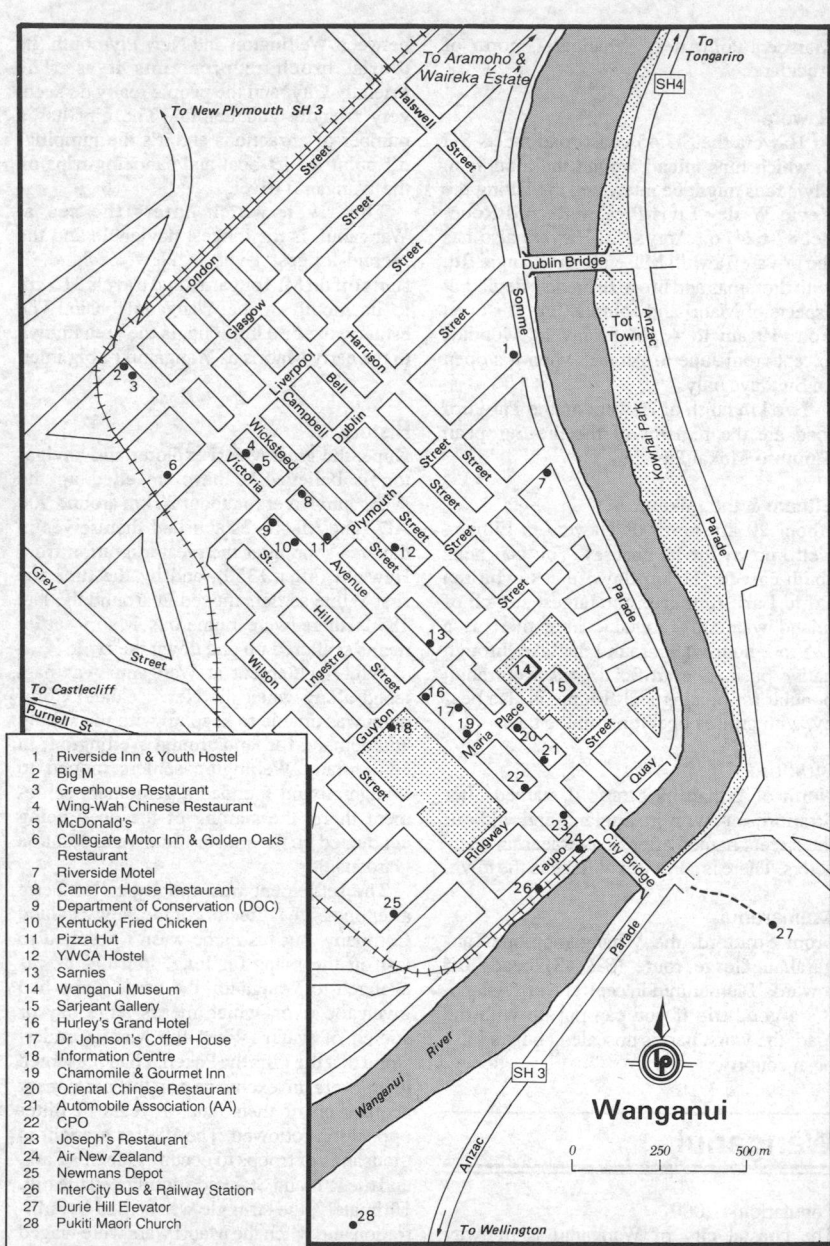

1   Riverside Inn & Youth Hostel
2   Big M
3   Greenhouse Restaurant
4   Wing-Wah Chinese Restaurant
5   McDonald's
6   Collegiate Motor Inn & Golden Oaks
    Restaurant
7   Riverside Motel
8   Cameron House Restaurant
9   Department of Conservation (DOC)
10  Kentucky Fried Chicken
11  Pizza Hut
12  YWCA Hostel
13  Sarnies
14  Wanganui Museum
15  Sarjeant Gallery
16  Hurley's Grand Hotel
17  Dr Johnson's Coffee House
18  Information Centre
19  Chamomile & Gourmet Inn
20  Oriental Chinese Restaurant
21  Automobile Association (AA)
22  CPO
23  Joseph's Restaurant
24  Air New Zealand
25  Newmans Depot
26  InterCity Bus & Railway Station
27  Durie Hill Elevator
28  Pukiti Maori Church

Wanganui

0          250          500 m

with the Taranaki tribes, the Wanganui Maoris actively assisted their Pakehas.

## Orientation
Victoria Ave is the main shopping street. You'll find most points of interest along or close to this busy avenue.

## Information
The Information Centre (tel 53-286) is on Guyton St, between St Hill and Wilson streets. It's open from 8.30 am to 5 pm Monday to Friday, and from 9 am to 2 pm on weekends and public holidays. The people there are very helpful and there's a great model of the country from Wanganui right up to the Tongariro National Park. The Information Centre can advise on jet-boat trips and canoeing.

The DOC office (tel 52-402), on the corner of Victoria Ave and Dublin St, is open from 8 am to 4.30 pm Monday to Friday. The CPO is on Ridgway St, and there's an AA office at 78 Victoria Ave.

## Wanganui Museum
The Wanganui Museum, opposite the Civic Centre on Wicksteed St, is the largest and one of the best regional museums in New Zealand, so if you've not had the chance to study Maori culture elsewhere, stop here. Apart from the Maori collection, which includes a fine war canoe and some nasty-looking meres – those elegant but lethal greenstone clubs – the museum also has a good wildlife collection, particularly the selection of moa skeletons. The giant moa is so tall its head disappears into a skylight! The museum is open from 10 am to 4 pm on weekdays and 1 to 4.30 pm on weekends and holidays; admission is $2 (children 60 cents, family $5).

## Sarjeant Gallery
Next to the museum is Wanganui's equally good art gallery, with an extensive permanent exhibition and frequent special exhibits. The gallery is open from 10.30 am to 4 pm Monday to Friday, 10.30 am to noon and

1.30 to 4 pm on Saturday, and 1.30 to 4 pm on Sunday. Admission is free.

## War Memorial Hall
Also in the Civic Centre area is the War Memorial Hall, comprising a concert chamber, convention hall and pioneer room. The public library is up behind the gallery.

## Parks
Wanganui has several parks right in the city centre including the pleasant little park in which the museum, gallery and library are situated. The complex is up a hill right beside the town centre and there are good views from the war memorial.

If you cross the City Bridge at the end of Victoria Ave and turn left, there's a very pleasant riverside park, Kowhai Park, extending all the way up to and beyond the Dublin Bridge, with an arboretum, plantings of exotic trees and a section with lots of entertainment for children, including a Tot Town Railway, bumper boats, mini-golf and a playground.

The Virginia Lake Scenic Reserve (Rotokawau) is about 3 km from the CPO on SH 3 heading towards New Plymouth. It's a beautiful 18.5 hectare reserve with a walk-in aviary, various theme gardens, a fountain, and several statues set around the lake, which takes about 25 minutes to walk around. The winter gardens and aviary are open from 10 am to 4 pm daily, and the rest of the reserve is always open.

## Durie Hill & Bastia Hill
Take Victoria Ave across the river from the town centre and immediately to the left you'll see the carved gateway entrance to the Durie Hill elevator. You follow a tunnel into the hillside then, for $1.75, ride up through the hill to the summit 65 metres above.

There are two viewpoints at the top: a lower one on the top of the lift machinery room, and a higher 31 metre watchtower built from fossilised shellrock. This higher one, the War Memorial Tower, closes at 6 pm, but you can go up the other one anytime. From here there's a fine view over the town and all the way to Mt Egmont, Mt Ruapehu or the South Island if the weather is clear.

In summer the elevator operates from 7.30 am to 7 pm Monday to Friday, 9 am to 8 pm on Saturdays, and 1 to 6 pm on Sundays. In winter it closes a bit earlier, at 6.30 pm, on weekdays and Saturdays.

Bastia Hill is another good lookout point, with a huge water tower that dominates the skyline view from anywhere in town. You can climb up the water tower on a spiral staircase, but only to the first couple of levels; after that a steel gate keeps you from reaching the top.

## Putiki Church

If you turn right after the Victoria Ave bridge and continue for a km or so you come to Putiki Church (St Pauls) – a plain enough little place from the outside but the interior is magnificent, completely covered in Maori carvings and Tukutuku wall panels.

## Waireka Estate

If you're in Wanganui at the height of summer, follow the Aramoho road 4 km past the Aramoho Park Camp to Upper Aramoho, where you'll find the Waireka Estate on Papaiti Rd. John and Margaret-Anne Barnett, the young couple who own the house, have been restoring the property and its grounds. In summer they open the gates to visitors and conduct tours around the curious museum collection housed in what was once the 'gentlemen's smoking room'.

Margaret-Anne's great-grandparents, who built the house in 1912, brought some of the items with them from England in 1876 and added others in New Zealand. John explains the various items, shows you how to handle a mere, and caps the visit by firing the cannon on the lawn. The estate is open from 9.30 am to 5 pm every day from 26 December (Boxing Day) to 29 January. The rest of the year it's only open for groups by arrangement (phone 25-729). Admission is $4 (children $1). There are donkey cart rides for the kids and Devonshire teas are served in the garden.

## Other Attractions

The Information Centre has maps outlining a Golden Arrow Scenic Drive (you can't miss the golden arrows as you explore around town) and several scenic walks in and near Wanganui. If you prefer sightseeing from the air, Mt Aero Tours (tel Wanganui 53-994 or Raetihi 54-349) has helicopter flights over the Whanganui and Tongariro National Parks, starting at about $85 per person.

The Splash Centre in the Springvale Park Sports Centre off London St is a large indoor heated swimming pool open all year round, from 6 am to 9 pm Monday to Thursday, 6 am to 8 pm on Friday and Saturday, and 8 am to 8 pm on Sunday. Admission is $2.50 (children $1.50).

The Donne Studio, 348 Somme Parade, at Cedar Drive, beside the river, shows the art of Peter Donne who has won many honours for his creations including bone carvings, paintings, and several other art forms, even including T-shirt art. The studio is open all day Sunday or whenever the sign says 'open', and at other times by request (phone 39-479).

## River Cruises

The historic 18 metre MV *Waireka* riverboat was built in England in 1905 and shipped to Wanganui in pieces, where it was reconstructed and has been in service continually ever since. From 26 December till the end of February it departs from Moutoa Gardens at 10 am and 2 pm daily for an Estate Cruise which visits the Holly Lodge Estate Winery, the Waireka Estate Museum and the Upokongaro Country Village. The fare is $11 (children $6). The Waireka also does moonlight cruises and rapids adventure trips, a memorable experience.

In summer you can have a 5 day trip on the MV *Wakapai* for about $517 (children $315), everything included. Phone Mr Winston Oliver (tel Raetihi 54-443) for schedule and bookings.

Holly Lodge operates the paddleboat *Otonui*, which departs from the City Marina beneath the City Bridge at 10 am on weekdays for a 3 hour return trip to Holly Lodge. On Saturdays and school holidays there are two trips, departing from the bridge at 10 am and 2 pm, and on Sundays it departs from Holly Lodge at 10 am and 2 pm for a 2 hour trip upriver. Jet-boat tours are also conducted from Holly Lodge twice daily (see Jet-boat Trips).

Holly Lodge Estate (tel Wanganui 39-344) is a pleasant and interesting place, being the only winery in New Zealand which can be visited by river. It has a porcelain doll factory that produces replicas of antique dolls, an aviary, many recreational facilities, a licensed restaurant, guided winery tours and, of course, free wine tasting. Cost for the wine trip is $11 (children $7) and if you book ahead you can enjoy a smorgasbord lunch for $12.50.

### Jet-Boat Trips

Before the Wanganui calms down on its way to the sea, it has a whole series of spectacular rapids – ideal for jet-boating. Jet-boats, an NZ invention, have an inboard engine but no propeller. Instead, water is drawn in and shot out the back, like a jet. Since there is no easily-damaged prop they can run in extremely shallow water – shooting rapids going upriver as well as down is a jet-boat speciality.

Several operators run jet-boat tours. Holly Lodge Estate (tel 39-344) do trips upriver to the Hipango Park Scenic Reserve, departing from the lodge at 10 am and 2 pm daily. They take 2 hours and cost $33 (children $25) including refreshments at the park. Longer or shorter trips can be arranged.

Eric Hammond (tel 27-796) does various trips including a 10 hour journey to the 'Bridge to Nowhere' for $94. Built in 1937, the bridge has hardly been used since. Shorter trips include a 6 hour excursion to Manganui-A-Te-Ao ($68), a 2½ hour trip to the Kawana Flour Mill ($44), and a 1 hour trip to Ahu Ahu ($22). All prices are return but can be greatly reduced by backloading. Hammond also hires canoes for half-day to 4-day trips, and does tramping, camping and horse trekking too.

It's 77 km upriver along a back road to Pipiriki from where you can make shorter trips, but although the road is scenic there is not much traffic and no regular public transport. You can, however, get to Pipiriki on the Monday to Friday mail run. See Getting There & Away and Around Wanganui for more on Pipiriki.

The section between Pipiriki and Drop Scene is the most exciting part of the river. Departing from Pipiriki, Pipiriki Jet Boat Tours (tel Raetihi 54-733) do half-hour return trips to Drop Scene for $25, 1 hour return trips to Manganui-A-Te-Ao for $30, or 4 hour return trips to Bridge to Nowhere for $55 (children half price on all tours). Ramanui Lodge (tel Raetihi 58-799), 21 km upriver from Pipiriki, also operates a variety of jet-boat tours from Pipiriki.

There are tours which combine a mail run bus trip to Pipiriki with a jet-boat trip from there. A minimum of three to four people is usually required and on all-day jaunts you'll need to bring lunch. Parkas and leggings are provided, but take warm clothing with you.

### Canoeing Trips

The Wanganui River is also popular for canoeing. Baldwin Canoe Adventures (tel 44-560) in Wanganui run trips for 2 to 6 days up the river and also hire kayaks and two-person canoes by the hour or the day. Yeti Tours (tel Ohakune 58-197) also run 6 day canoe trips up the river, departing weekly, December to March, from either Wanganui or Ohakune. The basic cost is $380 per person, but it's extra if they supply food, tent, or other items.

Yeti Tours also do shorter 2 day trips on the Rangitikei River and several others including a 2 to 3 hour action-packed rapids trip on the Lower Tongariro. They also hire canoes ($45 per day), kayaks ($25 per day) and tents ($18 per day) if you want to do your own trips, and can provide transport from Ohakune to the starting point at Taumarunui.

River Safaris/Rivercity Tracks (tel 58-395), 29 Ridgway St, Wanganui, is another outfit that offers 1 to 6 day canoe trips, hires kayaks ($19 per day) and canoes ($35 per day) and generally specialises in the outdoors.

Canoes can also be hired at Pipiriki (tel 54-635) and if you don't want to paddle upstream they will provide transport upriver and you can paddle back down. From Taumarunui, for example, it's about a 2 to 5 day trip. Pioneer Jet Boat Tours (tel 8074) in Taumarunui has jet-boats, kayaks and Canadian canoes and can arrange a variety of trips on the river.

### Other Tours

River City Tours (tel 32-529) operates from the Riverside Inn in Wanganui and has such a variety of jet-boat tours, canoe trips, bushwalks up to 4 days long, skiing trips, and so on that it's safe to say they'll do just about anything. Rates are about $88 to $100 per person per day (less 20% for children under 12) for a variety of 1 to 5 day pre-planned trips, but they will also make arrangements to do anything else you have in mind.

### Places to Stay

**Hostels** The *Wanganui Associate Youth Hostel* (tel 32-529), 2 Plymouth St, occupies three cabins, each sleeping three, in the rear part of the Riverside Inn by the river. The nightly rate is $13 and since it's an associate hostel you can stay there whether or not you're a YHA member.

For women only there's a small *YWCA* (tel 57-480) at 232 Wicksteed St – so small that you're unlikely to get in unless you book well ahead. It's a stately old home turned hostel, with single rooms at $10 per night if you bring your own bedding, $12 if you use theirs, or, on a permanent basis, $41 per week.

The *Alwyn Motor Court* has bunkroom accommodation for $14 per person (see Camping & Cabins).

**Guest Houses** There's been a spate of closures of the traditional old hotels but there are still some B&Bs. The *Riverside Inn* (tel 32-529), 2 Plymouth St, is a restored colonial building with B&B for $33/45 for singles/doubles. The Youth Hostel is in the rear part. Don't confuse it with the nearby *Riverside Motel* on Somme Parade.

**Hotels** The *Hurley's Grand Hotel* (tel 50-955) on Guyton St is about the only hotel of the old school still surviving in Wanganui. All rooms have private facilities and cost from $72/77. Suites are more expensive.

**Motels** There are plenty of motels in Wanganui including the *Alwyn Motor Court* and the more expensive *Avro Caravan Court* (see Camping & Cabins). Other cheaper motels include the *Acacia Park Motel* (tel 39-093), 140 Anzac Parade, with single/double units for $52/62, and the similarly-priced *River City Motel* (tel 39-107) on Halswell St, below St John's Hill. At 181 Great North Rd (SH 3), the *Oasis Motor Lodge* (tel 54-636) has singles from $58 to $68, doubles from $68 to $78. Wanganui has about 30 other motels; the Information Centre can supply details on all of them.

**Camping & Cabins** Most of Wanganui's camps and cabins are out at Castlecliff, 8 km from Wanganui. You can get there on the local Castlecliff bus any day except Sunday.

There's no camping at the *Alwyn Motor Court* (tel 44-500), 65 Karaka St, Castlecliff, but it has cabins for $14 per person, tourist flats for $28/40 for singles/doubles and motel units for $45/53. If you don't have your own bedding you can hire it there and on Sunday they provide free transport from Wanganui. It's a pleasant place right on the beach.

The *Castlecliff Camp* (tel 45-699, 42-227) in Castlecliff, by the beach on the corner of Karaka and Rangiora streets, has camping sites for $6 per person ($7 with power); cabins cost $11/18 for singles/doubles and on-site caravans cost $21 for doubles.

The *Aramoho Holiday Park* (tel 38-402) is at 460 Somme Parade, 6½ km north of the town centre on the town side bank of the Wanganui River. Aramoho buses run there but not on weekends. Camping is $8/14 for singles/doubles ($15 with power), and there are cabins from $23 to $25 for singles/doubles and tourist flats from $46.

Closest to the city is the *Avro Caravan Court* (tel 58-462), 36 Alma Rd, just 1½ km from the centre. Sites cost $15.50 for two, but unlike most motor camps there are no kitchen facilities. There are motel rooms here from around $54 to $60 single and $65 to $75 twin or double. *Gonville Caravan Park* (tel 42-012) is at 86 Bignell St, 3 km from town. Sites cost from $11 for two and on-site caravans sleeping two are also $11.

## Places to Eat

**Snacks & Fast Food** There's the usual collection of sandwich places along Victoria Ave but Wanganui's slightly old-fashioned air is seen at its worst in these places. Most of them have terrible, limp, junky white bread excuses for a sandwich. They're the sort of places that give McDonald's a good name.

Places a bit better than this dubious standard include *Chamomile* and the *Gourmet Inn*, both in the Maria Mall, just off Victoria Ave on Maria Place. *Erick's*, 178 Victoria Ave, is also pretty good. *Sarnies*, on Victoria Ave close to the Guyton St intersection, has a wide range of individually wrapped sandwiches. Or try *Dr Johnson's Coffee House* in the Tudor Court, Victoria Ave, for sandwiches and light refreshments.

Or give up on sandwiches and head for *McDonald's*, further down at 314 Victoria Ave. Before you come to it you'll pass the *Pizza Hut* and *Kentucky Fried Chicken*. The *Big M* all the way at the end of Victoria Ave, on the corner of London St, is another fast food outlet with burgers and the like.

**Pub Food** Wanganui is a long way from the best place in New Zealand for eating out but it does have a few good restaurants if you're prepared to pay the price. Hidden away in the innermost recesses of Hurley's Grand Hotel, on the corner of Guyton and St Hill streets, the *99 The Strand* bistro features the pub food regulars and there's also a more formal restaurant.

**Restaurants** The *Golden Oaks* restaurant at the Collegiate Motor Inn on Liverpool St is a bit on the expensive side for à la carte dining, but twice a week it has good-value smorgasbord dinners: Friday for $15.50 and Sunday for $17, served from 6 to 9 pm.

Also a bit pricey but good value is the award-winning *Bassano* Italian restaurant at the Bryvern Motor Inn, opposite McDonald's on Victoria Ave, with a plush atmosphere and main courses from $14 to $17. The Bryvern also has a cafe for daytime meals.

For Chinese food try *Wing-Wah*, also near McDonald's at 330 Victoria Ave, or if you don't want to walk the few blocks from the town centre there's the *Oriental Chinese Restaurant & Takeaways* at 5 Maria Place, near the Museum.

*Joseph's* at 13 Victoria Ave is also not bad, and *The Greenhouse* beside the Big M at the corner of Victoria Ave and London St is good for steak and seafood, but if you want to pull out all the stops and splurge then head for *Cameron House*, 281 Wicksteed St, on the corner of Dublin St, which is open for dinner every day except Sunday. In 1989 it won one of New Zealand's highest restaurant awards; it has an elegant atmosphere in a classic old converted home.

## Getting There & Away

**Air** Air New Zealand (tel 54-089), on the corner of Taupo Quay and Victoria Ave, has direct flights daily to Auckland, Wellington, Taupo and Whakatane, with connections to other centres.

**Bus** The InterCity depot (tel 54-439) is on Taupo Quay, and Newmans (tel 55-566) is at 156 Ridgway St. Both companies have services from Auckland through New Plymouth to Wanganui and on to Palmerston North, Napier and Wellington. They also have services north to Tongariro, Taupo and Rotorua, but you have to transfer at Bulls, on the way to Palmerston North. Wanganui is 2 to 3 hours by road from New Plymouth, Tongariro or Wellington, and about 1¼ hours from Palmerston North.

Check with the Wanganui Information Centre or with John Hammond (tel Wanganui 54-635) about the mail bus service on weekdays – it's $10 each way between Wanganui and Pipiriki and you can go and return in the same day or arrange to be picked up on another day for the return trip.

**Car** The road down from Tongariro (SH 4) passes through the Paraparas, an area of interesting *papa* hills with some beautiful views, and also passes close by the impressive Raukawa Falls.

Alternatively you can turn off at Raetihi, cross to Pipiriki and follow the Wanganui River to Wanganui. This is a popular scenic drive from Wanganui (see Around Wanganui), with points of interest marked along the way. It's not a very busy road and the Parapara route is much better if you're hitch-hiking and you want to actually get a ride!

**Getting Around**
**Airport Transport** A taxi to or from the airport is about $7.

**Bus** A suburban bus service is run by Greyhound Buses (tel 57-100), 160 Ridgway St, next to the Newmans depot. Buses run out to Aramoho and Castlecliff, but not on Sundays.

**AROUND WANGANUI**
**Whanganui National Park & Pipiriki**
The road from Wanganui to Pipiriki heads towards the Whanganui National Park. The DOC has dubbed it 'The River Road Scenic and Historic Drive'. You can get a brochure with details on the historic spots along the drive from either the Information Centre or the DOC office in Wanganui. It takes about 1½ to 2 hours to drive the 77 km to Pipiriki (that's not counting stops) – if you go on the mail bus it will take longer, but you'll have the benefit of lots of social and historical commentary. To make the full circle over from Pipiriki to Raetihi and back down SH 4 to Wanganui takes about 4 hours.

At Pipiriki are the Whanganui National Park office (tel 54-631), open from 8 am to 5 pm Monday to Friday, and the Colonial House, a historic house which is now a museum and information centre. There's also a public shelter opposite the Colonial House and both places have interesting photographic displays on the history of Pipiriki. Early this century it was quite a bustling place, with 12,000 tourists a year, and was served by several river steamers and paddleboats and the glamourous, 65 room Pipiriki House Hotel. The hotel burned down years ago and today all that can be seen are its stone steps and foundations. There are many good walks in the Whanganui National Park; the park office has brochures.

If you want to stay in the park there are huts or the Ramanui Lodge (tel Raetihi 58-799), with lodge accommodation for $42 per person, or $35 if you supply your own bedding. It's 21 km upriver from Pipiriki, in the heart of the national park near the Matemateaonga Track, and offers a variety of activities including canoeing, jet-boat trips, guided wilderness treks and hunting trips. It's accessible by tramping or boat. At Pipiriki there's a free camping site.

See the Wanganui section for details on jet-boat and canoeing trips on the Wanganui River, which depart from Wanganui, Pipiriki and Taumarunui.

**Walks** The Wanganui Information Centre and DOC have brochures on a couple of good walks, both starting from the Wanganui to Pipiriki Rd. The Atene Skyline Track is beside the Wanganui River at the southernmost end of the Whanganui National Park, 36 km north of Wanganui. It's a 6 to 8 hour track climbing 523 metres to the Taumata Trig, commanding broad views.

The Aramoana Walk, beginning 18 km north-east of Wanganui on the same road, is a 2 to 3 hour return walk from the Aramoana Lookout. It's part of the New Zealand Walkway system and is another place with great views, fossils and history. Take warm clothing and be prepared for mud after wet weather.

## Other Parks & Reserves

Bason Botanical Reserve is about 11 km from Wanganui. To get there, head east on SH 3 as if you were going to New Plymouth and turn off onto Rapanui Rd. You pass Westmere Lake before reaching the 25 hectare Bason Reserve. Attractions are a lake, conservatory, gardens including fern and camellia gardens, a deer park, a lookout tower and an old homestead. The reserve is open from 9.30 am until dusk every day; the conservatory is open from 10 am to 4 pm on weekdays and from 2 to 4 pm on weekends and public holidays.

Bushy Park is 24 km north-west of Wanganui. Take SH 3 to Kai Iwi, turn off where you see the signs, and go 8 km further on a sealed side road. Operated by the Royal Forest & Bird Protection Society, the park encompasses a 96 hectare scenic reserve and an historic homestead built in 1906. There's accommodation in the homestead (tel Wanganui 29-879) with everything you need. It's an interesting place to stay since it's like staying in a well-preserved museum. Single/double rooms are $35/40, but it's an extra $5 on Fridays and Saturdays. There are also a couple of caravan sites. For day use the park is open daily from 10 am to 5 pm.

Ashley Park (tel Waitotara 65-917), 34 km north of Wanganui on SH 3, is another attractive place for a country holiday. Cabins cost $11 per person, tent sites cost $6 per person and caravan sites cost $13.50 for two, plus B&B and farmstays. You can share in the farm activities with the sheep, cattle, deer and other animals, go hunting, visit the extensive park grounds with boating on a picturesque lake, and if you just want to come for the day there's an antique and craft shop and Devonshire teas.

# Coromandel Peninsula

To the north-east of the Hauraki Plains is the Coromandel Peninsula, a rugged, densely forested region with very little flat land where rivers force their way through gorges and pour down steep cliffs to the sea. The Coromandel State Forest Park stretches almost the entire length of the peninsula. It's an intensely scenic area, isolated and well worth going to before it becomes spoilt by tourism. There are a number of small towns scattered up and down both sides of the peninsula along the coast.

The Coromandel Peninsula is not the place to go if you're looking for entertainment, but if you're in the mood for lying around on beaches, fishing, lazing and walking it's superb.

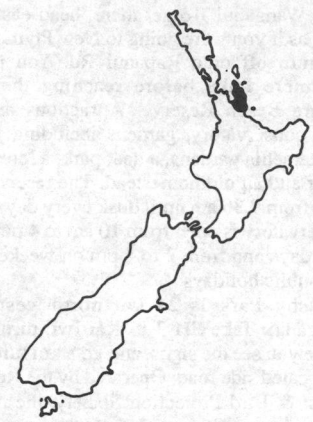

### History

The European history of the peninsula is steeped in gold-mining, logging and gum-digging. Gold was first discovered in New Zealand at Coromandel in 1852 by Charles Ring, but the rush was short-lived once the miners found it was not alluvial gold, instead having to be wrested from the ground by pick and shovel. More gold was discovered around Thames in 1867 and over the next few years other fields were proclaimed at Coromandel, Kuaotunu and Karangahake. In 1892 the Martha mine at Waihi began production; by the time it was closed in 1952, around $60 million of gold had been won. Interest in minerals is still strong today because the area is also rich in semi-precious gemstones like quartz, amethyst, jasper, chalcedony, agate and carnelian. In fact if you walk along Te Mata beach you will probably stumble over some agate.

Kauri logging was a big business on the peninsula for around 100 years. Allied to the timber trade was ship building which took off after 1832 when a mill was established at Mercury Bay. By the 1880s Kauaeranga, Coroglen (Gumtown) and Tairua were the main suppliers of kauri to the Auckland mills. Things got tougher once the kauri around the coast became scarce due to indiscriminate felling and the loggers had to penetrate deeper and deeper into the bush for the timber. The problems of getting it out became more and more difficult. Some logs were pulled out by bullock teams; others had to be hauled to rivers and floated out after dams had been built; tramways were built on the west coast; but by the 1930s the logging of kauri on the peninsula had all but finished.

### Information

There are Information Centres on the peninsula at Thames (tel 87-284), Coromandel (tel 58-598), Whitianga (tel 65-555), Tairua (tel 48-503), Waihi (tel 8386), Te Aroha (tel 48-052), Paeroa (tel 8636) and Whangamata (tel 58-340). The centres have an excellent series of leaflets on the peninsula.

### THAMES

If you're coming from Auckland, Thames is the first town you arrive at on the peninsula. The Maoris settled the region and lived on high land near Thames until the 1820s, returning about 10 years later to occupy a new pa site on the Thames flat. After the

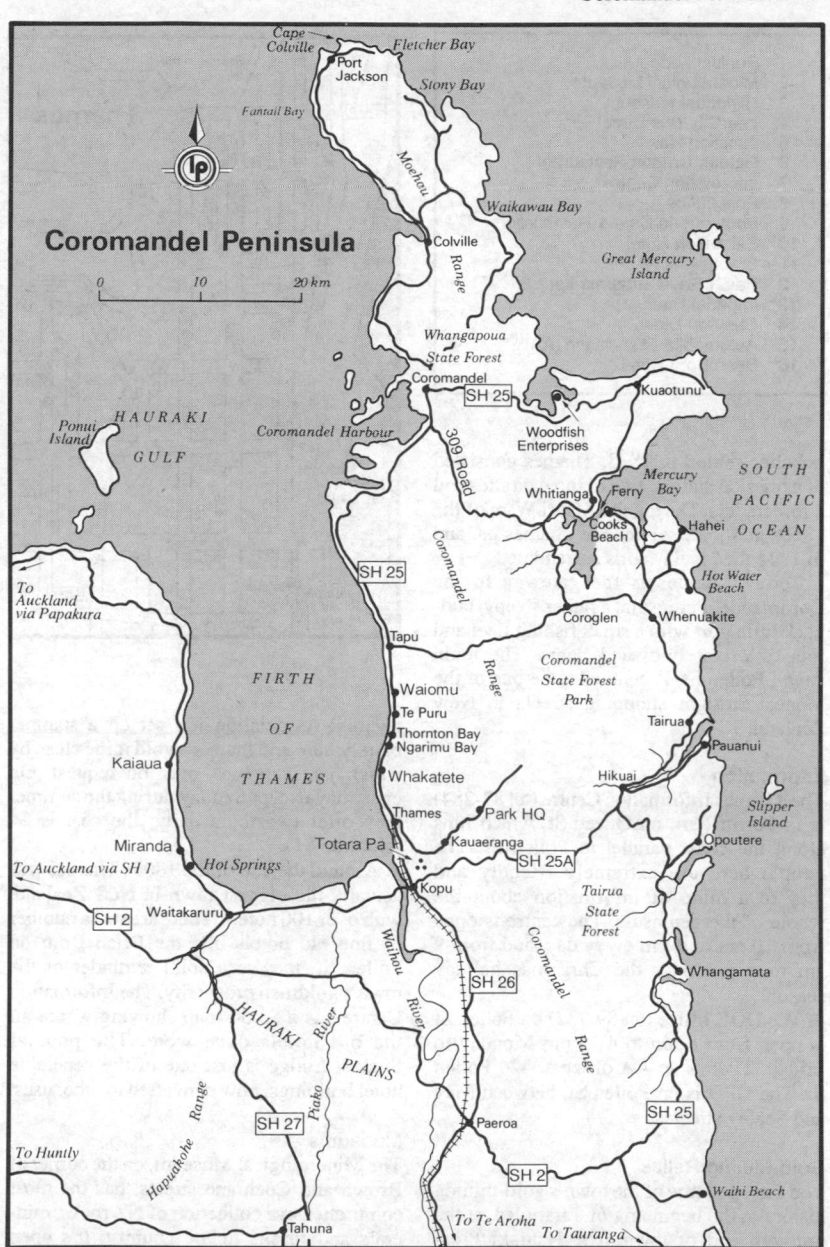

# Coromandel Peninsula

0    10    20 km

Cape Colville
Port Jackson
Fletcher Bay
Fantail Bay
Stony Bay
Moehau
Waikawau Bay
Colville
Colville Range
Great Mercury Island
Whangapoua State Forest
HAURAKI GULF
Ponui Island
Coromandel
SH 25
Kuaotunu
Woodfish Enterprises
Coromandel Harbour
309 Road
Whitianga
Ferry
Mercury Bay
SOUTH PACIFIC OCEAN
Cooks Beach
Hahei
To Auckland via Papakura
SH 25
Coromandel Range
Hot Water Beach
Coroglen
Whenuakite
Tapu
Coromandel State Forest Park
FIRTH
Waiomu
Te Puru
Tairua
OF
Thornton Bay
Ngarimu Bay
Pauanui
THAMES
Whakatete
Hikuai
Slipper Island
Kaiaua
Thames
Park HQ
Miranda
Totara Pa
Kauaeranga
Opoutere
To Auckland via SH 1
Hot Springs
Kopu
SH 25A
SH 2
Waitakaruru
Waihou River
SH 26
Tairua State Forest
HAURAKI
Piako River
Coromandel Range
Whangamata
SH 27
PLAINS
SH 25
To Huntly
Hapuakohe Range
Paeroa
SH 2
Tahuna
To Te Aroha
To Tauranga
Waihi Beach

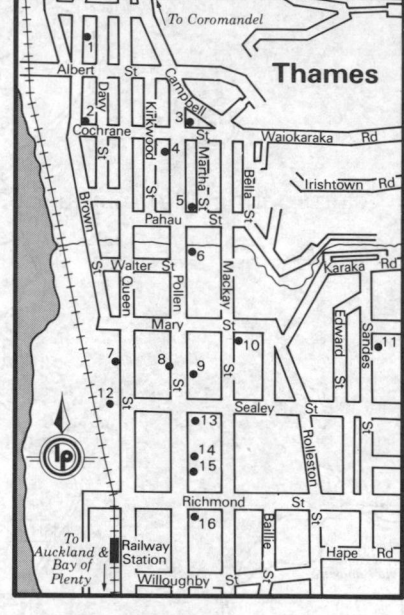

1  Sunkist Lodge
2  Mineralogical Museum
3  Historical Museum
4  InterCity Bus Depot
5  Junction Hotel
6  Golden Dragon Restaurant
7  Information Centre
8  Post Office
9  Boulangerie Cafe & Restaurant
10  Salutation Hotel
11  Brookby Motel
12  Pac'N Save Supermarket
13  Imperial Hotel
14  Chevron Diner
15  Automobile Association (AA)
16  Brian Boru Hotel

Pakehas settled in 1833, Thames consisted of a mission station, two or three pa sites and a few traders. During the Maori Wars of the 1860s gunboats shelled the Thames pa, and in 1864 the local Maoris surrendered.

Today Thames is the gateway to the Coromandel Peninsula, a rather sleepy, laid-back little port with a small fishing fleet and lots of privately-owned boats. The main street, Pollen St, is claimed to be one of the longest straight shopping streets in New Zealand.

### Information
The Thames Information Centre (tel 87-284) is in Porritt Park on Queen St, which runs along the coast parallel to Pollen St. The people here are extremely friendly and they're a mine of information about the whole of the peninsula. The centre is open from 10 am to 4 pm every day, and from 9 am to 5 pm over the Christmas holiday season.

The DOC office (tel 89-732) on Pollen St is open from 8 am to 4.35 pm Monday to Friday. There's an AA office at 424 Pollen St. The CPO is on Pollen St, between May and Sealey streets.

### Gold-Mining Relics
You can see some of the town's gold-mining history at the beginning of Tararu Rd, at the northern end of town. The Hauraki Pros-

pectors' Association has set up a stamper battery here and there's a gold mine close by which you can look over on request. On every day except Sunday during the summer they offer two tours daily; the cost is $4 (children $1).

Around the end of the 1800s Thames was actually the biggest town in New Zealand, with over 100 hotels. There are still a number of fine old hotels like the Brian Boru on Pollen St, they're a solid reminder of the town's goldrush prosperity. The Information Centre has a $3.50 map showing where all the old hotels once were. The popular Sunkist Lodge is just one of the venerable hotel buildings, now converted to other uses.

### Museums
The Mineralogical Museum, on the corner of Brown and Cochrane streets, has the most comprehensive collection of NZ rocks, minerals and fossils in the country. It's open

most of the year from Wednesday to Sunday, 11 am to 3 pm, daily during the summer; admission is $2 (children $1). Ask someone here and they may be able to put you in touch with one of the local prospectors so you can go fossicking. Next door is the Thames School of Mines which operated from 1886 to 1954. It is being restored by the Historic Places Trust.

The local Historical Museum, on the corner of Cochrane and Pollen streets, is open from 1 to 4 pm on Wednesday, Saturday and Sunday, and daily in summer. Admission is $2 (children 20 cents).

### Agatha Christie Weekends

Twice a month the Brian Boru Hotel becomes the scene of a murder, and each of the 30 to 45 guests is a suspect, when the Agatha Christie weekend takes place. Guests arrive on Friday evening for dinner and spend Saturday in guided visits around the Coromandel Peninsula. On Saturday evening they don fancy-dress costumes, and the mystery begins. Likely as not there will be a fire (with the cooperation of the local fire brigade), and with a dead body the race is on to guess 'whodunit'. The successful sleuth wins $200. On Sundays everyone joins in a 'post-mortem' over a big breakfast.

These weekends have been gaining local and international attention, winning awards for their entertainment value and attracting visitors from many countries. The price of $300 covers everything for the whole weekend, including the use of a fancy-dress costume if you don't have your own. Phone the hotel (tel 86-523) for reservations.

### Other Attractions

You can walk or drive up to Monument Hill – a WW I peace memorial – at the northern intersection of Pollen St and SH 25 (go up Waiotahi Rd) for a good view of Thames, the Hauraki Plains to the south and the Hauraki Gulf to the north.

Another good vantage point is Totara Pa Hill, a lookout over the Waihou Valley and the Hauraki Plains. Several Maori intertribal battles were fought in this area; if you look

carefully you will see the remains of fortifications and deep trenches. Nowadays there's a cemetery on the pa. Take Te Arapipi Rd to get there.

Scenic flights are offered by the Thames Air Service or you can go air gliding for about $30 per half-hour. Various horse treks go up into the bush. The Information Centre can recommend a good scenic drive around Thames, outlined on a map for 10 cents. There's also a nice drive to Kauaeranga Valley through bush country.

The Thames Society of Arts & Crafts is open on weekends in winter, longer hours in summer, showing locals' work at the Old North School on Tararu Rd, north of Thames. If you like arts and crafts ask the Information Centre for a map called the 'Coromandel Craft Trail', showing the locations of arts and crafts galleries all over the peninsula – there are many. For those who like a bargain Pollen St has an abundance of second-hand shops and also a book exchange.

The heated swimming pool at the southern end of Pollen St is covered in winter and open air in summer. In the park by the Information Centre are a mini-golf course and a children's playground.

Totara Vineyards at Totara, south of Thames on SH 25, has won awards for its wines. You can stop off for a tasting.

The Miranda Hot Springs (tel 73-055), reputed to be the largest thermal pool in the southern hemisphere, is a popular spot about 30 km from Thames, across the Firth of Thames. It's open from 10 am to 9 pm daily; admission is $5 (children $2.50), but it's free if you camp in the caravan park there.

### Places to Stay

**Hostels** The *Sunkist Lodge* (tel 88-808), 506 Brown St, is a pleasantly relaxed hostel. A dorm bed costs $12, a single room is $15, and twins or doubles (particularly the 'honeymoon suite') are $14 per person. The upstairs verandah is a fine place to laze on a sunny afternoon or to watch the sunset over the placid Firth of Thames. The fine old building was the Lady Bowen Hotel from 1868 to 1952 and it's reputed to have a resident ghost. The manager provides transport into the Kauaeranga Valley and also hires out mountain bikes for long or short-term explorations.

**Hotels** There are still enough hotels remaining from the goldrush days to give Thames a good representation in this category. Top of the heap is the *Brian Boru Hotel* (tel 86-523) on Pollen St. A single/double room costs $45/66, or $59/88 with a private bathroom. In the off season you might get budget rates if you ask.

The *Imperial Hotel* (tel 86-200), also on Pollen St, has rooms at $33/47 and a few double rooms with private bathrooms for $55.

The *Junction Hotel* (tel 86-008) is on the corner of Pollen and Pahau streets. The cheapest hotel of all is the *Salutation* (tel 86-488), 400 Mary St, where single/double rooms cost $24/42.

**Motels** There are plenty of motels in Thames and north along the coast towards Coromandel. None of them are bargains; count on at least $50 for a single or $60 for a double. You could try the *Brookby Motel* (tel 86-663) at 102 Redwood Lane or the *Crescent Motel* (tel 86-506) on the corner of Jellicoe Crescent and Fenton St. The *Coastal Motor Lodge* (tel 86-843), 3 km north of Thames on SH 25, is a bit more expensive at $66/78 for a single/double, but it's particularly attractive and pleasantly situated.

**Camping & Cabins** The *Dickson Holiday Park* (tel 87-308) is 3 km north of Thames, in an attractive quiet valley beside a stream 4 minutes from the beach. Camping costs $6.50 per person, or a bit more with power. Bunkroom accommodation costs $10, or there's shared accommodation in a tourist flat for $15 per person. Cabins start from $28.50 a double, a tourist flat with bathroom and colour TV costs $45 a double, and a motel unit costs $55. It's a pleasant site with a swimming pool and free bicycles. Telephone for courtesy pick-up.

There are other camping sites on the coast north of Thames – see the North of Thames section.

**Places to Eat**
**Snacks & Fast Food** The Pollen St takeaways and snack bars include the *Chevron Diner* at No 442 and *The Boulangerie* at No 523, opposite the CPO; and there are plenty more. *The Bakery* at No 326 is a bakery and coffee lounge open every day of the week where you can get baked goodies, light meals and takeaways.

The big Pac'N Save Supermarket on Queen St has the lowest prices in the area – a good place to stock up on provisions.

**Restaurants** The licensed *Old Thames Restaurant* on Pollen St has steak, seafood and various pizzas at $8 to $10 for a medium, $10 to $13 for a large. It also has Bluff oysters – not to be missed if you haven't tried them. It's open from 5 pm every day.

The Hotel Imperial, also on Pollen St, has the *Pan & Handle* restaurant and the more expensive *Regency Room*. The restaurant at the *Brian Boru Hotel* serves a fancy three-course dinner for $20, or you can have à la carte meals.

Thames has three Chinese restaurants, all serving food to take away or eat there. There's the *Sun Moon*, opposite the bus station, and the *Golden Dragon*. If you want a much better atmosphere try *New Seasons*, a licensed restaurant open for lunch and dinner every day, with a $10 smorgasbord lunch served Monday to Friday.

**Getting There & Away**
**Bus** The InterCity bus station (tel 86-074) is in Pollen St. InterCity operates buses between Auckland and Thames several times daily; it's a 2 hour trip. The bus continues north to Coromandel (1 hour) and Whitianga (2½ hours) every day except Saturdays. Another daily InterCity route goes from Auckland via Thames to Tauranga (1¾ hours) and Mt Maunganui (2 hours) on the Bay of Plenty. There's also a weekday bus between Thames and Hamilton (2½ hours).

**Hitching** Hitching is OK between Thames and Coromandel but can sometimes be difficult beyond there. Be prepared for long waits if you're heading up to Colville or across to Whitianga. Traffic is sparse on the east coast except at holiday periods, so hitching can be slow going.

## COROMANDEL FOREST PARK
There are over 30 walks and tramps through Coromandel State Forest Park, covering the area from the Maratoto Forest, near Paeroa, to Cape Colville; the most popular region is the Kauaeranga Valley which cuts into the Colville Range behind Thames.

### Information
Leaflets and pamphlets on walks through the Coromandel Forest Park – giving map references, general description and approximate walking times – can be obtained from the Information Centre and the DOC office in Thames, and from the Forest Park headquarters. Sunkist Lodge hostel in Thames also has lots of walking information. Be sure to ask for specific information on any tracks you're planning to use, as some are in very poor condition and may be hazardous.

The Coromandel Forest Park headquarters (tel 86-381), in the Kauaeranga Valley about 15 km from Thames, is open on weekdays from 8 am to 4 pm, as well as on weekends in season.

### Places to Stay
There are DOC camping grounds at various places throughout the Coromandel Forest Park. You'll find them on the west coast and northern tip of the peninsula at Fantail Bay, Port Jackson and Fletcher Bay and at Stony Bay and Waikawau Bay on the east coast. All have only a nominal fee, and you don't have to book.

### Getting There & Away
The headquarters and main entrance to the park are reached from the southern edge of Thames along Kauaeranga Valley Rd. There are other minor access points around the

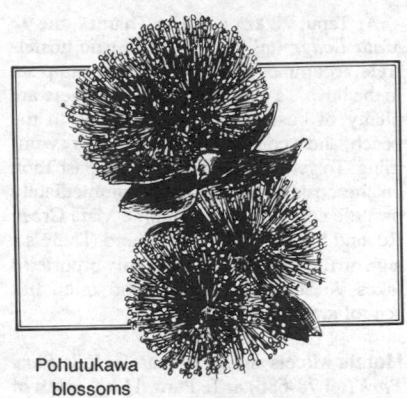

Pohutukawa blossoms

peninsula; ask at the DOC office in Thames for details.

## NORTH OF THAMES
North from Thames, SH 25 snakes along the coast for 32 km past lots of pretty little bays and beaches on one side and bush on the other. Fishing and shellfishing are excellent all the way up the coast, and the landscape turns crimson when pohutukawa trees bloom in the summer.

Along the way you pass through Whakatete, Ngarimu Bay, Te Puru, Tapu and other small settlements. The Rapaura Watergardens, 6 km inland from Tapu on the Tapu-Coroglen Rd, are open 10 am to 4 pm daily from 1 October to 30 April; admission is $5 (children $1).

### Places to Stay
There are two hostels and a number of motels and camping sites along the coast between Thames and Coromandel.

**Hostels** The *Glenavon* (tel 78-844) on SH 25 at Thornton Bay, 10 km north of Thames, is a small hostel with just one single room, one double room, one triple room and a flat. A room with a shared kitchen and bathroom costs $12 per person and the flat costs $15 per person. The hostel is right by the sea, with a sandy beach. The InterCity bus will stop at the door if you ask.

At Tapu, 22 km north of Thames, the *Te Mata Lodge* (tel 74-834) has rustic hostel-style accommodation for $11 in a camp set in the bush – a very woodsy place. There are plenty of bushwalks, including one to the beach, and a couple of rivers good for swimming. To get there go 1½ km north past Tapu on the coast road, turn inland immediately past the concrete bridge into Te Mata Creek Rd, and follow the road to the end. There's a sign on the gate. The very friendly proprietor takes guests on bushwalks and often has school groups in.

**Motels** Motels along the coast include *Puru Park* (tel 78-686) at Te Puru, 11 km north of Thames, the *La Casa Guesthouse* (tel 78-326), also in Te Puru, and the *Seaspray Motel* (tel 78-863), on the coastal road at Waiomu, 14½ km north of Thames.

**Camping & Cabins** The *Boomerang Motor Camp* (tel 78-879) in Te Puru, 11 km north of Thames, has camping facilities, cabins and on-site caravans. Another couple of km north is the *Waiomu Bay Holiday Park* (tel 78-777) which has camping, on-site caravans, cabins, tourist flats and motel units. Further north towards Coromandel, at Tapu, the *Tapu Motor Camp* (tel 74-837) has camping sites, on-site caravans and cabins; the backpackers rate is $9 per person in bunkrooms or caravans.

## COROMANDEL

When you get to Wilsons Bay the road leaves the coast and cuts through hills and valleys until you arrive at the next major town Coromandel, 55 km north of Thames, named after HMS *Coromandel* which visited the harbour in 1820 to pick up a load of kauri spars for the navy. It was here, on Driving Creek, 3 km north of the township, that kauri mill owner Charles Ring discovered gold in 1852. At the height of the goldrush the town's population rose to over 10,000 but today it's a soporific little township of less than 1000 souls which, like Rip van Winkle, seems to have been asleep for the past 100 years or so.

### Information
The Coromandel Information Centre (tel 58-598) is on the main road through town. In summer it's open from 9 am to 4 pm every day except Sundays; the rest of the year it's open from 10 am to 3 pm, Monday to Friday. The centre has many useful leaflets on the surrounding area, and makes bookings for all the accommodation in town.

A free leaflet, 'Historic Coromandel', guides you on a walking tour of the town and points out its historic attractions, including Charles Ring's cottage.

### Historic Buildings
The Coromandel Mining Museum (tel 58-825) on Ring's Rd is in a historic building erected in 1898 to house the Coromandel School of Mines. On display are exhibits pertaining to early gold-mining and the colonial era. In summer it's open daily from 10 am to noon and from 2 to 4 pm, admission $1 (children free). In winter it opens by arrangement.

The Coromandel Stamper Battery (tel 58-765), also on Ring's Rd, demonstrates ore-crushing to extract gold and shows various amalgamation processes. In summer it's open from 1 to 3 pm daily, and tours are offered for $2 or $3; in winter it's open by arrangement.

### Craft Gallery
Coromandel is a centre for potting and weaving. Go into the Coromandel Craft Gallery on Wharf Rd and, if you want to see more of any particular potter's or weaver's work, check whether you can go to their home – most of the local potters welcome visitors. Among the craft shops in the town, True Colours is a good place to see weaving in progress.

### Driving Creek Railway
Driving Creek, 3 km north of Coromandel, is where Charles Ring discovered gold. It is now the site of various fascinating enterprises masterminded by one of Coromandel's leading artists, Barry Brickell (tel 58-703).

Brickell is a potter who, upon discovering excellent clay on his land, had to find a way to get it down the hill; he built his own railway to do it. The Driving Creek Railway runs up steep grades, across three high trestle bridges, along a spiral and a double switchback, and through two tunnels! It's a 50 minute round trip and Brickell takes visitors up to the top at 5 pm daily from Christmas to Easter, on weekends, or by arrangement during the rest of the year. There's no charge, but a donation is politely requested at the end of the trip. Also at Driving Creek are Brickell's pottery stall, native forest restoration project, and a proposed environmental history museum at the top of the railway.

### Walks

Coromandel is smack in the middle of a region abounding in natural beauty, scenic reserves, and attractive bushwalks. The Information Centre has a big map on the wall showing all the scenic reserves, the two Farm Park Recreation Reserves with camping (at Cape Colville and Waikawau Bay), and a 'Walking in Coromandel' pamphlet.

A few of the more notable walks in the area include a 3 km walk from Coromandel to Long Bay through a grove of large kauris and a climb through Whangapoua State Forest to the 521 metre Castle Rock on 309 Rd. There are many old abandoned gold mines in the area and these, too, make for good explorations.

### Places to Stay

The Information Centre can make bookings for any accommodation in Coromandel.

**Hostels** The *Tui Lodge* (tel 58-237) is a small hostel in an orchard chalet, 10 minutes walk from town, 500 metres past where SH 25 heads east. The Whitianga bus will stop at the gate or there's free pick-up on request. It's $12 for a bunk in the backpackers' room, $15 per person in a twin room in the chalet when available, or $22 per person to have the chalet all to yourself. It's run by a friendly retired couple from whom you can borrow a

fishing rod, hire a bicycle, and find out all about the good things to do in the area.

**Guest Houses** There are a number of B&B places including the *Rose Cottage* (tel 57-047) on Pagitt St opposite the Mining Museum, where B&B in a private home is $25/45. The Information Centre has lots of other B&Bs on file.

**Hotels & Motels** The *Coromandel Hotel* (tel 58-760) is right on the main street and has rooms at $25 per person. There are many motels in Coromandel but most rooms cost at least $50. Possibilities include the *Wyuna Bay Motel* (tel 58-507), the *Harbour View Motel* (tel 58-690), the *Alpha Motel* (tel 58-709) and the *Colonial Cottages* (tel 58-856).

**Camping & Cabins** There are several motor camps in and around Coromandel. The *Coromandel Tourist Court* (tel 58-830), 400 metres from the post office, has camping sites for $8 per person (a bit more with power); cabins cost $20/32 for one/two people, and motel units cost $55/72. Off-season and family tariffs are available.

On the beachfront 3 km west of Coromandel there's camping at *Long Bay* and *Tuck's Bay* (tel 58-720 for both). Camping costs $6.50 per person; it's an extra $2.50 per site with power.

There are other camping possibilities around Coromandel. The *Oamaru Bay Tourist Flats and Caravan Park* (tel 58-735), on Oamaru Bay 7 km north of Coromandel, has camping sites, cabins and tourist flats. *Papa Aroha Motor Camp* (tel 58-818) at Papa Aroha, 12 km north, has camping sites and cabins. The *Angler's Lodge & Motor Park* (tel 58-584) at Amodeo Bay, 18 km north of Coromandel, is adjacent to both the beach and a river and has camping sites and one cabin.

### Places to Eat

Try the *Bakehouse* on Wharf Rd or the bistro bar at the *Coromandel Hotel*. The *Coro Cafe* near the Information Centre has sandwiches and hot meals and is open from 7 am on weekdays most of the year, as well as on weekends and in the evening during summer. The *Firlawn House* is a more expensive restaurant but it has good food.

The *Falls Restaurant* near the Waiau Falls Scenic Reserve, 7 km from Coromandel on SH 309, is in a lovely spot near a fine swimming hole. It has good, inexpensive food and outside service only. It's open in summer from 11 am until 8 pm daily.

If you're heading north from Coromandel you can't buy stores or food beyond Colville, so stock up here. There's an excellent market in Main St from 9 am to 3 pm every Saturday. Buy some fish from the local fishing fraternity and cook it yourself.

### Getting There & Away

InterCity buses serve Coromandel on the Auckland, Thames, Coromandel and Whitianga route once a day. Buses run every day except Saturday from Auckland to Whitianga, and Monday to Friday going the other way. It's about 1¼ hours from Coromandel to either Thames or Whitianga, and 3½ hours to Auckland.

### BEYOND COROMANDEL

From Coromandel you can continue north to Colville and Port Jackson or take either of two routes across to Whitianga and Mercury Bay on the east coast.

The road heading north is sealed to Colville, but it's rough going beyond that and hitching north of Colville may not be so easy.

The road ends at Fletcher Bay, from where it's about a 3 hour walk to Stony Bay where the road starts again. Sometimes groups who have access to transport drive as far as possible and walk the rest of the way, with a driver to meet them on the other side. There is camping at Port Jackson, Fletcher Bay, Stony Bay and Waikawau Bay.

From Coromandel south-east to Whitianga there are two possible routes. SH 25 is longer (46 km, 1¼ hours) but the road is sealed and it's also the more scenic route, going along the coast with exquisite beach views.

Highway 309 (locally known as 309 Rd)

is shorter (32 km, 45 minutes) but it's rather rough going as the road is unsealed. It's a bush road which is generally not as scenic as SH 25, unless you want to get out and do some walking. It does have some excellent spots including the Chiltern Scenic Reserve, Waiou Falls, a grove of large kauri trees, the unusual 'square kauri' with a square trunk, and a 40 minute walking track to the summit of Castle Rock.

### Places to Stay

The *Woodfish Enterprises* (tel 58-350, 58-370) is a 320 hectare farm on SH 25, 19 km from Coromandel and 27 km from Whitianga. It's on a beautiful promontory jutting out into Whangapoua Harbour – the farm is surrounded by water on three sides. Guests are welcome to stay in the flat behind the farmhouse for $6 per person, or to pitch a tent for $6 for any number of people. You have the run of the farm, boats and fishing tackle to use, fresh vegetables, tropical fruits, milk straight from the cow, Pacific oysters in the sand just outside the flat, a hill on the farm for a view of the entire bay, and even a swimming pool.

### WHITIANGA

The pleasant Whitianga area of Mercury Bay has a long history, by NZ standards. The Polynesian explorer Kupe landed near here around 950 AD and the area was called Te Whitianga A Kupe (the crossing place of Kupe). Prior to that the land was abundant with moas and there is evidence that there were early moa hunters here 2000 years ago.

Mercury Bay was given its modern name by Captain Cook when he observed the transit of Mercury while anchored in the bay in November 1769.

Whitianga is the principal town on Mercury Bay. The bay itself is attractive and there are seven good beaches all within easy reach of the town. Buffalo Beach, Whitianga's principal frontage onto the bay, takes its name from HMS *Buffalo*, wrecked there in 1840. Dolphins live in the bay and several frolic around Whitianga wharf in the summertime – if you take a boat trip out into the bay you'll see plenty more.

The town is a big game-fishing base for tuna, marlin, mako (blue pointer shark), thresher shark and kingfish. It is very much a tourist town, whose small population of about 2000 swells to mammoth proportions during the January holidays.

## Information

There's an Information Centre (tel 65-555) on the main street right in the centre of town. In summer it's open from 8.30 am to 5 pm every day. Winter hours are from 9.30 am to 2.30 pm Monday to Friday and 9.30 am to 12.30 pm on Saturdays. The centre closes for 3 weeks in July.

## Museum

The little Mercury Bay Historic Society Museum opposite the ferry wharf has some interesting exhibits, including many historic photos of Mercury Bay and the kauri logging era. Mining, blacksmithing, the colonial era, Maori carvings, and the story of the HMS *Buffalo* and other shipwrecks are also represented. The jaws of a 1350 kg white pointer shark caught in the Hauraki Gulf in 1959 hang on the wall overlooking all.

The museum is open in summer from 1 to 4 pm daily. Winter hours are shorter: 1 to 3 pm, 2 days a week. Admission is $1.50 (children 50 cents).

## Ferry Landing

From The Narrows on the southern side of town you can take a passenger ferry which takes 5 minutes to cross over to Ferry Landing, site of the original township on the southern side of Mercury Bay. A one-way crossing costs 70 cents (children 40 cents), with an extra 25 cents for bicycles. The ferry does not take cars, but you can drive to Ferry Landing on a circuitous route around the bay to the south, via Coroglen.

In summer the ferry runs continuously from 7.30 am to 6.30 pm, with evening crossings too from 7.45 until 8.30 pm and again from 9.30 to 10.30 pm. In winter the ferry runs from 7.30 am to noon and from 1 to 6.30 pm, with evening crossings by arrangement.

Bicycles can be hired from beside the store in Ferry Landing. You can walk, cycle or drive to a number of excellent spots on this side including Cook's Beach, Lonely Bay, Front Beach and Flaxmill Bay. The view from Shakespeare's Lookout, atop the white cliffs you see when you look across the river from Whitianga, is particularly lovely, a great spot to see all of Mercury Bay with its many beaches and coves.

The stone wharf at Ferry Landing was built in 1837 by Gordon Browne, who had a trading post, warehouse and boat building business. Stone for the wharf came from Whitianga Rock, a pa site of which Captain Cook said 'the best engineers in Europe could not have chosen a better site for a small band of men to defend against a greater number'.

## Purangi Winery

Purangi Winery (tel 63-724), 6 km south of Ferry Landing, is a mellow, rustic winery which makes wines (kiwi fruit, feijoa, passion fruit and apple) and liqueurs (kiwi fruit, feijoa and tamarillo) from a totally organic orchard. There's free tasting and also a good inexpensive restaurant with seating indoors or out under the vines, with lots of vegetarian dishes and summer barbecues with a big salad bar. The winery is open from 9 am to 9 pm daily. If you telephone ahead you can arrange to be picked up from the ferry at 11.30 am, 2.30 pm or 6.30 pm, and returned to the ferry after your visit.

## Other Attractions

Popular trips from Whitianga include Cathedral Cove and Hot Water Beach, where thermal waters are brewing just below the sand. You can go down on the beach 2 hours before and after low tide, dig a hole in the sand and sit in your own little natural spa pool.

## Activities

Whitianga has many activities for visitors and the Information Centre can supply details on all of them. On the water there are scenic yacht trips, mangrove cruises, kayak trips, fishing excursions, sailing, catamarans, jet-boating, water-skiing, and safe swimming. In summer you can fish off the wharf and see the dolphins playing in the river. River rafting is popular on the nearby Waiwawa River.

Back on land there are horse treks, bus tours, and numerous scenic drives and walks. The Buffalo Beach Tourist Park has a hot thermal swimming pool called Champagne Springs, due to open in mid-1991. It will be open to the public, except during January when it's for guests only. Admission will be about $5 per day.

If you don't want to spend all your time on water or land you can take to the air for 'flightseeing' excursions.

### Walks

Mercury Bay is rich in interesting walks. You can take a torch and visit several abandoned gold mines, but watch your step – some of the shafts are quite deep. One of the more popular gold mines is reached by an enjoyable 2 hour walk along a stream. The track starts on Waitaia Rd, about 14 km north-east of Whitianga. Many other good walks are across the river, 5 minutes away by ferry. The Information Centre has details on local walks.

### Places to Stay

**Hostels** The *Coromandel Backpackers Lodge* (tel 65-380), 46 Buffalo Beach Rd, is a converted seaside motel. Nightly cost is $12 in a dorm room or $14 per person in a double room. They have free kayaks, surfboards and dinghies, and you can also hire out bicycles, catamarans and a 4WD vehicle for tours of the region.

**Guest Houses** The small and pleasant *Cosy Cat Cottage* (tel 64-488), 41 South Highway, is an unusual B&B guest house – it's absolutely loaded with cat art. There are cats on everything from the sheets to the placemats at the dinner table, and literally hundreds of cat statues. Single rooms cost $40 and double

or twin rooms cost $35 per person, including a cooked breakfast.

*Esplanada 21* (tel 86-523, 65-209), 21 The Esplanade, opposite Buffalo Beach, has B&B for $30 per person.

The *309 Honey Cottage* (tel 65-151) is about 12 km from Whitianga on 309 Rd. It's a lovely place, relaxing and scenic, with 40 hectares of farm and bush. Cost is $10 a night in an old kauri cottage beside a river, or you can camp for $5 a night. There are plenty of farm animals about, and there's a glass beehive where you can see bees at work. Activities include rafting, horse-riding and bushwalking. There's no bus but they will pick you up in Whitianga if you phone.

**Hotels & Motels** The *Whitianga Hotel* (tel 65-818) on Blacksmith Lane has rooms at $22 to $45 for singles, $32 to $55 for doubles or twins; the more expensive rooms have private bathrooms.

Whitianga has a lot of motels. Most are in the $50 and up bracket but there are cheaper ones too.

On Buffalo Beach Road there are *Baileys' Motel* (tel 65-500) at No 66 on the beachfront and the *Seabreeze Motel* (tel 65-570) at No 71. The *Seafari Motel* (tel 65-263) is at 7 Mill Rd, and the *Central Park Motel* (tel 65-471) is nearby at 6 Mill Rd. Two others are the *Waters Edge Lodge* (see Camping & Cabins) or the *Bay View Motel* (tel 65-527) at 7 Mercury St.

**Camping & Cabins** At the *Buffalo Beach Tourist Park* (tel 65-854) opposite Buffalo Beach, camping costs $7 per person ($8 in summer); it's a couple of dollars more with power. On-site caravans cost $16.50/24 for singles/doubles, and shared accommodation costs $12 per person in bunkrooms or caravans. The enterprising management dug for thermal water and found it – effervescent thermal water, no less – and a large thermal swimming pool called 'Champagne Springs' is due to open in mid-1991. Park guests will be able to take a free swim anytime; for others there's a $5 fee.

Other similarly-priced camping sites

include the *Waters Edge Lodge* (tel 65-760) and the *Mercury Bay Motor Camp* (tel 65-579), both on Albert St; the *Whitianga Holiday Park* (tel 65-896) at the northern end of Buffalo Beach; and the *Aladdin Motor Camp* (tel 65-834) on Bongard Rd.

There's also camping at *309 Honey Cottage* (see the Guest Houses & Hotels section).

## Places to Eat
There's a choice of several takeaways: pizzas at *Napoli's Pizza*, good pub food at the *Whitianga Hotel*, or fresh seafood meals and the most popular takeaway fish & chips in town from *Snapper Jacks* seafood restaurant, opposite the Information Centre. The Purangi Winery south of Ferry Landing has excellent food and wine, great atmosphere, and it's not expensive. See the Purangi Winery section for details. There are also a number of more expensive restaurants – check with the Information Centre.

## Entertainment
There's a *Chinese Restaurant and Nightclub* beside the Information Centre. The *Whitianga Hotel* has live music in summer, and there is good pub entertainment in the nearby town of Coroglen.

## Getting There & Away
Whitianga is the end of the line for the Inter-City Auckland, Thames, Coromandel, and Whitianga bus route, running every day except Saturday from Auckland to Whitianga, and from Monday to Friday in the other direction. You can transfer at Thames to go to Hamilton instead of to Auckland. From Whitianga it's 1¼ hours to Coromandel, 2½ hours to Thames, 5¼ hours to Hamilton and 4 hours to Auckland on the express bus.

There are bus services between Waihi and Opoutere but there is no service between Opoutere and Whitianga.

## WHITIANGA TO WAIHI
The coast is wild and there are spectacular beaches all the way from Mercury Bay to Waihi, including Hahei, Hot Water Beach where thermal waters heat the sea, Tairua, Pauanui, Opoutere, Whangamata and Orokawa. There is a fascinating crafts shop, Easterly, in Tairua.

At Waihi, once a booming gold-mining town, there's a good museum with superb models and displays about Martha Mine. The large mine is now operating again after a long hiatus; ask locally if you can visit it. Railway buffs have acquired 8 km of track between here and Waikino and run trains between the two townships.

## Places to Stay
**Hostels** The *Opoutere Youth Hostel* (tel 59-072) is a fine place to get right away from it all. It's in a country setting overlooking Wharekawa Harbour, opposite a rare bird sanctuary which is roped off for the breeding season from November to January, but open the rest of the year. You can take one of the hostel's kayaks and paddle around, and there are plenty of bushwalks. The cost is $13 per night, or you can set up a tent on the lawn for a reduced rate.

The *Wilderland Community* (tel 63-848) is a large commune on SH 25 about 14 km south of Whitianga which takes in visitors for $5 per night. It has about 73 hectares of organic fruit and vegetable gardens so there's plenty of food around. The residents are vegetarians and alcohol and tobacco are not allowed, but if you like a natural life style, early-morning yoga and nude saunas, this is your spot. One-night stays are discouraged; they prefer visitors to stay a while and become acquainted.

Accommodation is in basic huts (no electricity) and there are usually a few visitors around for most of the year – sometimes as many as 300 in summer. The community runs a fruit stand on the road; the commune is about 1½ km behind it, over the hill.

**Camping & Cabins** There are camping sites and motels at various places down the east coast. Just down the road from the Opoutere Youth Hostel is the *Opoutere Park Beach*

*Resort* (tel 59-152) with camping sites at $7 per person.

Sites at the *Hot Water Beach Motor Camp* (tel 63-735) cost $7 per person (more with power), where there are thermal pools as well as the hot water under the sand. There's also the *Cook's Beach Motor Camp* (tel 65-469) and the *Hahei Tourist Park* (tel 63-889) which has camping sites, cabins and tourist flats.

# Bay of Plenty

Cook sailed into the Bay of Plenty aboard the *Endeavour* in October 1769, giving it that name because of the numbers of thriving settlements of friendly Maoris he encountered (and the amount of supplies they gave him). It was a sharp contrast to the 'welcome' he received from the Maoris of Poverty Bay several weeks earlier!

The Bay of Plenty region forms a rough triangle, with Rotorua, Katikati and Opotiki at its corners. The area is not as popular with tourists as the far more commercial Bay of Islands, but in summer it hums along rather nicely. It enjoys one of the highest proportions of sunny days in New Zealand, the climate is consistently mild all year round, and in summer the coastal towns and beaches are popular with Kiwi holiday-makers.

The region is rapidly becoming the horticultural centre of New Zealand, with its main exports being kiwi fruit and timber products, including logs and woodchips. There is a growing mineral water industry, with springs popping up everywhere. Naturally there are several hot mineral spas around.

## TAURANGA
Population 61,800

Tauranga, the principal city of the Bay of Plenty and the largest export port in New Zealand is – like the rest of the towns in the region – thriving economically. The rapidly growing town celebrated its 25th year in 1987.

Tauranga is a Maori name meaning 'resting place for canoes', and most appropriate it is; for this was where some of the first Maoris to arrive in New Zealand landed. Nowadays 530 cargo vessels dock there each year.

Tauranga is one of New Zealand's principal kiwi fruit and orchard regions. There's lots of work available when kiwi fruit is being picked (May and June) but you can probably find orchard work of some kind at almost any time of the year. Check with the hostels for orchard work contacts.

### Information
The Tauranga Information Centre (tel 788-103) is on The Strand by Coronation Pier. It's open from 8 am to 5 pm on weekdays, 8 am to noon on Saturdays, and from 8 am to noon and 2.30 to 4.30 pm on Sundays.

The DOC office (tel 787-677) on the corner of McLean and Anson streets is open from 8 am to 4.35 pm, Monday to Friday. There's an AA office on the corner of Cameron Rd and Hamilton St.

### Historic Attractions
The Historic Village (tel 781-302) on Seventeenth Ave features restored period buildings, vintage vehicles, farming equipment, an 1877 steam locomotive, an old tugboat, a Maori culture section, and relics from the gold-mining era. It's open from 10 am to 4 pm every day; admission is $5 (children $2).

Te Awanui, a fine replica Maori canoe, is on display in an open-sided building at the top end of The Strand, close to the centre of town. Continue uphill beyond the canoe to

Monmouth Redoubt, a fortified site during the Maori wars. A little further along is Robbins Park, with a rose garden and hot-house.

The Elms Mission Station House on Mission St was founded on the site in 1835 and the present house was completed in 1847 by a pioneer missionary. The grounds, containing gardens and several historic buildings, are open from 9 am to 6 pm daily except Sundays; admission is free. The mission house is still used as a private residence but you're welcome to wander around the gardens and chapel.

There's also the historic Brian Watkins House, built in 1887, near the corner of Elizabeth St and Cameron Rd. It's open from 2 to 4 pm on Sundays; admission is 50 cents.

### Mineral Pools
Fernland Natural Mineral Pools, 2 km down Cambridge Rd off Waihi Rd, has public and private hot pools. It's open from 10 am to 10 pm daily; admission is $3.50 (students $2.20, children $1.20). Therapeutic massages are $20 an hour, by appointment.

### Sea Activities
Tauranga is surrounded by water, so if you like the sea you'll find plenty to do. Charter and fishing trips operate from Tauranga all year round. During the summer the place comes alive with sea activities of all kinds including jet-skiing, water-skiing, windsurfing, parasailing, diving, surfing, swimming, fishing and harbour cruises. Ask at the Information Centre for the latest info, and see the Around Tauranga section for details about trips to Mayor Island.

### Wairoa River Rafting
White water rafting is a popular activity around Tauranga, particularly on the Wairoa River, which has some of the best falls and rafting in New Zealand. It's definitely a rafting trip for thrill-seekers – one highlight of the trip is a plunge over a 4 metre waterfall! The water level is controlled from a dam, so the Wairoa can only be rafted on

about 26 days in the year – usually about two or three weekends each month.

A number of rafting companies ply the Wairoa. The cost is about $55 and you should allow about 2½ hours. You can check with the Information Centre for info on rafting operators and the dates of upcoming trips. Operators who do trips on the Wairoa include Woodrow Rafting Expeditions (tel Tauranga 62-628, 789-555), Wet 'N Wild Rafting (tel Tauranga 884-093), River Rats (tel Rotorua 476-049) and White Water Raft Adventures (tel Rotorua 457-182). All of them do trips on other rivers too.

### Flying & Skydiving
Tauranga seems to be home to lots of air enthusiasts. The Tauranga Airport, just across the harbour in Mt Maunganui, is the base for a number of air clubs. Scenic flights can be arranged at the airport.

The Tauranga Glider Club (tel 756-768) flies every weekend, weather permitting. An instructor will take you gliding and give you a flying lesson as you go. The cost is $30 for a 15 to 20 minute trip. Phone between 9 am and 5 pm on weekends, or just show up at the airport.

You can also do a half-hour flight in a microlight (a sort of powered hang-glider) with the Bay of Plenty Microlight Association (tel 752-321, 67-717), operating from the airport's WPS hangar, or check with Airsports (tel 756-419), also at the airport. If these sports are not daredevil enough there's also skydiving (tel 410-069); you train in the morning and jump in the afternoon.

### Places to Stay
**Hostels** Tauranga's YHA hostel is called the *Waireinga Youth Hostel* (tel 785-064). At 171 Elizabeth St, it's superbly situated on the banks of the Waikareao Estuary, very close to the centre of Tauranga. It's a small, modern hostel with dorm, family and double rooms. Nightly cost is $13, or you can pitch a tent on the lawn for $9. There's a free dinghy, barbecue, bonfire and volleyball areas, bicycle hire, and they offer 20% discounts on the hot saltwater pools at Mt

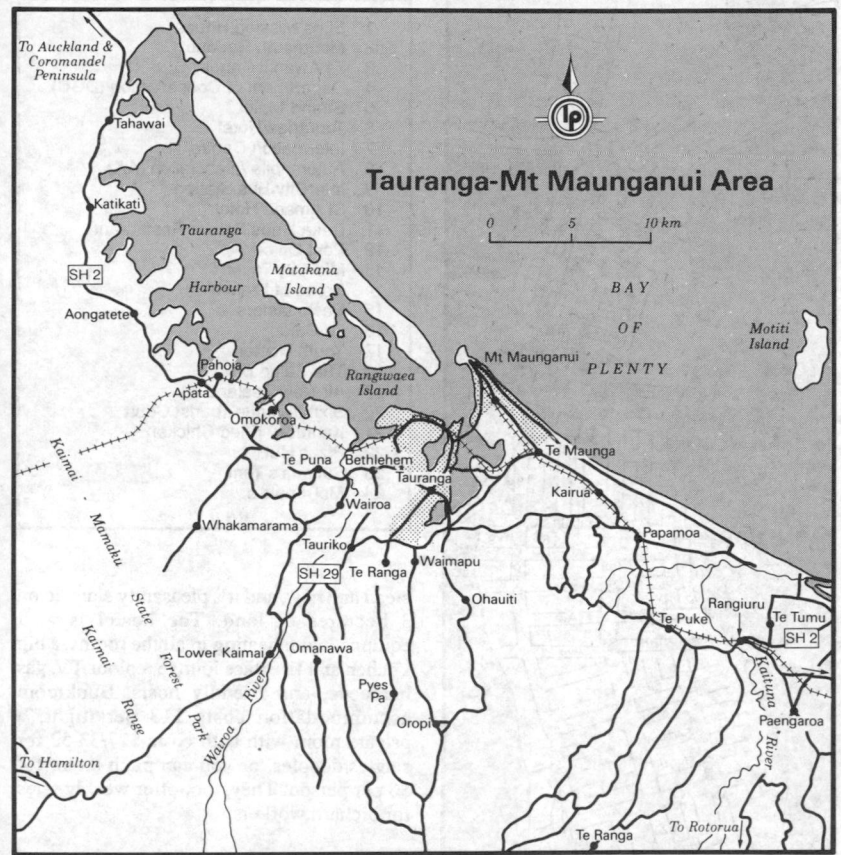

**Tauranga-Mt Maunganui Area**

To Auckland &
Coromandel
Peninsula

Tahawai

Katikati

SH 2

*Tauranga*

*Matakana
Island*

*Harbour*

Aongatete

0    5    10 km

*BAY*

*OF*

*PLENTY*

*Motiti
Island*

Pahoia

Apata

Omokoroa

*Rangiwaea
Island*

Mt Maunganui

Te Puna

Bethlehem

Tauranga

Te Maunga

Kaimai

*Kaimai*

Te Puna

Wairoa

Kairua

Whakamarama

Tauriko

SH 29   Te Ranga

Waimapu

Papamoa

*State*

*Forest*

*Park*

Lower Kaimai

Omanawa

Ohauiti

Rangiuru

Te Tumu

Te Puke

SH 2

*Kaimai*

*Range*

*Wairoa River*

Pyes
Pa

Oropi

Paengaroa

*Kaituna
River*

To Hamilton

Te Ranga

To Rotorua

Maunganui and Wairoa River rafting trips. If you're coming into town by bus, ask to get off at First Ave.

The *Backpacker Budget Tourist Lodge* (tel 782-382) is at 44-46 Botanical Rd, one block off Cameron Rd along Nineteenth Ave. The lodge offers courtesy pick-up when you reach town or you can take the local bus along Cameron St, and they have bicycles for hire. The hostel, recently redecorated and upgraded, is on the site of a former botanical garden. It has a lush garden of exotic plants, a beautiful sea view, and a free outdoor spa pool. There's plenty of space everywhere,

with a big two-storey building in front, another building out the back, several sitting areas and four separate kitchens. The cost is $12 in bunkrooms or $13 per person in double or triple rooms. They have work contacts if you're interested in orchard work, and if you're staying a while you can pay a weekly rate of $63.

The *Bell Travellers Lodge* (tel 786-344) at 39 Bell St is 4 km from the town centre. You can phone for a free pick-up when you arrive and get free transport to the bus or hitching spot when you leave. It's a purpose-built hostel opened in early 1989, so everything is

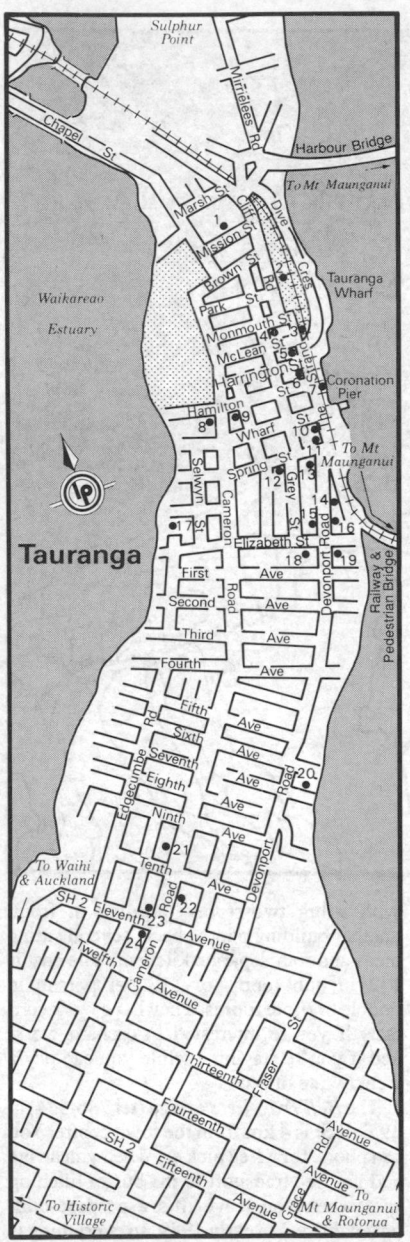

| 1 | Elms Mission House |
|---|---|
| 2 | Monmouth Redoubt |
| 3 | Te Awanui Canoe |
| 4 | Department of Conservation (DOC) |
| 5 | Strand Motel |
| 6 | Tauranga Hotel |
| 7 | Information Centre |
| 8 | Automobile Association (AA) |
| 9 | InterCity Bus Station |
| 10 | St Amand Hotel |
| 11 | Deka, Tops Family Restaurant |
| 12 | Post Office |
| 13 | Mid-City Tavern |
| 14 | Bread of France |
| 15 | Eastcoasters |
| 16 | Le Cafe |
| 17 | Youth Hostel |
| 18 | The Salad Bowl |
| 19 | Air New Zealand |
| 20 | Sixth Avenue Tourist Court |
| 21 | Kentucky Fried Chicken |
| 22 | Pizza Hut |
| 23 | Sultana's Tent |
| 24 | McDonald's |

clean and new, and it's pleasantly situated on 3 hectares of land. The hostel is well equipped with heating in all the rooms, a big kitchen and fireplace lounge, colour TV, gas barbecue, and friendly hosts. Bunkroom accommodation costs $13 per night, a private room with bath costs $27/33.50 for singles/doubles, or you can pitch a tent for $6 per person. They, too, offer weekly rates for orchard workers.

**Hotels** There are several traditional old hotels, particularly along The Strand. The *St Amand Hotel* (tel 788-127) on The Strand has single/double rooms with shared facilities for $35/50 or single rooms with a bath for $30. The St Amand has live bands at night in the Cactus Jack's Bar from Wednesday to Saturday, which is great for entertainment but a bit loud if you're trying to get some sleep.

Further down The Strand on the Harrington St corner, the *Tauranga Hotel* (tel 788-059) has single/double rooms for $33/44; some have private facilities, some are shared, all for the same price.

**Motels** There are plenty of motels around Tauranga, with prices averaging around $55/65.

The old *Strand Motel* (tel 785-807), 27 The Strand, right up at the Robbins Park end, is rather plain and straightforward but very conveniently located. Rooms are officially $55/68 for singles/doubles, but there are often discounts of $10 or $15.

The *Sixth Avenue Motel* (tel 785-709), on the waterfront next to the Sixth Ave camping ground, has doubles for $55.

The *Blue Water Motel* (tel 785-420), 59 Turret Rd, has single rooms for $43 and doubles and twins between $57 and $62. All the double rooms have a sitting room too and there's a tepid thermal swimming pool, private spa pool, children's play area, and a dinghy.

Nearby is the *Shoal Haven Motel* (tel 786-910), 67 Turret Rd, on the shore of the Hairini Estuary. It also has a spa pool and dinghy. Units with sitting rooms cost $48/55 for singles/doubles.

A similar place is the *Savoy Motel* (tel 786-435), 53 Turret Rd, with singles/doubles for $38/43.

**Camping & Cabins** The *Mayfair Caravan Park* (tel 783-323) is on Mayfair St, off Fifteenth Ave, beside the harbour. Tent facilities are limited. Powered sites cost $7 per person and cabins sleeping two cost $20 per night.

The *Silver Birch Motor Park and Thermal Pools* (tel 784-603) is at 101 Turret Rd (the extension of Fifteenth Ave) by the Hairini Bridge to Maungatapu. Sites here cost $8, cabins cost from $30 for two, and there are also tourist flats and motel flats. Campers have free use of the thermal mineral swimming pool, and there is also a boat ramp, canoes for hire, and lots of recreational facilities.

The small waterside *Sixth Avenue Tourist Court* (tel 785-709) is very close to the centre on Sixth Ave. Camping sites cost $16 for two and cabins cost $28 and $38 for two. You can hire bedding and cooking gear if you don't have your own.

At the *Palms Holiday Park* (tel 789-337), 162 Waihi Rd, about 4 km south of the town centre, caravan sites cost $7.50 per person and on-site caravans cost $29 for two.

The *Omokoroa Tourist Park* (tel 480-857) and *Plummer's Point Caravan Park* (tel 480-669), both 20 km out of Tauranga at Omokoroa, charge $7.50 per person for camping.

**Places to Eat**

There are all types of places to eat along Devonport Rd.

**Snacks & Fast Food** Tauranga has a *McDonald's* and a *Pizza Hut*, both on the corner of Cameron Rd and Eleventh Ave, and a *Kentucky Fried Chicken* a block north, between Ninth and Tenth avenues.

Other burger-style takeaways include *Fat Albert's*, open until midnight on the corner of Cameron Rd and First Ave, and *Big Al's* further south on the corner of Cameron Rd and Fourth Ave, which in addition to burgers has big submarine sandwiches for about $4. *Hatters*, 91 Devonport Rd, has burgers and other fast food to take away or eat there.

*The Deli*, at the northern end of Devonport Rd on the corner of the Spring St mall, makes sandwiches and snacks. You can sit and enjoy them at the tables in the mall in Tauranga's famous sunshine. The Deli is open from 8.30 am to 5 pm, Monday to Friday, and until noon on Saturdays.

**Cafes** Near the Deli, upstairs in the Deka department store, is the *Tops Family Restaurant*, an enjoyable and inexpensive cafeteria that serves tasty food at great prices with a sweeping harbour view. Lunch costs about $5. It's open from 9 am to 3.30 pm on weekdays, and until 2 pm on Saturdays.

Across the street and hidden back in an arcade, also with that lovely harbour view, is the *Top Tastes Cafe*, a fancy cafe open from 8 am to 4 pm Monday to Thursday, and until 7 pm on Fridays. The *Rendezvous Cafe* next door has good snacks, desserts, breakfasts for around $4, and espresso coffee. It's open from 6.30 am every day except Sundays.

Midway down Devonport Rd at No 58, *Bread of France* sells sandwiches, bread, rolls and French-style baked food; it's a good place for a takeaway breakfast.

The small but comfortable *Wok-Inn Cafe* in the Devonport Village mall serves lunch and dinner every day except Sunday; the set menu changes daily. Lunch is good value at just $3.50, and an ample four-course dinner is $14. The food is mostly Oriental with a few other styles thrown in for variety.

Further down at No 82 is the gourmet *Le Cafe*, an arty European-style cafe with attractive decor and umbrella tables on a terrace overlooking the bay. Prices are a bit higher; lunch starts at $6.50 for quiche and salad, and dinner main courses cost between $14 and $19. It's open from 8 am to 3.30 pm Monday to Friday and 10 am to 2.30 pm on Saturdays. It's also open for dinner from 6 pm on Friday, Saturday and Monday.

Around the corner at 32 Elizabeth St is the *Salad Bowl*, a good place for vegetarians; it has a variety of good-value salads.

The *Sultana's Tent* on the corner of Cameron Rd and Eleventh Ave is an enjoyable cafe, tiny and casual, with Middle Eastern food to eat there or take away. Mexican tacos or vegetarian or meat pita pockets cost between $3.50 and $4, and you can get good yoghurt shakes and desserts. It's open for lunch from 11 am to 2 pm on weekdays, and every night for dinner; later times can be arranged.

**Pub Food** The Hotel St Amand on The Strand has standard lunch and dinner pub meals in the sidewalk *Browsing Cafe/Bar*. The *Mainbrace Restaurant/Bar* inside the hotel is a bit more fancy, with lunch and dinner pub meals every day except Sunday, when they serve a smorgasbord dinner for $18.50 from 6 to 9 pm.

The *Boulevard Brasserie* at the popular Mid City Tavern, on the corner of Devonport Rd and the Spring St mall, is a big, bright place decorated in trendy pastel colours. It's open for lunch and dinner but it's on the expensive side.

There's also a *Cobb & Co* at the Greerton Motor Inn in Cameron Rd, south of the town centre.

**Restaurants** Upstairs at 77 Devonport Rd, *Eastcoasters* is a spacious and popular place specialising in Mexican and Tex-Mex food, light meals, burgers, and huge sandwiches, with something to please both vegetarians and meat-eaters. There's an obvious low-key effort to imitate the successful Armadillo places in Wellington and Auckland. It's not exactly cheap but the servings are huge and it's got great atmosphere.

For Italian food try the *Bella Mia* pizzeria restaurant at 73A Devonport Rd, with pizzas and pastas to eat there or take away. The Roman owner cooks authentic Italian food and he's put plenty of Italy into the decor.

More expensive restaurants include the quite fancy *Chez Panisse* Italian restaurant near the corner of Devonport Rd and First Ave – not connected with the Chez Panisse in Berkeley, California. Main courses cost around $20, although pasta main courses cost around $15.

At the northern end of The Strand there's the expensive but quite good *Staffords*.

*The Carvery* at the Otumoetai Trust Hotel in Bureta Rd is a bit inconvenient unless you have private transport, but it's good value. For $11 or $12 you can self-serve all the vegetables and salads you want from the long cafeteria line, then have a big serving of meat carved for you. It's open every night from 5 to 9 pm.

### Entertainment

Several hotel bars have live night-time entertainment from Wednesday to Saturday. *Cactus Jack's* is in the St Amand Hotel on The Strand. In Harrington St there's *Harrington's Nightclub. Alexander's Nightclub* at 132 Devonport Rd has music from 8 pm to 3 am Tuesday, Thursday, Friday and Saturday nights, with a happy hour from 8 to 10 pm. A sign at the door announces that a 'high standard' of dress is required – 'no denim, cords, track shoes or T-shirts'. The *Mid City Tavern* where The Strand meets the Spring St Mall has disco music upstairs on

Thursday, Friday and Saturday nights. It's popular and crowded, especially on Friday nights.

## Getting There & Away

**Air** Eagle Air and Air New Zealand (tel 780-083) share an office on the corner of Devonport Rd and Elizabeth St. Air New Zealand has direct flights to Auckland, Rotorua and Wellington, with connections to other centres. Eagle Air has direct flights to Auckland and Hamilton.

Tauranga's airport is actually not at Tauranga but at Mt Maunganui, just across the harbour.

**Bus** InterCity, Clark's Northliner and Newmans all have buses serving Tauranga. InterCity connects Tauranga with Auckland, Hamilton, Thames and Rotorua, and with Gisborne via Whakatane and Opotiki. All of these bus lines continue on to Mt Maunganui after stopping in Tauranga.

Newmans services are more limited, with buses to Hamilton and connections from there to Auckland, Rotorua and New Plymouth. Clark's Northliner has one bus to and from Auckland daily, except Saturdays.

The InterCity bus station (tel 782-839) is on the corner of Hamilton and Durham streets, close to the centre, but it may be moving to another location. Bookings for all three bus lines can be made through the Information Centre. Newmans and Clark's both operate from the Information Centre and InterCity will probably be picking up passengers from there as well.

By bus from Tauranga it's 2½ hours to Thames, 4½ hours to Auckland (via Thames), 2 hours to Hamilton, and 1½ hours to Rotorua.

**Car** The Bay of Plenty is about 200 km south-east of Auckland by the shortest route – SH 2 – which takes about 3 hours by car. From Rotorua it's a mere 55 minutes along SH 33 and from Hamilton it's a 2 hour drive down SH 1, turning onto SH 29 at Tirau.

## Getting Around

**Local Transport** Tauranga has two local bus companies which, between them, provide transport to all locations around the area, including Mt Maunganui. There used to be a ferry service to Mt Maunganui but it was discontinued when the new harbour bridge was built. The harbour bridge has a $1 toll in each direction for cars, but it's free for bicycles and pedestrians.

**Car Rental** Several rental car operators have offices in Tauranga. Probably the most economical is Rent-a-Dent (tel 781-772).

## MT MAUNGANUI

The town of Mt Maunganui stands at the foot of the 232 metre hill of the same name (also called The Mount). It's just across the inlet from Tauranga and its fine beaches make it a popular holiday resort for Kiwis. Like Tauranga, Mt Maunganui is built on a narrow peninsula. It has been recently joined to Tauranga by a new harbour bridge, making it much more accessible.

## Information

There's a small Information Centre (tel 755-099) on Salisbury Ave. It's open in summer from 10 am to 3 pm on weekdays and from 10 am to noon on Saturdays, and in winter it's open only from 10 am to 1 pm on weekdays. However, these times may change – they're thinking of going to the same full-time hours as the Information Centre in Tauranga. The Tauranga Information Centre also has information on Mt Maunganui.

## Attractions

There are hot saltwater pools at the foot of The Mount. Moturiki Island, which is actually joined to the peninsula, has an aquatic fun park called Leisure Island, with hot pools, a waterslide, bumper boats and race cars, and sailboards and catamarans for hire.

Walking trails go up and around Mt Maunganui and you can also climb around on the rocks on Moturiki. The beach between Moturiki and Mt Maunganui is good for surfing, bodysurfing and swimming.

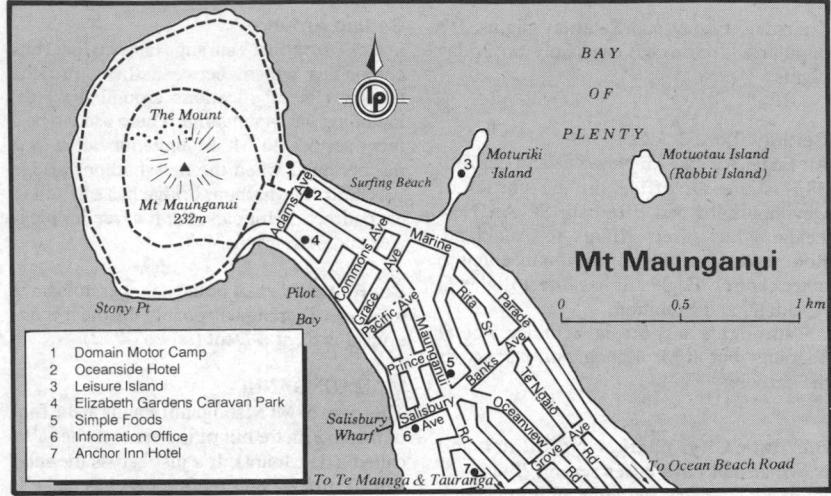

1 Domain Motor Camp
2 Oceanside Hotel
3 Leisure Island
4 Elizabeth Gardens Caravan Park
5 Simple Foods
6 Information Office
7 Anchor Inn Hotel

The Tauranga Airport, at Mt Maunganui, is the base for a number of airborne activities – see the Tauranga section for details.

## Places to Stay

**Hotels** The *Hotel Oceanside* (tel 753-149), pleasantly sited right below The Mount on the corner of Marine Parade and Adams Ave, has rooms from $35 to $49 for singles and from $49 to $70 for doubles or twins; the more expensive rooms have showers. The *Anchor Inn* (tel 753-135) is also fairly central on the corner of Maunganui Rd and Rata St. Single/double rooms there cost $22/40; the doubles have private bathrooms.

**Motels** There aren't as many motels in Mt Maunganui as there are in Tauranga. *Fawlty Towers* (tel 755-883) at 28 The Mall, facing the harbour, is expensive from Christmas to March but the rest of the year units cost $280 a week, or $45 per night for doubles.

The *Blue Haven Motel* (tel 756-508) at 10 Tweed St has single/double rooms for $53/63. *Wainui Thermal Motel* (tel 753-526) at 35 Maunganui St has similar prices. Prices are higher in summer.

**Camping & Cabins** Mt Maunganui is a popular summer resort so there are plenty of camping sites. At the foot of The Mount, the *Mt Maunganui Domain Motor Camp* (tel 754-471) has waterfront sites at $16 for two people, as well as a handful of on-site caravans at $38 for two; cheaper rates apply from Easter to late October.

At the *Cosy Corner* (tel 755-899), 40 Ocean Beach Rd, camping sites cost $8 per person and on-site caravans are $32 for two. The *Omanu Beach Holiday Park* (tel 755-968), 70 Ocean Beach Rd, is also conveniently central and has camping sites for $8 per person and a variety of cabins, cottages and tourist flats at $30 to $42 for two, with minimum charges at peak periods.

The *Ocean Pines Motor Camp* (tel 754-265) on Maranui St has camping sites for $8 per person. On-site caravans cost $24.50, and tourist flats cost $42 for two.

On The Mall, overlooking Pilot Bay on the Tauranga side of the peninsula, the *Elizabeth Gardens Holiday Park* (tel 755-787) has caravan sites for $8.50 per person. On-site caravans cost $12 per person and tourist flats cost $25/45 for singles/doubles.

There are more motor camps at Papamoa,

13 km south of Mt Maunganui, all of them along Papamoa Beach Rd. They are the *Papamoa Beach Holiday Park* (tel 420-816), *Beach Grove Holiday Park* (tel 421-337) and *Pacific Park Christian Holiday Camp* (tel 420-018).

## Places to Eat
There are many takeaways around town where you can get burgers, pizzas, Chinese and Mexican food, fish & chips and the like, particularly along Maunganui St. The *Anchor Inn* serves pub food.

## Getting There & Away
**Air** The Tauranga airport is actually at Mt Maunganui; see the Tauranga section for flight details.

**Bus** Long-distance buses serving Tauranga also stop at Mt Maunganui, in front of the Information Centre. Local buses cross the harbour bridge from Tauranga.

**Car** You can reach Mt Maunganui across the harbour bridge from Tauranga, or from the south via Te Maunga on SH 2. If you're driving across the harbour bridge there's a $1 toll in each direction.

## AROUND TAURANGA
### Mayor Island
Mayor Island is a dormant volcano about 40 km north of Tauranga in the Bay of Plenty. There are walking tracks through the now overgrown crater valley and an interesting walk around the island.

**Places to Stay & Eat** You need a permit from the Department of Maori Affairs in Tauranga to land on the island or to camp there, but you can arrange this through the boat company on Coronation Pier. Camping costs $3 per person and cabins cost $30 per night.

The Tauranga Game Fishing Club on Coronation Pier operates the *Mayor Island Lodge*, which has VIP cabins for $30 per person and more spartan cabins for $18. The canteen at the lodge has some food for sale

but you should bring most supplies with you. The camping site has a fireplace and barbecue facilities but you need all your own utensils.

**Getting There & Away** Cruises to the island operate from Coronation Pier in Tauranga, going out via Mt Maunganui at 7 am and returning at 7 pm. The trip takes about 3 hours in each direction. The cost is $35 (children $25) for a day trip, or $50 (children $30) if you go out on one day and return on another. A $3 landing fee is included in the cruise costs.

The cruises operate daily between Boxing Day (26 December) and 6 February. Between Labour weekend (at the end of October) and Boxing Day they go 3 days a week – usually Saturday, Sunday and Wednesday. The rest of the year they may operate only sporadically or not at all, depending on weather conditions. Private boats may sometimes take passengers, and there is speculation that a sea plane service may start up. Contact the Tauranga Information Centre for latest details.

### Minden Lookout
From Minden Lookout, about 10 km from Tauranga, there's a superb view back over the Bay of Plenty. To get there, take SH 2 to Te Puna and turn off south on Minden Rd; the lookout is about 4 km up the road.

### Katikati
Off SH 2 near Katikati, the Katikati Bird Gardens are a bird sanctuary and botanic gardens, open daily. The *Jacaranda Cottage* (tel 490-616), a couple of km up Thompson's Track, 5½ km south of Katikati, offers B&B, full board or just the bare necessities.

### Maketu
There's a Maori pa site at Town Point, near the township of Maketu, north-east of Te Puke (pronounced Pookay), where you can see some ancient carvings.

In Bledisloe Park, 3 km from Maketu, is the gun pit – still intact – from where, on 22 April 1864, Lieutenant-Colonel Thomas

McDonnell and 12 Europeans fought a pitched battle against 600 Maoris. To get to Maketu from Tauranga, take SH 2 through Te Puke and turn left into Maketu Rd just past Rangiuru.

### Kiwi Fruit Orchards & Wineries

The Bay of Plenty is kiwi fruit country and there are several places you can learn a little more about this fruit that is so important for New Zealand's economy.

Kiwi Fruit Country (look for the 'big kiwi fruit' sign) is on SH 33, 6 km east of Te Puke and 36 km from Tauranga. You can visit the orchards and shop, see a video about kiwi fruit and sample some kiwi fruit or kiwi fruit wine. There's no entry fee unless you want to take a kiwi-kart ride through the orchards and see how the fruit is grown and packed. The tours operate mostly during May and June when the kiwis are in fruit, and cost $7 (children $4). Kiwi Fruit Country is open daily from 10 am to 4 pm.

Prestons Kiwi Fruit Winery, on Belk Rd off SH 29, is another place where you can sample this uniquely NZ wine. They're open 10 am to 4.30 pm, Monday to Saturday.

Another kiwi fruit winery is Durham Light, in Glen Lyon Place off Oropi Rd in Greerton, right in Tauranga. It's open from 10 am to 5 pm, Monday to Saturday. Guided tours are taken through the winery at 10 am and 2 pm.

Longridge Park, 12 km south of Te Puke on SH 33, is a more extensive farm with tours, walks and other activities including jet-boating and white water rafting. It's designed to show the entire range of diversity of NZ farming and in addition to kiwi fruit and other orchards it has cattle, sheep, goats, and even forestry. It's open from 9 am to 5 pm; admission is $6 (children $2.80). The best time to see kiwi fruit picking and packing is during May and June.

Kaituna River Longridge Jets (tel Te Puke 31-515) does jet-boating on the Kaituna River near Te Puke, east of Tauranga.

### Walks

McLaren Falls, in the Wairoa River valley, 11 km from Tauranga just off SH 29, is worth a visit. There's good bushwalking, rock pools and, of course, the falls. It's picturesque, but not exactly awe-inspiring.

There's more bushwalking in the Kaimai Mamaku State Forest Park, which stretches south from Waihi to SH 5, near Rotorua. There are spectacular views from Kaimai Summit and Wairere Falls.

### WHAKATANE

Population 13,000

Whakatane, the principal town on the eastern side of the Bay of Plenty, is much smaller than Tauranga on the western side. It's on a natural harbour at the mouth of the Whakatane River and is the main centre of the Rangitaiki agricultural and milling district. In common with the rest of the Bay of Plenty, Whakatane has a favourable climate all year round and many visitors are attracted to the sunny beaches, especially in summer.

### History

The history of Whakatane began with the landing of the Mataatua canoe at the mouth of the Whakatane River in about 1350 AD, during the great Maori migrations. A Maori settlement was established and the site remained an important Maori centre. As late as the turn of the century there were still only a few White residents. However, when the Europeans realised the richness of the land they began to settle the area and in 1914

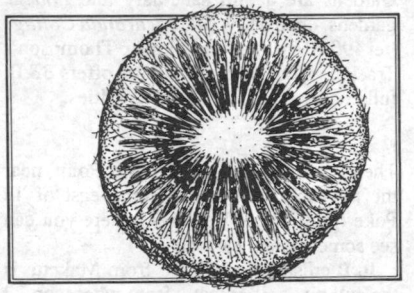

Kiwi fruit

Top: Brian Boru Hotel, Thames (TW)
Bottom: South of Coromandel, Coromandel Peninsula (TW)

Top:  Wellington (TW)
Left:  Viewing a Sperm Whale on a Nature Watch tour (BT)

Whakatane was formed into a town district, becoming a borough 3 years later.

## Information

There's a small but very well-organised Information Centre (tel 86-058) on Boon St half a block off The Strand, the town's tiny main street. The centre is open from 9 am to 5 pm on weekdays. From late October to Easter it also opens from 9 am to 2 pm on Saturdays. The AA office is opposite the Information Centre on Boon St and there's a DOC office (tel 87-213, 88-798) a block away at 28 Commerce St, open from 8 am to 4.30 pm, Monday to Friday.

## Whakatane Museum

The small Whakatane Museum is in Boon St beside the playground, about a block from the Information Centre. It has photographic and artefact exhibits on early Maori and European settlers, and the natural environment, including the smoking White Island volcano just offshore. It's also a centre of historical research, with an archives of historical publications. It's open from 10 am to 4 pm on weekdays and public holidays, and from 1.30 to 4 pm on weekends.

## Pohaturoa

Just to one side of the traffic circle on the corner of The Strand and Commerce St is Pohaturoa, a large rocky area which is an important Maori sacred site. The coastline used to come right up to here and there's a tunnel in the rock where baptisms and other rites were performed. Today the rock is set apart in a little park, with a plaque explaining its historical and religious significance. Also in the park are a Maori canoe, carved benches, and a monument to a chief of the Mataatua tribes.

## Other Attractions

The Whakatane Board Mills (tel 71-899) are working mills of NZ Forest Products Ltd, offering public tours at 10.30 am from Monday to Friday (minimum age 13 years), except during the Christmas season when it closes for a couple of weeks. The Tasman

Pulp & Paper Mill (tel 33-999) also has free public tours, starting at 2 pm weekdays.

The Whakatane Astronomical Observatory (tel 24-618) in Hurunui Ave, Hillcrest, opens to the public every Tuesday evening at about half an hour after sunset, weather permitting.

There's a botanical gardens at the river end of McGarvey Rd, beside a children's playground. Lake Sullivan, a swan lake, is on King St.

The Awakeri Hot Springs, 14½ km from Whakatane on SH 30, the main highway to Rotorua, has a hot springs, spa pools, picnic areas and a motor camp. Also nearby are the Tarawera Falls and Mt Edgecumbe, a nearly perfect archetype of a volcanic cone commanding a panoramic view of the entire Bay of Plenty from the top. You need a permit to climb it; contact Tasman Forestry (tel 34-599).

## Walks

The Information Centre and DOC have lots of info on walks. An interesting 2½ hour Town Centre Walk encompasses a number of scenic and historic spots including an historical cave, a waterfall, a lookout, a redoubt, the Pohaturoa rock and a big game fishing facility.

Other notable walks include the 3½ hour Kohi Point Walkway through the Kohi Point Scenic Reserve, passing many attractive sites including lookouts and the Pa of Toi, reputedly the oldest pa site in New Zealand. Other walkways are the Ohope Bush Walk, the Mokorua Scenic Reserve, Latham's Track and the Matata Walking Track. The 300 metre White Pine Bush Walk, beginning about 10 km from Whakatane, is suitable even for people in wheelchairs and the elderly.

## Other Activities

Check with the Information Centre about the wide variety of activities in and around Whakatane. Possibilities include 4WD mountain safaris to Mt Edgecumbe and the Tarawera Falls, hunting trips, horse treks and bushwalking. There are also numerous water activities including trout or sea fishing, diving and kayak trips, windsurfing and swimming. Jet-boat and white water rafting tours are made from Whakatane on the Rangitaiki, Wairoa, Motu, Whirinaki and Waimana rivers.

During January the Whakatane DOC offers a very cheap summer programme visiting many of the area's most interesting sites.

## Places to Stay
**Hotels** The old *Whakatane Hotel* (tel 88-199) on The Strand has single/double rooms for $35/45, or $5 more with private facilities. The *Bay Private Hotel* (tel 86-788) at 90 McAllister St has B&B for $37.50 or $42.50 per person. The more expensive rooms have private bathrooms.

**Motels** There are a number of motels around Whakatane and in Ohope Beach, 6½ km to the east. Rates begin at around $40/50 for singles/doubles. The best motel prices are at the three motor camps, all of which have motel units (see Camping & Cabins). The *Awakeri Hot Springs* has singles/doubles for $45/60, the *Ohope Beach Holiday Park* has doubles for $50, and *Surf 'N Sand* has units at $40 for a single and $50 to $55 for a twin or double. Otherwise there are no particular bargains.

**Camping & Cabins** The *Whakatane Family Motor Camp* (tel 88-694) in McGarvey Rd beside the Whakatane River has recreational facilities, a swimming pool and a spa pool. Tent or power sites are $6.75 per person, cabins and on-site caravans are $20 to $23 for two. The *Motor Lodge Park* (tel 85-189) in the south of town off Valley Rd has camping sites at $9 per person.

There are several other motor camps on Ohope Beach, 6½ km east of Whakatane. The *Ohope Beach Holiday Park* (tel 24-460), next to the golf course and harbour, has tent or caravan sites for $9 per person and cabins from $28 to $33 for two. The *Surf 'N Sand Holiday Park* (tel 24-884) on the Ohope beachfront, with a miniature golf course, bicycles and wave skis, has tent sites

and powered sites for $8 per person, on-site caravans for $18 per night, and tourist flats at $50 for two.

The *Awakeri Hot Springs* (tel 49-117), 16 km from Whakatane on SH 30, the main highway to Rotorua, is a popular hot springs and has a motor camp. Tent and caravan sites cost $7 per adult, cabins cost $30 for two and tourist flats cost $40 for two.

**Homestays & Farmstays** *Come 'N Stay Holidays* (tel 29-184, 87-955) has listings for homestays and farmstays on farms, orchards, in town, or out at Ohope Beach.

## Places to Eat
Most of Whakatane's eating places are in the shopping area along The Strand. You can get an adequate meal at the *Wedgewood Family Restaurant*, *Sammies Cafe* or the *Heidi Cafe*. Also along here is the *Mexican Restaurant*, open in the evenings, with dinner main courses costing $10 to $12. The *New Hong Kong Restaurant*, half a block off The Strand on Richardson St, has Chinese food, with a separate counter for takeaways straight back through the block in Boon St. The *New Rila Restaurant* in Commerce St is good for steak and seafood.

## Getting There & Away
**Air** Air New Zealand has daily flights linking Whakatane to Auckland, Wellington and Wanganui, with connections to other centres. The Air New Zealand office (tel 88-399) is at 129 The Strand.

A Whakatane-based airline, Bell Air (tel 86-656), has a weekday service to Auckland with two return flights daily. The office is at the Whakatane Airport, about 5 km west of Whakatane on SH 2.

**Bus** The InterCity bus depot (tel 88-208/9) is in Pyne St. InterCity has buses connecting Whakatane with Tauranga and on to Thames, Hamilton and Auckland. Other InterCity buses go to Rotorua and to Gisborne via Opotiki. It's 2 hours to Tauranga or Rotorua, about an hour to Opotiki, and another 2½ hours from Opotiki to Gisborne via the

Waioeka Gorge route (SH 2). Buses around the East Cape originate from Opotiki and Gisborne.

## WHITE ISLAND

White Island is an active volcano smoking and steaming away just 50 km off the coast from Whakatane. It's a small island of 324 hectares formed by three separate volcanic cones, all of different ages. Erosion has worn away most of the surface of the two older cones and the youngest cone, which rose up between the two older ones, now occupies most of the centre of the island. Hot water and steam continually escape from vents over most of the crater floor, and temperatures of 600°C to 800°C have been recorded. The highest point on the island is Mt Gisborne at 321 metres. Geologically, White Island is related to Whale Island and Mt Edgecumbe, as they all lie along the same volcanic trench.

### History

Before the arrival of Europeans the Maoris caught sea birds on the island for food. In 1769 Captain Cook named it White Island because of the dense clouds of white steam hanging above it.

The first European to land on the island was a missionary, the Reverend Henry Williams, who landed in 1826. The island was acquired by Europeans in the late 1830s and changed ownership a number of times after that. Sulphur production began but was interrupted in 1885 by a minor eruption, and the following year the island was hurriedly abandoned in the wake of the Tarawera eruption. The island's sulphur industry was resumed in 1898 but only continued until 1901, when production ceased altogether.

In the 1910s further mining operations were attempted and abandoned due to mud flows and other volcanic activity, and ownership of the island continued to change. In 1953 White Island was declared a Private Scenic Reserve.

The island is still privately owned and the only way you can land on it is with helicopter tours which have arranged permission. For a more detailed history of the island ask the Whakatane Information Centre for their excellent pamphlet, *History of White Island 1769-1966*.

### Getting There & Away

White Island Tours (tel 58-443, 84-188) has helicopter flights to White Island but they're not cheap. It's about $185 per person for a 2 hour excursion which includes a guided 1½ km walk exploring the craters, volcanic sites and the abandoned sulphur works. The helicopter flies you over both White and Whale islands, with magnificent views of the entire Bay of Plenty region. Bell Air (tel 86-656) does 45 minute scenic flights over White Island for $77 per person, but with no landing.

The cheapest way to get to the island is on a cruise with the *Island Princess*. It's a full-day cruise, departing Whakatane at 8 am and returning around 3 pm. The cost of $55 (children $30) includes cruises around both White and Whale islands, plus a big barbecue lunch. Book at the Information Centre.

## WHALE ISLAND

Whale Island, 9 km north of Whakatane, has an area of 414 hectares – somewhat larger than White Island. It was known to the Maoris as Motuhora Island and is still referred to by both the Maori and English names. Its English name comes from its shape, resembling a humpback whale. It's another volcanic island, on the same volcanic trench as White Island, and along its shore are hot springs which can reach 93°C. The summit is 350 metres high and several historic sites including an ancient pa site, an old quarry, and a camp are found around the island.

The Whakatane DOC office has free literature on the interesting history of Whale Island. A few notable events include pre-European Maori settlement, a 1769 landing by Captain Cook, and an 1829 Maori massacre of sailors from the trading vessel *Haweis* while it was anchored at Sulphur Bay. A whaling venture was started and abandoned in the 1830s. In the 1840s the island passed into European ownership and is still privately owned, although since 1965 it has been an officially protected wildlife refuge administered by DOC.

Whale Island is principally a haven for sea and shore birds, some of which are quite rare. Some of the birds use the island only for nesting at certain times of the year, while others are present all year round. The island's protected status means landing is restricted and there are also restrictions on what you can do there – smoking is not allowed, for example, due to the destruction a fire would wreak.

### Getting There & Away

The Whakatane DOC operates tours of Whale Island once a month during most of the year, more often in January. The cost is $30 and the trips last all day. These are the only trips which have permission to land on the island.

The *Island Princess* cruises to White Island also go around the bays of Whale Island, and there's a separate evening cruise to Whale Island only which, for $38, includes dinner and dancing. It leaves Whakatane around 6 pm and returns late in the evening. Ask the Information Centre about diving trips that take advantage of the excellent diving off Whale Island.

### OPOTIKI

Opotiki, the easternmost town of the Bay of Plenty, is the tiny centre of a prosperous dairying and sheep farming district. The town has nothing of particular interest to tourists, but people do come to visit the nearby beaches in summer – there are good surfing beaches at Ohiwa and Waiotahi. A road from Opotiki crosses over the Motu Hills through beautiful bush scenery – the road is unsealed and there's not much traffic.

Historically, Opotiki was the centre of Hauhauism, a doctrine advocating the extermination of Whites. In 1865 the Reverend Karl Volkner was murdered in his church, St Stephen the Martyr, which culminated in the church being transformed into a fortress by government troops.

Travelling east from Opotiki there are two routes to choose from. SH 2 crosses the spectacular Waioeka Gorge. There are some fine walks of 1 day and longer in the Waioeka Gorge Scenic Reserve; ask DOC for info. The gorge gets progressively steeper and narrower as you travel inland, before the route crosses typically green, rolling hills, dotted with sheep, on the descent to Gisborne.

The other route east from Opotiki is SH 35, around the East Cape.

### Places to Stay

**Hotels** Opotiki has two hotels, both in Church St. The *DB Opotiki Hotel* (tel 56-078) has single/double rooms for $22/40. The *Masonic Hotel* (tel 56-115) is slightly more expensive at $31/45. The *Patiti Lodge* (tel 56-834) at 112 Ford St has single/double rooms for $27/40.

**Motels** The *Ranui Motel* (tel 56-669) is at 36 Bridge St and the *Magnolia Court Motel* (tel 58-490) is on the corner of Bridge and Nelson streets.

**Camping & Cabins** The *Opotiki Holiday Park* (tel 56-050) on the corner of Grey St and Potts Ave, one block from the post office, has powered sites and tent sites for $6.50 per person and a bunkroom for $9 per person. For two people, cabins cost $23, tourist flats cost $32 and motel units cost $38.

There are several beachfront camping grounds near Opotiki. The *Island View Family Holiday Park* (tel 57-519), on Appleton Rd, 4 km from town, has camping sites, cabins and on-site caravans. The *Tirohanga Beach Motor Camp* (tel 57-942) on the East Coast Rd, 6 km from town, has camping sites, cabins and tourist flats. Also on the East Coast Rd, 12 km from Opotiki, the *Opape Motor Camp* (tel 58-175) has camping sites and on-site caravans.

### Getting There & Away

The InterCity bus depot (tel 56-146) is on Elliott St. InterCity has buses connecting Opotiki with Whakatane (1 hour), Tauranga

(3 hours), Rotorua (3 hours), and Auckland (7½ hours via Rotorua). You can also get to and from Auckland without going through Rotorua, but you have to change buses in Tauranga or Hamilton.

There are two InterCity routes from Opotiki to Gisborne. The shorter one (2½ hours) travels inland through the Waioeka Gorge once daily. The longer route (8 hours) goes along the coast around the East Cape and runs once a day, every day except Saturdays.

# Central North Island

The Central North Island region is famous throughout the world for its geysers, hot springs, mud pools, shimmering lakes, trout fishing, tramping, and a host of other activities. The region is also of great significance to the Maori population, whose presence there dates back to its discovery and exploration by Maoris in the 14th century.

It's still an active volcanic area and there have been some massive eruptions in the area in the last 100 years. The towns of Rotorua and Taupo are the centres of a thriving tourist industry that caters for the whole range of tastes.

## Rotorua

Population 53,000

Rotorua stands 280 metres above sea level on the shores of the lake of the same name. It's 109 km south-east of Hamilton, 368 km west of Gisborne, and 84 km north of Taupo. Rotorua is probably the most popular tourist area of the North Island, if not of New Zealand. Despite a strong smell of rotten eggs, Rotorua has a lot going for it, including:

- The most energetic thermal activity in the country – bubbling mud pools, gurgling hot springs, gushing geysers, evil smells. It's sometimes nicknamed 'Sulphur City' and some say it's sitting on a time bomb.
- A large Maori population with the most interesting cultural activities to be seen in New Zealand.
- The world's best trout fishing and some interesting trout springs and wildlife parks.

Despite all these attractions and the consequent hordes of tourists it's not too much of a rip-off. The blaze of signs outside the motels may be an assault on the senses but the assault on the wallet is not as devastating as you might think.

New Zealand's main belt of volcanic activity stretches in a line from White Island, north of the Bay of Plenty, down to the Tongariro National Park. At one time it must have continued even further, as Mt Egmont is a dormant volcano and Wellington Harbour is the flooded crater of a long extinct volcano. Rotorua is the most active area; all around the city steam drifts up from behind bushes, out of road drains and around rocks.

### Where Has All the Steam Gone?

The geysers, hot springs, bubbling mud pools and so on at Rotorua have performed faithfully as long as the Maori and Pakeha can remember but recently the geysers have erupted less frequently, the hot water hasn't been so hot, and some of the thermal attractions have simply dried up. There's considerable argument over the cause but undeniably a century ago there were not rows of hotels and motels all cashing in on the free hot water. Less obviously all that thermal activity is also widely tapped for industrial use, for heating and for power.

This is all fine, but Rotorua is built around tourism and if the geysers dry up so may the tourists. This fear has prompted all sorts of new rules about tapping Rotorua's steam potential. In particular the city government has capped all bores within a km of the Whakarewarewa reserve since this is the major Rotorua thermal attraction. A lot of residents blame the whole thing on the huge Wairakei thermal power station near Taupo.

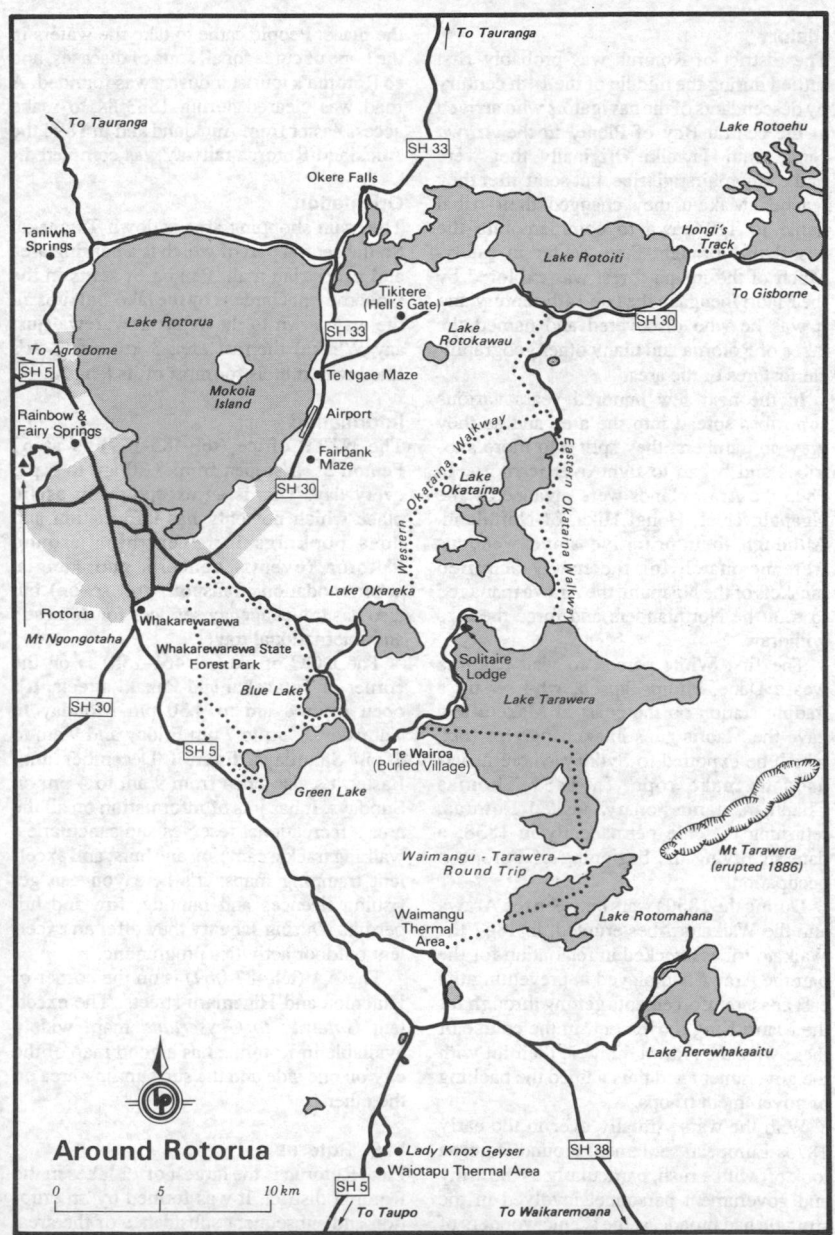

**Around Rotorua**

To Tauranga

To Tauranga

SH 33

Okere Falls

Lake Rotoehu

Lake Rotoiti

Hongi's Track

To Gisborne

Taniwha Springs

Tikitere (Hell's Gate)

SH 33

Lake Rotokawau

SH 30

Lake Rotorua

Te Ngae Maze

Airport

To Agrodome

SH 5

Mokoia Island

Western Okataina Walkway

Lake Okataina

Eastern Okataina Walkway

Rainbow & Fairy Springs

Fairbank Maze

SH 30

Lake Okareka

Rotorua

Whakarewarewa

Solitaire Lodge

Mt Ngongotaha

Whakarewarewa State Forest Park

Lake Tarawera

Blue Lake

SH 30

Te Wairoa (Buried Village)

SH 5

Green Lake

Mt Tarawera (erupted 1886)

Waimangu - Tarawera Round Trip

Waimangu Thermal Area

Lake Rotomahana

Lake Rerewhakaaitu

Lady Knox Geyser

Waiotapu Thermal Area

SH 38

0   5   10 km

SH 5

To Taupo

To Waikaremoana

## History

The district of Rotorua was probably first settled during the middle of the 14th century by descendants of the navigators who arrived at the central Bay of Plenty in the *Arawa* canoe from Hawaiki. Originally, they were of the Ohomairangi tribe, but soon after they reached Maketu they changed their tribal name to Te Arawa to commemorate the vessel that brought them so far in safety. Much of the inland forest was explored by the Maori Ihenga in the late 14th century and it was he who discovered and named the lakes of Rotorua and many other geographical features of the area.

In the next few hundred years various sub-tribes spread into the area and as they grew in numbers, they split into more sub-tribes and began to fight over territory. In 1823 the Arawa lands were invaded by the Ngapuhi chief, Hongi Hika, of Northland. Although their primitive stone weapons were no match for the newly acquired muskets of the Ngapuhi, the Arawa managed to rout the Northlanders and force them to withdraw.

The first White person to visit Rotorua was a Dane, Philip Tapsell, who set up a trading station on the coast at Maketu and gave the Maoris guns in exchange for flax, which he exported to Sydney where it was used to make rope. In 1831 Thomas Chapman, a missionary, visited Rotorua, returning to settle permanently in 1838; a date signifying the beginning of European occupation.

During the 1850s wars between the Arawa and the Waikato tribes erupted. In 1867 the Waikato tribes attacked in retaliation for the part the Arawa had played in preventing the east coast reinforcements getting through for the Maori King movement. In the course of these wars the Arawa threw in their lot with the government and thus gained the backing of government troops.

With the wars virtually over in the early 1870s European settlement around Rotorua took off with a rush, particularly as the army and government personnel involved in the struggle had broadcast the scenic wonders of the place. People came to take the waters in the hope of cures for all sorts of diseases, and so Rotorua's tourist industry was founded. A road was cleared during 1883-84 to make access easier from Auckland and in 1894 the Auckland-Rotorua railway was completed.

## Orientation

The main shopping area is down Tutanekai St, the central part of which is a parking area and pedestrian mall. Fenton St starts in the Government Gardens by the lake and runs all the way down to the Whakarewarewa (just say Whaka) thermal area 3 km away. It's lined with motels for most of its length.

## Information

The NZTP office (tel 485-179) is at 67 Fenton St. It's open from 8.30 am to 5 pm every day. This is an exceptionally useful place which not only has information and does bookings for everything around Rotorua (events, concerts and hangis, accommodation, transport, and so on) but also has travel agency services for domestic and international travel.

The DOC office (tel 461-155) is on the corner of Tutanekai and Pukaki streets. It's open from 8 am to 4.30 pm Monday to Thursday, 8 am to 7 pm Friday and 9 am to 4 pm Saturdays. From 1 December until Easter it's also open from 9 am to 4 pm on Sundays. It has lots of information on all the area's recreational reserves and sanctuaries, walking tracks, camping and huts, and excellent tramping maps; it's here you can get fishing licences and hunting, fire and hut permits. During January they offer an excellent outdoor activities programme.

The AA (tel 483-069) is on the corner of Hinemoa and Hinemaru streets. The excellent *Gateway to Geyserland* map, widely available in Rotorua, has a good map of the city on one side and the surrounding area on the other.

## Lake Rotorua

Lake Rotorua is the largest of 12 lakes in the Rotorua district. It was formed by an eruption and subsequent subsidence of the area.

There are various cruises on the lake – they depart from the jetty at the end of Tutanekai St. There are cruises every day to Mokoia Island on the *Ngaroto* from $20 (children free) for a 2 hour excursion or dinner barbecue. Or you can take the *Lakeland Queen* paddleboat for cruises, some with lunch or dinner included. You can also hire speed boats and jet catamarans, charter fishing yachts, go for a flight on the floatplane or simply pedal yourself around on the lake.

## Ohinemutu

Ohinemutu is a Maori village by the lake side with a finely carved meeting house and the historic Maori Church of St Faiths. In the church a Maori-cloaked Christ is etched on a window so that he appears to be walking on the waters of Lake Rotorua! Seen from this window, it's surprising how much Lake Rotorua does resemble the Sea of Galilee.

## Museum & Art Gallery

The Bath House, the small city museum and art gallery, is housed in Tudor Towers, an 'olde English' Tudor-style building in the Government Gardens, and yes, it was once used as a bath house, around the turn of the century. The museum displays interesting Maori artefacts and there's a fascinating model explaining the Tarawera eruption of 1886. Have a look at this before you do the Waimangu-Tarawera round trip covered later. The museum and art gallery are open from 10 am to 4.30 pm on weekdays and holiday weekends, and 1 to 4.30 pm on regular weekends; admission is free. In the gardens are typical English things like croquet lawns and rose gardens – not to mention atypical steaming pools!

## Te Amorangi Museum

Te Amorangi Museum has Maori and colonial artefacts, working demonstrations of agricultural machinery, and a miniature steam railway which is operated on the second Sunday each month. The museum is near the airport at Holdens Bay and is open from 1 to 4 pm on Sundays and holidays; admission is free.

## Whakarewarewa

Whakarewarewa is Rotorua's largest and best-known thermal zone and a major Maori cultural area. It's OK if you can't get your tongue around Whakarewarewa – it's known simply as Whaka.

The most spectacular geyser is Pohutu (Maori for 'big splash' or 'explosion'). It is also the most unpredictable, erupting anywhere from two to nine times a day. Pohutu spurts hot water about 20 metres in the air but sometimes shoots up over 30 metres in brief 'shots'. Each display lasts about 20 minutes, although one is reputed to have lasted 14 hours! You get an advance warning because the Prince of Wales' Feathers geyser always starts off shortly before Pohutu.

Other Whaka attractions are a nocturnal kiwi house, a replica Maori village, and Maori craftspeople working in the carving centre. There are lots of Maori concerts around Rotorua but the daily one at Whaka is rated one of the best.

Whaka is 3 km south of the town centre, straight down Fenton St. There's a bus roughly once an hour but on weekends the service is so infrequent you may have to walk or hitch. The reserve is open daily from 8.30 am to 5 pm; admission is $7.70 (children $2.25, family $19). The Maori concert is presented at 12.15 pm daily and costs $8.50 (children $2.25, family $20.50) or you can do the reserve and the concert for $15.20 (children $4, family $38.40).

## Hell's Gate

Hell's Gate, another highly active thermal area, is 16 km from Rotorua on the road to Whakatane (SH 30). The reserve covers 10 hectares, with a 2.5 km walking track to cover the various attractions including the largest hot thermal waterfall in the southern hemisphere. Guide sheets are printed in eight languages, including Australian! It's open daily from 9 am to 5 pm; admission is $7 (children $2.50).

George Bernard Shaw visited Hell's Gate in 1934. 'I wish I had never seen the place,' he said. 'It reminds me too vividly of the fate theologians have promised me.'

## Waiotapu

Waiotapu, 31 km south of Rotorua on SH 5, is another thermal area worth visiting. It has many interesting features including the large, effervescently boiling Champagne Pool, craters and blowholes, colourful mineral terraces and other rock formations, and the Lady Knox Geyser which spouts off (with a little prompting) punctually at 10.15 each morning and gushes until around noon. It's open daily from 8.30 am to 5 pm; admission is $6 (children $2.50).

### Performing to Schedule

How do the on-time geysers manage to perform so neatly to schedule? Simple – you block them up with some rags so the pressure builds up and you shove a couple of kg of soap powder in to decrease the surface viscosity. And off they go.

## Trout Springs

There are several trout springs around Rotorua – the springs run down to Lake Rotorua and the trout, lured perhaps by the free feeds waiting for them from the tourists, swim up the streams to the springs. They are not trapped there; if you watch you may see a trout leaping the little falls to return to the lake or come up to the springs. Try to latch on to a bus tour group or ask one of the people there to explain things – after about half an hour you'll be able to tell a rainbow trout from a brown trout, a male from a female, and a young one from an old one.

The Rainbow and Fairy Springs are the best known of the trout springs. There are a number of springs (one with an underwater viewer), an aviary and a nocturnal kiwi house. The first time I was there a male kiwi was being 'introduced' to a female kiwi and getting a damn good kicking for his troubles! Say 'hi' to Ray Punter, the knowledgeable 'keeper of the trout'. At the springs you'll also find eels, wallabies, deer, birds, sheep, wild pigs and other native and introduced animals, now all found wild in New Zealand. The springs are 4 km north of the city centre around the lake and they are open from 8 am to 5 pm daily; admission is $8 (children $3).

Across from the springs is Rainbow Farm, a farm show with sheep shearing, sheep dogs and a chance to try your hand at milking a cow. There are shows three times daily and entry is $8 (children $3, family $20).

Paradise Valley Springs are similar trout springs, set in an attractive 6 hectare park with various animals, including a pride of lions. If you've never been in a lion's cage this is your chance – the cubs, from a few weeks to a few months old, are kept in an enclosed area and you can go in and play around with them to your heart's content. The springs, 13 km from Rotorua on Paradise Valley Rd, at the foot of Mt Ngongotaha, open daily from 9 am to 5 pm; admission is $7.50 (children $3).

## Skyline Skyrides

At Skyline Skyrides you can take a gondola ride up Mt Ngongotaha for a wide view of the lake area and once up there go flying 900 metres back down the mountain on a luge (a sort of sled without snow) or a flying fox, coming back up again on a chairlift. Also up there are a cafe and a restaurant for twilight dining. The gondola costs $7.50 (children $2.50, family $16.50) for the return trip and the luge is $3.50 for one ride, less per ride for multiple trips.

At the entrance to the skyrides is a simulator, a new contraption introduced at the Brisbane Expo in 1988 and developed from the principles of flight simulators used in training military pilots. You can sample various thrills including downhill skiing, car and motorcycle speedway racing, jet-boating down the Shotover River, helicopter flying and, of course, a tear across the skies in a fighter plane. Each ride is about 4 minutes long and costs $5 (children $4.50). It operates daily from 9 am to 5 pm.

Also here is a herb shop where you can tour the herb gardens out the back for $3 (children free), or try your skill at mini-golf.

## Agrodome & Trainworld

If seeing the millions of sheep in the NZ countryside has stimulated your interest in these animals and their relation to New Zealand, visit Agrodome. Going to see a

superbly detailed model portrays the towns, villages, countryside and rail centres of Britain. It's open from 8.45 am to 5 pm daily; admission is $6 (children $3, family $14).

## Mazes

The NZ maze craze has spread to Rotorua and there are a couple of mazes near the airport. The Fairbank Maze, opposite the airport, is the largest hedge maze in New Zealand, with a 1.6 km pathway. There's also an orchard, gardens, ponds, picnic areas, birds and animals. The maze is open from 9 am to 5 pm daily; admission is $3 (children $1.50).

Te Ngae Park, 3 km beyond the airport, is a three-dimensional, 1.7 km wooden maze similar to the original Wanaka maze in the South Island. It's open every day from 9 am to 5 pm, admission is $4 (children $2).

## Thermal Pools

Of course you won't want to visit Rotorua without taking a dip in some thermal pools. The Polynesian Pools, in town off Hinemoa St, are open daily from 9 am to 10 pm. The first building in Rotorua, a bath house, was opened at these springs in 1882 and people have been swearing to the health-giving properties of the waters ever since. There are several pools in the complex including the Priest and Radium Hot Springs adult pools ($5.50), a separate pool for adults and children ($5.50, children $2), private pools ($6.50, children $2 for half an hour), and a sauna ($6). From 7.30 to 9.30 pm on Sunday evenings there's a poolside jazz band.

For ordinary swimming there's the Aquatic Centre, a non-thermal swim centre with a 50 metre outdoor pool, a 31 metre indoor pool, a recreational pool (all heated) and various activities for children. It's open daily from 6 am to 9 pm; admission is $2.25 (children $1). The centre is on Tarewa Rd, just behind the Thermal Lodge hostel.

## Orchid Gardens

The Orchid Gardens in Hinemaru St house not only an extensive orchid hothouse blooming all year round but also a

bunch of sheep seems a rather strange thing to do in New Zealand, but for $7 (children $3.50) you get an interesting, educational and entertaining 1 hour show at 9.15 am, 11 am and 2.30 pm daily. There's sheep shearing and sheep dogs displaying their expertise; by the time you're through you may even be able to tell the difference between some of the 19 breeds of sheep on show.

Outdoors are some life-size moa replicas and you can hire horses and minibikes for guided tours of the 120 hectare farm. Agrodome is 7 km north of Rotorua on SH 1.

Also in the Agrodome complex is Trainworld, an interesting little place with one of the largest '00' gauge model railways in the world. About 750 metres of track take 20 to 30 trains at a time whizzing around a 102 sq metre model which is as fascinating as the trains themselves. The whole thing is dubbed 'a journey through Britain' and the

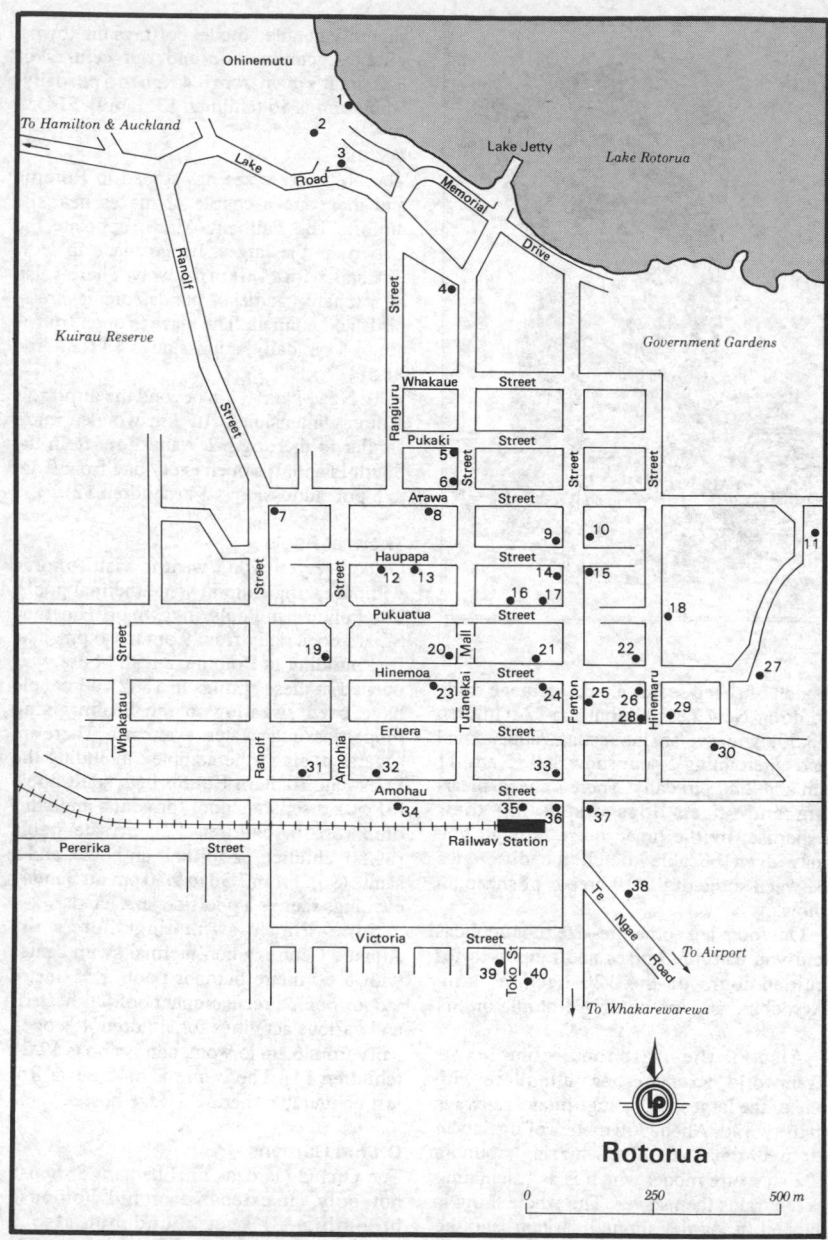

Ohinemutu

To Hamilton & Auckland

Lake Road

Lake Jetty

Lake Rotorua

Memorial Drive

Kuirau Reserve

Government Gardens

Ranolf Street

Rangiuru Street

Whakaue Street

Pukaki Street

Arawa Street

Haupapa Street

Pukuatua Street

Hinemoa Street

Eruera Street

Amohau Street

Railway Station

Pererika Street

Victoria Street

Whakatau Street

Tutanekai Street

Amohia Street

Ranolf

Mall

Fenton Street

Hinemaru Street

Toko St

Te Ngae Road

To Airport

To Whakarewarewa

**Rotorua**

0        250        500 m

| | | | |
|---|---|---|---|
| 1 | St Faiths Church | 21 | Grand Establishment, Cobb & Co |
| 2 | Ohinemutu Meeting House | 22 | Automobile Association (AA) |
| 3 | Lake Tavern | 23 | Smacker Jack's |
| 4 | Pizza Hut | 24 | Passage to India Cafe |
| 5 | Department of Conservation (DOC) | 25 | Chez Bleu |
| 6 | Bakers Butique & Coffee Bean | 26 | Eaton Hall |
| 7 | Arawa Lodge Motel | 27 | Polynesian Pools |
| 8 | Palace Tavern | 28 | Youth Hostel |
| 9 | NZTP Office | 29 | Hyatt Kingsgate |
| 10 | Municipal Council Chamber & Civic Theatre | 30 | Travelodge |
| 11 | Tudor Towers, Museum & Art Gallery | 31 | Kentucky Fried Chicken |
| 12 | Ivanhoe Lodge | 32 | Spa Tourist Hotel |
| 13 | Floyd's Cafe | 33 | Fentons |
| 14 | Cabbage Tree Cafe | 34 | InterCity Travel Centre |
| 15 | Police Station | 35 | Air New Zealand, Mt Cook & Gray Line |
| 16 | Gazebo Restaurant | 36 | McDonald's |
| 17 | Pizza Forno | 37 | Pac'N Save Supermarket |
| 18 | Orchid Gardens | 38 | YWCA |
| 19 | Zanelli's Restaurant | 39 | Tresco Guest House |
| 20 | CPO | 40 | Morihana Guest House |

Microworld display, where you can get a microscopic view of living reptiles and insects, and a big water organ.

Water organs are very unusual. There are only a half dozen or so in the world and this is the only one in the southern hemisphere. The sound is not actually produced by the water. The organ is really a huge fountain with over 800 jets putting on a magnificent 15 minute show of water swirling, leaping and making generally graceful, ballet-like movements up to 4 metres high, all choreographed to symphonic music and accompanied by a light show turning the water into changing colours.

The water organ plays every hour on the hour from 10 am to 5 pm. The complex is open from 8.30 am to 5.30 pm daily; admission is $6.60 (children $2.20, family $15). There's a very pleasant cafe at one end of the hothouse where you can enjoy classical music along with the orchids.

## Other Attractions

There's a Leisure World amusement park off Te Ngae Rd on the outskirts of town, with rides, a big waterslide and mini-golf. Nearby is a golf course with driving, rifle and pistol ranges. Little Village is an 'olde worlde'

village replica opposite the Rotorua International Hotel. On the outside wall of the police station opposite the NZTP office is an excellent mural depicting New Zealand's Maori and Pakeha heritage.

You can go horse-riding over farmland at The Farmhouse, off Sunnex Rd on the western side of Lake Rotorua. The Blue Lake has lots of summertime activities including water-skiing, jet-skis, parasailing, etc. The Green Lake, though, is sacred to the Maori people and you're not allowed to go on that one.

## Waimangu-Tarawera Round Trip

There are all sorts of tours and trips around Rotorua but this day trip is not to be missed. From Rotorua the tour takes you to the Waimangu Tearooms, where you can start the day off right with a Devonshire tea before you have to walk a km or two.

The walk, an easy downhill stroll, first passes the Waimangu Cauldron – a pale-blue lake steaming quietly at 53°C. In this valley the Waimangu Geyser used to perform actively enough to be rated the 'largest geyser in the world'. Between 1900 and its extinction in 1904 it would occasionally spout jets nearly 500 metres high!

The walk continues down to Rotomahana, 'warm lake', where a launch meets and carries you across the lake by the site of the Pink and White Terraces. These were one of the wonders of Rotorua but in 1886 nearby Mt Tarawera disastrously erupted. On 10 June, in the middle of the night, the eruption suddenly lit up the sky and by the time it was finished, 6 hours later, over 8000 sq km had been buried in ash, lava and mud, the Maori village of Te Wairoa was obliterated, the Terraces were destroyed, 153 people were killed and Lake Rotomahana was formed.

After you leave the launch it's a short walk – about 500 metres – across to Lake Tarawera where another launch takes you across to Te Wairoa, now known as the Buried Village – a sort of Maori Pompeii. At a waterfall nearby, your bus will collect you for the drive back to Rotorua. En route it stops at the Blue and Green lakes (usually the difference in colour is striking) and Whakarewarewa Forest Park where California Redwoods have been planted and, like the California rainbow trout, have done better than they ever did at home.

The tour, operated by InterCity Tours, departs daily at 9 am, returning at 5 pm. It'll set you back $54 (children $26). You have to take your own lunch as well but you'll probably reckon it was worth it by the time you get back.

If you don't go on the tour you can make the same trip on your own; you just have to arrange your own transport at both ends. If you join the tour at Waimangu the fee for the remainder of the trip is $25 (children $13, family $63). To visit the Waimangu Thermal Valley alone costs $7 (children $3.50, family $17.50) including a return uphill lift back to where you started. Or you can do the valley walk combined with a half-hour launch cruise on Lake Rotomahana for $13.50 (children $6.75, family $33.75). The cruise passes the Steaming Cliffs and the sites of the Pink and White Terraces. Waimangu is open daily from 8 am to 5 pm.

### Buried Village & Lake Tarawera

The Buried Village can be visited on the Waimangu-Tarawera Round Trip or as a separate trip. Coming from Rotorua it's a 15 km scenic drive along Tarawera Rd, passing the Blue and Green Lakes. On display are many artefacts unearthed from the village, displays on the Mt Tarawera eruption, and excavated buildings – you may see excavations still in progress.

Prior to the great eruption, Te Wairoa was New Zealand's principal tourist resort, being the starting point for excursions over Lake Tarawera to the famous Pink and White Terraces. Of particular interest is the story of the *tohunga*, Tuhoto Ariki, who foretold the destruction of the village – 4 days before the eruption occurred, a phantom Maori canoe was sighted on Lake Tarawera and the tohunga predicted that the village would be 'overwhelmed'. He was buried alive in his house (now excavated and on view) for 4 days before being dug out by Pakehas – the Maoris refused to rescue him, fearing that he had used his powers to cause the eruption! He died shortly thereafter, at over 100 years of age.

Many other interesting things are on view at the Buried Village and there's also a good bushwalk through the valley to Te Wairoa Falls, 83 metres high. The village is open from 8.30 am to 5 pm daily (9 am to 4.30 pm, June to August); admission is $6 (children $2).

At 11.30 am daily you can take the launch from the wharf at the foot of the Buried Village and cross over Lake Tarawera towards Lake Rotomahana, where it picks up the people coming from the Waimangu-Tarawera round trip. The boat stays on the other side for 1½ hours, making it a 3 hour trip in all, and the cost is $10 return. You could also take it over on one day, camp at Hot Water Beach on Te Rata Bay, and return on another day, for no extra cost.

### Other Trips & Tours

In the past couple of years two full-day tours have been developed specifically for backpackers and adventurous folk. They can be booked through any hostel in town. Both are good value and enormously popular.

Carey's Capers (tel 478-035) is a 'volcanic tour', visiting all of Rotorua's best thermal areas in 1 day including Waiotapu, the Lady Knox Geyser, Waimangu, Whakarewarewa, Hell's Gate and Hakereteke Stream (locally known as 'Kerosene Creek') where you can go for a swim in a lovely, naturally hot thermal swimming hole hidden away in the forest. The cost is $49 for the whole day. By the time you add up the entrance fees to all the various sites, this tour is a bargain. Colin Carey, who operates the tour, has received rave reviews from numerous travellers.

The other backpacker's tour, known simply as 'Doug & Mickey Rat's Tour' after the operators Doug Brownlie and his dog, takes a 4WD vehicle up Mt Tarawera (1111 metres), where you hike around the gigantic crater and then plunge right in, sliding down the ashy sides all the way to the crater's core. Of course there are great views from the top – on a clear day you can see all the way to Mt Egmont, nearly 250 km away to the south-west. All in all it's an outstanding experience. The tour also visits Waiotapu and the Lady Knox Geyser, and stops off at Kerosene Creek for a hot swim. The cost is $45; book directly with Doug (tel 461-000) or at any hostel.

The NZTP can advise on many other tours in and near Rotorua and further afield, and makes bookings for them. InterCity Tours (tel 481-039) offer city tours, tours to the thermal attractions, tours to the Buried Village, a visit to the Agrodome and so on, in addition to the excellent Waimangu-Tarawera day trip previously mentioned. Gray Line also does half-day tours around Rotorua and two other companies, Mt Tarawera Tours (tel 480-623) and Tarawera Mountain Sightseeing Tours (tel 485-179) make half-day 4WD trips up Mt Tarawera for $38.

Tours further afield include InterCity Waitomo Cave day trips for $50 (children $25) including the cave entrance fees and a full-day sightseeing trip to Taupo for $55 with Taylor's Tours (tel 461-333). Whirinaki Forest Tours (tel 65-235) offer full-day tours exploring the Whirinaki Forest for $62 (children $31). Whirinaki Wilderness Experience (tel Auckland 774-546) has 2 to 5 day wilderness, rafting, trekking and farm trips which depart from Rotorua, from October to May.

## Aerial Sightseeing

All Rotorua's attractions can be seen from the air and some, like the Tarawera volcano, are best observed from above. Flights depart either from the airport or by floatplane from the lake and are priced from around $35.

Volcanic 'Wunderflites' from Rotorua Airport (tel 456-079) are particularly popular. They will fly you up and over the awesome chasm of Mt Tarawera on a half-hour flight for $66 (children $44). For an additional fee you can land beside the volcano and wander over to look over the edge. They also have longer flights over the lakes, out to White Island, and even down to Mt Ruapehu and Mt Ngauruahoe in the Tongariro National Park.

My Rotorua flightseeing favourite is White Island Airways (tel 459-832) who operate an all-biplane fleet of Tiger Moths and Dragon Rapides. In their Tiger Moths they'll fly you over the city for $77, over Mt Tarawera for $135 or, if your stomach is strong, they'll take you up for some aerobatics for $99. You're out in the open air in a Tiger Moth but in your flight suit, leather helmet and goggles you'll feel as warm as the Red Baron. They also have a modern 10-seater de Havilland Dove; in this a Mt Tarawera trip costs $66 or you can take trips further afield, including to White Island, for $187 to $418.

Other operators include the Helicopter Line (tel 476-086) who operate from the City Helipad on Te Ngae Rd near the centre, Geyserland Airways (tel 456-749) who operate from the airport and Floatplane Airservices (tel 484-069) by the lake.

## White Water Rafting & Jet-Boating

There's white water rafting on the Rangitaiki River. Half-day trips, with a barbecue afterwards, cost around $55 to $65. The trips depart from the Rangitaiki River Bridge in

Murupara but if you don't have wheels they'll provide transport from Rotorua for an extra $5. Contact River Rats (tel 476-049), The Rafting Company (tel 480-233) or White Water Rafting Adventures (tel 457-182).

### Parks & Walks

Whakarewarewa Forest Park is just on the edge of town. This is a forest of non-native trees planted earlier this century as an experiment to find the most suitable species to replace New Zealand's rapidly dwindling and slow-growing native trees. The Forest Visitor Centre (tel 462-787) is open 9 am to 5 pm daily, with displays and an audiovisual on the history and management of NZ forests and forest industries. Check in here if you want to go walking – there are many walks ranging from half an hour to 4 hours in length, including routes to the Blue and Green lakes. Several walks start at the Visitor Centre, including a half-hour Redwood Forest Walk through a grove of large California Redwood trees.

About 50 km east of Rotorua is the Whirinaki Forest Park, a native podocarp (plum pine) forest with walking tracks, scenic drives, a 110 km motorcycle track, a recreation camp, other camping and huts, lookouts, waterfalls, the Whirinaki River, and some special areas including the Oriuwaka Ecological Reserve and the Arahaki Lagoon. The Park headquarters (tel Murupara 65-601) is adjacent to Minginui Village. It's open from 7.30 am to 4.30 pm on weekdays, and from 9 am to 4.30 pm on weekends and holidays. If you're there in January ask about the summer activities programme.

Other walks in the Rotorua area include the 22½ km Western Okataina Walkway from Lake Okareka to Ruato, through native bush. There's public transport past the Ruato end only; the whole walk takes about 6 hours, and you need boots or stout shoes.

There is now also an Eastern Okataina Walkway. It goes along the eastern shoreline of Lake Okataina to Lake Tarawera – about a 2-1/2 hour, 8 km walk. At one time you had to walk out the same way you walked in but recently a new connecting track has been added, making it possible to do a 2 day walk from either Lake Okataina or Ruato to Lake Tarawera, camp overnight at a DOC camping site ($5 per site) and the next day hike up Mt Tarawera, with a choice of three exit points. Get a map from the Rotorua DOC office before starting out.

Shorter walks can be made around Okataina, Mt Ngongotaha (just north of Rotorua), and Lake Rotorua. The DOC has info on these and other walks, and excellent maps. During January they have a programme of walks and other outdoor activities.

You can tramp up Mt Tarawera, but take some water as it's a scarce resource up there. Watch what streams you drink from anywhere in the area; being a thermal area much of the water isn't pure. Mt Tarawera is on private property so before you go you must obtain permission from the Te Arawa Maori Trust Board on Pukuatua St, or check at the NZTP office. It's not a hard walk (about 2½ to 3 hours each way) and no technical expertise is required.

### Fishing

And, of course, there's trout fishing. You can hire guides or go it alone, but remember you need a licence and there are various regulations about how you may catch them. The guided fishing trips aren't cheap (about $66 to $77 per hour) but they all but guarantee that you'll catch a fish. Get four people together to split the cost and it comes to just over $30 per person for a 2 hour trip. Ask at the NZTP office for fishing boat operators. Of course you can also just wander down to the lakefront and fish, as long as you have a fishing licence and you do it in the fishing season (October to June).

You can get your fishing licence directly from a fishing guide or from the DOC office. Rotorua district fishing licences cost $7 per day, $19 per week, $27 per month or $39 for the whole season. NZTP has special tourist fishing licences which, for $56.25, allow you to fish not only in the Rotorua district but anywhere in New Zealand for a whole month. Both places can tell you about fishing regulations.

## Places to Stay

With all the Rotorua region's tourist attractions, it's not surprising that it is well endowed with places to stay. Hot mineral pools are a Rotorua bonus in many establishments, no matter how humble, and almost every place is thermally heated.

**Hostels** The *Rotorua Youth Hostel* (tel 476-810) is on the corner of Eruera and Hinemaru streets, close to the town centre. Formerly known as the Colonial Inn, it's an excellent hostel, clean and bright, with plenty of twin and family rooms, a thermal spa pool, bicycles for hire, and it's open all day. Nightly cost is $15.

The *Ivanhoe Lodge* (tel 486-985) at 54 Haupapa St is also central. This popular, busy hostel has accommodation ranging from bunkrooms to heated cabins to rooms which come complete with bedding. Costs are $12.50 in a bunkroom, $17 in a cabin for singles, and $13 or $14 in a cabin for doubles or twins. Single/double rooms cost $20/34. There's a good communal kitchen, a comfortable lounge, a video, a house bar and billiard table, a spa pool (swimming gear unnecessary) and bicycles for hire.

The *Thermal Lodge* (tel 470-931) is at 60 Tarewa Rd, a km or so from the town centre. The cost per person is $17.50 in singles, $14 in doubles or $12.50 in larger rooms. There's also a big lawn area where tent and campervan sites are $6 per person. You can hire bicycles, and the lodge has a courtesy bus too.

The *YWCA* (tel 485-445) on Te Ngae Rd has casual accommodation for women and men in single and double rooms for $18 per person, or in a large dorm room for $12 ($1 more if you hire linen). Long-term accommodation is also available.

**Guest Houses** There are a number of guest houses and B&B places around Rotorua. The *Spa Tourist Hotel* (tel 483-486) is a simple little place at 69 Amohau St, opposite the InterCity Travel Centre. Singles are $28, twins and doubles $46 to $50, including a continental breakfast. All rooms have washbasins with hot and cold water. There are also cabins at $12 per person. Although this is a rather busy and noisy street during the daytime, Rotorua is a quiet place at night.

There are a couple of places on Toko St, off Victoria St which is just across the railway line from McDonald's. At 3 Toko St there's *Tresco Guest House* (tel 489-611), where B&B costs $36/55 for singles/-doubles. There are sinks in the rooms and it's a neat, tidy and comfortable place.

The same can be said for the *Morihana Guest House* (tel 488-511) a bit further down at 20 Toko St. Single/double rooms here cost $35/55, including breakfast. Both places have hot mineral pools. Although it's reasonably central, Toko St is a quiet street and well away from the tourist hustle of central Rotorua.

The *Traquair Lodge* (tel 486-149) at 126 Ranolf St is not quite as central. It's a homely though slightly scruffy and dog-eared sort of place, but breakfast is a major attraction there. 'The best breakfast we had in the North Island', reported one well-fed visitor. If you like to start the day with bacon & eggs and the other essentials of a truly British morning feast then this is the place. Singles/doubles, including breakfast, cost $27.50/44.

Other guest houses include *Eaton Hall* (tel 470-366) at 39 Hinemaru St, centrally located opposite the Hyatt Kingsgate, with single/double B&B for $35/57, lower in the off-season.

**Hotels** Right in the centre on the corner of Hinemoa and Fenton streets the *Grand Establishment* (tel 482-089) has single/-double rooms for $65/70. Rooms have tea and coffee-making equipment and there's a laundry, sauna and the Cobb & Co Restaurant. The *Australia Inn* (tel 488-516) at 15 Hinemoa St has hot mineral pools, à la carte restaurant and a lively Australian atmosphere, rooms are $42/55.

At the very fancy *Princes Gate* (tel 481-179), 1 Arawa St, singles/doubles are normally $82/94 (meals not included) but when it's not too busy they offer a B&B special at $65 for a double.

Rotorua has some big hotels, to cater for those big tour groups. There's a *Quality Inn*, *Rotorua Travelodge*, *Sheraton Rotorua*, *THC Rotorua*, *Geyserland Resort* and even the *Hyatt Kingsgate*. At these establishments even singles can cost $100 per night. Still, that's nothing on the *Solitaire Lodge* (tel 28-208) at Lake Tarawera where singles/-doubles including all meals cost around $450/650 a night, with a penthouse suite for $1000 a night!

**Motels** There are also plenty of motels in Rotorua and the competition has kept some of the prices down. Several of the camping sites have motel-style rooms as well as their cabins and tourist flats. Just a few of the cheaper places to try include:

*Aloha Motel* (tel 487-194), 105 Amohau St; singles $51 to $56, doubles $61 to $69
*Amber Lodge* (tel 480-595), 48 Hinemaru St; from $60/79
*Aywon Motel* (tel 477-659), 18 Trigg Ave; singles $50 to $60, doubles $60 to $80
*Bel Aire Motel* (tel 486-076), 257 Fenton St; from $50/59
*Colonial Motel* (tel 484-490), 22 Ranolf St; singles from $55, doubles $60 to $66
*Eruera Motel* (tel 488-305), corner Eruera & Hinemaru streets; from $49/64
*Havana Motor Lodge* (tel 488-134), 12 Whakaue St; singles $45 to $50, doubles $50 to $60
*Manhattan Motel* (tel 485-483), 130 Hinemoa St; singles $45 to $55, doubles $55 to $65
*Monterey Motel* (tel 481-044), 50 Whakaue St; doubles from $55
*Racecourse Motel* (tel 481-131), 258 Fenton St; from $36/42
*Tom's Motel* (tel 478-062), 6 Union St; doubles from $56
*Waiteti Stream Holiday Park* (tel 74-749), 14 Okono Crescent, Ngongotaha; from $50/60

**Camping & Cabins** Rotorua has a very good selection of camping sites, although some are 'caravan only' places. Almost all have cabins.

On Whittaker Rd (turn left towards the lake just before you get into town, coming from Auckland or Hamilton), *Cosy Cottage* (tel 483-793) has camping sites (only a limited number for tents) at $7.50 per person. Cabins cost $29 for two; tourist flats are $45 for two. The tourist flats have private bathrooms, heating and self-contained kitchens. There's a hot mineral pool, games room, trampoline and so on.

The *Lakeside Motor Camp* (tel 481-693) is also on Whittaker Rd, beside the lake and 2 km from the town centre. Sites here cost $15 for two and again there are cabins ($31 for two) and tourist flats ($42 to $46 for two), a hot mineral pool and various games.

The large *Rotorua Thermal Motor Camp & Lodge* (tel 463-140), on the southern end of the Old Taupo Rd near the golf course, has hot mineral pools and a heated swimming pool. Tent, caravan and campervan sites are $7.50, $8.50 and $10 per person. There's also bunkroom accommodation at $11 per person and a variety of cabins from around $26 to $35 for two. B&B at the lodge costs around $24 per person, linen included.

If you don't mind staying a little further out, there are many more camps and cabins in the area. The *Holdens Bay Holiday Park* (tel 459-925) is about 500 metres from the lake, 6½ km from central Rotorua on SH 30. Camping costs $8 per person, basic cabins cost $22 to $25 for two, fancier cabins with kitchens cost $35 and tourist flats cost $45. Peak season prices are about $10 higher. Again there's a swimming pool, hot mineral pools, billiard table, children's playground and so on.

The *Blue Lake Camp* (tel 28-120), 11 km from the town centre on Tarawera Rd on the shores of Blue Lake, has camping for $7 per person, cabins at $20 to $32 for two, and tourist flats at $36 to $42 for two, with higher rates at peak seasons. They hire canoes and ski-boats, and do horse treks.

There are a couple of places to camp at Ngongotaha, 8 km from Rotorua on the western shore of the lake, and plenty more places nearer and further from the city. All in all there's no shortage of camping sites:

*Moana Auto Park* (tel 456-240), 7½ km from the town centre on Lee Rd, Hannahs Bay, off SH 30; camping from $7.50 per person, also tourist flats

*Ngongotaha Caravan Park* (tel 74-289), 8 km from the town centre at 24 Beaumonts Rd, Ngongotaha; camping from $8 per person, also on-site caravans, cabins and tourist flats

*Waiteti Trout Stream Holiday Park* (tel 74-749), beside Waiteti Stream at 14 Okana Crescent, Ngongotaha; camping from $8.50 per person, also on-site caravans, cabins and tourist flats

*Willow Haven Holiday Park* (tel 74-092), 31 Beaumont Rd, Ngongotaha, on the lake side; camping from $8 per person, also cabins and chalets

*Lodge Motor Court* (tel 74-429), Hall Rd, Ngongotaha; camping from $7 per person, also cabins and tourist flats

*Redwood Park Caravan Park* (tel 459-380), 3 km from the town centre at 5 Tarawera Rd, Ngapuna; camping from $15 for two, also tourist flats

*Kiwi Ranch Holiday Camp* (tel 56-799), Rotokawau Rd, Tikitere, opposite Hell's Gate; camping from $5 per person, also cabins and tourist flats

*Merge Lodge* (tel Rotoma 831), SH 30 on the shores of Lake Rotoma; camping from $18 for two, also on-site caravans

*Taheke Lakeside Holiday Park* (tel Okere Falls 860), 21 km from Rotorua on Okere Rd, Okere Falls, on the shores of Lake Rotoiti, 1.5 km from Okere Falls; camping from $8.75 per person, also cabins

*Ohau Channel Lodge and Tourist Cabins* (tel Okere Falls 761 or 730), 17½ km from Rotorua on Hamurana Rd, at the northern end of Lake Rotorua between Lake Rotorua and Lake Rotoiti; camping from $5.50 per person, also cabins and tourist flats

**Farmstays & Homestays** There are many possibilities for staying on farms or in private homes around Rotorua. Ask at the NZTP office, which has listings and makes bookings.

**Places to Eat**

**Snacks & Fast Food** Rotorua has plenty of sandwich and fast food places. Try, for example, the *Bakery Boutique* up towards the lake end of Tutanekai St. At the nearby *Coffee Bean* you can sit down and enjoy your sandwiches; it's a good place for breakfast.

The *Taste Tease*, on Amohau St opposite Air New Zealand, has a bakery, open from 6 am to 6 pm every day, and a cafe with sandwiches, burgers and pizzas open 24 hours every day except Tuesday, when it closes at 6 pm. Another late-night fast food outlet is *Smacker Jack's*, on Hinemoa St opposite the CPO, with a takeaway counter and a slightly more expensive eat-in menu. It's open from 10 am to 11 pm Monday to Wednesday, till 4 am Thursday to Saturday, and from 9.30 am to 9 pm on Sundays.

*Pizza Forno* at 31 Pukuatua St is open every day but, apart from Friday and Saturday, it closes at 8 pm. Small pizzas cost from $4, large ones from $9, and pastas are around $8, all to eat in or take away. Two doors away, *Chez Maison* does good sandwiches.

The American Big Three are all represented in Rotorua. There's a large *McDonald's* on the corner of Fenton and Amohau streets. *Kentucky Fried* is further west on Amohau St, and *Pizza Hut* is right up at the lake end of Tutanekai St. There's even a poor little *Wimpy* as well, at the other end of Tutanekai St, near Amohau St. *Chez Bleu* is an imitation of the chain hamburger places, it's on Fenton St between Hinemoa and Eruera streets.

**Pub Food** Yes, there's a *Cobb & Co*, in the Grand Establishment on Hinemoa St, between Tutanekai and Fenton streets. It has the usual good-value Cobb & Co menu and it's open the usual 7.30 am to 10 pm hours – 7 days a week.

Other pub food alternatives include the bistro in *Fentons*, opposite McDonald's at the corner of Amohau and Fenton streets, the *Palace Tavern* on Arawa St and the *Lake Tavern* on Lake Rd near the lake in Ohinemutu. These latter two are rather basic, rough-edged grog houses although the bistro areas are peaceful enough.

**Restaurants** Naturally there are plenty of restaurants in Rotorua, particularly up at the lake end of Tutanekai St where the Pukaki St-Whakaue St block is real restaurant territory.

At 46 Haupapa St, just a few doors from the Ivanhoe Lodge, *Floyd's Cafe* is a pleasant, modern-looking, comfortable little BYO where dishes like moussaka or pastas cost around $8 for lunch and $13 to $16 for dinner. On Amohia St near the corner of Hinemoa St, *Zanelli's* has a somewhat similar mood but the food is strictly Italian and the colour scheme decidedly red, white and green. Pasta dishes cost around $8 as appetisers or $14 as main courses, other main courses cost around $17, and the gelati is great.

In that popular restaurant quarter on Tutanekai St, *Lewishams* is Eastern European – or Austrian-Hungarian as they say. For Indian food you can't beat the *Passage to India* on Hinemoa St opposite Cobb & Co. It has a pleasant atmosphere and a wide variety of both southern and northern Indian dishes to eat there or take away. Lunch and dinner are served every day except Sundays, when it's dinner only. Lunch costs around $6 and dinner main courses from $9.50 up to around $20 for the more exotic selections.

The *Cabbage Tree Cafe* at 87 Fenton St opposite the police station is a relaxing, inexpensive little BYO with vegetarian and Asian food, serving lunch, dinner and takeaways. *Gazebo*, on Pukuatua St is popular at lunch or dinner time, with main courses around $15 and a very straightforward menu.

Most of the tourist attractions have cafes but the one at the *Orchid Gardens* on Hinemaru St is especially enjoyable, and it's not expensive. It's at one end of the large indoor orchid garden; you can see the garden and listen to classical music while eating a light meal or tasty dessert.

## Entertainment

**Maori Concerts & Hangis** Maori culture is a major attraction in Rotorua, the unofficial Maori capital, and although it's decidedly commercialised it's a worthwhile investment to get out and enjoy it. There are two big activities – concerts and *hangi* feasts – and in many cases the two are combined. Some places simply put on the concerts and others combine them with a hangi although you can usually watch the concert without the feast to go with it.

A hangi is a Maori earth oven – a large pit is dug and a fire is lit to heat stones placed in the pit. Then food in baskets, covered with wet cloths, is buried with earth and steamed to perfection. Unfortunately the big hotels don't dig holes out the back and the flavour is consequently not the same but the traditional Maori foods – smoked eels, kumara (sweet potatoes), marinated fish and mussels are served, supplemented with dishes to the Pakeha taste (wild pork, lamb, venison stew) and dessert to follow; a full (and filling) evening.

The 12.15 pm Maori concert at Whakarewarewa is rated one of the best around. It costs $8.50 (children $2.25, family $20.50) or you can combine it with entry to the thermal reserve for $15.20 (children $4, family $38.40). Another popular concert is the one at the Civic Theatre, on the corner of Haupapa and Fenton streets, opposite the NZTP office. The concert starts at 8 pm daily, tickets cost $9 (children $2.50). The third concert-only performance is at the Ohinemutu Meeting House, also starting daily at 8 pm. Cost is $10 but they also sell discounted tickets through all the hostels for $5 or $6.

The combined concerts and hangis are generally at the big hotels. At any of them you can attend the concert only, skipping the hangi, but only if there's enough room available at the concert – book as early as possible if you want to attend the concert only. The concert at the Rotorua International Hotel has for some years had an excellent reputation. You should book ahead at any of these places, either directly with the hotels or through NZTP. Prices for concerts and hangis are:

*Geyserland Hotel* (tel 482-039); concert $10, concert & hangi $32

*Hyatt Kingsgate* (tel 471-234); concert $10, concert & hangi $35

*Rotorua International Hotel* (tel 481-189); concert $12, concert & hangi $33

*Sheraton* (tel 487-139); concert $17.50, concert & hangi $35

*Travelodge* (tel 481-174); concert $11, concert & hangi $33

The concerts are put on by local people and they seem to get as much of a kick out of them as you will. Chances are by the time the evening is over you'll have been dragged up on stage, experienced a Maori *hongi* (nose-to-nose contact), joined hands for a group sing-in, and thought about freaking out your next-door neighbour with a *haka* when you get home. Hakas are war dances which are intended to demonstrate how tough you are. The high point of the haka is to stick the tongue out as far as it will go, demonstrating derision and aggression. Other features of a Maori concert are *poi* dances, action songs and hand games.

Poi dances are performed by women only and consist of whirling round the poi (balls of flax fibre that are swung and twirled on lengths of string). Action songs are a recent addition to the Maori activities – story-songs illustrated by fluid hand and arm movements. There are also hand games – a reaction-sharpening pastime. The best game is where the two players make rapid gestures and try to catch their opponent making the same one!

**Pub Entertainment** Rotorua has the usual pub music – but not every night. Rock regulars include the rough-and-ready *Palace Tavern* on Arawa St and the *Lake Tavern* on Lake Rd near the hospital.

There's also the smaller and more intimate *Wheelers Bar* at the Cobb & Co in the Grand Establishment on Hinemoa St, with a jazz band and reasonably priced beer. Or try *Fentons* on the corner of Amohau and Fenton streets.

**Other Entertainment** Disco and nightclub-style activity can be found at *Tudor Towers* later in the evening.

### Getting There & Away

**Air** Air New Zealand's offices (tel 461-001) are at 38-42 Amohau St. They have direct flights to Tauranga and Wellington, with connections to other centres. Mt Cook Airlines (tel 477-451) shares the same office and has daily direct flights to Auckland, Welling-ton, Christchurch, Queenstown, Wanaka, Mt Cook, Taupo and the Bay of Islands, with connections to other centres. Ansett NZ (tel 455-348), 113 Fenton St, has daily direct flights to Christchurch with connections to Queenstown, Dunedin and Invercargill.

**Bus** InterCity long-distance and tour buses arrive and depart from the Travel Centre (tel 481-039) on Amohau St. InterCity has daily buses to and from Auckland (4 hours), Wellington (5½ hours), Taupo, Tauranga, Whakatane and Hamilton (all 1½ hours), Waitomo and Opotiki (both 2½ hours). On the east coast routes, InterCity goes daily to Gisborne (5 hours) via Opotiki and to Napier (3¼ hours) via Taupo. They also have services to Tongariro National Park (3½ hours) on Tuesday, Thursday and Saturday, and to Wairoa (5 hours) via the Urewera National Park and Lake Waikaremoana on Mondays, Wednesdays and Fridays.

Mt Cook buses also arrive and depart from the Travel Centre on Amohau St. Mt Cook has services to Auckland, Wellington, Napier, Hastings and Taupo.

Newmans buses go to and from Auckland, Hamilton, New Plymouth (6 hours), Palmerston North (5½ hours) and Napier. They arrive and depart from the NZTP office (tel 485-179), 67 Fenton St.

From Auckland there's a special back-packers tour bus to Rotorua via the Waitomo Caves; see the Tours section in the Auckland chapter. Rotorua is also the departure point for the 4 day East Cape Fun Etc bus tour; see the East Cape and Getting Around chapters for details.

**Hitching** Hitching to Rotorua is generally not bad except on SH 38 from Waikaremoana – once past Murupara heading out that way, count on about three cars per hour going past (that's if you're lucky!), although more people will stop than on the major roads.

The hitching problem out of Rotorua is often just the sheer number of backpackers leaving town. You may have to simply join the queue and wait.

## Getting Around

**Airport Transport** The airport is about 10 km out, on the eastern side of the lake. There is an airport shuttle bus service (tel 462-386); the one-way fare is $6.

**Bus** Suburban bus services operate from the InterCity Travel Centre on Amohau St but apart from a limited Saturday service they mainly operate Monday to Friday. There is nothing at all on Sundays. Route 3 runs to Whakarewarewa, route 2 along the lake side to Rainbow Springs.

**Car Rental** Rotorua has a host of rental car companies. The competition is fierce and they all seem to offer 'specials' to try to undercut the others. Check with the NZTP office for brochures and details on which ones are offering the best discount rates at any particular time.

**Motorcycle Rental** Rotorua Motorcycles (tel 489-385) at 65 Amohau St rent small-capacity Yamaha motorcycles, ideal for exploring the Rotorua area.

**Bicycle Rental** Rotorua is fairly spread out and public transport is not that good, so a bicycle is a nice thing to have. All the hostels have bicycles for hire.

You can hire bicycles, tandems and 10-speeds from Lady Jane's Ice Cream Parlour at the lake end of Tutanekai St for $5 per hour, $10 per day (returning it the same day) or $15 for 24 hours. It's open every day from 10 am to 9.30 pm. Blair's Mountain Bike Tours (tel 455-858/179) hires 18-speed mountain bikes at the NZTP office for $15 per day.

# Taupo

Taupo, 85 km south of Rotorua, is the world's trout fishing capital. If you thought those trout in the Rotorua springs looked large and tasty they're nothing compared to the monsters here. All New Zealand's rainbow trout are descended from one batch of eggs brought from California's Russian River nearly a century ago. The lakes here are everything a trout could dream of and they grow to a prodigious size.

Lake Taupo is in the geographical centre of the North Island. The largest lake in New Zealand, it is 606 sq km in area and 357 metres above sea level. The depression Lake Taupo occupies is thought to have been formed by a gigantic volcanic explosion and subsequent subsidence. Pumice from this explosion is found as far away as Napier and Gisborne and forms a layer – in some places just 1 cm thick, in others metres – over a vast area of central North Island.

## History

Back in the mists of time a Maori chief named Tamatea-arikinu visited the area and, noticing that the ground felt hollow and that his footsteps seemed to reverberate, called the place Tapuaeharuru – 'resounding footsteps'. Taupo, as it became known, was first occupied by Europeans as a military outpost during the Maori wars. Colonel J M Roberts built a redoubt in 1869 and a garrison of mounted police remained there until the defeat of Te Kuti.

In the 1870s the government bought the land from the Maoris who asked that it be named Bowen in honour of Governor Sir G F Bowen who visited the lake in 1872. While this was agreed to, it was never carried out. Taupo has grown slowly and sedately from a lakeside village of about 750 in 1945 to a resort town with a permanent population of 18,000 which swells to over 45,000 at peak holiday times. The town is on the lake side where SH 1, the main road from the north, first meets the lake.

## Information

The Taupo Information Centre (tel 89-002/3) is on Tongariro St and is open from 8.30 am to 5 pm every day except during the Christmas break. It may be moving to a new location but if so it shouldn't move far. The CPO, painted in amazingly un-post-office-

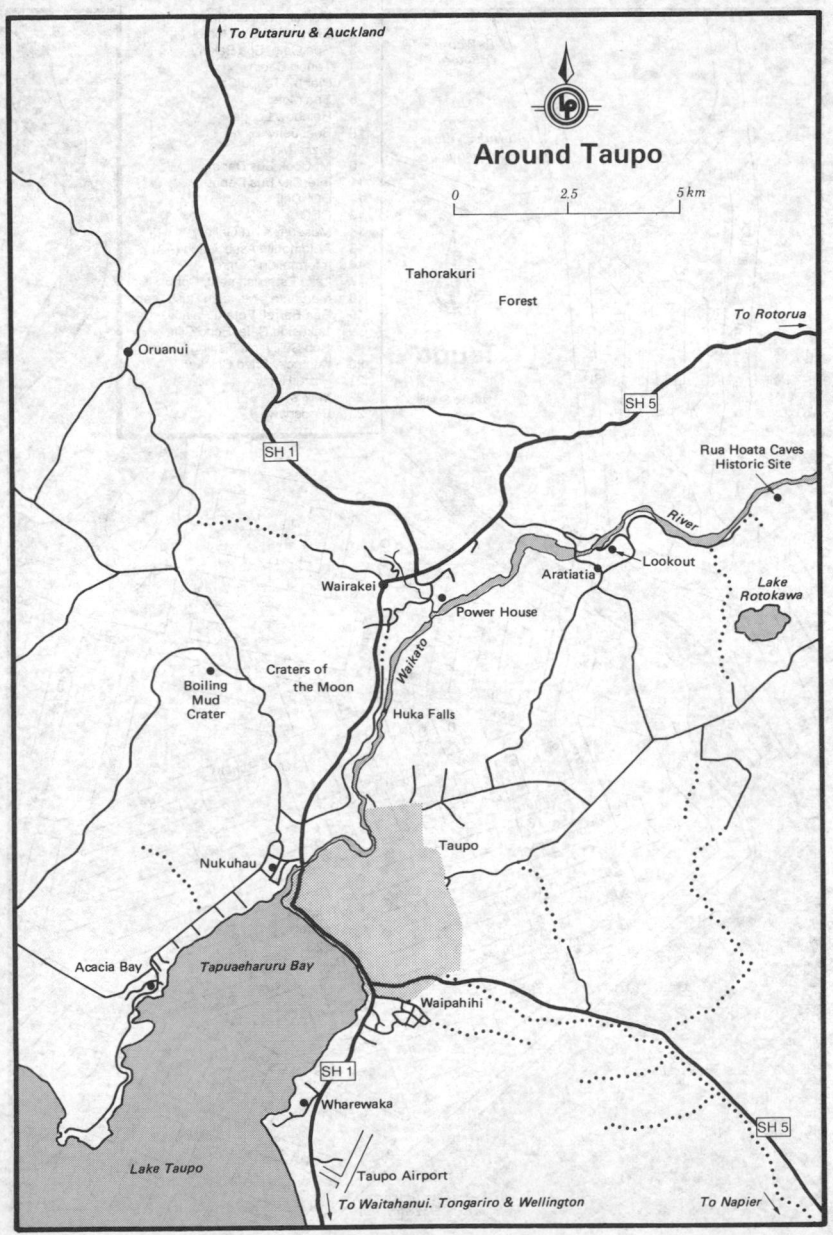

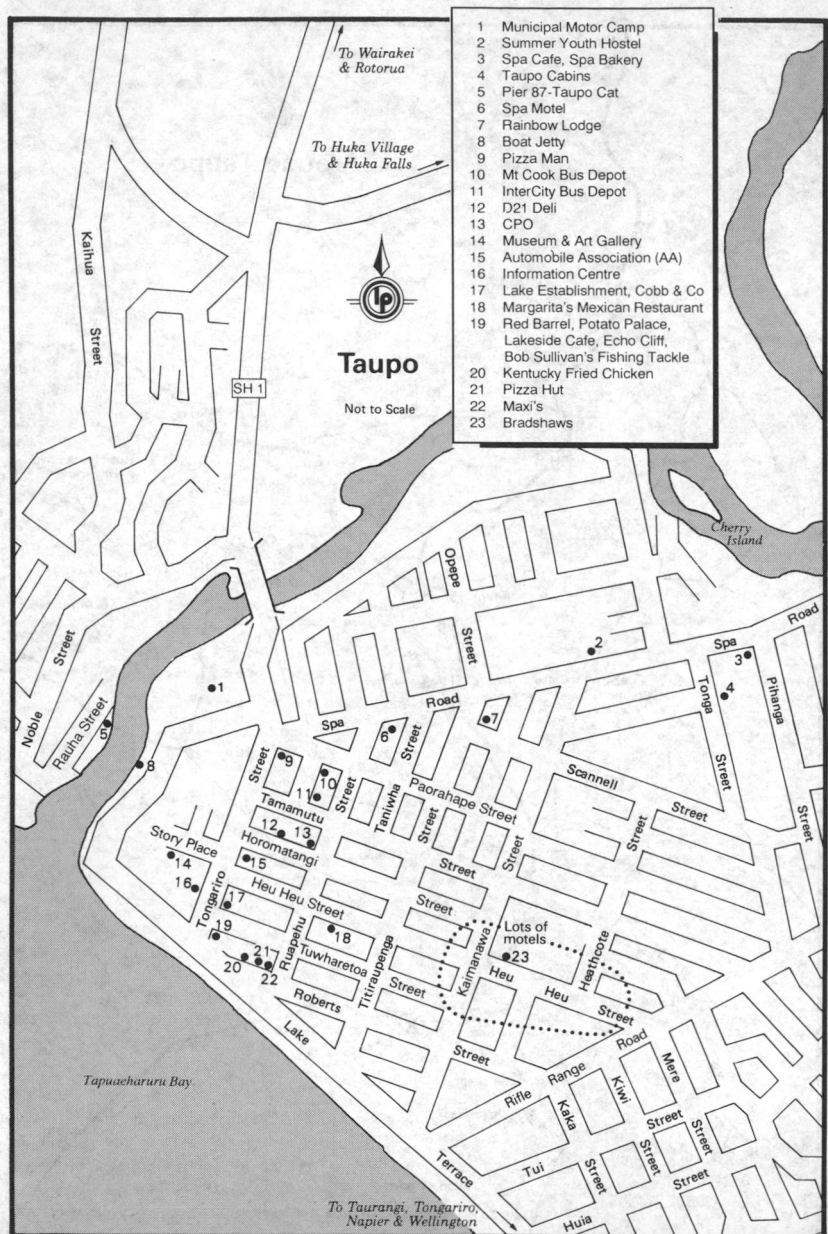

1 Municipal Motor Camp
2 Summer Youth Hostel
3 Spa Cafe, Spa Bakery
4 Taupo Cabins
5 Pier 87-Taupo Cat
6 Spa Motel
7 Rainbow Lodge
8 Boat Jetty
9 Pizza Man
10 Mt Cook Bus Depot
11 InterCity Bus Depot
12 D21 Deli
13 CPO
14 Museum & Art Gallery
15 Automobile Association (AA)
16 Information Centre
17 Lake Establishment, Cobb & Co
18 Margarita's Mexican Restaurant
19 Red Barrel, Potato Palace,
   Lakeside Cafe, Echo Cliff,
   Bob Sullivan's Fishing Tackle
20 Kentucky Fried Chicken
21 Pizza Hut
22 Maxi's
23 Bradshaws

like pastel shades of pink and blue, is on the corner of Horomatangi and Ruapehu streets.

## Orakei Korako

Between the main roads to Taupo from Hamilton and Rotorua is one of the finest thermal areas of New Zealand – Orakei Korako. Its remoteness is what stops people going there, but it's worth the trip if you can make it. It's 23 km off the Rotorua-Taupo highway and 14 km off the Hamilton-Taupo highway or 37 km from Taupo itself. You can visit it on a Taylor's bus tour from Rotorua, otherwise you can probably manage to hitch there. Admission is $9 (children $4, family $25), including a jet-boat ride across Lake Ohakuri, which was formed by a hydroelectric dam. It's open from 8.30 am to 4.30 pm (4 pm in winter) every day.

After the destruction of the Pink and White Terraces by the Tarawera eruption, Orakei Korako was possibly the best thermal area left in New Zealand and one of the finest in the world. Although three-quarters of it now lies beneath the waters of Lake Ohakuri, the quarter that remains is still worth seeing.

A well laid out walking track takes you around the large, colourful silica terraces for which Orakei Korako is famous, as well as geysers and Aladdin's Cave – a magnificent natural cave with a pool of jade green water. The pool is said to have been used by Maori women as a mirror during hairdressing ceremonies; the name Orakei Korako means 'the place of adorning'.

You can stay overnight at Orakei Korako in cabins for $14 per person, or if you have a tent or caravan you can stay for free. Canoes and dinghies are available for hire.

## Aratiatia

South of the Orakei Korako turn-off, on the road to Taupo, are a series of attractions along the Waikato River, at 436 km the longest river in New Zealand. The Waikato rises east of Ruapehu, flows into the southern end of Lake Taupo, where it's also known as the Tongariro River, leaves the lake at the township, and flows through the heart of northern North Island before finally reaching the west coast at Waikato Heads just short of Auckland.

The first attraction is Aratiatia; 2 km off the main road on your left just before Wairakei are the Aratiatia Rapids. Unfortunately the government, in its wisdom, went and plonked another power house and dam down here, shutting off the water to the rapids. To keep the tourists happy they open the control gates at 10 am and 2.30 pm daily. That's the time to be there to see the water flow through and there are three good lookout points to see it from. It's all open land, with no admission charge.

## Wairakei Thermal Valley

Just south-west of the Aratiatia turn-off, SH 5 from Rotorua meets SH 1 from Hamilton and Auckland, and then you're in Wairakei, 8 km from Taupo. If you are not too distracted by all the steam from the Geothermal Power Project, you'll see a 1½ km road on your right leading to the Wairakei Thermal Valley, where there are yet more mud pools.

This is the remains of what was once known as Geyser Valley. Before the geothermal power project started in 1959 this was one of the most active thermal areas in the world, with 22 geysers and 240 separate mud pools and springs. Now the neighbouring geothermal power project has sucked off the steam, and only eight or nine mud pools remain active. There's a bushwalk to the Huiata pools but they're only active after a heavy rain. Entry is $5 (children $1) and it's open from 9 am to 5 pm every day. There's a motor camp here too.

## Wairakei Geothermal Power Project

New Zealand was the second country in the world to produce power from natural steam. If you dive into all that steam you will find yourself at the Wairakei Geothermal Power Project which generates about 150,000 kW, providing about 5% of New Zealand's total electrical power.

There's a Geothermal Information Centre (tel 48-216) close to the road where you can make an educational stop between 9 am and noon, or 1 and 4.30 pm daily. Information on the bore field and power house is available and an audiovisual is shown up until half an hour before each closing time. You can drive up the road through the project and from a lookout see the long stretches of pipe, wreathed in steam.

### Huka Falls & Huka Village

Just south of Wairakei a road on your left (east) leads to the spectacular Huka Falls. A footbridge crosses the Waikato River above the falls, which plunge through a narrow cleft in the rock, dropping about 24 metres in all. The water here is incredibly clear and turquoise on a sunny day.

On the same spur road 2½ km before Taupo is Huka Village, a replica of an early NZ pioneer village. A number of historic buildings were restored and moved to the site and it functions as a working craft village with a ferrier, blacksmith, potters and other craftspeople. There's also an aviary, a deer park and a honey centre. Activities include horse-trekking, river rafting, farmstays, hunting, fishing and launch cruises. The village is open in summer from 9 am to 5 pm daily and in winter from 9 am to 4 pm; admission is $3.50 (children free).

### Craters of the Moon

Craters of the Moon is an interesting and unexploited thermal area where admission is free. It's signposted on the western side of the road about 5 km north of Taupo towards Wairakei. It's not too well publicised – the commercial thermal area operators would complain. The area is well fenced for safety purposes, but not overdone as commercially exploited thermal areas can be. Be careful when you leave your car as things have been stolen from cars here. It's run by the DOC and is open from dawn to dusk.

### Thermal Pools

The A C Thermal Baths (tel 87-321) are at the top of Spa Rd, about 2 km east of the town centre. There's a big swimming pool heated to 35°C with a 'Roaster Coaster' waterslide, private mineral pools and a sauna. It's open from 8 am to 9 pm every day and until 10 pm

over the Christmas holidays. Admission is $4 (children and pensioners $2, family $10) and for an extra $3 you can go up and down the waterslide all day long.

The De Brett Thermal Pools (tel 88-559) are on the Taupo-Napier Highway (SH 5), not far from SH 1. There's no waterslide, so the kids might prefer the A C Baths, but for adults a relax at De Brett's is pure heaven. The large outdoor pool is divided into two sections, one side at 36°C and the other at 40°C. There are also a number of private pools with different temperatures; the ones on the end are really quite hot. The pools are open from 8 am to 9.30 pm daily and admission is $3.50 (children $1.50); it's 50 cents more to use the private pools for as long as you want. The De Brett Thermal Hotel and Motor Camp are up here too.

### Other Attractions

Under the SH 1 bridge over the Waikato River in Taupo are control gates regulating the level of Lake Taupo and the amount of flow down the Waikato River through its string of hydroelectric power stations. Just up the hill from here is the turn-off to Acacia Bay, a pleasant peaceful beach a little over 5 km west of Taupo. There's a short walk from here to Little Acacia Bay.

Just off Spa Rd is a wildlife park, Cherry Island, in the middle of the Waikato River. About 1 km along Spa Rd turn left into Motutahae St then right into Waikato St. The island is open from 9 am to 5 pm daily; admission is $6 (children $2, students $4).

The small Taupo District Museum of Art & History is behind the Information Centre. It's open from 10 am to 3 pm, Monday to Saturday, and admission is free. Trainsville is an extensive model railway display at 35A Heu Heu St. It's open from 9.30 am to 4 pm Monday to Friday and 9.30 am to 12.30 pm on Saturdays; admission is $2.20 (children 80 cents, family $5.50). Lilliputt, on the corner of Ruapehu and Roberts streets (not far back from the lakeshore), is open from 10 am to 5 pm daily.

Opposite the golf course on SH 1, 5 km north of Taupo, Honey Village has three viewing hives (a glass hive, a commercial hive and a bush hive) set up for viewing, plus educational videos about bees and a number of honeys for tasting. It's open from 9 am to 5 pm every day; admission is free. Also here are other activities including horse-trekking and jet-boating, plus the New Zealand Country Music Hall of Fame. You can go in anytime to see the display of photos of country & western stars, but the place is most active on Friday nights when there's a big weekly dance.

### Lake Cruises

You can cruise the lake on the *Ernest Kemp* or the *Barbary*, a 60-year-old wooden yacht once owned by Errol Flynn. Don't ask me how it ended up on Lake Taupo! Cruises on the *Barbary* cost $15 (children $10) and typically last 2½ to 3 hours, on the *Ernest Kemp* it's a couple of dollars more. The cruises visit a modern Maori rock carving beside the lake. The carving can only be reached through private land so it's not easy to visit on foot. Both cruises take off in summer at 10.30 am and at 2 pm daily; in winter they go at 2 pm only. The *Ernest Kemp* requires a minimum of six people but the *Barbary* will take smaller groups.

The *Taupo Cat* is a large catamaran which makes 3½ hour morning and afternoon cruises of the northern and western sides of the lake which are inaccessible by road. It, too, visits the Maori carvings, plus many other sites, telling the historical and geographical facts along the way. Cost is $42.50 (children $15, family $99). It also does an evening cruise which for $53 (children $20) includes a smorgasbord dinner. The *Taupo Cat* (tel 86-052) departs from the docks at Pier 87, opposite the town centre.

### Fishing

There are a number of fishing guides and charter boat operators in Taupo, check with the Information Centre. A trip will probably cost about $60 per person. If you're staying at one of the hostels you can book fishing boat trips through them. They usually have the best prices around – around $45 an hour for the whole boat, which can hold up to six people sharing the cost.

If you go on a boat trip they'll supply all the gear. Otherwise you can hire tackle at Bob Sullivan's Taupo Sports Depot (tel 85-337) on Tongariro St, by the waterfront. The cost is $10 per day for spinning gear or $25 per day for fly gear. It's open during the normal business hours of 8.30 am to 5.30 pm Monday to Thursday, 8.30 am to 8.30 pm on Fridays, and 8.30 am to 12.30 pm on Saturdays; it's closed on Sundays. You can get your fishing licence there too, or from any other sports shop or the launch office at the harbour. Licences cost $7 per day, $19 per week or $26 per month.

### Walks

You can walk all the way from Taupo to Aratiatia. From the centre of town head up Spa Rd by Woolworths. Turn left at County Ave and continue through Spa Thermal Park at the end of the street, past the skateboard bowl and over the hill, following the rough roadway to the left until you hit the track.

The track follows the river to Huka Falls crossing a hot stream and riverside marshes en route. It'll take up to 2 hours from the centre of Taupo to Huka, depending on your walking speed. From Huka Falls you can cross the footbridge along the 7-km Taupo Walkway to Aratiatia (another 2 to 3 hours). There are good views of the river, Huka Falls, and the power station across the river. It's easy walking.

If you're going to Craters of the Moon as well you can make it a round trip, using the walkway in one direction between Taupo and Aratiatia, and the road in the other direction. You would need all day, and should time it so you're at Aratiatia at 2.30 pm when the control gates are open and at Wairakei when the Info Centre is open.

Another walk worth mentioning is Mt Tauhara, with magnificent views from the top. Take the Taupo-Napier Highway (SH 5) from just south of the Taupo town centre. About 6 km along SH 5, turn left into Mountain Rd. The start of the track is signposted on the right-hand side. It will take about 2 hours to get to the top, walking slowly.

A pleasant walkway goes along the lakefront to the south of town all the way from Two Mile Bay (3.2 km) to Four Mile Bay (6.4 km) – south of Taupo, just off SH 1, the lakeside road.

There are plenty of other good walks and tramps in the area, including river, lake, forest and mountain walks. Pick up a copy of the *Walking Trails* leaflet from the Taupo Information Centre.

### Other Activities

There's horse-riding at Huka Village and at Honey Village. Escape to the Wilderness does 1 to 5 day wilderness horse-trekking trips on private Maori land way out in the middle of nowhere (it's a couple of hours by 4WD just to get in). Out there is Wilderness Lodge, with bunkroom accommodation and all meals provided, plus plenty of horses, guides, and routes to explore. Book through the Huka Falls Stables (tel 80-356) or through any hostel (hostellers get a discount on price).

Bruce Webber Kayak Adventures (tel 84-715) offers numerous kayak trips, from the most peaceful lake and river paddles to challenging white water rapids trips. A 4 hour course for beginners costs $35; you can hire a kayak for $25 per day ($80 per week) or an open canoe for $40 per day ($140 per week). Once again you can book through the hostels.

Several white water rafting companies operate from Taupo with 1 day trips on the Tongariro and Rangitaiki rivers, longer trips on other rivers. Book these trips through the hostels or the Information Centre. There are plans for a combination trip that will include white water rafting on the Rangitaiki River, a bungy jump and a barbecue, with transport to and from Taupo.

During the summer there are lots of activities on Lake Taupo including swimming, water skiing, windsurfing, paragliding and sailing.

### Tours

Walter's Backpackers Tours are run by a delightful, spry old fellow who is also Taupo's radio weatherman and foremost cyclist. He does 3 hour tours of the local sights (Huka Falls, Aratiatia, Craters of the Moon, Mt Tauhara and so on) for $15, plus full-day trips further afield to Tongariro National Park for $35. Book directly with him (tel 85-924), through the hostels, or through the Information Centre.

Paradise Tours (tel 89-955) does 2½ hour tours of the Taupo sights for $24 (children $10).

### Aerial Sightseeing

If you're feeling affluent you can go for a scenic flight on the floatplane from the lakefront, next to Taupo Boat Harbour (tel 87-500, 89-441), or with Taupo Air Services (tel 85-325) from Taupo Aerodrome. They both have similar flights for similar prices, ranging upwards from about $20 (children $10) for a short flight around the Taupo area to about $96 (children $48) for flights across Lake Taupo over Tongariro National Park or north to Rotorua. At 11 am on Sundays you can arrange to go gliding from Centennial Park Airfield.

### Places to Stay

**Hostels** Taupo has two excellent private hostels. Both of them arrange a host of activities at significantly discounted prices. Be sure to ask about this when you check in; there are lots of possibilities!

*Rainbow Lodge* (tel 85-754) at 99 Titiraupenga St is a busy and popular hostel with an excellent reputation among travellers – so much so that it's often full and it's a very good idea to book ahead. There's a large communal area that's good for meeting other travellers, a sauna and games area, and they have camping gear hire and free luggage storage. The cost per night is $13 per person in bunkrooms or $15 in twin rooms.

The *Sunset Lodge* (tel 85-962) at 5 Tremaine Ave, about 2 km south of the town centre along the lakeside road, is another good hostel, with a comfortable atmosphere and friendly owners. They offer lots of free services including free pick-up, daily shuttles to Craters of the Moon and the De Brett thermal pools, bicycles, a surf ski and an inflatable boat you can take out on the lake, 100 metres away. The nightly cost is $12 per person in bunkrooms, $14 in double or twin rooms, and all rooms are heated in winter.

The summer *Youth Hostel*, open from mid-December to the end of January, is at Taupo Nui-a-Tia College, on Spa Rd. It costs $12 per night.

**Guest Houses** *Bradshaws* (tel 88-288) at 130 Heu Heu St has B&B for $30 to $35 per single and $50 to $55 for twins or doubles. Half the rooms have private facilities.

**Hotels** The *Spa Hotel* (tel 84-120) on Spa Rd has heated outdoor and thermal indoor pools, with rooms at $26/40, or $31/50 with breakfast. Suites are $5 more and there are also chalets at $50/68. It's a little far out from the centre. Before you decide that the Spa Hotel is your kind of place, see the description under Entertainment.

Right in the town centre, the *Lake Establishment* (tel 86-165) on the corner of Tongariro and Tuwharetoa streets has B&B for $39/65 for singles/doubles.

The *De Brett Thermal Hotel* (tel 87-080) is 3 km from the town centre on SH 5, 1 km from the lake. It's a grand old hotel which has just celebrated its centennial year. Single/double rooms cost $48/55 and there's entertainment in the lounge bar on weekends.

If money is no object, one of New Zealand's most expensive hotels is just outside Taupo. The *Huka Lodge* (tel 85-791) at Huka Falls has singles for $500 and doubles for over $700 a night!

**Motels** Taupo is packed with motels and, as in Rotorua, the competition tends to keep prices down although many of them have minimum rates during holiday periods. *Dunrovin* (tel 87-384) at 140 Heu Heu St, the *Continental Motel* (tel 85-836) at 9 Scannell St and the *Golf Course* (tel 89-415) on

Tauhara Rd are all similarly priced, with singles for $45 to $50 and doubles for $55 to $60. *Skipper's Motel* (tel 89-292) is very close to the centre at 69 Spa Rd and has rooms at $56/68. There are lots of motels along Heu Heu St.

**Camping & Cabins** Camping is free beside the river about 1½ km south of the Huka Falls towards Taupo. There are also lots of motor camps in Taupo including the *Taupo Motor Camp* (tel 79-889) on Redoubt St in the centre of town by the river, where camping costs $7 per person; $8 with power. There are also two-berth cabins for $26 and four-berth cabins for $38.

There is a variety of cabins at *Taupo Cabins* (tel 84-346) at 50 Tonga St, 1½ km from the CPO. The cost per night is $12 per person for the cheapies ($10 if you stay three or more nights), $32 for two in tourist cabins, or $43 for two in the fanciest tourist flats with kitchen and shower. *Auto Park* (tel 84-272) is on Rangatira St, also 1½ km from the centre. Camping costs $13 for two (about $2 more with power). Some cabins cost $9/16 for one/two people, others cost $30 for two, and tourist flats cost $38 for two.

The *De Bretts Family Leisure Park* (tel 88-559) is right beside the De Bretts Thermal Pools, 1 km from the lake on SH 5, the Taupo-Napier Rd. Camping sites are $7 per person (50 cents more with power) and there are also single/double motel units for $48/58. The De Bretts Thermal Hotel is next door (see the Hotels section).

There's also the *Hilltop Motor Caravan Park* (tel 85-247) at 39 Puriri St, where camping costs $7.50 per person and on-site caravans cost $30 for two. The *Lake Taupo Holiday Park* (tel 86-860) on Upper Spa Rd, Centennial Drive, also has camping sites, cabins and tourist flats.

*Acacia Holiday Park* (tel 85-159) on Acacia Bay Rd, west of the town centre, has camping for $7 per person. For two people, on-site caravans cost $30, cabins cost $23 and tourist flats cost $40. Other sites around Taupo include the *Wairakei Thermal Valley Motor Camp* (tel 48-004) at Wairakei and the

*Windsor Lodge Caravan Park* (tel 86-271) at Waitahanui, 12 km south of Taupo.

## Places to Eat

**Snacks & Fast Food** Taupo has the usual collection of sandwich places and takeaway bars. Down by the lakefront are a *Pizza Hut* and a *Kentucky Fried Chicken* side by side.

The *D21 Deli* on Horomatangi St has lots of sandwiches and snacks. Or try the *Pizza Man* on the corner of Tongariro St and Spa Rd. Up Spa Rd past the Rainbow Lodge and the summer hostel on the corner of Pihanga St, the *Spa Cafe* is a good place for fish & chips and the *Spa Bakery* in the same small shopping centre has good sandwiches and baked goods.

The *Potato Palace* on the lakefront at the corner of Lake Terrace and Tongariro St has baked potatoes with a variety of fillings from $2.50 for a basic one up to $5 for the 'Palace Pig'.

**Pub Food** There is a *Cobb & Co* in the Lake Establishment on Tuwharetoa St, open from 7.30 am to 10 pm daily with the usual menu and reasonable prices.

The *Red Barrel* is an enjoyable restaurant/pub on the lakefront. It's open daily, with bar meals served from 2 to 10 pm. The *Spa Hotel* has a bar menu with dishes like fish & chips, pie & chips, sausage & chips or steak & chips, each costing about $7 to $8.

**Restaurants** On the lakeside corner of Lake Terrace and Tongariro St are the *Lakeside Cafe* (daytime) and *Italian Connection* (evening), occupying the same dining room. The cafe serves breakfast and lunch from 7 am to 3 pm daily. Italian dinners are served from 6 pm every day except Sundays. Pasta dishes cost $13, while other mains cost from $11 to $16. A bit further down the lakefront *Maxi's* is a 24-hour dairy/cafe with takeaways and inexpensive sit-down meals.

*Margarita's* at 63 Heu Heu St has good Mexican food and great atmosphere, with a colourful Mexican decor featuring bright Aztec-style artwork and sombreros for lampshades. Main courses are $10.50 to $17.

It's open from 4.30 pm until about 1 am daily and there's jazz on Friday nights in the bar.

There are some other expensive restaurants like *Echo Cliff*, with good views over the lake, at the lake end of Tongariro St. *Manuel's* at the motor hotel of the same name on the lakefront is an expensive but top-notch award-winning restaurant specialising in NZ food.

## Entertainment

The *Red Barrel* on the lakefront near Tongariro St is a lively pub, good for socialising, dancing and meeting the locals. There's live entertainment on Thursday, Friday and Saturday nights, and sometimes on other nights too. The 1st floor *Waterfront Cafe* nearby has live or disco music. It's open later than the Red Barrel so often the crowd drifts over when the Red Barrel closes.

*Trumps* in the Lake Establishment on Tongariro St has a band on Thursday, Friday and Saturday nights. There's also entertainment in the bar of the *Sun Court Motor Hotel* in Northcroft St. There's live jazz at *Margarita's* in Heu Heu St on Friday nights from 10 pm on.

The *De Brett's Thermal Hotel*, 1 km down SH 5, has home-style country & western music on Thursday nights and other music on Friday and Saturday. Country & western fans will also enjoy the weekly Friday night dance at the *New Zealand Country Music Hall of Fame*, 5 km north of the centre on SH 1. The $5 admission includes a light supper and the band plays from 8 pm until midnight or 1 am.

There's also occasional entertainment at the *Spa Hotel*, some distance east of the town centre along Spa Rd. Actually the Spa Hotel is entertainment all by itself. The cavernous public bar is definitely a fishin', huntin' and shootin' hangout. There are trophy heads mounted around the wall and the toilets are labelled 'stags' and 'hinds'. Nobody seems to buy beer in less than a litre jug at a time but you feel unsteady on your feet even without any beer on board since the carpet seems to be underlaid with about 5 cm of foam rubber. Must make for softer landings when you fall over.

### Getting There & Away

**Air** Air New Zealand has daily direct flights to and from Auckland, Wellington and Wanganui, with connections to other centres. Mt Cook Airline also serves Taupo, with direct flights to Christchurch, Wellington and Rotorua. Both are handled by James Travel (tel 87-065) in Horomatangi St.

**Bus** Taupo is about halfway between Auckland and Wellington. Being at the geographical centre of the island, it's a hub for bus transport.

InterCity (tel 89-032) has several daily buses to Auckland (5 hours), Hamilton (2½ hours), Rotorua (1 to 1½ hours), Tauranga (2½ hours), Napier (2 hours), Wanganui (5 hours) and Wellington (7 hours).

Mt Cook (tel 89-030) also has daily buses to Auckland, Wellington, Rotorua, and Napier. Newmans has buses to Auckland, Hamilton, Palmerston North, Rotorua and Napier. The InterCity and Mt Cook stations are side by side on Gasgoigne St, off Ruapehu St. Newmans (tel 89-002) operates from the Information Centre on Togariro St.

To get between Taupo and the Tongariro National Park you can take an InterCity bus with stops at Turangi, Whakapapa, National Park and Ohakune, but only on Tuesdays, Thursdays and Sundays. Alternatively Alpine Scenic Tours (tel Turangi 68-392) provides transport to all points in the park including the walking tracks and will arrange to suit your schedule.

### Getting Around

The airport is 6 km south of Taupo; a taxi trip costs about $14. Bicycles can be hired from Roy's Cycle World (tel 86-117) in Ruapehu St for $6 an hour, $12 for half a day, $20 for a day (same day return) or $22 for 24 hours. Both of the hostels also have bicycles.

# Tongariro National Park

Tongariro, established in 1887, was New Zealand's first national park. It was given to the country by a far-sighted Maori chief who

Tongariro

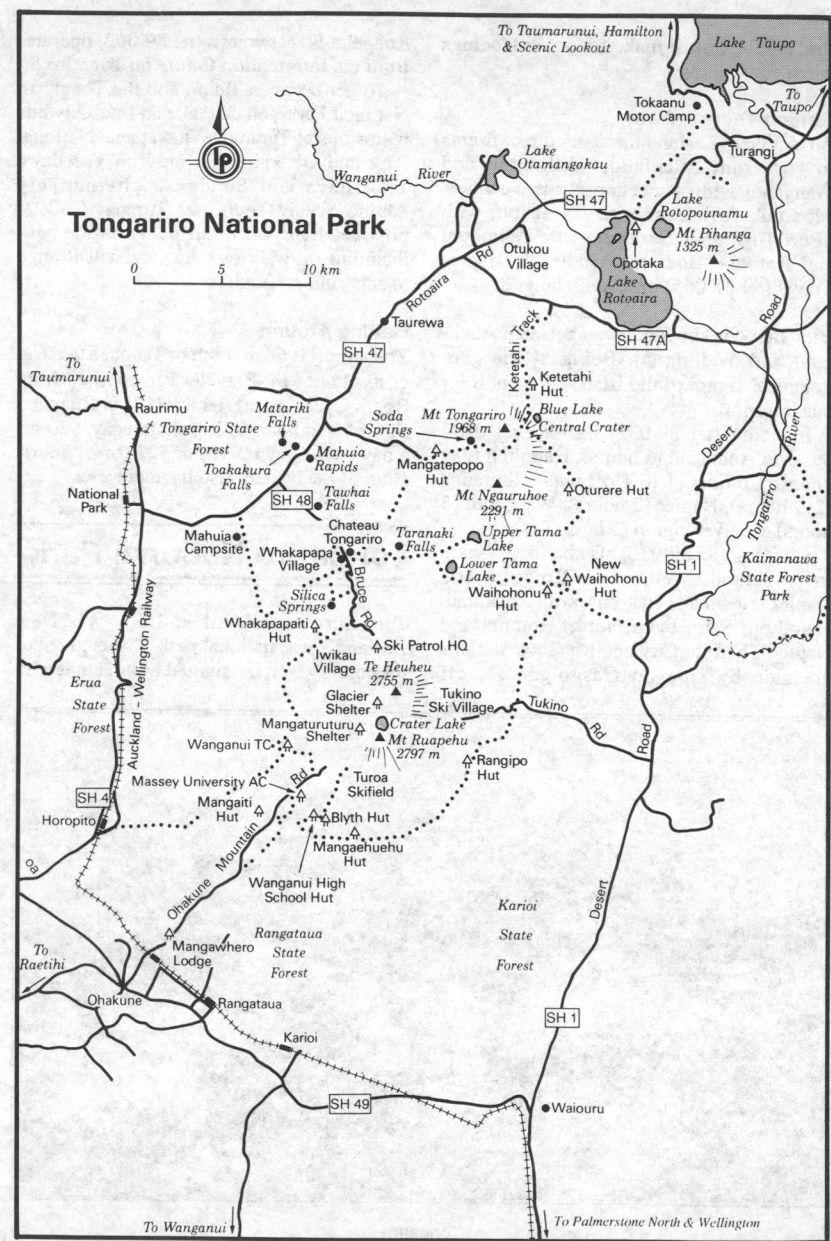

**Tongariro National Park**

realised that this was the only way to preserve an area of such spiritual significance in its entirety. With its collection of mighty (and still active) volcanoes, Tongariro is one of the most interesting and spectacular parks in New Zealand. In the summer it's got excellent walks and tramps and in the winter it's an important skiing area.

There are two main ski fields – the Whakapapa Ski Field up above the Chateau (the THC hotel) and the newer Turoa Ski Field near Ohakune. See the Skiing section in the Outdoor Activities chapter for more details. Clustered around the fine old Chateau are cabins and a 'skotel'. There are also huts scattered along the walking trails.

The Whakapapa Visitors Centre will supply you with lots of info on the park and its walks. Mt Ruapehu is the highest of the volcanoes at 2796 metres and is still active – it's also the site for all the ski runs! The upper slopes were showered with hot mud and water in the volcanic activity of 1969 and 1975, and in December 1988 the volcano threw out some very hot rocks. The long, multi-peaked summit of Ruapehu shelters Crater Lake which you can climb up to if you're well prepared. The route follows the Whakapapa Glacier for part of the way. Don't go too close to Crater Lake – it's surrounded by dangerous precipices.

From 1945 to 1947 the level of the lake rose dramatically when eruptions blocked the overflow. On Christmas Eve 1953 the overflow burst and the flood that resulted led to one of New Zealand's worst disasters. The torrent swept away a railway bridge moments before a crowded express train arrived and in the resulting crash 153 people lost their lives.

Mt Ngauruhoe is much younger than the other volcanoes in the park – it's estimated to have formed in the last 2500 years and the slopes to the 2291 metre summit are still perfectly symmetrical. It can be climbed by the experienced or with a guide although in winter it is definitely suitable only for experienced mountaineers. It's a very steep but rewarding climb. Mt Tongariro, at 1968 metres, is much older and considered

dormant. It has a number of coloured lakes dotting its uneven summit as well as hot springs gushing out of its side at Ketetahi. The Tama Lakes are crater lakes formed between Ngauruhoe and Ruapehu.

## Information
For information on Tongariro National Park, walks, tramps, huts, etc, see the Whakapapa Visitors Centre (tel Mt Ruapehu 23-729). It's behind the Chateau, opposite the motor camp, and is open from 8 am to 5 pm daily. There are also ranger stations at Ohakune (tel 58-578) and Turangi (tel 68-607).

The excellent DOSLI *Tongariro National Park* map is well worth purchasing before you go off trekking. It's available at the Visitors Centre for $11.

## Things to See
North of the main part of the park on the shores of Lake Rotoaira are some interesting excavations of a pre- European Maori village site. West of here is Te Porere Redoubt Historical Reserve, the site of the last pitched battle in the Maori wars in 1869. Very different from the ancient Maori pa, Te Porere was typical of the fortification that followed the introduction of firearms. The earthworks have been restored. It's a 22 km drive from the Chateau, and then another 15 minutes from the road.

To the east of Mt Ruapehu is an area known as the Rangipo Desert. It's not a desert in the true sense of the word, but was so named because of its desert-like appearance caused by its cold, exposed, windswept situation.

## Walks
The park has a number of interesting walks including a long one described in the Outdoor Activities chapter at the start of the book. The park ranger stations have brochures on the various short and long walks, and during the summer months there are regular, cheap guided walks. You can go on a walk to the Tama Lakes or climb to the summits of Mt Ngauruhoe and Mt Tongariro for only about $2.

Walks from the Visitors Centre include:

**Taranaki Falls** A 2½ hour walk to the Wairere Stream and along to the spectacular sheer drop of the Taranaki Falls.

**Silica Springs** Another 2½ hour trip to springs where the rocks are coloured by silica and other minerals carried in the water.

**Whakapapanui Track** Starting from the same point as the Silica Springs track, it takes 2 hours to follow this track alongside the Whakapapanui Stream downstream more-or-less parallel to the road.

**Whakapapanui Gorge** A full-day trip, for which you'll need boots. Follow the road above the Chateau up to the footbridge across the Whakapapanui Stream. Don't cross the bridge, but go to your left and follow the stream, rock-hopping up until you eventually enter the gorge itself with a sheer precipice at its head.

**Ridge Track** A 40 minute walk above the Visitors Centre.

**Whakapapaiti Valley** A day's round-trip walk from the Visitors Centre or Scoria Flat, about 4 km above Whakapapa on Bruce Road.

**Tama Lakes** To climb to these crater lakes takes 2 to 3 hours each way beyond Taranaki Falls.

Walks starting from other parts of the National Park include:

**Valley** From the end of the access road this 1½ hour walk (each way) leads to the valley between Tongariro and Ngauruhoe.

**Tawhai Falls** A 10 minute walk off the entrance road 4 km below the Visitors Centre.

**Waitongo Falls** Two hours return from the Ohakune access road.

**Mangawhero Forest** A 2½ hour walk through one of the few remaining original forests near Ohakune.

**Ketetahi Springs** The track starts about 30 km from the Chateau, on the northern side of Tongariro. It takes about 2½ hours to walk to the springs and you can bathe in the stream there. See the Outdoor Activities chapter.

**Mt Tongariro Traverse** It takes 6 to 8 hours to cross right across the mountain in what has been described as the finest 1 day walk in New Zealand. Come prepared for changeable mountain weather and you have to make transport arrangements at both ends. See the Tramping section in the Outdoor Activities chapter for details.

**Rotopounamu** A beautiful, secluded lake, 20 minute walk from the Te Ponanga Saddle road in a separate part of the Tongariro National Park between Mt Tongariro and Lake Taupo, which includes Pihanga. See the section on New Plymouth in the Taranaki chapter for the legend about Tongariro, Taranaki and Pihanga. You can walk around the lake in 1½ hours – no camping though.

**Places to Stay**
The choice at Tongariro is whether you want to stay actually in the National Park at one of the nine huts accessible only by walking tracks or at Whakapapa – where there is an expensive hotel, a rather expensive motel and a camping site – or whether you choose to stay outside the park in one of the surrounding towns. See the following sections on National Park, Ohakune and Turangi for accommodation details on the places outside the park boundaries.

**Hotels & Motels** The hotel is called the *Chateau* (tel Mt Ruapehu 23-809). Apart from the Hermitage at Mt Cook it is the best known hotel in New Zealand; and like the Hermitage, it's run by the THC. It was originally built in 1929 and is still in new condition, and priced accordingly. Rooms

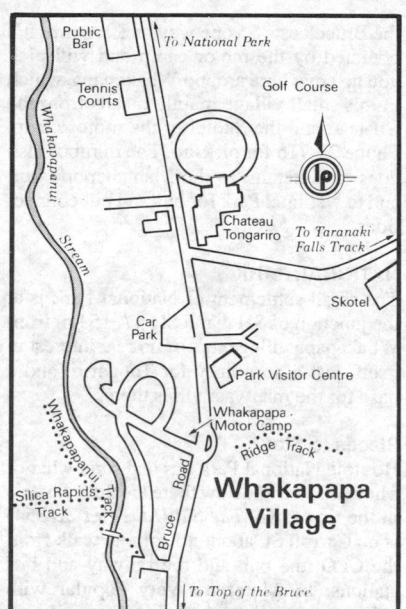

Public Bar
To National Park
Tennis Courts
Golf Course
Whakapapanui Stream
Chateau Tongariro
To Taranaki Falls Track
Skotel
Car Park
Park Visitor Centre
Whakapapa Motor Camp
Ridge Track
Whakapapaiti Track
Silica Rapids Track
Bruce Road
**Whakapapa Village**
To Top of the Bruce

**Camping & Cabins** The popular *Whakapapa Motor Camp* (tel Mt Ruapehu 23-897) is up the road from the Chateau, opposite the Whakapapa Visitors Centre. Camping in tents (not recommended in winter!) costs $6 per person. Caravan sites cost $8 per person, or $11 with power. There are also pleasant cabins for $9 per person but there's a minimum charge of $29. Tourist bungalows cost $12 per person but their minimum charge is $39. Similarly, tourist flats cost $15 per person with a minimum charge of $47. These rates apply all year, but from November to June there's also a $12 (cabins) and $15 (bungalows) backpackers' share rate, with no minimum charge.

Scattered around the park's tramping paths are nine huts, with access by foot only. Contact the Visitors Centre or the ranger stations about the tramping huts, which cost $8 per night – maximum stay two nights at busy periods.

### Places to Eat
There's a reasonable selection of food in the camp store if you're preparing your own – as usual it's more expensive than down the road. It's 16 km down the road to National Park, the nearest crossroads town. Milk and bread are sold at the store and the Chateau cafeteria, but can be difficult to get sometimes. The camp has kitchen facilities, of course, but so does the Skotel.

The camp store also has pies and light snacks. You can also get pies, sandwiches and the like in the public bar opposite the Chateau. Otherwise the *Skotel* has a family restaurant-bar with the pub regulars – main courses from around $8 to $15 at lunch and $15 to $18 at dinner; desserts for about $6. Breakfast costs between $8 (continental) and $13.50 (cooked).

Of course the fancy place to eat is at the *Chateau* where breakfast costs from $10 (continental) or at dinner main courses are around $21 to $30. Best deal of the week is the magnificently ample Sunday buffet lunch served from 12.30 to 2 pm, where for $20 (children $10) you can fill yourself up

cost between $85 and $280 in the low season (1 October to 15 July). In the high season you're looking at between $140 and $340. The Chateau is not for economising.

Round behind the Chateau is the *Skotel* (tel Mt Ruapehu 23-719) which has gone through a recent renovation and expansion. Accommodation here includes plain single/-double rooms at around $34/41, deluxe rooms for $47/56, and super deluxe rooms (with a video and other luxuries) for $59/72. These are the low season rates; in the ski season the rates jump about 50%. The Skotel also has chalets with kitchens and other goodies from about $72 for two. There's a communal kitchen for the regular rooms (you provide crockery and cutlery, they provide pots and pans), as well as a spa pool, gym, games room, restaurant and bar. From July to November there are special 'backpacker share' rates of $17 per person in the standard twin rooms.

on all kinds of wonderfully exotic and tasty foods that you usually can't afford.

During the ski season there is a takeaway food van, and if you're skiing there is food available up at the Top of the Bruce where the lifts and tows start.

### Getting There & Away

**Bus** An InterCity bus runs a route 3 days a week (Tuesdays, Thursdays and Sundays) which begins at Rotorua and stops at Taupo, Turangi, Whakapapa, National Park and Ohakune, and then returns along the same route to Rotorua. Daily Auckland-Wellington buses stop at National Park but not at Whakapapa.

Alpine Scenic Tours (tel Turangi 68-392) operate an inexpensive private bus which stops at Taupo, Turangi, Ketetahi, Mangatepopo, Whakapapa and National Park. You can take a taxi from Ohakune or National Park to Whakapapa but it isn't cheap.

**Car** The park is encircled by roads. SH 1 (at this point it's called the Desert Road) passes down the eastern side of the park. It was once a nightmare, but now it's a good sealed road, though sometimes temporarily blocked by snow in winter. SH 4 passes down the western side, SH 47 crosses the northern side and SH 49 the southern side. The main road up into the park is SH 48 which leads to Whakapapa Village, where the Visitors Centre and the Chateau are, and further up the mountain is Bruce Road to the 'Top of the Bruce' at Iwikau Village. The Ohakune Mountain Rd leads up to the Turoa Ski Field from Ohakune in the south-west.

**Hitching** From whichever direction you come, hitching to Whakapapa is never that easy because traffic is usually so light. If you're coming south from Turangi use the shorter saddle road, SH 47A – the locals no longer use the SH 1 to SH 47 route.

### Getting Around

The minibus shuttle service from Whakapapa up to the ski runs at the Top of the Bruce costs $5 one way or $9 return. It's operated by the motor camp and will pick you up anywhere around Whakapapa, which in this small village mainly means from the Chateau and the Skotel or the motor camp. Phone 23-716 for pick-up. The minibus also goes to Ketetahi, to the Mangatepopo hut, and to National Park for bus and rail connections.

### NATIONAL PARK

The small settlement of National Park is at the junction of SH 4 and SH 47, 15 km from Whakapapa village. It's of no real interest in itself, just a dormitory for Tongariro and a base for the many activities there.

### Places to Stay

**Hostels** National Park has had somewhat of a hostel boom and now there are three hostels in the tiny town. *The Ski Haus* (tel 22-854) is on Carroll St, about a 1 minute walk from the CPO, the pub and the railway and bus stations. In winter it's very popular with skiers, especially on weekends, so if you want to avoid the crowds, come during the week. Bunks cost $12 and double rooms cost $19 per person. In winter they also have a skiers' DB&B (dinner, bed & breakfast) package at $60 per person.

Campervan sites cost $5 per site plus $7 per person. There's a spa pool, recreation room, a sunken fireplace area in the attractive lounge and a house bar. The Ski Haus organises a variety of activities including horse treks, river rafting, trail bike trips, paragliding courses, skiing and tramping. They also operate a ski and bicycle hire shop, and provide daily transport to Ketetahi and Mangatepopo.

Nearby, *Howard's Lodge* (tel 22-827) has a variety of dorm, double, triple and quadruple rooms for $12.50 per person in summer (November to June) and $20 the rest of the year. They also offer B&B for $17.50 per person in summer and $30 in winter.

The *Macrocarpa Lodge* (tel 22-878), directly behind the BP petrol station at the junction of SH 4 and SH 47, has bunks for $10.50 during the November to June summer season and $15 the rest of the year. Double rooms are $35 in summer and $40 in winter. In summer they provide free transport to Tongariro walking tracks, and will arrange to pick you up from the tracks for a small fee, or to take you to Ohakune for bungy jumping.

**Hotels, Chalets & Motels** The *National Park Hotel* (tel 22-805) near the railway station has bunkrooms for two to six people at a cost of $12 in summer and $17.50 in winter if you bring your own linen, or $20 all year if you use theirs. Regular rooms are $15/65 in summer, $27.50/65 in winter, and there's a reasonably-priced restaurant and pub. You can walk across the road and use the spa pool at the Ski Haus lodge for $3 per half hour.

The *Discovery Best Western Motel* (tel National Park 22-744) is at the Discovery camping ground, about halfway between Whakapapa and National Park. Rates vary with the season, ranging from $34 to $60 single, $41 to $74 double during summer (November to June), upwards from $58/70 the rest of the year.

The *Buttercup Alpine Resort* (tel 22-702) at National Park has chalets for $60 per person, including breakfast and dinner ($35 per person for B&B only); the cost is the same all year. Activities organised from here include rafting trips on the lower Tongariro or volcano hikes that include lunch and transport to the start of the trail.

There are several other motels in National Park including the *Mountain Heights Lodge* (tel 22-833), open only from June to October (Christmas holidays by arrangement). DB&B costs $45 per person in bunkrooms and $48 in twin rooms.

**Camping & Cabins** The *Discovery Caravan Park* (tel National Park 22-744) is on SH 47 about midway between Whakapapa and National Park – which means it's effectively in the middle of nowhere! It has a covered swimming pool (heated in winter), two spa pools and a licensed restaurant, but no kitchen available to guests. Caravan sites

cost $6.60 per person. Cabins cost $24 per person during the ski season and $18 per person the rest of the year; you supply your own linen.

Six km south of National Park is *Erua Ski Lodge* (tel National Park 22-894, also New Plymouth 87-144, 84-216 for bookings), which can accommodate up to 100 people in bunks for $15 a night during the ski season. You supply your own bedding and blankets and the kitchen, dining room, showers and recreation area are communal. It's half price in the low season. In winter, on-site caravans sleeping four cost $55 a night. The management also organises summer camps which include windsurfing, horse-riding, sailing and climbing.

Six km north is the *Slalom Ski Lodge* (tel National Park 22-856) which has DB&B for $50 per person during the week and $56 on weekends. Sometimes they also have bunkroom accommodation for $15 to $20 per person and motel units for $55 per double.

**Getting There & Away**
**Bus** National Park is midway on the daily InterCity Auckland-Wellington bus route, about 5 hours from either city. Nearby towns served on this route include Ohakune, Raetihi, Taumarunui and Te Kuiti, near Waitomo. There's also a Tuesday, Thursday and Sunday InterCity bus with even more local stops, starting at Rotorua and calling at Taupo, Turangi, the Chateau, National Park and Ohakune, where it turns around and follows the same route for the return trip. See the Tongariro Getting There & Away section for even more bus options, with the private Alpine Scenic Tours buses.

**Train** Trains between Auckland and Wellington stop at National Park twice daily in each direction on weekdays, once daily on weekends.

**OHAKUNE**
In contrast to National Park, Ohakune is quite a pleasant little town with lots of motels and even more restaurants. It's very much a skiing town, a lot of effort goes into catering

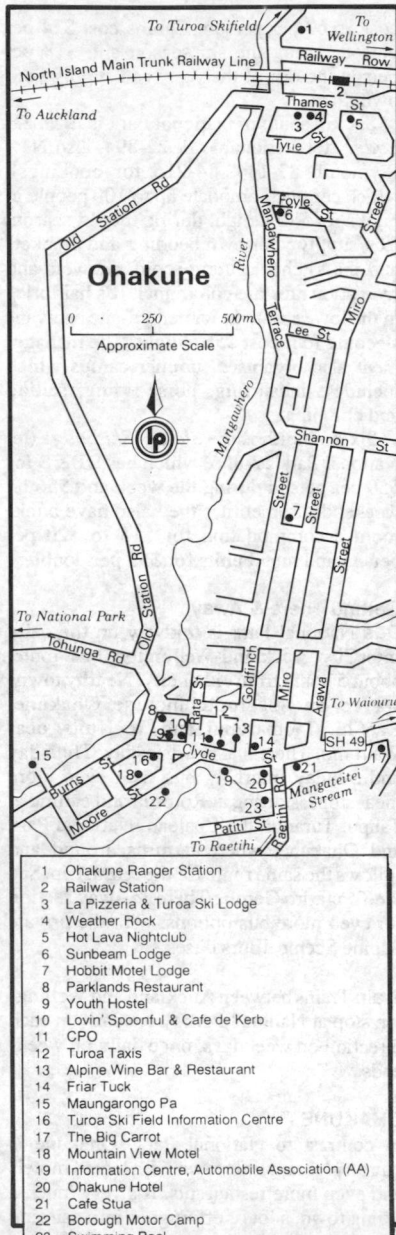

**Ohakune**

0        250        500 m

Approximate Scale

To Turoa Skifield

To Wellington

North Island Main Trunk Railway Line

Railway Row

To Auckland

Thames St

Tyne St

Foyle St

Shannon St

Old Station Rd

To National Park

Tohunga Rd

To Waiouru

SH 49

Clyde St

Burns St

Moore St

Patiti St

To Raetihi

Mangateitei Stream

River Mangawhero

Mangauhohu River

Terrace

Lee St

Miro

Street

Goldfinch

Arawa

1   Ohakune Ranger Station
2   Railway Station
3   La Pizzeria & Turoa Ski Lodge
4   Weather Rock
5   Hot Lava Nightclub
6   Sunbeam Lodge
7   Hobbit Motel Lodge
8   Parklands Restaurant
9   Youth Hostel
10  Lovin' Spoonful & Cafe de Kerb
11  CPO
12  Turoa Taxis
13  Alpine Wine Bar & Restaurant
14  Friar Tuck
15  Maungarongo Pa
16  Turoa Ski Field Information Centre
17  The Big Carrot
18  Mountain View Motel
19  Information Centre, Automobile Association (AA)
20  Ohakune Hotel
21  Cafe Stua
22  Borough Motor Camp
23  Swimming Pool

for those snow-season big-spenders. Most of the businesses in town either make it or break it during the few months of ski season, from late June to late October, and in fact many don't even bother opening up outside of this season.

Recently, though, there's been a push to try to attract tourists year-round, and there are many outdoor activities that can be enjoyed anytime. This is a great town for outdoors-loving people.

Ohakune is mainly a base for skiing or walking trips but while you're in town check the Big Carrot on the Waiouru road and the weather stone on Thames St. Kids will like the old tank in the children's play park by the Information Centre.

## Information

The Information Centre (tel 58-427) is at the southern end of town on SH 49. It has lots of brochures and an excellent three-dimensional model of Tongariro Park – great for tracing where you're going to walk. They also do bookings for all the area's activities and accommodation, and for InterCity buses. In ski season the office is open every day from 8.30 am to 5 pm, the rest of the year it's Monday to Friday, 9 am to 4.30 pm. The AA office is next door.

Also at this end of town is the Turoa Ski Field Information Centre (tel 58-456), a hexagonal office which provides up-to-the-minute info on ski conditions, road passability, etc. The CPO is nearby.

Up at the northern end of town by the railway line there's a sort of second centre with a number of restaurants along Thames St. Just north of the tracks is the Ohakune Ranger Station (tel 58-578) with info on walking in the park and a book to sign before you set off.

## Karioi Lakes

Lake Rotokuru is about 11 km south of Ohakune on SH 49, at Karioi in the Karioi State Forest, about 1 km from the Karioi turn-off. It's called Lake Rotokuru on the map but it's actually two lakes not one, and the locals call them the Karioi Lakes. They are two little jewels, one above the other, great for fishing and relaxing.

## Waiouru

If you're passing through Waiouru, at the junction of SH 1 and SH 49 east of Ohakune, the Army Memorial Museum makes an interesting stop. It's open from 9 am to 4.30 pm daily; admission is $6 (children $3, family $15).

## Bungy Jumping

There's bungy jumping off the 45 metre railway bridge over a canyon just out of town. A J Hackett, who achieved worldwide attention a few years ago with his famous bungy jump off the Eiffel Tower (see Queenstown in the Otago & Southland chapter) runs New Sensations (tel 59-189) from an office at 37 Thames St. In addition to bungy jumping they'll do just about anything for a thrill including parapenting, monoskiing, snowboarding and anything else you can think of. Bungy jumping costs $85, including a T-shirt. They usually jump all day every day during the busy winter season and on weekends only in summer, but when there's a demand, they go.

Queenstown is more famous for bungy jumping than Ohakune, but the jump at Ohakune is still high enough – in fact it's 2 metres higher than the Kawerau Bridge jump (43 metres) at Queenstown, which is the more popular jump. The 69 metre Skippers Canyon jump, though, outside of Queenstown, has both of them beat.

## Other Activities

Ask at the Information Centre about activities around Ohakune, there are many and they can give you the run-down on who is doing what. In addition to the many fine walks in the area, ranging in length from 15 minutes to several days, there are river activities including fishing, canoeing, jetboating and white water rafting on the Tongariro, Rangitikei and Maunganui-A-Te-Ao rivers.

A few operators to try are Yeti Tours (tel Ohakune 58-197), Pioneer Jet Boat Tours (tel Taumarunui 8074) and Ruapehu Outback Adventures (tel Ohakune 58-799). Ruapehu Outback Adventures also do horse treks for all ages and all levels of horse-riding expertise, they hire out 4WD and other vehicles, and they have homestead accommodation if you want to stay out of town. See the Wanganui section in the Taranaki chapter for more on Yeti Tours, which operate from Ohakune, Taumarunui and Wanganui.

Miro Park is a pleasant little park at the eastern end of Thames St and on weekends a 230 metre flying fox goes hurtling over the Miro Park Lake, rides cost $5 (children $3) or you can get a five-ride card for $18 (children $11).

## Aerial Sightseeing

Helicopter flightseeing trips over the Tongariro and Whanganui national parks are available from NZ Aero Tours (tel Raetihi 54-349, 54-538). Mountain Air (tel Taumarunui 22-812) does flightseeing trips over Tongariro in small aeroplanes with prices beginning at around $30 per person.

## Places to Stay

**Hostels** The *Ohakune Youth Hostel* (tel 58-724) is on Clyde St, near the CPO and Information Centre. It's a good hostel with lots of rooms, it's open all day and you have your own room key so you can come and go as you wish. During ski season it is very heavily booked so at that time you have to plan ahead. Nightly cost is $13.

A number of motels in town offer bunk-room accommodation, with lowest rates in the non-ski season. See Hotels & Motels.

**Hotels & Motels** Motel costs are usually higher during the ski season. At the *Hobbit Motel Lodge* (tel 58-248) on the corner of Goldfinch and Wye streets, singles/doubles are $60/70 in the low summer season, from $95 single or double in ski season. They also have bunkrooms where a bed costs $17 all year round if you bring your own bedding, $22 with linen provided.

The *Turoa Ski Lodge* (tel 58-274) at 10 Thames St is an attractive lodge with B&B

at $47.50 per person in the main lodge, which is open only during ski season. The bunkroom out the back, however, is open all year round – cost is $12.50 per person November to June, jumping to $32.50 in ski season, when breakfast is included.

At 2 Moore St, the *Ohakune Mountain View Motel* (tel 58-675) has rooms starting at $50 in summer, $70 in winter. They also have more economical cabins and a basic bunkhouse, where you provide your own sleeping bag and kitchen utensils. Cost is $10 in summer, $13 in winter. The cabins are also available on the same share basis and they're $12 per person during the summer, $16 in winter.

The *Ohakune Hotel* (tel 58-268) on Clyde St has rooms at $25/40, it's one place where prices remain the same all year.

The *Alpine Motel* (58-758) at 7 Miro St is highly recommended. It has all the usual motel facilities, is close to the centre of town and is reasonably priced. The people who run the motel are very friendly and do their best to make you feel welcome.

**Camping & Cabins** The *Ohakune Borough Camp* (tel 58-561) is on Moore St in the centre, with camping sites at $8 per person, power sites at $15.50 for two in summer, $18 in mid-winter. They offer caravan and vehicle storage for $11 a week while you're off trekking or doing other activities.

If you can't get in here, there's the *Raetihi Glow Worm Motor Camp* (tel Raetihi 54-176) with glow-worms on the premises, squash and tennis courts, swimming pools, a roller skating rink and a children's trampoline playground. Camping sites are $5 per person, $6 with power, and there's caravan storage at $5 per week.

**Places to Eat**
In the centre of town near the Information Centre, *Cafe Stua* has espresso coffee and light, simple breakfast and lunch. Nearby the *Alpine Wine Bar and Restaurant* is a good restaurant serving large portions of steak, seafood and the like. Lunch main courses are $10, dinner mains around $13 to $19.

At the Ohakune Hotel the *Griddlestone Restaurant* serves all three meals every day during ski season, closing on Sundays the rest of the year. Besides the à la carte menu there's a family smorgasbord dinner served Sunday evenings in winter, Saturday evenings in summer, cost is $16.

Up by the railway station are a number of restaurants along Thames St including *La Pizzeria* which does pretty good pizzas. Around the corner *Nobby's* is a local favourite with basic meals at $10, more exotic selections at $18, or snacks like nachos at around $7. It's a relaxed, comfortable place with seating indoors or out in the garden bar.

All of these places are open all year round but during the winter skiing rush the town fills up with skiers and many more options for dining. Worthy mentions open only in winter are *Margarita's* Mexican restaurant on Thames St beside La Pizzeria, and the licensed restaurant at the *Turoa Ski Lodge* next door.

About half a km out of town past the Big Carrot on the other side of Ohakune, the *Cajun Cafe* at Beecher's Lodge is worth the trouble to get out to it. It's a tiny restaurant with just a few tables and a delicious Cajun Creole cuisine. It's good value, with main dishes at $13, soups $3, entrees $5 and desserts $4. Unfortunately you'll only find it open if you're there in the winter.

**Entertainment**
The Hot Lava nightclub on Thames St is very popular, with live music on weekends all year round.

**Getting There & Away**
**Bus** InterCity buses serve Ohakune daily, arriving and departing from the Information Centre. See the National Park section for details on InterCity buses and bus routes – Ohakune is half an hour from National Park on the same bus lines.

**Train** The Auckland-Wellington trains stop at Ohakune twice daily in each direction on weekdays, once a day on weekends. Buy tickets at the Information Centre.

## Getting Around

There's plenty of transport available between Ohakune and the Turoa ski field during the winter. Best value are the Turoa Express bus (tel Ohakune 58-762) and Ruapehu Mountain Tours (tel Ohakune 59-045) who make the return trip for about $13. The Snowcruiser (tel 58-094) and Turoa Taxis (tel 58-573) are more expensive.

In summer a mountain road transport service departs from the Ski Field Information Centre (tel 58-456) opposite the youth hostel weekdays at 8 am (be there by 7.30 am), returning from the mountain around 4 pm. Cost is $5 and it's a useful service for hikers.

Turoa Taxis has summer transport to the various tracks – for one to four people it's $18 to the Blyth track, $25 to the Lake Surprise track, $60 to Pipiriki or the Chateau. YHA members get a discount.

## TURANGI

At the northern end of the park, beside Lake Taupo, Turangi is a new town, developed for the construction of the hydroelectric power station here. It's a good access point for the tracks at the northern end of the park.

## Information

There's an excellent Information Centre (tel 68-999) just off SH 1 by the town centre. It's an interesting place with several 3-D models including a detailed one of the Tongariro National Park and the power developments plus lots of photographic exhibits and information on the area's many activities. They also do activities and accommodation bookings, and they have many useful maps of the region including one showing all the trout pools on the Tongariro River. The centre is open from 9 am to 5 pm daily.

The DOC has a ranger station (tel 68-607) in Turangi at the southern end of town, open Monday to Friday from 8 am to 4.30 pm, with additional weekend hours during their January summer activity programme. If you're planning to walk into the park from the north fill in the walker's intentions book at the ranger station first.

| 1 | Swimming Pool |
| 2 | InterCity Bus Station |
| 3 | Shopping Centre |
| 4 | Information Centre |
| 5 | Tongariro Accommodation Centre |
| 6 | Turangi Holiday Park |
| 7 | Ranger Station |

Turangi

The AA agent is in the Chronicle office in the shopping mall.

## Trout Hatchery

Four km south of Turangi on SH 1 are the Tongariro Trout Hatcheries. They're open 9 am to 4 pm daily and entry is free. There's an underwater viewing area, keeping ponds, a pleasant picnic area and then you could try your hand on the real grown-up thing in the Tongariro River which runs close by.

**Trout** The Wildlife Service operates three trout hatcheries in New Zealand – one in Wanaka in the

South Island, one near Rotorua and the one in Turangi. The Wanaka hatchery is mainly for salmon while the two North Island hatcheries are almost exclusively for rainbow trout. There are other private hatcheries, some of which obtain their eggs from the Wildlife Service operations.

The first brown trout eggs arrived in New Zealand from Tasmania in 1867. They had originally come to Australia from England. Rainbow trout eggs first arrived from California in 1883. Hatcheries were established at that time to rear the first young fish and although many fish are hatched naturally there is still a need for artificial hatcheries. This is because New Zealand's lakes and rivers may be ideal for trout but some of them have insufficient good spawning grounds. Plus there's a hell of a lot of fishing going on!

In the wild fully grown trout migrate each winter to suitable spawning beds. This usually means gravel beds in the upper reaches of rivers and streams. Here a female fish makes a shallow depression and deposits eggs which are quickly fertilised by an attendant male fish. The female fish then sweeps gravel over the eggs. Over 2 or 3 days this process is repeated to create a *redd* with several pockets of eggs. All through this process the fish do not feed and a female fish may lose one-third of her body weight by the time she returns to the lake. Male fish are in even worse shape because they arrive at the spawning grounds before the females and leave afterwards.

Less than 1% of the eggs survive to become mature fish. The eggs may be damaged or destroyed by movement of the gravel and even when hatched they may be eaten by other fish, birds or rats. Even other trout will happily make a meal of them.

Because there were only a few shipments of eggs originally, from which all today's trout are descended, New Zealand's rainbow trout are considered to be a very pure strain. The hatchery eggs are collected by capturing fish during their spawning run. Eggs are gently squeezed from a female fish and milt from males added and stirred together in a container. Incubator trays containing about 10,000 eggs are placed in racks and washed over by a continuous flow of water.

After 15 days the embryo fish eyes start to appear and by the 18th day the embryo, previously very sensitive and frail, have become quite hardy. They'd better be because on that day the eggs are poured from a metre height into a wire basket. Any weak eggs are killed off by this rough treatment, ensuring that only healthy fish are hatched out. The survivors are now placed 5000 to a basket and about 10 days later the fish hatch out, wriggle through the mesh and drop to the bottom of the trough. They stay there for about 20 days, living off the yolk sac.

When they have totally absorbed their yolk sac they are known as fry and although they can be released at this stage they are normally kept until they are 10 to 15 cm long. At this time they are 9 to 12 months old and are known as fingerlings. They are moved outside when they are about 4 cm long and reared in ponds. Fingerlings are transported to the place where they will be released in what looks rather like a small petrol tanker, and simply pumped out the back down a large diameter pipe!

## Tokaanu

About 5 km out of Turangi on the road round the western side of Lake Taupo towards Taumarunui is this pleasant little pioneer settlement with an interesting thermal area. There's a posted walk around the bubbling mud pools and also hot pools and a sauna. The walk is free, the public pool costs $2.50 (children $1), private ones $3.50, and it's $6 for the sauna (children $2.50). There's not much in Tokaanu besides the hot pools but if you want to stay there are various accommodation possibilities including a motor camp, a lodge and a motel, all of which can be booked through the Turangi Information Centre.

## Other Attractions

Turangi is a popular base for lake and river fishing, walking and rafting. River Rats Rafting operate from the Tongariro Accommodation Centre (tel 67-492) and will take you on a half-day white water rafting trip down the Tongariro River for $70 per person. They go at 10.30 am midweek, 8.30 am and 1.30 pm on weekends. Other white water rafting trips also operate from Turangi and all trips can be booked through the Information Centre.

The Information Centre also arranges horse treks, hunting trips, cruises and charter boats, scenic minibus tours, and has good printed leaflets on the area's best trout fishing spots and walks.

Turangi Scenic Flights (tel 67-870) operate flights over Tongariro National Park, Lake Taupo and the Tongariro River. Prices begin at $25 per person.

On the slopes of Pihanga and near to Turangi it's a pleasant 1½ hour walk around Lake Rotopounamu which abounds in bird life.

## Places to Stay

**Hostels** Right in the centre the *Tongariro Accommodation Centre* (tel 67-492) on Ohuanga Rd was the single men's hostel during the construction of the power station. They have a number of accommodation blocks, each with 12 twin rooms, a TV room, kitchen and dining area. Cost is $13 per person if you bring your own bedding, $20 if you use theirs, or you can pay $5 per person to pitch a tent on the lawn. The kitchens may not be fully equipped with all the usual cooking utensils but you can get anything you need just by asking for it. They also have a central bar, garden bar, BBQ area and a restaurant serving a daily all-you-can-eat continental breakfast, plus other meals on weekends.

**Hotels, Motels & Lodges** There are plenty of motels and fishing lodges in Turangi. This is a very popular area for trout fishing and like the camping sites some of them are round the lakeshore towards Taupo. The Turangi Information Centre does bookings for all the area's accommodation.

The *Sportsmans Lodge* (tel 68-150) at 15 Taupehi Rd has rooms sharing a communal kitchen and TV lounge at $30/40 for singles/doubles. The *Turangi Motor Hotel* (tel 68-979) on Pihanga St has single and double rooms at $40, family suites at $60.

There's some interesting accommodation in nearby Tokaanu including the expensive *THC Tokaanu* (tel 68-873) with rooms at around $100 a night and a thermal swimming pool. Also at Tokaanu is the *Oasis Motel* (tel 68-569) with rooms at $55/60.

**Camping & Cabins** There are a number of camping sites in Turangi including *Turangi Holiday Park* (tel 68-754) on Ohuanga Rd, off SH 41. Power or tent sites are $7 per person. They also have cabins sleeping two at $14 per person and some on-site caravans. This was also at one time quarters for the construction workers, which accounts for the large number of cabins.

At Tokaanu the *Oasis Caravan Park* (tel Turangi 68-569) has camping sites at $6 per person, $7 with power, cabins at $14 per person with linen provided. They also have hot pools and spa pools.

There are several other camping sites out of Turangi on the road around the lake side to Taupo. They are the *Motuoapa Domain Camp* (tel 65-333), 8 km out at Motuoapa, the *Tauranga-Taupo Lodge & Caravan Park* (tel 68-385), 11 km out at Tauranga-Taupo, and the *Motutere Bay Caravan Park* (tel 68-963), 17 km out at Motutere Bay.

## Places to Eat

There are a scattering of coffee shops, takeaways and fast food places like *Golden Crust*, *Coffee Time*, *Kozy Kettle* and *Hong Kong Chinese Takeaways* in the modern little shopping centre. Upstairs is a comfortable, low-priced family restaurant open every day which serves meals and takeaways during the day, a restaurant menu in the evening. Or try *El Burcio*, a solidly Italian reminder of the many Italian construction workers at the time the power station was built.

## Getting There & Away

**Bus** InterCity buses (tel 68-918) stop beside the shopping centre, as do Mt Cook (tel 68-705) and Newmans buses. Daily Auckland-Wellington buses which run down the eastern side of the lake from Taupo, 1 hour to the north, all go through Turangi. On Tuesdays, Thursdays and Sundays there's an InterCity bus route beginning from Rotorua, stopping at Taupo, Turangi, Whakapapa, National Park and Ohakune, returning from Ohakune back the way it came.

## Getting Around

Alpine Scenic Tours (tel 68-392 at all hours) offer tours of the area but also provide transport for skiers and trampers. They'll take you to the start of the Ketetahi or Mangatepopo Trails, to Whakapapa, National Park or north to Taupo. Access to these northern trails used to be a real problem so this is an excellent service.

# Palmerston North

Population 69,000
Although Palmerston North is a major crossroads, few people pause there. It's basically just somewhere you pass through. The city is on the banks of the Manawatu River and is the site of the Massey University.

### Orientation
The wide open expanse of The Square is very much the centre of Palmerston North; it's a long way around it on foot on a wet and windy night! You can get your bearings from a lookout on top of the Civic Centre building in The Square. It's open 10 am to 3 pm on weekdays. Broadway Ave is the main street in the town.

### Information
There's an Information Centre (tel 85-003) in the Civic Centre on the south-western side of The Square. It's open from 8.30 am to 5.30 pm Monday to Friday and from 9.30 am to 1 pm on Saturdays. The DOC (tel 89-004) is in the Government Life Insurance Building on the corner of Queen St and Rangitikei St. The AA has an office on the corner of Broadway Ave and Amesbury St, two blocks from The Square.

The CPO is in Princess St between Main St and Broadway Ave, one block off The Square. Bennetts Bookshop on Broadway is one of the better bookshops in New Zealand.

Palmerston North is the home base of WWOOF (Willing Workers on Organic Farms, PO Box 10-037, tel 553-555). See Farmstays under Accommodation in the Facts for the Visitor chapter for details on WWOOF.

### Manawatu Museum & Art Gallery
At 221-225 Church St, only a few steps from The Square, the museum specialises in the history of the Manawatu region of which Palmerston North is the centre. It is open from 10 am to 4 pm Tuesday to Friday and from 2 to 4.30 pm on weekends and holidays;

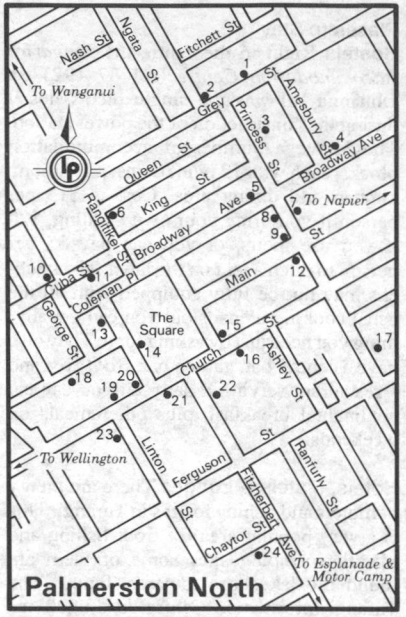

**Palmerston North**

1 Grey's Inn
2 Rugby Museum
3 Newmans Bus Depot
4 Automobile Association (AA)
5 Mid City Motel
6 Department of Conservation (DOC)
7 CPO
8 Ansett Airlines
9 Air New Zealand
10 Key West Restaurant
11 Costa's (upstairs)
12 Empire Establishment (Cobb & Co)
13 Pizza Piazza
14 Information Office
15 McDonald's
16 InterCity & City Bus Depot
17 Kentucky Fried Chicken
18 Manawatu Art Gallery
19 Manawatu Museum
20 Truelife Takeaways
21 Square Edge Arts Centre
22 Majestic Hotel
23 Youth Hostel
24 Chaytor House

closed on Mondays. Admission is free. Outside there are some old buildings including a schoolhouse and blacksmith's workshop.

Nearby on Church St is the town's spacious and modern Manawatu Art Gallery. It's open from 10 am to 4.30 pm Tuesday to Friday, and from 1 to 5 pm on weekends; closed on Mondays. Admission is free. The Square Edge Community Arts Centre, at the south-eastern corner of The Square, has exhibits, displays, workshops, shops and a pleasant little cafe.

### New Zealand National Rugby Museum
New Zealand's famous rugby mania is glorified in the New Zealand National Rugby Museum on the corner of Carroll and Grey streets. It's open from 1.30 to 4 pm daily; admission is $1 (children 20 cents).

### Esplanade Park
Esplanade Park, spread out along the Manuwatu River just a few blocks from The Square, includes gardens, bushwalks, a nature trail, an aviary, a conservatory, rose gardens and even a miniature railway. The Lido Swimming Centre and a mini-golf course are also there.

### Places to Stay
**Hostels** The *Palmerston North Summer Youth Hostel* (tel 64-347), at 10 Linton St, is open only during the summer, from about mid-November to mid-February. You can check at other YHA hostels for specific dates each year. The cost is $12 per night; there are plenty of twin and family rooms.

**Guest Houses** The *Chaytor House* (tel 86-878), 18 Chaytor St, has rooms at $34 to $39 for singles and $52 to $56 for doubles. The more expensive rooms have attached bathrooms. At the *Grey's Inn* (tel 86-928), 123 Grey St, B&B costs $40/60 for singles/doubles.

**Hotels** The *Majestic* (tel 80-079) on Fitzherbert Ave has rooms and suites from $45 to $69, some with private baths. The *Masonic* (tel 83-480) on Main St West has single/double rooms for $39/50.

**Motels** Palmerston North has a wide selection of motels. The *Consolidated Mid City Motel* (tel 72-184) at 129 Broadway Ave is very conveniently located, only a short walk from The Square. Singles/doubles cost $51/56. The *Broadway Motel* (tel 85-051), further along at 258 Broadway Ave, has single/double rooms for $57/68.

The *Central Motel* (tel 72-133) at 26 Linton St is also reasonably central and has single/double rooms for $45/56 and larger family rooms from $66. The *Always Inn* (tel 79-978) at 877 Main St is similarly priced. The *City Court Motel* (tel 72-132) at 451 Ferguson St has a swimming and spa pools; rooms are $63/74.

**Camping & Cabins** The *Palmerston North Holiday Park*, also called the *Municipal Camp* (tel 80-349) at 133 Dittmer Drive, off Ruha St and Park Rd, has camping sites for $6.60 per person and power sites that cost $14 for two. Cabins cost $19 to $26 and tourist flats cost $33 or $44, for two people. The site is very pleasantly situated beside the Lido Swimming Centre in Esplanade Park, about 2 km from The Square.

### Places to Eat
**Snacks & Fast Food** The *Pizza Piazza* on The Square does pretty good pizzas; small ones cost from $8, medium from $10, and large from $12. They also have a $5 pizza or pasta lunchtime special. *Sage*, in the Square Edge Arts Centre at the south-western corner of The Square, is a pleasant health food place for breakfast or lunch. It's open from 7.30 am.

*Truelife Takeaways*, at 47 The Square, is a good sandwich place. There's a *McDonald's* on The Square and a *Kentucky Fried Chicken* on Princess St.

**Pub Food & Restaurants** There are a number of pub food places around the centre, including the *Britannia Restaurant* in the Majestic Hotel, on Fitzherbert St near The

Square. It's open for lunch and dinner until 10 pm every day of the week (last orders 9.30 pm). The *Brasserie* in the same hotel is good for breakfast or lunch. There's a *Cobb & Co* in the Empire Establishment on the corner of Princess and Main streets, with the usual Cobb & Co menu, open 7 days a week.

Upstairs at 282 Cuba St is *Costa's*, a popular, good-fun Tex/Mex restaurant. It's open in the evenings from Tuesday to Saturday, serving ample, tasty dinners for around $13 to $16.

### Entertainment
Apart from pubs, Palmerston North now has several nightclubs. There's *Cheers* in the Masonic Hotel, *Madison's* upstairs on The Square near McDonald's, *Chantelle's* at the corner of Rangitikei and Featherston streets, and *Exchequers* on Cuba St near The Square. *Champers* upstairs over the Key West Restaurant on Cuba St may be in for a name change but it should still be going strong.

### Getting There & Away
**Air** Air New Zealand (tel 64-737) is on the corner of Princess and Main streets. It has several daily direct flights to Auckland and Wellington, with connections to other centres. Ansett NZ (tel 592-592) is at 50-52 Princess St and has direct flights to Auckland and Christchurch. Air Nelson (tel 82-028) has direct flights to Wellington and Nelson, while Eagle Air (tel 87-674) has direct flights to Hamilton.

**Bus** InterCity (tel 81-169) has a bus terminal right by The Square on Church St East. Newmans (tel 77-079) is on Princess St. Allans buses to Masterton also operate from the Newmans station. Mt Cook (tel 77-039) operates from the AA office on the corner of Broadway Ave and Amesbury St.

Most direct Auckland-Wellington services actually bypass Palmerston North, stopping instead at nearby Bulls. The Wellington-Napier buses do stop at Palmerston North. InterCity, Newmans and Mt Cook all have buses from Palmerston North to Wellington (1½ hours), Auckland (8 hours) via

Morepork owl

Taupo and Hamilton, Wanganui (1½ hours), New Plymouth (3½ hours), and Napier (3 hours).

**Train** Trains between Auckland and Wellington stop at Palmerston North, as do trains between Wellington and Napier. The railway station (tel 81-169) is on the outskirts of town, off Tremaine Ave. It's open from 10 to 11.30 am and 4 to 6 pm Monday to Friday, and from 10 to 11.30 am and 5 to 6.30 pm on Sundays; it's closed on Saturdays.

The Auckland-Wellington trains run twice daily (morning and evening), with stops at several places around Tongariro National Park. From Palmerston North it's about 2½ hours to Wellington and 9 hours to Auckland. The Wellington-Napier train runs once daily; on that train it's about 2 hours to Wellington and 3 hours to Napier.

### Getting Around
A taxi to or from the airport costs about $6. City buses go from the InterCity depot beside The Square on Church St. There's a flat fare system anywhere in town and the buses operate all weekend.

### AROUND PALMERSTON NORTH
### Steam Engine Museum
Outside the city you can visit the Tokomaru Steam Engine Museum with its display of working engines. It's 18 km south of Palmerston North and is open from 9 am to noon and 1 to 3.30 pm every day.

### Wildlife Centre

Also south of town is the Mt Bruce National Wildlife Centre, a preserve for native wildlife species, many quite rare. It has an aviary, streams and bush paths, and a Nocturnal Complex with kiwis, morepork owls and other nocturnal creatures. The centre is open in summer from 9 am to 4.30 pm (in winter until 4 pm) every day; admission is $5 (children 50 cents, family $10).

### Gardens

There are a number of gardens in the area, and you can make a garden tour of the Rangitikei; ask the Information Centre for their garden tour pamphlet. If you're in town in October or November when the rhododendrons are in bloom, check out the Cross Hills Gardens, open during those months from 10.30 am to 5 pm daily. The garden is in Kimbolton, about a 45 minute drive north of Palmerston North on SH 54, and there's also a Kimbolton Rhododendron Park.

### Walks

The Information Centre and DOC office in Palmerston North have leaflets detailing a number of scenic and nature reserves, walkways, lakes and so forth in the area, many with camping and huts.

### Jet-Boating

North of the town SH 2 to Hawke's Bay and Napier runs through the spectacular Manawatu Gorge. White Horse Jets (tel Woodville 48-118 or Dannevirke 47-882 after hours) operate jet-boat trips up the gorge from their docks at Ballance near Woodville, a 20 minute drive north of Palmerston North. The boats go every weekend from November to May and a half-hour trip up the gorge costs $33 (children $15). Additional trips may be made by request.

Himatangi Beach (29 km west of town) and Foxton Beach (40 km) are popular beaches near Palmerston North.

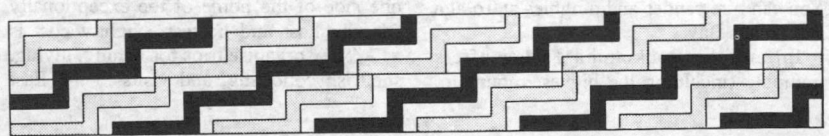

# East Coast

## EAST CAPE

The East Cape is one of the most scenic, isolated and least known regions of the North Island. The small communities scattered along the coast are predominantly Maori and the pace of life is peaceful and slow. Geographically, the area has few natural harbours and, until the road network was completed, goods had to be loaded off the beaches onto waiting barges. The interior is still wild bush, with the Raukumara Range extending down the centre of the cape. The western side of the range is divided into several state forest parks: Ruatoria, Raukumara, Urutawa, Waioeka and Mangatu.

The coast is now circled by 330 km of highway, SH 35, which took decades to build. It is an excellent road open all year round, making the coast more accessible than it ever has been before. The drive is worth it if only for the magnificent views of this wild coast, dotted with picturesque little bays, inlets and coves that change aspect with the weather – on a sunny day the water is an inviting turquoise colour, at other times a layer of clouds hangs on the craggy mountains rising straight up from the beaches and everything turns a misty green. Dozens of fresh clear streams flow through wild gorges to meet the sea. During the summer the coastline turns crimson with the blooming of the pohutukawa trees lining the seashore.

Along the first stretch of road from Opotiki there are fine views across to the steaming White Island volcano. The East Cape lighthouse is the easternmost point in New Zealand and it attracts early risers to view the sunrise. It's worth stopping at Tikitiki to see the wonderful Maori carvings inside the little church. Ruatoria is noted for its large community of Maori Rastafarians. You can hire canoes and dinghies at Tolaga BayTolaga Bay.

Inland the Raukumara Range offers tramping (including the highest mountain,

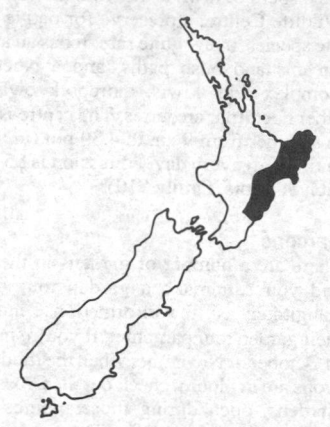

Hikurangi, at 1754 metres), hunting and white water rafting on the Motu River. Altogether the East Cape is great for bushwalking, fishing, shellfish collecting, and just relaxing.

### Places to Stay

On the way around East Cape there are various motor camps or you can camp for free almost anywhere if you have your own equipment. Along the cape's western side are *Te Kaha Holiday Park* (tel Te Kaha 894) at Te Kaha, with camping sites, cabins and tourist flats, and the *Heron Creek Holiday Park* (tel Waihau Bay 844) at Waihau Bay, with camping sites, cabins and on-site caravans.

On the northern tip of the cape are Hicks Bay and Te Araroa, both beautiful areas convenient for an overnight stopover. At Hicks Bay there's a private hostel, the *Hicks Bay Backpackers Lodge* (tel 44-731), on Onepoto Beach Rd fronting the sea. It's a small, simple place with a bunkroom off to one side of the home of the exceptionally friendly host and hostess. Nightly cost is $12. They organise trips for fishing, diving, shellfish collecting, and visits to the East

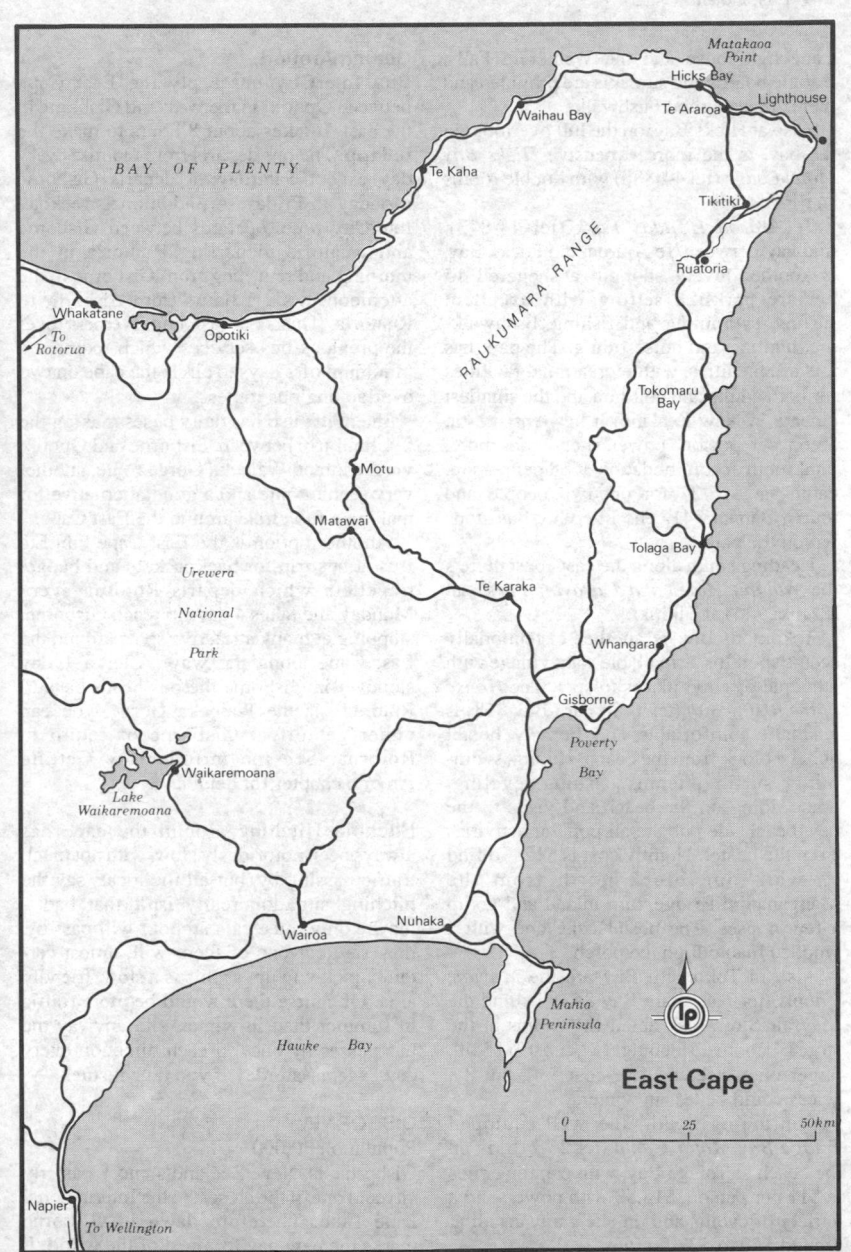

BAY OF PLENTY

Matakaoa Point
Hicks Bay
Waihau Bay
Te Araroa
Lighthouse
Te Kaha

RAUKUMARA RANGE

Whakatane
To Rotorua
Opotiki

Tikitiki

Ruatoria

Tokomaru Bay

Motu

Matawai

Tolaga Bay

Urewera
National
Park

Te Karaka

Whangara

Gisborne

Poverty Bay

Waikaremoana
Lake
Waikaremoana

Nuhaka
Wairoa

Mahia Peninsula

Hawke Bay

**East Cape**

0          25          50km

Napier
To Wellington

Cape lighthouse and the Waiherere Falls. Boogie boards and surf skis are provided and there are also good bushwalks.

Also at Hicks Bay, on the hill overlooking the bay, is the more expensive *Hicks Bay Motel Lodge* (tel 44-880) with double rooms starting at $59.

*Te Araroa Holiday Park* (tel 44-873), midway between Te Araroa and Hicks Bay, is another lovely spot, in a sheltered 15 hectare parklike setting with excellent surfing, swimming and fishing, bushwalking, hunting and horse-riding. The park has lots of amenities, with recreational facilities for both adults and children and the smallest cinema in New Zealand. It has tent sites at $5.65 per person, power sites at $1 more, bunkroom accommodation at $8 per person, cabins at $15/27 for one/two people and tourist flats at $41. The InterCity bus stops within the park.

Heading south along the east coast there's the *Waiapu Hotel and Caravan Park* (tel Tikitiki 745) at Tikitiki.

Tokomaru Bay is another exceptionally scenic spot. It's a small, pleasant village with a couple of good places to stay. The *House of the Rising Sun* (tel Tokomaru Bay 858) is a small, comfortable and homely hostel about a block from the beach. Hiking, swimming, surfing, tennis, fishing, cycling, horse-riding on the beach and visits to the new beachside pub are all popular activities from the hostel. Nightly cost is $12. To find it, walk one block north from the Mangahauini Bridge, turn inland and go up a few houses. The hostel's the one with a wooden man out on the porch.

Also in Tokomaru Bay are the *Mayfair Cabins* (tel Tokomaru Bay 843), behind the Mayfair Store (ask about the cabins at the store). Rooms sleeping two cost $18.50, larger ones sleeping five cost $30, but the prices could be less in winter.

Continuing south, the well-equipped *Tolaga Bay Motor Camp* (tel 26-716) is on the beach at Tolaga Bay, with camping sites at $11 per person, $13.50 with power, and a variety of cabins and on-site caravans all at around $20 to $22 for two.

## Getting Around

**Bus** InterCity buses ply the East Cape between Opotiki in the west and Gisborne in the east. It takes about 8 hours to make the full trip. The bus departs from Opotiki every day except Saturday; it departs Gisborne Monday to Friday. An additional weekday InterCity route operates between Gisborne and Ruatoria, departing Ruatoria in the morning and returning from Gisborne in the afternoon. It's 2½ hours from Gisborne to Ruatoria. This is a vast improvement over the previous bus services which required a minimum of 2 days to circle the cape on two overlapping bus routes.

InterCity also has daily buses making the 2½ hour trip between Gisborne and Opotiki via the inland Waioeka Gorge route, another very scenic route and a good alternative for making a full circle around the East Cape.

Another option is the East Cape Fun Etc Bus, a bus trip for backpackers and budget travellers which departs Rotorua every Monday and takes 4 days to reach Gisborne, stopping at many attractive spots around the East Cape along the way. After a 1 day stopover in Gisborne the bus heads back to Rotorua via the Waioeka Gorge, you can either get off at Gisborne or return to Rotorua. See the introductory Getting Around chapter for details.

**Hitching** Hitching around the cape has always been notoriously slow, with not much traffic passing by, but all the locals say the hitching situation really isn't that bad – maybe only three cars an hour will pass by, they say, but one of them will almost certainly pick you up, as this is a slow, friendly area. Of course there would be more traffic in summer than in winter, and anyway the bus passes by once in each direction every day except Saturday if you do get stuck.

## GISBORNE
Population 30,000
Gisborne is New Zealand's most easterly city and one of the closest to the International Date Line. Therefore dawn in Gisborne marks the new day for most of the world. It

is 368 km east of Rotorua and 220 km north of Napier. It was here that Captain Cook made his first landfall in New Zealand on 9 October 1769. He was distinctly unimpressed by what he saw and named it 'Poverty Bay' because, as he wrote in his log '...it did not afford a single article which we wanted, except a little firewood'.

Around Gisborne there are fertile alluvial plains which support intensive farming of subtropical fruits, maize and market-garden produce and vineyards. In fact, maize, citrus, maize, grapes, maize and more maize is just about all the eye can see. If such a sight doesn't have a great deal of appeal for you, remember that seasonal work is available if you're there at the right time – sweet corn is picked from around the second week in January, peas at the beginning of February. The city itself is right on the coast at the confluence of three rivers, the Turanganui, Waimata and Taruheru. Often described as the city of bridges, it is also noted for its fine parks and recreational facilities.

## History

European settlement of the region was very slow; much of the country was left unexplored until late in the 19th century. It was not until 1830 when whaling became increasingly popular that the missionaries began to move into the area. Two of them, Father Baty and Reverend William Colenso, were the first Europeans to tramp into the heart of Urewera and see Lake Waikaremoana.

Gradually more Pakehas arrived but there was no organised settlement. Several factors mitigated against it, the main one being that the Maoris were opposed to the idea. When the Treaty of Waitangi was signed in 1840 many chiefs from the east coast did not acknowledge the treaty, let alone sign it. Another was that the first governor of New Zealand to visit the region, Gore Browne, was not given much of a welcome and warned against unauthorised European settlement in the region. More important, during the 1860s numerous Maori wars broke out which further curbed White settlement, but by 1866 the government had crushed the rebels and transported most of the survivors to the remote Chatham Islands. This paved the way for an influx of Europeans who brought with them their flocks of sheep.

Even today, however, much of the pasture land is leased from the Maoris and a large part of it is under their direct control. Unfortunately, the pioneer farmers were so anxious to make a buck they ripped out far too much forest cover with disastrous results. Massive erosion occurred as the steeply sloping land was unable to hold the soil after heavy rains.

## Information

The Information Centre (tel 86-139) is at 209 Grey St. Look for the fine Canadian totem pole beside it. In winter (Easter to late October) it's open from 9 am to 5 pm on weekdays, 10 am to 5 pm on weekends. The rest of the year it's open from 9 am to 6 pm daily, except for the December-January school holidays when it's open from 9 am to 9 pm daily. The office has useful brochures and good city maps.

The DOC (tel 78-531) at 420 Palmerston Rd, on the corner of Disraeli St, is open from 8 am to 4.30 pm on weekdays. It has information on Urewera National Park, Lake Waikaremoana and the many walking tracks in that area. The AA is near the same corner of Disraeli St and Palmerston Rd, in the next block. There's a laundromat at the corner of Gladstone Rd and Carnarvon St.

## Museum & Arts Centre

That Gisborne and the surrounding district are strongly Maori is clearly exhibited at the small Gisborne Museum & Arts Centre at 18 Stout St. The gallery has changing exhibitions of local, national and international art, and the museum has numerous displays relating to the east coast Maori and colonial history, as well as geology and natural history exhibits. Outside there are more exhibits – a sled house, stable, Wyllie Cottage, and Lysnar House with working artists' studios you can visit. Lysnar House was the historic house on this site but only

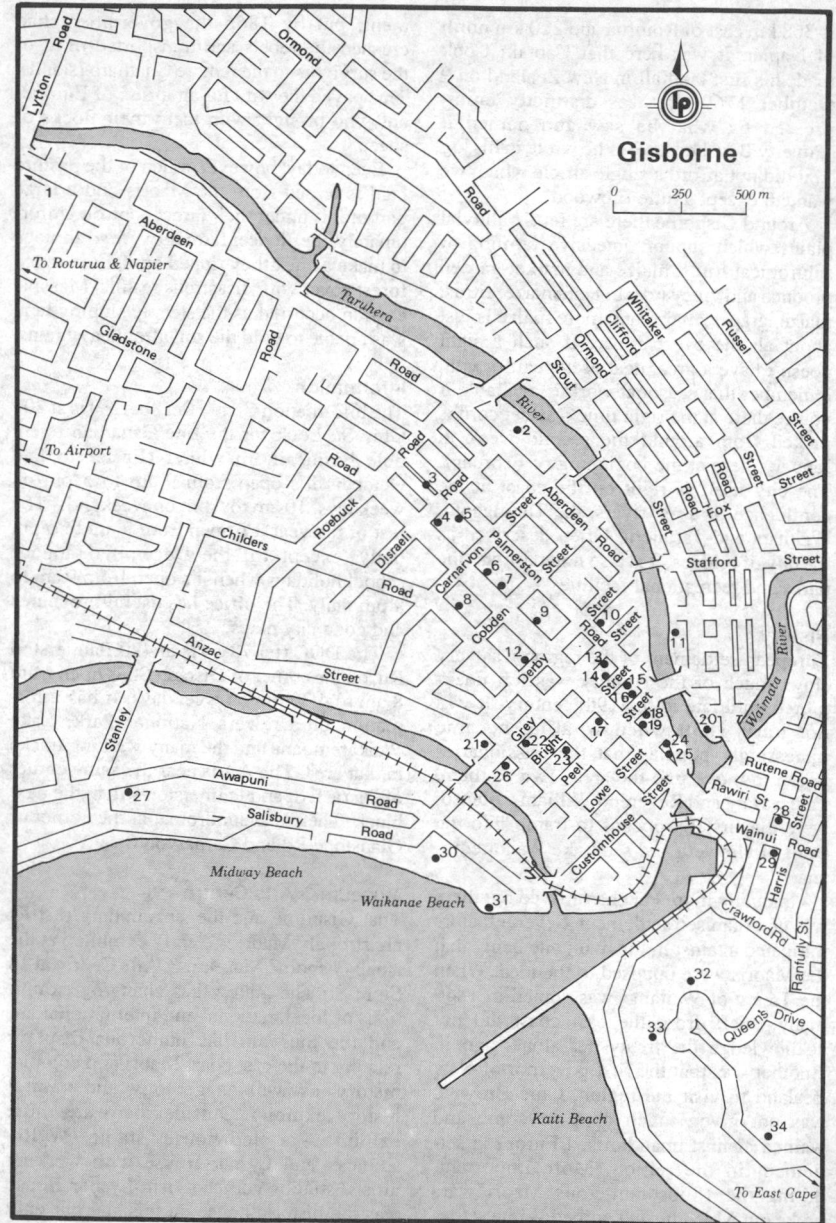

# Gisborne

1   To Showgrounds & Camp
2   Botanical Gardens
3   Department of Conservation (DOC)
4   Dominion Coachlines bus station
5   Automobile Association (AA)
6   Record Reign Hotel
7   Snackistaction
8   Aloha Travel Lodge
9   Royal Hotel
10  Dominion Bus Station
11  Museum, Art Gallery & Star of Canada
12  Meng Yee Restaurant
13  CPO
14  Air New Zealand
15  McDonald's
16  Robert Harris Coffee Shop
17  Lyric Cafe & Chanels Guest House
18  Scrumples
19  Regent Cafe
20  The Marina Restaurant
21  Information Centre
22  Kentucky Fried Chicken
23  InterCity Station
24  Bread & Roses Restaurant
25  Albion Hotel
26  Pizza Hut
27  Olympic Pool
28  Green Gables Travel Hotel
29  Youth Hostel
30  Waikanae Beach Camp
31  Statue of 'Young Nick'
32  Kaiti Hill Lookout
33  Captain Cook Memorial
34  Poho-O-Rawiri Meeting House

half of it is still here – the other half was cut off, moved down the river 500 metres or so, and now contains a restaurant!

The museum is open from 10 am to 4 pm Tuesday to Friday, 2 to 4.30 pm on weekends and public holidays; admission is $2.50 (children $1). The Star of Canada Maritime Museum (read on) is behind this one, the same ticket admits you to both museums. When you've had your fill of culture you can relax in the pleasant Deck Cafe.

## Maritime Museum

One wild night in 1912 the 12,000 ton ship *Star of Canada*, out of Belfast, Northern Ireland, was blown ashore on the reef at Gisborne, quite close to where Captain Cook made his landing. Although the ship was only 3 years old all attempts to refloat it failed and eventually whatever equipment could be salvaged was removed, including the ship's bridge and captain's cabin, which the salvager brought ashore to win a bet that it couldn't be done.

At the waterside he sold the 26-ton bridge for £104 and it was eventually installed on the corner of Childers Rd and Cobden St. It sat there for 15 years until in 1927 the second owner's daughter got married and needed a home. Additional rooms were added and the *Star of Canada* became the best known home in Gisborne.

When the owner died in 1983 she left her unique home to the city and it was moved to its present site, restored and made into a museum. There are displays on Maori canoes, early whaling and shipping and Captain Cook's Gisborne visit but the most interesting items relate, of course, to the *Star of Canada*.

The Star of Canada Maritime Museum is directly behind the Museum & Arts Centre. They're open the same hours, and one ticket admits you to both museums.

## Statues & Views

There's a statue of 'Young Nick', Cook's cabin boy, in a little park on the northern side of the rivermouth, just off Waikanae Beach. He was the first member of Cook's crew to sight New Zealand. Across the bay are the white cliffs which Cook named 'Young Nick's Head'.

Across the river on the foreshore at the foot of Kaiti Hill is a monument to Captain Cook, near the spot where he first set foot on New Zealand on 8 October 1769. Also at the foot of the hill is the Poho-o-Rawiri Maori meeting house, one of the largest meeting houses in New Zealand, and a little Maori church.

From the top of Kaiti Hill there's a fine wide-angle view of the area. There's a walking track up from the Captain Cook monument. If you're driving up, turn onto Queen's Drive from Ranfurly St. Near the top is another monument to Captain Cook, this one with a fine statue of the captain.

At the 135 metre summit is the James Cook Observatory, with a sign proclaiming it the 'World's Easternmost Observatory'. It's open to the public each Wednesday from 8.30 pm – viewing sessions begin promptly at 9 pm, weather permitting, and cost $1. The Gisborne Astronomical Society (tel 87-901) meets here at 7.30 pm on the last Wednesday of the month; all are welcome.

Another good view of Gisborne is from Gaddum's Hill. To get there head out to the suburb of Kaiti on Wainui Rd (SH 35 heading to East Cape), turn inland onto De Latour Rd and follow it up the hill. It's a short walk from here to the trig station, a 9 km return trip from Gisborne.

## Activities

You can swim right in the city at Waikanae Beach – in fact there's good swimming, fishing and surfing all along the coast. On Midway Beach there's an Olympic swimming complex with a big waterslide and children's playground. The Botanical Gardens are beside the river off Aberdeen Rd and there's mini-golf behind the Information Centre.

If you happen to be in Gisborne around the peak of the summer holidays, check out the DOC's programme of walks and talks. Transport to walks is by private car but sharing is encouraged so you should be able to get a ride without any trouble. The Gisborne Canoe and Tramping Club (tel 87-892, 84-741) also makes outings.

The Motu and Waioeka rivers are both in the Gisborne district; ask the Information Centre about white water rafting trips. The centre also has info on walks, horse-trekking, fishing and hunting, or more genteel pursuits such as visiting the many wineries and coastal home gardens around Gisborne.

## Tours

Tours around the Gisborne area are operated by Cosmac Tours (tel 84-139). Cost is $18 for a 3 hour morning or afternoon tour including most of the area's sights. They may also be starting up a winery tour. Other tours are operated by Sandown Safari (tel 79-299).

## Places to Stay

**Hostels** The *Gisborne Youth Hostel* (tel 83-269) is at 32 Harris St, 1½ km from the town centre across the river, in a big rambling old home with spacious grounds. Nightly cost is $13 and you can hire a bicycle to get around. Advance bookings are essential from Christmas to the end of January.

*A Home by the Sea* (tel 78-058), at 11 Wairere Rd, Wainui Beach, is 4 km north of the centre. It's a small, friendly hostel on one of the most beautiful sites in all New Zealand – the backyard verandah is practically right on the white sand of the 3 km long Wainui Beach. They have free surfboards and windsurfers, plus bicycles for hire. Cost is $13 in dorm or private rooms. They have free pick-up and drop-off services to town but it's a very easy hitch. This is a summer hostel, open only from Labour Weekend (in late October) to Easter.

**Guest Houses** Guest houses include the *Green Gables* (tel 79-872) at 31 Rawiri St, Kaiti, across the river from the city centre, with singles/doubles at $35/58, including breakfast. The *Channels Private Hotel* (tel 75-037) on the corner of Gladstone Rd and Peel St in the city centre has rooms at $30 to $35 for singles, $45 for doubles. Although it's more central it's not as good a place as Green Gables.

**Hotels** Gisborne once had several fine old hotels. Most of them have now closed down, but two of the oldest, both in Gladstone Rd, are still here. The *Royal* (tel 89-184) has single/double rooms at $26/38. The *Albion Club* (tel 79-639) is a bit cheaper at $22/28.

**Motels** Most Gisborne motels start from around $65 for doubles. Marginally cheaper ones include the *Coastlands Motel* (tel 86-464) at 114 Main Rd, the *Endeavour Lodge* (tel 86-075) at 525 Gladstone Rd, and the *Highway Motel* (tel 84-059) at 60 Main Rd.

**Camping & Cabins** The *Waikanae Beach Municipal Camp* (tel 75-634) is on Grey St at Waikanae Beach, very near the centre.

Sites cost $10 a night for two people, $12 with power. Cabins range upwards from $20 for two, tourist flats are $42.

The *Showgrounds Motor Camp* (tel 74-101), out at Makaraka near the showgrounds, is cheaper for camping – only $5.50 for two persons, $7.50 with power – but it's not so conveniently central. The cabins here are also cheap at $12 to $16 for two people but they're pretty spartan. This camp is closed during the month of October, at showtime.

### Places to Eat

**Snacks & Fast Food** There's the usual selection of sandwich places, particularly along Gladstone Rd, or try Peel St, up towards McDonald's, where there are two excellent up-market sandwich places. *Scrumples* has good hot lunches (quiche, samosas and the like) for $3 to $5, sandwiches, rolls, and drinks and is a relaxed and pleasant place to eat them.

Opposite this, in the centre leading through to McDonald's, is the *Robert Harris Coffee Shop* with an equally good selection of sandwiches. Here you can eat inside or out in the open air mall.

*Snackisfaction* in Gladstone Rd is a breakfast and lunch place open from 6.30 am weekdays (closed weekends) with good food at low prices. It has one picnic table if you want to eat there, otherwise it's takeaway.

Apart from the *McDonald's*, with its main entrance on Bright St, there are also a *Pizza Hut* and a *Kentucky Fried Chicken* on Grey St near the Information Centre.

As usual there are a number of Chinese takeaways. The most popular is *China Palace* in Peel St, where you can choose any three items for $5, any five items for $8, and eat there or take it away for the same price. It's open from 9.30 am to 11 pm Monday to Saturday, 4.30 to 11 pm on Sundays, and has a more expensive licensed restaurant upstairs.

**Light Meals & Pub Food** At 124 Gladstone Rd the *Lyric Cafe* is a fine, old-fashioned fish restaurant with a variety of seafood meals at around $10. They have a separate takeaways

counter. Across the road the *Regent* offers similar fare at similar prices.

The *Cooks Gallery Restaurant* in the Royal Hotel in Gladstone Rd between Cobden and Derby streets has the usual pub food menu, as does the *Record Reign Hotel* in the next block.

**Restaurants** The *China Palace* in Peel St is one of Gisborne's most popular restaurants. The upstairs licenced section is open nightly from 6 pm with main courses at around $14, or there's a Sunday smorgasbord for $19 (children half price). If you eat downstairs it costs much less.

*Bread & Roses* on the corner of Lowe St and Reads Quay has interesting meat or vegetarian main courses at about $17. *The Marina*, wonderfully situated beside the river – in the other half of the Lysnar House (see Museum & Arts Centre) – is very expensive.

### Entertainment

The *Sandown Park* on Childers Rd and the *Gisborne Hotel* on Huxley Rd have live music most weekends. Two nightclubs, *Crossroads* in Palmerston Rd and *Peaches* in Derby St, offer disco music and live stuff.

The *Tatapouri Hotel* on the main road in Tatapouri, about 12 km north of Gisborne, is one of the region's most popular and enjoyable nightspots, right on the beach with both indoor and outdoor bars.

During the summer holidays local bands, musicians and poets perform in the parks.

### Getting There & Away

**Air** The Air New Zealand office (tel 79-490) is at 37 Bright St. They have daily direct flights to Wellington and Napier, with connections to other centres. Eagle Air (tel 81-608) has several daily direct flights to Auckland and Napier, and a weekday service to Hamilton.

**Bus** The InterCity depot (tel 86-195/6) is on the corner of Bright St and Childers Rd. You can approach Gisborne from four directions.

From Napier in the south it's a pleasant 216 km, 3 hour trip on a road which runs close to, but rarely right on, the coast. Inter-City has buses along this route, originating in Gisborne and continuing south past Napier to Palmerston North and Wellington. Dominion Coachlines (tel 89-083), with a terminal on the corner of Gladstone Rd and Disraeli St, also has buses to Napier. Both lines stop at Wairoa.

Coming from Rotorua, Auckland and other points north, the most direct route is via Opotiki along the Waioeka Gorge. From Gisborne by this route it's 2½ hours to Opotiki, 5 hours to Rotorua, 10 hours all the way to Auckland. InterCity has two bus routes between Gisborne and Auckland via Opotiki, one through Rotorua and the other along the Bay of Plenty via Tauranga.

Alternatively, the East Cape Fun Etc bus has the cheapest bus transport from Gisborne to Opotiki, Whakatane and Rotorua along this route, departing only once a week (Sunday morning) on its way back to Rotorua to begin another East Cape tour. In Gisborne they operate from the Information Centre or the Youth Hostel.

An alternative but much longer route runs from Opotiki around the coast of East Cape. See the East Cape – Getting Around section for details on East Cape buses. The East Cape route, although longer, is one of the most scenic routes of the North Island.

The third route from Rotorua to Gisborne runs through the Urewera National Park, passing by Lake Waikaremoana and joining the Napier route at Wairoa, 97 km south of Gisborne. It's about 3½ hours by car between Gisborne and Waikaremoana but there is no direct bus. To travel this way by public transport involves connecting from the Napier-Wairoa-Gisborne InterCity or Dominion Coachlines bus to the Monday-Wednesday-Friday InterCity bus between Rotorua and Wairoa. Be sure to check the schedules to make the connection in Wairoa. If you do get stuck in Wairoa the *Riverside Motor Camp* (tel 6301) is a pleasant place on the banks of the Wairoa River with camping sites and cabins.

**Hitching** Hitching is OK from the south, not too bad through Waioeka Gorge to Opotiki (but it's best to leave early). To hitch a ride out head along Gladstone Rd to Makaraka a few km south, where you turn left for Wairoa and Napier, right for Opotiki and Rotorua. Hopefully you may get a ride before you walk as far as Makaraka but most of Gladstone Rd is a built-up area.

Hitching from Wairoa to Waikaremoana is hard going. Gisborne is actually just off SH 36 around East Cape so if you're hitching around East Cape head out along the Wainui road.

### Getting Around

There's a city bus service (tel 82-049) with an office in Carnarvon St. The buses run only on weekdays, and only until about 5 pm (some routes until about 8 pm on Friday only). A taxi to Gisborne airport costs about $9.

Corrin Motorcycle Service (tel 76-638) at 441 Gladstone Rd hires motorcycles and mopeds. There are various rental car companies including Budget, Avis and Hertz but also check Rent-a-Wreck (tel 78-164) for the lowest prices, with special one-way rates to Auckland.

### AROUND GISBORNE

At the A&P Showgrounds in Makaraka there's a Transport & Technology Museum. In summer it's open from 2 to 4.30 pm on Saturday and from 9 am to 4.30 pm on Sunday. In winter it's open on Sundays only, from 9 am to noon.

At Matawhero, a few km south along SH 2, there is an historic Presbyterian Church. It was built in 1865-66, originally as a schoolroom, but has also been a church, meeting place and hospital. It was the only building in the immediate vicinity to survive the Poverty Bay Massacre by Te Kuti and his band in 1868, and is one of a handful still standing from this period.

Other attractions in the Gisborne area include the Eastwood Hill Arboretum, a reserve with over 3000 species of plants and trees, including the largest collection of northern hemisphere plants in New Zealand. The arboretum, open daily from 10 am to 4 pm, is 35 km west of Gisborne on the Ngatapa-Rere Rd. About 10 km further along the same road are the Rere Falls.

The Morere Hot Springs, 56 km south of Gisborne (see Gisborne to Napier), are a popular day trip.

## UREWERA NATIONAL PARK

The Lake Waikaremoana turn-off (SH 38) is 97 km south of Gisborne at Wairoa, on the road towards Napier. This is a marvellous area of bush, lakes and rivers, with lots of tramps ranging from half an hour to several days, and plenty of birds, trout, deer and other wildlife. See the Outdoor Activities chapter for more on the Waikaremoana Track which circles the lake.

### Information

The Urewera National Park has three ranger stations. There's one in Taneatua, a few km inland from Whakatane (tel Whakatane 29-260), another at Murupara (tel Rotorua 65-641), and one within the park itself at Waikaremoana (tel Tuai 803). This one is the park's Visitor Centre and has interesting displays. They have information on the many walking tracks, camping sites and huts around the park, and during the summer they offer an excellent, inexpensive programme of guided walks and talks. The DOC office in Gisborne also has info on the park.

### Places to Stay

There are various camps and cabins spaced along SH 38, including a camp, cabins and motel 48 km inland from the Wairoa turn-off. At Galatea the *Urewera Lodge* (tel Rotorua 64-556) has a three-bedroom cottage with two to four bunks in each room. Cost is $19 per person, a bit less in the off-season from June to August, with discounts for weekly stays. They have good fishing, a variety of boats to hire and if you don't bring your own linen you can hire that too. It's on the shores of Lake Aniwhenua, 64 km south of Whakatane and 84 km east of Rotorua, just off the Whakatane-Murupara road.

There are several huts along the walking tracks, costing $4 per night. DOC also maintains a number of minimal-facility camping grounds around Lake Waikaremoana where it costs only $1 to camp, and there are many other free camping sites around the park too. All of the ranger stations have info on camping.

On the shore of Lake Waikaremoana the *Waikaremoana Motor Camp* (tel Tuai 826) has camping sites at $5 per person, $6 with power, plus cabins at $24 for two, chalets at $44 for two, motel units at $50 for two, and a family unit sleeping up to seven people at $65 for four adults. During the summer months Waikaremoana Launch Service (tel Tuai 871 or, in January only, Tuai 826) operates from the motor camp and offers boat trips for sightseeing, fishing, and transport around the lake.

### Getting There & Away

InterCity buses run the 5 hour trip between Rotorua and Wairoa on Monday, Wednesday and Friday. Most of the way between Frasertown and Murupara through the park, about 150 km, is unsealed, very winding and therefore very time consuming. There is very little traffic on this road, making it a slow go for hitching.

## GISBORNE TO NAPIER

Heading south towards Napier the bus follows the coastal SH 2 route. The road passes close to the Wharerata Forest Reserve where the Wharerata Walkway is a popular 10 km walking track.

The Morere Hot Springs, with various pools and bushwalks, is 56 km south of Gisborne on SH 2, a popular day trip from Gisborne. In summer (November to April) it's open from 10 am to 5 pm on weekdays, 10 am to 8 pm on weekends and holidays (including the December-January school holidays). Winter hours are the same except it closes an hour earlier on weekends. Cost is $3 (children $1.50) in the public pool, $4 (children $2) in private pools, and families get a 10% discount.

Beside the hot springs the Morere Tavern

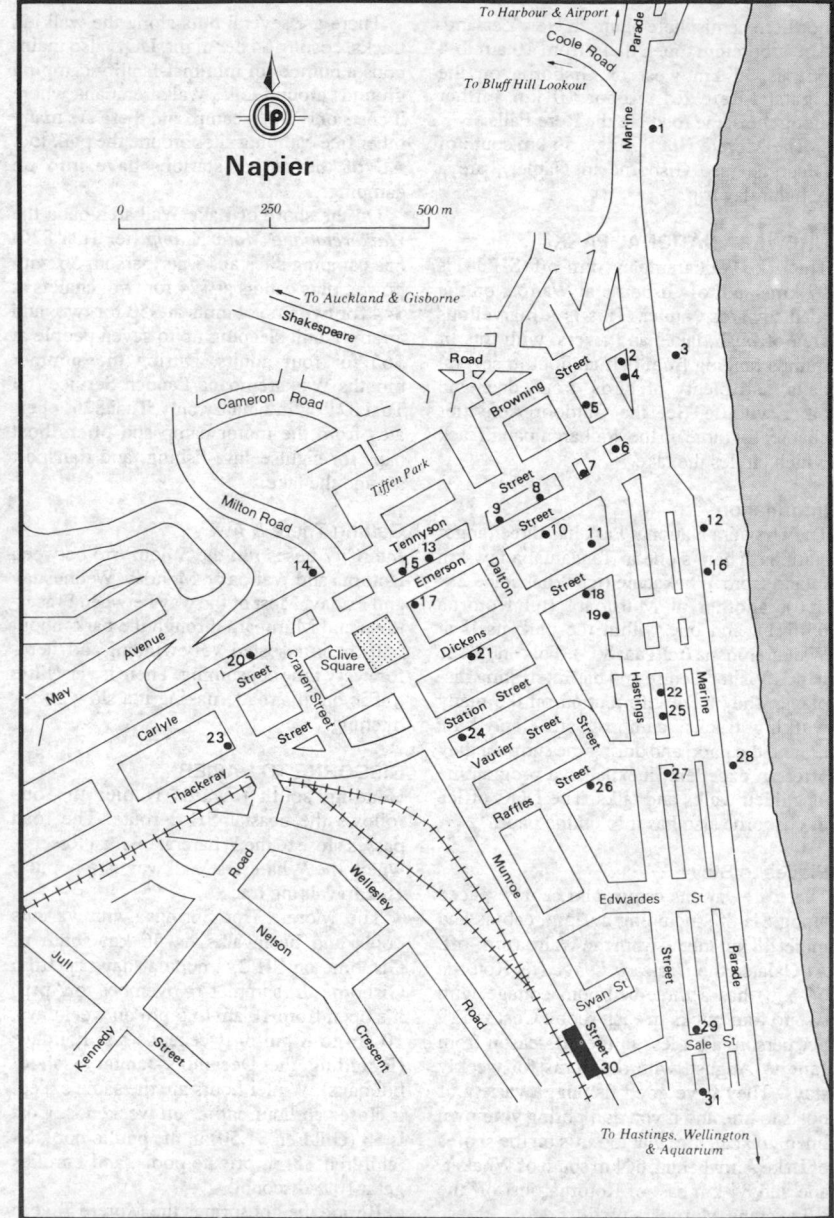

**Napier**

0    250    500 m

To Harbour & Airport
Coole Road
To Bluff Hill Lookout
Marine Parade

1

To Auckland & Gisborne
Shakespeare Road

Cameron Road
Milton Road
Tiffen Park
Browning Street

2
4
3
5
6
7
8
9
10
11
12
16

Tennyson Street
Emerson Street
Dalton Street
Hastings Street
Marine Parade

13
5
14
17
18
19
20
21
22
25
23
24
26
27
28

May Avenue
Carlyle Street
Craven Street
Clive Square
Dickens Street
Station Street
Vautier Street
Raffles Street

Thackeray
Road
Wellesley Road
Nelson Crescent
Jull Street
Kennedy Street
Munroe Road

Edwardes St
Swan St
Sale St
Parade Street

29
30
31

To Hastings, Wellington
& Aquarium

1 Kiwi House
2 Art Gallery & Museum
3 Pania of the Reef
4 Department of Conservation (DOC)
5 Ego's NightClub
6 Masonic Establishment Hotel
7 Criterion Backpackers Inn
8 Ziggurat Cafe
9 National Cafe
10 Ocean Blvd Mall
11 CPO
12 Information Centre
13 Food for Thought
14 Museum of Transport & Technology
15 Antonio's Pizza Parlour
16 Sunken Gardens
17 Juices & Ices
18 Golden Crown Restaurant
19 Air New Zealand
20 Kentucky Fried Chicken
21 Automobile Association (AA)
22 Waterfront Lodge
23 McDonald's
24 Mt Cook & Dominion bus depot
25 Pinehaven Private Hotel
26 Courtney's Cafe
27 Youth Hostel
28 Marineland of New Zealand
29 Pizza Hut
30 InterCity Travel Centre & Railway Station
31 Indonesian Restaurant

has a little restaurant. There are camping and cabins at the *Morere Camping Grounds* (tel Nuhaka 792) across the road (ask at the tearoom). You could probably camp for free at a little picnic area about 50 metres south of the springs, but it's right beside the road. The *Sunnyvale Motor Camp* (tel Nuhaka 777), about 1 km from the springs, has inexpensive camping, cabins and motel flats. A bit further on you reach Nuhaka and the turn-off to Mahia where there are good beaches and fishing. The *Mahia Beach Camp* (tel Mahia 830) at Mahia has camping, cabins and a motel.

Along SH 36, the inland route to Wairoa and Napier, there are also several things to see and do. You can climb up Gentle Annie Hill for a good view over the Poverty Bay area. Doneraille Park (53 km from Gisborne), a native bush reserve, is a popular picnic spot with good swimming when the water is clear. There's fine trout fishing at Tiniroto Lakes, 61 km from Gisborne, and about 10 km further on, the Te Reinga Falls are worth the few hundred metres detour off the main road.

## NAPIER
Population 52,100
In 1931 Napier was rather dramatically changed when a disastrous earthquake measuring 7.9 on the Richter scale virtually destroyed the city. In Napier and nearby Hastings over 250 people died, but in partial compensation the waterlocked city suddenly found itself 40 sq km larger. The quake heaved that amount of water-covered land above sea level! In places the land level rose by over 2 metres. The Napier airport is built on that previously submerged area.

### Orientation
Finding your way around Napier is slightly complicated by a lack of street name signs (pretty normal for New Zealand) but also by a lack of building numbers. People must simply know where places are; there are so few numbers on buildings that they don't even bother to list them in phone directories or other sources.

There is also a reconstruction going on, affecting almost everything in town. It took Napier only 2 years to rebuild after the 1931 earthquake and it seems the City Council is approaching the present reconstruction programme with equal zeal. The map in this book will certainly require some interpretation as straight streets are being curved, new street names (but not signs!) added and buildings moved.

All the address numbers on Marine Parade, for example, have recently been changed and all the letter boxes now display two separate numbers. Ask the proprietors which number is the correct one and they tell you, 'it's this one right now, but we think the City Council is going to change them all again soon!'

## Information

Napier's helpful and well informed Information Centre (tel 835-7182) is on Marine Parade close to the town centre. It's open from 8.30 am to 5 pm on weekdays, 9 am to 5 pm on weekends and public holidays. The AA office is a couple of blocks away on Dickens St.

The DOC office (tel 835-0415) is also on Marine Parade, in the Old Courthouse beside the museum. It's open from 8.30 am to 4 pm Monday to Friday, and has plenty of information on walkways around Napier, the Cape Kidnappers gannet colony, and the Kaweka and Ruahine forest parks, both about 50 km west of Napier and both with walking tracks and huts. If you're here in January ask about their summer outdoor activities programme. DOC is also a focal point for a wide range of outdoor activity organisations including tramping, canoeing, white water rafting, diving, angling and deerstalking clubs, any of which you're welcome to attend.

## Art Deco

The earthquake and fire of 1931 had a very interesting side effect. Most of the older brick buildings collapsed with the quake, while survivors were mainly new buildings of reinforced concrete. Two frantic years of reconstruction rebuilt Napier in the years from 1931 to 1933. The result is that much of the city architecture of Napier dates from the narrow period from the late '20s through early '30s – the peak years for art deco. In fact Dr Neil Cossons, past president of the British Museums Association, has stated:

Napier represents the most complete and significant group of Art Deco buildings in the world, and is comparable with Bath as an example of a planned townscape in a cohesive style. Napier is without doubt unique.

Napier has an Art Deco Trust which promotes and protects the city's unique architectural heritage and if you're in town on a Sunday you can take a guided 'art deco walk' starting from the museum at 2 pm for

$3 (children free). Ask also about midweek walks, which are sometimes available. If your Napier visit doesn't coincide with the guided walks you can guide yourself with a walk leaflet available for 50 cents from the Information Centre or the museum. There's also a $2 Scenic Drive map to guide you on a drive around many examples of Art Deco and Spanish Mission architecture around Napier and Hastings. The museum has a book on Napier's art deco architecture and some excellent post cards and posters. Many of the finest buildings are very well preserved and looked after.

As you walk around town look for art deco motifs on the buildings such as zigzags, lightning flashes, geometric shapes and rising suns. The soft pastel colours are another art deco giveaway. There are some excellent art deco buildings along Emerson St, check out the Ziggurat Cafe building or the Bank of New Zealand on the corner of Emerson St and Hastings St. On Dalton St the Central Hotel is a superb example of the style both externally and inside the foyer and stairs. Round the corner on Dickens St look for the extravagant Spanish-style building which used to be the 'Gaiety de Luxe Cinema'.

On Tennyson St see the Desco Centre facing Clive Square. It used to be the Napier Fire Station and the doors are now glassed in. The intersection of Tennyson and Hastings streets has more fine buildings, particularly the block of Hastings St from Tennyson St to Browning St. Look at Alsops storefront in particular, the window exhibit is terrific. On Marine Parade the Soundshell is art deco as is the paving of the plaza which used to be a skating rink. From here you can admire the art deco clocktower (neon lit at night) of the A&B building and the Masonic Hotel. Finally read the moving poem inside the colonnade beside the plaza.

## Marine Parade

Rubble from the destroyed buildings was used to form a new Marine Parade that runs along the seashore. Many of Napier's attractions are found along here and there are also parks, a sunken garden, a scented garden for the blind, amusements including a wax-works, mini-golf, a skateboard bowl and skating rinks, and Pania of the Reef, a sort of Maori equivalent of Copenhagen's Little Mermaid and a symbol of the town. The stony beach along Marine Parade has big waves but a strong riptide makes it unsafe for swimming.

## Marineland & Aquarium

On Marine Parade, Marineland of New Zealand has a collection of performing seals and dolphins. It is open daily from 10 am to 4.30 pm, with shows at 10.30 am and 2 pm (additional shows in summer). Admission is $7 (children $3.50, family $18.50) and includes entry to the Lilliput animated village.

Also on the parade the Hawke's Bay Aquarium is claimed to be the largest in Australasia. It has a wide variety of fish, sharks, turtles and other animals including New Zealand's unique tuatara lizards. It's open daily from 9 am to 5 pm, with extended hours in summer. Feeding time is 3.15 pm, admission is $6 (children $3, family $12.50).

## Hawke's Bay Museum

Also on Marine Parade is the excellent art gallery and museum. The museum has displays of Maori artefacts, European antiques, art deco items and they show a 20 minute audiovisual of the '31 earthquake and a 20 minute video on the reconstruction after the quake.

The museum's small exhibit of Maori art is one of the best in New Zealand, consisting entirely of the art of the east coast's Ngati Kahungunu tribe, one of New Zealand's largest tribes, and designed by a Ngati Kahungunu artist. Another 20 minute audiovisual shows the art and culture of this important tribe. The museum is open from 10 am to 4.30 pm on weekdays and from 1 to 4.30 pm on Saturday and Sunday; admission is $2 (children free).

Napier also has another museum, the Hawke's Bay Museum of Transport and Technology on Clive Square. It's open from 9 am to noon on Saturdays; admission is $2.50 (children 50 cents, family $6).

## Kiwi House

There are kiwis at nocturnal centres all over New Zealand but the Kiwi House in Napier is the only place in the world where you can actually touch a kiwi. Every day at 1 pm there's a half-hour show with an educational talk on kiwis and afterwards everyone gathers around for a feel of the unusual bird, which doesn't feel at all like you'd expect. After that, at 2 pm, it's feeding time and sometimes the children can come in to feed the birds.

The centre has other animals as well, including moreporks, barn owls, sugar gliders, night herons, bush geckoes and whistling frogs. It's open daily from 11 am to 3 pm; admission is $2.60 (children $1).

## Bluff Hill Lookout

There's an excellent view over all of Hawke's Bay from Bluff Hill, 102 metres above the Port of Napier. It's a sheer cliff face down to the port, however, and rather a circuitous route to the top. Coming from Marine Parade, turn inland onto Coole Rd, take the first right onto Pressley Rd, turn right onto Lighthouse Rd and follow it around until you reach the Bluff Hill Domain and Lookout. It's open every day from 7 am until 1 hour after sunset.

## Water Sports & Other Activities

Fishing trips and pleasure cruises from Napier are popular and there are night cruises when there's sufficient demand. There are also numerous other water activities including windsurfing, kayaking, canoeing, parasailing, jet-boating, jet-skiing, kneeboarding, water-skiing and so on – ask at the Information Centre to find the current operators, many of them operate from near the harbour. Although the beach along Marine Parade is not good for swimming, there's good swimming and surfing on the beach up past the port.

The swimming pool on Marine Parade costs just 80 cents. The Onekawa Pool

Complex is larger and fancier with waterslides and other attractions. Entry is 80 cents to the Olympic outdoor pool (open in summer only) or $1.60 (children $1) to the indoor pool, open all year.

Other activities around Napier are at Riverland (tel Te Poue 871), where there's horse-trekking and white water rafting. They have backpackers accommodation at $10 a night (camping $5 a night) if you want to stay overnight or longer.

## Tours

Bay Tours (tel 436-953) does 4½ hour Hawke's Bay tours including a scenic tour and a wine tour, each costing $32. The Information Centre has a leaflet with a map of 15 wineries in the Napier and Hastings area if you want to do a winery tour on your own.

The Leopard Brewery in Hastings conducts free tours on Monday, Wednesday and Friday, followed by a glass of the amber fluid. Or you could visit Classic Decor Sheepskins to see how sheepskins are processed. There are tours every day at 11 am and 2 pm and on weekdays they even provide free transport with a courtesy car; just book ahead.

## Places to Stay

**Hostels** The *Napier Youth Hostel* (tel 357-039) at 277 Marine Parade costs $13 a night. Close to the beach and opposite Marineland, it's more luxurious than most hostels because it is a converted guest house. Most of the 45 beds are in twin rooms and the kitchen, dining room and recreation area are all separate, making it more spacious. All rooms have their own keys, 24 hour access, and they also have bicycles for hire.

Right in the centre the *Criterion Backpackers Inn* (tel 352-059, 357-162) in Emerson St is upstairs in what was formerly the Criterion Hotel. It has the usual kitchen and dining facilities plus a large recreation area, and downstairs are a pizza parlour, bistro and bar. Nightly cost is $12 in the dormitory, $13 in twin rooms and $14 in double rooms. They have a few contacts for

local apple picking (January to April) and other agricultural jobs.

The *Glenview Farm Hostel* (tel 266-232, 266-234) is a peaceful and pleasant farm hostel on a 722 hectare hill country sheep and cattle station where horse-riding and walking are popular activities. You can join in the farm activities, and go hunting for geese or eels. Cost is $10 a night. The hostel is 31 km north of Napier off SH 2. A yellow AA sign at the junction of Arapaoanui Rd says 'farm hostel'; go 2 km towards the sea on this road and you're there. The owner provides free pick-up from this junction.

**Guest Houses** Since it is a summer resort of the old-fashioned school Napier has some good old guest houses, particularly along Marine Parade beside the beach. However, as this is a large and busy thoroughfare, it can be quite noisy. The *Pinehaven Private Hotel* (tel 355-575) at 259 Marine Parade has rooms at $36/48, breakfast is $6 extra and it's strictly a non-smoking place. The front rooms have fine views of the seafront. Or there's the cheaper *Waterfront Lodge* (tel 353-429) at 217 Marine Parade with rooms at $26/38 including breakfast.

**Hotels** Cheaper hotels include the *Provincial* (tel 356-934) on Clive Square with rooms at $24 a single, $40 to $44 a double. At the *Victoria Hotel* (tel 353-149) on Marine Parade, singles are $36 to $46, doubles $41 to $55.

The fine old *Masonic Establishment* (tel 358-689) on the corner of Marine Parade and Tennyson St is very central. There are a few cheaper singles for around $33 but rooms with bathroom are $77/94 for singles/-doubles. Although it's a comfortable and nicely situated place it's rather sombre and some parts are a bit scruffy.

**Motels** There are plenty of motels, particularly around Westshore, but most are around $65 or more for a double. The *Westshore Hotel/Motel* (tel 359-879) has twin rooms at $22/30 or larger rooms at $44 a double. The *City Close Motel* (tel 53-568) at 16-18

Munroe St is conveniently located and has budget rooms at $27/36, other rooms at $52/63. Some distance out, 2 km north of the airport, is the *Airport Boomerang Motel* (tel 266-828) on Main Rd at Bay View, with single/double rooms at $40/50.

**Camping & Cabins** Napier has a number of camping sites but none of them conveniently located if you don't have transport. Closest to the centre is *Kennedy Park* (tel 439-126) off Kennedy Rd at Marewa, 2½ km from the CPO. Sites cost $7 per person, $11 with power. There are also some basic huts at $28 for two, cabins at $34 for two, and tourist flats at $54 for two.

The *Westshore Holiday Camp* (tel 359-456) is on Main Rd near Westshore Beach, 4 km north of town. Camping sites here are $6 per person, $6.50 with power, cabins are $16 to $32 for two and there are also tourist flats.

Other sites include *Burden's Motor Camp* (tel Hastings 750-334) on the beachfront at Te Awanga, 19 km south of Napier towards Cape Kidnappers. Burden's Camp is the starting point for the tractor-trailer trip to the gannet sanctuary. Camping costs $10 for two, $11 with power, and there are cabins at $17 for two. The *Clifton Reserve Camp* (tel Hastings 750-263) has two beachfront areas 1½ km from Te Awanga, 22½ km from Napier. Camping is $11 for two, $4 for pup tents, $12 per person in bunkrooms or $15 for two in cabins.

At Taradale, 6½ km out, *Taradale Holiday Park* (tel Taradale 442-732) at 470 Gloucester St has sites at $6 per person, $6.50 with power, plus on-site caravans at $25 to $30 for two and a variety of cabins at $30 to $38 for two. Near Clive there's the *Clive Motor Camp* (tel 700-609) and there are also a couple of motor camps at Hastings.

**Places to Eat**
**Fast Food & Takeaways** There are plenty of sandwich places along Emerson St and the sandwiches here are often pretty good. Places to try include *Food for Thought* at 204 Emerson St with healthy sandwiches and snacks. Other Emerson St possibilities include the *National Cafe* for fish & chips and other snacks. A block behind the youth hostel *Courtney's Cafe* is a pleasant place for hot meals, sandwiches, snacks and desserts.

Back on Emerson St, the *Poppa's Bar & Pizzeria* below the Criterion Backpackers Inn is a popular place, with small/medium/large pizzas from $5/8/10 plus a salad bar and espresso coffee. Wednesday to Saturday nights the music drifts in from the Sportsmans Bar next door. *Antonio's Pizzas* is further down Emerson St near Clive Square. Right on the corner of Clive Square *Juices & Ices* has sandwiches and salads, plus sweet and savoury crepes and desserts including homemade ice cream, milkshakes and fruit smoothies.

Of course there are plenty of Chinese restaurants and takeaways in Napier. Try the *Golden Crown* on Dickens St which does both. Lunch here costs $5.50 or there's a Sunday smorgasbord with Chinese and European dishes for $16.50 (children $8). And yes, there is a *McDonald's* in Napier, it's on Thackeray St down past Clive Square, and nearby a *Kentucky Fried Chicken* on Carlyle St. There's also a *Pizza Hut* on Marine Parade.

**Pub Food & Restaurants** There's a *Cobb & Co* in the fine old Masonic Establishment looking out on to Marine Parade. It's open the usual 7 days a week, 7.30 am to 10 pm hours. The *Victoria Hotel* at 76 Marine Parade also has a restaurant with the pub food regulars.

Further out at 409 Marine Parade the *Restaurant Indonesia* is a small BYO with attractive decor and interesting food which makes a pleasant break from the sometimes bland NZ fare. Main courses are around $14 to $18 and they also do a variety of rijstaffels, that Dutch-Indonesian-smorgasbord blend. It's open from 6 pm every day

On Emerson St the 1st floor *Ziggurat Cafe* is a truly international licensed restaurant serving Italian, French, Chinese and Thai food. Not only is the food stylish, so is the art deco building itself and the internal fittings to go with it. Main courses are from $9 to $17 and it's open from 5.30 pm Tuesday to Sunday.

The *Harston's Cafe* at 17 Hastings St has a pleasant atmosphere and serves large portions of basic Tex-Mex food for about $12. The *Mexican Cantina*, also in Hastings St, offers the usual Mexican dishes at around $4.50 to $6.50 for lunch, $9.50 to $18 for dinner. There's live music at dinner time and it's open from Wednesday to Saturday.

### Entertainment
Popular rock pubs include the *Shakespeare Hotel* on Shakespeare Rd and the *Onekawa* in, you guessed it, Onekawa. The Criterion Hotel in Emerson St has bands in the *Sportsman's Bar* Wednesday to Saturday, the *Masonic* has jazz or guitars Thursday to Saturday, and out by the port the *Iron Pot Cafe* is also popular for jazz, blues and rock playing from 7 pm to 1 am Wednesday and Thursday, until 3 am Friday and Saturday nights.

Napier also has a couple of newer nightclubs. *Ego's* in Hastings St is popular with young people on Wednesday to Saturday nights. *Club Odyssey* in the Ocean Blvd Mall between Dickens St and Emerson St attracts a bit older crowd.

### Getting There & Away
**Air** Air New Zealand (tel 353-288) is on the corner of Hastings St and Station St. They have direct flights to Auckland and Wellington several times daily, with connections to other centres. Eagle Air (tel 389-501) has several direct flights daily to Gisborne and daily flights to Auckland and Hamilton, also with onward connections.

**Bus** InterCity buses (tel 353-199) operate from the railway station. They have services to Auckland (7 hours), Hamilton (4¾ hours), Rotorua (3¼ hours) and Tauranga (5 hours) via Taupo (2 hours). There's also a north-south route to Gisborne (3¾ hours), Palmerston North (3½ hours) and Wellington (6 hours).

Newman's (tel 352-009) has moved their depot out of town to Pandora Rd but they're planning to sell tickets and depart more centrally from the Information Centre on Marine Parade. They have one route heading north to Taupo, Hamilton and Auckland, another to Rotorua via Taupo, another heading through Palmerston North and Wanganui to New Plymouth, and yet another to Wellington via Palmerston North. Mt Cook (tel 351-063) has an office at 102-106 Station St. They operate an Auckland-Taupo-Napier-Hastings route.

Dominion Coachlines have regular buses between Gisborne and Napier with services on to Wellington. The service goes through Wairoa, from where you can catch an InterCity bus to Rotorua via Waikaremoana on Monday, Wednesday and Friday. The Dominion office (tel 83-231) is in Hastings; in Napier they go from the Mt Cook office.

It's 220 km north to Gisborne on SH 2. Taupo is 148 km north-west on SH 5. All the long-distance buses coming to Napier continue on for the extra half-hour ride to Hastings.

**Train** The railway station (tel 353-199) used to be on Station Rd, but in the urban reconstruction it's being relocated to Munroe St. The Bay Express train operates daily between Napier and Wellington, with several stops including Hastings and Palmerston North on the 5½ hour run.

**Hitching** Hitching is OK around here. If you're heading north catch a long distance bus and get off at Westshore, walk, or try thumbing closer in. If you're heading south stick to SH 2. The alternative inland route, SH 36, is much harder going with very little traffic.

### Getting Around
**Airport Transport** There's an airport shuttle bus (tel 700-700) which costs $7 (children $4). A taxi to the airport costs about $12.

**Bus** InterCity operates the suburban bus services on weekdays, with regular buses between Napier and Hastings via Clive and Taradale plus other local services. There's no

Art Deco Architecture, Napier (TW)

service at all on weekends. All the local buses depart from the State Theatre on Dickens St, between Dalton St and Munroe St.

**Bicycle Rental** Napier Cycle World (tel 359-528) at 104 Carlyle St hires 10-speeds and tandems at $12 for a half-day, $14 a day or $35 a week.

## AROUND NAPIER
### Gannets & Cape Kidnappers

From October to March one of Napier's unique sights is the Cape Kidnappers gannet sanctuary. These large, ungainly birds usually make their nests on remote and inaccessible islands but here they nest on the mainland and are curiously unworried by human spectators.

The gannets usually turn up in late July after the last heavy storm of the month. Supposedly, the storm casts driftwood and other handy nest building material high up on the beach so very little effort has to be expended collecting it! In October and November eggs are laid which take about 6 weeks to hatch.

Gannet

By March the gannets start to migrate and by April only the odd straggler will be left.

You don't need a permit to visit the gannet sanctuary but it can only be visited at certain times of the year. The best time to see the gannets is between early November and late February. The reserve is closed to the public from 1 July until mid-October each year to prevent disturbance to the birds during the early phases of nesting. From November to February a ranger is stationed at the reserve, available to answer questions and provide information.

You can get to Cape Kidnappers (so named because Maoris tried to kidnap an obviously tasty looking Tahitian servant boy from Cook's expedition here) by several methods. From Burden's Motor Camp at Te Awanga, 21 km from Napier, you can ride on a tractor-pulled trailer along the beach for $12 (children $8). The guided return trip takes about 4 hours altogether and departs about 2 hours before low tide at the cape. Phone 750-400 or 750-334 for details.

Alternatively you can walk along the beach from Clifton, just along from Te Awanga. The 8 km walk takes 1½ to 2 hours and you must leave no earlier than 3 hours after high tide and start back no later than 1½ hours after low tide. It's another 8 km back and there are no refreshment stops so come prepared!

You can also get to Cape Kidnappers with Gannet Safaris (tel Hastings 750-511) from Summerlee Station beyond Te Awanga. The tour travels 18 km over farmland in a 4WD coach, departing daily at 1.30 pm and taking about an hour each way with an hour at the sanctuary. A minimum of six people are required for the trip, cost is $34 (children $17). This trip operates only from October to April.

You can find out the tide schedule for Cape Kidnappers in Napier from the Information Centre or DOC, or ask at Clifton. There is a rest hut with refreshments available at the colony. This is also a place to see (or, even better, to avoid) New Zealand's only poisonous spider, the katipo. The natural habitat of this spider is in the driftwood above the high tide mark, so leave it alone!

DOC, which administers the reserve, has a handy leaflet on getting there and the gannets' habits. They also have booklets titled *The Cape Kidnapper Gannet Reserve* and *The Geology & Fossils of the Cape Kidnappers Area*. Whichever route you take to the gannets there is no public transport to Te Awanga or Clifton from Napier, but you should be able to hitch.

### Wineries

The Hawke's Bay area is one of New Zealand's premier wine producing regions and there are a number of vineyards you can visit and taste the wines. They include Brookfields Vineyards at Meeane, Mission Vineyards at Napier, Esk Valley Estate Winery in the Esk Valley, Vidal Wine and Ngatarawa Wines in Hastings, Te Mata Estate Winery and Lombardi Wines in Havelock North and McDonalds Wines in Taradale. Mission Vineyards is the oldest in the country. The Napier Information Centre has a booklet on the wineries and their opening hours. They are all closed on Sundays.

A fine way of visiting the wineries is on a bicycle, since most of them are within easy cycling distance and it's all flat land. Bicycles can be hired in Napier.

### New Zealand Walkway

The DOC in Napier has leaflets with maps and details on a number of New Zealand Walkway tracks in the Hawke's Bay area.

The Whaka Mahara Tanga Walk is an historical walk over Rorookuri Hill to the Otiere Pa, beginning from Ohehunga Rd just off SH 2 at the northern entrance to Napier. The Tangoio Walkway passes through the Tangoio Falls and White Pine Bush Scenic Reserves, beginning 25 km north of Napier on SH 2. The Tutira Walkway begins at the entrance to the Lake Tutira Recreation Reserve and Bird Sanctuary, 45 km north of Napier.

A beach walk, the Hawke's Bay Coastal Walkway, goes from the Aropaoanui River,

48 km north of Napier, to the Waikari River, 59 km north of Napier (or the other way around) – be sure to ask about tide times before you set out on this walk.

Other tracks include lake and lookout walks on the Opouahi Walkway, 57 km north of Napier, and the Boundary Stream Walkway through the Boundary Stream Scenic Reserve, 60 km north of Napier.

### Te Mata Peak

Te Mata Peak is about 31 km south of Napier, 11 km from Hastings. It rises up in some dramatically sheer cliffs to the Te Mata trig, 399 metres above sea level, commanding a spectacular view over the Heretaunga Plains to Hawke's Bay. On a clear day you can see all of Hawke's Bay up to the Mahia Peninsula, and to Mt Ruapehu in the Tongariro National Park. You can also see oyster shells in the rocks at your feet!

Te Mata Peak is part of the 98 hectare Te Mata Park, with several walkways including a branch of the New Zealand Walkway. You can drive right up to the trig at the summit. The park is closed every night from sunset to dawn.

If you're lucky you may see some highly skilled hang-gliders in action at Te Mata – the peak is a favourite spot for hang-gliding. In addition to the thrill of leaping straight out over a vertical cliff with nothing but fresh air under them for 399 metres or so, gliders get remarkable possibilities from the updraughts breezing in from the Pacific Ocean, just a few hundred metres away. A local reported that on one occasion a Te Mata Peak glider got stuck in an updraught for over 3 hours!

## HASTINGS

Population 55,400

Hastings, 20 km south of Napier, tends to get forgotten beside Napier but it also has some interesting examples of art deco architecture – it shared the same fate as Napier in the 1931 earthquake, the whole town was practically reduced to rubble and a similar rebuilding programme ensued.

Hastings is a flat country town but it does

have a few attractions worthy of mention, including several wineries and the Leopard Brewery (see Napier). Hastings is a centre for agriculture, particularly orchards, with numerous roadside stands on the outskirts selling fresh produce. At harvest season there's lots of agricultural work to be found.

Havelock North, just a few km from Hastings, also has some worthwhile attractions including wineries, craft studios and honey houses.

### Information & Orientation
The Hastings District Information Centre (tel 60-205) in Russell St is open from 8.30 am to 5 pm on weekdays and from 8.30 am until noon on Saturdays. It has a good city map outlining a scenic drive around Hastings, Havelock North and Flaxmere with many examples of art deco architecture and other points of interest including Te Mata Peak.

Walking around Hastings is easy, but its confusing pattern of one-way streets tends to make it a nightmare for drivers!

### Fantasyland
In the 27 hectare Windsor Park, 2 km from the town centre on Grove Rd, Fantasyland is an excellent old-fashioned children's amusement park. It has a miniature of the Disneyland castle, a Mother Hubbard's shoe, a merry-go-round, a pirate ship, Noddy Town, go carts, bumper boats, other boats you can take out on the swan lake fronting the castle, a flying fox, narrow gauge train rides, and much more. It's open every day and admission is $2.50 (children free).

Also in Windsor Park is a swimming pool with a waterslide, a skating rink, a motor camp and more.

### Exhibition Centre
The Hawke's Bay Exhibition Centre in Eastbourne St is associated with the Hawke's Bay Museum in Napier. The Exhibition Centre hosts a wide variety of changing exhibitions and the admission fee depends on what's showing at the time. It's open from 10 am to 4.30 pm on weekdays and from 1 to 4.30 pm on weekends and holidays.

### Places to Stay
In Windsor Park, adjacent to Fantasyland, the swimming pool and other attractions, *Hastings Holiday Park* (tel 86-692) has camping sites at $14 with or without power. Cabins are $18 to $25, tourist flats are $25, $35 or $42, a few dollars more in the summer high season. All of these prices are for two people. The camp is in Windsor Ave, 2½ km from the CPO.

The *Raceview Holiday Park* (tel 88-837, 66-623) at 307 Gascoigne St, adjacent to the jockey racecourse, has camping at $13, onsite caravans at $25, and tourist flats at $47, again all prices are for two people.

There are several hotels and motels, plus many home and farmstays available around Hastings. The Information Centre has listings.

### Places to Eat
Hastings has the usual assortment of takeaways, cafes, etc, but the ice cream at *Rush-Munro's Ice Cream Garden* is a real treat – home-made, loaded with fresh fruit, and very rich. People come from great distances for this ice cream, which you can only get at the garden itself, a local institution since WW II. If you're coming into town from Napier, you'll see it on your right at the entrance to town.

### Getting There & Away
It's easy to get to Hastings by bus from Napier, a half-hour away. InterCity operates a frequent local bus service from Napier but only on weekdays. All the long distance buses going to Napier continue to Hastings.

# Wellington

Population 325,200

Wellington, as the capital of New Zealand, takes part in friendly rivalry with larger Auckland, but it's quieter and not so speedy. The town is hemmed in around its magnificent harbour, the buildings marching picturesquely up the steep hills. It's a pleasant and lively city with plenty to see and do – so long as the wind isn't blowing. Many travellers pass through Wellington as, apart from its importance as the capital, it's also a major travel crossroads between the North and South islands.

## History

Traditionally, the Maoris maintain that Kupe was the first person to discover Wellington harbour. The original Maori name for the place was Te Whanga-Nui-a-Tara, Tara being the son of a Maori chief named Whatonga who had settled on the Hawke's Bay coast. Whatonga sent Tara and his half-brother off to explore the southern part of the North Island but it was over a year before they returned. When they did, their reports of the land were so favourable that Whatonga and his followers moved to the harbour, founding the Ngati-tara.

The first White settlers arrived on 22 January 1840 in the New Zealand Company's ship *Aurora*, not long after Colonel William Wakefield had arrived to buy land from the Maoris. The idea was to build two cities: one would be a commercial centre by the harbour and the other, further north, would be the agricultural hub. The settlers were to be allotted two blocks, a town section of an acre (less than half a hectare) and a back country block worth $2 an acre. But the Maoris denied they had sold the land at Port Nicholson, or Poneke as they called it. The settlement was the result of hasty and illegal buying by the New Zealand Company and the start of land rights struggles which were to plague the country for the next 30 years and still affect it today.

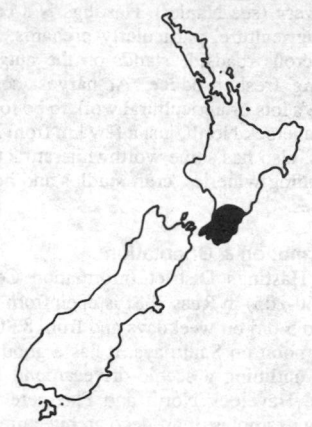

Wellington began as a settlement with very little flat land. Originally the waterfront was along Lambton Quay, but reclamation of parts of the harbour began in 1852 and has continued ever since. In 1855 an earthquake razed part of the Hutt Rd and the area around Te Aro flat to the Basin Reserve, which initiated the first major reclamation. The city is built around a fine harbour formed by the flooding of a long-extinct, and very large, volcano crater. The city runs up the hills on one side of the harbour, and so cramped is it for space that many Wellington workers live in two urban corridors leading northwards between the steep, rugged hills – one is the Hutt Valley and the other follows SH 1 northwards through Tawa and Porirua.

In 1865 the seat of government was moved from Auckland to Wellington and since then it has gradually become the business centre of the country – most major organisations operating in New Zealand have their head office here – and also the centre of the diplomatic corps.

## Orientation

Lambton Quay, the main business street, wriggles along, almost parallel to the sea-

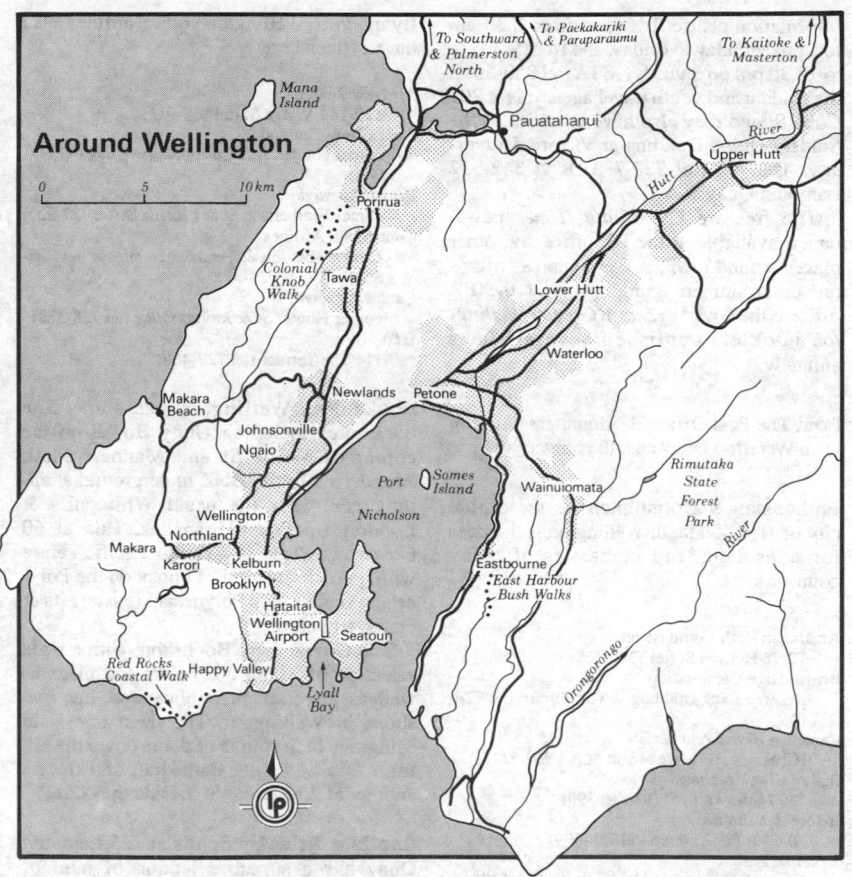

**Around Wellington**

0    5    10 km

To Southward & Palmerston North

To Paekakariki & Paraparaumu

To Kaitoke & Masterton

Mana Island

Pauatahanui

River

Upper Hutt

Porirua

Colonial Knob Walk

Tawa

Hutt

Lower Hutt

Waterloo

Makara Beach

Newlands

Petone

Johnsonville

Ngaio

Port Nicholson

Somes Island

Rimutaka State Forest Park

Wainuiomata

River

Wellington

Northland

Makara

Karori

Kelburn

Brooklyn

Hataitai

Wellington Airport

Seatoun

Eastbourne

East Harbour Bush Walks

Red Rocks Coastal Walk

Happy Valley

Lyall Bay

Orongorongo

front. Many of the older buildings in Wellington have been demolished in the past few years and modern concrete boxes have sprung up in their place. Thorndon is the area immediately north of the centre where you'll find a number of the major embassies and also the youth hostel. Mt Victoria is the area immediately south where you'll find a number of other hostels and cheap places to stay.

## Information

**Tourist Information** The PR office (tel 735-063) is in the Old Town Hall building, 101 Wakefield St on the corner of Cuba St, next door to the modernistic metal-and-glass Michael Fowler Centre. It's open from 9 am to 5 pm every day, with a wealth of information on Wellington and the surrounding area. The DOC Information Centre (tel 710-726) at 59 Boulcott St has information on walkways, parks and so on – much of their local information is available from the PR office. The office is open the usual DOC hours, from 8.30 am to 4.30 pm on weekdays.

The NZTP (tel 739-269) at 25-27 Mercer St is basically a travel agent rather than an information centre. It's open from 8.30 am to 5 pm Monday to Friday, and from 9.30 am to 12.30 pm on Saturday. STA (tel 850-561), the student and youth travel agency, is at 207 Cuba St and they also have an office in the Student Union Building at Victoria University. The AA (tel 738-738) is at 342-352 Lambton Quay.

The free weekly *Capital Times* newspaper, available at the PR office and other places around town, is Wellington's 'what's on' entertainment guide. Also at the PR office is the *Great Events in Greater Wellington* booklet, published several times annually.

**Post** The Post Office Headquarters building is on Waterloo Quay near the railway station.

**Embassies & Consulates** As the capital city of New Zealand, Wellington is the base for consulates and embassies of many countries.

Australian High Commission
    72-78 Hobson St (tel 736-411)
British High Commission
    Reserve Bank Building, 2 The Terrace (tel 726-049)
Canadian High Commission
    ICI House, 67 Molesworth St (tel 739-577)
Indian High Commission
    180 Molesworth St (tel 736-390)
Indonesian Embassy
    70 Glen Rd, Kelburn (tel 758-699)
Japanese Embassy
    Norwich House, 311 Hunter St (tel 731-540)
Netherlands Embassy
    corner Featherston St & Ballance St (tel 738-652)
Swedish Embassy
    39 The Terrace (tel 720-909)
Swiss Embassy
    22-24 Panama St (tel 721-593)
Thai Embassy
    2 Cook St, Karori (tel 768-619)
US Embassy
    29 Fitzherbert Terrace (tel 722-068)
West German Embassy
    90-92 Hobson St (tel 736-063)

**Airline Offices** Although Air New Zealand and Qantas are the only international airlines

flying into Wellington, other airlines also have offices here:

Air New Zealand
    129-141 Vivian St (tel 859-911)
Ansett New Zealand
    corner Hunter St & Customhouse Quay (tel 711-044)
British Airways
    corner Featherston St & Panama St (tel 727-327)
Continental Airlines
    corner Brandon & Featherston streets (tel 725-663)
Qantas Airways
    corner Hunter St & Jervois Quay (tel 738-378)
UTA
    114 The Terrace (tel 722-460)

**Bookstores** Wellington has some fine bookstores including Unity Books on the corner of Willis St and Manners Mall, Ahradsen's in the BNZ underground shopping centre or the usual Whitcoulls & London Bookshop branches. Tala at 60 Courtenay Place is a South Pacific centre with a good selection of books on the Polynesian region plus Polynesian music, arts & crafts, and cloth.

The Government Bookshop, with a wide selection of useful NZ books and maps as well as government publications, has two shops in Wellington. The main one is in Mulgrave St, a couple of doors down the hill from Old St Paul's Cathedral, and there's another at 25 Mercer St, beside the NZTP.

**Sports & Arts** Alp Sports at 125 Lambton Quay has a superb selection of outdoor equipment, as well as lots of Lonely Planet guidebooks. Second Wind Sports on Wakefield St opposite the PR office has good second-hand camping, skiing, surfing, diving and other sports equipment. Living Simply, which used to be in Wellington but has now moved about 9 km out of the centre to 326 Jackson St, Petone, has camping equipment, mountain bikes, maps, etc at lower prices than you'll find in town, making it worth the 15 minute bus trip (catch the Eastbourne bus) to get out there.

Several interesting annual events take place in Wellington. International tennis championships during January and February include the BP Nationals, the Fernleaf Women's Tennis Classic and the UDC Australasian Veterans Championships, and there are many other sports events held throughout the year. A Lampen Dragon Boat Festival is held in February. New Zealand's biggest car race of the year, the Nissan Mobil 500, roars through the streets of Wellington on the first weekend in December.

The arts are also well represented. Each summer from early December to the end of January the Summer City Festival sponsors a wide range of outdoor concerts, theatre, exhibitions, etc in parks and other open-air venues. Film festivals are held every March and July. The excellent, broad spectrum New Zealand International Festival of the Arts runs for 3 weeks in March in even-numbered years.

### Windy Wellington

Wellington really can get windy. When the sun's shining it can be a very attractive city but it's not called the windy city for nothing – one of the local rock stations even calls itself:

Particularly as winter starts to arrive you've got a fair chance of experiencing some gale-force days. The sort of days when strong men get pinned up against walls and little old ladies, desperately clutching their umbrellas, can be seen floating by at skyscraper height. Seriously the flying grit and dust can be uncomfortable to the eyes and the flying garbage can be a real mess. I was walking back from a restaurant late one windy night when a sudden gust blew several bags of garbage out of a doorway, a passing car hit one and a veritable snowstorm of soft drink cans, pizza boxes and assorted debris rushed down the street like tumbleweeds from an old western movie. The wind was blowing

☐ Yesterday's northerlies brought Wellington's strongest wind gust of the year, a Kelburn Weather Office spokesman said today.

The 76 knot (139km/h) gust shaded the year's previous best, recorded on February 4, by 13km/h, the spokesman said.

The strongest gust today, recorded just after midnight, was 113km/h.

so hard that this blizzard of rubbish actually overtook the offending car!

One blustery day back in 1968 the wind blew so hard it pushed the almost new Wellington-Christchurch car ferry *Wahine* on to Barrett's Reef just outside the harbour entrance. The disabled ship later broke loose from the reef, drifted into the harbour and then sank with the loss of many lives. The Wellington Maritime Museum has a dramatic model of the disaster.

### Old Government Building

At the northern end of Lambton Quay is the Old Government Building, one of the largest all-wooden buildings in the world – there's a wooden temple in Japan which beats it for 'the biggest' honours. Wood was widely used in the construction of buildings in Wellington's early days – there are some fine old wooden houses still to be seen.

### Parliament Building

Across from the Old Government Building is the very modern new parliament building known as the Beehive – because that is just what it looks like. You can arrange to take a free half-hour tour of the Parliament Buildings by phoning 719-999. The tours are held 7 days a week.

### Old St Paul's

One block away from Parliament in Mulgrave St, Thorndon (a couple of minutes walk from the railway station) is Old St

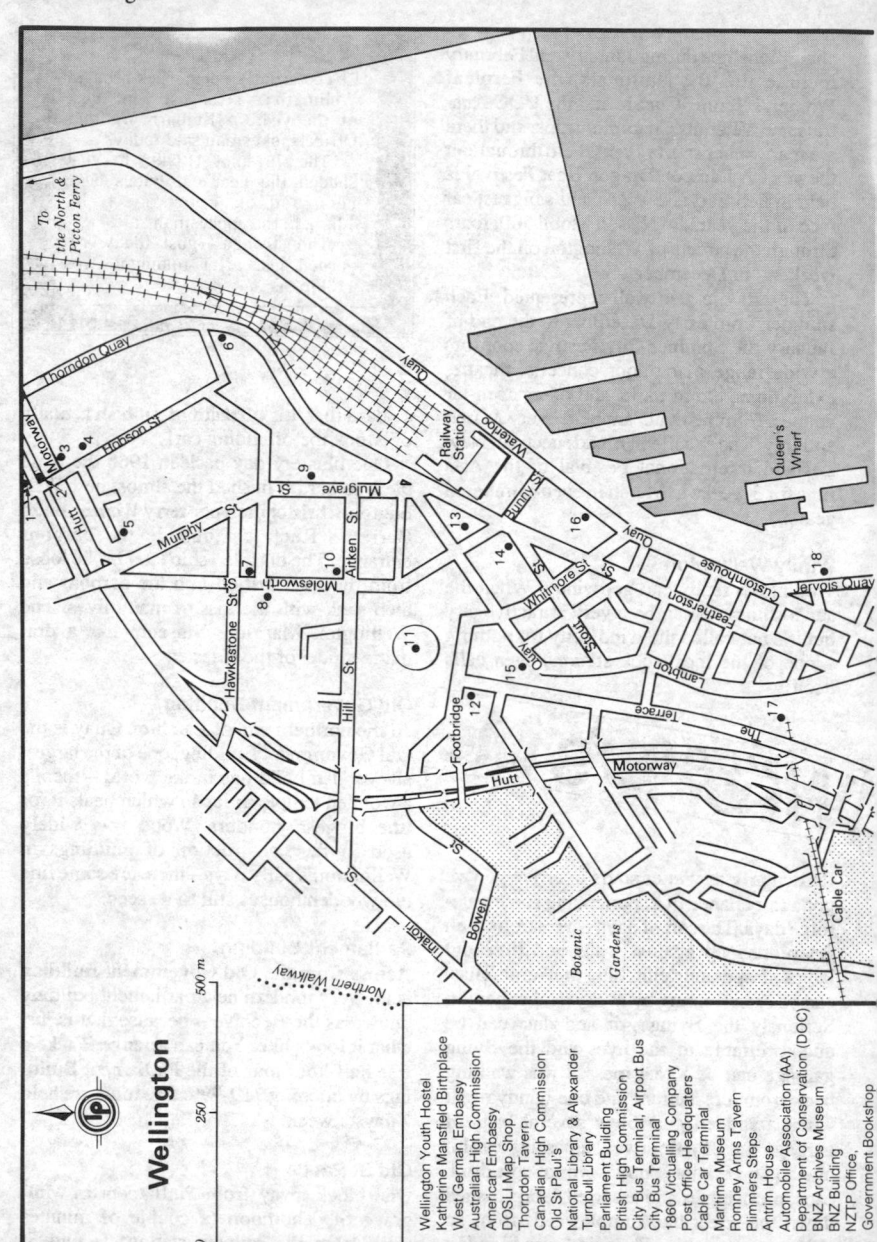

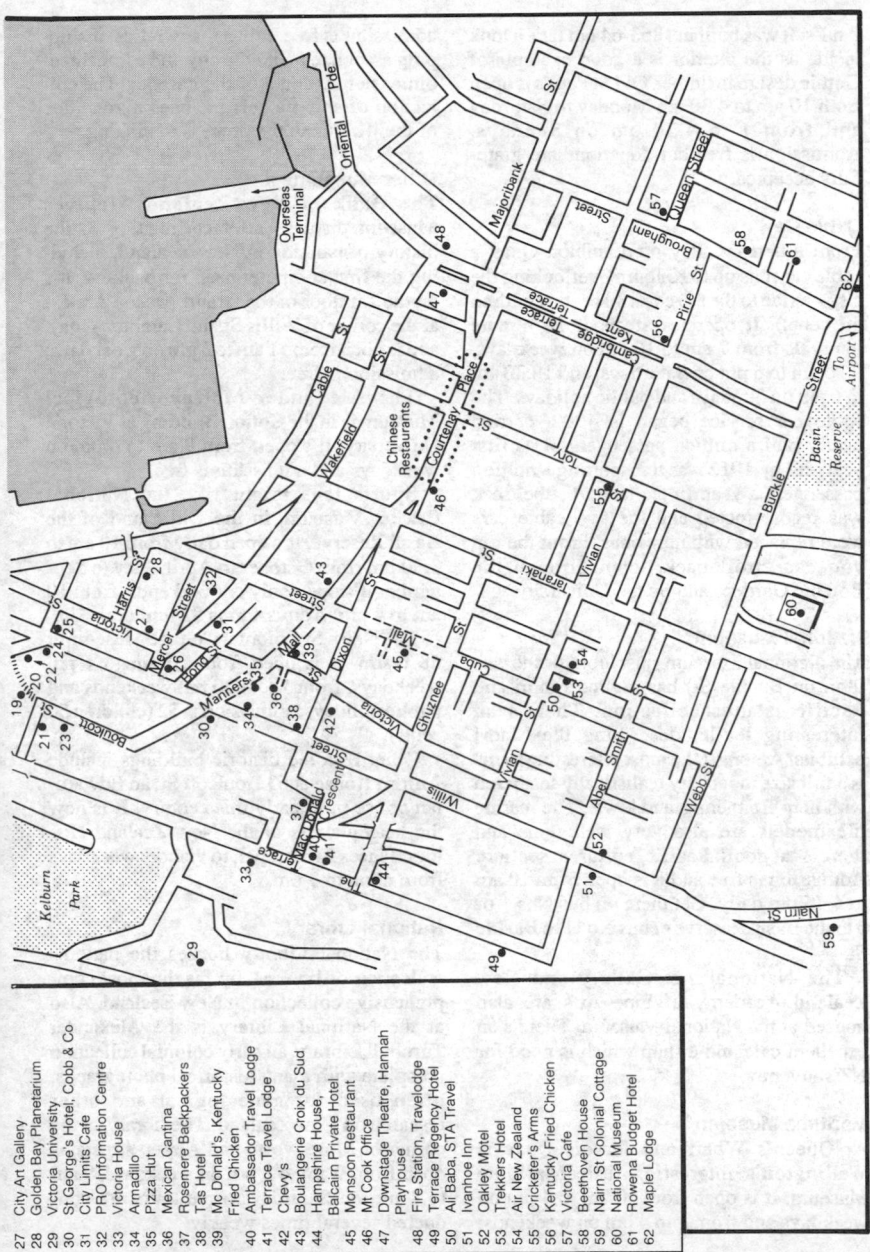

27 City Art Gallery
28 Golden Bay Planetarium
29 Victoria University
30 St George's Hotel, Cobb & Co
31 City Limits Cafe
32 PRO Information Centre
33 Victoria House
34 Armadillo
35 Pizza Hut
36 Mexican Cantina
37 Rosemere Backpackers
38 Tas Hotel
39 Mc Donald's, Kentucky Fried Chicken
40 Ambassador Travel Lodge
41 Terrace Travel Lodge
42 Chevy's
43 Boulangerie Croix du Sud
44 Hampshire House, Balcairn Private Hotel
45 Monsoon Restaurant
46 Mt Cook Office
47 Downstage Theatre, Hannah Playhouse
48 Fire Station, Travelodge
49 Terrace Regency Hotel
50 Ali Baba, STA Travel
51 Ivanhoe Inn
52 Oakley Motel
53 Trekkers Hotel
54 Air New Zealand
55 Cricketer's Arms
56 Kentucky Fried Chicken
57 Victoria Cafe
58 Beethoven House
59 Nairn St Colonial Cottage
60 National Museum
61 Rowena Budget Hotel
62 Maple Lodge

Paul's. It was built in 1863-64 but take a look inside as the interior is a good example of Gothic design in timber. Old St Paul's is open from 10 am to 4.30 pm Monday to Saturday and from 1 to 4.30 pm on Sundays. Admission is free but donations are gratefully accepted.

## Cable Car

From a narrow alley off Lambton Quay a cable car runs up to Kelburn overlooking the city – a ride to the top costs 80 cents (children 40 cents). It operates at about 10 minute intervals from 7 am to 10 pm on weekdays, 9.30 am to 6 pm on Saturdays, and 10.30 am to 6 pm on Sundays and public holidays. The cable car service began in 1902, carried nearly half a million passengers in its first year and by 1912 was transporting a million passengers a year. In the late '70s the track was reconstructed and the two cable cars were replaced with new ones. From the top you can stroll back down through the Botanic Gardens and by the University.

## National Museum

The National Museum (just look for the carillon on Buckle St) has a good Maori and Pacific Islands collection. There's an interesting leaflet describing the Maori exhibits. Amongst the most interesting items is a full size moa, very realistically feathered with help from emus and kiwis. The marine life models are also very well done and there's a good Pacific cultures section. Admission is free and it is open from 10 am to 4.45 pm daily. Get there on bus Nos 1 or 3 to the Basin Reserve or bus No 11 to Buckle St.

The National Art Gallery and New Zealand Academy of Fine Arts are also housed at the National Museum. There's an excellent cafe and a shop which is good for NZ souvenirs.

## Maritime Museum

At Queen's Wharf and Jervois Quay is Wellington's interesting little Maritime Museum. It is open from 10 am to 4 pm on weekdays and from 1 to 4 pm on weekends;

admission is free. It has many relics of shipping associated with the city and a fine three-dimensional model of the harbour. The collection of ship models includes a great one of the *Wahine* in the process of sinking.

## Other Museums

The Bank of New Zealand Archives Museum displays artefacts relating to the history of banking in New Zealand, including the first computer used for banking. It's on the 1st floor of the Grand Arcade Annex, at the corner of Willis St and Lambton Quay, and is open from 11 am to 3 pm on weekdays; admission is free.

The Alexander McKay Geological Museum is in the Cotton Building at Victoria University. It's open from 9 am to 4 pm on weekdays and admission is free.

Sports fans might like the National Cricket Museum, in the Old Stand of the Basin Reserve. It's open daily from 10 am to 3.30 pm from October to April; May to September it's open only on weekends, from 10 am to 4 pm. Admission is $2 (children $1).

The Nairn St Colonial Cottage Museum at 68 Nairn St is open from 10 am to 4 pm weekdays, from 1 to 4.30 pm weekends and public holidays; admission is $2 (children 50 cents).

Other restored historic buildings include Antrim House at 63 Boulcott St, an Edwardian house built early this century. It is now the headquarters of the New Zealand Historic Places Trust, open to visitors weekdays from noon to 3 pm.

## National Library

The National Library houses the nation's collection of books – by far the most comprehensive collection in New Zealand. Also at the National Library is the Alexander Turnbull Library, an early colonial collection complete with many historical photographs, often used for genealogical and other research on New Zealand. The library, at the corner of Molesworth and Aitken streets, is open from 9 am to 5 pm on weekdays, 9 am to 1 pm on Saturdays. Free tours are conducted several times weekly.

## Katherine Mansfield Memorials

The Katherine Mansfield Birthplace at 25 Tinakori Rd (opposite the YHA hostel) is the house where the author was born in 1888. It's been restored and is open from 10 am to 4 pm every day except Mondays; admission is $4 (children $2). Nearby, in the small park beside the fortress-like US Embassy building, is a memorial which Mansfield's father dedicated to her after her untimely death.

You can also visit Days Bay, where Mansfield's family spent their summer holidays (see Harbour Cruises).

## Zoo

Wellington Zoo has a nocturnal kiwi house and a wide variety of native fauna and other wildlife. The kiwis are on view from 10 am to 4 pm daily but the best time to see them is from 10 am to noon. The zoo is open daily from 8.30 am to 5 pm (last admission 4.30 pm), entry $5.50 (children $2.50, family $14). The zoo is 4 km from the city centre – you can get there on a bus No 11 marked Newtown Park Zoo, which leaves from the railway station at intervals of about 15 minutes on weekdays, 20 minutes on Saturdays and 30 minutes on Sundays.

## Walks

There are numerous walkways in the Wellington area, check at the PR office for a full range of brochures on walks in the city and surrounding areas. A Southern Walkway covers some 11 km and departs the city via Mt Victoria, Newtown, Melrose to Island Bay. You don't have to walk the whole 11 km as you can catch a bus at several points along the way.

There are several good walks around the harbour shore or outside the harbour – try the Red Rocks Coastal walk beyond the airport on the western side or the East Harbour Bush Walk above the harbour on the eastern side. The Colonial Knob walk near Tawa is also good. Longer walks can be found in the Rimutaka State Forest Park on the eastern side of the harbour.

## Other Attractions

For a great view of the city go to the top of Mt Victoria. A bus No 20 will take you there in 20 minutes; it starts from the railway station. City tour buses also stop at Mt Victoria.

The adventurous City Art Gallery is in Victoria St, at the corner of Chews Lane. It's open every day from 10 am to 6 pm, until 8 pm on Wednesdays; admission is free. Wellington has numerous other galleries and crafts shops.

The Golden Bay Planetarium on Harris St has sessions on Saturdays, Sundays and public holidays; admission is $4 (children $2, family $10). The Carter Observatory in the Botanic Gardens is open from 7.30 to 9.30 pm on Tuesdays from March to October and offers programmes featuring talks, slides, and telescope viewing. Admission is $5 (children $3). The observatory is opposite the upper cable car terminal.

## Harbour Cruises

Trips across the harbour to Days Bay are made on the *Government Print I* (tel 499-1273), an 18½ metre catamaran sponsored by the Government Printing Office. It's a 25 minute trip to Days Bay, where there are beaches, a fine park and a couple of houses which Katherine Mansfield's family kept for summer homes – her story 'At the Bay' recalls summer holidays at Days Bay. Eastbourne village, with lots of shops and restaurants, is a 15 minute walk from Days Bay. The catamaran goes to and fro on a regular daily schedule, one-way fare is $5.50 (children $2.50) or there's a $30 family return fare. Departures are from Queens Wharf.

Bluefin Launches (tel 698-203) does 3 hour evening meal cruises for $35, 2 hour smorgasbord lunch cruises for $26, and 2 hour scenic harbour cruises for $16 (children 66% fare on meal cruises, free to age 12 on scenic cruises). They depart from the end of Whitmore St. Harbour City Cruises (tel 499-5105) do 3 hour evening dine & dance cruises for $39, departing from Queens Wharf. Both companies operate 15 metre cruise launches and go on demand, not on fixed schedules, so phone ahead for reservations.

## Tours

Wellington City Transport's 2½ hour afternoon bus tour is a good city intro. It costs $17 (children $8.50), the bus departs from outside the PR office daily at 2 pm and after a circuit of the inner city it follows the Marine Drive out to Mt Victoria with fine views over the city and the airport. Phone Busline (tel 859-955) for bookings or for free pick-up from your hotel. Beware of higher priced private operators who try to hook people intending to take the city transport tour!

Wally Hammond (tel 720-869) does similar 2½ hour city highlight tours, departing at 10 am and 2 pm. The price is the same as for the city transport tours except YHA members receive a $5 discount. He does other tours on request but only for a limited number of people.

The Wellington Explorer is another service of Wellington City Transport. The bus stops at 13 of Wellington's prime tourist attractions. One $8 (children $4) ticket is good for the whole day – you get on and off wherever and whenever you like – and also entitles you to free cable car and city bus rides on the same day. No booking is necessary and you can catch the bus anywhere along its route. A route map is available at the PR office or phone Busline (tel 859-955) for info.

There are tours further afield, ask the PR office for current operators and details. Rimutaka Safaris (tel 643-066), operated by the DOC, have excellent 4WD Land Rover safaris in the Rimutaka Forest Park and beyond, departing from the park's Catchpool Visitors Centre.

## Places to Stay

Wellington's location, crowded in against the bay by the surrounding hills, means that building land is limited and this has an effect on the accommodation picture. There are no camping sites close to Wellington, the number of motels is very limited and even the guest houses, of which there are plenty, are comparatively expensive. Backpackers, at least, are fairly well catered for as there is a fair choice of hostels.

**Hostels** The Wellington Youth Hostel (tel 736-271) at 40 Tinakori Rd is conveniently situated only 10 minutes walk from either the ferry terminal or the railway station. Nightly costs are $15. It's a very popular hostel and it's often full up, so booking ahead is a good idea.

There's another YHA Youth Hostel (tel 267-251) 42 km north of Wellington at Kaitoke at the top of the Hutt Valley, in Marchant Rd just off the main highway. Nightly cost is $8 in this rather basic hostel. Kaitoke Regional Park, where there are bushwalking tracks and a river for swimming or canoeing, is nearby. Get there on an InterCity Wellington to Masterton bus.

The Rosemere Backpackers (tel 843-041) at 6 MacDonald Crescent is a short uphill walk from the centre, with good city views especially from the tiny 3rd-storey balcony. Cost is $13 for a bed in dorm, twin or double rooms; they also have B&B for $45/58 a single/double.

The Ivanhoe Inn (tel 842-264) at 302 Willis St is run by ex-hostel owners but it's not a regular hostel – it's a collection of six separate flats, each containing two bedrooms, a kitchen and a TV lounge. The rooms (with double, twin or dorm beds) are rented out hostel-style for $15 per person. Check in at the Oakley Motel across the road when you arrive.

Several other private hostels are found about 42 km south of the centre. The Beethoven House (tel 842-226) at 89 Brougham St, Mt Victoria, is known for its eccentric atmosphere. For a start you have to like Beethoven's music – there's rarely a moment when one or other of his works is not being played, beginning at around 6.45 am to wake you up for breakfast! And if you're a smoker, you'll have to give it up – at least temporarily – as there's no smoking allowed anywhere on the property and you'll encounter a great number of signs warning you of the evils of tobacco. All birthdays, including Beethoven's, the house's, yours and Christmas, are celebrated, and there are weekend excursions out to a house in the countryside. Allen Goh (don't mention my name), the hostel's manager, accounts for a large measure of the hostel's unusual personality.

Beethoven House is open 24 hours a day, nightly costs are $12 in winter, $13 in summer, although if you arrive *very* late you'll be charged more on night one. A light breakfast of toast and marmalade, tea and coffee is included; everybody breakfasts together at 7.30 am after waking up to Beethoven. It's hardly the tidiest hostel on earth – in fact a long way from it. Note that Beethoven House inspires love or hate and as many people positively hate it as love it!

To get there from the Railway Station end of town catch a bus Nos 2 or 5 to Brougham St, or a bus Nos 1 or 3 to the Kentucky Fried Chicken on Kent Terrace. From the Courtenay Place end of town it's only a 5 minute walk. There's no prominent sign outside, just a small 'BH'.

Close to Beethoven House are two places which are part hostel, part guest house. At 115 Brougham St the *Rowena Budget Hotel* (tel 857-872) is up above the street with fine views down over the city. It's a well kept place and you can't miss its amazing colour scheme. There are no less than 60 rooms, three lounges, kitchens, barbecue facilities, and costs of $13 for a dorm, $16.50 a single, $35 a double. Continental breakfast is available for $3 and a cooked breakfast is $5.

Just around the corner at 52 Ellice St is the *Maple Lodge* (tel 842-264), with single/double rooms at $16.50/22 as well as bunkroom accommodation at $12. It has the usual kitchen, lounge and laundry facilities.

The *Victoria House* (tel 843-357), a university hostel at 282 The Terrace, has accommodation available during university vacations (mid-November to late February, mid-May and late August to early September). Per-person cost is $15 for backpackers (with your own sleeping bag) in a share or twin room, $5 more with breakfast. Otherwise B&B is $30/35 for singles/doubles, or $40/45 with all three meals. The one drawback is there is no hostellers' kitchen.

**Guest Houses** Wellington has a limited number of conveniently situated motels but it has plenty of guest houses. A number of them are found along The Terrace where there are numerous attractive old wooden houses, many of them with great views over the city. The steep streets, the architecture of these old homes and the colours they're painted are all very reminiscent of similar areas in San Francisco.

The *Ambassador Travel Lodge* (tel 845-697) at 287 The Terrace has basic single/double rooms at $40/65 including breakfast, plus more expensive villa units, motel units and family rooms. At 291 The Terrace the *Terrace Travel Hotel* (tel 848-702) is a homely old building but well kept and costs $45/55, or there are some cabins at the back which are cheaper at $25/40 for singles/doubles, linen included. There's no guests' kitchen but a continental breakfast is available for $5.

On the corner of The Terrace and Ghuznee St is *Hampshire House* (tel 843-051) with rooms at $40/55; a continental breakfast is another $7. Right next door at 151 Ghuznee St is the *Balcairn Private Hotel* (tel 842-274). There are several other guest houses/private hotels along The Terrace.

Other guest houses include *Richmond House* (tel 858-529) at 116 Brougham St, with B&B at $40/55. Two hostels in this same area, *Rowena Budget Hotel* and *Maple Lodge*, also have private single and double rooms. Maple Lodge is cheap and pretty basic, while Rowena Budget Hotel is larger and a bit fancier. Another alternative is the *Clinton Private Hotel* (tel 859-515) in the southern part of the central area at 35 Thompson St, with B&B at $41/55.

At 182 Tinakori Rd the *Tinakori Lodge* (tel 733-478) is the historic home of an early prime minister. B&B here costs $66/77 for singles/doubles.

**Hotels** The *Trekkers Hotel* (tel 852-153) is on Dunlop Terrace, off Vivian St by Cuba St and right opposite the Air New Zealand office. It's a recycled old hotel and although the changes are mainly in the reception and restaurant area it's been quite attractively done. Rooms are \$40/50; with bathroom they're \$60/70. There are also some more expensive motel-style rooms. Or there's a backpackers share rate of \$15 per person with your own sleeping bag, \$20 if you use their linen. The hotel has a spa and sauna, restaurant and cafe, a house bar, and parking facilities.

There are some cheaper old hotels and also plenty that head up towards the sky pricewise. Cheaper ones which are also centrally located include the *Cambridge Establishment* (tel 858-829) on Cambridge Terrace with rooms at \$50/60 with shared facilities, or \$60/70 with private bathrooms. This is one of the nationwide Establishment chain. *Flanagan's Hotel* (tel 850-216) on Kent Terrace has rooms at \$64.

The *Tas Hotel* (tel 851-304) is very central at the corner of Willis and Dixon streets and has 37 rooms which cost \$110/118 from Monday to Thursday but drop to \$60 from Friday to Sunday. Also very central is *St George's Hotel* (tel 739-139) on the corner of Willis and Boulcott streets where the Cobb & Co Restaurant is located. It has a similar pricing arrangement: rooms are \$116/130 Monday to Thursday, \$62/77 from Friday to Sunday.

Much more expensive hotels include the *James Cook Hotel* (tel 725-865) on The Terrace, the *Terrace Regency Hotel* (tel 858-829) at 345 The Terrace, and the *Wellington Parkroyal* (tel 859-949) at 360 Oriental Parade. In these a double will probably be in the \$150 to \$200 range.

Wellington has some apartment hotels, a cross between an apartment and a hotel. Some of the fine old wooden houses along The Terrace are being converted into apartments for longer term stays – contact *City Life Apartments* (tel 723-413) but you're looking at a minimum of \$170 a night. At 140 Abel Smith St the *Iona Motels* (tel 851-569) has two bedroom apartments for \$112 a night.

**Motels** There are no motel bargains in Wellington. The *Oakley Motel* (tel 846-173) at 331 Willis St is an old wooden building but the rooms are all self contained and cost \$67.50. The *Aroha Motel* (tel 726-206) at 222 The Terrace is another old wooden building but with self-contained rooms from \$101. The *Wellington Luxury Motel* (tel 726-825) at 14 Hobson St has rooms from \$72. Otherwise you'll probably have to go out to the suburbs to find motels.

**Camping & Cabins** If you're looking for a camping site or cabins you'll find Wellington a tough place – there is no flat ground. The best you'll do is out at Lower Hutt in the *Hutt Park Holiday Village* (tel 685-913) at 95 Hutt Park Rd, 13 km from the Wellington CPO. Sites cost \$16 for two or \$18 with power. They warn that the site is not suitable for tent camping over the winter months. Cabins, tourist flats and motel units are also available starting from around \$23 for two in the plainer cabins. To get there without your own transport take an Eastbourne or Gracefield bus – they go at least hourly, every 20 minutes during rush hour. Then walk half a km. Or take a train to Woburn (faster at rush hour) and follow the signs for 2 km.

The *Harcourt Holiday Park* (tel 267-400) on Akatarawa Rd in Upper Hutt, about a 30 minute drive from Wellington, also has tent sites, caravan sites and tourist flats. There are more camping grounds up the west coast towards Paraparaumu. Out at the Rimutaka State Forest Park there's basic camping at Catchpool Valley, near the DOC's Catchpool Visitor Centre (tel 648-551); cost is \$3 per person.

### Places to Eat

Wellington probably has the widest variety of international cuisines to be found in New Zealand and there are plenty of restaurants to choose from. Courtenay Place and Willis St in particular are packed with restaurants.

**Fast Food** The American fast food giants are well represented in Wellington. *McDonald's*, *Kentucky Fried Chicken* and *Pizza Hut* can all be found in Manners Mall in the centre. There's another *Kentucky Fried Chicken* on Kent Terrace, near to the Brougham St/Ellice St accommodation places, and another *McDonald's* on Courtenay Place near the Cambridge Terrace junction.

**Takeaways** Wellington's a great place for a sandwich or snack at lunch time. You'll find lots of choices along Courtenay St and Manners Mall, up Plimmer's Steps and along Lambton Quay right in the centre, or along Cuba St and Cuba Mall.

Try the basement level under the BNZ (Bank of New Zealand) building at the Willis St/Lambton Quay junction. This is the Wellington equivalent of the underground shopping centres of Montreal but while the French-Canadians go subterranean to escape the cold, the Wellingtonians do it to escape the wind. Several places here sell sandwiches, tacos, pizzas, soup and other light meals.

Starting from the northern (parliament and railway station) end of town and moving south good sandwich places include *Stripes* in the Phoenix Centre on Lambton Quay. Or next door in the James Cook Arcade there's *Stickybun*. Climb Plimmer's Steps off Lambton Quay and you'll come to *Cafe Cuisine*, a more expensive sit-down place which is open for breakfast too, hours are from 7 am to 5 pm on weekdays, 9 am to 2 pm on Saturdays.

Along Cuba St, at No 157, there's *Food for Thought* with good wholefood sandwiches and snacks. At 101 Manners St, close to the Cuba St junction, there's a *Boulangerie Croix du Sud* French bakery with sandwiches and baked goods.

At 203 Cuba St *Ali Baba* is a great place for a doner kebab with salad and bread for around $6 or $7, add $1 more for hummus, kisir or fried zucchini. It's essentially a takeaway but there's an alcove at the back where you can sit at low tables, on Turkish

pillows of course. It's open from 10 am to 9 pm Monday to Saturday.

An important port like Wellington naturally has plenty of fish & chip specialists. On Courtenay Place near the corner of Cambridge Terrace are the *Capital Fish Shop* and *Courtenay Fish & Chips*. At 12 Bond St in the city centre the *Fisherman's Plate* will dish you up a fine fish & chips or other seafood meal on a paper plate, to eat there or take away. *Wellington Fish Supply* at 40 Molesworth St, opposite the Beehive, also has good fish & chips. On Wakefield St near the Information Centre and NZTP office *City Limits* is a pleasant and relaxing cafe for a coffee or light meal.

If you're staying in the Beethoven House area and need a quick meal there's a string of places providing pizzas, burgers and other takeaways nearby. They're all at the Ellice St/Kent Terrace junction. Finally if you're up at the *Dominion Museum* there's a coffee bar with excellent and economically priced sandwiches and snacks.

**Wholefood** The *Victoria Cafe* on the corner of Brougham and Queen streets, at the south end of town, is a pleasant, inexpensive vegetarian wholefood cafe with delicious food and live entertainment on weekend evenings. It's open for lunch and dinner every day except Sundays.

**Pub Food** Yes, there's a *Cobb & Co*, it's in the St George's Hotel on Willis St opposite the Manners Mall McDonald's. It's open the usual 7.30 am to 10 pm hours and serves the usual reliable Cobb & Co pub menu.

Other places with straightforward pub food include the *Victorian* on Lambton Quay. It has three bars, three menus, lunches from noon to 2 pm and the usual pub food, with a good choice of steaks, schnitzels, ham steaks and so on from around $10 to $15. It's open Monday to Saturday for lunch and dinner. Or move along Lambton Quay to the *Romney Arms* on Plimmer's Steps, with similar ambience, food and prices.

On Plimmer's Steps in *Plimmer's Tavern* there's the fairly smooth and slick *No Names*

*Bar* with main courses around $15 to $18. *Robbie Burns* on Kent Terrace also has pub food.

**Restaurants – Chinese** Wellington is positively weighed down with Chinese restaurants. They nearly outnumber everything else put together, in fact they probably outnumber all the rest of the Chinese restaurants in New Zealand put together. There are so many along Courtenay Place it's almost a Chinatown. The menus feature all the Cantonese regulars with main courses generally in the $10 to $16 bracket. Because of the great number of Chinese restaurants here there's a popular belief that the prices are lower and the quality higher than in New Zealand in general. My (admittedly limited) experience has been that Wellington's Chinese restaurants are very unexciting – the usual dollop of dull vegetables topped by the usual gluggy sauce. Why, when Cantonese food can be so terrific, is it almost always so dull?

Amongst the many, you might try the *Horn Kung* on Courtenay Place but Wellington's Chinese eating places all seem pretty similar.

**Restaurants – Other Cuisines** The *Mexican Cantina*, at 19 Edward St near the Manners Mall McDonald's, is great value. They have all the usual Mexican dishes – enchiladas, tacos, etc – from around $3.50 to $5 and some choice for vegetarians. Main meals are around $9 to $12. It's open for lunch from noon to 2 pm on weekdays, and every evening from 5.30 to 9.30 pm – get there early though as there may be a queue, it's a very popular spot.

Nearby at 95 Dixon St, *Chevy's* is a colourful pseudo-US restaurant with fancy burgers from $12 to $15 and plenty of other US-style fast meals including (for $12) a Ronald Reagan omelette. Made to Nancy's own recipe of course. It's licensed and wine costs $3.50 a glass, beers $3.50 to $5. The car on the menu is a '57 Chevy.

In the same area, more or less behind the Mexican Cantina, is another Wellington institution – *Armadillo* at 129 Willis St. It proved so popular that it's been exported (in a much larger but equally crowded version) to Auckland where the menu is identical. The food here is Texan. Or 'cowboy'. Which means ribs, southern chicken, burgers, etc. It's not cheap at $17 for main courses, $10 for starters, but you get plenty of food and the place, complete with its John Wayne decor, is lots of fun. 'At one point the patrons started batting around a beach ball,' reported one visitor. 'When the firecrackers started flying we left.'

There are all manner of 'ethnic' cuisines around Wellington including Burmese food at *Monsoon*, 124 Cuba Mall. Burmese cuisine is nothing to get too excited about – just straightforward curries – but the only other place in the whole world I've seen a Burmese restaurant (apart from in Burma of course) is San Francisco so this is a rare opportunity. Main courses range from $8.50 to $17.50 and they also have Singapore-Malaysian and Chinese food. They're open for lunch from noon to 2.30 pm on weekdays and for dinner from 5.30 to 10.30 pm Monday to Saturday.

Other ethnic restaurants around Wellington include the licensed *Genghis Khan* Mongolian barbecue restaurant with 'bottomless portions' at 25 Majoribanks St. The licensed *Middle East* restaurant, upstairs at the Regent Centre in Manners Mall, has belly dancing on Saturday nights. There's authentic Malaysian cuisine at *Yuyi*, 45 Ghuznee St; Indonesian food at *Toko Baru*, 146 Featherston St; Thai food at *Sala Thai*, 134 Cuba St; Greek food at *Emmanuel's*, 41 Vivian St; Indian food at *Shamiana*, on the corner of Victoria and Dixon streets; and Japanese food, with traditional tatami mat seating, at *Sakura*, up on the 3rd floor at 181-195 Wakefield St. And the list goes on! Check the *Capital Times* weekly for still more ethnic possibilities.

More familiar territory is covered by a number of Italian restaurants including *La Spaghettata* at 15 Edward St, beside the Mexican Cantina. The pasta is good and the setting pleasant. Or try *Mangiare* at 35

Dixon St, a long-standing favourite for pasta, open every evening except Monday with main dishes around $10. Nearby is the *Casa Cafe*, serving inexpensive Italian lunches, dinners and pizza.

Wellington has a number of other Indian restaurants including the licensed *Bengal Tiger* at the corner of Dixon and Willis streets. Tandoori food is a speciality here but we're getting into the expensive night out category by this time. Of course if you really want an expensive night out there's plenty of opportunity for that in Wellington.

## Entertainment

**Pubs** There are lots of pubs with music in the evenings and also good places just for a drink. In the centre the *Victorian* at the parliament end of Lambton Quay has three popular bars for a drink and they also have entertainment and food (see Pub Food).

Just off Lambton Quay beside the cable car entrance is the *Marble Bar*, a pleasantly relaxed after-the-office bar. There are lots of pubs along Lambton Quay. Further along Lambton Quay is the *Romney Arms Tavern* on levels one and two of the Williams Centre on Plimmer's Steps. It's a fairly new place, good for a drink or evening entertainment.

Further up Plimmer's Steps are the *No Names Bar* and the *Carpark*, a late-night licensed cafe with entertainment Tuesday to Saturday which could include rhythm & blues, jazz, comedy, dance or disco, with a weekly jam session. *Paisley Park* at 24 Taranaki St is a similar late-night cafe, it's open every night from 7 pm to 1 am and has entertainment several times weekly. More posh pubs include the *Oxford* on Lambton Quay and the *Arena* on Wakefield St.

If you're staying at the YHA hostel the *Thorndon Tavern* on Molesworth St is about halfway downhill towards the railway station. There's evening entertainment there too. Also near the youth hostel the *Western Park* at 285 Tinakori Rd is another place with music. Check the Thursday *Evening Post* entertainment section for current musical happenings around Wellington.

**Discos & Nightclubs** *Alfie's* is a disco on the 1st floor at the corner of Dixon and Cuba streets. Popular nightclubs include *Exchequer* on Plimmer's Steps, *Candyo's* in Manners St and *Spats* on the corner of Victoria and Harris streets.

**Theatre** Wellington supports a number of professional theatre companies. *Downstage Theatre* presents plays in the Hannah Playhouse on the corner of Cambridge Terrace and Courtenay Place. *Depot Theatre* at 12a Alpha St specialises in NZ drama, with new and Maori drama and local themes. *Circa Theatre* at 1 Harris St presents a variety of drama; *Bats Theatre* at 1 Kent Terrace is more avant-garde, alternative theatre. The *Wellington Repertory Theatre* at 13 Dixon St is a community theatre company.

**Shows & Films** The State Opera House in Manners St, the Michael Fowler Centre in Wakefield St, the Wellington Town Hall at Mercer and Wakefield streets and the Victoria University Theatre are all popular performance venues, check the newspapers for current shows.

The *Wellington Film Society* (tel 893-252) shows films at the Embassy, the University, and the National Museum Theatre.

**Vivian St** Vivian St around Cuba St is Wellington's very low key red light district with the odd extremely seedy strip joint or massage parlour. Plus, late at night, Kiwi ladies-of-the-night leaning acutely into the wind.

## Getting There & Away

**Air** Due to the lack of level land around the city Wellington Airport is very cramped and until recently this limited the number of international flights which could use the airport – it was simply too small for 747s. Now that Qantas and Air New Zealand both operate 767s there are regular flights to and from Australia.

Air New Zealand's travel centre (tel 859-922) is at 129-141 Vivian St. To get to the South Island you have to take the ferry or fly so there are many flights in and out of Wellington. Direct connections include Auckland, Blenheim, Christchurch, Dunedin, Gisborne, Hamilton, Invercargill, Napier, Nelson, New Plymouth, Oamaru, Palmerston North, Rotorua, Taupo, Timaru, Wanganui and Whakatane.

Other airlines serving Wellington include Air Nelson (tel 726-034) with direct flights to Blenheim, Motueka, Nelson, Palmerston North, Timaru and Westport. Mt Cook Airlines (tel 885-020) has direct flights to Christchurch, Nelson, Rotorua and Taupo. Ansett New Zealand (tel 711-044) has direct flights to Auckland and Christchurch.

There are also a couple of smaller carriers hopping across the Cook Strait to towns at the northern end of the South Island. They can make an interesting alternative to the ferry but note that the strait can be just as bumpy up above as it so often is at sea level. Skyferry/Outdoor Aviation (tel 888-380) has flights to Picton for $45 and other connections to places on the South Island close to the straits. This isn't that much more than the ferry fare but you do have to get to and from the airports at both ends. On the South Island the airport is 8 or 9 km out of Picton and the shuttle bus into town costs $2.75 (children $1).

Float Air Picton (tel Picton 36-433) operates a floatplane between Wellington and Picton, cost is $46. On the Wellington side it departs from Porirua Harbour.

**Bus** Wellington is an equally important junction for bus travel; all the services meet here whether you're coming south from Auckland and the central North Island attractions like Rotorua, Taupo and Tongariro; east from New Plymouth and Wanganui; or west from Napier and Gisborne. It takes about 12 hours to or from Auckland, 7 hours to Taupo, 8 hours to Rotorua, 6 hours to New Plymouth, 5 hours to Napier or 1½ hours to Palmerston North.

InterCity buses operate from the railway station (tel 725-399, 725-409) and go to all of these places.

Newmans (tel 851-149) have two routes

into Wellington – one from Napier, Taupo and Rotorua, the other from Wanganui, New Plymouth, Hamilton and Auckland. Newmans buses depart from the city bus terminal on Stout St, opposite the railway station.

Mt Cook have a service from Auckland via Taupo to Wellington, with connections from Taupo to Rotorua and Napier. Another route goes from Wellington to Napier via Palmerston North. The Mt Cook terminal (tel 885-020) is on the corner of Taranaki St and Courtenay Place but they also stop opposite the railway station.

The Kiwi Experience bus goes between Wellington and Auckland weekly. See the introductory Getting Around chapter.

**Train** Wellington Railway Station (tel 725-399, 725-409) is a travellers' centre and meeting place; it would be a bad day not to come across at least one backpacker here. You can leave gear in the left luggage area – it's a free service if you hold a train, ferry, or InterCity bus ticket; otherwise it costs $2 per item each day. The luggage area is open from 7 am to 8.45 pm on weekdays, and from 7.30 am to noon and again from 5 to 8.45 pm on weekends. Since the station's Information Centre closed, the luggage staff do their best to provide information to arriving travellers!

You can walk from the railway station to the ferry terminal in 20 minutes but there's also a free shuttle bus which goes from the railway station to the ferry terminal 35 minutes before each sailing.

The Silver Fern train operates between Wellington and Auckland Monday to Saturday, departing each end around 8.30 am and arriving around 6.30 pm. The Northerner train runs overnight between Wellington and Auckland, Sunday to Friday. The Endeavour train operates daily between Wellington and Napier, a 5½ hour trip.

**Sea** The Cook Strait ferry service shuttles back and forth between Wellington and Picton. There are usually four services daily in each direction and the crossing takes about

3 hours. Fares are $24.50 bargain fare, $30.50 standard fare. Bargain means most of the time, standard means holiday periods, including the May, August-September and December-January school holidays. Children travel at half price.

Day excursion return fares cost the same as one-way fares and there are a variety of short excursion fares, weekend saver fares, family fares, group fares and so on which provide a substantial discount. Cars or motorhomes cost from around $77 to $102 bargain fare, $102 to $132 standard fare. Bicycles cost $13, motorcycles $25 to $31.

At peak periods you must book well ahead, the ferries can be booked solid at certain popular holiday times. In fact it's not a bad idea to book ahead anytime to be sure of getting on, especially if you're taking a vehicle. All of the discount fares (except the day excursions) *must* be booked in advance, they are not available at the ferry terminal. You can book up to 6 months in advance at any InterCity bus or railway station or NZTP office and at many travel agents.

There are connecting buses to and from the ferry and in Wellington there's a free shuttle bus from the railway station to the ferry terminal, departing 35 minutes before each ferry sailing.

If you're planning to hitch out of Picton note that the cars are driving off the ferry almost as soon as the ferry docks. Foot passengers are likely to find every vehicle has gone by the time their feet hit terra firma! Try to hitch a ride while you're still at sea. Also keep your baggage with you or remove all valuables. Travellers have discovered their packs have been gone through and cameras or other items of value removed during the crossing.

**Hitching** It's not easy to hitch out of Wellington because that long stretch out of the city through Lower Hutt is built up all the way. It's probably best to catch a train at least as far as Porirua, or possibly to Paekakariki – it's an awkward road to hitch on wherever you are.

## Getting Around

**Airport Transport** Super Shuttle (tel 878-787) is a 24 hour door-to-door airport transport service. Cost is $8 for one person, $10 for two, and it also serves the bus and railway stations.

Tranzit Coachlines (tel 872-018) operate an airport express bus which runs along a convenient route through the city, beginning at the railway station. Cost is $4.50 one way or $7 return. It runs half-hourly from 6 am to 9.30 pm on weekdays, 7 am to 7.30 pm on Saturdays, and 7 am to 9.30 pm on Sundays. A taxi to the airport will cost around $11. There are left luggage lockers at the airport.

**Bus** Wellington City Transport runs the local central city bus services. Most local buses and the airport bus start from beside the railway station. Buses on most routes operate 7 days a week, and evenings too, with buses going as late as 11 pm – unlike most places in New Zealand! Phone Busline (tel 859-955) for all transport questions. There's a useful Bus Route Guide leaflet with a map showing the routes and information on which bus to use to get to the various attractions. A *Bus & Walk* leaflet describes how to bus to and from 16 different walkways and tracks. Bus leaflets and timetables are available at the PR office.

Bus fares start at 80 cents and step up to $2.40. A five-ride Downtowner ticket costs $2.20 and can be used on buses and cable cars, but only within the city centre. Or you can get a Daytripper ticket which covers an adult and two children for unlimited travel on buses and cable cars for one whole day (weekday rush hours excepted) for $5.50.

**Train** New Zealand Railways run the country's only electrified suburban train operation in Wellington, with quite good services along the two northern corridors.

**Bicycle Rental** Penny Farthing Cycle Shop (tel 852-279) at 65 Courtenay Place rents bicycles for $20 per day, or $15 per day if you keep it for a week. A $40 bond is refunded when you return the bike.

## AROUND WELLINGTON

### Tramway Museum

The Tramway Museum is 45 km north of Wellington in Queen Elizabeth Park, just past Paekakariki, where there are picnic and swimming spots. It's open weekends and holidays only from 11 am to 5 pm. You can have a ride for a small charge and there are static displays as well. The Engine Shed, a steam locomotive museum, is also at Paekakariki. It's open from 9 am to 5 pm on Saturdays.

An alternative way to get there is over the scenic Paekakariki Hill road. North of Paekakariki is a string of good, sandy beaches.

### Southward Car Museum

Also out of town the Southward Car Museum at Paraparaumu has one of the largest private car exhibits in the southern hemisphere, with nearly 100 cars on display. They include the three oldest cars in New Zealand including the 1895 Benz which is the oldest of the lot. Admission is $2.50 (children $1) and it's open from 9 am to 5 pm daily but getting there isn't too easy by public transport.

### Masterton

In the sheep raising Wairarapa area, Masterton has few notable attractions although it's a reasonable size town. The large Queen Elizabeth Park in Masterton has sports grounds, bowls and childrens' play-grounds, plus a fine miniature railway where trains are run on weekends. The Wairarapa Arts Centre has several galleries, including a former Wesleyan church and a Museum of Childhood. Trains and buses run frequently between Masterton and Wellington.

Just north of Masterton in the Tararua Forest Park at Mt Bruce there's the Mt Bruce Wildlife Centre, run by DOC. This native bird reserve has aviaries with examples of various rare or endangered species including the takahe and the black stilt. The centre is open from 9.30 am to 4 pm daily. There are several interesting places between Masterton and Napier. Mikimiki, 15 km north, has a pioneer museum.

**Places to Stay** Masterton has hotels, motels, camping sites and the pleasant and friendly *Okiokinga Guest House* (tel 82-970) at 88 Cole St. The *Victoria House Guest House* (tel 80-186) at 15 Victoria St and the *Station Hotel* (tel 89-319) at 145 Perry St are other possibilities.

### Other Attractions

Other attractions out of Wellington include the Gear Homestead at Porirua and Taylor Stace Historic Cottage at Pauatahanui. Ask at the Wellington PR office for the Visitors Guide to the Kapiti Coast, or stop by the Kapiti Information Centre (tel 88-195) in Paraparaumu. There are various scenic reserves and forest parks in the Wellington region, ask about them at the DOC.

# SOUTH ISLAND

# Marlborough & Nelson

To some people, crossing Cook Strait from Wellington to the South Island is like entering a new country. Many visitors strike out further afield immediately after crossing, but there is much of interest in this area, including of course the inlets and bays of Marlborough Sounds.

## Marlborough Sounds

The convoluted waterways of the Marlborough Sounds are the first sight of the South Island from the ferry. To get an idea of how convoluted the sounds are, Pelorus Sound is 42 km long but has 379 km of shoreline!

### History

The first European to come across the Marlborough district was Abel Tasman, who spent 5 days sheltering under the eastern coast of D'Urville Island in 1642. It was to be over 100 years before the next White man, James Cook, turned up in January 1770, remaining there for 23 days. Between 1770 and 1777 Cook made four visits to the stretch of water he named Queen Charlotte's (now Charlotte) Sound. Near the entrance of Ship Cove there's a monument which commemorates the explorer's visits. Because Cook spent so much time there he was able to make detailed reports of the area which made it the best known haven in the southern hemisphere. In 1827 the French navigator Jules Dumont D'Urville discovered the narrow strait now known as French Pass, and his officers named the island just north of there in his honour.

In the same year a whaling station was set up at Te Awaiti in Tory Channel, which brought about the first permanent European settlement in the district. There was much activity in the next few decades until the arrival, in June 1840, of HMS *Herald* with Governor Hobson's envoy, Major Bunbury, on the hunt for Maori signatures to the Treaty of Waitangi. On 17 June Bunbury proclaimed the Queen's sovereignty over the South Island at Horahora Kakahu Island. Towards the end of that year a Wesleyan mission was set up at Ngakuta Bay in the north-western corner of the port.

In spite of this, the Marlborough area was not the site of an organised company settlement; it was more an overflow of the Nelson colony. Around 1840 the opportunistic and unscrupulous New Zealand Company attempted to settle part of the Wairua Plain after buying the alleged rights from the widow of a trader, John Blenkinsopp. He claimed to have bought the land from the Maoris for one 16-pound gun, and obtained a dubious deed signed by illiterate Maori chiefs. The gun is now on display in Blenheim.

By 1843 the pressure for land from the Nelson settlers was so great that it led to conflict with the Maoris, who denied all knowledge that any part of Wairau was sold. Two Maori chiefs, Te Rauparaha and Te Rangihaeata, arrived from Kapiti to resist survey operations. The Whites sent out a hurriedly co-opted armed party led by Arthur

Wakefield and Police Magistrate Thompson to arrest the chiefs. The party was met peacefully by the Maoris at Tuamarina, but the Pakehas precipitated a brief skirmish during which Te Rangihaeata's wife was shot. The Pakehas were forced to surrender and Rangihaeata, mad with rage, demanded vengeance. Twenty-two of the party, including Wakefield and Thompson, were axed to death or shot; the rest escaped through the scrub and over the hills.

Te Rauparaha was a distinctly unsavoury character and indirectly was a major reason for the British government taking control of New Zealand. He cultivated the captains and crews of visiting whaling ships (they nicknamed him the 'old sarpint') and, with muskets and other weapons he acquired, set out on the wholesale and horrific slaughter of other South Island tribes. In his most gruesome raid he was aided by a White trader who transported his warriors and decoyed the opposing chiefs on board where they

were set upon by Te Rauparaha's men. The ensuing slaughter virtually wiped out the tribe. When news of this event, and the captain's part in it, reached Sydney the British Government finally decided to bring some law and order to New Zealand and to their unruly citizens operating there.

At least, that is the reputation that has been ascribed to Te Rauparaha – a reputation that has been questioned in a biography entitled *Te Rauparaha: A New Perspective*.

In March 1847 Wairau was finally bought and added to the Nelson territory. It was not long before the place was deluged by people from Nelson and elsewhere. However, when the Wairau settlers realised that revenue from land sales in their area was being used to develop the Nelson district they petitioned for the separation and independence of the area. The appeal was successful and the colonial government called the new province Marlborough and approved one of the two settlements, Waitohi (now Picton) as the capital. At the same time, the other settlement known as 'The Beaver' was renamed Blenheim. After a period of intense rivalry between the two towns, including legal action, the capital was transferred peacefully to Blenheim in 1865.

## THE SOUNDS

The convoluted waters of the Marlborough Sounds have many bays, islands, coves and waterways, formed by the sea invading its deep valleys – an ideal holiday area. Parts of the sounds are now included in the Marlborough Sounds Maritime Park. The park is actually many smaller reserves separated by private land.

### Information

The best way to get around the sounds is by boat, but the road system has been extended. Permits are required for hunting or camping and there's lots of good swimming, tramping and fishing. Information on the park is available in Picton from the Information Centre and the DOC.

### Activities

Marlborough Sounds Adventure Company (tel Picton 42-534, 42-301) organises sea-kayak trips and bushwalks around the sounds. The kayak trips range from 2 days ($190) or 3 days ($290) up to expeditions of 4 to 10 days (from $390). Prices include the kayak, guide, camping equipment and all meals. They also hire kayaks for solo trips at a daily cost of $30 for a single kayak or $45 for a double kayak; the rates are $10 less per day after 3 days.

### Places to Stay

There are various places to stay on the sounds, some of them accessible only by boat or floatplane. Prices are usually fairly reasonable, and practically all offer free use of dinghies and other activities.

**Hostels** Various other places around the sounds offer cheap backpackers' accommodation and do their bookings through the Pavlova Backpackers Hostel in Picton. They include the *Resolution Bay Camp & Cabins* in Resolution Bay and the *Ferneaux Lodge* on the Endeavour Inlet section of the Queen Charlotte Sound Walkway, both charging just $10 a night. The *Lazy Fish Hostel* (tel Picton 36-055) on Queen Charlotte Sound, 12 km from Picton, is accessible only by boat. Cost in this homestead-turned-hostel is $15 per night and includes free use of windsurfer, dinghy, canoe, fishing gear, snorkels, volleyball, barbecue and so on. The front deck is just 7 metres from the secluded beach. There are only 15 beds here, so be sure to book ahead. In summer lots of boats will take you out there.

**Guest Houses** The *Bulwer Guest House* (tel Rai Valley 26-285) is on Waihinau Bay on Pelorus Sound and has self-contained units and flats for $12 per person or guest house accommodation including all meals for $48 per day. Road access is via Rai Valley.

**Hotels & Lodges** They include the well-known *Portage Hotel* (tel Lochmara 34-309) on Kenepuru Sound. Double rooms here cost at least $92 per night but there is also bunkroom accommodation for $22 per person which still allows you to use all the resort's facilities. The hotel has all sorts of attractions such as sailing, windsurfing, fishing, spa, gym, and tennis. It can easily be reached by road, boat or floatplane from Picton.

The *Raetihi Lodge* (tel Lochmara 34-300), also on Kenepuru Sound, costs $70 per night including all meals. *Hopewell Cottages* (tel Lochmara 34-341) has self-contained cottages ranging from $33 to $41 for two, and the *St Omer Guest House* (tel Lochmara 34-086) has cottage accommodation from $18 to $22 per person, or chalets for $65 per person including all meals. There's road access to all of these places on Kenepuru Sound.

At the *Te Pangu Bay Lodge* (tel Picton 39-755) on Te Pangu Bay, Tory Channel, self-contained units for two to seven people cost $20 per person (minimum unit charge $30). The *Tira-Ora Lodge* (tel Lochmara 34-253) on Northwest Bay, Pelorus Sound, is more expensive; rooms there cost $88 per night for one or two people. Both lodges can only be reached by boat or floatplane.

**Resorts & Cabins** There are cabins at *Gem Resort* (tel Picton 39-245) at the Bay of Many Coves. Cabins for two cost between $42 and $56; there's no road access. The *Te Rawa Boatel* (tel Lochmara 34-285), 27 km by launch from Havelock, is a bit cheaper, with rooms between $36 and $45 for two people. *Punga Cove Tourist Resort* (tel Lochmara 34-561) on Endeavour Inlet, Charlotte Sound, is more expensive; double rooms cost between $60 and $100 per night.

### Getting Around

The 'mail run' boat runs to the Lazy Fish Hostel on Queen Charlotte Sound all year round on Mondays, Tuesdays, Thursdays and Fridays, and costs about $15. A water taxi costs about the same if you have a group of four to split the $60 fare. See the Picton and Havelock sections for information about transport around the sounds.

### PICTON

The ferry from the North Island comes into Picton, a pretty little port at the head of Queen Charlotte Sound. Picton, a small borough with a population of about 4000, is a hive of activity when the ferry is in and during the peak of summer, but rather slow and sleepy any other time.

### Information

The Information Centre (tel 37-513) is in the car park between the ferry terminal and the town centre. From mid-December to Easter it's open from 9.30 am to 4.30 pm Monday to Friday and from 10 am to 3 pm on weekends. During the holiday period from mid-December to the end of January it's also open from 7 to 8 pm every day. During the slower period between Easter and mid-December it's open from 10 am to 3 pm every day. It has good maps, information on boats and walking in the sounds area, and some interesting exhibits.

The DOC (tel 37-582) offices, on the 1st

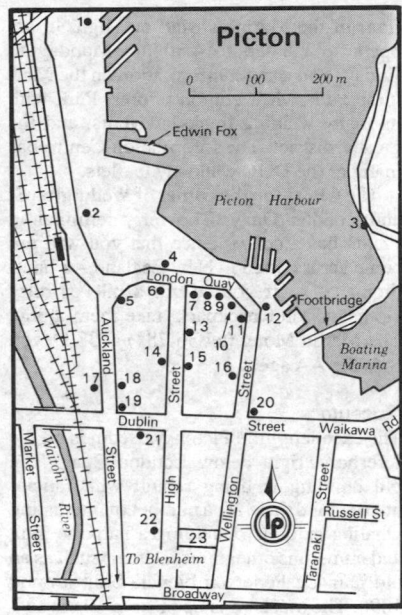

| | |
|---|---|
| 1 | Cook Strait Ferry Terminal |
| 2 | Information Centre |
| 3 | 'Echo' Marlborough Cruising Club |
| 4 | Museum |
| 5 | New Zealand Experience |
| 6 | Terminus Hotel |
| 7 | Dairy & Tea Rooms |
| 8 | Hotel Federal |
| 9 | Seaspray Cafe |
| 10 | Oxley's Hotel |
| 11 | Village Cafe |
| 12 | CPO |
| 13 | Marlborough Fare |
| 14 | Ship Cove, Tides Inn |
| 15 | Book Exchange |
| 16 | 5th Bank Restaurant |
| 17 | Southern Cross Car Rental |
| 18 | Pavlova Backpackers Hostel |
| 19 | Picton Bakery |
| 20 | Whalers Inn |
| 21 | Youth Hostel |
| 22 | Picton Seafoods |
| 23 | Mariners Mall, Department of Conservation (DOC) |

floor of the Mariners Mall on High St, are open from 8 am to 4.30 pm Monday to Friday. You can get information on the Maritime Park, Mt Richmond Forest Park with its many walking tracks and huts, and the greater district. The Information Centre has many of the DOC walkway leaflets.

The CPO is on the corner of Wellington St and London Quay. The ferry terminal in Picton has a convenience that you will not come across often in New Zealand – a laundromat – so if you've got a pile of dirty clothes in your backpack, take them along. The Marlin Motel (tel 36-784) at 33 Devon St is the AA agent.

### Museum

The excellent little Picton Museum is on the foreshore, right below London Quay. The old building is being rebuilt with fancier quarters and there are a number of interesting whaling exhibits, including a harpoon gun, and numerous other unusual items such as an old Dursley Pederson bicycle built around 1890. The museum is open from 10 am to 4 pm daily; admission is $1 (children 50 cents).

### The Edwin Fox

Between the museum and the ferry wharf is the battered, but still floating, hull of the old East Indiaman *Edwin Fox*. Built of teak in the Bengal region of India the 48 metre, 760 ton vessel was launched in 1853 and in its long and varied career carried convicts to Perth, troops to the Crimean War and immigrants to New Zealand. Later she was one of the first vessels to operate as a cold store with the most up-to-date freezing machinery in its time. The ship arrived in Picton in 1897 and was used as a coal hulk for the Picton Freezing Works until the mid-1950s. It sat unused next to the freezing works until it was towed to Shakespeare Bay in 1967. The *Edwin Fox* remained a hulk on the beach there until 1986 when it was refloated and towed back to Picton.

Plans for the restoration of the *Edwin Fox* have now been drawn up. Progress has been impeded by lack of funding but work will begin when the funds are raised. The project will take at least 10 years to complete, and may cost several million dollars – but that should keep the boat in the water for another 200 years! All the original methods and materials will be used to restore the ship to its original condition, and it will remain open throughout the restoration process so you can see the work actually under way. The metal-sheathed hull is open to visitors from 8.45 am to 5 pm every day (closing at 4.30 pm in winter) and admission is $2 (children $1, family $5). A small maritime museum has been started upstairs.

### The Echo

On the other side of Shakespeare Bay, across the inlet from the town centre via the footbridge, is the scow *Echo*, now used as the clubrooms of the Marlborough Cruising Club. Built on the Wairau River in 1905, the *Echo* traded between Blenheim and Wellington, shipping around 14,000 tons of freight a year, and was only retired in 1965 after the railway ferries were introduced.

### Walks

There are many scenic bushwalks around Picton as well as longer tramps. The Information Centre has a map showing several good walks in and near town, as well as others further afield in the sounds and the Maritime Park. The DOC also has plenty of maps and leaflets on walks in the area.

An easy 1 km track runs along the eastern side of Picton Harbour to Bob's Bay where there's a barbecue area in a sheltered cove. There's also the Tarahunga Walkway, beginning in Newgate St behind the hospital, which takes about 45 minutes each way and offers a good view of Picton and the sounds.

Queen Charlotte Drive, the road between Picton and Havelock, has nice scenery but hostile sandflies. Walk up Queen Charlotte Drive for about 5 minutes for an excellent lookout over Picton.

### Other Attractions

The New Zealand Experience is a multi-screen show and assorted amusements on the corner of London Quay and Auckland St. It's open daily from 9.15 am to 5 pm with shows every 30 minutes; admission is $6.50 (children $3.50, family $14).

Creek Pottery on High St has interesting pottery and other local crafts.

Out of Picton is Port Underwood, the scene of great whaling activity in the 19th century. The narrow winding road from Waikawa to Rarangi has magnificent views of the North Island silhouetted against the horizon.

Near Koromiko, 6 km south of Picton, is one of the ubiquitous deer parks – complete with picnic area and children's playground – that are scattered around both islands. Tuamarina, 13 km further on, is historically interesting as the site of the Wairau Massacre. The tree near where the skirmish started still stands on the riverbank. In the cemetery, just above the road, is a White monument designed by Felix Wakefield, the youngest brother of Arthur Wakefield who was killed in the affray.

## Tours

The main access around Queen Charlotte Sound is by water, which means there are innumerable cruises and fishing trips. Ask about them at the Information Centre, or take a stroll down by the wharf, where every operator seems to have a little office set up.

Out on the water there are round-the-bay cruises on the MV *Swansong* including a stop to feed the tame fish at Double Cove. The trips take about 2 hours and cost $25 (children $12.50). The *Swansong* also has luncheon cruises to Punga Cove, lasting from around 10 am to 3 pm. The cost is $38; there's an optional smorgasbord lunch for $13 or you could take a picnic lunch.

Beachcomber Fun Cruises have a number of popular cruises on the MV *Beachcomber* including an all-day 'mail run' cruise around the sounds on Mondays, Tuesdays, Thursdays and Fridays for $36, 2 hour scenic cruises for $25, and evening cruises for $22. Full day trips to the Portage Hotel on Kenepuru Sound are another possibility;

they cost $28. Children travel for half price on all the *Beachcomber* tours.

Picton has several water taxis that can take you anywhere you want to go around the sounds, including the various out-of-the-way hotels and walking tracks that can be reached only by water. Check first, though, with the tour boat operators. Most tour boats will gladly take you along on the tour, dropping you off and picking you up wherever and whenever you wish; they're cheaper than the taxis.

On land, Marlborough Scenic Tours (tel 36-262) and Bramley's Mini Bus Service (tel 37-866) are two local tour operators; winery visits are a speciality. Deluxe Coachlines (tel Blenheim 85-467, 89-539) operate all-day wine trail tours from Blenheim but they also make pick-ups in Picton. Skyline Horse Treks (tel 36-844, 37-787) have 2 hour scenic horse treks for $24 (children $18).

Or you can get up above it all on floatplane flights. Float Air Picton (tel 36-433), between the *Edwin Fox* and the ferry terminal, does scenic flights and normal transport trips to any point around the sounds and also to Lake Rotoiti and Wellington.

The Picton Underwater Centre at 41 Wellington St hires diving equipment for underwater explorations.

## Places to Stay

**Hostels** The *Wedgwood House* (tel 37-797) is an Associate Youth Hostel at 10 Dublin St, close to the centre of town. It's a converted guest house with two, four or six beds to a room; the cost is $13 per night. YHA members get 'mail run' discounts (see the Tours section). You can stay here with or without a YHA card.

The *Pavlova Backpackers* (tel 573-6598) at 34 Auckland St has dorm beds for $13.50 or $15 each in double rooms. It's a well-equipped hostel which also serves as a centre for information and bookings for backpackers' activities around Marlborough Sounds. As at all the other Pavlova hostels, a piece of the famous dessert is served here in the evening.

**Guest Houses** Picton has a number of guest houses and private hotels, including the *Marineland Private Hotel* (tel 36-429) at 28 Waikawa Rd which has a 'shark-free swimming pool'. Single/double rooms are $38/55 with breakfast or there are four self-contained motel units at $66 for two. The *Admiral's Lodge* (tel 36-590) at 22 Waikawa Rd has single/double rooms for $34/50; low-season discounts.

**Hotels** The *Federal Hotel* (tel 36-077) on the waterfront has single/double rooms at $28/40.

**Motels** Picton has plenty of motels, most priced at around $60 for two. The *Tourist Court Motel* (tel 36-331), in the centre of town at 45 High St, is a simple place with studio units from around $52 for two or two-bedroom units for $62; low-season discounts might be available. The *Sunnyvale Motel* (tel 36-800), 5 km out at Waikawa Bay, is also good value at $56 for two.

**Camping & Cabins** The *Blue Anchor Holiday Park* (tel 37-212), on Waikawa Bay Rd about 500 metres from the town centre, has sites at $18 for two, various cabins for around $26 to $39 for two, and more expensive tourist flats. The *Alexander's Motor Park* (tel 36-378) is a km out on Canterbury St and has sites at $8 per person, plus a variety of cabins and on-site caravans at $22 to $32 for two.

The *Parklands Marina Holiday Village* (tel 36-343) is on Beach Rd at Waikawa Bay, 3 km from town. Other possibilities include *Waikawa Bay Caravan Park* (tel 37-434) and *Momorangi Bay Motor Camp* (tel 37-865), on Queen Charlotte Drive 13 km from Picton. The Momorangi Bay site has dinghies for hire.

## Places to Eat

**Snacks & Fast Food** Most food would be better than the junk you get on the ferry, but you're unlikely to find much on offer early in the morning or late at night. In any case Picton doesn't offer many real taste treats

although there are plenty of takeaways and fast-food places around the town centre. Try the *Village Cafe* on Wellington St; the sign announces 'A Good Eating Place'. There are several cafes along the waterfront including the attractive little *Seaspray Cafe*. Or there's the *Sandwich Maker* on High St, the *London Quay Dairy & Tea Rooms* on the corner of London Quay and High St, and the *Carousel* takeaway next door.

The *Marlborough Fare* coffee lounge-restaurant on High St has strong coffee, good sit-down lunchtime specials, and takeaways.

Further down High St, *Picton Seafoods* has good fish & chips and pizzas, and it's one of the few places open late – until 8 pm from Sunday to Wednesday, 11 pm on Thursdays, and until midnight on Fridays and Saturdays. The Picton Bakery is on the corner of Auckland and Dublin streets.

**Pub Food** There are three pubs along London Quay and all three – the *Terminus*, the *Federal* and *Oxley* – have pub food, with bistro meals from about $6 to $8.

**Restaurants** The *5th Bank* on Wellington St is an expensive restaurant; seafood, steak or vegetarian main courses cost from $14 to $22. A block away at 33 High St, the licensed *Ship Cove* and the BYO *Tides Inn* in the same arcade are both rather fancy, with main courses from about $12 to $16. Across the road is the simpler *Americano Restaurant* where main courses are around $10 to $12. The *Terminus*, the *Federal* and *Oxley* hotels on London Quay also have licensed restaurants.

## Getting There & Away

**Air** Skyferry (tel Picton 37-888, Wellington 888-380) has a regular service across the strait to and from Wellington. The short flight costs $45 and operates about six times a day. The Picton airstrip is at Koromiko, 8 km out of town, and a shuttle bus connects to the flights for $2.75 (children $1).

The floatplane operated by Float Air Picton (tel 36-433) also flies to and from Wellington, where it lands at Porirua

Harbour. The one-way fare is $46. It also does local and scenic flights around the Marlborough Sounds and to Lake Rotoiti.

**Bus** Delta Landline (tel Blenheim 81-408) has a daily service between Picton and Blenheim and on to Greymouth via Wairau Valley, Lake Rotoiti (St Arnaud), Murchison and Reefton. Deluxe Coach Services (tel Blenheim 85-467, 89-645) runs a bus from Picton to Blenheim at least three times daily on weekdays and once or twice a day on weekends.

All and sundry seem to have services from Picton south to Christchurch. Mt Cook Landline buses (tel 37-277) continue all the way to Dunedin and Invercargill. Newmans (tel 36-687) has services through Blenheim around the northern coast to Havelock, Nelson, Motueka and Takaka with connections to Collingwood. They also have buses heading south-west through Nelson to Westport and Greymouth, and south through Kaikoura to Christchurch and Dunedin.

InterCity (tel 37-515) has a bus route south to Christchurch with connections on to Dunedin and Invercargill, and another route east to Nelson via Blenheim and Havelock with connections to Greymouth and the glaciers. At least one bus daily on each of these routes connects with a ferry sailing to and from Wellington.

A small private bus company, Picton Connections, has daily buses between Picton and Nelson, stopping at Havelock and Rai Valley. Unlike InterCity and Newmans, which go via Blenheim, this bus takes the more scenic Queen Charlotte Drive route. There's also the Corgi Passenger Truck (tel 37-125), a new shuttle service providing cheap transport from Picton to Nelson, Kaikoura and other places. The shuttle holds four to nine passengers; the larger the group, the less each person pays.

The Flying Kiwi bus departs from Picton once a month for a tour of the South Island. See the Bus section in the Getting Around chapter for details.

All buses serving Picton operate from the ferry terminal, except for InterCity which operates from the railway station nearby. It takes about 3 hours by bus from Picton to Nelson, 2 hours to Kaikoura, and 5 or 6 hours to Christchurch.

**Train** The train between Picton and Christchurch, via Blenheim and Kaikoura, operates daily in each direction and takes about 5½ hours. The train connects with the ferry and a free shuttle service is provided between the railway station and ferry terminal on both sides of the strait.

**Car** There are basically two directions you can take to the rest of the South Island from Picton: the west coast route and the east coast route. If you opt for the east coast route it's a straight run south from Picton through Blenheim and on down SH 1. If you're heading west, you can either take the scenic Queen Charlotte Drive westwards from Picton, or go south to Blenheim and head west from there.

**Ferry** The inter-island ferry service shuttles back and forth between Wellington and Picton. There are usually four services daily in each direction and the crossing takes about 3 hours. See the Getting There & Away section in the Wellington chapter for fares and details.

**Hitching** Hitching out on SH 1 towards Blenheim is possible if you've got patience. It can take a few hours to get a ride or at other times you may not get one at all. Most traffic is on the road just after a ferry arrives – there is not much between sailings. The trouble with being on the road just after the ferry docks is that every other hitchhiker is there as well, so it doesn't necessarily make for easier hitching at that time.

If you're heading west, the best bet is to go south to Blenheim and head west from there.

On average it will take a day to reach Christchurch or Nelson. Queen Charlotte Drive between Picton and Havelock is the shortest way to Nelson but has little traffic so it's easier to hitch via Blenheim on the

Spring Creek bypass: follow the Blenheim road (SH 1) 22 km to Spring Creek, where you turn right towards Renwick.

## Getting Around
**Airport Transport** A shuttle bus connects Picton with flights to and from the Picton airstrip at Koromiko for $2.75 (children $1).

**Car Rental** Avis, Hertz, Thrifty, Budget and Avon all have rental offices at the ferry terminal. Southern Cross has an office at 27 Auckland St.

**Motorbike Rental** 'Nifty fifty' 50 cc motorbikes (no motorcycle licence needed) can be hired from the kiosk beside the CPO. The cost is $12 for the first hour and $8 per hour thereafter.

## BLENHEIM
Population 23,000
The largest town in the Marlborough Sounds region, Blenheim is 29 km south of Picton, on the Wairau Plains – a contrasting landscape to the sounds – at the junction of the Taylor and Opawa rivers. The town is particularly well laid out, but more by accident than design as the early development was confined to the high ground to avoid the swamp in the centre. The swamp has been reclaimed and is now Seymour Square with its attractive lawns and gardens.

## Information
The Information Centre (tel 84-480) is on the corner of Queen and Arthur streets. It has a number of DOC maps and leaflets on the many walkways around the Marlborough Sounds and environs. The centre is open from 9 am to 5 pm Monday to Friday. The AA office (tel 83-399) is at 23 Maxwell Rd on the corner of Seymour St. The DOC (tel 88-099) has an office on the same corner at 68 Seymour St.

## Parks & Museums
The 5½ hectare Brayshaw Museum Park, off New Renwick Rd, has several attractions including a reconstructed village of colonial

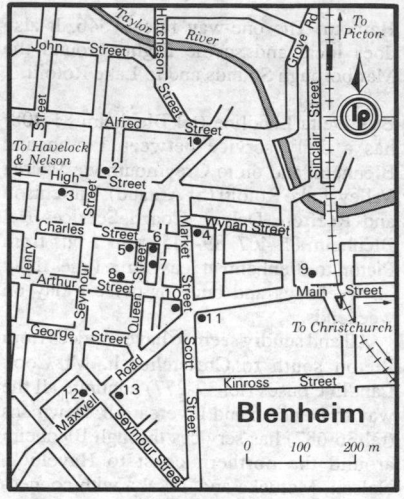

| | |
|---|---|
| 1 | Criterion Hotel |
| 2 | Blenkinsopp's Cannon |
| 3 | Cobb & Co |
| 4 | Raffles |
| 5 | Supermarket |
| 6 | Louie's |
| 7 | Air New Zealand |
| 8 | Information Centre |
| 9 | Pizza Hut |
| 10 | Cafe Marlborough |
| 11 | CPO |
| 12 | Department of Conservation (DOC) |
| 13 | Automobile Association (AA) |

buildings designed to recreate colonial Blenheim, early farming equipment, a miniature railway, a model boating pond, and the Museum and Archives Building. The park is open during daylight hours and admission is free.

Pollard Park and Waterlea Gardens, off Parker St, has a children's playground and a fitness trail; there are flowers blooming all year. The Blenheim Recreation Centre, near the centre on Kinross and Scott streets, has large indoor and outdoor swimming pools, a sauna, mini-golf and a roller skating rink.

Near Seymour Square are relics of Blenheim's violent early history, including the old cannon known as Blenkinsopp's gun which is on the corner of High and Seymour streets. Originally part of the equipment of the whaling ship *Caroline* which Blenkinsopp captained, this is reputedly the cannon for which Te Rauparaha was persuaded to sign over the Wairau Plains and is thus one of the causes of the subsequent massacre at Tuamarina (see the History entry at the start of the Marlborough Sounds section).

### Walks

The Information Centre has details of some interesting walks in the Blenheim area, most some distance from town. About 4 km from the town centre the Wither Hills Walkway, off Taylor Pass Rd, has a viewpoint about 20 minutes from the roadside starting point with excellent views of the Wairau Plains and Cook Strait; on a clear day you can see all the way to the North Island.

### Rainbow Ski Field

Rainbow ski field, 130 km (1½ hours) west of Blenheim, has good skiing for families and beginners. Delta Landline buses from Blenheim stop at the ski field turn-off during the ski season, and a shuttle bus takes you from there up to the slopes.

### Tours

Deluxe Coachlines (tel 85-467) has a 6 hour 'Scenic Wine Trail' tour of local wineries which costs $32 (children $16). If you have your own wheels you can construct your own wine trail tour – pick up a copy of the *Marlborough Wine Trail* map from the Information Centre, showing the location of nine wineries around the Blenheim district.

### Places to Stay

**Guest Houses & Hotels** There are a couple of guest houses to choose from. The *Maple Guest House* (tel 87-375) at 144 High St offers B&B for $25 per person. The more expensive *Koanui Guest House* (tel 87-487) at 33 Main St has B&B for $33 per person.

Rooms at the *Criterion Hotel* (tel 83-299) on Market St cost $50/66 for singles/twins.

**Motels** Reasonably priced motels include the *Raymar Motor Inn* (tel 85-104) at 164 High St, where double rooms cost $55, and the similarly priced *Alpine Motel* (tel 81-604) at 148 Middle Renwick Rd. At most other motels doubles cost from about $60.

**Camping & Cabins** The *A1 Holiday Park* (tel 83-667), at the northern end of town at 78 Grove Rd (SH 1), has sites for $8 per person, cabins from $21 for two and tourist flats from $41. The *Blenheim Motor Camp* (tel 87-419) at 27 Budge St is 1 km from the town centre off SH 1. Sites cost $6 per person ($7 with power), cabins cost from $22 for two, and tourist flats cost $40.

Camping sites further from town include *Duncannon Caravan Park* (tel 88-193), 1.2 km south of town, where caravan sites cost $7 per person and on-site caravans $15 per person. *Grenfelt Caravan Park* (tel 81-259) at 173 Middle Renwick Rd, another caravan park, charges $12 for two people. The *Spring Creek Holiday Park* (tel 25-893), on Rapaura Rd 6 km out towards Picton and about 500 metres off SH 1, has camping sites and cabins.

### Places to Eat

There's a supermarket on the corner of Charles and Queen streets. Otherwise, there's the usual choice of takeaways, pubs and restaurants.

**Snacks & Fast Food** There are plenty of takeaways and cafes around the centre, but this is another Kiwi town where they produce the sort of sandwiches and snacks that give McDonald's a good name. No, McDonald's hasn't got to Blenheim (yet) but there is a *Kentucky Fried Chicken* on the northern side of town and a *Pizza Hut* on Main St near the town centre.

**Pub Food** There's a *Cobb & Co* in the Grosvenor Establishment at 91 High St, on Seymour Square. It's open from 7.30 am to

10 pm every day. Cheaper bar meals are available there at lunch time. The *Criterion* on the corner of Market and Alfred streets also does pub food.

**Restaurants** An exception to the generally low standards of eateries in Blenheim is *Raffles* in the Raffles Hotel at 59 Market St, corner of Wynen St, which serves a variety of international dishes on a constantly changing menu. Lunch (from $5) and dinner (from $10) are served every day. The *Cafe Marlborough*, also on Market St, is a licensed restaurant with a good reputation.

Several of the wineries around Blenheim also serve meals. The *Grove Mill Winery* north of town in Dodson St, off Grove Rd, has pretty good food, as does the *Rocco's* licensed Italian restaurant next door. The *Hunters* and *Merlen* wineries on Rapaura Rd also serve food; at Hunters you can barbecue your own lunch.

### Getting There & Away
**Air** Air New Zealand (tel 85-299), at 29 Queen St, has direct flights to Wellington with connections to other centres. Air Nelson (tel 84-059) has direct flights to Nelson and Wellington, also with connecting flights to other centres. Skyferry (tel 37-888) has flights to and from Wellington from Blenheim and Picton. The Marlborough Aero Club (tel 85-073), which operates from the Omaka Aerodrome, has cheap charter flights to Wellington and other places.

The Picton airstrip at Koromiko is about half way between Blenheim and Picton. The Blenheim airport is on Middle Renwick Rd, about 6 km west of town.

**Bus** See the Picton Getting There & Away section for details on bus services. Deluxe Coachlines (tel 85-467) at 45 Main St has regular services between Blenheim and Picton. Delta Landlines (tel 81-408) at 53 Grove Rd operates a daily service from Picton through Blenheim and on to Greymouth via Lake Rotoiti (St Arnaud), Murchison and Reefton, with connections to Nelson and Westport.

Newmans (tel 80-959), also on Grove Rd, operates on the Picton-Blenheim-Nelson route and the Picton-Blenheim-Christchurch route. From Nelson and Christchurch you can connect to centres further afield.

Mt Cook Landline (tel 85-299) operates from the Delta office on Grove Rd and has a Picton-Blenheim-Christchurch service with connections on to Dunedin and Invercargill.

InterCity (tel 87-049) buses operate from the railway station with services from Picton through Blenheim to Christchurch, Dunedin and Invercargill. West-bound InterCity buses from Picton stop at Blenheim on their way to Havelock, Nelson, Greymouth and the West Coast glaciers.

**Train** The daily Picton to Christchurch train stops at Blenheim.

### Getting Around
You can get a taxi to Blenheim airport from the town centre for about $15.

## HAVELOCK
Population 360
Heading west from Picton or Blenheim, the first town of any size you'll come to is Havelock.

Founded around 1860 and named after Sir Henry Havelock of Indian Mutiny fame, this attractive little town is situated at the confluence of the Pelorus and Kaituma rivers, 43 km from Blenheim and 73 km from Nelson. It's the only place where a main road touches the Pelorus Sound.

Havelock was once the hub of the timber milling and export trade and later became the service centre for gold-mining activites in the area. Today it's a thriving small-boat harbour and a pleasant place to drop off the planet for a couple of days. Havelock is also proud to be the 'green-lipped mussel capital of the world'; you can buy these mussels very cheaply at the packing plants down on the wharf.

### Information
Glenmore Cruises (tel 42-276) in the centre of town acts as the tourist information centre

Top: Picton Harbour (TW)
Bottom: Mutton Cove, Abel Tasman National Park (VB)

for Havelock. The Youth Hostel also has a wealth of information about the area. The DOC (tel 42-019) has a small office on Mahakipawa Rd. The tiny museum is a good source of information on the local history.

### Walks

There's not much to do in the town itself but there are a number of good walks, including the 4 hour return walk to Takorika Summit behind the township and the half-hour walk to Cullen Point from where there are good views of Havelock and the sunset. Glenmore Cruises in Havelock provides boat access to the popular 2 day Nydia Track. The Youth Hostel can supply information on these and other walks.

### Mail Boat Trips

Glenmore Cruises takes passengers along on the mail run boat, stopping at isolated homesteads to deliver mail and supplies. Tea and coffee are available free on board and fishing enthusiasts can try their hand with the bait and handlines which are supplied. If you want to camp or tramp anywhere along the way you can get dropped off and collected again on a specified day. You're on your own, so take what you need. Fresh water is available in some places; ask the locals whether you need to take any.

The trips depart at 9.30 am on Tuesdays, Wednesdays and Thursdays, returning between 5 and 6 pm. Between Christmas and Easter, Glenmore Cruises has various other trips every day except Mondays, including an additional Friday sailing of the mail run boat. The round-trip mail run fare is $40 (children $20) and there's a generous discount to YHA members staying at the Havelock Youth Hostel.

For information and bookings check with the Glenmore Cruises office. If it's shut, try the tearoom across the road or the Youth Hostel. Various other cruises and fishing trips are also available from Havelock, with costs ranging from $18 to $25.

### Places to Stay

**Hostels** The *Havelock Youth Hostel* (tel 42-104) is on the corner of Lawrence St and the main road through town. Nightly cost is $13 in dorm or twin rooms. The hostel occupies an 1881 schoolhouse once attended by Lord Ernest Rutherford, who discovered the atomic nucleus. The manager has information on walks and other local activities including fishing, farmstays, explorations around the Sounds, and more. The hostel is well-equipped with bicycles, billiards, volleyball, piano, guitar and so on.

**Motels** Havelock has a couple of small motels, both on the main road through town. The *Havelock Garden Motel* (tel 42-387) has units at $46 to $56 for two people, with low-season discounts available. The *Pelorus Tavern* (tel 42-412), which has a restaurant and pub, has motel units for $55.

**Camping & Cabins** The *Havelock Motor Camp* (tel 42-339) on Inglis St has camping sites from around $13 for two people ($15 with power). The *Chartridge Tourist Park* (tel 42-129), 6 km south of Havelock on SH 6, has camping sites at $7 per person.

### Places to Eat

The *tearoom* on the main road has snacks and light meals. You can get counter or restaurant meals at the *Pelorus Tavern* and dine overlooking the Havelock marina.

### Getting There & Away

Newmans and InterCity buses both have Picton-Blenheim-Nelson buses that stop at Glenmore Cruises in the centre of Havelock at least once each day. There's a minibus mail service along the Queen Charlotte Drive 'scenic route' between Picton and Havelock, making the return trip in the morning, Monday to Friday. Check at the tearoom or the Youth Hostel for departure times. A private bus company, the Picton Connection, also stops at Havelock on its Picton-Nelson run.

### HAVELOCK TO NELSON

SH 6 from Havelock to Nelson is 75 km of scenic highway, passing the Wakamarina

Valley, Pinedale (also known as Canvastown), the Pelorus Bridge Scenic Reserve and Rai Valley.

### Pinedale (Canvastown)

The tiny township of Pinedale, in the Wakamarina Valley 8 km west of Havelock, got the nickname Canvastown back in the 1860s – gold was discovered in the river in 1860 and by 1864 thousands of canvas tents had sprung up as miners flocked to the prosperous working goldfield, one of the richest in the country. By 1865 the boom was over. Nevertheless gold is still reputed to be in the area and in 1986 a tourist staying at the motor camp panned a 5 gram nugget from the river!

### Activities

Visits to the interesting indoor-outdoor gold-mining museum, gold panning, bush-walking, horse-trekking and trout fishing are all popular activities. The Wakamarina Track, an old gold-miners' trail which passes through the Mt Richmond State Forest Park, begins from Butchers Flat, 15 km into the Wakamarina Valley on the metalled road from Pinedale.

Gold-panning

### Places to Stay

The *Trout Hotel* (tel Havelock 42-120) has single/double rooms at $25/40 and motel units at $50 for two. The *Pinedale Motor Camp* (tel Havelock 42-349) has camping sites for $6 per person and cabins at $20 for two; you can hire gold pans and other equipment there.

### Pelorus Bridge

The Pelorus Bridge Scenic Reserve, 18 km west of Havelock, has interesting walks of between 30 minutes and 3 hours on the Pelorus and Rai rivers, with waterfalls, a 417 metre trig point, a suspension bridge, and the Pelorus Bridge itself. Within the reserve are a tearoom, camping and caravan sites at $3 to $5, and some cabins for about $20 for two people. You can find the ranger at the Rai Valley Tearoom (tel 26-019).

### Rai Valley Pioneer Cottage

At Carluke, 1½ km from the Rai Valley township on the road leading to Tennyson Inlet, is the Rai Valley Pioneer Cottage, a restored pioneer's cottage built in 1881 when the area was still virgin bush. The cottage served as a home to its owner for 28 years and had been used as a sheep shed and chicken house before being restored in 1969 and given to the Historic Places Trust in 1980. There's no charge to see the cottage, but donations are appreciated.

# Nelson

Population 45,200

Nelson is a pleasant, bright and active town. The surrounding area has some of the finest beaches in New Zealand and more sunshine than any other part of the country so it's not surprising that it's a popular holiday area. Apart from beaches and bays, Nelson is noted for its fruit-growing industry and its very energetic local arts and crafts.

### History

The Maoris began to migrate to the South

Island during the 16th century, and among the first to arrive in Nelson were the Ngati-tumatakokiri, or Tumatakokiri. By 1550 this tribe occupied most of the province, as Abel Tasman was to find out to his cost when he turned up at the place he later named Murderers' Bay. Other tribes followed the Tumatakokiri, settling at the mouth of the Waimea River. The Tumatakokiri remained supreme in Tasman Bay until the 18th century when the Ngati-apa from Wanganui and the Ngati-tahu – the largest tribe in the South Island – got together in a devastating attack on the Tumatakokiri, who virtually ceased to exist as an independent tribe after 1800.

The Ngati-apa's victory was short-lived, because between 1828 and 1830 they were practically annihilated by armed tribes from Taranaki and Wellington who sailed into the bay in the largest fleet of canoes ever assembled in New Zealand.

By the time the European settlers arrived there were no Maoris living at Te Wakatu – the nearest pa being at Motueka – and the population of those that remained was so decimated they put up no resistance. The first White settlers sailed in response to advertisements by the New Zealand Company, which was set up by Edward Gibbon Wakefield to colonise the country systematically. His grandiose scheme was to transplant a complete slice of English life from all social classes. In reality 'too few gentlemen with too little money' took up the challenge and the new colony almost foundered in its first few years from lack of money.

The settlement was planned to comprise small but workable farms grouped around central towns. However, the New Zealand Company's entitlement to the land was disputed and it was almost a year before this problem was sorted out. So while the land around the town had been distributed early, the farmland was not available for such a long time that landowners and labourers forced to live in town had whittled away their capital simply to survive.

The Wairau massacre (described in the Marlborough Sounds History section) resulted in the deaths of 22 of Nelson's most able citizens, including Captain Wakefield whose leadership was irreplaceable, and plunged the colony into deep gloom. To make matters worse the New Zealand Company was declared bankrupt in April 1844 and, since nearly three-quarters of the population were dependent on it in some way or another, particularly for sustenance, the situation was so grim as to be near famine. Only the later arrival of hard-working German immigrants saved the region from economic ruin.

## Information

The PR office (tel 82-304), on the corner of Trafalgar and Halifax streets, is open from 7.30 am to 5 pm on weekdays and from 7.30 am to 1 pm on Saturdays. From December to February it's open from 7.30 am to 5 pm every day, including Sundays. This office also acts as a travel agent and makes bookings for everything in town – accommodation, transport, tours and so on. It also serves as Nelson's Transit Centre – all buses serving Nelson arrive and depart from this office. Trafalgar St, which crosses the river just before the Information Centre and runs straight up to the cathedral, is the main street in Nelson.

The DOC (tel 69-335) is a couple of blocks away in the Monroe Building at 186 Bridge St. It has information and good topographical maps on the Nelson and Marlborough area, the Abel Tasman, Heaphy and Wangapeka tracks, and Nelson Lakes National Park. The office is open from 8 am to 4.35 pm Monday to Friday. The AA office is nearby at 45 Halifax St.

If you are on a working holiday there's fruit and tobacco picking and other agricultural work from February to May and there may be some casual daily work at fisheries at the port. Contact the Employment NZ office or individual growers about picking work.

## Cathedral

The focal point of Nelson is its cathedral, at the top of Trafalgar St. The present building

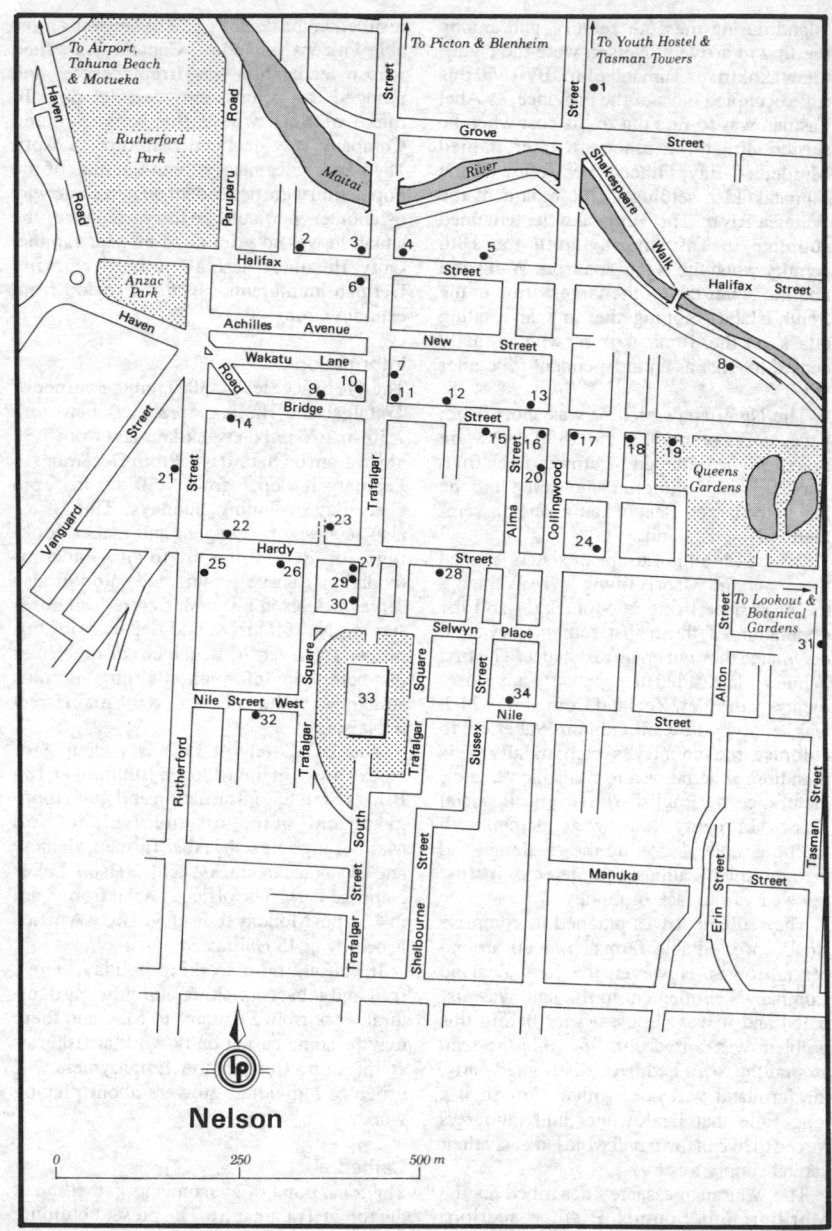

**Nelson**

0          250          500 m

| | |
|---|---|
| 1 | California Guest House |
| 2 | Horatio's Nightclub |
| 3 | Air New Zealand |
| 4 | Information Centre |
| 5 | Automobile Association (AA) |
| 6 | CPO |
| 7 | Pizza My Heart |
| 8 | Riverside Pool |
| 9 | Suburban Bus Company |
| 10 | Cafe de Curb |
| 11 | Pavlova City Hostel |
| 12 | Metropolitan Hotel & Maxine's Night-club |
| 13 | Hitching Post Pizza |
| 14 | Bumbles Hostel |
| 15 | Colonial Restaurant |
| 16 | Royal Hotel |
| 17 | Hotel Wakatu, Cobb & Co |
| 18 | Department of Conservation (DOC) |
| 19 | Suter Art Gallery |
| 20 | Asian Gardens Restaurant |
| 21 | InterCity |
| 22 | Limbo's Nightclub |
| 23 | Cultured Cow Yoghurt |
| 24 | Public Library |
| 25 | McDonald's |
| 26 | City Lights Cafe |
| 27 | Traffers |
| 28 | Pegasus Coffee Bar |
| 29 | Zhivago's |
| 30 | Chez Eelco |
| 31 | 125 Hostel |
| 32 | South St Gallery |
| 33 | Cathedral |
| 34 | Bishop School |

has had a somewhat chequered career. The foundation stone for the cathedral was laid in 1925 but construction dragged on for many years and in the 1950s arguments raged over whether the building should be completed to its orginal design. Eventually construction recommenced to a modified design in the 1960s and was completed in 1967. When the cathedral was finally consecrated in 1972 no less than 47 years had passed since the foundation stone was laid! The cathedral is open from 8 am to 7 pm daily.

## Bishop's School

For about 90 years from 1840, Bishop's School served Nelson as a school. It's on Nile St East and it's open from 2 to 4 pm on Sundays, and on Tuesdays and Thursdays during holiday periods. If you don't find it open during these hours, ask at 28 Nile St. You can read some of the notes and text-books used in the old days.

## Arts & Crafts

The Suter Art Gallery adjoins Queen's Gardens on Bridge St and is open from 10.30 am to 4.30 pm every day. Entry is $1 (children 20 cents, family $2.20). As well as having a permanent art collection it has musical, theatrical and dance performances, art exhibitions, films and craft displays. The gallery takes its name from Bishop Suter, who formed the Bishopdale Sketching Club back in 1889.

Seven Weavers at 36 Collingwood St is a cooperative weavers' workshop where hand-woven articles are designed and made on the premises, many with handspun wool. It's open from 10 am to 4 pm on weekdays.

If you're interested in pottery, visit the South St Gallery, close to the Cathedral on Nile St West. It's open from 10 am to 5 pm Monday to Thursday, 10 am to 7 pm on Fridays, and 10 am to 4 pm on weekends and public holidays.

There are numerous other galleries in the area. Nelson's artistic reputation is partly due to the local clay which attracted many potters to the town. The Nelson Potters Association has a guide leaflet showing where to find the potters in the Nelson area.

## Museums

Founders Park, at 87 Atawhai Drive, is a collection of old Nelson buildings, reflecting the town's early history. It's open from 10 am to 4.30 pm daily and admission is $4 (children $2).

The Nelson Provincial Museum, at Isel Park in the nearby town of Stoke, has an important photographic collection and exhibits on local and Maori history. It's open from 9.30 am to 4.30 pm Tuesday to Friday and from 2 to 5 pm on Saturdays, Sundays and holidays; it's closed on Mondays. Admission is 50 cents on weekends and holidays, but on weekdays it's free. Also in Isel Park is the historic Isel House, open from 2 to 4 pm on Saturdays and Sundays, but only from late October to Easter.

### Gardens & Walks

Nelson has some fine gardens, including the beautiful Botanic Gardens and Queens Gardens. There's a good lookout at the top of Botanical Hill with a spire proclaiming it as the exact geographical centre of New Zealand.

The riverside footpath makes a pleasant stroll through the city and there are many other fine walks and tramps. The Maitai Valley is a particularly restful and beautiful area and the Maungatapu Track leads from here across to the Pelorus River. The PR office has a leaflet called 'Nelson, the City of Walks' outlining 17 good short walks in and around town, many of them good for an evening stroll.

### Beaches

The best-known beach near Nelson is Tahuna, 5 km from the town centre. Rabbit Island is another popular beach, with 13 km of undeveloped beach backed by forest. There's road access to the island but it's closed off after 6 pm daily, and camping is not allowed.

### Other Activities

The Riverside Pool on Halifax St, right beside the river, is within walking distance of the town centre. It costs $1.80 (children $1) to swim in the large indoor heated pool, and there's also a spa pool which costs $3 (children $2) for 20 minutes. The pool is open from 7.30 am to 6 pm on Mondays, Wednesdays and Fridays, from 7 am to 8 pm on Tuesdays and Thursdays, and from 11 am to 5 pm on weekends and holidays. It closes for 6 weeks in July and August.

Nelson offers a wide variety of outdoor activities. At Tahunanui Beach windsurfers, wave skis and body boards can be hired, and there's also a windsurfing school. The Rapid River Rafting Company (tel Nelson 23-110)

and the Ocean River Adventure Company (tel Motueka 88-823) both do white water rafting on the Buller and Gowan rivers. You can go parapenting with Sky High Parapentes (tel 68-711), and the Nelson Aero Club (tel 79-643) offers a variety of scenic flights, very reasonably priced at $20 to $65 for 20 to 60 minutes of flying. The PR office has information on these and many other activities around Nelson.

Camping gear for trips on the Abel Tasman or other tracks can be hired in Nelson from many, in fact most, of the hostels, or from Alp Sports at 123 Bridge St (tel 68-536). Bruce Rollo Ltd (tel 82-363) on Bridge St also has a more limited selection of gear for hire. Prices are usually quite reasonable, around $5 a day for packs and boots, $8 a day for tents. Just about every hostel will also store your excess luggage while you're away on the track, some for free and some for a small fee.

### Tours

There are many tours around Nelson, all of which can be booked through the PR office. Some of the more popular are the Wine Trail tours ($30 to $35), Craft and Scenic Tours (from $18), and the Motueka Horticultural Tour ($18) which visits a number of unusual agricultural operations including tobacco, hop, green tea, kiwi fruit, nashi pear and other fruit farms, with their accompanying tobacco kilns, hop harvesters and packing houses. Farewell Spit Safari Tours ($33) are another popular attraction, departing from Collingwood; transport can be arranged from Nelson (see the Collingwood entry in the Nelson to Golden Bay section).

Backpackers Nelson Trips has a variety of popular cheap day trips, including all-day guided tramps around places such as Lake Rotoiti, Cable Bay, the Wangapeka Valley or Mt Arthur for $22, plus transport and lunch.

During the summer, day trips from Nelson to the Abel Tasman National Park are popular and good value. See Abel Tasman National Park entry in the Nelson to Golden Bay section later in this chapter for details.

## Festivals

The New Year Mardi Gras used to be one of Nelson's prime annual attractions, but excessive rowdiness put an end to this popular celebration. Nevertheless Nelson still has many noteworthy events throughout the year. There's the Christmas Carnival in Founders Park, the New Year Hops Festival, the Kaiteriteri Carnival in the first week of January and, in late February or early March one of the most interesting of all, the 'Wearable Art Award' competitions. Also in early March is the Taste Nelson Festival for locally produced food and beverage, and an Agricultural and Pastoral (A&P) show on the third weekend in November.

## Places to Stay

**Hostels** Hostels have been popping up like the proverbial mushrooms around Nelson, and there are now at least eight to choose from in this not-so-large town!

The YHA hostel and a good private hostel are close to each other on Weka St about 1 km north of the town centre. The neat, clean and friendly the *Nelson Youth Hostel* (tel 88-817) at 42 Weka St has room for 32 people at $13 per night. The hostel is in one of Nelson's original homesteads and it's loaded with information about tracks, transport and things to do in the area – the walls of the foyer are covered with information, and even as you sit on the toilet you can read a sign about transport to the Abel Tasman Track! The hostel hires out bicycles and camping equipment and will store your luggage if you go off tramping.

The *Tasman Towers* (tel 87-950) at 10 Weka St is a spacious, new purpose-built hostel. Rooms are mainly for two, three or four people and there are plenty of doubles for couples. The cost is $14 per night in any room and there are good kitchen and lounge facilities. The people who operate it are ex-YHA and have made a real effort to cater for travellers' needs.

You can't miss the brightly coloured *Pavlova City Hostel* (tel 548-9001), right in the centre of town on the corner of Trafalgar and Bridge streets. There's room for 58 people in dorm, double and twin rooms and every bed costs $13 per night. There's a special 'Party Room' where wild parties take place several times weekly and they give talks on the Abel Tasman and Nelson Lakes National Parks every evening at 8 pm. The Pavlova hires out bicycles and camping equipment, stores your excess luggage, and sells passes for the Abel Tasman Track.

There's also a *Pavlova Farm Hostel* (tel 548-9906) at 328 Brook St, 3 km from the town centre. It's unusual in that this 40 hectare farm is actually within the town boundaries. It costs $13 per night in dorm rooms (just one double room here) and apart from the farm animals they also have free rides to town, bicycles to borrow, camping equipment to rent, lots of tramping advice and they'll pick you up from Nelson. The pavlovas are pretty good too!

In the centre of town at 8 Bridge St is *Bumbles* (tel 82-771), a former hotel with dorm and double rooms for $11 to $13 per night and several self-contained units with B&B at $50 for two.

There are also two smaller hostels – *Nelson Backpackers 125* and *Alan's Place* – set up in private homes. Each can accommodate a maximum of 10 people and although they are licensed hostels they have a more homely, personal atmosphere, with helpful and friendly hosts. Both have free bicycles to get around on, free luggage storage and so on. The owners work during the day; you can phone them in the evening and on weekends, but you're welcome to arrive anytime.

*Nelson Backpackers 125* (tel 87-576) at 125 Tasman St is conveniently located and has beds for $12 in the recently renovated downstairs of a pleasant two-storey older home. *Alan's Place* (tel 84-854) at 42 Westbrook Terrace is a bit further out, but still a reasonable walk from town, and offers beds for $12 the first night, $10 each night after that, plus all the free coffee and tea you can drink. Alan even takes you for a free tour of town when you arrive, ending up at Chez Eelco where he treats you to one of his favourites, hot chocolate!

Even smaller is *Dave's Place* (tel 84-691)

at 29 Wellington St, the private home of an extremely friendly and hospitable fellow who has achieved an excellent reputation on the travellers' grapevine. Beds in twin or double rooms are $12 per person and Dave often does free impromptu wine or town tours, beach trips and so on. It's a relaxed and personal place, just a short walk from the cathedral. Phone for free pick-up.

The *Backpackers Beach Hostel* (tel 86-817) at 80 Tahunanui Drive, Tahuna Beach, is about a 1 minute walk from the beach and shops. It's an enjoyable hostel, with free windsurfers, bicycles and luggage storage, and although it's 4 km from the town centre it's not inconvenient. Local and long-distance buses stop right outside the door, it's an easy hitch to town, and the friendly owner takes people along in the van whenever he goes to town. Phone for free pick-up when you arrive. All beds are $13 a night in double, twin and triple rooms.

**Guest Houses** Nelson has plenty of B&B places, but you might still have difficulty finding somewhere to stay in the high season. Best known and probably most expensive is *California House* (tel 84-173) at 29 Collingwood St, just across the river from the centre. It's run by Carol Glen, who is (would you believe it) a Californian, from the tiny town of Elk in Mendocino County. She provides a real Californian breakfast that might include orange juice, fresh berries and cream, ham and sour cream omelettes, apricot nut bread, apple and cheese blintzes, pancakes with maple syrup and coffee. Cost is $80 to $110 for a couple including that hearty breakfast. There are only double rooms; if you're by yourself it's going to cost $60, but you do get a double bed. California gets lots of recommendations but it's only open from September to May.

California is definitely an upper class B&B but there are various other more conventional places in Nelson, all of which include breakfast in their tariff. *Palm Grove* (tel 84-645) at 52 Cambria St costs $25.50 per person. The *Alpha Inn Private Hotel* (tel 86-077) at 25 Muritai St has doubles at

around $54. The *Abbey Lodge* (tel 88-816) at 84 Grove St and *Hunts Home Hosts* (tel 80-123) at 15 Riverside St both charge $30/50 for singles/doubles. There are several others in the area including the *Willowbank Modern Guest House* (tel 85-041) at 71 Golf Rd, Tahunanui, and the *Bridge Guest House* (tel 23-301) at 141 Lightband Rd in Brightwater.

For real Kiwi hospitality stay with *Kay Morrison* (tel 87-993) at 81 Cleveland Terrace, on the eastern side of town, 10 minutes walk from the town centre. There's a self-contained unit set aside for guests, with two double bedrooms, for $14 per person.

**Hotels** There are plenty of regular hotels around Nelson. They include the *Dominion* (tel 84-984) at 2 Nile St West where singles cost $28 to $31 and doubles cost $42 to $45, and the *Metropolitan* (tel 69-224) at 131 Bridge St, where singles/doubles cost $32/46. The *New Royal Hotel* (tel 69-279) at 152 Bridge St has rooms at $51 to $59 for doubles.

The more expensive 115 room *Quality Inn* (tel 82-299) is on Trafalgar St and has everything from a sauna and swimming pool to a spa and gym. The cheapest rooms cost about $120, with discounts on weekends.

**Motels** There are a great number of motels in Nelson, many of them near the airport at Tahunanui. Motels that are both fairly central and reasonably priced include the *Lynton Lodge Motel* (tel 87-112) at 25 Examiner St with double rooms for $68. The *Riverlodge Motel* (tel 83-094) is at 31 Collingwood St, on the corner with Grove St; double rooms cost $67 to $70. At the *Trafalgar Lodge Motel* (tel 83-980), 46 Trafalgar St, motel units cost $50/60 for singles/doubles and B&B costs $33/50.

The *Mid City Motor Lodge* (tel 83-595), in the centre of town at 218 Trafalgar St, has rooms priced from $55 to $80 for doubles. By the river at 8 Ajax Ave the *AA Motor Lodge* (tel 88-214) is very conveniently located with rooms around $72 to $78 for two people.

## Camping & Cabins

There are plenty of camping sites around Nelson, including the *Tahuna Beach Holiday Park* (tel 85-159) near the airport and Tahuna Beach – the largest motor camp in Australasia! It can accommodate 4500 people and there are lots of camping places at $14 for two, cabins and lodges from $22 to $33 for two, and tourist flats from $38 for two. Linen can be hired. The site is 5 km from the city centre and just a couple of minutes from the beach – but light sleepers, beware! It's also very near the airport. The convenient camp supermarket is open to campers and to the public every day of the year.

The *Brook Reservoir Motor Camp* (tel 80-399) in the upper Brook Valley is situated in a superb position near a stream and surrounded by rolling pastures and forested hills. It's about the same distance from the centre as Tahuna, but rather smaller and more personal. Camping costs $6 per person, or $7.50 with power. There are cabins from very basic four-bunk ones at $18.50 for two up to more luxurious ones at around $32 for two. The camp is a long way uphill if you're walking.

The *Maitai Reserve Motor Camp* (tel 87-729) on Maitai Valley Rd is operated by the city council and is on the riverbank, 6 km from the centre. Sites are $11 for two people, or $7.50/12 for a powered site for one/two people. They also have cabins at $28.

The *Nelson Cabins & Caravan Park* (tel 81-445) at 230 Vanguard St has cabins at $32 for two with cutlery and cooking utensils supplied, and you can hire linen too if needed. Tourist flats are $43 for two. It's very central but there are no tent sites; powered caravan sites are $13.50 for two.

Other sites in the area include the *Richmond Holiday Park* (tel 47-323), 13 km from Nelson at Richmond, and the *Waimea Town & Country Club Caravan Park* (tel 46-476), also in Richmond. There's also camping, caravan sites and cabins around Mapua (see the Motueka Places to Stay section for details).

## Homestays

Nelsonians are a friendly lot, and a number of private homes in the area offer accommodation for a maximum of four guests at a time, with rates usually about the same as the hostels. Ask for a referral at the PR office.

## Places to Eat

### Snacks & Fast Food

There are plenty of sandwich specialists around the centre and, a little further out, a *Pizza Hut* and a *Kentucky Fried Chicken*. *McDonald's* has also appeared in the centre of Nelson, it's on Rutherford St near the Hardy St corner.

At 147 Trafalgar St, down at the river and CPO end, *Pizza My Heart* sells takeaway pizzas, including individual slices for $3. The *Pegasus Coffee Bar* on Hardy St is a good place for sandwiches and snacks. For a more expensive but pleasant lunch, the cafe at the *Suter Art Gallery* is worth considering – good food in a pleasant setting; it's open daily.

The *Cafe de Curb* is a big white pie cart that has been serving mobile fast foods in Nelson since 1933. It's reputed to have the 'biggest burgers in New Zealand'. You can find it parked on Trafalgar St near Bridge St after 6 pm every day except Sundays. It's open until midnight on Mondays and Tuesdays, until 1.30 am on Wednesdays and Thursdays, and until 3.30 am on Fridays and Saturdays!

### Pub Food

There's a *Cobb & Co* in the Wakatu Hotel on the corner of Collingwood and Bridge streets, with the usual Cobb & Co menu and the usual opening hours – 7.30 am to 10 pm daily. *Traffers*, on the corner of Trafalgar and Hardy streets, also has a fairly standard pub-style menu.

Other hotels with pub food include the *Royal Hotel* with its Dixies Restaurant opposite Cobb & Co, a rather trendy eatery where main courses cost $10 to $20. The *Metropolitan Hotel* on Bridge St also has a bistro menu with most meals costing $9 to $14. It's open for lunch and dinner daily and has a relaxed, old-fashioned atmosphere.

**Restaurants** The *Chez Eelco*, near the cathedral at 296 Trafalgar St, is a Nelson institution. It's a relaxed coffee bar and restaurant which stays open from 6 am to 11 pm, 7 days a week. Apart from those wonderful hours it also has tables and chairs out on the sidewalk which makes it one of the few (if not the only) sidewalk cafes in New Zealand. They serve everything from strong coffee, croissants, sandwiches and fruit juices to regular restaurant meals. It's a popular meeting place and the front window is an equally popular local notice board. Give it a try.

If you want good pizzas, try the popular *Hitching Post* at 145 Bridge St which has 13 choices in three sizes; prices start at around $8. The menu goes much further, however, with main courses from $9 to $15, smorgasbord salads for $3.50, drinks, desserts and so on. The Post has a rustic decor and an open air courtyard out the back.

*City Lights* at 142 Hardy St is a glossy modern restaurant with a decidedly international menu including Greek, Californian, Mexican, Chinese – you name it – influences. Main courses cost $15 to $18, and it's open every day.

The *Asian Gardens* at 94 Collingwood St serves selections from a number of Asian countries including India, Malaysia, Thailand, Indonesia and China. Main courses cost around $18, with starters and desserts around $5. It's a cosy, enjoyable BYO, open for dinner from 6.30 pm Tuesday to Saturday.

The *Samadhi*, an Indian vegetarian restaurant at 30 Washington Rd on the corner of Hastings St, isn't right in the town centre but it's well worth the short walk to reach it. Classic North Indian dishes are served in the traditional thali style – all you can eat! – and cost from $12 to $19, with a good selection of sweets and drinks too. It's a non-smoking BYO which has become one of Nelson's favourites, open from 6 pm every day except Sundays.

### Entertainment

**Pubs** Various pubs have entertainment including the *Turf Hotel* at Stoke or the *Ocean Lodge Hotel* at Tahunanui, both with discos. The *Royal Hotel* and the glossy new *Traffers* in the central city have entertainment on weekends.

**Nightclubs** Nelson also has several nightclubs. There's *Horatio's* in Halifax St near the CPO, *Zhivago's* on the corner of Trafalgar and Hardy streets, or *Limbo's* on Hardy St near Rutherford. In New St off Trafalgar are three good places – *Maxine's*, the *Cactus Club*, and near these the *Bridge Cafe* also becomes a nightclub in the evening. Most nightclubs in town have one night during the week when they offer a special deal and become packed out with locals out for a good time – both Maxine's and the Cactus Club had '$1 Night' on Wednesdays on our last visit.

**Other Entertainment** Wherever you're drinking in Nelson make it a point to try a Mac's beer. Nelson's own beer is brewed by an independent brewery and it's not bad. The Wine Trails Tour includes a tour of the brewery.

Also worth a mention is the evening entertainment at the *Suter Art Gallery* on Bridge St. Besides the theatre, music, dance and so on mentioned previously, they have the *Stage Two* theatre with a top selection of popular and international art films, changing frequently.

### Getting There & Away

**Air** Air New Zealand (tel 82-329, 69-300) is on the corner of Trafalgar and Halifax streets, by the river and opposite the CPO and PRO. It has daily direct flights to Wellington, Auckland and Christchurch, with connections to other centres. Most flights, even those to Auckland and Christchurch, go via Wellington.

Air Nelson (tel 76-066) has direct flights to Wellington, Auckland, Christchurch, Motueka, Westport, Palmerston North and Timaru, again with connections to other cities. Mt Cook Airline (tel 69-300) operates from the Air New Zealand office and has direct flights to Wellington, Christchurch, Queenstown, Te Anau and Mt Cook, once again with connecting flights.

**Bus** All buses serving Nelson arrive and depart from the PR office (tel 82-304) on the corner of Trafalgar and Halifax streets. The office sells tickets for all bus lines. InterCity (tel 81-539) also has a Travel Centre at 56 Rutherford St.

InterCity buses run daily east to Picton and south to Greymouth via Murchison and Reefton, with connections to the Franz Josef and Fox glaciers.

Newmans (tel 88-369) also has daily buses from Nelson to Picton, continuing south to Christchurch. They also have buses to Christchurch via the Lewis Pass, and to Greymouth on a more interesting route than InterCity takes, going via the Buller Gorge and the scenic coastal route with a stop at Punakaiki (the Pancake Rocks).

Besides these two major bus lines, Nelson has a surprising number of more local operators.

From Nelson to Picton there's the Picton Connection, with one bus daily in each direction. Unlike Nelson and InterCity, which go via Blenheim, the Connections bus goes via the scenic Queen Charlotte Drive coastal route, making stops at little towns and bays all along the way. The Corgi Passenger Truck (tel Picton 37-125) takes groups of four to nine people from Picton to Nelson, and you could probably arrange to take it from Nelson to Picton too.

Heading west to Motueka and Golden Bay there's quite a variety of transport. Newmans has buses to Motueka and Takaka. Collingwood Bus Services (tel Collingwood 48-188) has services from Nelson to Collingwood via Motueka and Takaka, connecting with Newmans buses at Takaka. They and other companies provide transport from Nelson, Motueka and Takaka to the Abel Tasman Track (see Abel Tasman National Park in the Nelson to Golden Bay section for details).

Several local companies have buses to the Nelson Lakes National Park. Nelson Lakes Transport (tel St Arnaud 36-858) runs a return bus between Nelson and St Arnaud daily except Sunday, connecting with Delta Landline buses between Picton and Greymouth. Wadsworths Motors (tel Tapawera 34-248) has thrice-weekly buses from Nelson to Lake Rotoiti and Tadmor, plus buses to Tapawera on weekdays.

Finally, Southern Sights (tel 88-901) is a good private bus and tour company providing transport to the Abel Tasman Track (northern or southern end), Nelson Lakes, the West Coast glaciers, Pancake Rocks, or any other place. It goes on demand, usually quite frequently – it serves the Youth Hostel and Tasman Towers regularly but you can use the service no matter where you are staying; it will come to pick you up. Southern Sights goes anywhere, all year round, and provides not only transport but a scenic tour as well, stopping to see interesting things along the way. Trampers can arrange to be picked up at the end of a track at a specified time.

Two alternative buses, the West Coast Express and Magic Bus, depart from Nelson for 6 day trips down the West Coast to Queenstown, with plenty of stops along the way. Since hitching is notoriously slow and seeing all the sights can be difficult travelling by public bus, these are a good way to see the West Coast if you don't have your own wheels. See the Getting Around chapter for details.

**Hitching** Getting out of Nelson is not easy as the city sprawls so far. It's best to take a bus out to the outskirts. Hitching to the west coast can be hard going, so take a bus as far as Tapawera.

**Getting Around**
**Airport Transport** The Nelson Shuttle Service (tel 82-304, after hours 521-151) offers door-to-door service to and from the airport for $4.50. It operates from about 7 am to 6 pm on weekdays and from 8 am to 2 pm

on Saturdays, but not at all on Sundays. A taxi to the airport costs about $12.

**Bus** The Suburban Bus Company operates local services from its terminal on Lower Bridge St. They run out to Richmond via Tahuna and Stoke, and also to Wakefield. Buses operate during the day until about 5 or 6 pm on weekdays, with one later bus at about 7 pm on Friday nights. On Saturdays a couple of buses run in the morning but there are no buses on Sundays.

The Nelson Shuttle Service (see Airport Transport) was set up to provide airport transport, but since it makes continuous return trips from Nelson to Tahuna Beach and on to the airport, many people use it to go just between Nelson and Tahuna. You can catch it from the PR office or the Quality Inn.

**Bicycle & Motorbike Rental** Bicycles can be hired from Stewart Cycles (tel 84-344) at 126 Hardy St by the half-day, day, week or month, or from Greg Fraine Cycles Ltd (tel 83-877) at 101 Bridge St. Beachcrafts (tel 86-155) operates Sun City Scooter Hire at 5 Tahunanui Drive, hiring 50cc motorcycles (no special motorcycle licence needed) by the hour, half-day or full day.

## AROUND NELSON
### Nelson Lakes National Park
Nelson Lakes National Park is 118 km south-west of Nelson. There's good tramping, walking, lake scenery and also skiing (in winter) at the Rainbow and Mt Robert ski fields. Rainbow in particular is a good ski field for families and beginners. Information on the park is available at the Park Visitors Centre (tel 36-806) in St Arnaud or at the Lake Rotoroa Ranger Station (tel Murchison 369) near the northern end of Lake Rotoroa.

An excellent 3 day tramp from St Arnaud takes you south along the eastern shore of Lake Rotoiti to Lake Head Hut ($4), across the Travers River and up the Cascade Track to Angelus Hut ($8) on beautiful alpine Lake Angelus. The trip back to St Arnaud takes you along Roberts Ridge to the Mt Robert ski field. On a clear day this ridge walk

affords magnificent alpine views all along its length. The track descends steeply to the Mt Roberts car park, from where it's a 7 km road walk back to St Arnaud.

For information on other walks in Nelson Lakes National Park, ask at the ranger stations or refer to *Tramping in New Zealand* by Jim DuFresne (Lonely Planet).

**Places to Stay & Eat** The *Yellow House Guest House* (tel 36-898) in St Arnaud has hostel-style accommodation for $12 per night. *Alpine Lodge* (tel 36-869), a 10-minute walk from the lake, has rooms for $77, but also some backpackers accommodation. There are also several camping grounds and lodges within the park itself, contact the Park Visitors Centre. There's a restaurant at the Alpine Lodge, and a snack bar at the petrol station, which also sells limited supplies of groceries.

**Getting There & Away** Delta Landline buses stop at St Arnaud on the daily Picton-Blenheim-Westport-Greymouth run. Wadsworth Motors of Tapawera operate a service between Nelson and St Arnaud on Mondays, Wednesdays and Fridays. Nelson Lakes Transport, based in St Arnaud, also has daily buses between St Arnaud and Nelson.

### Wakefield
South of Nelson, at Pigeon Valley, Wake-field, is the Waimea Steam Museum, with an interesting collection of vintage steam-driven machinery. It's open daily from 9 am to 4.30 pm.

### Moutere Eels
On the back road route along Wilson's Rd to Motueka are the tame eels of the Moutere River. They're about 11 km from Upper Moutere village – look out for the signpost. Patient feeding over the years has made them so tame that they'll actually slither out of the water to take bits of meat from your hand. It's an unusual sight! Entry is $2 (children 50 cents) and feeding times are supposedly 10 am to noon and 1 to 4 pm, but they're fairly

flexible. The eels hibernate over winter, from about late May to early August.

## Wineries

There are a number of vineyards on the Nelson Wine Trail which you can follow by doing a loop from Nelson through Richmond to Motueka, following the SH 60 coast road in one direction and the inland Moutere River road in the other. Wineries which are open for visitors include Korepo Wines, Neudorf Vineyards, Weingut Seifried, Redwood Cellars, Ranzau Winery, Robinson Brothers and Laska Cellars. You can get a Wine Trail map from the information centres in Nelson or Motueka.

# Nelson to Golden Bay

## MOTUEKA

Population 5000

Motueka is the centre for a tobacco, hops and fruit-growing area. People often come here for the summer picking work and it's also a popular base for trampers en route to the walks in the Abel Tasman National Park and the Heaphy Track. In summer it's a bustling place, but in winter they say you could shoot a gun down the main street and not hit a thing!

## Information

Motueka is essentially one long main street, High St, and just about every business in town is found along it.

At the Tourist Information Centre (tel 87-660), in the Museum building right in the centre of town, you can get information, make bookings and buy tickets for most things happening around town, including tours, kayaks, launches, transport and so on. It's open from 9 am to 5 pm every day, except during the Christmas holidays when it's open from 8.30 am to 5.30 pm on weekdays and 9 am to 4 pm weekends. There's an AA agent at 115 High St.

The DOC office (tel 89-117) is on the corner of High and King Edward streets, and is open from 8 am to 4.30 pm on weekdays, and on weekends during the Christmas holidays. The office is an excellent source of information and maps on the Abel Tasman National Park and the North-West Nelson State Forest Park, which contains the Heaphy and Wangapeka tracks.

Facilities Use Passes for the Abel Tasman Track can be bought in Motueka at either the Information Centre or the DOC. Check with the DOC for tide info.

## Things to See & Do

The interesting little Motueka District Museum is at 140 High St, in the same building with the Information Centre and the Gallery Cafe. It's open weekdays; admission is $1 (children 50 cents).

The Motueka Recreation Centre (tel 88-560) on Old Wharf Rd has lots going on including skating, a gym, aerobics, sports, summer minibus tours, and a cinema which shows a frequently-changing schedule of sometimes surprisingly good films.

Pretty's Tours (tel Motueka 89-480) offers a horticulture tour around Motueka – see the Nelson Tours section for details. They operate from the Old Cederman House in Riwaka but will pick you up in Motueka. The tour costs $18 (children $10, discounts for families) and they also have a wine tour for $23.

The Information Centre has a *Motueka Valley Craft Trail* pamphlet with a map and details on where to visit many artists and craftspeople in the area, and also a *Wine Trail* map.

There are good beaches near Motueka at Kaiteriteri, Marahau, and the dress optional Mapua Leisure Park. The best beach in the area is Kaiteriteri, north of Motueka on the road in to Abel Tasman National Park. At Ruby Bay, south of Motueka, a rock concert is held in March each year. The beaches along the Abel Tasman National Park coast can be easily reached on day launch trips, see the Abel Tasman National Park section.

## Rafting, Kayaks & Cruises

Ocean River Adventures (tel 88-823) is

based in Motueka and does white water rafting trips on the Buller and Gowan rivers. There's a half-day trip for $56 or an all-day trip for $90. There's also an easier 1½ hour trip on the Motueka River that's good for families, costing $26 (children $11.25).

Launch trips and sea kayaking off the Abel Tasman National Park coast are popular and good value; see the Abel Tasman National Park entry in this section for details.

### Camping Gear

The Motueka Hire Centre (tel 87-426) beside the Shell service station hires tents and backpacks for use on the Abel Tasman Track. Sleeping bags and cooking gear can be hired from the White Elephant hostel.

### Places to Stay

**Hostels** There's a YHA *Summer Youth Hostel* (tel 86-094) at Motueka High School on Whakarewa St. It's just a few hundred metres from the centre of town but it's only open for a very short time, from mid-December to late January – check the specific dates at other hostels. The cost is $12 per night.

Opposite this is a good private hostel, the *White Elephant* (tel 86-208) at 55 Whakarewa St. It has room for 20 people in a big, comfortable old house set on almost 1 hectare of land. It costs $13 in dorm rooms and $15 per person in double rooms, including linen, and there are also a few tent sites at $7 per person. Bicycles and camping gear can be hired here for a minimal cost.

The *YMCA* (tel 88-652) has a hostel at 500 High St, on the Nelson side of town. Nightly cost in this pleasant and modern hostel is $10 per night plus a $5 key deposit, mostly in twin rooms. They also have tent sites at $7/12 for one/two people and if you don't have your own tent you can hire one for $1 per day. Bicycle hire costs $2 per day.

The *Riverside Community* (tel Lower Motuere 758), 7 km out of Motueka on the Moutere Highway, is a well-organised community that's been going since 1941. Anyone can stay here for $10 a day, or $6.50 per person if you pitch your own tent, and the cost includes fresh milk and apples in season.

Community meals are held several times weekly and they welcome visitors' involvement in the community. There's no difficulty in finding it – all the locals know it and there's a sign on the road.

**Guest Houses** The *White's Guest House* (tel 87-318) at 430 High St is a friendly B&B in what used to be a nunnery! All rooms have a wash basin and there's a lounge with pleasant views. The cost is $33/55 per night for singles/doubles, with a substantial continental breakfast. You can get dinner here for another $16.50, with vegies fresh from their organic garden.

**Hotels & Motels** The *Post Office Hotel* (tel 89-890) in the centre of town has single/double rooms at $35/50. Other alternatives include the *Abel Tasman Motel* (tel 87-699) at 45 High St with single/double rooms at $49/56, and the *Motueka Garden Motel* (tel 89-299) at 71 King Edward St, near the clocktower, where rooms cost $62 to $66 for two.

**Camping & Cabins** The *Vineyard Tourist Units* (tel 88-550) are at 328 High St, near the centre of town. There's a variety of cabins and flats which are simple but good value, each with its own kitchen. Small cabins sleep up to four people for $20 to $24 for two, tourist units with private toilet facilities cost $33 for two, and motel units cost $45 for two.

Camping sites include *Fearon's Bush Motor Camp* (tel 87-189) at the northern end of town, where tent and powered sites cost $9/14 for one/two people and cabins are $20 for two. The *Motueka Beach Reserve Camp* (tel 87-169) at Port Motueka has camping sites at $8/12 for one/two people.

The *Marahau Beach Camp* (tel 78-176) at Marahau, 18 km north of Motueka, has tent and caravan sites for $9/14 for one/two people; cabins cost $25 for two and a self-contained flat is $35 for two.

The *Peninsula Lodge* (tel 68-740) is a pleasant lodge on the bank of the Motueka River at Ngatimoti, 19 km from Motueka in the Motueka Valley. There's trout fishing, tramping, rafting and swimming. The cost is $30 per night for two people.

The *Mapua Leisure Park* (tel Mapua 666) at 33 Toru St, Mapua, 21 km south of Motueka, is 'New Zealand's first clothes-optional leisure park'! They have a private beach, nine-hole golf course, tennis and volleyball courts, swimming pool, sauna and spa, and a children's playground. Camping costs $8.50 per person for tent or power sites and there are cabins for $14.50/29 for one/two people, on-site caravans and chalets at $40 for two, or more expensive tourist flats at $52 for two, with off-season reductions. Many people come over here just for the day, to enjoy the lovely beach.

The *McKee Memorial Reserve*, 2 km north of the leisure park and 19 km from town, is a very basic camping ground right on the water's edge. Water, toilets and barbecue pits are the only amenities, but rates are cheap at $4 per camping site.

### Places to Eat
**Snacks & Fast Food** There's the usual string of takeaways and sandwich bars along Motueka's endless main street including The *Wheelhouse*, opposite the CPO, a three part operation with takeaways at one end, fish & chips at the other, and an eat-in space in the middle. They have Chinese food as well as burgers and they're open until at least 8.30 pm every day; on Fridays and Saturdays they're open until midnight. For sandwiches and snacks try the *Silver Spoon Bakery* at 105 High St or the fancier *Sandwiched Eaterie* at 219 High St.

**Pub Food** Opposite the CPO, next to the Wheelhouse, is the *Post Office Hotel*, serving lunch and dinner every day except Sundays. There's the regular pub menu with lunches for around $7.50 and dinners from $10 up to $16.50 for a big steak. The other two hotels – the *Motueka* and the *Swan* – also have pub food but the Post Office Hotel is the most serious about it, with a large dining area.

**Restaurants** Motueka's most interesting food question, however, is how did a little Kiwi country town end up with not one but four such interesting restaurants. Any of these restaurants would be an asset to most small NZ towns, Motueka's very lucky to have them all!

Smallest of all is the *Theatre Cafe* on High St, with some of the best pizza in New Zealand. The owners, Richard and Melanie, have travelled in 35 countries and the hundreds of photos and mementos of their travels that decorate the little place can keep you entranced for hours – a true travellers' rest. On our last visit we found an eclectic display on Richard's most recent journey among the head-hunting tribes of Sarawak in Borneo! It's open every day from 5 pm, with medium pizzas from $10 to $15 and large ones from $14 to $20.

Equally unusual is the *Gothic Gourmet* in the town centre. You can't miss the place; it's in what was formerly a Gothic-style Methodist church, now painted shocking pink from steps to steeple! Walk in the side door and you enter the bar. The dining room is in the old sanctuary with its towering ceiling, and there's also a garden courtyard out the back. Decor aside, the gourmet-style meat and vegetarian dishes would be notable anywhere. Lunches are served daily and prices range from $7.50 to $10.50; dinners are served from Tuesday to Sunday, with main courses from $13 to $17; and there's a bar menu with selections from $4 to $10. The Sunday smorgasbord for $17.50 is good value.

At the southern end of the shopping area at 265 High St is *Mottandoor*, where the menu features a diverse array of Asian dishes. You can try a Burmese or Malay curry, an Indonesian satay, a Korean fried rice, or Indian dishes prepared in the tandoor oven. Starters cost $4 to $8, main courses $16 to $20, and desserts (also from all over Asia) $7. It's open from 6 pm every night (licensed or BYO) and has takeaways too.

Finally, the *Gallery Cafe* in the Museum and Information Centre building in the centre of town is both a cafe and an art gallery, with dining inside or out on the covered patio. They have particularly good salads, desserts and coffee – you can get a whole pot for $4.40 – and other tasty selections for lunch ($5 to $8) and the evening meal (main courses $12.50 to $16), with plenty for both meat-eaters and vegetarians. In summer it's open every day and evening except Sundays; in winter it's open from Monday to Friday.

### Getting There & Away

**Air** Air Nelson (tel 88-772) has direct flights to Nelson, Takaka and Wellington, with connections to other centres.

**Bus** Newmans and Collingwood Bus Services (tel Collingwood 48-188) both operate buses from Nelson through Motueka to Takaka. The Collingwood buses go straight through to Collingwood, with additional Takaka-Collingwood connections with the Newmans buses. The Newmans office (tel 87-280) is on High St at the northern end of town.

Skyline Travel (tel 88-850) on Wallace St has daily buses to Nelson, Takaka, Totaranui, Kaiteriteri and Marahau, but only in summer. Also during the summer, Abel Tasman National Park Enterprises (tel 87-801) has buses linking Motueka with Nelson and Kaiteriteri, connecting in Kaiteriteri with their launch going up and down the coast following the Abel Tasman Track – but with this company you *must* book ahead.

Motueka Taxis (tel 87-900) provides cheap transport all year round to the Abel Tasman track on their weekday mail run to Marahau. See the Abel Tasman National Park entry in this section for more info on transport to and from the track.

### Getting Around

Holliday's Cycle Centre at 227 High St hires mountain bicycles for $15 per day, 10-speeds for $12. The White Elephant and YMCA hostels also hire bicycles.

### MOTUEKA TO TAKAKA

From Motueka, SH 60 continues on over Takaka Hill to Takaka and Collingwood.

Before ascending Takaka Hill you pass a turn-off on your right to Kaiteriteri and the southern end of Abel Tasman National Park, then a turn-off on your left to Riwaka Valley, a good area for picnicking, swimming in river pools, and walks. You can walk to the spring that is the source of the Riwaka River.

Takaka Hill, 791 metres high, separates Tasman Bay from Golden Bay. Near the summit are the Ngarua Caves where you can see moa bones. The caves are open from 10 am to 4 pm daily except Friday but are closed from mid-June to August. Takaka Hill is also known as Marble Mountain due to the large amounts of marble buried beneath the limestone that forms the hill's surface.

As you cross the crest of the hill there are fine views from Harwood Lookout down the Takaka River Valley to Takaka and Golden Bay. There's an interesting explanation of the geography and geology of the area at the lookout.

### Abel Tasman National Park

The coastal Abel Tasman National Park is a popular tramping area and the various walks include one around the coast (but beware of the sandflies!). The park is at the northern end of a range of marble and limestone hills extending up from North-West Nelson State Forest Park, and the interior is honeycombed with caves and potholes. There are other tracks in the park, including an inland track, but the coastal track is the popular one. See Tramping in the Outdoor Activities chapter for more information.

Some people prefer to follow the track around the coast by sea kayak! A traveller from Denmark, Steen Rasmussen, wrote to say:

I did the Abel Tasman National Park kayaking instead of walking, and can definitely recommend it. No overfilled tracks or huts, and you're alone with nature all the time. There're plenty of secluded beaches where trampers can't get access. No tiring hills, and possibility of bringing all you want. The beauty and the silence of the sea beats everything, and the seals playing below and around your boat is just amazing.

Kayak hire costs about $25 per day for a

single and $50 per day for a double, including all gear. There are also guided sea kayaking trips at about $30 for half a day or $45 for a full day, including lunch. Two kayak operators are Ocean River Adventure (tel Motueka 88-823) and Abel Tasman Kayaks (tel Marahau 78-022).

Abel Tasman National Park Enterprises (tel Motueka 87-801) has 6½ hour launch services departing from Kaiteriteri at 9 am, dropping off trampers in Totaranui (the northern end of the track) at 12.15 pm and picking up returning trampers, and arriving back at Kaiteriteri at about 3.30 or 4 pm.

The launch service doubles as trampers' transport and also a pleasant day cruise. Along the way it stops at Tonga Bay, Bark Bay, Torrent Bay and Tinline Bay. You can easily combine a walk along part of the Abel Tasman track with the cruise, being dropped off at one bay and picked up later at another. There are several such options, the most popular being to disembark at Bark Bay, walk the track 2½ hours to Torrent Bay, have time on the beach for swimming, and be picked up there. The cost for either the full day cruise or a walk/cruise option is $33 (children $16.50).

The launch service operates on a scheduled route from 1 October to 31 May each year, but will go at any time of the year if they have enough bookings. From 26 December to 15 January there's also an evening cruise for $25 (children $12.50) and you can go in the morning, returning in the evening, to spend more time in the park.

All launch trips must be booked in advance, either directly with Abel Tasman National Park Enterprises or at the information centres in Nelson or Motueka. The same company operates a bus service from Nelson and Motueka which connects with the launch, making it an easy day trip from either town.

**Getting There & Away** Abel Tasman National Park Enterprises (tel Motueka 87-801) operates buses from Motueka and Nelson to Kaiteriteri, from where their launch departs. You can take either the bus or the launch separately, but you must book this bus, as well as the launch, in advance.

There's also land transport to either end of the track. Skyline Travel (tel Nelson 80-285 or Motueka 88-850) operates buses between Nelson, Motueka, Kaiteriteri and Marahau from 1 November until 31 March. From 1 December until 31 March they also have services to and from Takaka and Totaranui. Motueka Taxis (tel Motueka 87-900) have an inexpensive service to Marahau on their weekday mail run from Motueka, all year round.

Collingwood Bus Services (tel Collingwood 48-188) has services to and from the Totaranui end of the track which run on demand and can be timed to connect with bus services to Nelson, Motueka, Takaka and Collingwood. You can phone them collect from Totaranui.

## TAKAKA
Population 1200
The small centre of Takaka is the last town of any size as you head towards the northwest corner of the South Island. It's the main centre for the beautiful Golden Bay area. It's also quite a hip little community – lots of '60s and artistic types have settled there. Pohara Beach is a popular summer resort near the town.

### Orientation
Just about everything in Takaka is found along Commercial St, which is the main road through town, only a few blocks long.

### Information
On the Motueka side of town there's a very helpful Information Centre (tel 59-136) open from 9 am to 5 pm in summer and 10 am to 4 pm in winter, 7 days a week. Pick up a copy of their free promotional booklet which has interesting articles about the many points of interest around Golden Bay.

There's a DOC office (tel 58-026) with information on the Abel Tasman, Heaphy and Kaituna tracks, Farewell Spit, Cobb Valley, the Aorere Goldfields and the Pupu Springs Scenic Reserve. It's open from 8.30

am to noon and 1 to 4 pm, Monday to Friday. There's an AA agent in the centre of town.

Facilities Use Passes for the Abel Tasman track are available in Takaka from the DOC office, the Information Centre, the Shady Rest Hostel, the Pohara Beach Camp and the bus depots.

## Attractions

Takaka has a small museum, open daily (entry $1, children 50 cents). The Village Theatre brings in top quality popular and international art films, with several different films showing each week. The Whole Meal Trading Company sometimes has live music. The Begonia House is open in summer to show off its colourful flowers.

Windsurfing is a popular activity on Golden Bay – all the local beaches are excellent – and windsurfers are available at the Shady Rest Hostel and the Pohara Beach Camp. There are tame eels in the Anatoki River, 6 km south of Takaka.

## Arts & Crafts

Many artists and craftspeople are based in the Golden Bay area, including painters, potters, blacksmiths, screen printers, silversmiths and knitwear designers. Right in town, a cooperative of the Golden Bay craftspeople has established the large Artisans Shop to display their wares. Many other artists and craftspeople are tucked away all around the Bay. The *Golden Bay Craft Trail* leaflet gives directions to the galleries and workshops. The Whole Meal Trading Company also has art on display.

## Rawhiti Caves

The Rawhiti Caves near Takaka are among the largest in New Zealand, well worth a look. A 2½ hour guided tour of the caves costs $8 (children $4). It's an enjoyable and popular tour that's good value. Phone 59-061 for bookings.

## Pupu Springs

Pupu Springs (the real name is Waikoropupu, but everyone calls it simply Pupu) are the largest freshwater springs in New

Zealand and among the largest in the world. Many springs are dotted around the Pupu Springs Scenic Reserve, including one with 'dancing sands' thrown upwards by the great volume of incredibly clear water emerging from the ground.

Walkways through the reserve take you to the various springs, passing by gold-mining works from last century – gold was discovered in Golden Bay in 1865, 4 years after the first NZ discovery in the Coromandel. The DOC produces an excellent leaflet about the reserve. To reach Pupu from Takaka, go 4 km north-west on SH 60, turn inland at Waitapu Bridge and continue another 3 km.

## Places to Stay

**Hostels** The *Takaka Summer Youth Hostel* (tel 59-067) is in the Golden Bay High School on Meihana St. It's only open over the Christmas holiday period and costs $12 a night.

The *Shady Rest Hostel* is a hospitable and relaxed hostel in a big historic home on the main road, 400 metres from the town centre, on the Collingwood side. Dorm or double rooms cost $12 per night. The hostel has windsurfers for hire, and you can spend some enjoyable hours feeding the tame eels, pukekos and ducks in the creek behind the house. There's no telephone, so just show up.

**Hotels & Motels** The *Junction Hotel* (tel 59-207) and *Telegraph Hotel* (tel 59-308) are both on the main road in Takaka and have rooms for around $28/40 for singles/-doubles. A few km on the Motueka side the *Upper Takaka Hotel* (tel 59-411) is better known as the Rat Trap! It costs $30/45 per night for singles/doubles.

There are a number of motels in or around Takaka, particularly at Pohara Beach, all charging around $60 to $65 for two people. The *Golden Bay Motel* (tel 59-428) is on the main road in Takaka, and there's the *Tata Beach Motel* (tel 59-712) on Tata Beach. At Pohara the *Pohara Beachfront Motel* (tel 59-660) has units at $54 to $62 for two.

**Camping & Cabins** The *Pohara Beach*

*Camp* (tel 59-500) is 10 km from Takaka, right on the beach. Camping sites are $14 for two ($1 more with power), and there are cabins at $22 and $32 per night for two. On Tukura Beach, 18 km north of Takaka and 8 km south of Collingwood, the *Golden Bay Holiday Park* (tel 59-742) has camping sites at $7.50/13 for single/doubles ($1 more with power) plus cabins at $15/24 for one/two people. Minimum unit rates apply during holidays.

The *Totaranui Beach Camp* (tel Takaka 58-026, Motueka 88-083/4) at Totaranui, 33 km from Takaka in the Abel Tasman National Park, is administered by DOC, with camping sites at $5 per person. Sites for the Christmas holidays can be reserved from July onwards.

### Places to Eat

The *Whole Meal Trading Company* in the town centre is a local institution, an enjoyable wholefoods cafe, restaurant and art gallery which also sells bulk natural foods, has a community bulletin board, and sometimes has live music in the evenings. The *Cabbage Tree Cafe* further down the main road is another good spot with a relaxed atmosphere. The *Takaka Restaurant & Tearooms* has an inexpensive Chinese takeaway to one side. The *Junction* and *Telegraph* hotels both have pubs with bistro meals.

### Getting There & Away

**Air** Air Nelson (tel 76-066) has direct flights to Motueka, with connecting flights to Wellington and Auckland.

**Bus** The Newmans bus service from Nelson through Motueka terminates at Takaka. Collingwood Bus Services connects with these buses to continue to Collingwood. There's also a Collingwood bus which goes the entire way from Nelson through Motueka and Takaka and on to Collingwood. See the Abel Tasman National Park entry in this section for details on bus services to and from the Abel Tasman Track.

## COLLINGWOOD

Population 200

The tiny township of Collingwood is the end of the line, which is really why people come here. For most it's simply the jumping-off point to the Heaphy Track. From here you can head south-west to more caves and the Heaphy Track in the North-West Nelson State Forest Park, or north-east to Farewell Spit.

### Tours

Collingwood Motors (tel 48-131) organises 5 hour Farewell Spit Safari Tours for $34 (children $20), going up the beach in a 4WD vehicle – it's the only way you can visit the Spit, as it's a protected wildlife sanctuary and only this tour has permission to go onto it. Tours leave daily on demand, timed to the tides. Collingwood Motors also does 2½ to 3 hour trips to the Rebecca and Te Anaroa Caves for $11 (children $7).

Collingwood Bus Services (tel 48-188) also does a couple of good tours. The Scenic Mail Run tour visits isolated farming settlements and communities around Cape Farewell and the west coast. The driver points out many points of historical and contemporary interest along the way. The tour lasts 5 hours, departing from the Collingwood CPO at 9.30 am Monday to Friday, and the cost of $22 (children $14) includes lunch on a 1000 hectare farm.

Collingwood Bus Services also offers a tour of the Cobb Valley, departing from the Collingwood CPO at 9.30 am and from the Takaka Information Centre at 10 am. The cost of $35 (children $20) includes lunch.

### Aorere Goldfields

The Aorere Goldfield was the first major goldfield in New Zealand. In February 1857, 5 ounces (142 grams) of Collingwood gold were auctioned in Nelson, precipitating a gold rush which lasted 3 years, although various companies continued to wrest gold from the soil by sluicing and stamping batteries right up until WW I. The old goldfields are now overgrown but the more durable features such as terraces, water races and mine shafts can still be seen.

The DOC in Takaka has an excellent eight page pamphlet detailing the history of the goldfields and guiding you on a historical walk, with directions beginning from Collingwood. The walk takes most of a day to complete.

You can learn more about the local history at the small museum in town.

### Places to Stay
**Chalets & Motels** The *Collingwood Vacations Chalets* (tel Takaka 48-221) in Tasman St has self-contained units at $40 for two. The *Collingwood Motel* (tel Takaka 48-221) in Haven Rd has two units at $57 for two.

**Camping & Cabins** The *Collingwood Motor Camp* (tel Takaka 48-149) near the centre of the tiny township has sites for $10 for two ($12 with power). Cabins cost $18 for two and tourist flats cost $30 for two. The *Pakawau Beach Motor Camp* (tel Takaka 48-327) is 13 km north of Collingwood, which means it's even closer to the end of the road. Camping sites cost $6 per person ($7.50 with power), and there are also self-contained cottages at $30 and $35 for two.

### Places to Eat
If you're not fixing your own food there's a pub opposite the CPO or the *Collingwood Cafe*, a dairy and cafe that's open from 7.30 am to 8 or 9 pm every day.

### Getting There & Away
Collingwood Bus Services (tel 48-188) behind the CPO is the key to all local transport. Its bus comes from Nelson to Collingwood in the morning every day except Saturdays, returning in the afternoon. They also have twice-daily buses from Collingwood connecting with Newmans buses in Takaka and buses from Collingwood northwards around Cape Farewell or inland to Bainham, every day except Sundays.

Collingwood Bus Services also provide transport to and from the Totaranui (northern) end of the Abel Tasman Track and to the Browns Hut end of the Heaphy Track, 35 km from Collingwood. These services run on demand; the cost is about $50 per trip for the minibus, or $10 per person if there are more than five people. Inward and outward trips can be arranged to connect with their buses onward to Nelson.

# South Marlborough

Many travellers head west or north-west from Picton to the walking tracks or the West Coast glaciers, but there are also a number of points of interest along the route south from the Marlborough district across the Canterbury Plains to Christchurch.

### KAIKOURA
Kaikoura is on SH 1, 133 km south of Blenheim and 180 km north of Christchurch. Shortly south of Kaikoura the road splits, SH 1 continuing along the coast while SH 70 branches off inland and later merges with SH 7 crossing over from the West Coast.

Until early 1988 the sleepy little seaside town was noted mainly for its fishing and its fine setting on an incredibly beautiful bay backed by the steeply rising foothills of the Seaward Kaikoura Range, snow-capped in winter. It was also known for its fine crayfish (lobster) – Kaikoura means 'to eat crayfish' in Maori.

At Christmas 1987, Nature Watch Charters began making whale-watching trips – the first such commercial operation in New Zealand. The tours quickly became famous and put Kaikoura on the tourist map. With the rapid influx of visitors, Kaikoura, whose economy until 1987 was based solely on fishing and farming, is now experiencing a boom.

Two whale-watch companies are now operating very successfully. The host of other things to do in the area, and the simple beauty of the town keep visitors around for days after they've gone to see the whales. There are many enjoyable and inexpensive tours, an interesting museum and some caves, and if you walk out to the end of the peninsula to the seal and seabird colony and a small aquarium you'll also pass some historic buildings. Other good walks in the area include Mt Fyffe and tracks in the State Forest, and there's skiing in winter at the newly opened Mt Lyford ski field.

## History

In Maori legend, the tiny Kaikoura Peninsula (or Taumanu-o-te-waka-a-Maui) was the seat upon which the demi-god Maui sat when he fished the North Island up from the depths of the sea. The area was heavily settled before Europeans came – at least 14 Maori pa sites have been identified on the peninsula.

Excavations near the Fyffe House show it was a moa-hunter settlement about 800 to 1000 years ago, even before the advent of the Maoris. In 1857 George Fyffe came upon an early moa-hunter burial site near the present Fyffe House and among other things he found was an almost complete moa egg shell. It is the largest moa egg ever found (240 mm long and 178 mm in diameter) and is housed at the National Museum in Wellington. You can see a replica at the Kaikoura Museum.

In 1828 the beachfront of Kaikoura, now the site of the Garden of Memories, was the scene of a tremendous battle when a Ngati Toa war party led by the chief Te Rauparaha from Kapiti, an island off Wellington, bore down on Kaikoura armed with muskets, killing or capturing several hundred people of the local Ngati Tahu tribe.

Captain Cook passed by here on 15 February 1770, but did not land. His journal states that 57 Maoris in four double-hulled canoes came out from shore towards the *Endeavour*, but 'would not be prevail'd upon to put along side'. Cook called the peninsula 'Lookers on', a name later mistakenly ascribed to the Seaward Kaikoura Range.

The first European to settle in Kaikoura was Robert Fyffe, who established a whaling station in 1842. Kaikoura was a whaling centre from 1843 until 1922. Meanwhile the land had been discovered to be rich for settlement and sheep-farming; even after

Kaikoura's whaling era ended, the sea and the farmland continued to support the community.

## Orientation

Kaikoura is a little town facing the sea. The main street curves along the seafront and is known variously as Beach Rd, West End, and The Esplanade; it's all one road. Kaikoura is on a peninsula and most of the town is built on the northern side. The southern side is called South Bay, and the main street over there is South Bay Parade – again, running right beside the sea.

## Information

The Information Centre (tel 5641), in the Memorial Hall on The Esplanade, is open from 9 am to 5 pm Monday to Friday and from 9 am to 1 pm on Saturdays. In summer from December to February it's also open from 10 am to 2 pm on Sundays. This is a very good information centre with lots of posters and displays on things to do in Kaikoura. They can make bookings for any tour.

The DOC office (tel 5714) is on Ludstone Rd. Most of its information on walks, camping and so on is available at the Information Centre.

## Museum

The Kaikoura Historical Society Museum on Ludstone Rd is not as small as it looks; it has several big sections out the back, including the old town jail, built in 1910. There are also many historical photographs, Maori and colonial artefacts, and an exhibit on the region's whaling era. The museum is open from 2 to 4 pm on weekends and during school holidays. If it's not open and you want to have a look, there is a list of telephone numbers on the door – someone will gladly come and open it up. Admission is $1 (children 50 cents).

## Fyffe House

George Fyffe, cousin of the first European settler, Robert Fyffe, came to Kaikoura from Scotland in 1854 and built Fyffe House around 1860. It is the only building remaining from the whaling days and is now under the protection of the Historic Places Trust. The house, on The Esplanade about 2 km east of the town centre, is open from 10 am to 4 pm every day except on some Mondays. The curator, who lives in the house, will show you around at no charge; donations, however, are gratefully accepted.

## Sea Aquarium

There's a tiny Sea Aquarium beside the Youth Hostel on The Esplanade, with a single tank of sea animals and a video presentation on Kaikoura's ocean wildlife. It's run by the University of Canterbury Research Centre and is open most days; admission is free.

## Maori Leap Cave

Tours of Maori Leap Cave, a limestone cave formed by the sea and discovered in 1958, take place several times daily and depart from the Caves Restaurant, south of the town centre on SH 1. The 40 minute tour costs $6 (children $2).

## Other Attractions

On the Esplanade beachfront, opposite the Information Centre, is the Garden of Memories, a pleasant garden with a walkway arched by giant whalebones. Further east along The Esplanade there's a seaside outdoor swimming pool.

Up on the hill at the eastern end of town there's a water tower which is a great lookout point; you can see both sides of the peninsula and all down the coast. Take the walking track up to the tower from The Esplanade or drive up Scarborough Terrace.

There are a few interesting art galleries, including a Maori gallery at the railway station run by the people who run Kaikoura Tours (both are operated by the local marae). The Sealside Gallery at 17 West End is a cooperative presenting the work of a number of Kaikoura artists, with a variety of arts and crafts. There are other galleries and workshops in town; ask the Information Centre for a list.

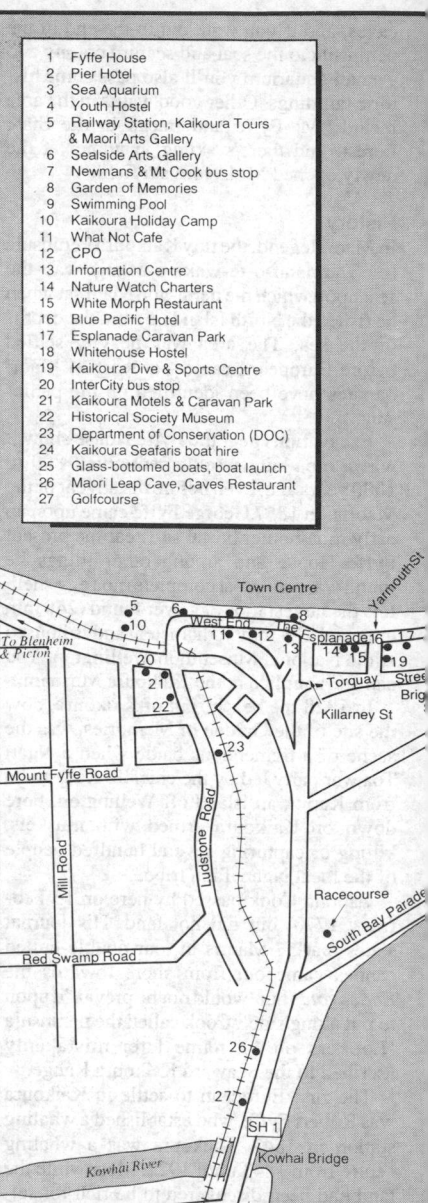

1 Fyffe House
2 Pier Hotel
3 Sea Aquarium
4 Youth Hostel
5 Railway Station, Kaikoura Tours & Maori Arts Gallery
6 Sealside Arts Gallery
7 Newmans & Mt Cook bus stop
8 Garden of Memories
9 Swimming Pool
10 Kaikoura Holiday Camp
11 What Not Cafe
12 CPO
13 Information Centre
14 Nature Watch Charters
15 White Morph Restaurant
16 Blue Pacific Hotel
17 Esplanade Caravan Park
18 Whitehouse Hostel
19 Kaikoura Dive & Sports Centre
20 InterCity bus stop
21 Kaikoura Motels & Caravan Park
22 Historical Society Museum
23 Department of Conservation (DOC)
24 Kaikoura Seafaris boat hire
25 Glass-bottomed boats, boat launch
26 Maori Leap Cave, Caves Restaurant
27 Golfcourse

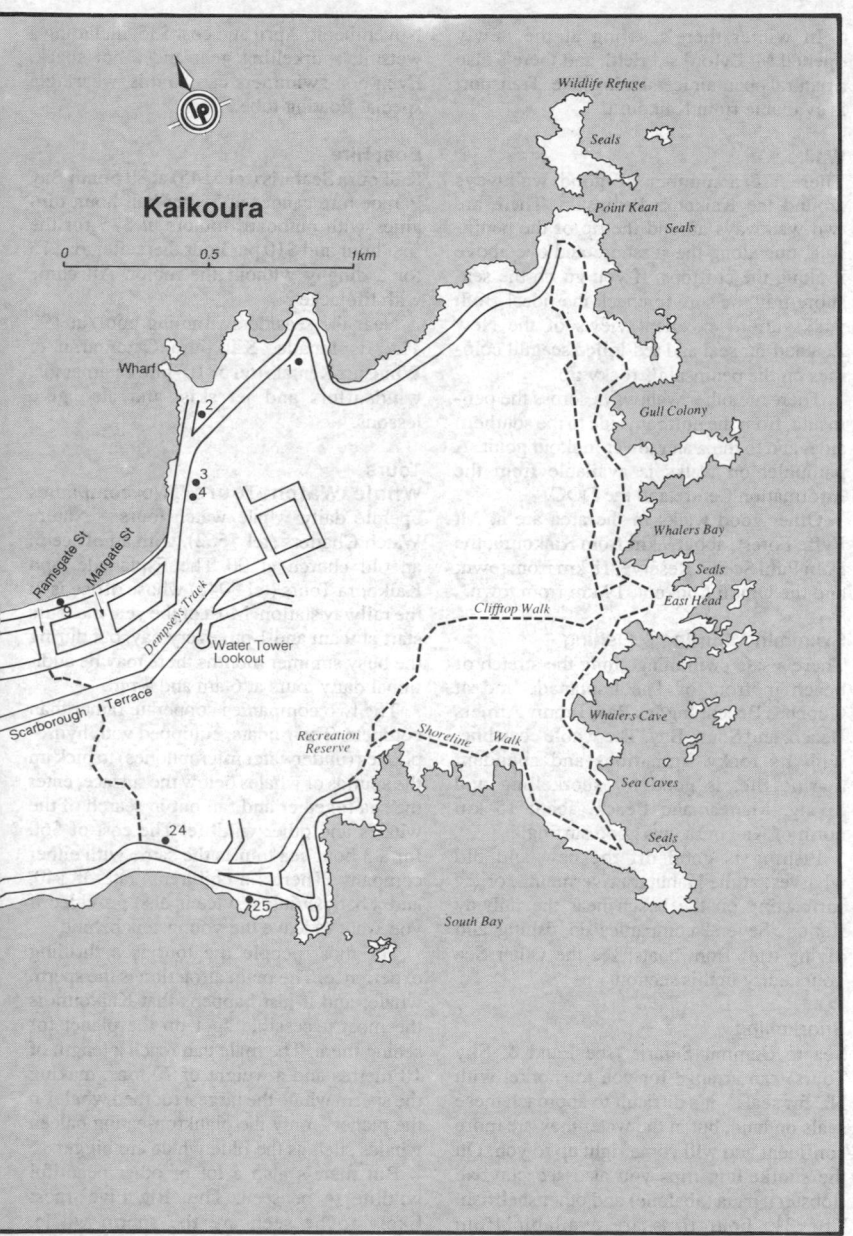

**Kaikoura**

0        0.5        1km

Wildlife Refuge

Seals

Point Kean

Seals

Wharf

Gull Colony

Whalers Bay

Seals

East Head

Clifftop Walk

Ramsgate St

Margate St

Dempseys Track

Water Tower Lookout

Scarborough Terrace

Recreation Reserve

Shoreline Walk

Whalers Cave

Sea Caves

Seals

South Bay

In winter there's skiing at the newly opened Mt Lyford ski field, and there's also a natural open-air ice-skating lake. Transport is available from Kaikoura.

### Walks
There are a number of good walkways around the Kaikoura Peninsula. There are two walkways around the tip of the peninsula, one along the seashore and one above it along the clifftops. If you go on the seashore trail, be sure to check the tides! Both walks afford excellent views of the New Zealand fur seal and red-billed seagull colonies on the peninsula's rocky tip.

There are other walkways across the peninsula, from the northern side to the southern side, and to the water tower lookout point. A pamphlet on walks is available from the Information Centre and the DOC.

Other good walks in the area are at Mt Fyffe Forest, about 9 km from Kaikoura; the Puhi Puhi Scenic Reserve, 18 km from town; and the Omihi Lookout, 19 km from town.

### Swimming, Surfing & Fishing
There's safe swimming along the stretch of beach in front of The Esplanade and at Gooches Beach, Ing/les Bay, Jimmy Armers Beach, and South Bay. The whole coastline, with its rocky formations and abundant marine life, is good for snorkelling and diving. Mangamanu Beach, about 15 km north of Kaikoura, has good surfing.

Fishing is good off the new and old wharves, at the Kahutara rivermouth, or try surfcasting on the beach near the railway station. Several companies do fishing and diving trips from boats; see the Other Sea Tours entry in this section.

### Snorkelling
Sea to Summit Safaris (see Land & Sky Tours) can arrange for you to snorkel with NZ fur seals – it's difficult to approach these seals on land, but in the water they are more confident and will come right up to you. On the snorkelling trips you also see crayfish (lobster), paua (abalone) and other shellfish. The 3½ hour trips are available from November to April and cost $35, including a wetsuit, snorkelling gear and a hot snack. Even non-swimmers can do this, wearing a special floating tube.

### Boat Hire
Kaikoura Seafaris (tel 5145) at 89 South Bay Parade hire canoes at $5 per half hour, dinghies with outboard motors at $25 for the first hour and $10 per hour thereafter, or $15 for a dinghy without the motor. All come with lifejacket.

Near the seaside swimming pool, at 192 The Esplanade, Kaikoura Catamaran & Windsurf Rentals (tel 5810) hire catamarans, windsurfers and jet skis, and also give lessons.

### Tours
**Whale Watch Tours** Two companies operate daily whale watch tours – Nature Watch Charters (tel 5662), with an office in an old church at 90 The Esplanade, and Kaikoura Tours (tel 5045) whose office is in the railway station. Most of the year the tours start at 9 am and 1 pm every day, but during the busy summer months there may be additional daily tours at 6 am and 4 pm.

The two companies cooperate rather than compete. Their boats, equipped with hydrophones (underwater microphones) to pick up the sounds of whales below the surface, enter the sea together and fan out in search of the whales and other wildlife. The cost of $60 for a 3 hour sea tour is the same with either company. There's a childrens' rate of $40, and a babysitting service is also provided if you want to leave the youngsters behind.

For most people the tour is a thrilling experience. The main attraction is the sperm whale; and it just happens that Kaikoura is the most accessible spot on the planet for seeing them. The male can reach a length of 18 metres and a weight of 70 tons, making the sperm whale the largest toothed whale on the planet – only the plankton-eating baleen whales such as the blue whale are bigger.

But there's also a lot of other beautiful wildlife to be seen. The 'Big Five' most likely to be seen are the sperm whale,

Little blue penguin

Hector's dolphin (the smallest and rarest of all dolphins, found only in NZ waters and now on the list of endangered species), the dusky dolphin (found only in the southern hemisphere, often in herds of more than 100 dolphins), the NZ fur seal, and the royal albatross. Other animals frequently seen include the orca or killer whale (the largest of all dolphins), common dolphins, pilot whales, blue penguins, mollymawks, and many other sea birds.

Nature being what it is, there's no guarantee of seeing any specific animal on any one tour, but it's fairly certain that something of interest will be out there any time you go. In general, the sperm whales are most likely to be seen from October to August, and orcas from December to March. Most of the other animals are seen all year round.

There's a reason why all of these animals are found at Kaikoura. It is here that the continental shelf comes closest to land, just about 800 metres off the coast. From land, the shelf slopes gradually to a depth of about 90 metres and then drops abruptly to a depth of over 800 metres. Warm and cold currents converge here, and when the southerly current hits the continental shelf it creates an upswelling current, bringing nutrients up from the ocean floor and into the light zone. The nutrients attract small marine animals, which in turn attract larger fish and squid – the sperm whale's favourite food!

**Other Sea Tours** Kaikoura Seafaris (tel 5145) have 2½ to 3 hour sea canoe safaris for $30 per person. They also have a 6 metre glass-bottomed boat which departs daily from the Coast Guard station on South Bay. A 1 hour trip to experience this 'window on the undersea world' costs $15 (children $8). Seafaris also have 2 hour fishing trips for $25 per person, diving trips for $30 per person, and half-day or all-day boat charters. They also offer a variety of minibus tours and transport to walking tracks.

Kaikoura Water Recreation Tours (tel 5920) is another operator offering a variety of sea tours. A 2 to 3 hour sightseeing adventure by boat costs $40. You can also go on a fishing trip; the cost per person is $40 for half a day or $73 for a full day, with gear and bait provided. Three hour diving trips for divers or snorkellers are also $40 per person, and there are longer scallop diving trips north to the Marlborough Sounds.

The Kaikoura Dive & Sports Centre on Yarmouth St is another place to ask about diving – it does diving trips, hires tanks, and has an air-filling station.

**Tours on Land** Sea to Summit Safaris (tel 5676, after hours 6182), based at the White Morph Restaurant on The Esplanade, operates 4WD adventures on Mt Fyffe, up to a point 1080 metres above sea level, with a view of the sea and a portable telescope for spotting whales. In summer there are 3 hour trips up there during the day, or sunset 'Alpine Wine & Dine Barbecues'. In winter they take up a toboggan for fun in the snow. Cost is $35, with a discount for hostellers and students. They also do visits to the seal and gull colonies and in winter 4WD trips to the Mt Lyford ski field for skiing, ice-skating and tobogganing.

Rakanui Scenic and Farm Tours (tel 5987)

have a 4WD farm tour on a coastal hill country farm for $20. Or you can tour on horseback with Fyffe View Horse Treks (tel 5069, 5641), which runs half-day guided horse treks for $30, and all-day adventure rides up Mt Fyffe. Kaikoura Tours (tel 5045) do guided wilderness tramping treks in addition to their whale-watching trips.

### Aerial Sightseeing

The Kaikoura Aero Club (tel 6132, 5371) has air tours ranging from 15 minutes to over 1 hour, carrying up to three passengers. A 15 minute flight costs around $47 and a 40 minute flight costs about $125 – not bad if split between two or three people.

### Places to Stay

**Hostels** The *Maui Youth Hostel* (tel 5931) at 270 The Esplanade is an attractive, modern hostel beside the sea about 1½ km from the town centre. The common room is open all day and has a superb view along the bay to the mountains beyond. The cost is $13 per night. Mt Cook buses drop off and pick up passengers at the door, and Newmans buses will do so on request. The hostel will send someone to pick you up if you come in by train if you arrange it in advance. They also hire bicycles for $5 for half a day or $10 for a full day.

The *Whitehouse* (tel 6042) at 146 The Esplanade is a private hostel in a large two-storey building by the sea which was built as a guest house about 100 years ago. Renovations are coming along a little at a time but it's open for business now. The cost is $14 per person in bunkrooms or $15 per person in double rooms, including a light breakfast of toast and coffee or tea. Cooked meals are available each night for around $6. There are bicycles for hire and a courtesy car to pick you up when you arrive in town.

Each of these hostels is licensed to accommodate 20 guests, but both can arrange accommodation in private homes when they're full.

**Hotels** The *Adelphi Hotel* (tel 5141) on West End is an older hotel. Single/double rooms cost $20/40 with shared bathrooms or $35/46 with private facilities. At the *New Commercial Hotel* (tel 5018) on the corner of Torquay and Brighton streets, B&B costs $33/54 for singles/doubles.

The *Pier Hotel* (tel 5037) on Avoca St, near the wharf, has rooms for $23 per person, B&B for $30 per person, and B&B with dinner for $42 per person. Or there's the more modern *Blue Pacific Hotel* (tel 5017) at 114 The Esplanade, where B&B costs $35/65 for singles/doubles.

**Motels** There are plenty of motels in Kaikoura, especially along The Esplanade. Most charge at least $50 per night for two, including the *Kaikoura Motels & Caravan Park* mentioned under Camping & Cabins. *Panorama Motel* (tel 5053) at 266 The Esplanade, *Clearwater Motel* (tel 5326) at 168 The Esplanade, and *Oregon Court Motel* (tel 5623) at 169 Beach Rd are all similarly priced.

At the *Norfolk Pine* (tel 5120), 124 The Esplanade, studio units cost $57 for two, two-bedroom units cost $68 for two, and a three-bedroom house sleeping eight people costs from $72 for two plus $14 for each extra adult and $10 for each extra child.

**Camping & Cabins** *Kaikoura Motels & Caravan Park* (tel 5999) at 11 Beach Rd, near the railway overpass, has tent sites costing $12.50 for two (power sites $1 more), and on-site caravans at $30 for two. They also have a budget lodge with six rooms, each sleeping five people, at a cost of $25 for two plus $8 for each extra adult. Motel units at the park cost $50 for two.

The *Kaikoura Holiday Camp* (tel 5362), on Beach Rd beside the railway station, has camping sites for $5.50 per person (power $3 extra). A two-berth cabin costs $15 and a four-berth cabin costs $30.

At the *Esplanade Caravan Park* (tel 5947), 126 The Esplanade, powered camping sites cost $14 for one or two people, cabins cost $23 for two, and on-site caravans cost $27 for two.

The DOC has three seaside camping

grounds near Kaikoura: *Puketa Camping Ground* (tel 6299), 8 km south of Kaikoura, with 100 tent sites, 100 power points, 10 cabins and a camp shop; *Goose Bay Camping Ground* (tel 5348), 18 km south of Kaikoura, with 100 tent sites, 90 power points, and five cabins; and *Waipapa Bay Camping Ground* (tel 6307), 32 km north of Kaikoura, with 25 tent sites and 26 power points. The Goose Bay camp is actually several camping areas spread over a 5-km stretch of coastline. The camping sites at each camping ground cost $5 per adult (an extra $4 for power), and the cabins cost around $20 for two people.

The *Waitane Cabins* (tel 5494) at Oaro, 22 km south of Kaikoura off SH 1, has just two self-contained cabins (you only supply linen), each costing $26 for two people. Also at Oaro is the *Ocean View Motel* (tel 5454), where caravan sites cost $10 for one or two people and motel units cost $45 for two.

### Places to Eat

When in season, crayfish (lobster) are often featured in Kaikoura restaurants; you even find it in the local takeaways. Before the whale-watching boom, the crayfish alone made Kaikoura a worthwhile stop! If you want to provide your own food you can try your luck fishing from the wharf.

**Snacks & Fast Food** There are many takeaways and coffee shops around town. The *What Not Cafe* in the town centre specialises in home-made food, with takeaways, pizza, sandwiches, salads and some health food selections. The fish shop down on the wharf sells cooked crayfish and many kinds of fish.

**Pub Food** Various hotels serve standard pub fare including the *Pier Hotel* near the wharf, the *Adelphi Hotel* and the *Commercial Hotel*.

**Restaurants** The *White Morph Restaurant* at 94 The Esplanade, beside the Nature Watch tours office, is housed in a stately old home and has both indoor and garden tables. It's open Wednesday to Sunday, in summer

from 9.30 am to 9.30 pm (to 8 pm in winter), with a break from 4 to 6 pm to prepare for dinner. Devonshire teas are served all day, and there's seafood fresh from the local fishing boats for lunch and dinner. Main courses are $10.50 to $14 and there's a salad bar for $5.50.

The *Caves Restaurant*, next to the Maori Leap Cave 3 km south of the centre on SH 1, is open admirably long hours – from 7 am to 10 pm every day except Christmas. Steak ($13) and seafood ($8.50 to $15) are served in the restaurant, and there's also a separate takeaways counter.

### Getting There & Away

**Air** There are no commercial airlines serving Kaikoura but the local Aero Club will do flights to Wellington and other places. Contact the Information Centre for details.

**Bus** The daily InterCity, Mt Cook and Newmans bus services operating between Picton and Christchurch all stop at Kaikoura. From Kaikoura it's about 2½ hours to either Picton or Christchurch.

InterCity buses arrive and depart from the Searles Four Square grocery (tel 6160) on Beach Rd; tickets are sold at the shop. Mt Cook Landline and Newmans buses arrive and depart from the car park on the beach side of West End in the centre of town. Mt Cook tickets are sold by PGG Travel (tel 5012). Newmans tickets can be purchased from The Coffee Shop (tel 5221) and The Office (tel 5359), both on West End in the centre of town, and Kaikoura Auto Care (tel 5419) at 68 Beach Rd.

**Train** One north bound and one south bound Coastal Pacific train between Picton and Christchurch stops at Kaikoura every day.

### Getting Around

The Whitehouse Hostel rents out bicycles; a single-speed costs $2 for half a day and a 10-speed costs $5 for half a day. The Maui Youth Hostel also hires out bicycles.

## HANMER SPRINGS

Hanmer Springs, the main thermal resort on the South Island, is about 10 km off SH 7, the highway to the west coast. It's popular for a variety of outdoor activities including forest walks, horse treks, river and lake fishing, jet-boating, rafting, skiing in winter and golfing at the 18 hole course. And of course, the hot pools!

### Information

There's an Information Centre (tel 7193) on Conical Hill Rd. It's open from 9 am to 5.30 pm Monday to Friday and 9 am to 1 pm on Saturdays.

### Places to Stay

**Hotels & Guest Houses** *The Lodge* (tel 7021) is a fine old hotel right in the centre of town. Rooms cost $35 to $45 for singles and $50 to $75 for doubles; some with private facilities. There's also a swimming pool. The *Shining Cuckoo Guest House* (tel 7095) at 6 Cheltenham St has B&B for $29/49. It's conveniently close to the town centre and just a 3 minute walk from the hot pools.

**Motels** There are numerous motels, most costing at least $65 per night. The *Willowbank Motel* (tel 7211) on Argelins Rd is less expensive; units cost from $45 to $55 for two. At the *Torquay Motel* (tel 7132) on Bristol St rooms cost $50 for two.

**Camping & Cabins** The *Mountain View Holiday Park* (tel 7113), on the edge of town, has camping sites at $8/14 for one/two people ($1 more with power). There's also a variety of cabins at $29 to $35 for two people and fully equipped tourist flats at $45 to $49 for two.

The *AA (Central) Tourist Park* (tel 7112) is on Jacks Pass Rd, 3 km from the town centre, with camping sites at $15 for two, cabins at $35 for two and tourist flats at $50 for two, with a small discount for AA members. Also on Jacks Pass Rd, adjacent to the golf course, is the *Pines Motor Camp* (tel 7152) where camping sites cost $5 per person ($7 with power). At the *Hanmer Alpine Village* (tel 7111), 6 km from town, on-site caravans cost $22 for two people, cabins cost $30 for two, and tourist flats cost $35 for two.

### Places to Eat

The *Alpine Restaurant*, around the corner from the CPO, is good for basic takeaways.

### Getting There & Away

InterCity buses run twice daily (once on Sundays) between Hanmer Springs and Christchurch; it's a 2 to 3 hour trip depending which bus you take! Newmans buses go to and from Christchurch Monday to Friday, connecting at the Hanmer Springs junction with Cunninghams 'Buller Connection' buses to and from Westport (2 hours) and Karamea (4 hours). These buses, unlike the InterCity ones, just drop you at the junction and you have to make your own way into the town.

# West Coast & Glaciers

The two glaciers, the Fox and the Franz Josef, are the major west coast attractions but the whole stretch of the coast is worth exploring. The road hugs the coastline most of the way from Westport in the north to Hokitika, then runs inland until it finally joins the coast again for the last stretch, before turning east and heading over the Haast Pass. Not far inland from the coast, but a long way by road, is Mt Cook with the Tasman Glacier.

Most visitors come to the west coast in summer, and the area is heavily visited at the height of the summer season from December to January. However, locals say that May to September is an excellent time to be on the coast. The days are warm and clear, with views of snow-capped peaks (but see the Weather section below!), there are no crowds and you can often get off-peak accommodation rates. Also there are no sandflies in winter!

Along the coastal beaches, the Fiordland Crested Penguin is found from June to November, and the seal colonies have the most seals from April to November. On the other hand, White Herons are in residence from November to February! Some of the organised activities take place only in summer, when the tourists are there in numbers. All in all, the west coast is definitely worth a visit at any time of the year.

## Weather

Westland could aptly be 'Wetland'. It rains a lot on the west coast, 5 metres (200 inches) or more a year. A poetically inspired visitor to Hokitika earlier this century summed up the Westland weather situation pretty well:

It rained and rained and rained
The average fall was well maintained
And when the tracks were simply bogs
It started raining cats and dogs
After a drought of half an hour
We had a most refreshing shower
And then the most curious thing of all
A gentle rain began to fall

Next day also was fairly dry
Save for a deluge from the sky
Which wetted the party to the skin
And after that the rain set in

## Glaciers

Some glacial terminology for visitors to the Fox or Franz Josef glaciers which are discussed in this chapter, or the glaciers of the Mt Cook region (see the Canterbury chapter):

*Accumulation zone* – where the snow collects

*Ablation zone* – where the glacier melts

*Bergschrund* – large crevasse in the ice near the headwall or starting point of the glacier

*Blue ice* – as the accumulation zone or névé snow is compressed by subsequent snowfalls it becomes firn and then blue ice

*Crevasses* – as the glacial ice moves down the mountain it bends and cracks open in crevasses as it crosses irregularities

*Dead ice* – as a glacier retreats isolated chunks of ice may be left behind. Sometimes these can remain for many years

*Firn* – partly compressed snow on the way to becoming glacial ice

*Glacial flour* – the river of melted ice that flows off glaciers is a milky colour from the suspension of finely ground rocks

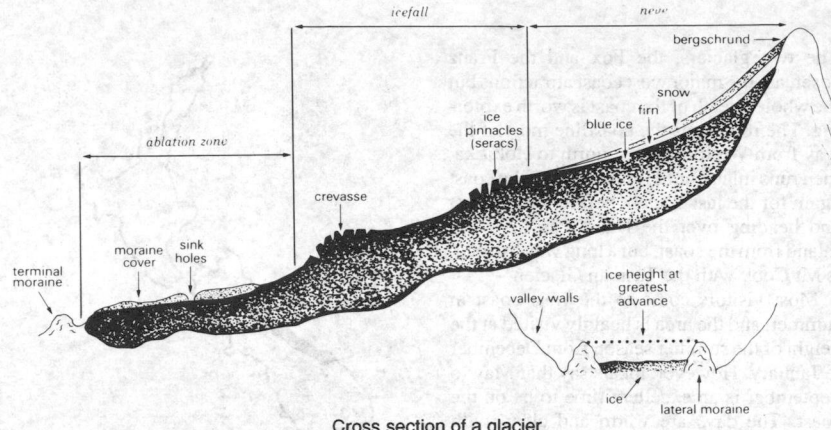

Cross section of a glacier

*Icefall* – when a glacier descends so steeply that the upper ice breaks up in a jumble of iceblocks

*Kettle lake* – lake formed by the melt of an area of isolated dead ice

*Lateral moraine* – walls formed at the sides of the glacier

*Névé* – snowfield area where firn is formed

*Seracs* – ice pinnacles formed, like crevasses, by the glacier bending over irregularities

*Terminal* – the final ice face at the end of the glacier

*Terminal moraine* – mass of boulders and rocks marking the end point of the glacier, its final push down the valley

# Westland

You can approach the northern end of the west coast from three directions – coming south from Nelson or the two crossings from Christchurch, the northern one passing close to Hanmer Springs while the southern one runs through Arthur's Pass.

## NELSON TO THE COAST

The road across from Nelson in the north to the coast is interesting and scenic. The Buller area is still scarred from the 1929 Murchison and 1968 Inangahua earthquakes. From Inangahua junction you can head through the Lower Buller Gorge to the coast, or you can

go on to Greymouth via Reefton on the inland route. The coastal route has more to offer but is a fair bit longer.

## WESTPORT
Population 4660

Westport is the major town at the northern end of Westland. Its prosperity is based on coal mining although the mining activity takes place some distance from the town.

### Information

Palmerston St is the main street of Westport. There's an Information Centre (tel 6658) in Brougham St, a couple of doors off Palmerston St, open from 9 am to 5 pm every day. The DOC office (tel 7743) in Palmerston St is open from 8 am to 4.30 pm on weekdays. It has information on the seal colony and the many tracks and walkways in the area. The AA office is on the corner of Russell and Wakefield streets.

### Coaltown Museum

Coaltown on Queen St is a well laid out museum reconstructing aspects of coal-mining life, including a walk through a simulated coal mine complete with authentic sound effects, two audiovisual presentations, coal-mining artefacts and some excellent

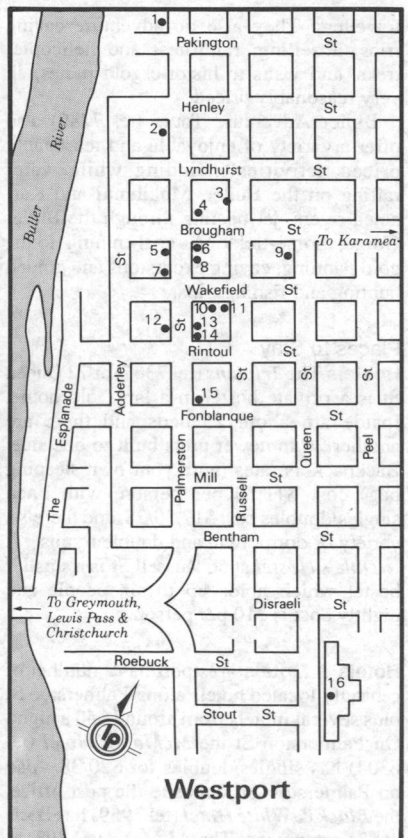

1 Wagon Wheel Restaurant
2 Mandala Coffeehouse
3 Dale's Hostel
4 Information Centre
5 Black & White Hotel
6 Post Office
7 Bonanza Takeaways
8 Department of Conservation (DOC)
9 Tripinns Hostel
10 Cristy's Restaurant
11 Automobile Association (AA)
12 Newmans Coachlines
13 Cunningham's Coachlines bus depot
14 InterCity bus depot
15 DB Westport Motor Hotel
16 Coaltown Museum

photographic exhibits. It's open every day from 9 am to 4.30 pm; admission is $4 (children $2).

## Cape Foulwind Walkway

The 4 km, 1½ hour Cape Foulwind Walkway is part of the New Zealand Walkway system and extends along the cape down to Tauranga Bay, passing by a lighthouse site, a replica of Abel Tasman's astrolabe and a seal colony. A brochure describing the walk is available from the Information Centre or the DOC office in Westport.

The Maoris knew the cape as Tauranga, meaning 'a sheltered anchorage or landing place'. The first European to discover the cape was the explorer Abel Tasman, who sighted it in December 1642 and named it 'Glyphaygen Hock' or Rocky Point. When Captain Cook anchored here in March 1770 his ship *Endeavour* was rocked by a furious storm and he named it 'Cape Foulwind' – a cape of foul winds.

## Seal Colony

There's a seal colony at Tauranga Bay, 12 km from Westport. It is on the southern end of the Cape Foulwind Walkway, which follows the coastline for 4 km from Cape Foulwind to Tauranga Bay. If you have wheels and you're not doing the walkway you can drive to this end of the walkway (follow the signposted road to Carters Beach) and simply scale the bluff to look down on the colony.

Depending on the time of the year there may be anywhere from 20 to over 100 seals down on the rocks. Pups are born in late November-early December and for about a month afterwards the mothers stay on the rocks to tend the young before setting off to sea on feeding forays. Lookouts have been built to give you a good view of the seals; beware of venturing past the marked areas as the cliffs can be dangerous.

Fur seal

### Other Attractions

From Denniston, 27 km north-east of Westport and 600 metres up in the hills, there are magnificent views if you're lucky enough to get a clear day. Coal from here used to be taken down the Denniston Incline, a railway with a gradient of one in one (yes!), to Waimangaroa below. The complete 5 km walk takes about 2 hours downhill or 3 hours if you do it uphill.

Charming Creek Walk is another interesting Westport walk through a mining area. The complete walk takes over 4 hours but it can be done in sections. The Lyell Walk is a 1½ hour return walk departing from the town of Lyell in the Buller Gorge, 64 km from Westport, once again through a mining area, this time gold-mining. The Information Centre has brochures describing all of these and other mining walks.

Other Westport activities include jet-boating on the Buller River or tramping, caving or fishing trips. Norwest Adventures (tel 6686, 8922) do 4 to 5 hour 'underworld rafting' trips through caves, passing by stalactites, stalagmites and glow-worms, for $45. These tours are highly recommended by travellers. They also do adventure caving trips, abseiling, rainforest and helicopter treks, and visits to historic gold mines, all very reasonably priced.

Buller Adventure Tours (tel 7286) also offer a variety of enjoyable and reasonably priced activities including white water rafting on the Buller, Mokihinui and Karamea rivers, jet-boating through the Buller Gorge, horse-trekking, coal-mining tours, gold panning, caving excursions and guided hunting and fishing trips.

### Places to Stay

**Hostels** The *Tripinns* (tel 7367) at 72 Queen St is a private hostel in a large old home. Inside are about 25 beds and there are another 20 in newer units built to one side. Backpackers rates (with your own sleeping bag) cost $11.50 per person, with linen singles/doubles cost $17.50/28, and there's a variety of dorm, twin and double rooms.

*Dale's Hostel* at 56 Russell St is a smaller hostel which holds up to six people and nightly cost is $10 per person.

**Hotels & Motels** Westport has a number of centrally located hotels along Palmerston St plus several motels from around $50 a night. On Palmerston St the *McManus Hotel* (tel 6304) has singles/doubles for $20/38. Also on Palmerston St, opposite the post office, the *Black & White Hotel* (tel 7959) has B&B at $25 per person. The *Al Motel* (tel 808) at 63 Queen St has self-contained units at $55 to $65 for two.

**Camping & Cabins** The *Howard Park Holiday Camp* (tel 7043) is on Domett St only a km from the post office. Camping costs $7/12.50 a night for one/two people, or $9.50/14 with power. They also have chalets at $23 for two, on-site caravans at $26 for two and bunkroom accommodation at $9 per person.

The *Seal Colony Tourist Park* (tel 8002) is 6 km from Westport, out towards (yes) the seal colony. Rates here for tent or power sites are $15 for two, cabins are $32 for two and

Top: The Post Office, Cathedral Square, Christchurch (TW)
Left: The Wizard, Cathedral Square, Christchurch (TC)
Right: Scott Monument, Christchurch (TW)

Top: Antigua Boathouse, Christchurch (TW)
Bottom: Airforce Museum, Christchurch (TW)

tourist flats are $46 for two, with discounts in the low season.

## Places to Eat

There are a number of takeaways and sandwich places along Palmerston St including *Bonanza Takeaways* near the Wakefield St corner where you can take the food out or sit down and eat there. It's open from 8 am to 10 pm on weekdays, until midnight on Fridays and Saturdays, and noon to 10 pm Sundays. There's pub food at several of the hotels including the *Black & White* on Palmerston St or the *Wagon Wheel Restaurant* in Larsens Tavern.

The *Mandala* on Palmerston St is a pleasant coffee house restaurant serving pizzas and takeaways, vegie or meat burgers and dinner meals with main courses from around $12.50 to $16. They also have good coffee, cold fruit drinks and desserts, and they're open every day of the week from 7 am until 10.30 pm. Up market *Cristy's* on Wakefield St is Westport's flashy licensed restaurant.

## Getting There & Away

**Air** Air Nelson (tel 7209) have daily direct flights to Wellington, with connections to other centres including Auckland, Christchurch, Dunedin, Nelson and Blenheim.

**Road** InterCity buses make return trips between Westport and Greymouth (2 hours) with a rest stop at the Pancake Rocks (Punakaiki) every day but Sundays. From Greymouth they have connecting buses heading north to Nelson and south to the glaciers, and both a bus and train to Christchurch. The Christchurch bus goes via Hanmer Springs, the largest thermal resort in the South Island.

Newmans have a Nelson-Westport-Greymouth service, also running daily except Sundays. From Nelson they have connections to Motueka and Takaka, to Picton or to Christchurch.

Heading north to Karamea for the Heaphy Track, Cunningham's buses make the return trip Monday to Friday, leaving Karamea in the morning and returning from Westport in the afternoon. They also go to the Hanmer Springs junction, connecting there with Newmans buses to Christchurch, from Monday to Friday.

## Getting Around

A taxi to the airport costs around $12. Bicycles are hired from Beckers Cycles & Sports on Palmerston St.

## KARAMEA

From Westport, SH 67 continues 100 km north to Karamea, near the end of the Heaphy Track and the Wangapeka Track. Many good day walks are in the area too, including the 5 hour Fenian Track and the 8 hour return trek to the 1084 metre Mt Stormy. There's another walk to Lake Hanlon and the first leg of the Wangepeka Track also makes a good day walk.

Several spectacular limestone arch formations are found in the Karamea area, 15 km from the North Beach turn-off. The Honey Comb Caves are also magnificent, with a collection of bones of moa and other extinct species. Access is restricted to protect the caves, but you can go through them on a guided tour.

The Karamea River offers good swimming, fishing and canoeing. There are also good swimming holes on the Wanganui, Oparara and Kohaihai rivers. Swimming is dangerous in the open sea but there are tidal lagoons 1 km north and 3 km south of Karamea where swimming is good at high tide. There are lots of beautiful beaches around but the only drawback is millions of sandflies. A long-running local joke is that 'sandflies work in pairs – one pulls back the sheets, while the other eats you alive'.

Information on these and other natural attractions is available in Karamea at the DOC office (tel 26-852).

## WESTPORT TO GREYMOUTH

The coast road has some most unusual bridges – not only are they one-lane, so traffic can only pass in one direction at a time, but they also share the bridge with the railway line. It's best to give way to trains!

### Paparoa National Park & Punakaiki
Midway between Westport (57 km north) and Greymouth (47 km south) is Punakaiki, better known as the Pancake Rocks. These limestone rocks have formed into what look like stacks of pancakes just waiting for a hungry sea giant. If there's a good tide running here, the water surges into caverns below the rocks and squirts out in impressive geysers. There's a 15 minute walk from the road, around the rocks and geyser, and back again. It's best to go at high tide when the blowholes really perform. Be sure to heed the signs warning you to keep on the track – people have been killed when they wandered off the track and fell over the cliffs.

There was pressure for years to have this area declared a national park and this was finally accomplished in December 1987 when the 30,000 hectare Paparoa National Park became the twelfth national park in New Zealand. In addition to the rocks at Punakaiki it has many other natural attractions including mountains (the Paparoa Range), rivers, wilderness areas, limestone formations including cliffs and caves, diverse vegetation, and a black petrel colony, the only nesting area of this rare albatross-like bird. If you plan to go caving you need to know what you're doing – in some caves the water rises so fast after rain that you'd drown before you had a chance to get out.

The park has a number of interesting walks including the Inland Pack Track, a 2 day track along a route established by miners around 1867 to circumvent the more rugged coastal route. Also notable are the Croesus Track, a full day or 2 day tramp over the Paparoa Range from Blackball to Barrytown, and the Moonlight Track – both tracks pass through historic gold-mining areas. There are also many shorter river and coast walks. If you're planning on walking or caving, register your intentions at the Park Visitor Centre. Guides are available for many activities within the park and environs.

The Paparoa National Park Visitor Centre (tel Barrytown 895) is next to the highway and it's open every day from 8 am to 4.30 pm. In summer it may stay open later, until around 6 or 6.30 pm. It has interesting displays including an audiovisual, pamphlets and maps on all the park's walks and attractions, and can supply information on tides and current conditions throughout the park. Many of the inland walks are subject to river flooding and other conditions, so check here before setting out.

**Places to Stay & Eat** The *Punakaiki Camping Ground* (tel Barrytown 894) has tent sites at $6 per person, power sites at $14 for two, cabins at $24 for two, and bunkroom accommodation at $10 per person. It's operated by the DOC, in conjunction with the National Park.

The Pancake Tearooms opposite the Pancake Rocks are open from 9 am to 5 pm daily all year round. Also here is the very pleasant natural-foods *Nikau Palms Cafe* which is only open seasonally from around November to Easter.

At Barrytown, 16 km south of Punakaiki, the *All Nations Tavern* (tel Barrytown 812) has bunkroom accommodation at $12 per person, double and twin rooms at $35, which one person can take for $17 if it's not busy. There's a fully-equipped kitchen for guests' use and they also serve takeaways, breakfast and bistro meals.

**Getting There & Away** InterCity and Newmans buses between Westport and Greymouth stop at Punakaiki every day except Sundays.

### GREYMOUTH
Population 11,200
It's another 47 km to Greymouth, a town with a long gold-mining history and still a bit of gold town flavour today. It's the largest town on the west coast despite its small population. It's located at the mouth of the Grey River – hence its name – and despite the high protective wall along the Mawhera Quay the river still manages to flood the

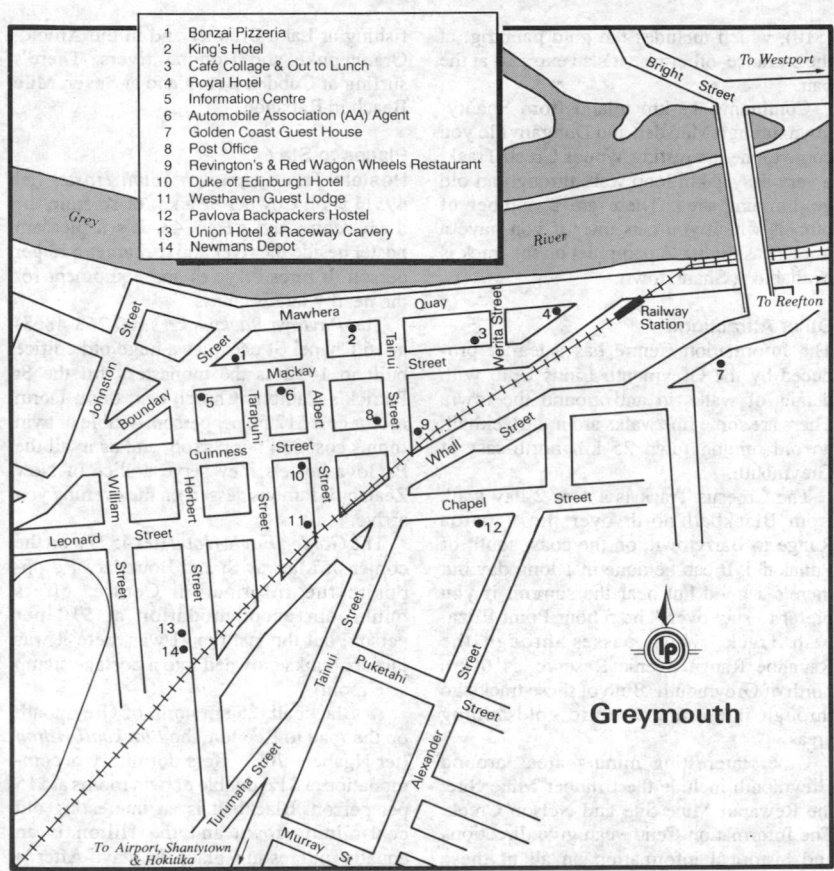

1   Bonzai Pizzeria
2   King's Hotel
3   Café Collage & Out to Lunch
4   Royal Hotel
5   Information Centre
6   Automobile Association (AA) Agent
7   Golden Coast Guest House
8   Post Office
9   Revington's & Red Wagon Wheels Restaurant
10  Duke of Edinburgh Hotel
11  Westhaven Guest Lodge
12  Pavlova Backpackers Hostel
13  Union Hotel & Raceway Carvery
14  Newmans Depot

Greymouth

town once in a while after periods of heavy rain.

### Information

There's an Information Centre (tel 5101) in the Regent Theatre on the corner of Herbert and Mackay streets. It's open from 8.30 am to 5 pm on weekdays only. There's an AA agent about a block away on Mackay St.

### Shantytown

Greymouth's major tourist attraction is 8 km south of the town and then 3 km inland from the main road. Shantytown is a fine repro-

duction of west coast life in the gold rush days, with all the buildings a town of that era would have had. For many the prime attraction will be the two 1897 steam locomotives taking you out for a short trip into the bush. You can also have a go at gold panning, there's an old fellow there to give you pointers and everyone is assured of coming up with at least a few flakes to take away in a little bottle.

Shantytown is open 8.30 am to 5 pm daily and entry, including train rides, costs $7 (children with family $2). If you want to try panning for gold buy a combined ticket

($10), which includes the gold panning, at the entrance, otherwise it's an extra $4 at the pan.

Continuing 17 km inland from Shantytown through Marsden and Dunganville you come to the interesting Woods Creek Track, a very easy 1 km loop walk through an old gold-mining area. There are a number of tunnels which you can enter if you have a torch (flashlight). A pamphlet on the track is available at Shantytown.

## Other Attractions

The Information Centre has a leaflet produced by the Greymouth Lions Club with details of walks in and around the town. There are some fine walks around Blackball, an old mining town 25 km north-east of Greymouth.

The Croesus Track is a 1 or 2 day walk from Blackball north over the Paparoa Range to Barrytown, on the coast south of Punakaiki. It can be done in 1 long day but there's a good hut near the summit if you prefer to stay over. The 5 hour Point Elizabeth Track, which passes through the Rapahoe Range Scenic Reserve, is 6 km north of Greymouth. Both of these tracks go through interesting historic gold-mining areas.

Other interesting mining areas around Greymouth include the Brunner Mine Site, the Rewanui Mine Site and Nelson Creek. The Information Centre can give directions and historical information on all of these sites, and on good spots where you might try panning for gold – there are many places along the west coast where gold is still found. They also have details on many good scenic drives near Greymouth.

Off Beat Tours (tel Ngahere 842) does reasonably priced tours of gold and coal-mining sites, ghost towns, fishing, scenic rafting, transport to and from walking tracks, sailing trips on Lake Brunner, pub crawls off the main routes, and more. The Greymouth Aero Club (tel 80-407) does scenic flights around the area with rates starting from $20.

Fishing safaris are especially popular activities from Greymouth, there's good fishing at Lake Brunner and in the Arnold, Orangepuke and Hohonu rivers. There's surfing at Cobden Beach and at Seven Mile Beach in Rapahoe.

## Places to Stay

**Hostels** The *Greymouth Youth Hostel* (tel 4951) is on Cowper St a km or so from the town centre and sleeps 43. It's a pleasant hostel beside the river and it charges $13 per person. It hires bicycles and equipment for the nearby tennis courts.

The *Pavlova Backpackers* (tel 768-4868) at 16 Chapel St occupies a huge old edifice built in 1912 as the monastery for the St Patrick's Catholic Church next door. Dorm rooms cost $12.50 per person, double or twin rooms cost $14 per person, and as in all the Pavlova hostels they serve a slice of New Zealand's famous dessert on the evening you arrive.

The *Golden Eagle Hotel* (tel 4577), on the corner of Mackay St and Boundary Rd opposite the Information Centre, offers bunkroom accommodation at $10 per person, but the last time I was there it was just six bunks crowded into a postage stamp size room!

At Blackball, 25 km north of Greymouth on the road to Reefton, the *Blackball Hilton* (tel Ngahere 705) offers dormitory accommodation at $12, double or twin rooms at $15 per person. Blackball is an interesting old coal-mining town and the Hilton is an equally interesting place to stay. After a period of disrepair it now has new owners who have lovingly restored it to some of its old glory and it's recently been designated a New Zealand Historic Place. David and Linda are friendly hosts with lots of information on the history of the Hilton, the town, and things to do around Blackball. The Hilton is full of character and also has a billiards room, a TV lounge, a sauna and spa pool. They offer an economical breakfast and dinner, or you can cook your own.

**Camping & Cabins** The *Greymouth Seaside Motor Camp* (tel 6618) is 2½ km south of the centre on Chesterfield St. Camping charges for two people are $13.50 or with power $15. Cabins cost $26 to $33 for two, on-site caravans $29, and tourist flats $48. There's also bunkroom accommodation at $11. It's right beside the beach and right at the end of the airport runway.

The *South Beach Motor Park* (tel 26-768) about 5 km south of Greymouth has camping sites at $5 per person, $6 with power, but it lacks the usual kitchen and shower facilities. At Rapahoe, 11 km north of Greymouth, the *Rapahoe Motor Camp* (tel Greymouth 7337) also has camping sites at $5 per person, $7 with power, and cabins which cost $15 to $20 for two.

**Guest Houses** There are three guest houses close to the town centre. The *Westhaven Guest Lodge* (tel 5605) is at 65 Albert St beside the railway line. Nightly cost in this pretty basic sort of place is $18 per person or $23 with breakfast. The *Golden Coast Guest House* (tel 7839), at 10 Smith St overlooking the river, is a bit up-market from the West Haven and singles cost $42 to $50, doubles or twins cost $60, including breakfast. The *High Street Guest House* (tel 7444) at 20 High St offers B&B at $47/68.

**Hotels** That gold-mining history shows in the number of hotels you'll find around central Greymouth. None of them are particularly special. You could try the *Duke of Edinburgh* (tel 6302, 4020) in Guinness St with singles/doubles from $31/40 or the *Australasian Hotel* (tel 4023) on Main South Rd about 2½ km south of town, where singles/doubles cost $35/50 or $44/65 for B&B.

There are other hotels around Greymouth but they are more expensive. The *Revington's Hotel* (tel 7055) on Tainui St has the Red Wagon Wheels Restaurant and rooms with attached bathroom cost $63/73. The *King's Hotel* (tel 5085) on Mawhera Quay has doubles ranging from around $75 to $95.

**Motels** There are plenty of motels in Greymouth but there's hardly anything

under $65 a night! The *Willowbank Motor Lodge* (tel 5339), 2 km from Greymouth on SH 6, has two studio units at $58 for two but their larger units cost $65 to $75. The *Ace Tourist Motel* (tel 6884) on Omoto Rd, also 2 km from the centre has rooms from $64 to $70 for two. Others are the *South Beach Motel* (tel 26-768) at 318 Main South Rd and the *Greymouth Motel* (tel 6090) at 195 High St, both with rooms at around $65 for two.

### Places to Eat
There's the usual selection of cafes and sandwich places around the town centre. You could try the *Hideaway Tea & Coffee House* on Albert St or the *Out to Lunch* sandwich bar on Mackay St. The *Bonzai Pizzeria* at 29 Mackay St is a pleasant little place with 16 varieties of quite good pizza. Medium pizzas cost $8 to $15, large ones are $12 to $20, and they have tempting desserts too. They open at 11 am weekdays, 5 pm on weekends, and stay open every night until 10 or 11 pm.

At the *Union Hotel* on Herbert St near the railway line the *Raceway Carvery* is something of a local institution. The front is very unpromising but it's quite reasonable inside. The accent here is on low prices and big quantities, cuisine highlights are a definite second. It's open for breakfast, lunch and dinner daily. Dinner is served from around 5 to 8 pm Sunday to Thursday, to 9 pm Friday and Saturday. The menu has all the pub regulars from T-bones to chicken kiev at prices around $7 to $11.

Alternatively there's the *Red Wagon Wheels Restaurant* in the Revington's Hotel on Tainui St, serving breakfast, lunch and dinner every day except Sundays. It was formerly a Cobb & Co and still has the same decor and a similar menu, with dinner main courses from $10 to $16 and a special children's menu. Quite a few other pubs offer food including the *Royal Hotel* on Mawhera Quay. For a fancier night out try the *Cafe Collage* on Mackay St.

### Getting There & Away
**Air** Air Nelson flights operate from Hokitika

although there is a small airport in Greymouth.

**Bus** Delta Landline has daily buses between Picton and Greymouth, via St Arnaud, Murchison and Reefton. It's 4 hours to St Arnaud or 5½ hours to Blenheim, from where you transfer to Picton. Tickets are sold at the House of Travel (tel 4479) in Mackay St but the Delta buses come and go from opposite Revington's Hotel on Tainui St.

Newmans (tel 6118) are on Herbert St near the railway line. They have a Monday to Saturday Greymouth-Westport-Nelson service. From Nelson they operate to Motueka and Takaka, Picton and Christchurch.

InterCity buses go from the railway station (tel 4199) and they have daily services north to Westport and Nelson and south down the coast to the glaciers. Buses to Christchurch go four times a week. Travel times are 2 hours to Westport, 5 hours to Nelson, 4 and 5 hours to the glaciers, and 4½ hours to Christchurch.

**Train** The Tranz Alpine Express operates daily between Christchurch and Greymouth. The trip takes about 5 hours and is notable for its spectacular scenery – it crosses some remarkable gorges on its climb through the Southern Alps, passing over numerous viaducts and bridges and 19 tunnels, including the 8½ km Otira Tunnel. Between Arthur's Pass and Greymouth the road and railway line take quite different routes.

### Getting Around
Kitchingham's Cycles (tel 6559) on Mackay St rents bicycles for $10 a day, tandems for $20 a day, or baby push chairs for $2. Greymouth Taxis (tel 7078) goes to the airport for $10.

### ARTHUR'S PASS
The small settlement of Arthur's Pass is 4 km from the pass of the same name. The 924 metre pass was on the route used by the Maoris to reach the Westland, but its European discovery was made by Arthur Dobson

in 1864, when the gold rush on the Westland created enormous pressure to find a crossing over the Southern Alps from Christchurch. A coach road was completed within a year of Dobson's discovery. Later on the coal and timber trade demanded a railway, which was completed in 1923.

The town is a fine base for the walks, climbs, views and winter-time skiing of Arthur's Pass National Park and you can go there on a day trip from Greymouth or Christchurch.

### Information
There's a National Park Visitor Centre (tel 89-211) in the town, open from 8 am to 5 pm every day. It has information on all the park walks, with pamphlets on many good day walks and also topographical maps and route guides for 11 longer tramps with huts. They can also offer valuable advice on the park's often savagely changeable weather conditions – check here before you go on any walk, and fill out an intentions card. Be sure to sign out again when you leave, otherwise they'll send a search party out to find you! The rangers can help you to choose a walk that is safe at the time and suitable for your experience and abilities.

The Visitor Centre is also a park museum, with excellent displays, an audiovisual presentation, and a three-dimensional model of the park. In January there's a summer programme of guided walks and evening talks, discussions, films and slide shows.

### Arthur's Pass National Park
There are day walks in the park which offer 360° views of snow-capped peaks. Many peaks are over 2000 metres, the highest being Mt Murchison at 2400 metres.

The park has huts on the tramping tracks and also several areas suitable for camping. The day walks leaflet from the Visitors Centre lists half-day walks of 1 to 4 hours and day walks of 5 to 8 hours. The 2 hour (one-way) walk to Temple Basin provides superb views of the surrounding peaks. There's skiing at Temple Basin; the ski season is usually from June to September.

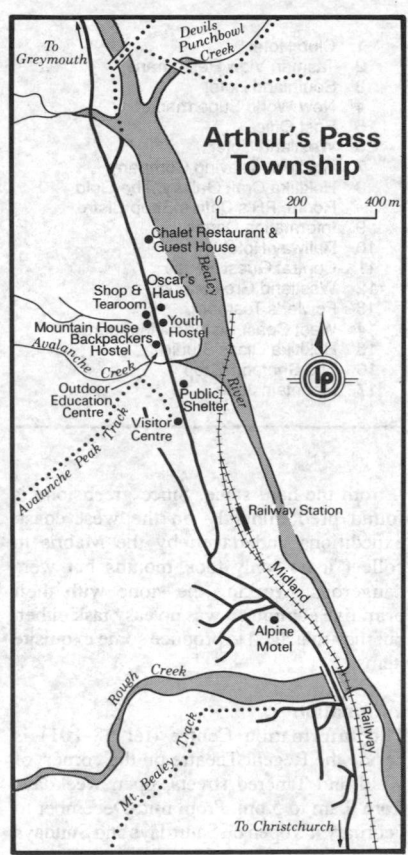

## Arthur's Pass Township

*To Greymouth*

*Devils Punchbowl Creek*

0    200    400 m

Chalet Restaurant & Guest House

Oscar's Haus

Shop & Tearoom

Mountain House
Backpackers
Hostel

*Avalanche Creek*

Youth Hostel

Outdoor Education Centre

Public Shelter

Visitor Centre

*Avalanche Peak Track*

*Bealey River*

Railway Station

*Midland*

Alpine Motel

*Rough Creek*

*Railway*

*Mt. Bealey Track*

*To Christchurch*

## Places to Stay & Eat

The *Arthur's Pass Youth Hostel* (tel 89-230) has bunkroom accommodation at $13 a night. Across the road is *Mountain House* (tel 89-258), a good private hostel which also has bunks for $13. The *Alpine Motel* (tel 89-233) has double rooms at $58 and some simpler rooms from $45. The *Chalet Guest House* (tel 89-236) offers B&B for $65 double with shared facilities or $75 double with private facilities.

The *Oscar's Haus Alpine Crafts* (tel 89-234) has a fully equipped Alpine-style house behind the shop with double rates of $65 for the first night, $55 the second night and $50 for each night thereafter. They also have a few campervan sites at $15 and tent sites at $5 per site.

You can also check with the Park Visitor Centre for other accommodation in and near town. They have listings of club and social huts and private baches which are sometimes available for hire. Usually this must be arranged in advance and it's an especially good option for groups.

Outside of town, the *Otira Hotel* (tel 802) in the township of Otira, 14½ km west of Arthur's Pass, has single/double rooms at $20/30.

The *Flock Hill Lodge* (tel Darfield 88-196) is a high country sheep station 35 km east of Arthur's Pass on SH 73, adjacent to Lake Pearson and the Craigieburn Forest Park. It can accommodate 36 people in twin or bunkrooms for $18 per person and there's a fully equipped communal kitchen. Activities include tramping and forest walks, canoeing, windsurfing, swimming, fishing, horse-riding, skiing and ice skating.

You can eat in the *Arthur's Pass Store & Tearoom* or in the *Chalet Restaurant* which has a cheaper coffee bar beyond its restaurant area. If you're preparing your own food bring it in with you if possible, as groceries are more expensive in Arthur's Pass than elsewhere.

## Getting There & Away

You can get to Arthur's Pass by road or rail. InterCity buses going between Greymouth and Christchurch on Sunday, Monday, Wednesday and Friday stop at Arthur's Pass. The Tranz Alpine Express daily train between Greymouth and Christchurch also stops here. Both are priced about the same. Bus and train tickets are sold at the Arthur's Pass Store.

Between Arthur's Pass and Christchurch, the train takes the more scenic route; on to Greymouth they both offer great views of the Otira Gorge, although the road goes over the top of the pass, rather more spectacular than the rail route which goes through the 8½ km Otira tunnel immediately upon leaving town.

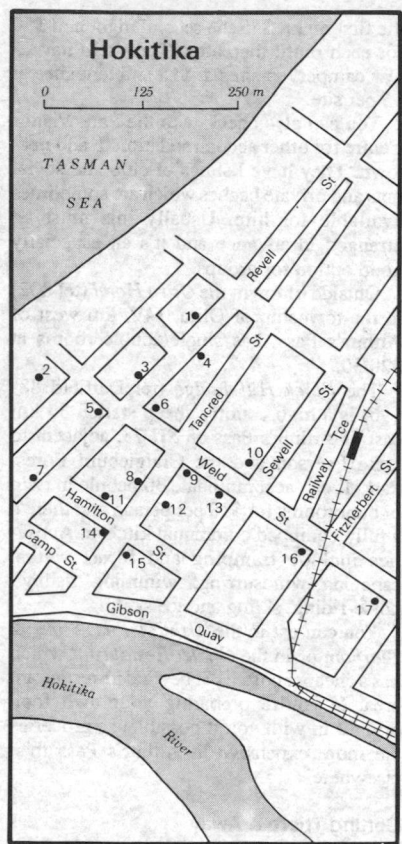

| | |
|---|---|
| 1 | Club Hotel |
| 2 | Tasman View Restaurant |
| 3 | Southland Hotel |
| 4 | New World Supermarket |
| 5 | Post Office |
| 6 | Westland Hotel |
| 7 | Hokitika Weaving Company |
| 8 | Hokitika Craft Gallery, The Gold Room, PR's Coffee Shop Bistro |
| 9 | Information Centre |
| 10 | Railway Hotel |
| 11 | Central Guest House |
| 12 | Westland Greenstone |
| 13 | Fowler's Tearoom |
| 14 | West Coast Historical Museum |
| 15 | Hokitika Glass Studio |
| 16 | The Seafood Shop |
| 17 | Mountain Jade |

### Getting Around

The Arthur's Pass Passenger Service (tel 89-233) offers minibus transport to the ski fields and walking tracks. If you're going tramping you can arrange with them to pick you up at the other end when you finish.

### HOKITIKA

Hokitika, 40 km south of Greymouth, is a major centre for greenstone. Historically, greenstone or jade was much treasured by the Maoris who used it for decorative jewellery – tikis – and for carving their lethal weapons – the flat war clubs known as meres – from the hard stone. Since greenstone is found predominantly on the west coast, expeditions undertaken by the Maoris to collect it not only took months but were dangerous. Working the stone with their primitive equipment was no easy task either, but they managed to produce some exquisite items.

### Information

The Information Centre (tel 58-101) is beside the Regent Theatre on the corner of Weld and Tancred streets, open weekdays from 9 am to 5 pm. From mid-December to February it's open on Saturdays and Sundays too, also from 9 am to 5 pm.

Hokitika has several banks but except for one branch of the Westland Bank in Harihari there are no more banks further south until you reach Wanaka. There's an AA agent beside the Hokitika Motel in Fitzherbert St, on the outskirts of town.

### Museum

The West Coast Historical Museum, on Tancred St, has many gold-mining relics and various other interesting exhibits. It's open 9.30 am to 4.30 pm weekdays most of the year and daily from Christmas to Easter. Admission is $2.55 (children $1) including an audiovisual presentation.

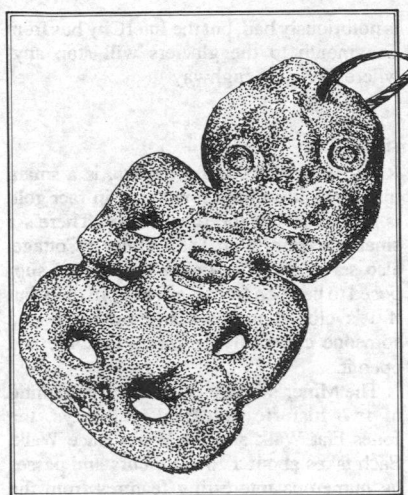

Tiki

## Crafts

You can buy jewellery, tikis of course, and other greenstone ornaments from Westland Greenstone on Tancred St. It's open from 8 am to 5 pm daily. Whether you're buying or not you can visit the workshop and see greenstone being cut and carved. Even with modern tools and electric power, working greenstone is not simple and good greenstone pieces will not be cheap. Mountain Jade in Weld St specialises in jade sculpture as well as jewellery and is also open daily from 8 am to 5 pm.

There are several other craft outlets in Hokitika including the Hokitika Craft Gallery opposite Westland Greenstone. Next door, The Gold Room sells handcrafted gold jewellery made from locally mined gold, with many specimens of the distinctively flat gold nuggets found in the region. Also in Tancred St is the Hokitika Glass Studio. All of these shops are open daily from 8.30 am to 5 pm. A block over on Revell St is Genesis Creations.

The Hokitika Weaving Company in Revell St also does some interesting work,

weaving on Dobcross 1955 model looms imported from England. You'll find them weaving from 9 am to 4 pm on weekdays.

## Other Attractions

There's a glow-worm dell right beside the road on the northern edge of the town. Hokitika has a number of historically interesting old buildings and a leaflet describing a historic walk is available at the information centre or the museum. In 1866 Revell St had no less than 84 hotels! Only six are left.

The Heritage Hokitika group has recently renovated the historic old wharf along Gibson Quay, where there are historical buildings and various water activities including daytime or evening jet-boat rides for $15. Heritage Hokitika has also produced a leaflet outlining an 'Old Pub Walk', available at the Information Centre.

Scenic Rafting (tel 57-114, 58-481) offers various rafting trips including an all-day 'thrill seeker' trip down one of New Zealand's steepest rafting rivers, where you helicopter to the top of Frisco Canyon and raft down through harrowing rapids, ending up with a barbecue, all for $120. They also do family rafting and Canadian canoeing in the Hokitika Gorge, Grey River, Lake Mahinapua and Mahinapua Creek, with trips priced from $25 to $55.

There are a number of scenic areas around Hokitika including Lake Kaniere, Lake Mahinapua, the Hokitika Gorge, and Goldsborough, with many interesting walking tracks, gold panning, camping, fishing, and so on. The Information Centre has details on the many things to do in the region.

## Places to Stay

The *Hokitika Holiday Park* (tel 58-172) is on the corner of SH 6 and Livingstone St and has a variety of accommodation possibilities. Camping is $11.50 a night for two people, $2 more with power. They also have a bunkhouse costing $8 per person, a selection of cabins priced from $15 to $32 for two, and tourist flats at $36 for two.

Hokitika has a number of motels, all from

around $60 a night. There are also several hotels around the town centre. The big *Westland Hotel* (tel 58-411), on the corner of Weld and Revell streets, has rooms at $30/40 or with attached bathroom at $40/50. The *Club Hotel* (tel 58-170) on Revell St has rooms at $20/36. The *Southland Hotel* (tel 58-334), also on Revell St, has budget rooms at $32/42 in addition to their more expensive 'de luxe' rooms at $72/82.

The pleasant *Central Guest House* (tel 58-232) at 20 Hamilton St is a cosy place with rooms at $29/44 for singles/doubles. Meals are extra, but inexpensive and good value. The Information Centre has listings for farmstays around Hokitika and all around the South Westland.

### Places to Eat
For snacks and sandwiches you can try the *Preston Bakery & Tearoom* on Revell St or *Fowler's Tearoom & Restaurant* on Weld St has good pies and light meals, as does *PR's Coffee Shop Bistro* in Tancred St. The *El Jebel* in the mall near the New World supermarket in Revell St serves pizza, and the *Seafood Shop* by the railway tracks does fish & chips.

In the pub food category, the *Westland Hotel* has a carvery for lunch and dinner. Overlooking Hokitika's windswept and grey beach is the *Tasman View* restaurant.

### Getting There & Away
**Air** Air Nelson (tel 58-134) has three daily direct flights to Christchurch and weekday direct flights to Wellington and Nelson, with connections to other centres.

**Bus** The InterCity services down the coast from Greymouth to Fox Glacier stop through Hokitika at least once a day. Travel time is 40 minutes to Greymouth, 4 hours to Fox Glacier.

### SOUTH FROM HOKITIKA
It's about 140 km south from Hokitika to the Franz Josef Glacier but you can make a few stops on the way. Hitching along this coast

is notoriously bad, but the InterCity bus from Greymouth to the glaciers will stop anywhere along the highway.

### Ross
Ross, 30 km south of Hokitika, is a small, historic gold-mining town, and in fact gold is still mined in the town today. There's a small museum in an 1885 Miner's Cottage, also serving as the Visitor Centre. It's supposed to be open from 8 am to 4 pm daily but if it's closed just ask around town and someone can easily be found to come and open it.

The Miner's Cottage sits at the beginning of two historic goldfield walkways, the Jones Flat Walk and the Water Race Walk. Each takes about 1 to 1½ hours and passes by numerous interesting features from the gold rush days. In the evening there are glow-worms on these walks but at any time, be very careful to stay on the walkway or you could find yourself down a mineshaft!

A long area along Jones Creek is open to the public for gold panning and pans may be hired from several businesses in town. Near the car park in front of the Miner's Cottage is a new working gold mine where you can stand and watch the operations from above for as long as you like. There's also a small, but unusual, museum on the main street, but it may be closed in winter. Also centrally located is a display of old gold-mining equipment and buildings.

At the Waitaha Valley, a few km south of Ross, South Westland Saddle Safaris (tel Ross 54-182) does horse treks. Full-day treks cost $60 and they also do excursions up to 12 days long.

**Places to Stay & Eat** The atmospheric *Empire Hotel* (tel 54-005) has camping sites, cabins at $8 per person, rooms at $20/40 for singles/doubles, B&B at $25/50, or $32/60 with both breakfast and dinner. Around the corner the Ross Motel (tel 54-022, 54-153) has motel units at $50 double, ask about them at the Manera Store.

The *Empire Hotel* has bar meals at lunch and dinner time. Or there's the *Nicada Tearooms & Restaurant* on the main street.

## Pukekura to Okarito

From Ross it's another 109 km to Franz Josef, but there are plenty of bush tracks and lakes along the way if you want to break the journey and can stand the sandflies. Heading southwards the vegetation becomes more and more dense rainforest, in many parts it looks like you could walk right over the top of the forest easier than you could find a way through it! There are also many places along here where you can find low-cost accommodation.

About 20 km south of Ross the *Lake Ianthe Cabins* (tel Ross 54-032) near Pukekura has cabins at $15/25 for one/two people, with activities including boating, sailing, fishing and hunting.

In the small town of Harihari, 22½ km further south, the *Harihari Motor Inn* (tel 33-026) has centrally heated bunkrooms at $10 per person, motel units at $50 double, and campervan sites at $10 per van, with free use of the hot spa pool. Across the road the *Tomasi Motel* (tel 33-116) has cabins with private bathroom at $10 per person and motel units at $40 double. Neither one has kitchen facilities for the budget rooms, but there are several places in town where you can get inexpensive meals including a tearoom, a fish & chips shop, and the motor inn, which has pub meals and takeaways plus a separate restaurant and two bars.

There are several interesting things to do around Harihari. The 2 to 3 hour Harihari Coastal Walk (also called the Doughboy Walk) is a popular local attraction, with a lookout over the coastline, forest and mountains. An old goldminers' pack track, or rivermouth trout and salmon fishing and exploring of the estuaries and wetlands of the Poerua and Wanganui rivers, are other possibilities.

Near Whataroa, 35 km south of Harihari, is a sanctuary for white herons, which nest here from November to February. White Heron Sanctuary Tours (tel Whataroa 34-120) at Whataroa operate jet-boat tours to see the birds in their colony beside the Waitangi-Taona River. Cost is $50 (children $25) for the 2 hour return trip and they provide free transport from Whataroa or Franz Josef. You can go in on your own but you must get permission from the DOC and check in with the warden at the sanctuary.

There is year-round accommodation in Whataroa in a large house behind the tours office. Shared accommodation is $10 (you supply your own linen), motel-style doubles cost $55, or you can camp in a tent for $8 per person or $12 for two in a campervan. Scenic jet-boat tours of the river operate all year round.

Another 15 km south of Whataroa is The Forks. From here it's just 17 km to Franz Josef, but if you turn off here you will find peaceful Okarito, 13 km away on the coast. Okarito Lagoon is the feeding ground for the white heron (kotuku) and it's a good place for watching all kinds of birds in their natural habitat including kiwis. There are lots of walks along the coast from Okarito – get hold of leaflets from the DOC in Hokitika or Franz Josef.

The small *Okarito Youth Hostel* (tel Whataroa 34-082) is a shelter hostel – no electricity, spartan facilities, just $5 a night and room for only 10 people. Originally it was the schoolhouse, built in the 1870s when Okarito was a thriving gold town. Opposite the hostel is a very basic camping ground with just barbecues and toilets, but it's a pleasant location and the price is right, just whatever you care to donate to the camp's upkeep. If you plan to stay at Okarito, bring your own food and sleeping bag, supplies out there are limited.

Back towards the Forks turn-off, 3 km in from the highway, *The Forks Lodge* (tel Whataroa 34-122) is an attractive little lodge with shared accommodation at $10 per person. It has everything you need – fully equipped kitchen, showers, etc – but bring your own bedding and food. They also have caravan power points which you can pull up to for $12 for two.

Soon after The Forks you reach Franz

Josef, Westland National Park and the magnificent peaks of the Southern Alps.

# The Glaciers

The two glaciers of the Westland National Park – the Fox and the Franz Josef, 25 km to the north – are amongst the most interesting sights in New Zealand. Nowhere else in the world, at this latitude, do glaciers approach so close to the sea. Unlike the Tasman Glacier, on the other side of the dividing range in Mt Cook National Park, these two are just what glaciers should be – mighty rivers of ice, tumbling down a valley towards the sea. From many viewpoints you can admire them from lookouts fringed with subtropical vegetation. There are visitors' centres at both townships with maps, leaflets, evening slide shows and much useful information.

The reason for the glaciers' unusual development is three-fold. The wet west coast weather means there's a lot of snow on the mountain slopes. Secondly the zone where the ice accumulates on the glaciers is very large, so there's a lot of ice to push down the valley. Finally, they're very steep glaciers – the ice can get a long way before it finally melts. The rate of descent is staggering – a plane that crashed on the Franz Josef in 1943, 3½ km from the terminal face, made it down to the bottom 6½ years later – a speed of 1½ metres a day. At times the glacier can move at up to 5 metres a day, over 10 times as fast as glaciers in the Swiss Alps. More usually it moves a metre a day.

### Advance & Retreat
Glaciers always advance, they never really retreat. The word 'retreat', with its image of the glacier pulling back up the valley, is rather a misnomer. The ice is always advancing, it's just that sometimes it melts even faster than it advances. And in that case the terminal or end face of the glacier moves back up the mountain.

Glacial ice, pushed by gravity, always advances downhill, but at the same time it melts. When advance exceeds melt the whole length of the glacier increases, when melt exceeds advance the length decreases. The great mass of ice higher up the mountain pushes the ice down the Fox and Franz Josef valleys at prodigious speeds but like most glaciers in the world this past century has been a story of steady retreat and only the odd short advance.

The last great ice age of 15,000 to 20,000 years ago saw the glaciers reach right down to the sea. Then warmer weather came and they may have retreated even further back than their current position. In the 14th century a new 'mini ice age' started and for centuries the glaciers advanced, reaching their greatest extent around 1750. At both the Fox and Franz Josef the terminal moraines from that last major advance can be clearly seen. In the nearly 250 years since then the glaciers have steadily retreated and the terminal face is now several km back from its first recorded position in the late 19th century or even from its position in the 1930s.

From 1965 to 1968 the Fox and Franz Josef Glaciers made brief advances of about 180 metres but in 1985 they once again started to advance and have been moving forward steadily and fairly dramatically ever since. Nobody is quite sure why this advance is taking place. It could be cooler or more overcast summers or it could be the result of heavy snowfalls 10 or 15 years ago which are now working their way down to the bottom of the glacier. It's a pity this interesting natural phenomenon is not being more carefully chronicled. An advance of up to 20 metres a month would make a fascinating photographic subject simply by taking the same photo daily or weekly from the same spot.

### FRANZ JOSEF GLACIER
The Franz Josef was first explored in 1865 by Austrian Julius Haast, who named it after the Austrian emperor. Apart from short advances from 1907-09, 1921-34, 1946-59 and 1965-67 the glacier has generally been in retreat since that time although in 1985 it started advancing again and in early '90 it was still moving down. It has progressed well over 1000 metres, moving forward by about 30 cm a day, although it is still several km back from the terminal point Haast first recorded.

### Information
The Westland National Park Information Centre (tel 796) is open 8 am to 5 pm daily. The centre has leaflets on the many short walks around the glacier. In the summer they operate a free programme of guided walks and evening lectures and slide shows.

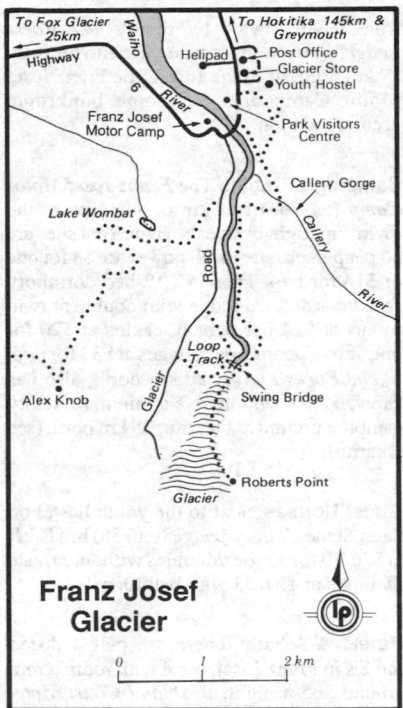

## Franz Josef Glacier

road up to the glacier car park – including one from where the first photo of the glacier was taken, with a reproduction of that historic photo there, so you can check how things have changed.

You can walk to the glacier from the car park, or you may find it worthwhile to fork out $21 (children $12.50) for a guided walk on the glacier ice with an experienced guide. In the high season there are guided walks departing twice daily from the Trips & Tramps office (tel 718); equipment, including boots, is included.

Other walks require a little worthwhile footslogging. The loop track is a short 15 minute stroll by the terminal moraine from the 1750 advance and Peter's Pool – a small 'kettle lake' formed by the melting of ice buried and left by a retreating glacier. It's a longer walk (3½ hours) to Roberts Point, overlooking and quite close to the terminal face.

There is a pleasant 1 hour round trip around the Terrace Track, which starts on the old Callery Track, scene of much goldmining activity in earlier days, and leads up onto a terrace at the back of the village, giving pleasant views down the Waiho River.

### Aerial Sightseeing
Mt Cook Airlines (tel 714) have skiplane flights over both glaciers. You can fly over both glaciers for $88 (children $66), land on one of them for $90 ($68), visit the Tasman Glacier on the other side as well for $150 ($113) including a landing or make that same Grand Circle route but without the landing for $154 ($116).

The Helicopter Line (tel 767) flies from Franz Josef and has glacier flights from $50 (children $40) up to $80 (children $60) for a snow landing, $120 ($100) for both glaciers and a landing on one or $160 ($140) for the full Grand Circle across the divide and a landing. Glacier Helicopters (tel 755) fly from both Fox and Franz Josef with roughly the same flights for the same prices. Flights up and over the glaciers are expensive but they're a superb experience, it's money well spent. You can also make helihikes with a

### Keas
There's plenty of opportunity to observe these large, cheeky parrots at the Fox and Franz Josef Glaciers. At the car park at the terminal of the Fox Glacier they hang around waiting for tourist handouts. Signs warn you of their destructive tendencies and they make concerted assaults on campervan roof hatches as soon as the passengers have wandered off. Or they ride nonchalantly on the spinning roof ventilators on tourist buses.

Down at the Franz Josef motor camp one evening we watched two keas methodically moving through the park, knocking each bin over in turn and plundering the contents.

### Walks
There are many walks to do around the glacier. Ask at the Information Centre for their excellent walk leaflets. There are several good glacier viewpoints close to the

flight up to the glacier and then a guided walk across the ice.

On the Grand Circle flights, done by several companies at both Franz Josef and Fox, you get to see not only the most famous glaciers but a number of others as well. The route passes over at least nine glaciers including the Fox, Franz Josef, Balfour, La Parouse, Hooker, Tasman, Rudolph, Bauman, and Victoria glaciers!

### Glacier Rafting

From November to March there's rafting on the Waiho River, conducted by Buller Adventure Tours (tel 704). A 1½ hour trip costs $24 (minimum age 13) and wetsuits, etc are provided.

### Tours

Stan Peterson operates Westland Guiding Service (tel 750), with a number of interpretive tours to interesting places including Franz Josef Glacier (35 minutes, $8), Fox Glacier and Lake Matheson (3½ hours, $30), both glaciers (3½ hours, $30) or to Okarito Beach and Lagoon (4 hours, $30) plus guided fishing and hunting safaris. The fishing trips for salmon and trout are a good deal, the hourly cost of $45 for the boat can be shared by up to four people.

White Heron Sanctuary Tours (tel Whataroa 34-120) offer free transport from Franz Josef for their tours of the white heron sanctuary near Whataroa which take place during the herons' breeding season from November to February. See Whataroa in the South from Hokitika section for details.

### Places to Stay

Hostels The *Franz Josef Youth Hostel* (tel 754) is at 2-4 Cron St, just off the main road. It's a pleasant and fairly new hostel and costs $13 a night. All rooms are centrally heated, with twin and family rooms available, and it's open all day. They have a small shop, pool table, videos in the evenings, and a budget priced meal service from September to April.

Okarito, with its small YHA shelter hostel, is only 25 km north but it's a 13 km walk

from the highway. Or there's *The Forks Lodge*, 3 km from the same Okarito turn-off, 17 km north of Franz Josef. The Franz Josef Motor Camp also has some bunkroom accommodation.

Camping & Cabins The *Franz Josef Motor Camp* (tel 766) is a km or so south of the township, right beside the river. Tent sites are $6 per person, sites with power are $8 for one or $14 for two. There's a 12-bed dormitory with beds at $8, a lodge with double or twin rooms at $14 per person, cabins at $20 for one or two people, or cottages at $33 for two.

*The Forks Lodge*, 20 km north, also has caravan sites, and there's a minimal-facility camping ground at Okarito, 25 km north (see Okarito).

Guest Houses Next to the youth hostel on Cron St the *Callery Lodge* (tel 738) has B&B at $26/40 for singles/doubles without private facilities or $51/53 with bathroom.

Hotels & Motels There are half a dozen motels in Franz Josef, most with rooms from around $65 a night. *Bushland Court Motel* (tel 757) at 10 Cron St is the most economical of the lot, with units from $52 to $66 a night for two people. The *Westland Motor Inn* (tel 728) is rather more expensive as is the *THC Franz Josef* (tel 719) which is about a km north of the township and has rooms from $72 to $99.

### Places to Eat

The shops at Franz Josef have a good selection of food supplies. You can eat at the *Glacier Store & Tearoom* or at *DA's Restaurant & Tearoom*. Curiously at DA's the cafe and takeaway section offers much the same menu as the proper restaurant side but at higher prices! In the restaurant there's a standard pub-style menu from chicken kiev to ham steak at around $14 to $20 including serve-yourself salads. Main courses in the coffee shop at the *THC Franz Josef* are also in the $14 to $20 range.

you're not you could well stand on the same spot for 3 days.

## FOX GLACIER

If time is short seeing one glacier may be enough but if you have the time it's interesting to see both. Basically the same activities are offered at both glaciers – walks, glacier walks, flights and so on. Like the Franz Josef the Fox Glacier has, despite the consistent retreat throughout this century, been on the advance since 1985. In 1987 it had moved forward something like 1000 metres, and from May '87 to October '89 it advanced another 210 metres.

### Information

The Visitors Centre (tel 807) is open from 8 am to 5 pm daily. In the summer and during the holiday season there are evening slide shows and sometimes there'll be a quick walk down to the glow-worm grotto organised afterwards. The centre has displays on the glaciers and natural environment of the area and leaflets on a number of interesting short walks around the glacier.

There's a petrol station in the town and if you're driving south, take note, this is the last fuel stop until you reach Haast, 120 km further on.

### Walks

The shortest and most popular walk at the Fox Glacier is the couple of minutes stroll from the centre to the glow-worm grotto. It's close to the roadside just opposite the garage. Of course, you have to go in the dark of night in order to see the worms glowing! See the Waitomo section in the South of Auckland chapter for more information on glow-worms.

Head towards the coast from the township for a viewpoint with superb views of the glacier and the whole mountain range. Before this viewpoint is the turn-off to Lake Matheson and one of the most famous views in New Zealand. It's an hour's walk around the lake and at the far end you'll get a spectacular view of the mountains and their reflection in the lake. The best time to see the

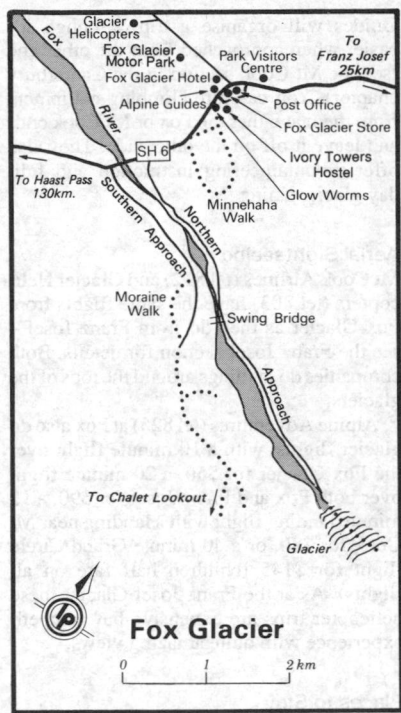

**Fox Glacier**

Map labels: Glacier Helicopters, Fox Glacier Motor Park, Fox Glacier Hotel, Park Visitors Centre, To Franz Josef 25km, Fox River, Alpine Guides, Post Office, Fox Glacier Store, SH 6, Ivory Towers Hostel, To Haast Pass 130km, Glow Worms, Southern Approach, Northern Approach, Minnehaha Walk, Moraine Walk, Swing Bridge, To Chalet Lookout, Glacier

0    1    2 km

### Entertainment

There's a bar at the *Franz Josef Hotel* but it's some distance from the town centre.

### Getting There & Away

The northbound and southbound InterCity bus services overlap between the two glaciers, with daily buses south to Fox Glacier and Queenstown and north to Greymouth. The connections are such that Nelson to Queenstown (or vice versa) by bus along the west coast takes a minimum of 2 days. In the high season (in summer) buses along the coast can be heavily booked, plan well ahead or be prepared to wait until there's space.

Hitching along the west coast can be very bleak. If you're lucky you might do Greymouth to Queenstown in 3 days – if

famed reflection is very early in the morning, when the lake is at its most mirror-like calm.

An almost equally famous viewpoint can be found by making the short climb up to Cone Rock, overlooking the glacier from a green and leafy lookout point, or the easier walk to Chalet lookout. Mt Fox is another excellent viewpoint – a 3 hour walk one way.

There are many other interesting walks around the glacier including the short moraine walk over the advance of 200 years ago or forest walks on the Ngai Tahu Track, the short Minnehaha Walk or the River Walk. It takes something over an hour to walk from town to the glacier – it's 1½ km from town to the turn-off, and the glacier is another 5 km back from the main road.

A particularly interesting walk is the 1½ to 2 hour coastal walk to the seal colony at Gillespies Beach. Up to 1500 seals can be seen here and the walk also passes an old miners' cemetery and the remains of gold dredges from the gold- mining days.

The walk up to Welcome Flat Hot Springs, at the first hut on the Copland Track when entered from this side, is another good walk. It starts from the Copland Valley sign on the main road, 26 km south of town, from where it's an easy 6 hour walk up the valley to the hot springs. The Welcome Flat hut at the hot springs is an excellent modern hut, sleeping 40 people, and costs $8 per night.

As at the Franz Josef you can make guided walks up onto the glacier ice with Alpine Guides (tel 825). They leave at 9.30 am and 2 pm daily and boots and other equipment are included in the $25 (children $15) cost. From December to April they also have full day guided glacier walks for $40. Of course you can just follow the marked track to the glacier from the car park although they officially disapprove of unguided walkers going up on the ice.

Alpine Guides also have half-day and full-day helihikes and an overnight trip to Chancellor Hut. The overnight trip includes hut fees, food and the flight up for $415 each for three people, $495 each for two, including a helicopter trip on each end. If you want to cross the Copland Pass to Mt Cook, Alpine Guides will organise a trip, although it's easier when approached from the other end (see the Mt Cook section in the Canterbury chapter). You can hire climbing equipment from them at either the Fox or Mt Cook ends and leave it off on the other side. They also offer mountaineering instruction and full-day glacier skiing.

### Aerial Sightseeing

Mt Cook Airlines (tel 812) and Glacier Helicopters (tel 803) have the same flights from Fox Glacier as they do from Franz Josef – see the Franz Josef section for details. Both companies do landings around the tops of the glaciers.

Alpine Adventures (tel 825) at Fox also do glacier flights, with a 10 minute flight over the Fox Glacier for $50, a 20 minute flight over both Fox and Franz Josef for $90, a 15 minute landing flight with a landing near Mt Cook for $80, or a 40 minute Grand Circle flight for $145 (children half fare on all flights). As at the Franz Josef Glacier these helicopter trips are expensive but a superb experience with quite amazing views.

### Places to Stay

**Hostels** The *Fox Glacier Associate Youth Hostel* (tel 847) is in one wing of the Golden Glacier Motor Inn, on the main road near the town centre. Nightly cost is $13 or, in double rooms, $16.50 per person. Most rooms sleep four, with private bathroom and TV, and hostellers have access to all the facilities including games room, videos, etc. Because it's an associate hostel, you don't need a YHA card to get the hostel rates.

The *Ivory Towers* (tel 838) on Sullivans Rd, behind the Golden Glacier Motor Inn, is a friendly, well-equipped private hostel with rates of $11 a night in rooms sleeping four, or $12 a night in twin rooms. They hire mountain bikes for $10 a day or $6 half a day.

The motor camp has bunkroom accommodation and inexpensive cabins, and you can also find cheap accommodation at the Fox Glacier Hotel (see Hotels & Motels).

**Hotels & Motels** The elderly *Fox Glacier Hotel* (tel 839) has rooms with facilities for $62/79 plus a smaller number of cheaper rooms without attached bathrooms at $23.50 per person, or share budget rooms at $12.50 per person.

The *Golden Glacier Motor Inn* (tel 847) on the main road has hostel-style accommodation at $13, or $16.50 per person in budget double rooms (see Hostels). They also have more expensive rooms from $50/55 up to $50/72.

At the *Alpine View Motel* (tel 821) in the motor camp units cost $48/55. The small *Halseys Motel* (tel 833) is right in the township and a little cheaper, with rates at $45 for two.

**Camping & Cabins** The *Fox Glacier Motor Park* (tel 821) is 400 metres down the Lake Matheson road from the town centre. Tent sites cost $7.50/$13.50 for one/two people, power sites are $11.50/$15. It also has bunkroom accommodation at $10 per person, small cabins at $12/20, standard cabins at $16/24, tourist cabins at $36/45 and motel units at the Alpine View Motel.

**Places to Eat**
The shop has a reasonable selection of essentials although not as wide a choice as you'll find at the Franz Josef Glacier. You can eat at the *Fox Glacier Restaurant & Tearoom* or there are pretty good sandwiches and light meals at the *Hobnail Coffee Shop* in the Alpine Guides building. At the *Fox Glacier Hotel* there's a bar with good value bar meals from $5 to $11 and a restaurant with dinner main courses for $14, breakfast from $9 to $12.

**Entertainment**
Unlike at the Franz Josef Glacier the *Fox Glacier Hotel* is wonderfully central and you can sit with a jug of beer and talk about where you've been and what you've seen during the day.

**Getting There & Away**
The InterCity bus services overlap – south-bound services from Greymouth start and finish at Fox Glacier, northbound ones from Queenstown continue to Franz Josef. Buses run every day to and from Greymouth (4 hours) and Queenstown (8 hours). From Greymouth there are onward connections to Westport, Nelson, Picton and Christchurch.

See the Franz Josef section for the sad news on hitchhiking and a warning about the heavily booked bus services.

**Getting Around**
Mountain bicycles can be hired from Alpine Guides for $5 an hour, $15 for half a day or $25 for a full day. The Ivory Towers hostel also hires mountain bikes, at $6 for half a day or $10 for a full day – you can rent them whether or not you're staying there, but their guests get first grabs.

Glacier Ventures (tel 849) provides minibus transport to the glacier ($6 return), Lake Matheson ($6 return) and to Gillespies Beach and the seal colony ($12 return), dropping you off and picking you up again at a specified time. They will also do special trips to the Copland Track and other places.

**SOUTH TO HAAST**
South of the glaciers the road (SH 6) eventually departs from the coast and climbs over the Haast Pass and on down to Wanaka. It's a longish, all day drive, presenting a remarkable variety of scenery as you cross over from one climatic zone to another. Heading south from the glaciers, the rainforest is so dense on both sides of the road that you can barely see a couple of metres into it. Further on, it opens up to reveal broad sweeps of coastline.

Just 26 km south of Fox Glacier is the Copland Valley. This is the end of the Copland Track, coming over from Mt Cook. It's a very pleasant 6 hour walk up the valley from the highway here to the first hut at Welcome Flat, where there is a hot springs. See the Fox Glacier – Walks section for details. A sign on the road marks the entrance to the valley and the track. There's transport from Fox Glacier to the Copland Valley by either InterCity or private bus.

There are several possibilities for places to stay on the stretch of road between Fox Glacier and Haast to break up the journey. The *Pinegrove Motel* (tel Fox Glacier 898), 35 km south of Fox Glacier, has a variety of accommodation including campervan sites at $7 per person, basic cabins at $12 per person, fancier cabins at $35/40 for one/two people, and motel units at $40/45.

### Lake Paringa

Lake Paringa, about 70 km south of Fox Glacier and 50 km north of Haast, is a tranquil little trout-filled lake surrounded by forest, right beside the road. The *Lakeside Motel* (tel Fox Glacier 894) is on the lakeshore and has boats and canoes for hire. Rates are $15 per person in self-contained cabins if you supply your own bedding, or $59 for two in the larger motel units. About 1 km further south, still on the lakefront, is a free DOC camping area with just basic facilities – toilets and picnic areas.

The historic Haast-Paringa Cattle Track begins from the main road 43 km north of Haast, coming out at the coast by the Waita River, just a few km north of Haast. Before the Haast Pass road was opened in 1965, this trail was the only link between the Southland and the west coast. It is being developed for tramping, with some huts already in place and others planned in the near future. The first leg of the track makes a pleasant day hike. Information on the track is available in Haast or at the Lake Moeraki Wilderness Lodge.

### Lake Moeraki

Lake Moeraki, 31 km north of Haast, is another peaceful forest lake with good fishing, not far off the highway. It's also not far from the coast – just a 40 minute walk along a stream brings you to Monroe's Beach, where there's a breeding colony of Fiordland Crested Penguins, standing 70 cm tall, found there from July to November. Also at Monroe's Beach are fur seals and good snorkelling.

There are many other good short and long walks around the lake and the Moeraki River

which runs from the lake to the sea. Fishing tackle, canoes and rowboats are available from the Lake Moeraki Wilderness Lodge.

The *Lake Moeraki Wilderness Lodge* (tel Haast 32-881), right on the highway and just 20 metres from the lakeside, has a variety of accommodation including lodge rooms at $55/60 for one/two people, motel units at $5 more, a self-contained cottage at $45 for two (you supply bed linen), and caravan sites at $10 per person. There's a restaurant, lots of help in organising outdoor and nature activities, and special indoor activities on rainy days. The owner, Dr Gerry McSweeney, is the director of the New Zealand Forest and Bird Society, the country's largest conservation group.

### Haast

The tiny community of Haast is on the coast where the wide Haast River meets the sea, 120 km south of Fox Glacier. There's really not much to the town, although this is an area which has been targeted for tourist development, in connection with efforts to declare the area a National or World Heritage Park. Probably in the very near future there will be activities including white water rafting, horse-trekking and so on, and more options in places to stay.

A series of tracks are being developed, including the Hapuka Estuary Walk leading from the motor camp, and a rainforest, seacoast and wetland walk along Ship Creek, halfway between Haast and Lake Moeraki. The aforementioned Haast-Paringa Cattle Track is also being upgraded.

A new DOC Visitor Centre should be open in Haast by the end of '90, at the junction of SH 6 and Jackson Bay Rd on the southern bank of the Haast River. It will have more current information on the area and on things to do, especially on nature-related activities.

### Places to Stay & Eat

The *Haast Motor Camp* (tel Haast 860) is at Okuru, 11 km south of Haast township on the road to Jackson Bay. Camping sites cost $12 for two, $14 with power, and there are various cabins at $18, $23, or $32 for two, with linen for hire if needed. In the township itself, the *Haast Hotel* (tel 827, 828) has share-facility rooms at $10 per person ($15 in a single room) if you supply your own linen, $45 or $50 for two in the regular rooms with private facilities. Or there's the Lake Moeraki Wilderness Lodge, 31 km north at Lake Moeraki.

Meals are served at the restaurants of both the Haast Hotel and the Lake Moeraki Wilderness Lodge.

## HAAST PASS

Turning inland at Haast, snaking along beside the wide Haast River and climbing up the pass, you soon enter the Mt Aspiring National Park and the scenery changes again – the vegetation becomes much more sparse the further inland you proceed, until beyond the 563 metre summit you reach snow country covered only in tussock and scrub. Along the Haast Pass are many picturesque waterfalls, most of them just a couple of minutes walk off the road.

The roadway over Haast Pass was opened in 1965. Prior to that the only southern link to the west coast was by the Haast-Paringa Cattle Track, walking or on horseback! The cattle track is now a historical walkway.

Heading south, the next town of any size you come to after Haast is Wanaka, a distance of 145 km, about 3½ hours by road (see the Otago & Southland chapter).

If you're driving north, check your fuel gauge – the petrol station at Haast is the last one you'll come to until you reach Fox Glacier, 120 km north.

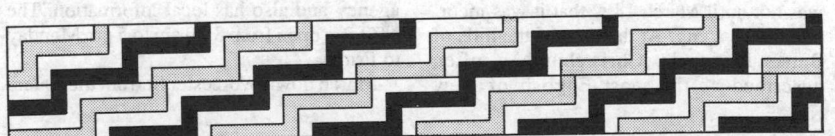

# Canterbury

The South Island's large Canterbury region extends all the way from near Kaikoura in the north to near Oamaru in the south, and from the Pacific coast all the way to the Southern Alps.

This is one of the driest and flattest areas of New Zealand. The moisture-laden westerlies blowing in from the Tasman Sea are swept upwards by the Southern Alps, causing heavy rainfall on the South Island's West Coast – over 5 metres a year! When the winds continue east over Canterbury, they have lost most of their moisture, and the Canterbury region – not so far from the West Coast distance-wise – has a markedly different climate, with an annual rainfall of only around 75 cm.

The predominant feature of the region is the Canterbury Plains, a large, flat area primarily devoted to farming and agriculture. Christchurch, New Zealand's third largest city, is the centre for the region.

# Christchurch

Population 300,700
Since I was born outside Christchurch, England, I find it rather curious that New Zealand's Christchurch isn't named after the English one and the fact that the River Avon flows through both cities is also unconnected. The rivers are remarkably similar – placid and picturesque – but the down-under Avon is named after a Scottish Avon not the English one. The name Christchurch comes from Christ Church College at Oxford University – one of the leaders of the early settlers was educated there.

The first Europeans in Christchurch began building huts along the Avon in 1851 but it was not until March 1862 that it was incorporated as a city. At the base of the hills of Banks Peninsula, Christchurch is often described as the most English of New Zealand's cities. True or not it's a lovely city, relaxed, picturesque and with that pretty-as-a-postcard river winding its way right through the centre.

### Orientation
The Cathedral Square (just look for the spire) is very much the centre of town. Climb to the top to get your orientation. The NZTP and the CPO are both on the square. Christchurch is a pleasantly compact city and walking is a pleasure although slightly complicated by the river which twists and winds through the centre and crosses your path in disconcertingly varied directions. The network of one-way streets adds even more excitement if you're driving. Colombo St, running north-south through Cathedral Square, is a main shopping street.

### Information
**Tourist Information** The NZTP (tel 794-900) is right on Cathedral Square in the Tower Court Building. It operates as a travel agency and also has local information. The NZTP is open from 8.30 am to 5 pm Monday to Friday.

March down Worcester St from the square

to the Information Centre (tel 799-629) by the riverside, on the corner of Oxford Terrace. It's open from 8.30 am to 5 pm Monday to Friday and from 9 am to 4 pm on Saturdays and Sundays. This is a better bet for local information.

The DOC (tel 799-758) at 133 Victoria St has leaflets and information on most national parks, walkways and other outdoor attractions around the South Island. Opening hours are 8 am to 4.30 pm, Monday to Friday. The AA District Headquarters (tel 791- 280) is at 210 Hereford St.

**YHA** The YHA national headquarters is in Christchurch. The office and Travel Centre (tel 799-970) are at the corner of Gloucester and Manchester streets and handles YHA membership, takes passport photographs, sells camping equipment, packs, clothes and books and makes domestic and international travel reservations.

**Consulates** Consulates in Christchurch include those of Denmark (tel 895-134), France (tel 516-259), Japan (tel 665-680), the Netherlands (tel 669-280), Sweden (tel 650-000), the UK (tel 796-100) and the USA (tel 790-040).

**Airlines Offices** Airline offices are generally close to Cathedral Square.

Air New Zealand
    156 Armagh St (tel 795-200)
Ansett New Zealand
    Clarendon Towers Building, corner Worcester St
    and Oxford Terrace (tel 791-300)
Mt Cook Airlines
    91 Worcester St (tel 790-690)
Qantas
    CML Building, Cathedral Square (tel 793-100)
Singapore Airlines
    AMP Building, Cathedral Square (tel 668-099)

**Bookstores** Christchurch has numerous bookstores including the government run GP Book Shop at 159 Hereford St which carries government publications, DOSLI maps and books about New Zealand including specialised guidebooks. Scorpio Books at the corner of Hereford St and Oxford Terrace has a wide range of books.

### Cathedral Square
Christchurch is calm, orderly and pancake flat so it's a good place to explore by bicycle. Start from the Cathedral Square where, for $1 (children 50 cents), you can climb 133 steps to the viewing balconies 30 metres up the 63-metre-high spire. There you can study the cathedral bells and look around while you reflect that earthquakes have damaged the spire on several occasions, once toppling the very top into Cathedral Square! The pointed stone top was replaced with the green copper-skinned one after that incident. The cathedral is open from 9 am to 4 pm weekdays, 12.30 to 4 pm on Sunday afternoons.

### The Wizard
Make sure you're around to hear the Wizard – he attempts to conquer gravity through levity – spouting in Cathedral Square at 1 pm from Monday to Friday. One of New Zealand's more amusing eccentrics, he dresses the part – long black velvet robes and cape in winter and white robes in summer – and plays it to the hilt. An extremely eloquent man, the Wizard has a line of glib patter – pet subjects are bureaucracy and feminism – and a skilful way of playing with the hecklers. Whether you like what he has to say or not, it's a production you shouldn't miss.

### Canterbury Museum
The fine Canterbury Museum on Rolleston Ave, at the entrance to the Botanic Gardens, is open daily from 10 am to 4.30 pm and admission is free. Free guided tours are held at 10.15 am, 1.15 pm and 2.30 pm, and on Sundays there's a planetarium show at 3 pm.

Particularly interesting are the early colonists' exhibits featuring a century old Christchurch street reconstruction, and the Antarctic exhibit. Christchurch is the HQ for 'Operation Deep Freeze' and supplies are ferried from Christchurch Airport to US bases in the Antarctic although the USA is still making noises about shifting the opera-

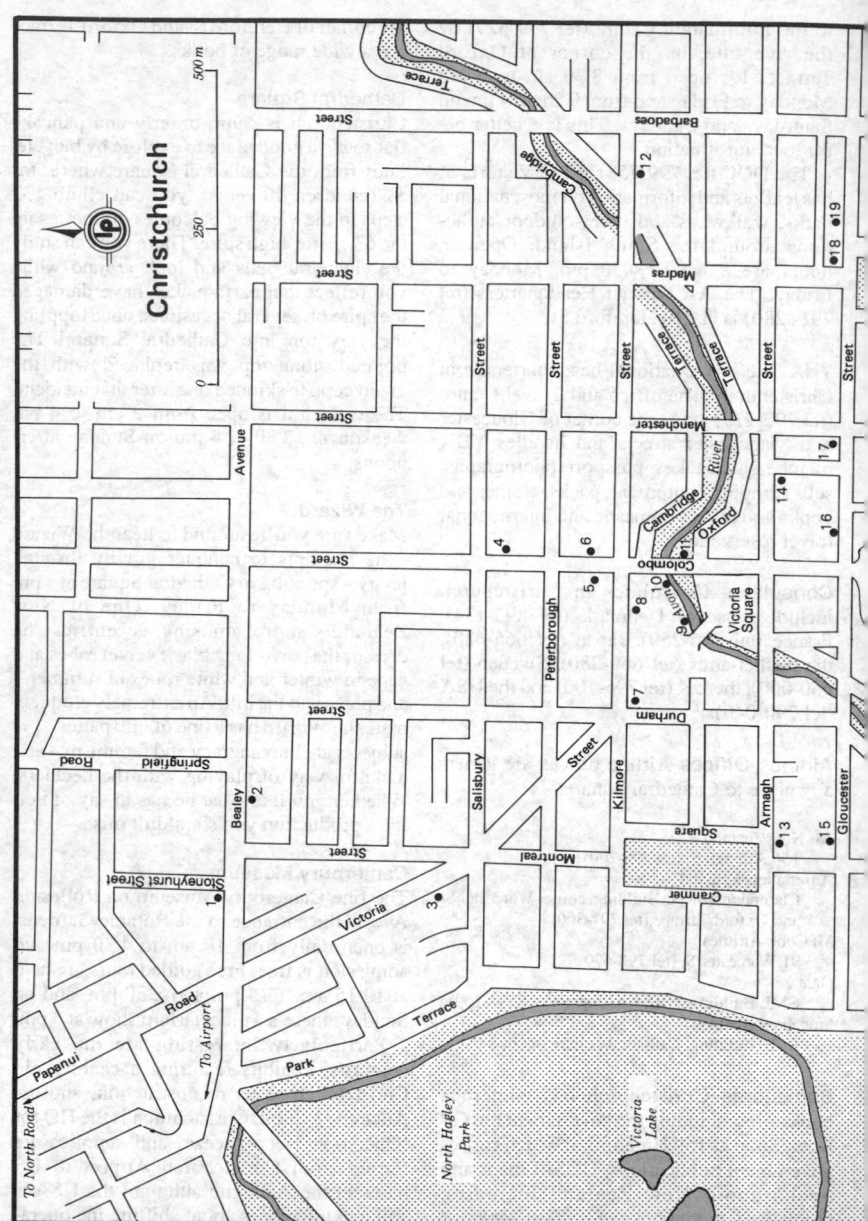

| | | | |
|---|---|---|---|
| 1 | Bealey Lodge | 23 | Chung Wah II Restaurant |
| 2 | Bealy Ave International Backpackers Hostel | 24 | Information Centre |
| 3 | Department of Conservation (DOC) | 25 | Noah's Hotel |
| 4 | Off the Wall & Mainstreet Cafes | 26 | NZTP Office, The Greek Recipe |
| 5 | Cafe Revere | 27 | Bus Information Kiosk |
| 6 | Spagalimi's Pizzas & Marco Polo Restaurant | 28 | Cathedral |
| 7 | Park Royal Hotel | 29 | Warners Hotel, Pavlova Hostel |
| 8 | Town Hall | 30 | Gopal's |
| 9 | Dandelions Fountain | 31 | Dux de Lux Restaurant |
| 10 | Town Hall Restaurant | 32 | CPO |
| 11 | Oxford Tavern | 33 | Great Sights Buses |
| 12 | Foley Towers Hostel | 34 | Mediterranean Take Away |
| 13 | Windsor Private Hotel | 35 | YMCA Hostel |
| 14 | Air New Zealand | 36 | Hereford Private Hotel |
| 15 | Hotel Melville | 37 | Scorpio Books |
| 16 | Rent-a-Bike | 38 | Automobile Association (AA) |
| 17 | Youth Hostel (YHA) Headquarters | 39 | Antigua Boat Sheds |
| 18 | Latimer Hostel | 40 | Mt Cook H & H Bus Station |
| 19 | Stonehurst Hotel | 41 | Tre Gatti's |
| 20 | Gaslight Cafe | 42 | Craft Gallery |
| 21 | Museum & Art Gallery | 43 | The Excelsior |
| 22 | Rolleston House Youth Hostel | 44 | Ambassadors Hotel |
| | | 45 | Newmans Bus Station |

tion to Tasmania in Australia in protest against New Zealand's antinuclear stance.

### Art Galleries

Behind the museum is the Robert McDougall Art Gallery. It has an extensive collection of NZ and international art and is open from 10 am to 4.30 pm daily.

Other galleries are the Canterbury Society of Arts Gallery at 66 Gloucester St which sprecialises in New Zealand's arts & crafts, the Brooke/Gifford Gallery at 112 Manchester St which has contemporary NZ art and the Gingko Gallery in the Arts Centre which has original prints and drawings. There's also the GEFN Crafts Co-Op on Cashel St Mall and a Crafts Gallery on Oxford Terrace near the boat sheds.

### Arts Centre

The University of Canterbury town site has been transformed into the biggest Arts Centre in New Zealand. It's worth a look, even if just to see the beautiful old buildings. New Zealand has a lot of good handicraft centres making some fine pottery, jewellery and other crafts and Christchurch is particularly well represented. The Arts Centre has everything from galleries to handmade toys to Maori carvings and a couple of good restaurants. An arts, crafts and antiques market, with live entertainment and plenty of exotic food is held here Saturday and Sunday over the summer, usually just one or the other day in winter.

There are some beautiful old (by NZ standards, anyway) stone buildings around Christchurch, especially around the Arts Centre.

### Botanic Gardens

Beside the museum off Rolleston Ave the Botanic Gardens, open 7 am to sunset, has 30 hectares of greenery with the Avon River burbling gently by. The many floral show houses are open daily from 10 am to 4 pm while the electric 'toast rack' operates tours from the cafe between 11 am and 4 pm when the weather is fine. There's an Information Centre open daily from 10.15 am to 4 pm September to April, noon to 3 pm May to August.

## Town Hall

Christchurch citizens are justly proud of their modern riverbank town hall. Visitors are welcome from 9 am to 5 pm on weekdays, 11 am to 5 pm on weekends and holidays and guided tours can be arranged. Outside is a fountain by the same designer as Sydney's Kings Cross el Alamein Fountain. It goes two better by having three dandelions.

## Avon River

That invitingly calm Avon River obviously requires canoes so head to the Antigua Boatsheds by the footbridge at the bottom of Rolleston Ave. One-person canoes are $4 an hour, two-person canoes $8 an hour. They also have paddle boats for $8 a half-hour. The boatshed is open from 9.30 am to 4 pm daily and there's a pretty good sandwich bar right by it.

If paddling a canoe sounds like too much effort you can relax and be punted along the river. Punts depart from the Worcester St Bridge Information Centre at the corner of Worcester St and Oxford Terrace, with departures and landings also available opposite the Town Hall Restaurant and the Band Rotunda Restaurant. For a 20 minute trip it's $5 per person (family $15); for 45 minutes it's $10 (family $30). The punts ply the river daily from 10 am, stopping at 6 pm from October to March, 5 pm in April and September, and 4 pm from May to August. Punts also operate from Mona Vale, on Fendalton Rd about 1½ km from the city centre.

## Air Force Museum

Opened in 1987 the RNZAF Museum is exceptionally well presented. There are a variety of aircraft used by the RNZAF over the years, convincingly displayed with figures and background scenery. Antarctic aircraft sit in the snow, aircraft are serviced, a Canberra bomber of the '50s taxis out at night, a WW II fighter is hidden in the jungle. There are also displays of air force memorabilia and many exceptionally good models.

The museum is at the Wigram airport, quite close to the city centre, and can be reached by a Hornby bus No 25 from Cathedral Square. It's open from 10 am to 4 pm Monday to Saturday, and from 1 to 4 pm on Sunday. Entry is $7 (children $2).

## Other Museums

South-east of the city centre is the 40 hectare Ferrymead Historic Park at 269 Bridle Path Rd, Heathcote. It's a working museum of transport and technology with incredibly varied exhibits including electric and steam locomotives, household appliances, cars and machinery of all types, plus hundreds of mechanical musical instruments. It's open from 10 am to 4.30 pm daily. Entry is $6 (children $3, family $16) including a ride on a steam train or tram. Bus Nos 3G, 3H, 3J or 3K all come from Christchurch.

The Yaldhurst Transport Museum opposite the Yaldhurst Hotel on the Main West Rd, 12 km from the city centre, is open daily between 10 am and 5 pm. Displayed on the 3 hectare grounds of an attractive 1876 homestead is some of New Zealand's earliest transport, including horse-drawn vehicles, vintage cars, racing cars, motorcycles, steam engines and aircraft. Admission is $5.50 (children $2).

## Orana Park Wildlife Trust

The Orana Park Wildlife Trust, with its drive-through lion reserve (the first one in New Zealand), also has a kiwi house and lots of other animals including tigers, camels and water buffalo. Feeding times for the various animals are scheduled throughout the day. It's open from 10 am to 5 pm daily (last admission at 4.30 pm) and entry is $8 (children $3). It's on McLeans Island Rd, Harewood, beyond the airport. There's no public bus but tour buses do come here.

## Willowbank Wildlife Reserve

This reserve also has exotic and local animals including a variety of domestic animals. There's also a pre-European Maori village model and a nocturnal kiwi house. The reserve is open daily from 10 am to 11 pm and entry is $6.50 (children $3). The reserve is on Hussey Rd, with a public bus

Kiwi

running from outside the Information Centre daily from December to March, on weekends and holidays the rest of the year.

## Queen Elizabeth II Park
Near New Brighton and 8 km from the centre of Christchurch, this huge sports complex, with four indoor pools, two waterslides and seven squash courts was the venue for the 1974 Commonwealth Games. The Leisure Centre has a variety of amusement park attractions. QE II Park is open daily, take bus Nos 19M, 29M or 10N from Christchurch.

## Mona Vale
The grounds of Mona Vale, an Elizabethan-style riverside homestead with 4½ hectares of richly landscaped gardens, ponds and fountains, are open every day from 8 am to 6.30 pm October to March, and from 8.30 am to 5.30 pm April to September. Tea and a smorgasbord lunch are served Sunday to Friday, and there's punting on the Avon River here. It's just 1½ km from the city centre on Fendalton Rd (bus No 9).

## Other Attractions
There's an aquarium and zoo at 155 Beach Rd, North Beach. It's open daily from 10 am to 5 pm, admission is $3 (children $1.50) and you can get there on bus Nos 19M, 29M or 10N.

Just over the Ferrymead Bridge on the main road to Sumner, Cob Cottage is a restored sod hut from the 1860s. Deans Bush and Homestead on Kauri St, built in 1843, is the oldest building in the province and is now a private museum, standing amidst a native bush reserve.

The Waimakariri River, about 15 km north of the city centre, is a popular river for jet-boating. Day trips to the Waimakariri Gorge are made from Christchurch. Longer rafting trips are also made on this river.

## Beaches
The closest beaches to the city are North Beach (10 km, bus No 19), South Brighton (10 km, bus No 5S), Sumner (11 km, bus No 3), Waimairi (10 km, bus No 19), New Brighton (8 km, bus No 5) and Taylors Mistake – a pleasant sheltered beach further out from Sumner and popular for surfing. All bus numbers refer to Christchurch Transport buses.

## Walks
Visit the Information Centre for details and leaflets about walks around Christchurch. The bus information kiosk has a leaflet on bus access to the various walks.

Starting in the city are the Riverside Walk – the leaflet on this is packed with information – and various city historical walks. From the Sign of the Takahe there is a walkway up to the Sign of the Kiwi through Victoria Park, and then along near the Summit Rd to Scott Reserve – good views from many points. The walk is accessible by bus from Victoria Square near the Town Hall.

How about walking one way to Lyttelton on the Bridle Path? It leads from Heathcote Valley to Lyttelton and takes 1 to 1½ hours at a reasonably easy pace. The Godley Head Walkway is a 2 hour round trip from Taylors Mistake, crossing then recrossing Summit

Rd with beautiful views on a clear day. The Rapaki track is an excellent walk taking just a couple of hours and offering fine views of the whole city and of Lyttelton.

The Crater Rim walkway around Lyttelton Harbour goes some 14 km from the Bridle Path to the Ahuriri Scenic Reserve, passing through a number of scenic reserves along the way, plus the Sign of the Bellbird and the Sign of the Kiwi. The walkway can easily be done in several short stages.

### Skiing
Skiing is a popular NZ sport, and there are 11 ski fields in the Canterbury area within a 2½ hour drive of Christchurch. They are:

Porter Heights – near Porters Pass, 89 km (1 hour drive from Christchurch)

Mt Hutt – near Methven, 104 km (1½ hours)

Broken River, Craigieburn Valley and Mt Cheeseman – all between Porters Pass and Arthur's Pass, 122 km (1½ hours)

Mt Olympus – near Lake Ida, 132 km (2 hours)

Amuri – near Hanmer Springs, 150 km (2 hours)

Fox Peak – near Fairlie, 153 km (2½ hours)

Temple Basin – near Arthur's Pass, 163 km (2 hours)

Erewhon – Upper Rangitata River, 185 km (2¼ hours)

Mt Dobson – near Fairlie, 200 km (2½ hours)

Information on these ski fields is available in Christchurch from the NZTP, the Christchurch Information Centre, or the New Zealand Snow Centre (tel 665-022). The ski season is generally from June to November at Mt Hutt, from June or July to September or October at the other fields.

### Tours & Trips
**Bus Tours** There are a variety of bus tours around Christchurch and the surrounding country. Christchurch Transport operate four tours through Great Sights which are good value. There's a 10 am 2 hour tour of the city which costs $14 (children $7), and a 3 hour afternoon tour of the hills, coast and harbour including a short harbour cruise and a stop for tea at the Sign of the Takahe. This one costs $20 (children $10), tea extra! They also have a 5 hour wildlife tour to the Orana Park and Peacock Springs animal reserves,

departing daily (except Christmas day) from November to March. Cost is $22 (children $11) including admission to the reserves. Finally there's a full day tour to Akaroa for $26 (children $13), with the option of taking a cruise on the *Canterbury Cat*. Bookings can be made at the Bus Information Kiosk (tel 794-600) in Cathedral Square.

From December to February the English Connection red double-deck bus does a couple of very economical short city tours. The 40 minute Inner City tour departs daily at 10.30 am, 11.30 am and 2.30 pm, and if you like you can jump off at the Canterbury Museum, Arts Centre or Botanic Gardens, rejoining the bus when it comes past again. Cost is $3 (children $1.50). Their 2 hour Mona Vale tour combines the Inner City tour with a visit to Mona Vale. Cost for this one is $4 (children $2) and it departs daily at 12.30 pm. The English Connection buses depart from bus stop No 16 in Cathedral Square and bookings can be made at the Bus Information Kiosk in the square.

**Other Tours** Gray Line (tel 790-690) does 3 hour tours of the Christchurch highlights for $16 (children $8). Canterbury Scenic Tours (tel 669-660) offer half-day city tours ($22) and full day tours to Akaroa ($72) or Hanmer Springs ($73).

InterCity Thrifty Tours (tel 799-020) does a number of economical full day tours by coach or train to places further afield including Akaroa ($23), Timaru ($28), Hanmer Springs ($28), Mt Cook ($65), Lake Tekapo ($45), Arthur's Pass ($45), Greymouth ($77), and Kaikoura ($34 or $73, depending on what you want to do in Kaikoura).

### Places to Stay
Christchurch is the major city and the only international arrival point on the South Island. As a result it has far more accommodation in every category than you might expect – there are lots of hostels, camping sites, guest houses, hotels and motels.

**Hostels** Christchurch is well equipped with hostels including two youth hostels and some popular private ones. *Rolleston House Youth Hostel* (tel 666-564) at 5 Worcester St is opposite the Canterbury Museum, the Arts Centre and the Botanic Gardens, and only 700 metres from the city centre (about 8 minutes walk to Cathedral Square) so it's very conveniently located. There are 48 beds at $15 a night. The hostel and office are open all day but it's very popular so booking ahead is a good idea.

The other youth hostel, *Cora Wilding* (tel 899-199), at 9 Eveleyn Couzins Ave, is 5 km from the city centre (about a 25 minute walk along the river) and has 40 beds. To get there catch a bus No 10 from Cathedral Square to Tweed St. Cost here is $13 a night and the place is quite elegant, being a former mansion in a well-cared-for city park. The office shuts during the day but the rest of the hostel remains open.

The popular *Foley Towers* (tel 669-720) is at 208 Kilmore St near the Madras St end. It's a straightforward travellers' hostel (no children or groups their card announces) with plenty of space. You may have trouble getting a bed here so phone ahead. There's a pleasant little garden at the back, the usual kitchen and laundry facilities and a bed costs $12 a night, with a $1 discount for paying in advance. The rooms are for two to five, with plenty of twin and double rooms at $13 per person. It's run by ex-YHA people who are very *au fait* with travellers' needs.

*Bealey Ave International Backpackers* (tel 666-760) at 70 Bealey Ave is a similar sort of place, with a friendly atmosphere, an outdoor garden and barbecue area and a cosy log fire in winter. They offer a free pick-up service, luggage storage, and morning drop-offs at the train/bus station. Rates are $12 for a share room, or $13 per person for a double.

The *Pavlova Backpackers* (tel 665-159; 366-5159 as of July 1992), located in the old Warners Hotel right in Cathedral Square, has accommodation starting at $13 per person (some equipped with bed linen). The hostel is open 24 hours.

The *YMCA* (tel 650-502) is at 12 Hereford St, a few steps from the Botanic Gardens, the Arts Centre and Canterbury Museum. The old YMCA hostel was getting a bit worn but in early '90 a brand new five storey hostel was completed and there are now 154 rooms with over 250 beds! There's a wide variety of accommodation with bunks at $14, single rooms at $25 ($17 in the older section), twin or double rooms at $35. With bathrooms, the singles/doubles are $45/60. They also have one and two bedroom apartments, and substantially discounted rates for stays of 2 weeks or longer. There's a cafeteria serving inexpensive meals (breakfast $4, dinner $7), plus a hostellers' kitchen to do your own cooking. During the school terms most of the single and double plain rooms may be full up with students, but there should always be some room for casuals. The hostel is open 24 hours a day and they take both men and women.

The *YWCA* (tel 522-725) at 93 Harewood Rd is away from the city centre, about 5 km from the airport, but bus Nos 1 and 4 run frequently from Cathedral Square, stopping at the gate. The cost of $20/30 for single/twin rooms includes a light breakfast, or there's a weekly rate of $80/120. You can get both lunch and dinner for an extra $7 per day, or cook in the hostellers' kitchen. The hostel is in a quiet area, with a park-like setting and, like most YWCAs, it takes women only.

*Latimer Hostel* (tel 798-429) is centrally located on the corner of Madras and Gloucester streets. Unfortunately it's become so old and run-down that it generates many complaints from travellers. Cost in crowded bunkrooms is $11, or $21/30 for single/double rooms.

## Rooms & Hostel-Style Accommodation

There are several places providing good accommodation at hostel rates as well as regular rooms.

The *Hereford Private Hotel* (tel 799-536) at 36 Hereford St is opposite the Arts Centre and very close to the YMCA and youth hostel. Bunkroom accommodation is $13, singles $22, doubles or twins $32, and all rooms come equipped with bed linen, towels and soap. It's very plain and straightforward but excellent value. There are laundry facilities for guests' use but no kitchens. This is made up for by a restaurant which serves very economical meals – continental breakfast for $4, dinner for $6.50. This place has had strong recommendations from several travellers.

The *Ambassadors Hotel* (tel 667-808) at 19 Manchester St is a 5 minute walk south of the city centre and very close to the railway station and InterCity and Newmans bus depots. It's quite a flash old hotel, with leaded cut-glass windows, a lovely lounge area and deep velvety carpets. Upstairs the B&B rates are $39/60 for single/double rooms ($33/48 without breakfast), but downstairs there's another section where beds in a five bed dorm are $12.50, or $15 per person in single, twin or double rooms. All the beds are nicely made up – no need for your own linen! The one drawback is that there's no kitchen although there's free tea and coffee anytime, and continental breakfast for $2.50 or a giant cooked breakfast for $6.

*Bealey Lodge* (tel 666-770) is at 69 Bealey Ave on the corner of Stoneyhurst St, near the Bealey International Backpackers Hostel. It's a small, quiet and very pleasant guest house with B&B at $32/54. If you provide your own bedding it's just $16 per person in twin rooms and they'll provide breakfast for an extra $4 or you can cook in the upstairs kitchen.

*Thistle Guest House* (tel 481-499) at 21 Main South Rd, near the junction of Riccarton and Yaldhurst roads, is near the airport, with frequent buses to town. Rooms are $27/41, but if you provide your own bedding it's $15 per person in singles or doubles. Breakfast is available and there's a kitchen.

A couple of other places have separate hostel and regular sections. *Aarangi Backpackers Hostel* (tel 483-584) is at 15 Riccarton Rd, adjacent to Hagley Park, and offers free pick-up and luggage storage. Rates are $13 per person in rooms for two to four people. There's also a B&B guest house section upstairs, where the cost is $48/58 for singles/doubles.

*Stonehurst Hotel* (tel 794-620) at 241

Gloucester St is just around the corner from the Latimer Hostel, very close to the city centre and has a separate building with all the usual hostel facilities (kitchen, laundry, etc). Bunkroom beds are $12.50 per person (provide your own bedding) or there are double rooms (linen provided) at $30 for two. Hostellers are welcome to use the garden, house bars and TV and billiards rooms of the hotel next door. There's a courtesy van and the hostel is open 24 hours. Although it looks great from the outside, it's a bit shabby around the edges inside – the owners put more care into the hotel than the hostel side of the business. Room rates in the hotel are $37/50 for singles/doubles.

As in other major cities it may be possible to find accommodation at the university during student vacations. You can call the student association on 487-069.

**Guest Houses** The *Windsor Private Hotel* (tel 661-503) at 52 Armagh St is just 5 to 10 minutes walk from the city centre. It's meticulously clean and orderly and rooms cost $49/72 including a traditional cooked breakfast.

There are other places near the Windsor, such as the *Hotel Melville* (tel 798-956) at 49 Gloucester St. It's not quite as neat and tidy but most rooms have washbasins, unlike the Windsor. B&B costs $20/30 in the more basic detached rooms at the back, $30/50 in the main building.

Two km north-west of Cathedral Square the *Wolseley Lodge* (tel 556-202) at 107 Papanui Rd is a pleasantly old-fashioned place in a quiet setting with rooms at $35/50 including breakfast. A few doors down at No 121 the *Highway Lodge* (tel 555-418) has rooms at $25/45 plus $5 for breakfast. It's also a pleasantly olde-worlde place and you can get to both these places on a No 1 bus.

Closer in, the *New City Hotel* (tel 660-769) at 527 Colombo St offers rooms including breakfast at $40/60, or $45/65 with bathrooms. See the Rooms & Hostel-Style Accommodation section for other good guest houses.

**Hotels** *Warners Hotel* (tel 665-159; 366-5159 as of July 1992) is an old landmark right in Cathedral Square. Singles/doubles cost $25/50 with a washbasin, $56/84 with bathroom. Breakfast is $6 (continental) or $10 for Warners' 'hearty English-style breakfast'. See the Rooms & Hostel-Style Accommodation section for more economical hotel possibilities.

Top bracket Christchurch hotels include the *Avon Hotel* (tel 791-180) at 356 Oxford Terrace, the *Quality Inn Chateau* (tel 488-999) on the corner of Deans Ave and Kilmarnock St, *Noah's* (tel 794-700) on the corner of Worcester St and Oxford Terrace, and out at the airport the *Christchurch Airport Travelodge* (tel 583-139). At all these hotels doubles are in the $150 and up range, a long way up at Noahs. Right at the top of the price scale is the imaginatively designed and wonderfully situated *Park Royal Hotel* (tel 657-799) where a double costs nearly $300! It's worth a look even if you don't aspire to staying there.

**Motels** Christchurch is as well equipped with motels as in the other categories. Most of them start from $60 a double. As in other towns there are bargains to be found at the camping sites, which often have motels, tourist flats and cabins as well as sites for camping or campervans.

Better priced motels include:

*Adorian Motel* (tel 667-626), 47 Worcester St, singles/doubles $69/75
*Avon City Motel* (tel 526-079), 402 Main North Rd, singles/doubles $56/60
*Bucklands Motel* (tel 889-442), 525 Pages Rd, near New Brighton, swimming pool, singles/doubles $40/50
*Canterbury Court Motel* (tel 388-351), 140 Lincoln Rd, swimming pool, singles/doubles $70/82
*Cashel Court Motel* (tel 892-768), 457 Cashel St, swimming pool, doubles $58 or $64 with cooking facilities
*City Court Motels* (tel 669-099), 850 Colombo St, centrally located at corner of Salisbury St, doubles $50
*Colombo Travel Lodge* (tel 663-029), 965 Colombo St, 1 km north of Cathedral Square, singles/doubles $55/60
*Fairlane Court* (tel 894-943), 69 Linwood Ave, singles or doubles $48
*Hillvue Court Motel* (tel 385-112), 37 Hillier Place, singles/doubles $50/58
*Holiday Lodge Motel* (tel 666-584), 862 Colombo St, doubles $50
*Middle Park Kowhai Lodge* (tel 487-320), 120 Main South Rd, Upper Riccarton, singles $50, doubles $52 to $66
*Riccarton Motel* (tel 487-126), 92 Main South Rd, Upper Riccarton, doubles $60
*Salisbury Motel* (tel 668-713), 206 Salisbury St, centrally located, singles/doubles $43/55

**Camping & Cabins** There are plenty of camping sites, some very conveniently located. *Addington Park Motor Camp* (tel 389-770), at 47-51 Whiteleigh Rd off Lincoln Rd, is only 3 km from the city centre and has camping sites at $5.50 per person, or $9/13 for one/two people with power. It also has a variety of cabins from as little as $15/20 for one/two people. Other cabins are $26 for two, or $42 with fully equipped cooking facilities, private shower and toilet. It's conveniently located, comfortable and cheap – but closed for 2 weeks during the show in early November. Get there on bus No 7.

*Riccarton Park Motor Camp* (tel 485-690) at 19 Main South Rd, Upper Riccarton, is 6 km from the city centre. Tent sites are $6, cabins are $18/22 for one/two people, or there are on-site caravans at $15 for two. Take bus No 8H.

*Meadow Park Motor Camp* (tel 529-176), at 39 Meadow St off the Main North Rd, is 5 km out. Camping costs $7.50 per person, or $13/16 for one/two people with power. There are cabins from $28 to $47 for two. The camp has a covered heated swimming pool, a spa, children's playground equipment and a recreation hall. Take bus No 4.

*Russley Park Motor Camp* (tel 427-021) is at 372 Yaldhurst Rd, opposite Riccarton Racecourse about 10 km from Cathedral Square or 5 km from the airport. At this pleasant camp tent sites cost $7.50 per person, or $12/16 with power. The camp also has on-site vans at $28 to $32 for two, chalet cabins from $32 to $36 and some fancier tourist flats from $45. Take bus No 8G.

*South New Brighton Park* (tel 889-844),

in Halsey St off Estuary Rd, is another pleasant park, also 10 km out. Caravan sites cost $8/15 or there are a few on-site caravans at $15 plus the site charges. Take bus No 5S.

*Amber Park Caravan Park* (tel 483-327) is conveniently located at 308 Blenheim Rd, only 5 km south of the city centre. There are no tent sites here, caravan sites cost $16 for two. Tourist flats, which share the camp kitchen facilities but have their own showers and toilets, cost $40 to $44 for two. Any bus No 25 will get you there.

Other camping grounds include the *Rawhiti Domain Camp* (tel 887-408) in Shaw Ave, New Brighton, 9 km out; *Prebbleton Holiday Park* (tel 497-861) at 18 Blakes Rd, Prebbleton, 12 km out; and *Spencer Park Holiday Camp* (tel 298-721) in Heyders Rd, Spencerville, 14 km north (all distances from The Square).

## Places to Eat

These days you can eat in Christchurch all days and at all hours. There are a number of restaurants, luncheon places and takeaways around Cathedral Square and the two block stretch of Colombo St just north of the river has interesting restaurants.

**Fast Food & Takeaways** There are various places around Cathedral Square, including *Warners*, a 24-hour takeaway bar right behind Warners Hotel, in the north-east corner. *Leo Coffee Lounge* near the square is open 7 days a week until late.

Apart from the usual sandwich places there are some more exotic takeaways around Cathedral Square. *The Greek Recipe* at 55 Cathedral Square, beside the West End Theatre, has authentic, inexpensive Greek takeaways and is open from 10 am to 10 pm every day but Sunday. Only a block from the square at 176A Manchester St the *Mediterranean Take Away* has that eastern Med blend of Turkish/Greek/Lebanese food including doner kebabs. It's a good place to get food to eat in the square.

*Gaslight Cafe* in the Chancery Lane Arcade is a cosy little cafe, open from 6 am to 4 pm Monday to Thursday, until 9 pm on

Friday. The *Victoria Coffee Gallery* on the corner of Oxford Terrace and Montreal St by the river is also good for lunch. There's an economically priced cafeteria at the *YMCA*, opposite the Arts Centre on Hereford St. The pleasant coffee bar in the foyer of the *Town Hall* is open every day and in the evening whenever there's a concert.

**Pub Food** On Colombo St by the river the conveniently located *Oxford Tavern* has a family restaurant dubbed the *Major Bunbury*. It's open daily from 11 am to 9 pm, until 10 pm on Friday and Saturday. Main courses, which span the pub-food universe from family roasts to T-bone steaks, are in the $9.50 to $14 range and there's also a $5 children's menu.

Other places with pub food include the *Excelsior* on the corner of High and Manchester streets with main courses in the $12 to $15 range and again it's open for lunch and dinner 7 days a week.

There are *Cobb & Co's* at the *Caledonian Hotel*, 101 Caledonian Rd, north of Cathedral Square, and at the *Bush Inn Courts*, 364 Riccarton Rd, south of the square. Cobb & Co's are all open 7 days a week until 10 pm at night and have a standard and highly consistent pub food menu. Other pub food possibilities include the *Carlton Hotel* on the corner of Papanui Rd and Bealey Ave.

**Restaurants** The *Gardens Restaurant* in Christchurch's wonderful Botanic Gardens is renowned for its excellent smorgasbord which costs $12 including coffee. It's served from noon to 2 pm daily and also from 5.30 to 7.30 pm during the summer. The restaurant is open from 10 am for snacks and other light meals.

The riverside setting of the *Town Hall Restaurant* makes it a popular place to eat. There's a weekday lunchtime smorgasbord for $20, a Sunday smorgasbord lunch or dinner for $22, and a regular à la carte menu for dinner or late supper, with main courses from $12 to $30. Across the plaza at the ultra-modern, ultra-expensive *Park Royal Hotel*, the inner courtyard is given over to a rather elegant cafe/restaurant which is not as expensive as it looks – main courses, both meat and vegetarian, cost around $9 to $16, and there's an attractive salad bar. The wine list is about as long as the menu!

The riverside *Band Rotunda Restaurant* is housed in what used to be a band rotunda by the river on Cambridge Terrace. It's a great position and you could complement the romantic atmosphere by arriving by punt! It's reasonably priced with main courses for lunch at around $6.50 to $8, for dinner from $6.50 to $12, with both meat and vegetarian selections. It's open for lunch from Tuesday to Friday and again on Sunday; in the evening from Wednesday to Sunday.

*Speakers' Corner* at 139 Worcester St on the corner of Manchester St is a good BYO but it's particularly popular for delicious breakfasts from Tuesday to Sunday. Count on around $12 for cereals, fruit, toast, juice and tea or coffee.

The restaurant blocks of Colombo St, just north of the river, offer good dining possibilities. At the river end try *Spagalimi's Italian Pizza Restaurant* at No 798. It's a very popular place with takeaways as well. Pizzas range from $4 to $5.50 for the little ones up to $16 for the fanciest large pizza. It's open every night, and for lunch on Thursday and Friday.

Other possibilities in the same few blocks include the *Oxford Tavern* just south of the river (see Pub Food) and the *Mainstreet Cafe* further north (see Vegetarian). Or try *Marco Polo's* at No 812 with an interesting mix of Indonesian and Indian dishes. It's open from Monday to Saturday evenings, with main courses from $15.50 to $18. At No 834 the *Off the Wall Cafe* is a trendy looking place with starters from $6 to $9 and main courses from $10 to $16.

*Cafe Revere* at 813 Colombo St is a casual restaurant with a spacious woodbeam and brick decor. It has an eclectic international menu of seafood ($7.50 to $16), vegetarian ($6.50 to $8.50), hot & spicy ($7.50 to $12.50) and meat ($16) dishes, with starters from around $4.50 to $6. All their food is homemade and includes varied selections

like Indian vindaloo, Sri Lankan chicken curry, lamb shwarma, hummus, terrine or nachos. It's open Tuesday to Sunday from 5.30 pm until late, with live music on Friday and Saturday. *Strawberry Fare* at 114 Peterborough St, a few steps off Colombo St, is a restaurant for desserts only. They're expensive but definitely mind blowing!

At 76 Lichfield St, just south of the city centre, *Tre Gatti's* has pretty reasonable standard Italian dishes and is open commendably late at night. There are plenty of Chinese restaurants around Christchurch including the imposing *Chung Wah II* at 61-63 Worcester St. *Kim's* at 805 Colombo St is a lower key Chinese place, with both restaurant and takeaway sections; it's open every day from 11.30 am to 8.30 pm, until midnight on Friday and Saturday.

The *Sign of the Takahe*, out of the city at Cashmere Hills, is in an impressive old stone building, has fine views of the city, a great setting, careful service and high prices to go with it. It's open daily for Devonshire teas and smorgasbord lunches, Tuesday to Saturday for dinner. You can get there on bus No 2D.

**Vegetarian** Vegetarians are well catered for in Christchurch with good food in all price categories. *Gopals* at 143 Worcester St is another of the excellent Hare Krishna-run restaurants. It's open for lunch on weekdays and on Friday evenings.

Exceptionally good vegetarian food can be found at the *Mainstreet Cafe* on Colombo St by the corner with Salisbury St, in the restaurant blocks north of the river. Mainstreet is a pleasantly relaxed and very popular place with an open-air courtyard at the back. Imaginative main courses are around $16.50 or you could have bread and salad for $5. The salads are good and the desserts, particularly their varied selection of cheesecakes, are mouthwatering. It's open long hours, from 7 am to 11 pm daily.

*Dux de Lux* is another very popular place for gourmet vegetarian taste treats. It's in the Arts Centre, on Montreal St near Hereford St. There's a pleasantly green outdoor court-

Top: Glacier landing, Fox Glacier (TW)
Bottom: Fox Glacier Walk (TW)

Top:  Lake Tekapo (TW)
Left:  Mt Cook (TW)
Right:  Copland River (VB)

yard and service is counter style, with main courses around $7 or $8 (lunch) or $13.50 (dinner). They're licensed, with their own bar and brewery, and live music 4 nights a week. Dux de Lux is open from around 11.30 am until midnight, 7 days a week.

## Entertainment

**Pub Music** There are a few pubs with rock music at night, particularly on the weekends. Popular ones include *Dux de Lux* with its own brewery and bar (see Vegetarian Restaurants) and *Bush Inn Courts* at 364 Riccarton Rd, which has a small cover charge. The *Carlton*, on the corner of Bealey Ave and Papanui Rd, also has weekend entertainment. Or there's the *Star & Garter* at 332 Oxford Terrace, the *Imperial* on the corner of St Asaph and Barbadoes streets, the *Ferrymead Tavern*, the *Bishopdale Tavern*, the *Lancaster Park Hotel* and plenty others.

**Dance & Music** There's rock all week at *The Playroom* on the corner of Cuffs Rd and Pages Rd. The *Firehouse* at 293 Colombo St in the city centre is a nightclub. Other Christchurch nightclubs are *Romanov's* and *Cats*, both on Manchester St, and the *Palladium* on Gloucester St. *Warners*, in Cathedral Square, has folk music.

## Getting There & Away

**Air** Christchurch is the only international arrival and departure point on the South Island. Qantas, Air New Zealand, British Airways, Singapore Airlines and Thai Airlines all fly here. Safe Air fly between Christchurch and the Chatham islands.

Air New Zealand have their Christchurch office (tel 795-200) at 156 Armagh St. There are connections between Christchurch and most destinations in the North and South islands including Auckland (1½ hours), Dunedin (45 minutes), Invercargill (1 hour) and Wellington (45 minutes). There are as many as eight to 10 flights daily to Auckland or Wellington.

Ansett New Zealand (tel 791-300) and Mt Cook Airlines (tel 790-690) also fly into and out of Christchurch. Ansett have flights to Auckland, Dunedin, Invercargill, Queenstown and Rotorua. Mt Cook fly between Christchurch and Auckland, Wellington, Mt Cook, Nelson, Queenstown, Rotorua, Taupo, Te Anau and Wanaka at similar fares. Air Nelson (tel 585-112) have flights to Nelson, Hokitika, Oamaru and Timaru.

Smaller airlines operating out of Christchurch include Associated Air which fly to Blenheim and on to Paraparaumu near Wellington on the North Island. Wairarapa Airlines fly between Christchurch and Nelson or Masterton on the North Island.

The airport is modern and has an information centre (tel 537-854) open every day. There are luggage lockers at 50 cents for 8 hours, $1.50 for 24 hours. Ask about storing luggage for longer periods. Don't forget your $15 departure tax on international flights.

**Bus** InterCity buses (tel 799-020) depart from the InterCity Travel Centre at the railway station on Moorhouse Ave. Newmans buses (tel 795-641) leave from 347 Moorhouse Ave, opposite the railway station. Mt Cook/H&H buses (tel 482-099) go from 40 Lichfield St, near Cathedral Square.

Christchurch-Picton is about 5 to 6 hours, with Kaikoura an interesting midway stopping point. InterCity, Newmans and Mt Cook/H&H all do this route. All three also operate south to Dunedin – about 6½ hours. InterCity and Mt Cook/H&H continue south from Dunedin to Invercargill, another 3 hours.

Newmans have a Christchurch-Nelson service (via either Lewis Pass or Picton) with connections through to Westport and Greymouth on the west coast, or another route to Westport running more directly across the island. InterCity has more direct services to the west coast, with a bus to Greymouth via Arthur's Pass four times weekly. They also have services from Greymouth south to the glaciers three times weekly but this requires a layover in Greymouth as the schedules of the two routes are not timed to connect. The trip across the South Island via Arthur's Pass is a stunningly beautiful journey, not to be missed. From Christchurch it's about 2½ hours to Arthur's Pass, and another 1¾ hours on to Greymouth.

InterCity and Mt Cook also have daily bus services to Mt Cook (5 hours) and Queenstown (almost 10 hours). From November to April Mt Cook has an additional daily Christchurch-Queenstown excursion bus which makes a 3½ hour stopover at Mt Cook; this can make either a day trip (Christchurch-Mt Cook-Christchurch) or an attractive way of getting to Queenstown. InterCity buses take the same route daily all year round (to Queenstown via Mt Cook) but with only a 40 minute stopover at Mt Cook. Mt Cook's year-round daily buses from Christchurch to Mt Cook connect through Twizel; their year-round buses to Queenstown continue on to Te Anau. Another bus to Queenstown with a brief stopover at Mt Cook is operated by Great Sights (tel 661-999).

Other InterCity services from Christchurch include buses to Akaroa (2 hours), Hanmer Springs (2 hours), Tekapo (3½ hours) and Wanaka (9 hours).

The Shoestring Travel bus departs from Christchurch, and the Flying Kiwi bus can also be picked up here as well as from Picton. See the Getting Around chapter for details on these 'alternative' buses.

**Train** The railway station (tel 799-020) is on Moorhouse Ave, quite a long walk south of Cathedral Square. There are luggage lockers in the station costing $1 for 24 hours.

Trains run daily each way between Christchurch and Picton, connecting with the ferry across to Wellington. There's also a Monday to Saturday service each way between Christchurch and Invercargill via Dunedin. The TranzAlpine Express train runs daily between Christchurch and Greymouth via Arthur's Pass. Crossing over to the west coast the section of railway through the Waimakariri Gorge (above Springfield) has interesting scenery, but the road follows a different and even more spectacular route.

**Driving** From Christchurch it's 340 km north to Picton, 362 km south to Dunedin, about 4 or 5 hours drive in either direction. Westbound it's 150 km to Arthur's Pass, 248 km to Greymouth, 331 km to Mt Cook or 486 km to Queenstown.

**Hitching** It's pretty good hitching on the whole but Christchurch-Dunedin can be a long day. Generally it gets harder the further south you go, then easier as you approach Dunedin. Catch a Templeton bus (Nos 25L, 25K, 8L or 8K) to get out of the city. It's also possible to hitch between Christchurch and Picton in a day although there can be long waits in some places. If you're hitching northwards take a Christchurch bus to Woodend to get you on your way.

To hitch west take a bus No 8G (Yaldhurst) – then keep your fingers crossed; it can be a long hard haul, say a 2 day trip. Pick up the train somewhere along the way if you become despondent. The first part of this trip is easily hitched, but once you leave SH 1 it gets steadily harder.

**Getting Around**
**Airport Transport** The public bus service to the airport is operated by Christchurch Transport from Worcester St, just off Cathedral Square. Going out to the airport it's bus No 24, coming in it's bus No 28. Buses go about every half-hour from around 6 am to nearly 6 pm then less frequently until 9.45 pm on weekdays; they're less frequent on Saturdays and even worse on Sundays. Cost is $3.

There are several door-to-door airport shuttle buses. Super Shuttle (tel 655-655) operates 24 hours a day, serving not only the airport ($5) but also the bus and train stations. Another shuttle is operated by Canterbury Scenic Tours (tel 669-660) and also costs $5. A taxi to or from the airport will cost about $14 to $18 depending on the time you go, so it can work out cheaper than the shuttles with several people.

**Bus** Most city buses are operated by Christchurch Transport and run from Cathedral Square. Unlike most NZ urban bus services, Christchurch's is good, cheap and well organised. There's a Bus Information Kiosk (tel 794-600) in the square; it's open daily but at variable hours. Fares start at 50 cents and step up 50 cents at a time to $2.50. Note the Christchurch tradition of hanging baby strollers and pushchairs off the back of the buses.

**Taxi** There are plenty of taxis in Christchurch but, as with other places in New Zealand, they don't cruise. You have to find them on taxi ranks or phone for them.

**Car & Campervan Rental** The major operators all have offices in Christchurch as do numerous smaller local companies. With the smaller operators, unlimited km rates start from around $50 a day plus about $12 per day for insurance for rental periods of 3 days or more.

Avis
    26 Lichfield St (tel 793-840)
Avon Rent-a-Car
    339 Moorhouse Ave (tel 793-822)
Budget Rent-a-Car
    corner Oxford Terrace & Lichfield St (tel 660-072)
Economy Rent-a-Car
    518 Wairakei Rd (tel 597-410)
Hertz
    44-46 Lichfield St (tel 660-549)
Letz Rent-a-Car
    200 Yaldhurst Rd (tel 796-880)
Percy Rent-a-Car
    154 Durham St (tel 793-466)
Renny Rent-a-Car
    156 Tuam St (tel 666-790)
Southern Cross Rental Group
    105-107 Victoria St (tel 794-547)
Thrifty Car Rental
    574 Wairakei Rd (tel 587-533)

Wheels (tel 664-855) at 20 Manchester St hires cars at about $250 per week, everything included, but they also have a programme whereby they sell you a car and buy it back again at a pre-agreed price.

There are also many campervan rentals available in Christchurch. Campervan companies include:

Horizon
    530-544 Memorial Ave (tel 535-600)
Maui Campavans
    530 Memorial Ave (tel 584-159)
Mt Cook Line Motorhomes
    47 Riccarton Rd (tel 482-099)
Newmans
    530-544 Memorial Ave (tel 535-800)

**Motorcycle Rental** Motorcycles can be hired from Phil Payne's Cycletreads (tel 797-382) at 50 Tuam St, or from Te Waipounamu Motorcycle Tours (tel 523-541, 794-320).

**Bicycle Rental** Bicycles are ideal for Christchurch as it is nice and flat. There are cycling lanes on many roads and Hagley Park, which encompasses the Botanical Gardens, has many cycling paths. You can pedal away from Rent-a-Bike (tel 657-589) in the Avon Carpark Building, 139 Gloucester St; it's open from 8.30 am to 6 pm Monday to Thursday, 8.30 am to 11 pm on Friday. Single-speed bikes rent for $2 an hour, $10 a day, or $54 a week. Three-speed bikes are $3/15/70.

Sam's Bike Shop (tel 485-811) at 81A Riccarton Rd has 18-speed mountain bikes at $7 an hour, $20 a day or $90 a week. Insurance is $1.50 a day. Contact the Recreational Cycling Club if you'd like to join the club's Sunday tours.

There's also a Penny Farthing bike shop in Christchurch.

## KAIAPOI

Kaiapoi, on the coast 20 km north of Christchurch, is noted for its wool mills. The Kaiapoi Museum in the Old Courthouse on Williams St has exhibits on local history. It's open from 2 to 4 pm on Sundays and Thursdays; entry is $1 (children 20 cents or free with an adult).

From Kaiapoi you can make trips on the MV *Tuhoe* which sails most Sundays to Kairaki and back. The round trip costs $8 (children $4) and takes 1¼ hours. There's fishing for trout, salmon and whitebait on the Kaiapoi River. You can reach Kaiapoi from Christchurch on a Kaiapoi bus Nos 1R or 4R,

Waikuku bus Nos 1T or 4T, or Rangiora bus No 4V; it's a 35 minute trip.

## LYTTELTON

To the south-east of Christchurch are the hills, and behind them Lyttelton Harbour, Christchurch's port. Like Wellington Harbour it is the drowned crater of a long extinct volcano.

### Harbour Trips

There are all sorts of boat trips on Lyttelton Harbour, starting from as low as $4 (children $2) for the one-way trip to Diamond Harbour and Quail Island. The turn-of-the-century steam tug *Lyttelton* does 2 hour harbour cruises from January to April every Sunday at 2 pm. It departs from No 2 Wharf and the cost is $12 (children $6). There are also cruises every day at 2 pm from Jetty B to Ripapa Island Historic Reserve, also for $12 (children $6).

### Museum

The Lyttelton Museum has displays on colonial Lyttelton, a maritime gallery and an Antarctic gallery. It's in the centre of Lyttelton on Gladstone Quay and is open from 2 to 4 pm on weekends all year round, plus from 2 to 4 pm on Tuesday and Thursday from December to February. A self-guided historic walk begins from the museum and guided tours are available.

### Timeball Station

In Reserve Terrace, Lyttelton, is the Timeball Station, one of the few remaining in the world. Built in 1876, it once fulfilled an important maritime duty as all ships sailing from Lyttelton Harbour relied on it to set their chronometers. It's open from 10 am to 4 pm on weekdays, 10 am to 5 pm on weekends and public holidays, and entry is $3 (children $1, family $6).

### Getting There & Away

Bus Nos 28G or 28H from Cathedral Square take you to Lyttelton. From Christchurch there are three roads to Lyttelton. The quickest way is through the road tunnel (12 km). Alternatively, you can go via Sumner and Evans Pass (19 km) or head straight down Colombo St from the square, and continue up over Dyers Pass (22 km). The Dyers Pass route passes the Sign of the Takahe, an impressive Gothic-style stone building, now housing an olde-English tea house. It's a popular stop for bus tours (bus No 2 goes to the hills). There is also a road along the summit of the hills.

# Banks Peninsula

Near Christchurch, Banks Peninsula makes an interesting side trip. Not as flat as the area around the city itself, the hilly peninsula was formed by two giant volcanic eruptions in the distant past. The many tiny inlets and bays all around the peninsula's coast make for some pleasant explorations.

The peninsula was first sighted by Captain Cook in 1770 and named after naturalist Sir Joseph Banks. The Maori Ngati Tahu tribe, who then occupied the peninsula, were attacked by Te Rauparaha in 1831 and suffered a severe decline in numbers. A few years later, in 1836, the British established a whaling station at Peraki.

Two years later, in 1838, the French captain Jean Langlois chose the site of Akaroa as an attractive spot for French settlement. He returned to France and in 1840 a group of 63 French settlers set out from Rochefort. Meanwhile, also in 1840, the Treaty of Waitangi was signed, bringing all of New Zealand under British sovereignty. The French, however, did go ahead with their plans and settle at Akaroa. In 1849 the French land claim was sold to the New Zealand Company and the following year the French were joined by a large group of British settlers.

Originally heavily forested, the land was cleared for timber, and dairy farming, later supplanted by sheep farming, became the main industry of the peninsula.

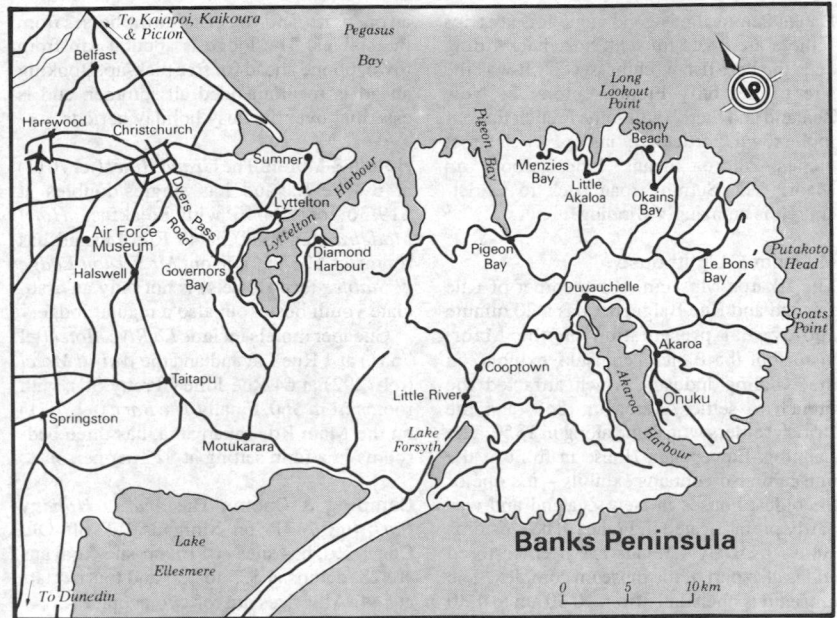

**Banks Peninsula**

## Places to Stay

Most of the places to stay on the Banks Peninsula are in or near Akaroa, the peninsula's principal (though tiny) town, but a few other possibilities are scattered around the various bays.

**Hostels** Six km south of Akaroa at Onuku, the *Onuku Farm Hostel* (tel Akaroa 7612) is beside the bay on a 400 hectare sheep farm. You'll recognise it by the antinuclear sign on the roof! It's a friendly and relaxed place with a good library. Nightly costs are $12 in the house, $8 in summer huts, or $7 for tent sites. They will pick you up from Akaroa.

At Okains Bay, 1 km from the beach, *Hua Whenua Backpackers* (tel 514-8647) has caravans with electricity at $10 per person. It's a small organic farm, opposite the Maori/Early Settlers Museum.

The *Kukupa Hostel* (tel Pigeon Bay 8823) at Pigeon Bay was the first Youth Hostel in New Zealand, though it's now privately owned. There are just two bunkrooms at this small hostel; cost is $9 for YHA members, $10 for everyone else, or $30 for families. Set in magnificent bush land, it's a bit far from everything if you don't have your own wheels – Pigeon Bay is about 35 km from Akaroa and very remote. To get there from Christchurch, take a bus to Duvauchelle or Akaroa and then transfer to the Eastern Bays bus, which operates every day except Sunday and stops near the hostel.

**Camping & Cabins** *Duvauchelle Reserve Board Camp* (tel 813) is 8 km from Akaroa off SH 75. Tent sites are $3.50 per person, add an extra $2.20 per site for power.

The *Le Bons Bay Motor Camp* (tel 8533), on Le Bons Bay Valley Rd about 22 km from Akaroa, has tent and power sites at about $7 per person, on-site caravans at $28 for two.

## AKAROA

Akaroa, 82 km from Christchurch on the

Banks Peninsula, is good value for day trips – there are boats for rent, horseback riding and 'the best fish & chips in NZ'. It was the site of the only French colony in New Zealand and there's still some French flavour in the town, particularly in the French street names. Akaroa means 'long harbour' in Maori. The Summit road back to Christchurch is amazingly winding.

### Museum & Lighthouse

The Akaroa Museum, at the corner of Rue Lavaud and Rue Balguerie, has a 20 minute audiovisual presentation on the Maori history of the Banks Peninsula, exhibits on the whaling industry which attracted the French to settle Akaroa in 1840, and the British settlers who came along in 1850. The Langlois-Eteveneaux House in front of the museum also contains exhibits – it's one of the oldest houses in New Zealand and was partly prefabricated in France. The Customs House by Daly's Wharf has been restored and is also part of the museum complex. The museum is open daily from 10.30 am to 4.30 pm (4 pm in winter); admission is $1 (children 50 cents).

The historic Akaroa Lighthouse is open on Sundays from 1 to 4 pm, daily during January.

### Harbour Cruises

Daily harbour cruises are operated on the *Canterbury Cat*, departing the Main Wharf at 1.30 pm. Cost is $18 (children $9). You can buy tickets from their office opposite the wharf at the Akaroa Village Inn (tel 7641).

### Places to Stay

**Hostels** The *Mt Vernon Lodge & Stables* (tel 7180) on Rue Balguerie is a combination hostel and guest lodge. Rates are $13 per person in a four-bed room if you supply your own bedding, or $35 per person in double rooms with linen provided. The rooms have a mezzanine floor over the main area and there are share-kitchen facilities. The lodge is in a deer farm overlooking Akaroa and the harbour; there's a swimming pool, barbecue and a large comfortable common room with

an open fire, and you can ride the horses from the stables. The lodge is about 1 km from town, phone ahead for free pick-up. Booking ahead is recommended all summer, and is essential over the busy holiday periods.

**Hotels & Motels** The *Grand Hotel* (tel 7011) at 6 Rue Lavaud has singles/doubles at $19/36, or $24/46 with breakfast. *Hotel Madeira* (tel 7009) at 48 Rue Lavaud has rooms at $23 per person. *Mt Vernon Lodge & Stables* (see Hostels) is not only an associate youth hostel but also a regular lodge.

Cheaper motels include *La Rive Motel* (tel 7651) at 1 Rue Lavaud and the *Wai-iti Motel* (tel 7292) at 64 Rue Jolie ('Pretty St'), with rooms from $60. Finally *The Barn* (tel 7671) on the Main Rd, Takamatua, has three bedrooms in a farm setting at $25 per person.

**Camping & Cabins** The *Akaroa Holiday Park* (tel 7471) on Morgans Rd, off Old Coach Rd, has sites at $16, on-site caravans at $28, cabins at $33 to $35 and tourist flats at $44. All prices are for two people.

### Getting There & Away

Akaroa is only 82 km from Christchurch and there are regular buses as well as daily Inter-City and Great Sights/Christchurch Transport day excursions. Akaroa Tours (tel Akaroa 7421; Christchurch 799-629) operate an Akaroa Shuttle minibus, departing from the post office in Akaroa and from the Information Centre in Christchurch. The InterCity depot in Akaroa is on Aubrey St close to the centre.

# South Canterbury

Heading west from Christchurch on SH 73, it's about a 2½ hour trip to Arthur's Pass and the Arthur's Pass National Park, at the summit of the Southern Alps. If you keep on going west past the summit, you're in Westland. (See Arthur's Pass in the Westland chapter.) The route from Christchurch to Greymouth, crossing the Alpine summit at

Arthur's Pass, is a spectacular route covered by buses and the Tranz Alpine Express train.

On the other hand, if you head south from Christchurch there are basically two routes through the South Canterbury region. Taking SH 1 straight south along the coast you come to Timaru, Oamaru and then Dunedin. Or you could head inland, crossing the MacKenzie Country and heading towards the Southern Alps. This route between Christchurch and Queenstown, passing Lake Tekapo and Mt Cook along the way, is a much travelled road.

Methven and Geraldine are each a short distance off the road, whether you're taking the inland or coastal routes.

## METHVEN

Inland from Ashburton below Mt Hutt is Methven, a good centre for the Canterbury Plains or the mountains. A small town, Methven is very quiet for most of the year, coming alive during the winter when it fills up with skiers using it as a base for Mt Hutt and other ski fields.

### Places to Stay

The *Mt Hutt Accommodation* (tel 28-508, 28-585) at 32 Lampard St in central Methven has hostel-style accommodation from $14 ($16 in winter), with facilities including twin, double and multiple-bed rooms in lodges, cottages and bunk houses. If you don't have your own bedding you can hire it for $2. They have another site at 177 Rakaia Gorge Rd.

*Methven A&P Showgrounds* (tel 28-005) on Barkers Rd has tent sites at $10 for two, power sites at $12, and cabins at $10 per person. You can hire bedding and cooking utensils if you don't have your own.

*Pudding Hill Chalets* (tel 28-416) on SH 72 has tent sites at $8/11 for one/two people, caravan sites for $2 more, and chalets where B&B is $35 per person in twin rooms, $30 per person in larger rooms (lower off-season, June to September). They have lots of enjoyable extras including sauna, spa pool, swimming pool, a children's play area, billiards, a ski room and drying room.

*Aorangi Lodge* (tel 28-482) is at 38 Spaxton St and has rooms at $60 during ski season, with off-season reductions. *Mt Hutt Homestead* (tel 28-130) is part of a high country sheep and deer station just outside Methven. It's not cheap at $189/243, including breakfast and dinner, but the food is excellent and it's an interesting place to stay. There are other motels and hotels.

## GERALDINE

Off the main Christchurch-Timaru road on the road inland to Mt Cook is Geraldine, a picturesque town with an interesting Vintage Car & Machinery Museum. The collection includes a couple of 1910 Model Ts and lots of cars from the '10s, '20s and '30s. The huge shed at the back houses about 60 tractors, dating back to the 1920s; tractors are entered in the annual Geraldine tractor races and competitions. There's also a single aircraft and a large amount of rather rusty agricultural machinery. The museum is open from 10 am to 4.30 pm on Saturday and Sunday all year, daily during school holidays, and entry is $2 (children free).

Barker's Wines (tel 38-969) is 8 km out of Geraldine, off SH 79 towards Mt Cook, and is open for tasting Monday to Saturday until 6 pm. It specialises in elderberry and other berry fruit wines.

## MACKENZIE COUNTRY

The high country from which the Mt Cook park rises is known as the MacKenzie country after a legendary sheep rustler, Jock MacKenzie, who ran his stolen flocks in that uninhabited region around 1843. When he was finally caught other settlers realised the potential of the land and followed in his footsteps. The first people to traverse the MacKenzie were the Maoris who used to trek across the country from Banks Peninsula to Otago hundreds of years ago.

## TEKAPO

At the southern end of Lake Tekapo the small settlement of Tekapo is a popular rest stop for buses heading to or from Mt Cook or Queenstown. There's a little cluster of businesses by the main road from where there are sweeping views across the lake with the hills and mountains as a backdrop. The lake, walks and, in winter, skiing are the Lake Tekapo attractions.

### Church of the Good Shepherd
The picturesque little church beside the lake was built of stone and oak in 1935. Further along is a statue of a collie dog, a touching tribute to the sheep dogs which made the development of the MacKenzie country possible.

### Walks
It's an hour's walk to the top of Mt John and you can continue on to lakes Alexandrina and McGregor, an all day walk. Other walks are along the eastern side of the lake to the ski field road, the 1 hour return walk to the Tekapo lookout or 1½ hours to the power station.

### Aerial Sightseeing
Air Safari (tel 880) operate flights from Tekapo over Mt Cook and its glaciers for $105 (children $70). The flights do not land on the glacier but Air Safari's 'Grand Traverse' takes you up the Tasman glacier, over the upper part of the Fox and Franz Josef glaciers, and by Mt Cook and Mt Tasman. Air Safari operates the same flights from Glentanner, near Mt Cook for the same price ($105, children $70), but YHA members can get a 10% discount from Tekapo, not available from Glentanner. They are much cheaper than similar flights offered by other airlines from Mt Cook itself.

### Other Activities
Other popular activities around Lake Tekapo include fishing, boating, kayaking and bicycle touring, horse trekking and hanggliding. From October to May you can tour the Mt John observatory, phone 813 for details. It's also possible to tour the hydroelectric power station.

In winter, Tekapo is the base for downhill skiing at Round Hill (beginners) or Mt Dobson (intermediates), or cross-country skiing on Two Thumb Range. There's ski field transport and ski hire in season. Tekapo also has an open-air ice skating rink.

### Places to Stay
**Hostels** The *Tekapo Youth Hostel* (tel 857) is beyond the post office, restaurants and shops on the Mt Cook side of town. It's a well-equipped, friendly little hostel sleeping 28 people and has great views across the lake to the mountains beyond – this is the hostel with the 'million dollar view'. It's open all day and nightly cost is $13, or there are limited tent sites beside it for about half that price.

**Hotels & Motels** The *Lake Tekapo Hotel* (tel 808) has backpackers accommodation at $12, single/double rooms with private facilities at $25/55, and one motel unit at $65. The *Lake Tekapo Alpine Inn* (tel 848) has budget rooms at $51, standard rooms at $73, and superior (lake view) rooms at $96, all for two people. The *Tekapo Camp* also has motel units, see Camping & Cabins.

**Camping & Cabins** Beside the lake the *Tekapo Camp* (tel 825) has tent or power sites at $6.50 per person, cabins at $10 per person, cottages with cooking facilities (everything supplied except bed linen) at $40 for two, and motel units from $56 for two.

### Places to Eat
There are takeaways and cafes as well as a bakery in the business centre by the main road. The *Lake Tekapo Hotel* has reasonably priced bistro meals for lunch and dinner every day except Sunday. The *Alpine Inn Family Restaurant* is open daily for all three meals. During the summer season they serve a daily hot buffet lunch ($13.50) and dinner ($23).

### Getting There & Away
The InterCity and Mt Cook Landline southbound services to Queenstown (3½ hours), Wanaka (5 hours) and Mt Cook (1¼ hours) come through every day, as do the northbound services to Timaru (3 hours) and

Christchurch (3½ hours). Book at the petrol station.

Hitching in or out of Tekapo can sometimes be difficult as there is not much traffic; but once you've got a ride it will probably be going a fair way.

## TWIZEL

Slightly south of Lake Pukaki, Twizel is at a conveniently central location for the whole area. By car it's only about 30 minutes from Mt Cook. Nearby Lake Ruataniwha has an international rowing centre, fishing, boating and windsurfing. There's a huge hydroelectric power station, you can arrange a free tour from the town's Information Centre.

### Information

The Twizel Information and Display Centre (tel 802) on Wairepo Rd is open from 9 am to 4 pm Monday to Friday, 10 am to 3 pm on Saturday and Sunday. It also houses the DOC.

### Places to Stay

The *Basil Lodge* (tel 671) has all sorts of accommodation starting with hostel-style bunks (only two beds to a room, though) at $12, singles/doubles at $27/39, and family rooms at $39 plus $5 per child.

On the edge of town the *MacKenzie Country Inn* (tel 869) has standard rooms at $38/45 a single/double, 'superior' rooms at $79/90. Right beside the lake, 4 km out of town, the *Ruataniwha Motor Camp* (tel 613) has tent or power sites at $7 per person and cheap although fairly basic cabins at $11 per person.

*Glenbrook Station* (tel Omarama 407) is a high-country sheep station between Twizel and Omarama on SH 8, 8 km south of Twizel and 22 km north of Omarama. It offers a variety of accommodation including four bunkrooms, each with kitchen and bathroom and sleeping up to 10 people, at $12 per person; motel units each sleeping up to six people at $50 per unit, or at $75/125 for one/two people including breakfast and dinner. It's an interesting place to stay, with

horse riding, cross country trail riding, bushwalks and hunting among the activities.

There's also homestead accommodation on the 72 sq km *Rhoborough Downs Sheep Station* (tel Twizel 509), 15 km from Twizel near the SH 8 and SH 80 junction. Here there's just one twin room and one double room, and rates including breakfast and dinner are $100 a night for two people.

### Places to Eat

The licensed *Basil Lodge* restaurant serves breakfast ($5.50 to $11.50), lunch ($5 to $7) and dinner (main courses $10 to $17.50). They also have a cheaper takeaway counter.

In the small shopping centre the plain *Black Stilt Cafe* offers takeaways, burgers at $2.50 to $4, cooked breakfast at $7 and meals at around $10. Also in the shopping centre the *Lunch Box* has takeaways and outdoor tables. For higher class dining there's the restaurant at the *MacKenzie Country Inn*, which also serves less expensive bistro meals.

### Getting There & Away

The InterCity and Mt Cook Landline buses serving Mt Cook all stop at Twizel, with additional buses shuttling between Twizel and Mt Cook; it's about a 50 minute bus ride.

## MT COOK

The Mt Cook National Park is almost 700 sq km in size and one of the most spectacular parks in a country famed for them. Encompassed by the main divide, the Two Thumb, Liebig and Ben Ohau Ranges, more than one third of the park is in permanent snow and glacial ice.

Of the 27 NZ mountains over 3050 metres, 22 are in this park including the mighty Mt Cook – at 3765 metres the highest peak in New Zealand and Australasia. Known to the Maoris as Aorangi – cloud piercer – the tent-shaped Mt Cook was named after Captain James Cook by Captain Stokes of the survey ship HMS *Acheron*. It was first climbed on Christmas Day 1894 and many famous climbers (including Sir Edmund Hillary) learned to climb on this

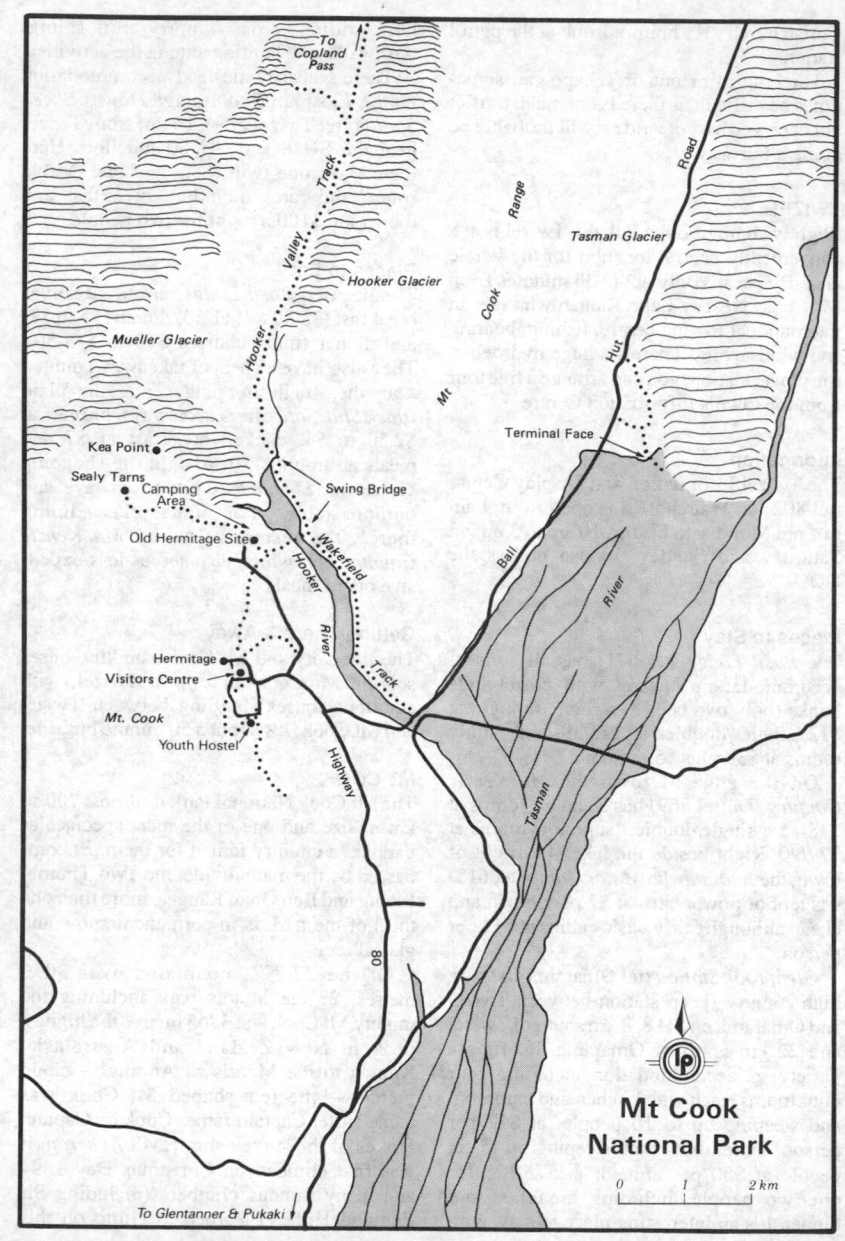

Mt Cook
National Park

formidable peak. It towers over the park and provides a fine view from the famed Hermitage Hotel.

## Information

The Park Visitor Centre (tel 818/9), open daily from 8 am to 5 pm, will advise you on what guided tours are available and on tramping routes. For information before you arrive write to: The Chief Ranger, PO Box 5, Mt Cook. There's a post agency (not a complete post office, but you can buy stamps and send letters) at Mt Cook and travellers' cheques can be cashed at the Hermitage.

Alpine Guides Mountain Shop (tel 834) sells skiing and mountaineering equipment or you can rent a variety of equipment including boots, parkas, ice axes, crampons, packs, rain pants, day packs and gaiters. It's open every day from 8 am to 5.30 pm.

Alpine Guides have ski-touring and mountaineering courses but the costs are almost as steep as Mt Cook itself. A 1 week Mountain Experience course is $1075, a 10 day Technical Mountaineering Course $1975, other courses and expeditions are around $2000. Want a private guide for the day? Well, by yourself that will be $240, between four of you it's $80 each. They also provide guides for the Copland Track, see the Outdoor Activities chapter. Heliskiing in the Ben Ohau Range is $440, and to go skiing on the glacier it's a cool $425 by skiplane.

## The Hermitage

Skiing on the Tasman Glacier and the Copland Pass Track (see the Outdoor Activities chapter) over the main divide to Westland National Park are two of the energetic attractions of the park, but one of the park's chief attractions is rather more sedentary: The Hermitage is the most famous hotel in New Zealand – principally for its location and the fantastic views out to Mt Cook. Originally constructed in 1884, when travel up here from Christchurch took several days, the first hotel was destroyed in a flash flood in 1913. You can see the foundations about a km from the current Hermitage. Rebuilt, it survived until 1957 when it was totally burnt

out and the present Hermitage was built on the same site.

## Tasman Glacier

Higher up, the Tasman is a spectacular sweep of ice just like a glacier should be, but further down it's ugly. Glaciers in New Zealand (and elsewhere in the world) have generally been retreating all this century. Normally as a glacier retreats it melts back up the mountain but the Tasman is unusual because its last few km are almost horizontal. In the process of melting over the last 75-or-so years it has contracted vertically rather than horizontally: the stones, rocks and boulders it carried down the mountain are left on top as the ice around them melts. So the Tasman in its 'ablation zone' (the region it melts in) is covered in a more or less solid mass of debris – which slows down its melting rate and makes it look pretty unpleasant.

Despite this considerable melt the ice by the site of the old Ball Hut is still estimated to be over 600 metres thick. In its last major advance, 17,000 years ago, the glacier crept right down to Pukaki, carving out Lake Pukaki in the process. A later advance didn't reach out to the valley sides so the Ball Hut Rd runs between the outer valley walls and the lateral moraines of this later advance.

Like the Fox and Franz Josef glaciers on the other side of the divide the glaciers from Mt Cook move fast. The Alpine Memorial, near the old Hermitage Site on the Hooker Valley Walk, illustrates the glaciers' speed. The memorial commemorates Mt Cook's first climbing disaster when three climbers were killed by an avalanche in 1914. Only one of the bodies was recovered at the time but 12 years later a second body melted out of the bottom of the Hochstetter Icefall, 2000 metres below the spot where the party was buried.

## Walks

There are various easy walks from the Hermitage area. The Visitors Centre can give you all the info including leaflets that list the main attractions, describe the degree of difficulty and tell you about the flora and fauna in the area. If you're there in the summer keep a look out for the large mountain buttercup, often called the Mt Cook lily. There are also mountain daisies, gentians and edelweiss. Among the animals you may see are the thar, a goatlike mammal and excellent climber; the chamois, smaller and of lighter build than the thar but an agile climber; and red deer.

**Kea Point** An easy 1½ hour walk with much native plant life and fine views of Mt Cook, the Hooker Valley and the ice face at Mt Sefton.

**Sealy Tarns** This is a 2½ hour walk that branches off the Kea Point track. If the weather is warm and you're feeling brave you can swim in the tarns.

**Red Tarns** This is a good way to spend 1½ hours and if you climb for another half-hour the views of Mt Cook and along the valley are spectacular.

**Hooker Valley** It is a 2 hour walk up the valley across a couple of swing bridges to Sefton Stream. After the second swing bridge Mt Cook totally dominates the valley and there are superb views. From here the alpine route climbs up and over the Copland Pass to the other side of the divide but crossing this high pass is for the experienced or well-guided only. Alpine Guides will guide you up to the top of the pass. The walk down the other side to the west coast road doesn't require expert assistance.

**Other Walks** The 2 hour Wakefield Track follows the route used by early mountaineers and sightseers then returns by the Hooker Valley track. Governors Bush is a short 1 hour walk through one of the last stands of silver beech in the park.

Shorter walks include the 10 minute Bowen Bush Walk through a small patch of totara trees near Alpine Guides. The 15 minute Glencoe Walk, beginning from the rear of the Hermitage, ascends through totara forest to a lookout point facing Mt Cook and the Hooker Valley.

**Tasman Valley Rd Tracks** A number of short tracks branch off from the Tasman Valley Rd including a track to view the Wakefield Falls, another to overlook the five Blue Lakes, and various tracks providing different viewpoints of the Tasman Glacier.

**Overnight** If you're well enough equipped you can tramp up to Hooker or Mueller hut, the closest hut to the village, and spend the night there.

### Climbing

There is unlimited scope here for climbing for the experienced, but beware, there have been over 160 people killed in climbing accidents in the park, with an average of five deaths each year! The Copland Pass track is a particularly problematic track, as it is well known and is too often attempted by people who are not sufficiently experienced to handle it safely.

Ice axes and crampons are a necessity, but you must have the knowledge of how to use them. Ropes are recommended, but there have been cases of several climbers tying themselves together and when one falls over a ledge, they all have been pulled over.

The highly changeable weather is an important factor around here – Mt Cook is only 44 km from the Tasman coast, catching the weather conditions blowing in over the Tasman Sea. The weather can change abruptly and a storm be upon you before you know it. Unless you are experienced in these types of conditions, don't attempt to climb anywhere without a guide.

It's important to check with the park rangers before attempting any climb, and not only to check with them, but to heed their advice! Fill in a climber's intentions card before starting out on any climb, so that someone can check on you if you are overdue coming out.

## Aerial Sightseeing

The skies above Mt Cook are alive with the sound of aircraft. This is the antipodean equivalent of the Grand Canyon in the USA although fortunately the skies are not yet that crowded. The views are superb and glacier landings are a great experience.

Air trips are operated by Mt Cook Airlines from Mt Cook, or by Air Safari and the Helicopter Line from Glentanner. Air Safari operate the same trips at the same fare from Tekapo. YHA members get a 10% discount on the flights if taken from Tekapo, a saving not offered from Glentanner.

The Mt Cook skiplane landing flights are the most expensive. They have a 30 minute 'skiplane fun' flight at $120 (children $89), a 40 minute 'glacier highlights' flight at $167 ($125) and a 55 minute 'grand circle' flight at $237 ($178).

The Helicopter Line has a 30 minute 'trans glacier' flight at $84, a 30 minute flight over the Richardson glacier at $140, and a 45 minute 'mountains high' flight over the Tasman Glacier and by Mt Cook with a glacier landing for $196. These flights go from Glentanner Park as do the Air Safari flights which are probably the best value although they do not actually land on the glacier. Air Safari's 'Grand Traverse' takes you up the Tasman Glacier, over the upper part of the Fox and Franz Josef glaciers, by Mt Cook and Mt Tasman and generally gives you your fill of mountain scenery for $105 (children $70). Transport is available to Glentanner Park from Mt Cook village.

## Other Activities

From the Glentanner camp you can go on horse treks from $14 for half an hour to $72.50 for 4 hours. There are 4WD trips for $22 per person, lasting about an hour. They also do an hourlong tour of the Glentanner Station farm, which for $14 includes a sheep shearing and sheepdog demonstration. Or you can combine the farm tour and the 4WD trip and pay $35 (children $17.50), the whole thing takes about 2½ hours. They also do fishing safaris. A minimum of four people is required for all the Glentanner trips.

## Tours

The interesting (but at $24 rather expensive) 2 hour Tasman Glacier Guided Coach Tour is operated two or three times a day in season – check at the Hermitage or Glencoe Lodge about bookings and tour times. The rocky road follows the lateral moraines of the Tasman Glacier and the bus stops several times to see this mighty river of ice. Part of the tour involves an optional 15 minute walk.

## Places to Stay

Mt Cook is a resort and priced accordingly. Despite the prices, demand has been running ahead of supply so it's wise to book in advance, particularly during the summer high season. Apart from the Youth Hostel all the places are operated by the THC.

**Hostels** The excellent *Mt Cook Youth Hostel* (tel 820) has lots more room than the small old one. Nevertheless it can still get crowded in the high season – booking ahead is essential from December to April, when you should try to book at least 4 days in advance. It's well equipped, with a sauna, barbecue, and disabled facilities. It's also conveniently located, has a friendly atmosphere, and is open all day. Cost is $15 per night.

**Chalets, Hotels & Motels** These are all run by the THC and booked by phoning Mt Cook 809, Wellington 729-179, Christchurch 790-718 or Auckland 773-689.

At the bottom of the price range are the *Mt Cook Chalets* which cost $85 for two, then $17 for each extra adult. They have two mini-bedrooms and a fold-down double bed-sofa, so between six people they can be reasonably economical. Well-equipped kitchens and a dining table add to the convenience. They may be closed in the winter season though.

Above this, the prices become expensive. The *Glencoe Lodge*, open only during the summer season from September to April, costs $158/169 for singles/doubles; the rooms have no cooking facilities but the price includes breakfast. The *Hermitage* (well it is nice to stay there) has prices in line with its fame – about $210 for a single or double, $282 for a suite.

**Camping & Cabins** Camping is allowed at the White Horse Hill camping area at the old Hermitage site, the starting point for the Hooker Valley track, 1.8 km from Mt Cook Village. There's running water and toilets but no electricity, showers or other luxuries you find at motor camps. It's run by the DOC on a first come, first served basis (no advance bookings) and cost is $3 per night for each adult (children $1). For more information contact the Park Visitor Centre.

The nearest motor camp to the park is 23 km down the valley on the shores of Lake Pukaki at *Glentanner Park* (tel Mt Cook 855). Facilities are good and campervan sites with power cost $6 per person. There are also on-site vans at $12 per person, basic cabins at $30 for two, and deluxe cabins at $50 for two. Note that the camp store here is only open from 8 am to 5 pm. The only other store is up at Mt Cook so if you're going to arrive late bring supplies with you, or prepare to starve!

If you are hiking or mountaineering there are many huts scattered around the park, but some are only accessible to the experienced climber. The Park Visitor Centre can tell you where they are and advise you on good walks. Hut fees are generally $12 a night, except for the very basic shelters, which are free.

### Places to Eat

The only way to eat economically at Mt Cook is to fix your own food. There's a small, but well-stocked, store and prices aren't too out of line, although you'll save a bit by bringing food up with you. The Glentanner motor camp has a small store and cafe. There's also a little coffee shop at the Mt Cook airport.

Otherwise you have three choices at the Hermitage and one at the Glencoe Lodge. The Hermitage base line is their *coffee shop* which is usually open from 9 am to 5 pm but sometimes closes earlier. It does very unexciting sandwiches and pies. By the end of the day they can look very tired and even more unexciting than they did at the beginning of the day!

Then there's the *Alpine Room* where main courses are around $15 to $19 (but if you want vegetables or a salad, that's a few dollars extra!) and desserts are around $6. For breakfast and lunch the Alpine Room does buffets – $17 for breakfast, $25 for lunch. The Glencoe Lodge has a similarly priced restaurant but it's open only for dinner in the evening. Finally there's the Hermitage's *Panorama Room* where two people can spend well over $100 – starters are $9 to $13.50, main courses $20 to $40, desserts $7.50 to $11.

### Entertainment

You can drink at the bar, sit around and talk or there's a disco at *Glencoe Lodge* on Friday evenings during the busy season. The Hermitage has a resident pianist.

### Getting There & Away

**Air** Mt Cook Airlines (tel 849) have daily direct flights to and from Queenstown, Christchurch and Rotorua, with connections to other centres. At certain times of the year they also have daily flights to and from Te Anau. Mt Cook provides bus services to and from the airport.

There's no scheduled air service to Fox or Franz Josef but you can fly over one way if you like. It's a way of combining transport with a scenic flight and means you can avoid the difficult Haast route if hitching. But you can't rely on the weather and may get held up at Mt Cook for quite a while waiting for suitable conditions to get across.

**Bus** Mt Cook Landline (tel 849) has daily buses to Queenstown, Te Anau, Christchurch, and Timaru. Most of their services connect with the longer routes through Twizel, 70 km (an hour's drive) from Mt Cook. There are year round daily buses, but in summer they add extra, more direct services, making travel time quicker. From November to April they run special excursion buses between Christchurch and

Queenstown, or day trips out of Christchurch, all allowing about 3½ hours stopover time at Mt Cook.

InterCity also has a daily Queenstown-Christchurch route with a 40 minute stop at Mt Cook. The Mt Cook and InterCity buses both stop at the front door of the Mt Cook Youth Hostel.

**Hitching** It's over 5 hours drive from Christchurch or Queenstown. Hitching is hard – expect long waits once you leave SH 1 if coming from Christchurch or Dunedin and long waits all the way if coming from Queenstown. Hardest of all, though, is simply getting out of Mt Cook itself since the road is a dead end. It's worth considering taking the bus down to Twizel, where there's much more traffic.

# Christchurch to Dunedin

SH 1, south of Christchurch, is very flat and boring for many km as you cross the Canterbury Plains. There are long straight stretches and one town looks much like another. Being in a truck, or even a bus, makes all the difference to your view, allowing you to see over the nearby hedges and obstructions. In clear weather there are some magnificent views of the distant Southern Alps and their foothills.

South of Christchurch you drive through artificial forests that were flattened by a storm some years ago. The remnants of these forests are still being picked through, though much has merely been bulldozed into long mounds and new trees planted.

There are many wide, glacial-fed rivers to be crossed – quite a sight in flood, though you don't see much water at other times. The Rakaia River Bridge is about 2 km long and this river is popular for jet-boating – contact White Water Jets (tel Glenroy 898) or Windwhistle Jets (tel Glenroy 850), both

based at the Rakaia Gorge. Salmon fishing is popular in South Canterbury.

## TIMARU
Population 28,400
Timaru is a pleasant little port about halfway between Christchurch (164 km) and Dunedin (202 km), a convenient stopping point with an especially attractive beach at Caroline Bay. The Christmas Carnival at Caroline Bay, beginning on 26 December and continuing for about 10 days, is superb.

Timaru comes from the Maori name Te Maru, the place of shelter, but there was no permanent Maori settlement here when the first Europeans, the Weller brothers of Sydney, set up a whaling station in 1839-40. The *Caroline*, one of the sailing ships which picked up whale oil, gave the picturesque bay its name.

### Information & Orientation
Timaru's main road, SH 1, is a road of many names – the Hilton Highway north of town, Evans St as it enters town and Stafford St as it goes through the town centre. Most businesses are on or near Stafford St. Continuing south, it becomes King St and then Main St as it emerges from town heading south.

The Information Centre (tel 688-6163) is at the corner of Stafford and Sefton streets, near Caroline Bay. It's open from 8.30 am to 5 pm Monday to Friday. The AA is at the corner of Church and Bank streets.

### Caroline Bay & Other Parks
Caroline Bay is one of the few safe, sheltered beaches along the east coast and it attracts windsurfers, swimmers and sunbathers. The park along the beach has a walk-through aviary, a maze, a pleasant walkway and other attractions. The Christmas Carnival is held here. A pleasant walk heads north from town along Caroline Bay, past the Benvenue Cliffs and on to the Dashing Rocks and rock pools at the northern point of the bay. Caroline Bay is sheltered and calm but there's good surfing south of town.

Timaru has other good parks including Centennial Park along the Otipua Creek with

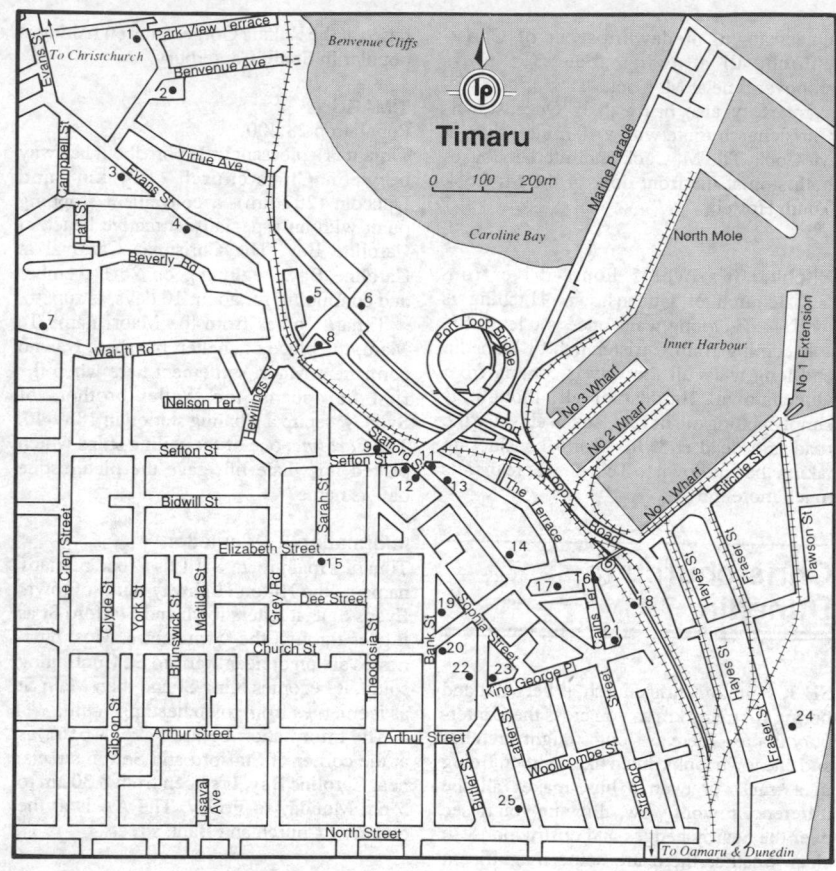

Timaru

0   100   200m

Benvenue Cliffs
Caroline Bay
North Mole
Inner Harbour
Port Loop Bridge

a pleasant 3½ km walkway along the stream bed. Timaru Gardens has gardens, duck ponds and a statue of Robert Burns overlooking the Queen St entrance. The Information Centre has leaflets for a historical walk and a scenic drive.

## Museum & Art Gallery

The South Canterbury Museum, in the Pioneer Hall on Perth St, is the main regional museum, with exhibits on the whalers and early settlers. Admission is free and it's open daily from 1.30 to 4 pm except Monday and Saturday.

Over 900 works of art, plus changing exhibits, are featured at the Aigantighe Art Gallery at 49 Wai-iti Rd. The gallery is open from 11 am to 4.30 pm from Tuesday to Friday, and from 2 to 4.30 pm on Saturday and Sunday; admission is free.

## Activities

The DB Brewery on the northern outskirts of town gives free tours at 10.30 am and 2 pm Monday to Thursday. Phone ahead (tel 688-2059) to reserve a spot.

The town freezing works also offers free tours, arranged through the Information

| | |
|---|---|
| 1 | Ashbury House |
| 2 | Maori Park Swimming Pool |
| 3 | Anchor Motel |
| 4 | Major's Bed & Breakfast |
| 5 | Tennis Courts |
| 6 | Amusement Playground |
| 7 | Aigantighe Art Gallery |
| 8 | Aviary |
| 9 | Hydro Grand Hotel |
| 10 | Information Centre |
| 11 | The Boat House Restaurant |
| 12 | Dominion Hotel |
| 13 | Expastriates Cafe |
| 14 | George's Restaurant |
| 15 | Traveller's Rest Hostel |
| 16 | Grosvenor Hotel |
| 17 | Vienna Cafe |
| 18 | InterCity Travel Centre & Railway Station |
| 19 | Library |
| 20 | Automobile Association (AA) |
| 21 | The Kitchen |
| 22 | Museum |
| 23 | Post Office |
| 24 | Mt Cook bus station |
| 25 | Cobb & Co |

per person. *Ashbury House* (tel 684-3396) at 30 Te Weka St has rooms at $30/55 including a big cooked breakfast. *Majors Guest House* (tel 688-0871) at 24 Evens St costs $20 per person with a continental breakfast or $25 with a cooked one.

The *Dominion Hotel* (tel 688-6189) on Stafford St North has rooms at $25 per person or $30 with breakfast. On the same street the *Hydro Grand Hotel* (tel 684-7059) is somewhat grander and costs $28/36 or $40/46 with bathroom. The *Grosvenor Hotel* (tel 688-3129) on Cains Terrace is more expensive at $74/80.

**Motels** Timaru has numerous motels, especially along Evans St (SH 1) on the northern end of town. Most cost from around $60 a night but the *Anchor Motel* (tel 684-5067) at 42 Evans St is marginally cheaper, as are the *Bay Motel* (tel 684-3267) at 9 Hewlings St, the *White Star Motel* (tel 684-7509) at 12 White St, and the *Wai-iti Court Motel* (tel 688-8447) at 5 Preston St.

**Camping & Cabins** The *Selwyn Holiday Park* (tel 684-7690) on Selwyn St, 2 km north of the town centre, has sites from $5.50 per person, power sites at $7.50/12.50 for one/two people, cabins at $17 for two, cottages and on-site caravans at $23 for two, and tourist flats at $48 for two. There's also the *Glenmark Motor Camp* (tel 684-3682), on Beaconsfield Rd south of the town centre, where camping sites are $12 for two ($2 more with power), cabins and on-site caravans are $25 for two.

**Homestays & Farmstays** The Information Centre has listings for private homestays and farmstays.

**Places to Eat**
There are the usual takeaways and coffee shops around town, with a few interesting cafes. The American-run *Expastriates Cafe* at 329 Stafford St makes burgers, salads and sandwiches. The *Vienna Cafe* at 17 Biswick St is a pleasant European-style coffee shop, with fresh flowers on red-checked table-

Centre or the Travellers Rest Hostel. There are also outdoor and indoor swimming pools and horse-riding, or Mt Cook flights can be arranged.

Interesting day trips can be made from Timaru if you have private transport. There are Maori rock carvings on the back road from Pleasant Point to Fairlie, an interesting 2 hour round trip. The winery and museum at Geraldine are popular excursions while Peel Forest Park Scenic Reserve and Mt Nimrod have camping and many good bushwalks.

**Places to Stay**
**Hostels** The quite good *Travellers Rest Hostel* (tel 688-4685) at 14 Elizabeth St, close to the centre and two blocks from Caroline Bay, sleeps 20 at $12.50 a night. It has bicycles and tennis rackets for hire and the manager is friendly and informative.

**Guest Houses & Hotels** *Jan's Place* (tel 688-4589) at 4A Rose St offers B&B at $25

cloths, serving good cappuccino but rather bland lunches and light meals. The *Richard Pearse Restaurant* in *The Tavern* on Le Cren St and the *Cobb & Co* at 4 Latter St offer pub food.

Near the railway station *The Kitchen* at 5 George St is an excellent licensed vegetarian restaurant with main courses from $7 (lunch) and $12.50 (dinner), starters and desserts at $4.50. It's open from 8 am to 3.30 pm Monday to Friday, from 11.30 am for brunch on Sunday, and from 6.30 pm for dinner Wednesday to Saturday.

For a more expensive night out *George's* at 247 Stafford St is operated by a Swiss couple and has an accent on French cuisine. At *The Boat House*, 1st floor at 335 Stafford St on the corner of Sefton St, seafood and steak are the specialities and it has a great view all the way from the bay to the mountains. Both are licensed.

### Getting There & Away
**Air** Air New Zealand and Air Nelson have daily flights to Christchurch, Oamaru and Wellington with onward connections.

**Bus** The InterCity depot (tel 684-7199) at the railway station has buses through Timaru on their Christchurch-Dunedin-Invercargill route at least twice daily. Mt Cook/H&H also use the railway station on their daily Picton-Christchurch-Dunedin-Invercargill and Christchurch-Tekapo-Mt Cook routes, but their tickets are sold from the Mt Cook office (tel 688-3159) at 41-46 Fraser St.

Newmans stop at Timaru on their Christchurch-Dunedin run and they depart from either the railway station or the Grosvenor Hotel.

From Timaru it's 2 to 2½ hours to Christchurch, 3 hours to Dunedin, and 4 hours to Mt Cook.

**Train** Timaru is on the Christchurch-Dunedin-Invercargill railway route, with a train in each direction daily except Sunday.

**Hitching** For hitching north get a Grants Rd bus to Jellicoe St and save yourself a walk.

### Getting Around
A taxi to Timaru airport costs about $16.

## OAMARU
Population 14,050
Oamaru is a quiet, rural sort of town with beaches, the Forrester Art Gallery, a museum, a heated swimming pool and the large Oamaru Gardens. A colony of the rare yellow-eyed penguins lives on one of the beaches – ask at the Information Centre for directions to a hidden observation spot. They also have maps for the Oamaru Walkway and for directions to the Parkside Quarry, 7 km out of town at Weston, where you can make a self-guided tour to see how the soft, white Oamaru limestone is quarried.

Totara Estate Centennial Park is about 2 km south of Oamaru and it was from here that the first NZ frozen meat was shipped in 1882. It took over 3 months to reach England but arrived in good condition and thus began New Zealand's most important industry. It's a New Zealand Historic Place and is open from 1 to 4 pm on Sunday, 10 am to 4 pm on school and public holidays. Admission is $2.50 (children 50 cents). There's a 30 minute walkway to Brydone Monument on nearby Sebastopol Hill.

### Information & Orientation
Thames St is the main street through town. The Information Centre (tel 45-643) on Severn St, opposite the police station, is open from 9 am to 5 pm Monday to Friday. There's an AA agent at the corner of Thames and Usk streets.

### Places to Stay
**Hostels** The Oamaru *Red Kettle Youth Hostel* (tel 47-348) is a seasonal hostel open approximately from mid-October to mid or late April. It's on the corner of Reed and Cross streets and the nightly cost is $13.

**Guest Houses** The *Anne Mieke Travel Hotel* (tel 48-051) at 47 Tees St has B&B at $32 per person while at *Totara Lodge* (tel 48-332) at 299 Thames St it's $35.

Yellow-eyed penguin

**Motels** The *Alpine Motel* (tel 45-038) at 285 Thames St is conveniently located and has units sleeping one to seven people from $60 to $65 for two. The *Thames Court Motel* (tel 46-963) at 252 Thames St is similarly priced. At the *Avenue Motel* (tel 70-091) at 473 Thames St rooms range from $49 to $64 a night for two, while the *Tui Travel Inn Motel* (tel 71-443) at 469 Thames St charges $46.

**Camping & Cabins** The *Oamaru Gardens Holiday Park* (tel 47-666) is in Chelmer St, adjacent to the large Oamaru Gardens domain. Tent or power sites cost $7.50 per person and there are various cabins from $22 to $37 per night for two.

### Getting There & Away
**Air** Air New Zealand has daily direct flights to and from Timaru and Air Nelson has direct weekday flights to Christchurch. The House of Travel (tel 49-960) at 61 Thames St is the centre for air reservations.

**Bus** The InterCity, Mt Cook/H&H and Newmans bus services between Christchurch and Dunedin all stop at Oamaru.

From Oamaru it's 1 hour to Timaru, 3 hours to Christchurch and almost 3 hours to Dunedin.

**Train** The Christchurch-Dunedin-Invercargill rail services also stop at Oamaru, with a train in each direction every day except Sunday.

### Getting Around
A taxi to Oamaru airport costs about $20.

### TAKIROA
There are Maori rock drawings at Takiroa, 50 km east of Oamaru on SH 83. The sandstone cliff drawings were done with red ochre and charcoal and may date back to the moa-hunting period. Some were cut out of the sandstone in 1916 and are now in museums at Dunedin, Wanganui and Auckland.

Other rock art sites in the region portray humans, moas, dogs, birds and fish as well as unrecognisable or simple geometrical shapes. Most of the sites are on private land and can only be visited with permission from the owners but there are several on public land, in addition to the ones at Takiroa. These include Timpendean, at the Weka Pass in North Canterbury; Raincliff and Frenchman's Gully in South Canterbury; and Maerewhenua which, like Takiroa, is in North Otago. Local information centres can give directions or you can contact the New Zealand Historic Places Trust in Wellington.

### MOERAKI & SOUTH
At Moeraki, 30 km south of Oamaru, there are extraordinary spherical boulders rather like giant marbles. There are others further south at Kaitiki and Shag Point. The friendly *Moeraki Motor Camp* (tel Hampden 759), is less than an hour's walk from the boulders.

Past Shag Point the high, pointed hill with a phallic-shaped symbol on top is a monument to Sir John MacKenzie, the MP responsible for splitting large farms into smaller holdings, farms that are now being bought up again. The hill is called Puketapu and there's a track to the top signposted from the northern end of Palmerston. Every Labour Weekend there is a race up the hill (19 minutes is the record), known as 'Kelly's Canter' because, during the war, Kelly, the local policeman, had to climb it every day to keep an eye out for shipping.

As you approach Dunedin it gets hillier. You pass over the Kilmog, then the Northern Motorway hill, and you're in Dunedin.

# Otago & Southland

Otago and Southland make up the southernmost part of the South Island. If you've come down the west coast and over the Haast Pass, the first town you'll reach is Wanaka.

## Wanaka

Wanaka is just over 100 km from Queenstown, at the southern end of Lake Wanaka. It is the gateway to the Mt Aspiring National Park and the Cardrona, Harris Mountain and Pisa Range Nordic ski fields.

The first step to set aside this glacier country for a park took place in 1935, but it was not until December 1964 that around 200 hectares in north-western Otago and southern Westland were earmarked. The park, named after its highest peak, 3027 metre Mt Aspiring, now extends over 2900 sq km along the Southern Alps between the Haast and Te Anau highways.

### Information

Wanaka Lake Services (tel 443-7495) in the small building beside the jetty has information about the town and things to do. It's open from 8.30 am to 6 pm daily. The Wanaka Booking Centre (tel 443-7277, 443-7930) is opposite the jetty on Ardmore St. It operates more as a travel agency but also has lots of information on things to do in Wanaka.

The Mt Aspiring National Park Visitors Centre (tel 443-7660) on the corner of Ballantyne and Main roads is open from 8 am to 5 pm Monday to Friday all year, as well as on weekends from mid-December to mid-January. It has displays and an audiovisual presentation on the park.

### The Maze

On the road to Cromwell, 2 km from Wanaka, is the maze and puzzle centre. Three-dimensional mazes have become

quite a craze in New Zealand and they're now exporting them overseas, but this was the original one. It's a series of fenced-off corridors and alleys with a confusing number of dead ends, further complicated by several 'bridges' that carry you from one quadrant to another.

The idea is to find your way to the towers at each corner and then back to the exit. And it's more difficult than you think. Tashi and I finally gave up after an hour, we'd found our way to three of the corners but it was starting to get dark! The maze complex, which includes a puzzle centre and mini-golf course, is open from 8.30 am to 5.30 pm and admission is $4 (children $2, family $12). If you're still lost when it closes you can keep on searching all night – there are emergency exits if frustration sets in.

### On the Water

Wanaka offers lots of activities on its beautiful lake. Check with Wanaka Lake Services by the waterfront. A hovercraft makes trips over the lake twice daily – $16 (children $8) for a 15 minute trip, $55 (children $27) for an hour. The Wanaka Riverjet does 50 minute jet-boat trips on the lake for $38. Or take lake cruises from 1 to 4 hours on the MV

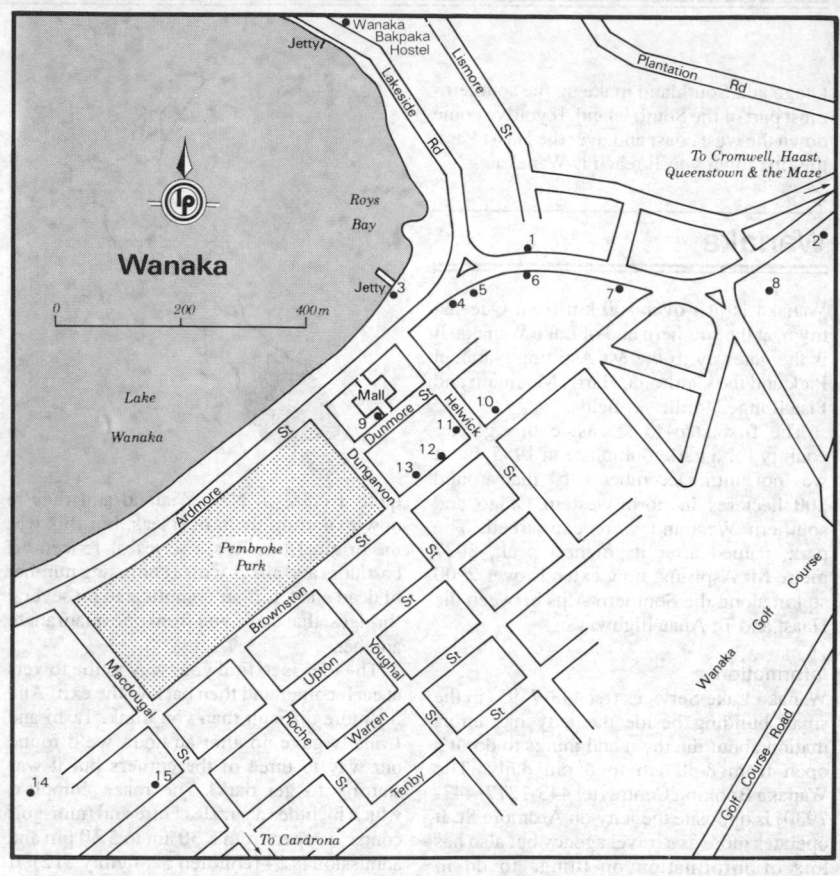

*Ena-De* – trips to Pigeon Island (4 hours) and Ruby Island (2 hours) are popular.

Guided fishing trips cost $110 for 2 hours. They're not too bad if you get four people together ($27.50 each). Alternatively, you can hire a boat and go fishing on your own. Alpine Safaris (tel 443-8446) has jet-boat trips on the lake and up the Clutha River. Makaroa River Tours (tel 433-8351) does 1¼ hour jet-boat rides on the Wilkin River for $36.

There are plenty of other seasonal activities on the lake in summer, including windsurfing, water-skiing, jet-skiing, and so on. Good Sports (tel 443-7966) on Dunmore St hires an array of sports equipment including windsurfers, kayaks, fishing tackle, water skis and other water paraphernalia in addition to camping equipment, skiing and mountain climbing gear, and anything else you can think of that has to do with sports.

### Kayaks & Rafts

Down to Earth Adventures (tel 443-7405), operating from the youth hostel, offer kayak trips and kayak hire, and do river raft trips on local rivers and in Mt Aspiring National Park. There are 4 hour kayak trips on the

| 1 | InterCity bus depot & First Cafe |
| 2 | Best Western Fairway Lodge |
| 3 | Wanaka Lake Services |
| 4 | Wanaka Travel Centre & Mt Cook bus depot |
| 5 | Relishes Cafe |
| 6 | THC Wanaka Hotel |
| 7 | CPO |
| 8 | Mt Aspiring National Park HQ |
| 9 | Good Sports |
| 10 | Mc Thrifty's Motel |
| 11 | Chiu Po Restaurant |
| 12 | Te Kano Cafe |
| 13 | Laundromat |
| 14 | Wanaka Motor Camp |
| 15 | Youth Hostel |

Motatapu River for $45. For a longer, more scenic trip try either the Matukituki or Makarora rivers in the park, both of which take the better part of the day. All trips are suitable for beginners. Raft trips are also available on the Hawea and Clutha rivers.

### Walks & Tramps

You don't have to be a physical fitness freak to attempt the fairly gentle climb up Mt Iron (527 metres) near the Maze. It is 45 minutes from the road to the top and the view of the rivers, lakes and mountains is worth the effort.

More exhausting is the trek up Mt Roy (1585 metres). It will take about 3 hours from the road to the top if you're fit – longer if you're the sedentary type. The track winds every step of the 8 km from base to peak, but Mt Aspiring is quite a knockout from here.

The 2½ to 3 hour Rob Roy Walk is a popular bush walk with good views. It's a 1 hour drive up the Matukituki Valley (in summer you can bus up there with Matuki Services), from where the walk goes up the Rob Roy Stream to a point below the Rob Roy Glacier.

There are lots of places to go tramping in Mt Aspiring National Park and the Matukituki, Motatapu, Makarora, Blue and Wilkin valleys. You can get all the info you need on these walks and tramps from the National Park Visitors Centre.

Easiest of all is the lakeside walk which starts along the grassy lakefront in town and runs around to Eely Point and on to Bremner Bay, about a 30 minute walk from town.

### Horse-Riding

NZ Backcountry Saddle Expeditions (tel 443-8151), based 26 km from Wanaka on the Cardrona Valley Rd (SH 89), offer 2 hour horse treks for $30 (children $18) and overnight wilderness pack trips from $95. Diamond Horse Treks (tel 443-8614), also on the Cardrona Valley Rd but just 3 km from town, do 2 hour horse treks for $35 (children $25). Both offer a 10% discount if you're staying at the youth hostel.

### Aerial Sightseeing

Aspiring Air (tel 443-7942/3) has scenic flights ranging from a 15 minute jaunt over Ruby Island, Glendhu Bay, Matukituki River and other local beauty spots costing $50, to a 45 minute flight over Mt Aspiring and the glacier and alpine country for $100. There are also flights to Mt Cook for $195 or Milford Sound for $180. With a launch trip as well the Milford trip costs $205. Children travel for half price on all these trips.

The Helicopter Line also has flights in the Wanaka area.

### Other Activities

Matuki Services (tel 443-7135) offers various bus trips and provides access to the tramping tracks. Edgewater Resort Adventures (tel 443-8311) does 4WD trips in the area at a cost of around $60. Explorer Tours (tel 443-8130) does scenic tours all year round. Makarora River Tours (tel 433-8351, 443-8372) has an interesting trip for $85 which includes a flight into Siberia Valley, a guided 3 hour walk into the Wilkin Valley, and a jet-boat ride down the Wilkin River. The Wanaka and Hawea lakes, about 16 km from Wanaka, are good for trout and salmon fishing.

Down to Earth Adventures offers instruction in mountain-climbing and does climbing expeditions. Good Sports also offers mountaineering instruction and they have a 'climbing wall' for practising your climbing techniques. They also give lessons in windsurfing and kayaking. Cycling is another popular activity around Wanaka and mountain bikes can be hired at many places around town.

Wanaka is near several good ski fields – Treble Cone, Cardrona, the Pisa Range Nordic Ski Area for cross-country skiing, and Harris Mountain heli-skiing. Cardrona has the longest ski season in New Zealand (June-July to September). Wanaka is the base for all of these fields during the ski season, with ski hire, ski field transport, etc readily available. Daily shuttle buses also operate from Queenstown, 1½ hours away, to these slopes during ski season. See the Skiing section in the Outdoor Activities chapter for more details.

## Places to Stay

**Hostels** The *Wanaka Youth Hostel* (tel 443-7405) at 181 Upton St has a relaxed, friendly atmosphere and its facilities are open all day. The cost is $13 per night. Mountain bikes are available from the hostel, which also sponsors many other activities. YHA members receive discounts on various activities around town.

The *Wanaka Bakpaka* (tel 443-7837) at 117 Lakeside Rd is opposite the jetty on the northern side of Roys Bay, just a few metres from the lake. It's on a hill with a great view of the lake, town, and mountains. Formerly a hotel, it opened as a private hostel in April 1990. There's a hot spa pool and you can hire mountain bikes. The cost per person is $13 in dorm rooms or $14.50 in twin or double rooms.

**Guest Houses** There are several small B&B places in Wanaka. *Wanaka Lodge* (tel 443-7837) at 117 Lakeside Rd is pleasantly situated beside the lake; B&B costs $39/55 for singles/doubles. A three-course dinner is served in their restaurant every night for $17.50. The small *Creekside Guest House* (tel 443-7834) at 84 Helwick St has just three rooms with B&B at around $25/50.

**Hotels & Motels** There are plenty of places in this category in Wanaka and you can also find such accommodation at the camping sites.

At *McThrifty's Motel* (tel 443-8333), on the corner of Brownston and Helwick streets, you can get a room with a private bathroom, fridge, and tea and coffee-making facilities at $44 for one to four people. It's run by the *Brookvale Manor* next door, where double rooms cost $66.

Other cheaper motels include the *All Seasons Motel* (tel 433-7530), 5 km from town on the Haast Highway. Rooms there cost $54 for two. More centrally located are the similarly priced *Wunderview Motel* (tel 433-7480) and *Pembroke Inn* (tel 433-7296), both on Brownston St.

At the top of the market are the *THC Wanaka Hotel* (tel 433-7826) on Ardmore St with rooms for $77 and the *Edgewater Resort* (tel 433-8311) on Sargood Drive with singles/doubles for $115/135.

**Camping & Cabins** The *Wanaka Motor Camp* (tel 443-7883) is on Brownston St, about 1 km from the town centre. Camping costs $7.50 per person with power. A bunkroom costs $11 per person, cabins cost $26 for two and tourist flats cost $38 to $48 for two. The *Pleasant Lodge Holiday Park* (tel 443-7360), 3 km from Wanaka on Glendhu Bay Rd, has cabins and tourist flats at similar prices.

Adjacent to Lake Wanaka, 13 km out of town on the Treble Cone road, is the *Glendhu Bay Camp* (tel 443-7243), again with camping and cabins. Finally, *Penrith Park* (tel 443-7009) is at Beacon Point and has camping, cabins and a bunkroom.

## Places to Eat

**Snacks & Fast Food** The *Snack Shack* on Ardmore St, by the Mall, has pizzas and the usual takeaway food. Next door is *Julie's Cafe*, a pleasant cafe which also has takeaways. In the Mall are the *Freshwater Cafe*, the *Coffee Shop* which is open reasonably early for breakfast, and the *Doughbin* for bread and baked food. *Chiu Po* on

Helwick St has a Chinese and English takeaway counter and a restaurant to one side.

**Pub Food & Restaurants** The *THC Wanaka Hotel* has a bistro restaurant with pub-style meals, and a restaurant with a Sunday 'surf & turf' buffet for $19.

Wanaka is surprisingly well equipped with restaurants, including the superb *Te Kano Cafe* on Brownston St. This atmospheric little cottage has wonderful vegetarian food – well prepared, imaginative, filling and delicious. This was the best meal I had in New Zealand! Soup costs $4.50, starters around $7.50, and main courses $13.50 to $17.50. In winter you can get gluhwein (hot spiced red wine).

The *First Cafe* on Ardmore St is an interesting little place where the menu includes spaghettis, dishes with an Indonesian or Chinese flavour, and steaks. Starters cost around $5.50 and all the main courses cost either $10 or $17.50. *Relishes Cafe* on Ardmore St is also pleasant and has dinner main courses for around $15; lunches are cheaper.

In the Mall, the up-market *Ripples Restaurant* offers 'al fresco' dining on the verandah with good views of the lake and mountains. The food here has a good reputation. *Capriccio* is a licensed Italian restaurant, also in the Mall, which sometimes has intriguingly un-Italian 'Chinese nights'! It's not cheap, though – main courses are in the $20 to $27 range.

Finally there's the well restored *Cardrona Restaurant* (tel 8153), 30 km from town in the Cardrona Valley. This is a place for splurges – it's licensed.

## Getting There & Away
**Air** Aspiring Air (tel 443-7942/3) has flights to Queenstown up to four times daily, connecting there with Mt Cook Airlines and Ansett New Zealand flights to other centres.

**Bus** The InterCity bus depot is on Ardmore St, opposite the THC Wanaka Hotel. Daily buses from Queenstown stop at Wanaka on the way to the glaciers via Haast Pass, as does a connecting bus from Tarras on InterCity's daily service from Queenstown to Christchurch via Mt Cook. InterCity also has a connecting bus from Cromwell on the Queenstown to Dunedin route every day except Sundays. Travel times from Wanaka are: Queenstown (2 hours); glaciers (6 hours); Mt Cook (4¼ hours); Christchurch (10 hours); and Dunedin (7 hours).

Mt Cook Landline buses operate from the Wanaka Travel Centre (tel 443-7414) on Dunmore St in the town centre. Buses run every day to Christchurch, Dunedin and Mt Cook, daily except Saturdays to Queenstown, and on weekdays to Invercargill.

**Car** Although the Cardrona road to Queenstown looks much shorter than the route via Cromwell on the map, it's a winding, twisting, climbing, unsealed mountain road so travel is unlikely to be quicker. Rental cars and campervans are banned from this road, and a large sign at each end announces that caravans are also banned.

**Hitching** If you're heading out of Queenstown to the Haast Pass and glacier country you could try hitching to Wanaka, but you will have to be very patient. Hitching out of Queenstown is difficult and hitching through the Haast Pass to Fox or Franz Josef is almost impossible because of the light traffic, although once you're offered a lift you're more than likely to get one going the whole way. The Haast Pass road branches off the Cromwell road about 2 km from Wanaka, just beyond the Maze. Hitchhikers have written the sorry stories of their long waits on stones by the roadside.

## Getting Around
Matuki Services (tel 443-7135) offers minibus transport to various places within Mt Aspiring National Park, including the Matukituki Valley and Cameron Flat. There are regular services from mid-December to mid-March, but minibuses also go at other times (and to other places) if there are at least three passengers. From the town centre to

Matukituki Valley costs $17 one-way, $30 return, or $25 for a scenic round trip. Wanaka Taxis (tel 443-7804, 443-8565) also offer trampers transport, local scenic trips, airport transport and ski field transport in winter.

A few years ago somebody got the idea of hiring mountain bikes in Wanaka and now there are about as many mountain bikes for hire as there are people in the town! You can hire them from the youth hostel (whether or not you're staying there) for $20 per day or $15 for half a day. In the town centre, Good Sports, Racer's Edge and Ski 47, to name a few, also hire mountain bikes.

### CROMWELL

This pleasant little town on the main route between Wanaka and Queenstown is a good place for a short pause. The Cromwell Information Centre (tel 50-011) is in the Cromwell Mall, with some excellent displays and slide presentations on the hydroelectric power projects in the Clutha Valley. It's open from 9 am to 5 pm Monday to Friday and from 10 am to 4 pm on weekends.

Cromwell has a museum with artefacts of local mining, including a section on the Chinese miners. It's open from 10 am to 4 pm daily. Several historic buildings, some of stone, are being restored to recreate a main street of 'Old Cromwell'. You can see the old buildings in Melmore Terrace.

The gorge between here and Queenstown is often spectacular and you can pause to watch the bungy jumping at the interesting old Kawarau suspension bridge. The bridge was built in 1880 for access to the Wakatipu goldfields and used right up until 1963.

### Places to Stay & Eat

The Sunhaven Motor Camp (tel 50-164) on Alpha St, about 2 km from the town centre, has camping sites and cabins; camping costs $6 per person ($7 with power) and cabins cost $20 to $30 for two. There are also hotels and motels.

There are a number of sandwich places in the Cromwell Mall. You can try the Gold Mine Restaurant, which has good food, or the pricier Daniel's. The Golden Gate Lodge has bistro food in the pub and also a restaurant.

# Queenstown

Close to what many say is the finest skiing in New Zealand, on a beautiful lake with a variety of summer cruises, handy to some of the best walking country, with a good vintage car museum, some exciting shoot-the-rapids expeditions and bungy jumping thrown in for good measure – it's no wonder Queenstown is one of the most popular vacation areas in the country. If it sounds like a tourist trap, it is, but if you want to have a good time this is a great place to be.

It's extremely easy to go through a lot of money here but Queenstown is a 'doing' place and sometimes you just have to forget the cost and 'do' it. So relax and enjoy the fantastic setting; there's lots to do, a large and friendly transient work population and more nightlife than most places in New Zealand.

### History

There is evidence that Queenstown was once the site of a Maori settlement. However, when the Pakehas began arriving in the mid-1850s the region was deserted. The first Pakehas to settle the area were sheep farmers, but in 1862 two shearers, Thomas Arthur and Harry Redfern, discovered gold on the banks of the Shotover River, precipitating a rush of prospectors to the area. Queenstown quickly developed into a mining town and by early 1863 streets had been laid out and permanent buildings established. Then the gold petered out and by 1900 the population had dropped from several thousand to a mere 190 people.

During this era the lake was the principal means of communication and at the height of the mining boom there were four paddle steamers and about 30 other craft plying the waters. One of those early steamers, still in use today, was the TSS Earnslaw, which was prefabricated in Dunedin, carted overland in sections, and rebuilt at Kingston in 1912. The highway skirting the lake between Queenstown and Glenorchy was only completed in 1962, the centenary of the founding of the township. There are several theories on how Queenstown got its name, but the most popular is that it commemorates the town of the same name on Great Island in Cork Harbour, Ireland, probably because most of the diggers were Irish.

## Orientation

Queenstown is a tiny, compact township on the shores of beautiful Lake Wakatipu, and backed by equally beautiful hills. The main street is the pedestrians-only Mall.

## Information

**Tourist Information** The NZTP (tel 442-8238) is at 49 Shotover St, opposite the Mountaineer. It makes local, national and international bookings and has plenty of local information. The office is open from 8.30 am to 5 pm Monday to Friday, and from October to April it's also open from 8.30 am to 12.30 pm on Saturdays.

The Queenstown Information Centre (tel 442-7318) on the corner of Shotover and Camp streets is another source of information and also makes bookings for local activities. The office is open in winter from 7.30 am to 8 pm and in summer from 7.30 am to 10 pm, every day. There's an AA agent in the SMIU office about four doors away, on Shotover St. Also on Shotover St is the Information and Track Walking Centre (tel 442-7867).

The DOC (tel 442-7933) is on the corner of Ballarat and Stanley streets, a block behind the CPO. It has information on the many natural attractions of the area, long and short drives and walks, including the Milford, Kepler, Routeburn and other tracks. It has interesting displays and a summer programme of nature walks. It's open from 9 am to 4.30 pm Monday to Friday all year round, and also from 10 am to 3 pm on Saturdays and Sundays from mid-December to mid-February.

**Tour Agents** Plenty of places make bookings for Queenstown's multitude of activities, including the NZTP office and the Queenstown Information Centre already mentioned, or there's Fiordland Travel and the InterCity office by the *Earnslaw* wharf, Mt Cook Travel at the end of the Mall and plenty of others. The Newmans office is on Church St opposite the Mt Cook Landline depot.

**Other Information** There's a useful notice stand right in the middle of the Mall. If you've got plenty of dirty clothes and nowhere to wash them head for the Alpine Laundrette on Shotover St near the Athol St junction.

## Views

Try starting at, literally, the top of the town. Catch the Skyline Gondola to the summit of the hill overlooking the town for incredible views over the lake – well worth the $8.50 (children $2, family $19). There's a licensed cafe up at the top which is not bad and a more expensive restaurant for dinner. If you're more energetic you can walk up the vehicle track to Skyline from Lomond Crescent, but the ride is worth experiencing. The lift operates from 10 am to 10 pm daily.

Another good viewpoint is Coronet Peak, 18 km from the town centre. There's skiing in winter but it also stays open in summer, when you can ride the chairlift to the top for $12 (children $6) and shoot back down in a little cart on the Cresta Slide. One ride down is $4 (children $3), five rides are $12 ($8), and you can go up and down the chairlift as many times as you like.

What really makes Queenstown's setting is the Remarkables. A written description can hardly do them justice, but you can easily spend a day just watching the constant changes in their appearance in different lights. They're especially beautiful capped with snow, at sunrise or in the after-glow of dusk. If you're super fit it's a long, hard, steep climb to the top, 2000 metres above the lake level – very energy-sapping in the hot Central Otago sun.

## Queenstown Motor Museum

The motor museum just below the lower gondola terminal has a fine collection of cars, all well restored and in running order. There's also a motorcycle collection upstairs and a fine old Tiger Moth suspended overhead. The museum is open 9 am to 5.30 pm daily, admission is $5 (children $2.50).

## Kiwi & Birdlife Park

Also below the gondola terminal is the kiwi house and birdlife park. It has what is becoming a NZ standard – the nocturnal kiwi house. Keas and a variety of other birds can also be seen in the pleasant park. The park is open from 9 am to 5 pm daily and admission is $6 (children $2.50, family $16).

There's a maze between the kiwi park and the motor museum, but it's open only during the school holidays; hours are 10 am to 9 pm and admission is $4.50 (children $3.50, family $11).

## Underwater World

On the pier at the end of the Mall in the centre of Queenstown is Underwater World, a submerged observation gallery where you can look out and see eels and trout in the clear waters of Lake Wakatipu. The agile little scaup or 'diving' ducks also make periodic appearances outside the windows. Regular feedings attract the fish and eels, you can add to them for 50 cents. Underwater World is open daily; in summer the hours are 8.30 am to 8 pm and in winter they're 9 am to 5.30 pm. Entry is $5 (children $2.50).

## The Earnslaw

The stately old coal-burning TSS (Twin Screw Steamer) Earnslaw is the most famous of Queenstown's many lake cruise boats. There's a daily 3 hour cruise at 2 pm which goes out to the Mt Nicholas sheep station and back. On the way you can sip a beer, watch the activity in the immaculate engine room or sing along with a pianist. At the station you see a sheep dog demonstration and sheep shearing. Cost is $30 (children $10).

The Earnslaw also operates a short lunchtime cruise at 12.30 pm which costs $19 ($10), not including lunch, which is available on board for an additional $2 to $6. There's also an evening dinner cruise at 6.30 pm, cost is $22 ($10) for the 1½ hour cruise and the buffet is an extra $16 ($12). In winter the expensive-to-run Earnslaw used to be parked in favour of a smaller modern boat but these days it only takes one month off in June for its annual overhaul.

The Earnslaw is steel-hulled and weighs 330 tons. At full speed she churns across the lake at 13 knots, burning a ton of coal an hour. Measuring 51 metres in length and 7.3 metres across the beam, she is licensed to carry 810 passengers and at one time was the major means of transport on the lake. The development of modern roads ended her career with New Zealand Railways and she has been used for lake cruises since 1969.

## The City of Dunedin

The City of Dunedin was the sole NZ craft in the 1982 single-handed round the world yacht race. She was one of only a few vessels to complete the 43,470 km (27,000 mile) voyage, taking 9 months to reach the finish line, with many adventures along the way. The City is now based at Queenstown and does 2 hour sailings in which every passenger (maximum 19) can become part of the crew and participate in the sail. She sails at 10.30 am, 1 and 4 pm daily from the water taxi jetty opposite the Park Royal Hotel; the cost is $29 (children $15).

## Other Lake Cruises

There are various other lake cruises to choose from, including a half-hour zip round the lake by hydrofoil every hour for $22 (children free). It departs from the pier at the end of the Mall. There's also a 3 hour catamaran cruise to Walter Peak twice daily for $30 (children under 12 free).

## Jet-Boat Trips

Hurtling up the rivers around Queenstown in jet-boats or down them in inflatable rafts are popular activities. The Shotover and Kawarau rivers are the popular jet-boat rivers, with the Dart River less travelled but also good. Trips either depart straight from Queenstown or go by minibus to the river and then by boat. The jet-boat trips generally take about an hour and cost around $35 to $50.

The Shotover Jet is one of the most popular; the narrow and shallow Shotover River is particularly exciting for jet-boating. Be prepared to get wet but it's great fun. The Twin Rivers Jet operates on the Upper Kawarau and Lower Shotover rivers but I've got to give it the thumbs down. The ticket warns you that they may cancel their trips without prior warning but fails to add that they may not bother to tell you that they've done so.

The Kawarau Jet departs from the town wharf and crosses the lake to the Kawarau River; the trip costs $35. People who really want to do everything can combine helicopter and jet-boat rides (from $75) or three-in-one trips combining helicopters, jet-boats and raft rides ($110 on the Kawarau River, or from $139 to $154 on the Shotover).

Trips on the Dart River with Dart River Jet-boat Safari are also excellent, passing parts of the Routeburn and Dart-Rees tracks. They depart at 8.15 am and 2.15 pm daily and cost $95 for a 5 hour trip.

### Raft Trips

Although jet-boating up the rivers is popular, they're equally good for rafting down. Again the Shotover and Kawarau rivers are the primary locations. The rivers are graded, for rafting purposes, from one to six, with six meaning 'unraftable'. The grading of the Shotover canyon varies from 3 to 5+ depending on the time of year, the Kawarau River is rated 4. On the rougher stretches there's usually a minimum age limit of 12 or 13 years. The rafting companies supply wet suits and life jackets.

Trips on the Shotover typically take from 4½ hours ($85 per person) to a whole day ($130), or even longer. If you opt to helicopter in rather than go by minibus you can pay even more. On the Kawarau you can do a

3½ hour rafting trip ($65) or a jet-boat and raft combination ($85) or, on both rivers, the three-in-one jet-boat, raft and helicopter combination trips.

Rafting companies include Danes (Shotover 4½ hours or full day, Kawarau 3½ hours, Landborough 3 days), Kawarau Raft Expeditions (Kawarau 3½ hours, Shotover 4½ hours or full day) and Kiwi Discovery Tours (Kawarau 3½ hours, Shotover 4½ hours).

### Skiing

The Remarkables and Coronet Peak ski fields operate from Queenstown. The Treble Cone and Cardrona fields operate from Wanaka, but from Queenstown they are just about 1½ hours away, with shuttle buses running daily from Queenstown during the ski season. There's also excellent heli-skiing at Harris Mountain and Southern Lakes, both accessible from Queenstown. The Remarkables and Cardrona both have excellent beginners' fields. See the Outdoor Activities chapter for more details.

### Bungy Jumping

Of all the things to do around Queenstown, probably the one that sparks people's interest the most is bungy jumping. The A J Hackett Queenstown Bungy Centre (tel 442-7100) is beside the Information Centre on the corner of Shotover and Camp streets. You can book jumps there or at any local booking office. When you get to the jump site you can arrange to have photographs or a video taken of your jump to amaze your friends afterwards.

A J Hackett became world-famous for his 1986 bungy jump off the Eiffel Tower. Since he began operating at Queenstown in November 1988, over 20,000 people have leapt off two bridges, over the Shotover and Kawarau rivers, hurtling earthward with nothing between them and kingdom come but a gigantic rubber bungy cord tied to their ankles.

The jump begins when you crawl out onto the jumping platform, get your ankles strapped up with a towel for padding, and stand out over thin air, ready to jump. The crew shout out 'five, four, three, two, ONE!' and you're off and flying. Likely as not you will dunk head first into the river below before soaring upwards again on the bungy.

After bobbing up and down like a human yo-yo, you finally settle down, grab the pole held up to you by the crew down below, and are pulled into a rubber raft. There you're unstrapped and towed back to dry land. No doubt about it, it's a daredevil sport, and the adrenalin rush can last for days. But it's all very well organised, with every possible precaution and attention to safety.

The historic Kawarau Suspension Bridge, 23 km from Queenstown on SH 6, attracts the most jumpers; it's 43 metres from the special bungy platform to the Kawarau River below. Observation platforms have been built to accommodate all the viewers who come to watch, and even if you don't jump yourself, you can enjoy seeing others do it. The jump at Karawau costs $85, including a bungy T-shirt which you can only get if you've jumped.

The Skippers Canyon Bridge, towering 69 metres over a narrow gorge above the Shotover River, is the more spectacular site. It's also more difficult to reach, about an hour's ride down a tortuous road from Queenstown.

Several packages have been arranged for jumping at Skippers. The 'Barefoot Special – Big Thrills, No Frills' package costs $129, with a shuttle van taking you out to the bridge and back, and the optional T-shirt is an extra $25. Other packages include the 'Heli-Bungy' for $199 where you helicopter to and from the bridge, or the 'Canyon Classic' for $245 where you do basically the same but with a champagne lunch thrown in. Or there's the 'White Water Bungy' for $241 where you shuttle into the canyon, do the jump, and then do some white water rafting out down the Shotover River, with a lunch stop on the way. Finally there's the 'Bungy Overnight', in which for $273 you can take the shuttle van to the bridge, do the jump, have an evening barbecue party, overnight there with breakfast the next morning, and

| 1 | Pinewood Lodge |
| 2 | Creeksyde Campervan Park |
| 3 | Skyline Gondola Terminal |
| 4 | Kiwi House |
| 5 | Queenstown Guest House |
| 6 | Redwood Lodge |
| 7 | Hulbert House |
| 8 | Car Museum |
| 9 | The Bakery |
| 10 | Alpine Laundromat |
| 11 | Queenstown Information Centre & AJ Hackett Bungy Centre |
| 12 | Information & Track Walking Centre, Magic Bus |
| 13 | Department of Conservation (DOC) |
| 14 | Melbourne House |
| 15 | NZTP Office |
| 16 | Newmans Office |
| 17 | Upstairs, Downstairs, Gourmet Express |
| 18 | Mt Cook Landline Office |
| 19 | Park Royal Hotel |
| 20 | Wharf, InterCity Office & Fiordland Travel |
| 21 | Queenstown Motor Camp |
| 22 | Vacation Inn |
| 23 | FAB - Families & Backpackers Hostel |
| 24 | Goldfields Guest House |
| 25 | Mountain View Lodge |
| 26 | Bumbles Hostel |
| 27 | Lakeside Motel |
| 28 | Hotel Esplanade |
| 29 | Down to Earth & Saguaro Restaurant |
| 30 | Wicked Willies |
| 31 | Mt Cook buses |
| 32 | CPO |
| 33 | The Mountaineer |
| 34 | Cardrona's Cafe |
| 35 | The Cow |
| 36 | Avanti Restaurant |
| 37 | Mt Cook Airline & Travel Office |
| 38 | Eichardt's Hotel |
| 39 | Underwater World |

then white water raft out the next day with a lunch stop on the way.

### Aerial Sightseeing

No possibility is ignored at Queenstown – if you can't boat up it, down it or across it, walk around it, or get a chairlift over it, then you can still fly above it. There are all sorts of flights from short helicopter flights over Queenstown (from $55) to flights to Milford

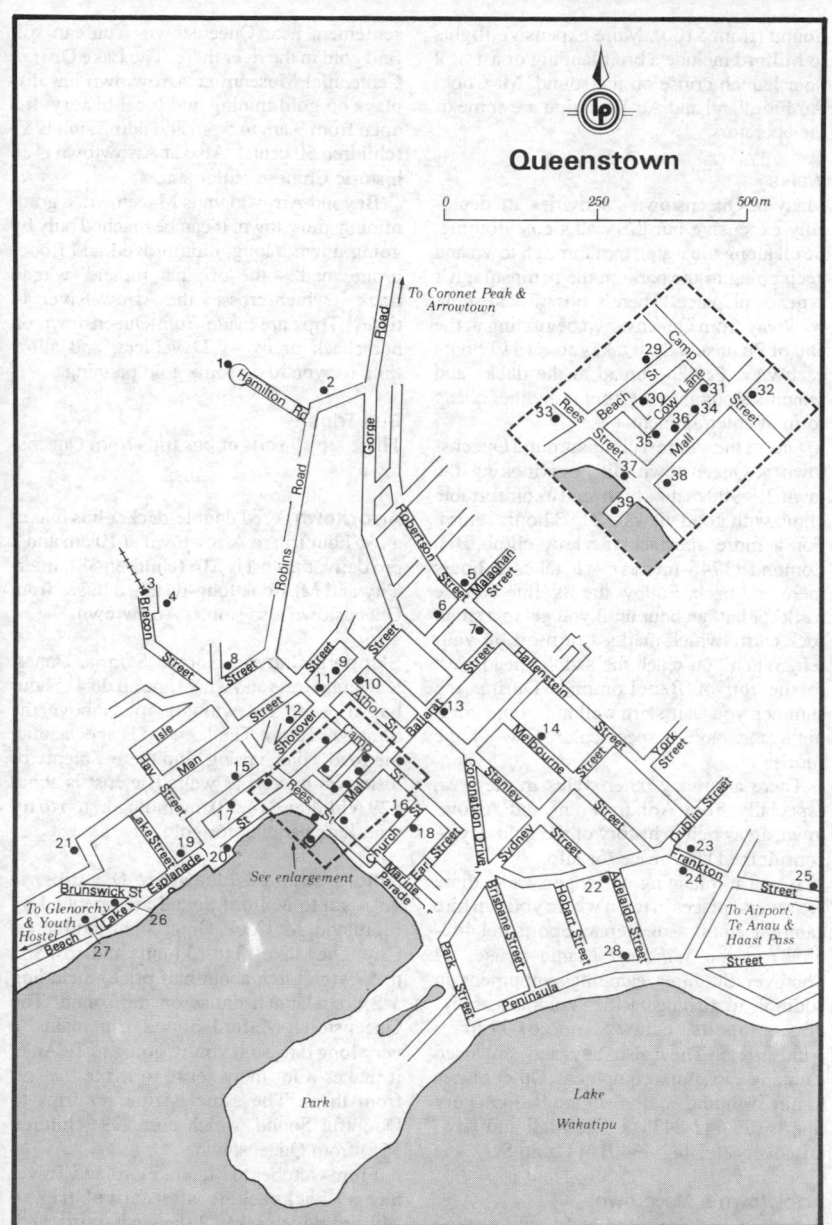

# Queenstown

0    250    500 m

To Coronet Peak &
Arrowtown

Hamilton Rd

Gorge Road

Robins Road

Brecon Street

Isle Street

Hay Street

Man Street

Shotover Street

Athol St

Ballarat St

Camp St

Rees Street

Mall

Church Street

Earl Street

Marine Parade

Beach Street

Lake Esplanade

Brunswick St

To Glenorchy
& Youth
Hostel

Lake Beach

Robertson Street

Malaghan Street

Hallenstein Street

Melbourne Street

Stanley Street

Coronation Drive

Sydney Street

Brisbane Street

Hobart Street

Adelaide Street

Park Street

Peninsula Street

York Street

Dublin Street

Frankton Street

To Airport,
Te Anau &
Haast Pass

Camp St

Rees Street

Beach Street

Cow Lane

Mall

Street

See enlargement

Park

Lake
Wakatipu

Sound (from $100). More expensive flights to Milford include a brief landing or a 1 or 2 hour launch cruise on the sound. Mt Cook, Air Fiordland and Air Wakatipu are some of the operators.

## Walks

Many of Queenstown's activities are decidedly expensive but the walks cost nothing. Stroll along the waterfront through town and keep going to the park on the peninsula. It's a peaceful place. There's now a lakeshore walkway from Queenstown beginning at the end of Peninsula St; it takes about 1¼ hours each way. Feeding bread to the ducks and seagulls along the lakefront is another cheap form of entertainment.

One of the shortest climbs around Queenstown is Queenstown Hill, overlooking the town. It's 900 metres high, and a comfortable climb with good views – 2 to 3 hours return. For a more spectacular view, climb Ben Lomond (1746 metres) – it takes 5 hours there and back. Follow the Skyline vehicle track for half an hour until you get to a small rock cairn, which marks a turn-off on your left. When you reach the saddle, head west to the top of Ben Lomond. During the summer you can start walking about midnight and have a spectacular view of the sunrise.

There are many other walks in the area, especially from Arthurs Point and Arrowtown, areas rich in history of the gold days – consult the DOC office for info.

If you're planning on longer walks there are several places in town where you can hire camping equipment. Replay Sports (tel 442-6590) at the Windsurf Mania house, 27 Shotover St, hires camping equipment in addition to fishing tackle, goldpans, bicycles, mopeds, canoes and, of course, windsurfers. They also buy and sell used camping and sports equipment. Other places to hire camping equipment are Bill Lachery Sports (tel 442-8438) in the Mall and Kiwi Discovery (tel 442-7340) in Camp St.

## Arrowtown & Macetown

Arrowtown is a restored early gold-mining settlement near Queenstown. You can still find gold in the river there. The Lake District Centennial Museum at Arrowtown has displays on gold-mining and local history. It's open from 9 am to 5 pm and admission is $2 (children 50 cents). Also at Arrowtown is an historic Chinese settlement.

Beyond Arrowtown is Macetown, a gold-mining ghost town. It can be reached only by going down a long, unimproved and flood-prone road – the original miners' wagon track – which crosses the Arrow River 44 times! Trips are made from Queenstown on horseback or by 4WD vehicle, and allow time for you to do some gold panning.

## Bus Trips

There are all sorts of bus trips from Queenstown:

**Arrowtown** A red double-decker bus makes a 2½ hour trip to Arrowtown at 10 am and 2 pm daily; the cost is $16 (children $8). Inter-City and Mt Cook long-distance buses from Queenstown also stop at Arrowtown.

**Skippers Canyon** Nomad Safaris, Danes, Kawarau Rafts and Gray Line all do 4½ hour bus trips up the winding road above the Shotover River. The scenery is spectacular, the road's hair-raising, and there's plenty of historical interest as well. The cost is about $29 (children $14.50), including a stop to try your luck panning for gold.

**Milford Sound & Elsewhere** Day trips via Te Anau to Milford Sound are operated by Fiordland, Mt Cook, Great Sights and Inter-City. They take 12 to 13 hours and cost $85 to $99 (children about half price) including a 2 hour launch cruise on the sound. The Queenstown-Milford Sound trip makes a very long day, so if you're going to Te Anau it makes a lot more sense to make the trip from there. The same is true for trips to Doubtful Sound, which cost $99 (children $55) from Queenstown.

From October to March, Fiordland Travel has a 'backpackers alternative' trip to Milford which takes 2 days and costs $85.

Top:  Near Queenstown (TW)
Left:  View of Queenstown from the gondola (TC)
Right:  Jet-boat on the Shotover River, near Queenstown (JL)

TSS *Earnslaw*, Queenstown (TW)

The first day you go from Queenstown to Walter Peak on the TSS *Earnslaw* steamship, then a bus takes you to Te Anau via the back road; you stay there overnight at your own expense (see the Te Anau section for possibilities). On the second day the bus takes you from Te Anau to Milford for a 2 hour cruise on the Milford Sound, then back to Te Anau and Queenstown via the back road and the TSS *Earnslaw* again. You can opt to stay longer in Te Anau or Milford, returning to Queenstown on a later day.

You can also do the 3 hour steamship and back road trip one way between Queenstown and Te Anau for $30 (children $15).

Magic Bus has trampers' transport to the Routeburn, Greenstone, Caples and Dart-Rees tracks. If you're not tramping you can still go along on the bus and make a day trip of it. They also go between Queenstown and Milford, leaving in the morning and arriving in the afternoon, with a stopover in Te Anau.

## Other Activities

Still more Queenstown activities? Well you can go fishing, water-skiing, windsurfing, paraflying or parapenting, charter a yacht, hire a catamaran, ride a horse, play squash, try a simulator, ride a water-bike, visit the amusement park, or hire a moped or mountain bike.

The Ultimate Game, a few km out of town, is a simulated strategic war game played in teams, complete with camouflage clothing and rifles that shoot gelatine capsules.

Out towards Cromwell there's the Kawarau Gorge Mining Centre with an operating stamper battery, sluicing, gold panning, walks, a flying fox across the river and more; it's open from 9 am to 5.30 pm daily.

You can see how dried flowers are grown, harvested and processed at Sheds of Flowers, near the Shotover River; guided tours commence around mid-November.

The Skyline Showscan Theatre at the top gondola terminal shows 'Kiwi Magic', a film on the scenery of New Zealand. The wrap-around screen and a dynamic sound system give the feeling of being inside the action.

## Places to Stay

Despite the multitude of accommodation in Queenstown you may still have trouble finding a room at peak periods. Try the NZTP or the Queenstown Information Centre if you're stuck. Prices vary with the season, they go sky high at the peak summer period or in the middle of the ski season, then drop in-between. I've tried to give high-season prices for Queenstown. There's a lot of overlap between accommodation types in Queenstown – some of the guest houses and camping sites also have cabins, bunkrooms and motel rooms for example.

**Hostels** The *Queenstown Youth Hostel* (tel 442-8413) is right by the lake at 80 Lake Esplanade. It's a large hostel with beds for 100 people; cost is $15 per night. The night-time curfew at the hostel has been extended until 3 am and you can also get tasty food here – a huge lasagne, for example, for $6.50. In winter the hostel can get hopelessly booked out due to all the skiers.

Also along Lake Esplanade beside the lake are two other hostels. *Bumbles* (tel 442-6298), on the corner of Brunswick St, has dorm beds for $13, and twin or double rooms for $15 per person. It's a comfortable, friendly hostel with good cheap meals. This is the closest hostel to town, and it's enormously popular.

The *Lakeside Motel* (tel 442-8976) at 18 Lake Esplanade has hostel-style accommodation in the buildings behind the large and fancy motel. The cost is $11 per person for one to four people in a room.

There are a couple of other private hostels close to the town centre. The *Redwood Lodge* (tel 442-9116), just above the town centre at 8 Lower Malaghan St, has great views over the town and lake. It's a small place with beds for $12 – supply your own bedding as usual – or fancier rooms upstairs for $15 or $20 per person, linen included.

The *Pinewood Lodge* (tel 442-8273) is a little further from the centre at 48 Hamilton Rd. It used to offer motel-style accommodation but it's now a hostel with several units of two or three rooms that share a lounge, kitchen and bathroom. If you supply your own bedding the nightly cost is $12 per person in a dorm room or $13 per person in a twin or double room; you can hire linen and blankets if needed. There's a free pick-up service from all transport terminals.

Just a bit further out, *FAB – Families & Backpackers* (tel 442-6095) at 42 Frankton Rd is also a former motel; in fact it still has some motel units, at $50 for doubles. Shared accommodation is $14 in dorm rooms (up to five people) or $15 per person in twin rooms. Each room has its own fully-equipped kitchen and bathroom with shower and tub.

A final possibility is the *Contiki Lodge* (tel 442-7107) on Sainsbury Rd in Fernhill, about 2 km from the centre, with a magnificent view of the lake. There are several types of accommodation, and all prices include a cooked breakfast. Shared accommodation with four to a room costs $20 per person if you supply your own bedding, or $30 per person if you use theirs; $33 per person in a shared twin room; or $70 per couple in a double room. The Contiki has budget meals, a licensed restaurant and bar, games and various activities including party nights.

**Guest Houses** At *Melbourne House* (tel 442-8431) at 35 Melbourne St, B&B costs $45/68 for singles/doubles, studio units cost $68/79, and larger kitchen units cost from $77/96 up to $132, depending on the size. Cooked or continental breakfasts and dinners are available with these rooms. It's a friendly and well-organised place with laundry facilities and a guest lounge, and it's conveniently close to the town centre.

The pleasant *Queenstown House* (tel 442-9043) at 69 Hallenstein St, on the corner of Malaghan St, has B&B for $36/55. There are good views over the town and lake from the balcony and it's close to the town centre.

The *Goldfields Guest House* (tel 442-7211) is at 41 Frankton Rd, just beyond the Vacation Inn. Like Melbourne House it has a variety of accommodation. B&B costs $69 to $72 for two, pleasant A-frame chalet rooms cost $77 including a continental

breakfast, and regular motel rooms cost $77 without breakfast.

Between Melbourne House and Queenstown House is the wonderful old *Hulbert House* (tel 442-8767) at 68 Ballarat St. This is upper class B&B; just a handful of very gracious rooms, wonderful views and a cost of $88 to $121 for a single and $121 to $143 for a double per night. There is, however, just one very cheap cabin-style room separate from the main house.

**Hotels** At the *Hotel Esplanade* (tel 442-8611), overlooking the lake at 32 Peninsula St, a room with a bathroom costs $24/38 for singles/doubles. Breakfast is available for $5 (continental) or $7 (cooked) and there's an indoor pool and sauna.

The *Mountaineer Queenstown Establishment* (tel 442-7400) is on Beach St right in the town centre. Rooms with private facilities are $50/88, and there are a few rooms without private bathrooms for $32/41. The rooms have tea and coffee-making facilities.

**Motels** Queenstown has plenty of motels and motel flats including some at the various camping sites and guest houses; see those sections for details. Motel prices in Queenstown are not cheap but they tend to fluctuate with the seasons. The *Mountain View Lodge* (tel 442-8246) on Frankton Rd is a good example – there are cabins and motel-style rooms as well as the adjoining camping facilities. The main building is known as the bottle house – nearly 15,000 bottles (none of them beer bottles!) are set into the walls. Moderately priced motel rooms are attached to *Melbourne House* and the *Goldfields Guest House* (see Guest Houses). The A-frame chalet rooms at Goldfields are very pleasant. *Mountain View Lodge* (see Camping & Cabins) also has motel units.

There are quite a few other motels around Queenstown, generally costing around $60 or $70 per night.

**Camping & Cabins** There are plenty of camping sites in and around Queenstown, all with cabins. The closest in is The *Queens-*

*town Motor Park* (tel 442-7252/4), less than 1 km from the town centre. Camping costs $7.50 per person ($8.50 with power). There are also cabins from $31 for one or two people, tourist flats from $45, and motel flats from $56. As well as being so conveniently located, the camp is very well equipped – good kitchen, coin-operated laundry, TV room and so on – but it's also coldly efficient, regimented and off-hand. You may be charged a $20 refundable deposit when you check in.

The *Creeksyde Campervan Park* (tel 442-9447) on Robins Rd has campervan sites for $9 per person, and a very limited number of tent sites for $8 per person. There's also just one self-contained cottage for $30 per night for one or two persons, with the possibility of a cheaper rate for families.

The *Mountain View Lodge Holiday Park* (tel 442-8246) is on Frankton Rd, just over 1 km from the town centre on the Frankton side. Camping costs $9 per night for two, with or without power. There's also a lodge with 10 rooms, each sleeping two to four people, that cost $36 for two. Bedding is supplied in the lodge and you have your own toilet but you need your own cooking equipment for the communal kitchens. The camp also has a restaurant and bar.

At *Frankton Motor Camp* (tel 442-7247), 6 km from town, camping costs $5 per person ($6 with power). Cabins cost $34 for two in the simpler units and $45 for two in the fancier ones with a shower and kitchen. The *Kawarau Falls Lodge* (tel 442-3510), also at Frankton, has camping sites for $6 per person ($8 with power) plus a variety of indoor accommodation including wooden huts for $8 or $15 per person, a hostel-style lodge at $11 per person, cabins for $12.50 per person, and chalets for $15 per person. *Queenstown Holiday Park* (tel 442-9306) at Arthurs Point has camping for $7.50 per person and cabins for $31 for two.

The *Closeburn Alpine Park* (tel 442-9474, 442-6073) is about 7 km south of town in a particularly peaceful and attractive forest setting overlooking the lake. Its camping sites cost $8 for two people ($13 with power)

or $18 with private toilet and shower. On-site caravans with attached bathrooms cost $25 for two, and a hostel-style lodge with bunks costs $11 per night.

Further out is the *Glenorchy Holiday Park*, which offers camping either by itself or in combination with transport to various walking tracks; see Tramping Transport in the Getting There & Away section for details.

## Places to Eat

Queenstown has its share of pretentiously over-priced restaurants (well it is a ski resort) but there are plenty of places with reasonably priced good-value food. The centre is very compact so it's no problem walking to any of these places.

**Snacks & Fast Food** There is an assortment of the usual snacks – sandwiches, fish & chips, and the like. For coffee-bar food, pancakes and light meals (breakfast, lunch and early dinner) try *Cardrona's* in the Mall where you can sit down and watch the Mall activity. Next door is *Sweet Memories*, a patisserie and chocolate shop with tasty baked goods and sandwiches.

A block away at 5 Beach St, *Down to Earth* has good sandwiches and excellent wholemeal munchies. *The Bakery*, on Shotover St just beyond Camp St, has baked food, sandwiches and pizzas. Round the corner on Camp St is the *Town Fish Shop*, which is not bad for fish & chips. The tiny *Habebe's Lebanese Takeaways* is near the waterfront in the arcade on the corner of Rees and Beach streets (opposite the Mountaineer).

The ground floor of *O'Connells Pavilion*, on the corner of Camp and Beach streets, has a number of international takeaway counters (Italian, Mexican and so on) with a dining area in the middle. It's open from 9 am to 9 pm daily.

The *Pizza Hut* on the corner of Camp and Church streets is so far the only one of the American fast food giants to make an appearance in Queenstown, although the *Gourmet Express*, on Shotover St towards the waterfront in the Bay Centre, looks very American

– like a Denny's. It's very popular for breakfast; you can get pancakes or a continental breakfast for $5. The menu features the fast food regulars including a variety of tasty-looking burgers from $3.75 to $7. It's open from 7 am to 9 pm daily.

**Restaurants** The restaurant in the *Mountaineer* used to be a Cobb & Co. It still serves basically the same menu and stays open the usual long hours. Across the road in the corner arcade, the *Lakeside Cafe* has good lunch-time dishes and some tables have pleasant views over the lake.

The *Cow* in Cow Lane is something of a Queenstown institution, a tiny old stone-walled building with a roaring fire (in winter) and excellent pizzas and pastas. It's an atmospheric little BYO with the emphasis on little. You'll probably have to queue for a table although they do takeaways as well. The pizzas cost $8 to $11 for small ones and $11 to $17 for the large size. Either way they're substantial, so bring an appetite. Spaghetti costs around $9 to $13.

Over on the Mall is *Avanti*, a straightforward Italian BYO with pizzas from $5 to $22, pastas and Italian main courses from $9.50 to $12.50, and desserts for $4 – nothing special but good value and with a pleasant courtyard at the back. Directly opposite, the *Stonewall Cafe* is a pleasant place for snacks, lunch, dinner, desserts and cappuccino. Tasty food with a variety of international dishes is served at tables inside, out on the Mall, and in the little rear courtyard. It's a good place for people-watching.

Upstairs in the Trust Bank arcade in Beach St, *Saguaro* has Mexican food – enchiladas, tacos, burritos, fajitas – for around $16, with lunch-time specials for $5.50, all served with Mexican rice and beans. It's open until late every night.

There are plenty of more expensive restaurants. Facing each other across Shotover St are *Upstairs Downtairs* and *Roaring Megs*, two of Queenstown's better and pricier BYO eating places with main courses in the $18 to $25 range. Roaring Megs is an old miner's cottage.

Right at the top, altitude-wise at least, would have to be dinner at the *Skyline Restaurant*. Including the gondola ride to the top, a big carvery buffet dinner costs $35 (children $17.50). It has great views and nightly entertainment.

### Entertainment

Queenstown is a small place but there's a reasonable variety of night-time activities. In the Mall near the waterfront is *Eichardt's*, which has been around for a long time – during the 1879 floods, hard-drinking miners are said to have paddled up to the bar in rowboats! During the Franco-Prussian war Herr Eichardt, being a good Prussian nationalist, ran the German flag up the flagpole after every German victory. Meanwhile, down the road at Monsieur Francois St Omer's bakery, the tricolour flew every time the French won. The public bar is a popular local meeting and drinking place. Upstairs you'll find activity until late at night in the *Penthouse* nightclub.

Only a block away is the *Mountaineer*, near the site of the old bakery. You may also find some night-time activity in this more family oriented pub. The *Wicked Willies* on Beach St has recently had a major rebuild. On Shotover St there's the *Dolphin* nightclub. Or you can ride the gondola to the *Skyline Restaurant* where there's entertainment with dinner each night.

### Getting There & Away

**Air** Mt Cook Airlines and Ansett New Zealand both fly into Queenstown. Mt Cook (tel 442-7650) has daily direct flights to Auckland, Christchurch, Dunedin, Te Anau, Milford Sound, Wanaka, Mt Cook, Nelson, Alexandra and Rotorua, with additional connecting flights from Christchurch to Wellington, Auckland and Nelson, and also has scenic flights to Milford Sound. Ansett New Zealand (tel 442-3010) has daily direct flights to Christchurch with connections to Wellington, Auckland and Rotorua. The Mt Cook office is next to the pier at the end of the mall; Ansett New Zealand is at the airport.

**Bus** The InterCity depot (tel 442-7420) is on Beach St beside the steamship wharf. Mt Cook buses leave from the depot on Church St (tel 442-7650/3). Great Sights buses (tel 442-7028) depart from 37 Shotover St. Magic Bus (tel 442-7867) departs from the Information and Track Walking Centre on Shotover St.

InterCity buses have several daily routes to and from Queenstown. The route to Christchurch (10 hours) goes via Mt Cook (4¼ hours). Other routes are to Te Anau (2½ hours) and Milford Sound (5 hours), Invercargill (3½ hours) and Dunedin (5¼ hours).

InterCity also has a daily west coast service to the west coast glaciers via Wanaka and the Haast Pass, taking 2 hours to Wanaka, 7½ hours to Fox Glacier and 8 hours to Franz Josef Glacier. If you want to continue up the coast from the glaciers you have to stay overnight at Fox or Franz Josef. It takes a minimum of 2 days (longer if you want to see anything except a bus window) to get up the west coast to Nelson.

If you want to go up the coast to Nelson by bus, the West Coast Express or the Magic Bus are probably the best alternatives, if you have the time and you want to get out and see things. The Shoestring Travel bus is another alternative travel option from Queenstown, heading first to Christchurch and then doing a circle via Arthur's Pass and the glaciers back down the west coast to Queenstown again. See the Getting Around chapter for details on these 'alternative' bus lines.

Mt Cook Landline also has several bus routes from Queenstown, with daily buses to Christchurch, Wanaka, Mt Cook and Te Anau. From November to April it has a special daily bus route to Christchurch which includes a 3½-hour stopover at Mt Cook. Mt Cook buses to Dunedin run daily except Sundays, and to Invercargill daily except Saturdays. Great Sights operates tourist buses to Christchurch.

From early October to late March Fiordland Travel (tel 442-7500) has a 3 hour bus and steamship route between Queenstown and Te Anau. It departs Queenstown on the TSS *Earnslaw* steamship, landing at Walter Peak and continuing from there to Te Anau by bus via the back road. You can go from Te Anau to Queenstown on the same route. The cost is $30 (children $10). The same service can also be taken all the way to Milford as a round-trip sightseeing tour from Queenstown (see the Bus Trips section for more details).

Several companies have buses to Milford via Te Anau, including InterCity, Magic Bus and Fiordland Travel.

**Tramping Transport** Magic Bus runs to and from the Routeburn, Greenstone, Caples, and Dart-Rees tracks, all via Glenorchy. The service between Queenstown and Milford via Te Anau can be used for track transport or simply as a way to get to or from Milford. Buses generally run two or three times weekly but the schedule varies according to demand, with extra trips in summer and possibly none at all in winter. Fiordland Travel and InterCity also have buses to and from the Routeburn, Greenstone, Caples, Hollyford and Dart-Rees tracks during the tramping season. Transport to the Milford track departs from Te Anau.

The Glenorchy Holiday Park (tel 442-9939) is conveniently near many of the walks and offers packages of transport to their camp, overnight accommodation and transport the next morning to the walks. Glenorchy is near the start of the walks so this is a good way to make an early start. The cost for the Routeburn or Dart-Rees packages is $25 if you're camping and $30 in their lodge. For the Greenstone/Caples package the cost is $30 and $35. If you get to Glenorchy on your own, camping costs $5.50 per person ($7 with power) and bunkrooms or cabins cost $12 per person.

**Hitching** Hitching into Queenstown is relatively easy, but getting out may require real patience. Be prepared for very long waits.

### Getting Around
**Airport Transport** The Airporter Shuttle (tel 442-9803) meets all incoming and outgoing

flights and costs $6 per person, picking you up and dropping you off wherever you wish. A taxi (tel 442-7788) is just as good a deal for two people and even better for a larger group, charging $12 for up to five people.

**Bicycle Rental** You can rent bicycles at Queenstown Bike Hire at 23 Beach St. They have single-speed and 10-speed bikes, tandems, triples, side by side bikes, and 10, 12 and 18 speed mountain bikes. Rates start at $4 an hour, $14 a day, $22 for 2 days or $40 a week for single speed bikes. Mountain bikes are $6 per hour, $21 per day, $34 for 2 days or $70 per week. Mountain bikes can also be hired from Replay Sports in the Windsurf Mania house at 27 Shotover St and from Kiwi Discovery in Camp St.

**Moped Rental** Queenstown Bike Hire at 23 Beach St also hires mopeds. Prices including a full tank of petrol and unlimited km are $20 for 2 hours, $30 for half a day, $40 per day, $65 for 2 days or $120 for a week. Replay Sports at 27 Shotover St, and Letz Rent-a-Car on Camp St near the corner of Shotover St, beside the Information Centre, also hire mopeds.

# Te Anau & Fiordland

Te Anau is the jumping-off point for visits to the Fiordland National Park and for some of New Zealand's most famous walks, including the best known of the lot, the Milford Track. Information on these walks can be found in the Outdoor Activities chapter. The two main towns in the area are Te Anau and, a little to the south, Manapouri on Lake Manapouri.

### Annoying Weather & Wildlife
Once you leave Te Anau, you hit two of the menaces of Fiordland: rain and sandflies. Some definitions might be in order. Rain, for those Australians who haven't come across it, is water falling from the sky – Milford gets over 6 metres (20 feet) annually! Sandflies, for those who haven't met them, are nasty little biting insects, smaller than mosquitoes with a similar bite – you will see clouds of them at Milford. Don't be put off sightseeing by rain, the masses of water hurtling down the sheer walls of Milford Sound are an incredible sight and the rain tends to keep the sandflies away. For walking and tramping it is a different story, causing flooded rivers and poor visibility.

## TE ANAU
Beautifully situated on the shores of Lake Te Anau, the town of Te Anau is like a smaller, low-key version of Queenstown. Like Queenstown there are all manner of activities and trips to keep you busy, although for many visitors the town is just a jumping-off point for trips to Milford and the Milford Track. Lake Te Anau is the second-largest lake in New Zealand (after Lake Taupo) and the largest in the South Island. It's 53 km long and 10 km across at its widest point, with three fiords stretching westwards in long arms off the lake.

### Orientation
Most of the activities and businesses in Te Anau are found along two streets – Te Anau Terrace, which runs along the lakefront, and Milford Rd.

### Information
The Fiordland National Park Visitors Centre and Museum (tel 7921) is on Te Anau Terrace, beside the lake. You can get all your information on tramping or shorter walks there. It's open from 8 am to 5 pm daily. As well as the Milford Track, Te Anau is also the jumping-off point for walking the Greenstone, Caples, Routeburn and Hollyford tracks, so it's a very popular walking locale. See the Outdoor Activiites chapter for more details.

Fiordland Travel (tel 7419), which operates the lake cruises and tours, is on the corner of Te Anau Terrace and Milford Rd. YHA members are eligible for 10% discounts. The Mt Cook Airlines Travel Office is on Te Anau Terrace.

### Cruises & Trips
There are all manner of cruises and trips from

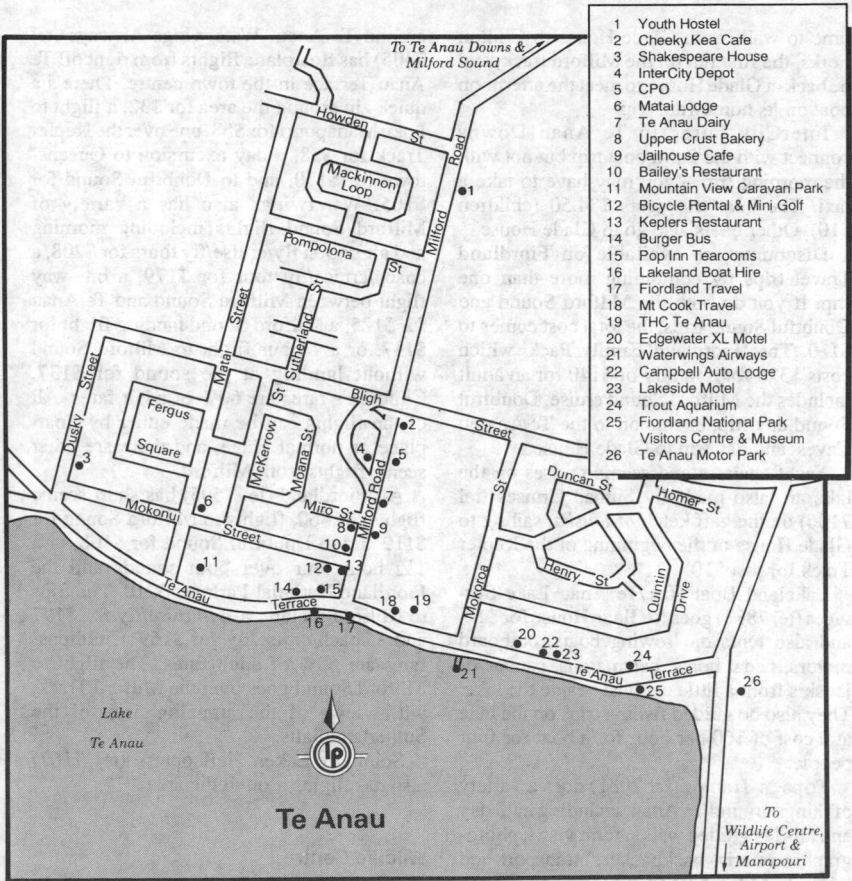

1   Youth Hostel
2   Cheeky Kea Cafe
3   Shakespeare House
4   InterCity Depot
5   CPO
6   Matai Lodge
7   Te Anau Dairy
8   Upper Crust Bakery
9   Jailhouse Cafe
10  Bailey's Restaurant
11  Mountain View Caravan Park
12  Bicycle Rental & Mini Golf
13  Keplers Restaurant
14  Burger Bus
15  Pop Inn Tearooms
16  Lakeland Boat Hire
17  Fiordland Travel
18  Mt Cook Travel
19  THC Te Anau
20  Edgewater XL Motel
21  Waterwings Airways
22  Campbell Auto Lodge
23  Lakeside Motel
24  Trout Aquarium
25  Fiordland National Park
    Visitors Centre & Museum
26  Te Anau Motor Park

**Te Anau**

Te Anau. Fiordland Travel has trips to Milford Sound, Doubtful Sound, the Manapouri Power Station and the Te Ana-au Caves, all of which can be taken from Te Anau. See the following sections on Milford Sound and Manapouri for details of the trips in these areas.

Cruises on Lake Te Anau are very popular. One of the cheaper trips goes to the unique Te Ana-au Caves, which were mentioned in Maori legends and rediscovered in 1948. On the shores of the lake and accessible only by boat, these caves, whose name means 'cave of swirling waters', are magical with their waterfalls, whirlpools and glow-worm grotto. The 2½ hour trip costs $27 (children $10).

You can also go to Glade House at the northern end of the lake, the starting point for the Milford Track. From November to April, when the Milford track is open, Fiordland Travel boats run from Te Anau Downs to Glade House at 8.30 am three times a week and at 2 pm every day for the Milford Track trampers. You can go on the 2 pm boat only if there is extra space, and you'll have to come straight back if you're not doing the track. However, going on the morning boat gives you about a 5 hour stopover – enough time to walk from Glade House to Clinton Forks, the first hut on the Milford track, and be back at Glade House to meet the afternoon boat on its homeward trip.

InterCity buses to Te Anau Downs connect with the 2 pm boat trip but not with the morning trip – you may have to take a taxi. The boat trip costs $34.50 (children $10). Other boats also go to Glade House.

Discounts are available on Fiordland Travel trips by combining more than one trip. If you do both the Milford Sound and Doubtful Sound trips, the total cost comes to $110. The 'Fiordland Family Pack' which costs $325 for a family or $140 for an adult includes the Milford Sound cruise, Doubtful Sound day trip, excursion to the Te Ana-au Caves, and day trip to Glade House.

Yacht charters and scenic cruises on the lake are also made by Sinbad Cruises (tel 7106) on the gaff ketch *Manuska*, sailing to Glade House or the beginning of the Kepler Track for just $10.

Lakeland Boat Hire/Te Anau Lake Services (tel 7883) goes to Glade House for $10, and also rents out rowing boats, outboard motors, pedal boats, catamarans, canoes or jet skis from a little caravan beside the lake. They also do guided fishing trips on the lake at a cost of $60 per hour for a boat for four people.

Trips 'n Tramps (tel 7081) does a variety of things around Te Anau, including half-day and all-day guided walks, farm visits, photographic safaris, backpackers' transport and leisurely Milford Road explorations.

Milford Sound Adventure Tours (tel 7227) has full-day mountain bike trips, beginning from the Homer Tunnel on the road to Milford, descending to the Cleddau Valley and then going on a cruise of the sound. Cost is $55 (children $32) including mountain bikes and gear.

There are many interesting things to see along the road to Milford. Fiordland Travel has a free map pointing out the many scenic wonders along the route.

### Aerial Sightseeing

There are lots of flightseeing opportunities around Te Anau. Waterwings Airways (tel 7405) has floatplane flights from right off Te Anau Terrace in the town centre. There's a quick zip around the area for $32, a flight to Lake Manapouri for $58, one over the Kepler Track for $58, a day excursion to Queenstown for $150, and to Doubtful Sound for $105. Waterwings also has a variety of Milford Sound flights including morning and afternoon fly/cruise/fly tours for $208, a coach/cruise/fly tour for $179, a one-way flight between Milford Sound and Te Anau for $125, a Milford Sound landing flight for $147, or a 1 hour flight to Milford Sound without landing at the sound for $137. Children's fares are 60% of adult fares. All of the flights can be made either by floatplane or normal plane, and there are other scenic flights from Milford.

Air Fiordland (tel 7505) has short scenic flights for $60, flights to Milford Sound for $119 and to Doubtful Sound for $108, or a 1½ hour tour over both sounds and the Fiordland National Park for $210. The trips to Milford include a fly/cruise/fly for $197 and a coach/cruise/fly for $169. Childrens' fares are 60% of adult fares. The flight to Milford Sound goes over the Milford Track, with views of the amazing drop of the Sutherland Falls.

Southern Lakes Helicopters (tel 7167) also has flights around the area.

### Wildlife Centre

Just outside Te Anau, on the road to Manapouri, is the compact and nicely laid out Te Anau Wildlife Centre, run by the DOC. It concentrates on native birds but also has a trout hatchery. Admission is free. It's worth taking time out if only to see the rare takahe, one of New Zealand's species of flightless birds, considered extinct until a colony was discovered in 1948. There are still less than 200 in the wild in the Murchison Mountains but the ones here are so tame that you won't have to wait long to see them. The centre has a variety of other NZ birds both common and rare. A sign next to the keas warns trampers that keas:

Takahe

...enjoy the following sports: ripping tents, flys and sleeping bags, trying on tramping boots (if they don't fit they usually cut a bit off here and there), eating your supplies, criticising alpine landscape artists...

In the town, opposite the National Park Visitors Centre on Te Anau Terrace, is an underground trout aquarium. Admission is two 50-cent coins which you place into a turnstile. Between Te Anau and Manapouri there's a wildlife park with wapiti, red deer and a few fallow deer.

### Places to Stay

**Hostels** The *Te Anau Youth Hostel* (tel 7847), about 1½ km out of town on Milford Rd, has room for 40 people. The cost is $15 per night and you can hire camping equipment, leave gear here while you're away tramping, and get YHA discounts on cruises, bus trips and so on.

The *Fiordland Resort Hotel* (tel 7511) has accommodation in triple rooms for $11 if you bring your own sleeping bag or $14 using the hotel's linen. Double rooms with linen supplied cost $28.50 for two. The resort has plenty of more expensive rooms as

well. All rooms have private bathrooms and you can do your own cooking or eat in the licensed restaurant. A swimming pool, spa pool and sauna all make this an enormously popular place, so it's a good idea to book ahead. It may close in winter from May to October.

**Guest Houses** Te Anau has a couple of well kept B&B places. *Shakespeare House* (tel 7349) at 10 Dusky St offers B&B accommodation 'as you like it'. The quiet and pleasant rooms are off a bright, covered-in verandah and the breakfast is a substantial one – you're fixed up for the day! Rooms cost $50 for a single and $64 to $68 for doubles from December to March. At other times of the year they're a bit cheaper.

At the *Matai Lodge* (tel 7360), on the corner of Matai and Mokonui streets, B&B costs $55/60 for singles/doubles in the high season and a bit less during the rest of the year.

**Motels & Hotels** The *Edgewater XL Motel* (tel 7258) at 52 Te Anau Terrace has rooms for $60 to $68 per night. There's a small 1 night surcharge and lower off-season rates. The *Lakeside Motel* (tel 7435) at 36 Te Anau Terrace is similarly priced.

Another moderately priced motel is the *Anchorage* (tel 7256) at 47 Quintin Drive. There are numerous other motels at similar or higher prices. If you're aiming for the top, the *THC Te Anau Hotel* (tel 7411) is on Te Anau Terrace right in the town centre; rooms start around $200!

**Camping & Cabins** The *Te Anau Motor Park* (tel 7457, 7695), opposite the lake just 1 km from Te Anau on the road to Manapouri, has sites for $7 per person ($8 with power). There's also a bunkhouse with beds for $11, cabins at $25 for two, tourist flats from $45, and motel units. It's a large, well-equipped camp with attractive surroundings and a very pleasant atmosphere. Car, van and gear storage is available for trampers.

The *Mountain View Cabin & Caravan*

*Park* (tel 7462) on Mokonui St has cabins and on-site caravans from $25 for two, but there are no facilities for tent campers. Powered caravan sites cost $8 per person.

## Places to Eat
**Snacks & Fast Food** The *Pop Inn Tearoom*, close to Fiordland Travel near the lakefront, has light snacks and sandwiches; there's a pleasant outdoor eating area looking out over the lake. The *Burger Bus* appears nearby at night to dispense burgers and other fast food.

There are several places along Milford Rd in the town centre with snacks and takeaways – try the *Jailhouse Cafe* which has good sandwiches, the popular *Te Anau Dairy*, or the *Upper Crust Bakery*. The *Cheeky Kea Cafe* has pizza, sandwiches and takeaways.

If you're going to Milford take some supplies with you, there's not much available there in the cheap eats department.

**Pub Food & Restaurants** *Henry's Family Restaurant & Bar* at the THC Hotel has main courses for $12 to $18 and a Sunday evening buffet for $17.50 (children $8). *Keplers* on Milford Rd features venison and seafood on its menu, with main courses from $14 to $21.

*Bailey's Restaurant & Coffee Shop* on the corner of Milford Rd and Mokonui St serves breakfast all day, bistro lunches, morning and afternoon teas, and an evening menu with selections which can be ordered as a starter for $8 to $11 or as a main course with potatoes and salad bar for $14 to $22.

## Getting There & Away
**Air** Mt Cook Airlines (tel 7516) has daily flights to Queenstown and Mt Cook, with connections to other centres. Waterwings Airways (tel 7405), an agent for Ansett New Zealand, has flights to Queenstown and Milford. Air Fiordland (tel 7505) also has flights to Queenstown, Milford and Mt Cook.

**Bus** InterCity (tel 7559) has daily bus services between Queenstown and Milford via Te Anau, taking 2½ hours from Te Anau to

either Queenstown or Milford. There's also a daily service to Invercargill (3 hours) and Dunedin (6 hours), involving a half-hour transfer stop in Lumsden. Buses arrive and depart from the InterCity depot on Milford Rd.

Mt Cook Landline (tel 7516) also has daily buses between Queenstown and Milford via Te Anau, and a weekday bus from Te Anau to Invercargill.

Magic Bus also operates buses between Queenstown and Milford via Te Anau. Depending on the time of year they may go daily, a few times a week, or not at all in winter. They specialise in doing trampers' transport to the walking tracks.

Fiordland Travel (tel 7419) on the lakefront has buses to Queenstown and Milford. It also has a bus and steamship combination which goes between Te Anau and Queenstown, making part of the journey by coach on the back road from Te Anau to Walter Peak and continuing from there to Queenstown over Lake Wakatipu on the TSS *Earnslaw*. The cost is $30 (children $15) each way.

**Hitching** Hitching in and out is a bit easier than to Milford, though still fairly hard. Hitching between Manapouri and Te Anau is good if you go there for a day trip.

## Getting Around
You can hire bicycles from the mini-golf course just off Milford Rd for $4 per hour for single-speed bikes or $8 per hour for tandems.

## MANAPOURI
If Te Anau is a low-key version of Queenstown then Manapouri is a low-key version of Te Anau. Just 19 km south of Te Anau, on the shores of Lake Manapouri, it's also a popular centre for trips, cruises and walking expeditions.

## Information
Even more so than at Te Anau, Fiordland Travel (tel 7416) is the main information and tour centre – the office on the waterfront

organises most of the trips. Although the Manapouri Power Station and Doubtful Sound trips depart from Manapouri, there are connecting buses from Te Anau for these trips.

### Cruises & Trips

There are two popular cruises from Manapouri with Fiordland Travel. One takes you across the lake to visit the hydroelectric power station on West Arm. The Doubtful Sound trip follows the power station visit with a drive over Wilmot Pass to Deep Cove on Doubtful Sound and then a cruise on Doubtful Sound up Hall Arm.

The power station on West Arm was built primarily to provide power for the Comalco aluminium smelter near Bluff. It generates 760,000 kW and discharges 19 million litres of water per minute from Lake Manapouri into Doubtful Sound. Not surprisingly, the project was the focus of intense environmental battles. At one time it was planned to considerably raise the level of the lake but this plan was defeated by the Save Manapouri Petition – the longest petition in NZ history. When you see the beauty of what has been described as 'New Zealand's loveliest lake' it's hard to imagine that anyone would want to destroy it. Lake Manapouri is the second-deepest lake in New Zealand with a greatest depth of 443 metres.

The cruise across the lake from Manapouri is followed by a bus trip down a 2 km spiral tunnel to the power station machine hall, about 2 km underground – a long way! From there the water is passed through a 10 km long trail-race to Deep Cove in Doubtful Sound. The road from West Arm over the Wilmot Pass to Doubtful Sound, built during the construction of the powerhouse, is totally isolated from the rest of the NZ road system.

Before the road was built in 1959 only the most intrepid tramper or sailor entered the inner reaches of Doubtful Sound. Even Captain Cook, who named it, did not enter it – when he observed it from off the coast in 1770 he was 'doubtful' whether the winds in the sound would be sufficient to blow the ship back out to sea. He named the place Doubtful Sound and continued sailing up the coast.

Today Doubtful Sound is an exquisitely peaceful place. Bottlenose and dusky dolphins can be seen in its waters, and there's also a small colony of fur seals. The Fiordland crested penguin nests in the sound for about 6 to 8 weeks in October and November. Life is also abundant below the surface, with black coral growing at an unusually shallow depth due to the fresh water on the surface, brought down by the power station and darkening the water.

The power station visit takes about 3 hours and costs $37 (children $10). If you want to continue on to Deep Cove and go on the Doubtful Sound cruise it'll cost you $91 (children $46) for the all-day excursion. You can order lunch on the trip when you book or take your own. It costs less if you combine several Fiordland Travel trips; see the Te Anau section for details.

### Walks

The National Park Visitors Centre in Te Anau has a leaflet on short Manapouri walks ranging from 1 to 4 hours. They're all across the Lower Waiau River from Manapouri, so you have to row across to the starting point.

### Places to Stay

**Hostels** There are no hostels in Manapouri but you can stay at the *DOC Hostel* at Deep Cove on Doubtful Sound for $12 per person. The hostel has dinghies, fishing lines, lifejackets and wet-weather gear for hire, and there are a number of good walks in the area of the hostel. For most of the year the hostel also hosts school groups, which come for 4 day park outings. Arrangements must be made through the Fiordland National Park Visitors Centre in Te Anau. The only way to get there is with Fiordland Travel.

**Guest Houses & Motels** The fine old *Murrell's Grand View* (tel 642), built in 1889, has B&B at $50/90 for singles/doubles with a shared bathroom or $60/110 with a private bathroom.

There are motels next to both camping

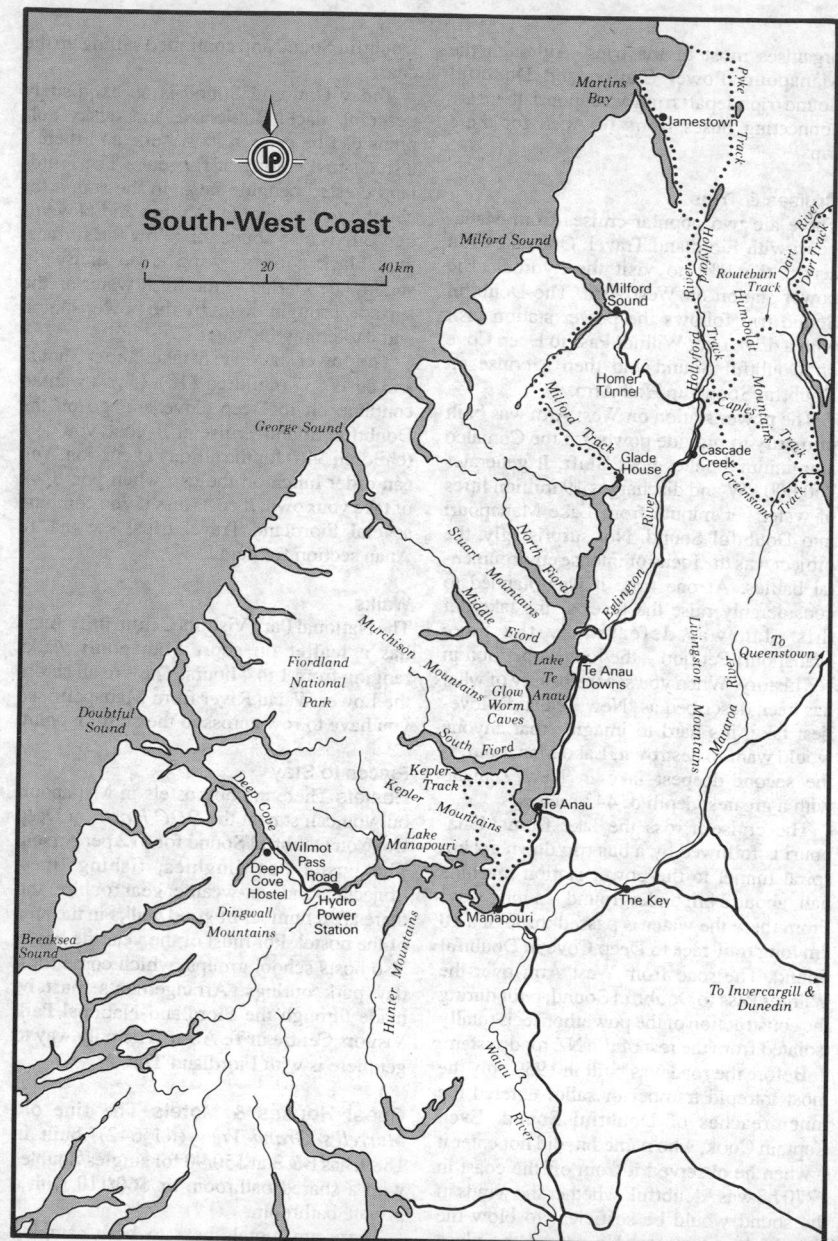

**South-West Coast**

0    20    40 km

grounds. The *Lakeview Motel* (tel 624) has units for $60 to $64 and the *Manapouri Glade Motel* (tel 623) has units for $55.

**Camping & Cabins** The *Lakeview Motor Park* (tel 624), 1 km from the CPO on the Te Anau road, has camping sites at $14 for two ($16 with power) and cabins from $27 for two. The motor park has a sauna and spa pool.

The *Manapouri Glade Caravan Park* (tel 623), on a stunning site adjacent to the river and lake, has sites at $15 per night for two and cabins at $24 for two. There's a spa pool here, too.

### Places to Eat

The coffee lounge at *Fiordland Travel* has good sandwiches and other snacks. If you're going on a day trip it's probably better putting something together here (or before you arrive) rather than paying $7.50 for a Fiordland Travel lunch pack. Meals are available at *Murrell's Grand View*.

### Getting There & Away

InterCity used to have buses to Manapouri but they seem to have been discontinued. Fiordland Travel has lots of people going from Manapouri to Te Anau to hook up with their Te Anau trips and vice versa so they operate a Te Anau-Manapouri bus service for $4.50 (children $2.25) one way.

### Getting Around

You can rent rowing boats from Manapouri Stores for $3 per person, plus $2 a night if you keep it overnight, while you go on the walking tracks across the river.

### MILFORD SOUND

Whether or not you walk the Milford Track, you should make a visit to Milford Sound, the 22 km long fiord that marks the end of the walk and beside which rises the beautiful, 1695 metre high Mitre Peak. The fiord is really breathtaking. The water, usually calm, mirrors the sheer peaks that rise all around.

There's a small but very interesting display on the history of Milford Sound in the foyer of the THC Hotel, with photographs and stories relating to the geology and the glacial formation of the fiords, the long efforts to find a pass and then to construct a roadway from Te Anau to Milford, and the arduous construction of the Homer Tunnel. There are also photographs and stories of Donald Sutherland, 'the Hermit of Milford' – you can see his grave out behind the hotel.

### Cruises & Trips

Cruises on Milford Sound are very popular so it's a good idea to book a few days ahead. The Fiordland Travel cruise on the MV *Milford Haven* lasts a little over 1½ hours and costs $30 (children $10). You can have a buffet lunch for $17 (children $10) or you can get a packed lunch for $7.50 from Fiordland Travel, or bring your own. Free tea and coffee are served on all the Fiordland Travel cruises.

Fiordland Travel also has a fishing cruise on a smaller boat, which goes on exactly the same route as the *Milford Haven* – all the way out to the Tasman Sea – but is a more relaxed cruise lasting for 3 hours, with the opportunity to catch some fish along the way. The cost is the same as for the *Milford Haven* cruise.

The THC Hotel at Milford also operates cruise boats on the sound. They take basically the same route as the Fiordland Travel boats and they cost the same. Most people say they prefer the Fiordland Travel boats, which are newer and have more amenities such as free tea and coffee.

The prices quoted here are for the simple cruise. Various cruise packages involving busing or flying into and out of Milford are available from Queenstown and Te Anau; see those sections for details.

### Places to Stay

**Milford Sound** Accommodation at Milford Sound is very limited, so it's a good idea to book ahead if you want to stay there.

The hostel-style *Milford Lodge* (tel 8071) has beds for $15 in two to six-person rooms, tent sites for $6 per person, and campervan sites for $8 per person. It's open all year but it's especially busy from December to April, when there's a free sauna, daily budget transport to and from walking tracks, and the evening meal is served from a little cafe counter (or you can cook your own). The hostel shop provides basic supplies and trampers congregate in the dining area; all in all it has a very agreeable atmosphere.

The other accommodation option at Milford is the *THC Milford Hotel* (tel 7926), where even the 'economy' rooms are $57/85 for singles/doubles and the standard rooms are $147 for one, two or three people. The hotel is attractively situated at the tip of the sound and has great views, but it's becoming rather elderly and frayed and its future is uncertain, since it's up for sale along with all the other THC hotels.

**Along the Road** There are a number of camping areas along the Milford road between Te Anau and the Eglinton Valley – check with the Park Visitors Centre in Te Anau.

You can camp at *Gunn's Camp* (also called *Hollyford Camp*) in the Hollyford Valley for $3.50 per person. The camp also has primitive cabins (a mattress and wood-burning stove; you supply the rest) at $11/20 for one/two people. The camp has a shop with basic trampers' supplies, and also an interesting little museum, the very personal creation of owner Murray Gunn, who has been finding things in the hills around here for years and saving mementos of the area's history. On our last visit he had become alarmed that deer hunters were 'shooting anything brown that moves' and so he had painted the sides of his 33-year-old brown horse in big white letters saying 'HORSE' on one side and 'COW' on the other! A few km up the road from Milford there's a very basic little camping site.

**Places to Eat**
The *THC Hotel* has a restaurant and the pub serves basic pub food. The *Milford Lodge* serves good evening meals at its little restaurant counter from December to April and it also has a small shop.

**Getting There & Away**
You can reach Milford Sound by four methods, all interesting: hike, fly, bus, and drive or hitch. The first, the Milford Track route, is detailed in the Tramping section in the Outdoor Activities chapter.

**Air** Probably the most spectacular way to go is to fly there. Flights operate from Queenstown and Te Anau; see those sections for details. A good combination trip is to go to Milford by bus and return by air.

**Bus** You can do the round trip by bus from Te Anau or further afield. Making the round trip from Queenstown in 1 day involves a lot of bus travel, so Te Anau is a better jumping-off point; a day trip from Queenstown means about 10 hours of bus travel, but from Te Anau it's only about 5 hours. The 120 km trip by road is spectacular, and InterCity, Mt Cook Landline and Fiordland Travel all run daily bus services from Te Anau for $27 one way or $34 return (children half price).

The 1 day Fiordland Travel coach-/cruise/coach excursion, leaving Te Anau at 8 am and returning at 5 pm, costs $64 (children $32). From Queenstown it departs at 7.15 am and returns at 7.45 pm. InterCity has basically the same excursion at the same price, except the cruise is on the THC Red Boats. It's essential to book in advance for the Milford excursions during the high season.

Magic Bus also goes to Milford, stopping at the Divide for the Routeburn and other walks. In Te Anau it departs from the Te Anau Motor Camp, the Mountain View Caravan Park and the Youth Hostel, or you can take it all the way from Queenstown. It usually runs only during the summer tramping season (October to April) when it may go several times a week or even daily, depending on demand.

**Car** If you're driving to Milford, stop by Fiordland Travel for a copy of their free map of the road to Milford, which points out sights along the way including the Mirror Lakes (58 km from Te Anau), the Avenue of the Disappearing Mountain (63 km), Homer

Tunnel and walks (101 km), the Chasm (109 km) and many other interesting spots and nature walks.

The Homer Tunnel, which made the road possible, was started in 1935 as a major depression works project but proved too big a task and was not opened to vehicles until 1953. The 1.2 km tunnel, with a gradient of one in 10, goes through solid rock – best appreciated as you approach the massive, forbidding cliffs from the Milford side.

Until recently the tunnel was too narrow to allow traffic to travel in both directions at the same time. Now it has been widened and sealed and you no longer need to plan your trip to arrive at the tunnel at the right time to be able to go straight through without waiting. The road is normally open all year, but may occasionally be closed due to heavy snow and avalanches in winter. If you go by car the drive itself should take about 2½ hours but make sure you allow extra time to stop off on the way, especially if you're planning to take photographs.

**Hitching** Hitching on the Milford road is possible but hard going. There's little traffic and nearly all of it is tourist traffic which is unlikely to stop. There are walks off the Milford road including walks close to both ends of the tunnel and also walks off the Lower Hollyford road which branches off the Milford road.

# Dunedin

Population 106,600
There's a distinct Scottish feeling about Dunedin – not surprising considering the name is Celtic for Edinburgh. It's a solid, no nonsense sort of place – second city of the South Island, home of New Zealand's first university and at one time (during the gold rush days) the largest city in New Zealand.

The city is situated in a kind of natural amphitheatre at the head of Otago Harbour, a long fiord-like inlet. It is the gateway to Otago with its many lakes and mountain resorts.

## History
The first Europeans arrived at Port Chalmers in March 1848, six years after the plan for a Presbyterian settlement on the east coast of the South Island was initially mooted. Not long after the settlers' arrival in Dunedin gold was discovered in Otago and the province quickly became the richest and most influential in the colony.

## Orientation
The eight-sided Octagon – really more of a circle – marks the centre of Dunedin. The main street runs through it, changing name from Princes St on the southern side to George St on the northern side.

Being very much a university town, Dunedin becomes rather dead (or peaceful, depending on your viewpoint) during university vacations.

## Information
The well-organised and extremely helpful Dunedin Visitors Centre (tel 774-176) is at 48 The Octagon. It's open from 8.30 am to 5 pm on weekdays and from 9 am to 5 pm on weekends, with extended hours in summer. Apart from providing a great deal of information and advice, the centre books tours.

The NZTP (tel 740-344) at 131 Princes St is open from 8.30 am to 5 pm Monday to Friday but this is another NZTP office which is essentially a travel agent. You can book domestic and international travel here, but the Visitors Centre is the place to go for local information and bookings.

The DOC (tel 770-677) is at 77 Stuart St, opposite the Cobb & Co. It has pamphlets and information on walking tracks but most of their information is also available from the Visitors Centre. The AA (tel 775-945), at 450 Moray Place just east of Princes St, is open from 8.30 am to 5 pm Monday to Friday.

**Brochures** Various *Know the City* and *Know the Region* brochures for around 70 cents each help you to explore on foot or by

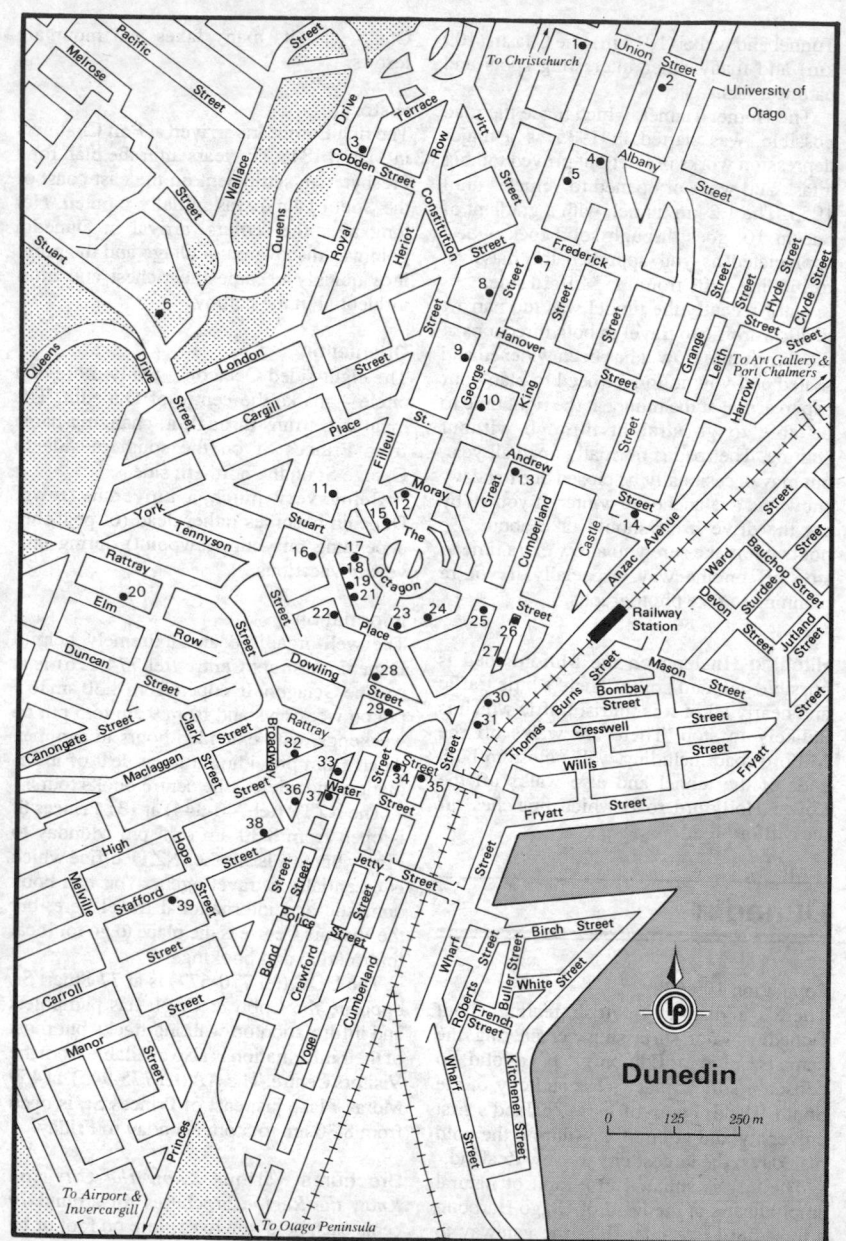

**Dunedin**

0  125  250 m

To Airport &
Invercargill

To Otago Peninsula

| | |
|---|---|
| 1 | Sheldon House |
| 2 | Otago Museum |
| 3 | Olveston |
| 4 | Captain Cook Hotel |
| 5 | Blades, Governors & Epi d'Or |
| 6 | Moana Swimming Pool |
| 7 | Robbie Burns & The Larder |
| 8 | Partners & Ritchies |
| 9 | Upper Crust |
| 10 | McDonald's |
| 11 | Quality Inn |
| 12 | Library |
| 13 | Mt Cook H & H Bus Terminal |
| 14 | Newmans Bus Terminal |
| 15 | Visitors Centre |
| 16 | Stage Left Cafe & YWCA |
| 17 | Friendship Centre & Los Gatos |
| 18 | Carnegie Centre & Terrace Cafe |
| 19 | Miniature World |
| 20 | Elm Lodge Hostel |
| 21 | YMCA |
| 22 | Ma Cuisine |
| 23 | Sidewalk Cafe |
| 24 | Automobile Association (AA) |
| 25 | Potpourri, Department of Conservation (DOC) |
| 26 | Law Courts Establishment |
| 27 | Leviathan Hotel |
| 28 | NZTP Office |
| 29 | Palms Cafe |
| 30 | Early Settler's Museum |
| 31 | InterCity Travel Centre |
| 32 | Southern Cross Hotel |
| 33 | Air New Zealand |
| 34 | Doug's Diner |
| 35 | Pavlova Backpackers Hostel |
| 36 | Wains Hotel |
| 37 | CPO |
| 38 | Provincial Hotel |
| 39 | Youth Hostel |

car – there's a whole series of these interesting do-it-yourself guides, all of them available at the Visitors Centre. Walk No 1 takes you from The Octagon that marks Dunedin's centre, past the many old buildings close to the city centre, the port, many elderly churches, the fine old railway station, a plaque marking the landing place of the first settlers, and back to your starting point.

The Visitors Centre also has other interesting pamphlets on places you can visit including *Historic Dunedin* published by the New Zealand Historic Places Trust. There

are many other old churches and stone buildings worth a look. The new library at the back of the Octagon is quite impressive.

### Olveston

Olveston is a fine old turn-of-the-century house at 42 Royal Terrace, preserved as it was when lived in by a wealthy and cultured family of the early 1900s. The guided tour is a real education. There are five tours a day from Monday to Saturday, the first one at 9.30 am and the last at 4 pm. On Sunday there are only three tours: 1.30, 2.45 and 4 pm. Phone ahead (tel 773-320) to reserve a place on the tour; admission is $6 (children $2).

### Chocolate Factory

A tour of the Cadbury's chocolate factory is a major attraction – in fact it's so popular that you have to book well in advance and you can give up all hope during school vacations! The 1 hour tour shows you how all the chocolates are made and concludes with a free sample of the delicious stuff. Tours are held twice daily from Monday to Thursday and can be booked at the Visitors Centre or by phoning 741-126. The entrance to the factory is on Cumberland St. The factory closes to give its workers a break over the Christmas holiday period.

### Speight's Brewery

When you've overdosed on chocolate you can head to Speight's Brewery for a tour at 10.30 am Monday to Friday. It costs $4 (children free), and you must book in advance by phoning 779-480. Tours start from the visitors centre in Rattray St. The brewery is one of the smallest in the country and the 1¾ hour tour concludes with a glass of beer in the company board room!

### Otago Museum

The Otago Museum on the corner of Great King and Union streets has a large and varied collection including Maori and South Pacific exhibits; items from ancient Egypt, Greece, Rome, Japan, China, Tibet, Southeast Asia, a marine and maritime hall; wildlife and ceramics exhibits; jewellery and art; and a lot more. Exhibits relate to the present as well as the past. Admission is free and it's open from 10 am to 5 pm on weekdays, 1 to 5 pm on Saturdays, and 2 to 5 pm on Sundays.

### Early Settlers Museum
The Early Settlers Museum at 220 Cumberland St, between the railway station and the InterCity bus depot, has a fine collection relating to the early settlement of the region. At the railway station end of the museum there are a couple of old steam locomotives in glassed-in display rooms. The museum's open from 8.30 am to 4.30 pm on weekdays, 10.30 am to 4.30 pm on Saturdays, and from 1.30 to 4.30 pm on Sundays. Admission is $4 (students $3, accompanied children free).

### Other Museums & Galleries
The Dunedin Public Art Gallery is in Logan Park, near the university at the northern end of Anzac Ave. It's open from 10 am to 4.30 pm on weekdays and 2 to 5 pm on weekends; admission is free. It's the oldest art gallery in New Zealand and has an extensive collection of international and NZ art.

The Carnegie Centre at 110 Moray Place is a complex of craft shops and galleries including an interesting toy shop and the excellent Press Gallery which specialises in original prints by local NZ artists. Also at the centre is Miniature World – A Museum of Childhood and Toys. It's open from 9.30 am to 6 pm every day; admission is $4 (children $2).

The Otago Military Museum is at the Army headquarters Drill Hall in Bridgman St. Admission is free, and the museum is open by arrangement (tel 551-099).

The Transport & Technology Museum on Russell St in Seacliff is open from 11 am to 5 pm on Sundays, or by arrangement (tel 465-7775, 881-048). Admission is $2.50 (children 50 cents).

### University of Otago
The Geology Museum of the University of Otago has displays illustrating mineral types and NZ fossils. Admission is free and it's open from 9 am to 5 pm on weekdays during term time, and by arrangement at other times (tel 791-100).

The university itself is worth a walk around. It was founded in 1869, 25 years after the settlement of Otago, with 81 students. Today it has 7000; more than two-thirds come from outside Otago. There's a wide variety of old and new styles of architecture on the campus. Dunedin, more than any other NZ city, is a university town.

### Parks & Pools
Dunedin has plenty of parks, including the Botanical Gardens at the northern end of the city on the lower slopes of Signal Hill. The hothouse there is open from 10 am to 4.30 pm. Rhododendron Week, the third week in October, is a big deal at the gardens. The gardens also have an aviary with keas and other native birds.

In Upper Stuart St on the corner of Littlebourne Rd is a fine Olympic swimming pool, Moana Pool (tel 743-513), heated to 27°C. There's a waterslide maze associated with the pool. It's best to phone first to check on hours as they're rather complex and further complicated by the fact that some of the time it's open only for school or university parties, not the public. Admission is $2.25 (children $1), and the waterslide costs $5 (children $4).

### Stargazing
If the night is clear it's possible to do a little stargazing at the Beverley Begg Observatory (tel 777-683), in the Robin Hood Ground – it's off to your left across the lawn when you reach the top (western end) of Rattray St. There's usually viewing on clear Sunday nights at around 8 pm, but may be later or not at all during summer when it gets dark as late as 10 pm. The cost is only around $2. Public meetings are held at the observatory on the first and third Tuesdays of every month, and visitors are welcome.

The Southern Skies Astronomy Centre (tel 770-621) at the Carnegie Centre, 110 Moray Place, has a planetarium theatre operating throughout the day and exhibits on the history of astronomy, astronomical tools, science fiction, holograms, and 'hands-on science'. The centre is open from 10 am to 5 pm on weekdays, 10 am to 1 pm on Saturdays, and 1 to 4 pm on Sundays. The admission fee of $4.50 (children $2, family $9.50) includes a ticket for night-time viewing through the 20 cm (8 inch) telescope nearby.

### Other Attractions

There are 4 hour train excursions through the Taieri River Gorge from October to April, departing from Dunedin Station on various days at 3.30 pm and returning by 7.30 pm. The cost is $39.50 (student or YHA cardholders $28.50) and two children can ride for free with each paying adult. Phone 774-449 for a schedule and reservations.

Other activities around Dunedin include golf (there are two 18 hole golf courses), tennis, 10 pin bowling, horse trail riding, and flightseeing with the Otago Aero Club. Or enquire at the Otago Tramping & Mountaineering Club – they have regular weekly meetings – about their walking and climbing trips. You can get info on all these activities through the Visitors Centre.

### Cruises

You can make 2½ to 4 hour boat trips with Otago Harbour Cruises (tel 774-215) on the MV *Monarch* from Rattray St Wharf. Among the *Monarch* cruises is one out along Otago Harbour, passing seal, shag and gull colonies and the royal albatross colony at Taiaroa Head. This half-day cruise costs $24 (children $12).

The 17½ metre *Southern Spirit* (tel 771-031) sails daily on a similar 5 hour harbour cruise to Taiaroa Head, departing from the Harbour Board Basin Marina in Birch St. The cost is $40. Also available are 2 hour ($45) and 4 hour ($75) salmon fishing trips.

The *Samara* (tel 763-745, 727-287) does salmon and game fishing. The cost is $75 per person for a 4 hour morning or afternoon salmon fishing trip, or $575 per day (which can be shared among up to six people) for off-shore angling for mako sharks, thresher sharks and tuna.

### Beaches & Walks

On the headland at the end of St Clair Beach is a heated outdoor saltwater pool. It's open only in the summer – catch bus No 7. St Clair and St Kilda are good beaches to walk along or if you happen to be there on the shortest day (the middle of the winter) you can join the famous Shortest Day Swim (in the sea, not the heated pool!).

There is a walkway to Tunnel Beach. Catch a Corstorphine bus from the Octagon to Stenhope Crescent and walk along Blackhead Rd till you reach a 'no exit' road leading towards the coast. Head towards the triangular promontory, where you'll find a hand-carved stone tunnel leading towards a secluded beach. The walkway is closed in September and October for lambing season. For more information see the Visitors Centre.

If you catch a Dunedin City Council Normandy bus to the start of Norwood Rd, you can walk up the road to the Mt Cargill-Bethunes Gully Walkway. It takes 2 hours uphill, 1½ down. The highlight is the view from Mt Cargill, which is accessible by car. Take warm clothes as it gets very windy at the top. The walkway continues from Mt Cargill to the Organ Pipes.

Up behind Dunedin is the Pineapple Flagstaff Walk, which is not accessible by public transport. You can get leaflets on these walks from the Visitors Centre.

### Tours

Dunedin Unlimited (tel 774-176; 740-198 after hours) does 2 hour guided walking tours of the city whenever there are three or more people who want to go. Further afield Silverpeaks Tours (tel Mosgiel 896-167) has jet-boating and white water rafting trips on the Taieri River. See also the bus tours detailed in the Otago Peninsula section.

### Places to Stay

As well as the following places to stay in Dunedin, there are a few places on the Otago Peninsula; they're listed in the Otago Peninsula section.

**Hostels** The *Stafford Gables Youth Hostel* (tel 741-919) is at 71 Stafford St, only about a 5 minute walk from the CPO. It's a very elegant and sprawling old building, once used as a private hotel before being converted to a hostel. The cost is $15 per night. There's room here for 62 including a number of family and twin rooms. Cheap meals are available in the evening. The hostel rents out 10-speed bikes and runs tours of the Otago Peninsula. The hostel and office are open all day.

The *Elm Lodge* (tel 741-872) at 74 Elm Row, 10 minutes uphill (five going back down) from the Octagon, is a private hostel situated in a fine old family home, with a smaller, homely atmosphere. It costs $13 in dorm rooms and $15 in double rooms. There's free pick-up, and the lodge rents out bicycles. Despite its central location, Elm Lodge has great harbour views.

Right in the centre of Dunedin is *Pavlova Backpackers* (tel 479-2175) on the corner of Rattray and Vogel streets, a city-style hostel with accommodation for 54 people for $13 in dorms or $14 in double or twin rooms. You can't miss it – the outside is painted bright lavender and green! It's very close to various attractions including the brewery and the chocolate factory. Pavlova is served in the evening.

The *YMCA* (tel 779-555) at 54 Moray Place, just off the Octagon, is also very centrally located. It generally caters for permanents, but will take casuals when there's room. It's shared accommodation – six people to a flat in singles and doubles, sharing a lounge and kitchen. The nightly cost is $12/20 for one/two people if you use your own bedding, or $14/22 with sheets supplied (blankets are free). There's also a weekly rate of $80 per person. The Y takes in both men and women, and doesn't segregate them.

**Guest Houses** The *Sahara Guesthouse & Motel* (tel 776-662) is at 619 George St, just off the northern end of the map and quite close to the university. Singles/doubles cost $38/58, including breakfast, and there are

some motel units for $46/56. The nearby *Sheldon House Lodge* (tel 775-435) at 597 George St, on the corner of Union St, has B&B for $48/52.

At *Magnolia House* (tel 467-5999), a Victorian villa on Grindon St, B&B costs $35/60 for singles/doubles. It's a very pleasant place but all bookings must be made by phone – don't just turn up – and it's strictly non-smoking.

**Hotels** Cheaper hotels in Dunedin include the small *Hotel Branson* (tel 778-411) at 91 St Andrews St. Single/double rooms cost $25/50 although they may sometimes have special deals. Breakfast is an extra $5 (continental) or $10 (cooked) and cheap bistro meals are also available. The *Wharf Hotel* (tel 771-233) at 25 Fryatt St offers B&B for $30/50.

The *Beach Hotel* (tel 554-642), on the corner of Prince Albert and Victoria roads at St Kilda, has single/double rooms with private facilities for $36/50. *Wains* (tel 779-283) at 310 Princes St is a great-looking old place close to the town centre, with B&B at $60/75 for singles/doubles. Out at Port Chalmers, *Chicks Hotel* (tel 728-736) at 2 Mount St is a classic old stone building with B&B at $25 per person.

The solid, reliable, old-fashioned and central *Leviathan Hotel* (tel 773-160) on the corner of Cumberland and High streets, opposite the railway station, is a Dunedin landmark. Singles/doubles cost $64/69 and all rooms have attached bathrooms; there are also motel units for $76. The Leviathan is tourist licensed (ie for guests only), unlike the other fully licensed hotels. Also in the city centre, the *Law Courts Establishment* (tel 778-036) on the corner of Stuart and Cumberland streets has singles/doubles for $62/70.

Right up at the top of the Dunedin hotel list are the *Quality Inn* (tel 776-784) on Upper Moray Place and the *Southern Cross* (tel 770-752) at 118 High St. Both start from the high side of $100 and both are centrally located.

**Motels** There are a number of moderately priced motels along Musselburgh Rise, on the Otago Peninsula side of town. They include the *Arcadian Motel* (tel 42-000) at Nos 85-89, the *Chequers Motel* (tel 45-244) at No 119, and the *Bayfield Motel* (tel 45-648) at No 210. Double rooms cost around $52 to $59 at each of these places.

Others to try include the *Aaron Lodge Motel* (see Camping & Cabins) and the *Sahara Motel* (see Guest Houses). The *Dunedin Motel* (tel 777-692) at 624 George St has double rooms from $57. The *Argyle Court Motel* (tel 779-803) on the corner of Duke and George streets is in the same price range, as is the *St Kilda Motel* (tel 551-151) on the corner of Victoria Rd and Queens Drive. There are plenty of other motels.

**Camping & Cabins** The *Tahuna Park Seaside Camp* (tel 54-690) is by the beach, near the showgrounds at St Kilda. You can get there on a St Kilda bus. Sites cost $6.50 per person, powered sites are $13.50 for two. There is a variety of cabins from $22 for two in the simplest ones to $40 in the best ones.

At the *Aaron Lodge Motor Camp* (tel 64-725), 162 Kaikorai Valley Rd, sites cost $13.50 for two ($15 with power). Cabins there are $25 to $28 for two and blankets and utensils are available for hire. They also have motel units at $52 for two. You can get there on a Bradford bus, and the Brockville bus also goes nearby on some runs.

The *Leith Valley Touring Park* (tel 741-936) is at 103 Malvern St, Woodhaugh. Powered sites are $7.50 per person and there are on-site caravans which cost $12, plus the basic camping site fee, you supply your bedding but everything else is provided.

The *Farmlands Caravan Park* (tel 822-730) is on Waitati Valley Rd, 13 km north of Dunedin off SH 1. Camping costs $6 per person ($7 with power), cabins cost $24 for two, and on-site caravans cost $26 for two. There's an adventure playground with pony rides, a flying fox and farm animals.

The *Brighton Caravan Park* (tel 811-404) is at 331 Main Rd, Brighton, about 10 km south of Dunedin. Cost is $7 per person in

tent or power sites and there are boats available for hire.

**Places to Eat**
Dunedin's a surprisingly good place for eating out in just about all categories. In fact there are so many dining out possibilities there's even a guide to *Eating Out in Dunedin*, available from the Visitors Centre. The centre also has free leaflets on restaurants and on places which are open on Sundays.

**Snacks & Fast Food** Dunedin has an excellent selection of places for a sandwich or for lunch. There are lots along George St and around Moray Place. If the weather's lousy and you need a place to eat your sandwiches head for the *Friendship Centre* at the Central Methodist Mission, just up Stuart St from the Octagon. It's a very considerate public service; you can get tea and biscuits for 90 cents or a bowl of soup for 80 cents. The centre is open from 9 am to 4 pm daily.

Around Moray Place are several excellent places for lunch. At No 45 is *Ma Cuisine*, a wholefood cafe with quiches, spinach pies, sandwiches and so on. A mixed salad costs $4 and there are also inexpensive rolls and vegetarian pizzas. Only a few steps away is the spacious *Stage Left Cafe*, equally well priced and also a pleasantly relaxed place to sit and eat.

You might also try the *Sidewalk Cafe* at 480 Moray Place. It's open from 10 am to 4 pm daily and on Wednesday to Saturday nights for dinner. The cafe has an excellent selection of sandwiches and light meals and it's a popular and pleasant place to eat them. *Potpourri* at 97 Stuart St is another good wholefood place open for lunch Monday to Saturday, and also for dinner from 5 to 8 pm Monday to Friday. It has salads, tacos, quiche and other light meals.

There are several other sandwich or light lunch possibilities in George St. The *Upper Crust* at 263 George St is open for lunch every day except Sundays and has salads, sandwiches and baked food. A bit further down at 351 George St is *Partners*. It's a bit more expensive than some of the other lunch-time cafes but the food is excellent. You can have a big bowl of soup with French bread, open sandwiches, larger meals and diet-blowing (but superb-looking) cakes.

The *Larder* at 388 George St has a big selection of takeaway sandwiches, and there's *Epi d'Or*, a French bakery at 430 George St. At the other end of the George St culinary spectrum is the *McDonald's*, just north of The Octagon. *Stewarts Coffee House*, downstairs at 12 Lower Octagon, has cheap sandwiches and excellent coffee. The *Bakers Oven* at 11 Lower Octagon is a big bakery. Good food is also available in the *Botanic Gardens Restaurant*, open from 10 am to 4 pm daily.

The *Deli Cafe* on the ground floor of the Southern Cross Hotel at 118 High St is open 24 hours. *Doug's Diner* at 116 Lower Rattray St is a straightforward place for grilled food and takeaways but it opens early and closes late. If you want to start the day with bacon and eggs and finish it with a late-night burger then this is the place.

**Pub Food** The *Rhumbline* bistro in the Provincial Hotel, at 6 Stafford St near the youth hostel, is open for lunch or dinner. Burgers cost around $3.50, light meals cost $5 to $6, and main courses cost $10 to $12. And there's the *Bowling Green* at 71 Frederick St, open for lunch from Monday to Saturday and for dinner on Fridays, Saturdays and Sundays.

There's a *Cobb & Co* in the Law Courts Establishment on the corner of Stuart and Cumberland streets. It has the standard Cobb & Co menu and is open their commendably generous hours.

Well north at 370 George St, *Foxy's Cafe* in the Robbie Burns Hotel has pub food regulars for $15 to $18 or cheaper dishes like curried lamb or pasta. *Zapatas* at the same address has tacos, pastas, enchiladas, quiches and other varied but definitely un-Dunedin-like food!

The *Captain Cook* is a popular student pub and has good food upstairs – if you can get in the door – and also a beer garden. It's round the corner from the Robbie Burns at the intersection of Albany and Great Kings streets.

**Restaurants** *Palms Cafe* on the corner of Dowling and High streets is a very pleasant and deservedly popular place, open from 6 to 9 pm Wednesday to Sunday. It has good salads, pastas for $8 to $10, main courses for $10 to $14 and desserts for around $5.

At *Los Gatos*, just off The Octagon at 199 Stuart St near the Friendship Centre, you can get some of the most authentic Mexican food in New Zealand. It's reasonably priced too but it's also so popular that unless you book you may not get a table, particularly on weekends. The restaurant is open from 5.30 pm Tuesday to Saturday; main courses cost from around $11 to $19. There's also a cafe alongside, open for lunch from Tuesday to Saturday and for dinner from 5.30 pm on Fridays. You can put together a meal there for around $7 to $9, depending on your appetite, and add a dessert for $2.50.

The *Terrace Cafe*, around the corner from Los Gatos at 118 Moray Place, is also very popular. The menu is an imaginative blend of cuisines as diverse as Italian and Indian. Main courses cost around $14, including some interesting vegetarian dishes.

If you're looking for an expensive night out at the best Dunedin has to offer then two places to try are *Blades*, way up at 450 George St, or *95 Filleul* at 95 Filleul St. *Yope's* at 401 Moray Place does Indonesian food for around $15 to $20 or rijstaffel for two from $40 to $45.

## Entertainment

**Pubs** Dunedin is a drinkers' town and there are plenty of places to slake that thirst. They include several of the places mentioned under Pub Food, such as the *Provincial* or the *Law Courts Establishment*.

The *Captain Cook*, on the corner of Albany and Great Kings streets near the university, is a very popular student pub. It gets so crowded that you can hardly get in the door sometimes. It has a pleasant garden bar which is great in summer.

Pubs with music, particularly in the evenings, include the *Beach Hotel* at St Kilda, *Hotel Branson*, the *Provincial*, *Foxy's Cafe* at the Robbie Burns and a great many others. Check the *Otago Daily Times* on Sundays for what's on. The *Sands* bar at the *Beach Hotel* is popular for its satellite dish reception of US TV stations, something of a rarity in New Zealand.

**Other Entertainment** *Sammy's* and the *Tai-Pei Cabaret* are nightclubs. Dunedin has a number of theatres including the professional *Fortune Theatre* and several amateur companies. The *New Edinburgh Folk Club* meets at 6 Carroll St at 8 pm on Fridays.

### Getting There & Away
**Air** Air New Zealand's office (tel 775-769) is in John Wickliffe House at 263 Princes St. There are daily direct flights to Auckland, Christchurch, Invercargill and Wellington, with connections to other centres. Air New Zealand is also the agent for Mt Cook Airlines which flies from Dunedin to Alexandra and Queenstown with connections to Te Anau, Milford, Mt Cook and other places. Ansett New Zealand (tel 790-123) at 1 George St (on The Octagon) has flights to Auckland, Christchurch and Wellington.

**Bus** InterCity buses depart from the Inter-City Travel Centre (tel 772-640) on Cumberland St, only a couple of blocks from The Octagon and a short distance from the railway station. It's a fine example of art deco architecture. They have services north to Christchurch, south to Invercargill and west to Queenstown, Te Anau, Milford Sound, Wanaka and the west coast. There are several buses daily to Christchurch and Invercargill. Travel times from Dunedin are 6 hours to Christchurch, 3½ hours to Invercargill, 6 hours to Queenstown, 6 hours to Te Anau and 5 hours to Wanaka.

Mt Cook/H&H Coachlines (tel 740-674), at 67 Great King St, has daily services up and down the east coast of the South Island, all the way from Picton to Invercargill via Christchurch and Dunedin. It takes 15½ hours from end to end.

Newmans (tel 773-476) is at 205 St Andrew St. They have a twice daily service on weekdays and a daily service on weekends between Dunedin and Christchurch with connections from Christchurch to Picton, Nelson and Westport.

**Train** Stuart St, which runs through The Octagon, continues down to the railway station on Anzac Ave. The Christchurch-Invercargill train passes through in both directions every day except Sundays. The train to Christchurch takes about 6 hours, to Invercargill about 3½ hours. The railway station is a local landmark, an example of Dunedin architecture at its most imposing and confident. No tickets are sold at the train station; buy train tickets at the InterCity Travel Centre (tel 772-640) about a block away.

**Hitching** To hitch northwards you can get a Pinehill bus to the beginning of the motorway or a Normandy bus to the Gardens from The Octagon, or walk there in about 30 or 40 minutes. You can get an InterCity Cherry Farm bus to Waitati and avoid the city and the motorway. Hitching south, you can take an Otago Road Services bus from Lower High St (opposite Queens Gardens) to Fairfield. Alternatively take an InterCity bus to Mosgiel, alighting at the turn-off or, if it's a long-distance bus, at East Taieri.

### Getting Around
**Airport Transport** Three companies offer door- to-door service to and from the airport. Dunedin Airport Shuttle (tel 792-481) and Ritchies Coachlines (tel 779-238) both cost around $9 per person, the Airporter Express (tel 892-758) costs $12. The 31 km trip to the airport takes around 40 minutes. If you have a long wait at the airport you can eat at the airport restaurant, which is better than most.

**Bus** City buses leave from The Octagon or from the intersection of High and Princes streets. The local buses are operated by the

Dunedin City Council. Unlike most places in New Zealand, they run every day including weekends, although buses are more frequent during the week.

**Bicycle Rental** You can rent bicycles from Recycled Recreation (tel 741-211) at 77 Lower Stuart St at $10 for half a day or $15 for a full day. Little Rainbow Bikes (tel 774-176; after hours 876-067) operates from the Visitors Centre and rents bicycles for $4 per hour or $15 per day, with a 15% discount if you hire them for 3 days or longer. From Dunedin down the peninsula all the way to the albatross colony is a good ride.

## OTAGO PENINSULA

You can spend a pleasant afternoon or longer tripping around the Otago Peninsula. Stops can be made at Glenfalloch Woodland Gardens, the Portobello Aquarium and Marine Biological Station, and Otakou where there's a Maori church and meeting house with a small museum. There are many other historical sites, walkways, natural formations, and so on dotted around the peninsula, making for an interesting trip. The *Otago Peninsula* brochure and map, published by the Otago Peninsula Trust and available at the Dunedin Visitors Centre for 80 cents, lists 41 different things to see and do on the peninsula.

## Glenfalloch Woodland Gardens

About 9 km from Dunedin, the Glenfalloch Woodland Gardens are noted for their rare rhododendrons and azaleas and for the peacocks and domestic birds which wander freely in the grounds. The gardens are open from 9 am until dusk every day; admission is $2.50 (children free). There's a restaurant and tearoom there too. You can get to Glenfalloch on a Portobello bus.

## Larnach Castle

The highlight of the peninsula is probably Larnach Castle (tel 761-302), a conglomeration of architectural styles and fantasies on the highest point of the peninsula. It's open to the public from 9 am to 5 pm (longer from December to May). Built by J W M Larnach in 1871, it is said to be the most expensive house in the southern hemisphere – its construction cost over $10 million by today's standards. Its owner, an able politician, committed suicide in a Parliament House committee room in 1898.

You can get to Larnach Castle, 15 km from central Dunedin, by taking the Ritchies Peninsula bus to Company Bay, from where it's a 4 km uphill walk, or you can come on a tour from Dunedin. Entry to the castle and gardens is $8 (children $3.50), or $3.50 (children $1) to visit only the gardens, stable and ballroom. A cafe in the castle ballroom does Devonshire teas or light lunches. Accommodation is also available (see Places to Stay).

## Taiaroa Head & Albatross Colony

At the end of the peninsula is Taiaroa Head where the only royal albatross colony in the world close to human habitation can be seen. Public access is allowed only by purchasing a permit for $12 (children $6) from the Visitors Centre in Dunedin, entitling you to a 1

Albatross

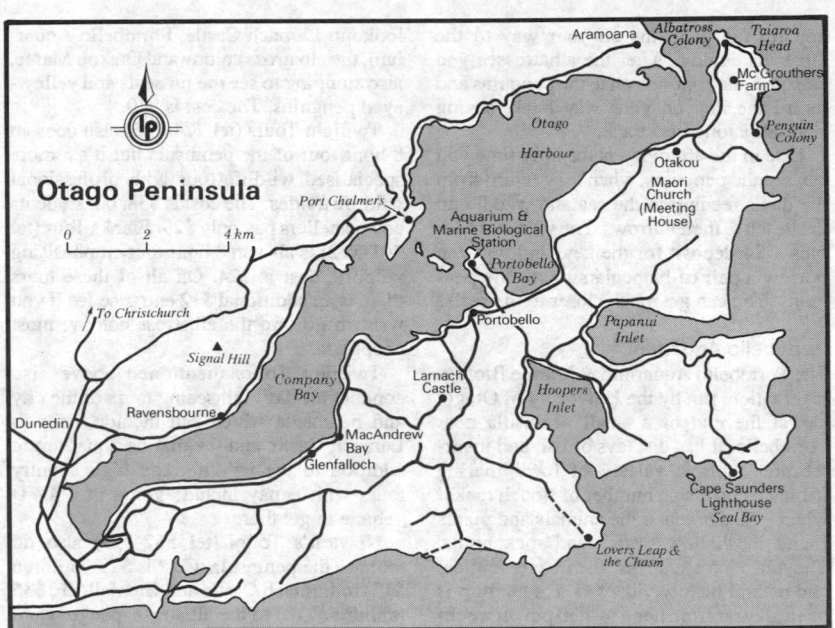

**Otago Peninsula**

0    2    4 km

To Christchurch

Dunedin

Signal Hill

Ravensbourne

Company Bay

Glenfalloch

MacAndrew Bay

Larnach Castle

Port Chalmers

Aquarium & Marine Biological Station

Portobello Bay

Portobello

Aramoana

Otago Harbour

Albatross Colony

Taiaroa Head

McGrouthers Farm

Penguin Colony

Otakou

Maori Church (Meeting House)

Papanui Inlet

Hoopers Inlet

Cape Saunders Lighthouse Seal Bay

Lovers Leap & the Chasm

hour conducted visit. Visiting hours are from 10 am daily except Tuesdays, when it's open only in the afternoon. The colony is closed between 31 August and 24 November, and the DOC may close it at other times during the year. A tour to the historic Armstrong Disappearing Gun can be combined with the visit to the albatross colony.

To get to the albatross colony, catch a Ritchies Peninsula bus to Portobello, then walk or hitch the remaining 11 km through beautiful scenery to the colony. Otherwise you can come on any of various tours from Dunedin. There is an element of chance in what you will see – in calm weather it's unlikely you'll see an albatross flying. The later you get there the more likely you are to see them fly as there's usually more wind later in the day.

The royal albatross is the largest sea bird in the world with a wingspan which can exceed 3 metres. Because of their great size, these birds nest only where there are the high winds and favourable updrafts that they need to get airborne. The birds arrive at the nesting site in September, court and mate in October, lay eggs in November, then incubate the eggs until January when the chicks hatch. Between March and September the chicks are left alone at the colony while their parents collect food for them, returning only for feeding. By September the fully grown chicks depart, and the cycle begins again.

### Penguins & Seals

Penguins and seals are also to be found on the peninsula. The local yellow-eyed penguin is the rarest penguin on earth! To visit the penguin and seal colony you have to pick up a gate key from McGrouther's Farm (tel 780-286) down Harrington Point Rd on the Otago Peninsula. You can't miss it – there's a big sign for the 'Penguin Place'.

The penguin colony is not at the farm, but further on down the road past the albatross colony. If you plan to see both, pick up the key for the penguins on your way to the albatross colony. After the albatrosses you can then just continue on to the penguins and return the key on your way back, saving yourself a long backtrack.

Late in the afternoon is the only time you can see the penguins, when they return from the day's feeding in the sea and waddle up the beach to their burrows. The visit costs $4, plus a $4 deposit for the key, and you can borrow a pair of binoculars to see the penguins. You can get much closer to the seals.

### Portobello Aquarium
The Portobello Aquarium & Marine Biological Station, run by the University of Otago, sits at the end of a small peninsula near Portobello. It has displays of fish and invertebrates from a variety of local marine habitats, and also a number of 'touch tanks' where you can touch the animals and plants found in shallow waters and rock pools. They also have tuataras (the native reptiles) and natural history videos. The aquarium is open all year from noon to 4.30 pm on weekends. It's also open every day from November to February and during school holidays. Admission is $2 (children $1, family $5).

### Museum & Historical Society
The Otago Peninsula Museum & Historical Society at Portobello is open from 1.30 to 4.30 pm on Sundays, or on weekdays by arrangement (tel 780-294).

### Ocean Beach Railway
During the week you can sometimes see restoration work in progress at the Ocean Beach Railway (tel 552-798). From 2 to 5 pm on certain Sundays you can have a ride but phone and check what's going on before you go out. Catch the St Kilda bus from John Wickliffe House in town to its terminus.

### Tours
Several companies do full day minibus tours of the Otago Peninsula. The Stafford Gables Youth Hostel (tel 741-919) does an 8 hour tour which includes visits to the Mt Cargill

lookout, Larnach Castle, Portobello Aquarium, the albatross colony and Otakou Marae, also stopping to see the fur seals and yellow-eyed penguins. The cost is $30.

Twilight Tours (tel 774-176) also does an 8 hour tour of the peninsula but it's a more specialised wildlife tour with professional wildlife guides. The cost is $38, but students and hostellers pay only $29. Franks Tour (tel 741-872) is also an 8 hour tour emphasising wildlife, cost is $24. On all of these tours there is an additional $12 entrance fee if you want to go into the albatross colony; most people do.

Twilight Tours mentioned above also conduct all-day sightseeing tours of the city and peninsula which can include visits to Larnach Castle and the marine aquarium in addition to the wildlife, and high country tours which may include going in a 4WD vehicle to get there.

Newton's Tours (tel 552-199) also do tours to the peninsula. Cost is $23 (children $12) to Larnach Castle and Glenfalloch, $35 (children $18) to the albatross, penguin and seal colonies. The Newton's city sights tour includes an escorted tour of Olveston and costs $17 (children $8). Unlike the other, smaller tours, this one is on a regular standard-size tour bus.

### Places to Stay
There are a few places where you can stay on the peninsula. You can camp at the *Portobello Domain* (tel 780-899) for a nightly cost of $5 per person in a tent or campervan site. It has a facilities block with kitchen and ablutions facilities, and power points are expected to be installed during 1990.

At *McGrouther's Farm* (tel 780-286) you can stay in former army barracks which have everything you need including a lounge and fully equipped kitchen; you only need supply your bedding and food. Cost is $7 per person.

The *Larnach Castle Lodge* (tel 761-302) is on the grounds of the famous castle. Bunks in the historic stable building cost $20 per person and hotel-style rooms cost $48, or

$69 with private facilities. There are also a few campervan sites at $18 for two.

## Getting Around

As well as the tour bus services already mentioned under Tours, Ritchies Coachlines (tel 779-238) runs buses up as far as Portobello.

## DUNEDIN TO INVERCARGILL

If you've got your own transport and you're travelling between Dunedin and Invercargill, consider taking the coastal route. The distance is pretty similar to the inland route although it's somewhat slower since some of the road is unsealed.

The route goes through the region known as the Catlins, including the Catlins Forest Park and a number of other forests and scenic reserves. Some interesting features are Jacks Blowhole (best at high tide), the Cathedral Caves (which can only be entered at low tide), and a number of waterfalls – including one named Niagara! There are many good beaches and bush, forest, waterfall and coastal walks. Slope Point is the southernmost point of the South Island.

There are several camping grounds and motor camps along the route, and a lodge at the Lenz Scenic Reserve. Information on the Catlins is available at the information centres in Dunedin and Invercargill.

# Invercargill

Population 52,200

Invercargill, the southernmost city in New Zealand, is very much a farm-service community, with a surprising amount of wealth (you notice more Jags here than anywhere else in New Zealand). To most travellers coming here it's just a jumping-off point for the tramping tracks of Stewart Island. Invercargill is surprisingly far south, although relative to South America it's at the northern end of Patagonia rather than the southern end.

## History

When the Chief Surveyor of Otago, J T Thomson, travelled south to settle on a site for Invercargill the region was uninhabited and covered in a dense forest known as Taurakitewaru Wood, which stretched from the Otepuni Stream (then known as the Otarewa) in the south to the Waihopai River in the north. Realising that ships of 500 tons could sail up the estuary to the mouth of the Otepuni Stream, Thomson chose Taurakitewaru Wood as the best site for the new town. It was laid out over 'a mile square' with four reserves just inside its boundaries and a fifth one running down the banks of the Otepuni Stream. Originally, Queens Park was just over the northern boundary and 200 acres (80 hectares) of forest was set aside for it. Today the only part of the forest that remains is a small area known as Thomsons Bush.

## Orientation

The locals staunchly defend their city, despite snide comments from the rest of the country about its backwardness. There are minor variations in speech and language throughout New Zealand, but in Southland the difference is most marked. Listen for the 'Southland drawl', with its rolled 'r' – more pronounced in the more isolated rural areas.

The two major streets are Tay St, which is the main road in from Dunedin and the east, and Dee St which meets Tay St at right angles. The shopping centre is between them, north of Tay and east of Dee St. Invercargill really sprawls – they had lots of room to build it and they used it all!

## Information

There's a Visitors Information Centre (tel 86-091) at 82 Dee St. For most of the year it's only open from 9 am to 5 pm on weekdays, but during holiday periods it's also open from 9 am to 12.30 pm on Saturdays and Sundays. The CPO, with its strange purple and white colour scheme, is at the bottom of Dee St, but postal services are in a separate building on Spey St, between Dee and Leven streets.

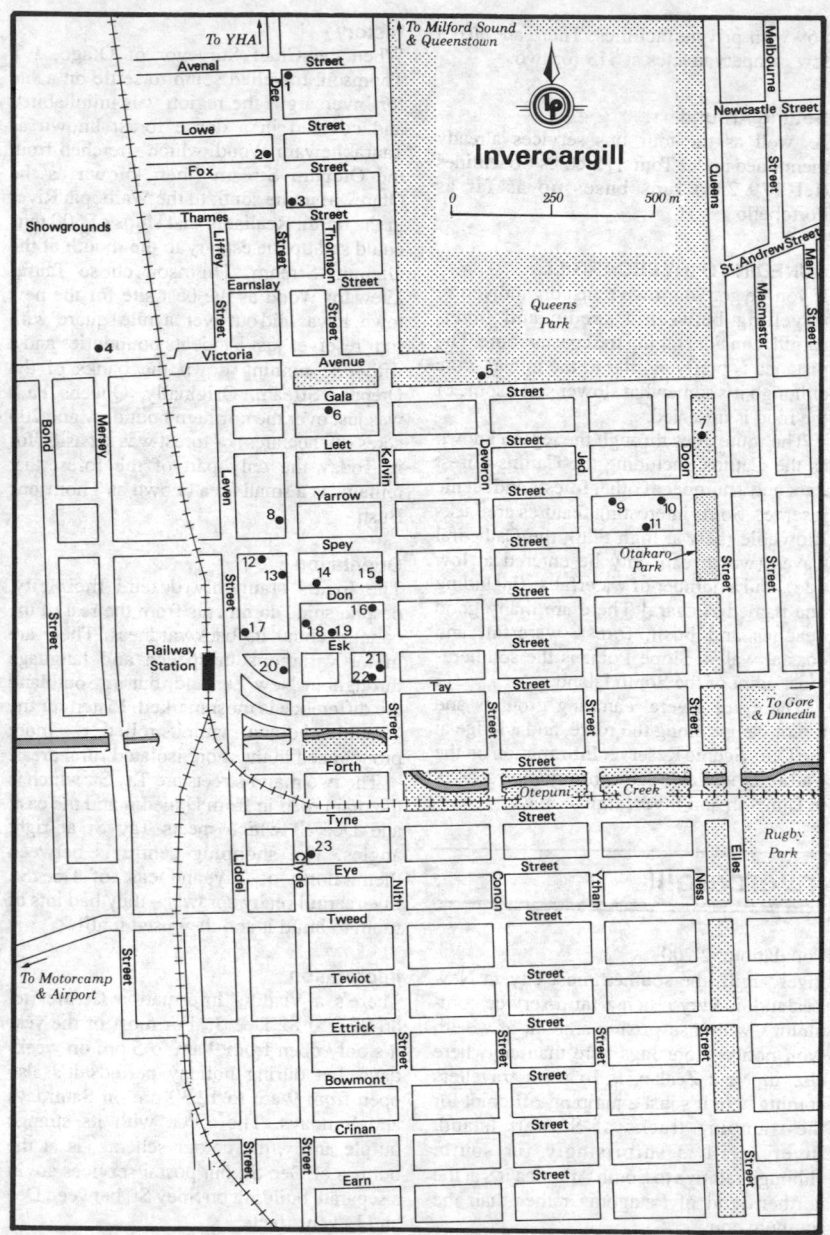

**Invercargill**

0        250        500 m

To YHA

To Milford Sound
& Queenstown

To Gore
& Dunedin

To Motorcamp
& Airport

Showgrounds

Queens
Park

Otakaro
Park

Rugby
Park

Railway
Station

Otepuni Creek

Avenal Street
Lowe Street
Fox Street
Thames Street
Earnslay Street
Victoria Avenue
Gala Street
Leet Street
Yarrow Street
Spey Street
Don Street
Esk Street
Tay Street
Forth Street
Tyne Street
Eye Street
Tweed Street
Teviot Street
Ettrick Street
Bowmont Street
Crinan Street
Earn Street

Dee Street
Thomson Street
Kelvin Street
Deveron Street
Jed Street
Doon Street

Bond Street
Mersey Street
Leven Street
Liddel Street
Clyde Street
Nith Street
Conon Street
Ythan Street
Ness Street
Ellis Street

Melbourne Street
Newcastle Street
Queens Street
St Andrew Street
Macmaster Street
Mary Street

Liffey Street

| | |
|---|---|
| 1 | Avenal Homestead |
| 2 | Pizza Hut, Willow Chinese Restaurant |
| 3 | Kentucky Fried Chicken |
| 4 | Showground Motor Camp |
| 5 | Southland Museum & Art Gallery |
| 6 | Automobile Association (AA) |
| 7 | Water Tower |
| 8 | Moa's Restaurant, Joy's Gourmet Kitchen & Fresh Sea Food |
| 9 | Aachen Motel |
| 10 | Yarrow Motel |
| 11 | Montecillo Travel Hotel & Motel |
| 12 | Postal Services |
| 13 | Southland Information Centre & Grand Hotel |
| 14 | Tillerman's Restaurant |
| 15 | Mt Cook/H&H Bus Station |
| 16 | Department of Conservation (DOC) |
| 17 | Gerrard's Railway Hotel |
| 18 | Nobles |
| 19 | Air New Zealand |
| 20 | CPO & Telecom |
| 21 | Kelvin Hotel |
| 22 | Boulevard Hotel |
| 23 | Clyde Tavern |

The AA Southland office (tel 89-033) is at 47 Gala St and the DOC (tel 44-589) is in the State Insurance Building on Don St. If you're going to Stewart Island it's a good idea to drop in at the DOC office to pick up all the info on walks. The Visitors Information Centre also has information on Stewart Island.

## Museum & Art Gallery

Invercargill's main attraction is the Southland Museum & Art Gallery, near the entrance to Queens Park in Gala St. It's undergoing a major redevelopment and should have world-class exhibits on view by the end of 1990 or early 1991.

The building itself is of interest. It's been rebuilt in the shape of a pyramid, and they say that at 24 metres high, with a base of 42 by 52 metres, it's the largest pyramid to be constructed since the ones in Egypt thousands of years ago – even larger than the glass one in Paris. There are plans for audiovisual and laser shows on the front face, visible from outside the museum.

Probably the most interesting of the new exhibits will be the 'Roaring 40s' gallery, recreating the experience of being on sub-Antarctic islands – a walk-through exhibit complete with forest, trails, icy winds, lightning and thunder! This exhibit will begin with an audiovisual presentation simulating the boat voyage down to the frigid islands. Set up in conjunction with the DOC, it will be the first of its kind in the world and has been receiving international interest even before its completion.

There's also a tuatara house, where several of the ancient and rare NZ reptiles are on display. Some are over 100 years old (they can live to about 150 years), and new ones are being born here too. Other features include a Maori gallery, a natural history gallery, a gallery on the history and technology of the Southland, two art galleries, and a special children's gallery.

The museum's astronomical observatory is open from 7 to 9 pm on Wednesday nights from April to September – good fun on a starry night.

The museum itself is open from 10 am to 4.30 pm Monday to Friday and from 1 to 5 pm on weekends. Admission is free, but all the restoration is costing a lot of money and donations are very gratefully accepted. While you are there, the 80 hectare Queens Park itself is worth a quiet wander. You can pick up a walking-tour leaflet of Invercargill's historical places from the museum.

There is another Art Gallery (tel 57-432) at Andersons Park, 7 km north on the main road to Queenstown. It's open from 2 to 4.30 pm daily except Mondays and Fridays.

## Beaches & Pools

There are two heated indoor swimming pools in Invercargill, one on Conon St, just off Tay St, and one on Queens Drive at the end of Queen's Park. The one on Queen's Drive has a waterslide too.

Invercargill's beach is Oreti, 9½ km west of the city. It's a long sweeping beach and the water is much milder than in most of the South Island beaches because a warm current sweeps across from Australia.

The Riverton Rocks area is a popular local beach and holiday resort. Riverton, 38 km west of Invercargill, is considered to be one of the oldest settlements in New Zealand, dating from the sealing and whaling days. It's quite interesting if you can get out there.

### Bluff

Invercargill's port, and the departure point for the Stewart Island ferry, is Bluff, 27 km to the south. There's an observation point at the top of 265 metre Bluff Hill – you can drive all the way to the top, or walk it in a half hour or so – from where you can see the Island Harbour, Foveaux Strait, Stewart Island and the Tiwai Point aluminium smelter. Hills being quite a rare physical feature in this area, it's one of the better vantage spots.

Also at Bluff is Fred & Myrtle's Paua Shell House, at 258 Gore St. It has an amazing array of shells collected from all over the world, and the entire front room is lined from floor to ceiling with brilliantly polished paua (abalone) shells. It's all set up in the friendly old couple's private home and Fred, who personally collected the shells from more countries than he can remember, is on hand to show you around. Visitors are welcome from 9 am to 5 pm every day; there's no admission fee, but you could make a donation.

Further on past the Paua Shell House is an ocean lookout with a sign telling your distance to the south pole, the equator, and many other places around the world.

Across the harbour from Bluff is the Tiwai aluminium smelter, eighth largest in the world. The overseas owners were attracted to Bluff by promises of cheap power; the Manapouri Power Scheme was built to feed it, and if there hadn't been such a public outcry Lake Manapouri would have been raised and destroyed to cater for the hunger for electricity. The smelter is now a major source of employment for Invercargill's citizens – around 1600 jobs – and they get mighty sensitive to any hint of criticism about it. Free tours can be arranged by phoning 85-999 in advance. The tours are at 2 pm on Tuesdays and Thursdays, and daily during holiday periods, but you need your own transport to get out there.

### Other Attractions

Queens Park is the town's principal park. Among its attractions are various animals, an aviary, duck ponds, rose gardens, a tea kiosk open daily from 10 am to 5 pm, and a swimming pool and waterslide complex, in addition to the Museum & Art Gallery mentioned earlier. The curious water tower at the bottom of Leet St was built in 1888.

If you want to go horse-riding contact the Otatara Riding Centre (tel 331-127) on Oreti Rd. It's open every day, but bookings are essential. There's 10 pin bowling at Super Bowl, on the corner of Kelvin and Leet streets.

### Walks

The main attraction is Foveaux Walk, a 6.6 km walkway from the southern end of SH 1 to Ocean Beach, where it emerges at a bus stop. It takes about 2½ hours. Don't be misled by the name 'Ocean Beach' – what you will find there is a smelly freezing works. Glory Track leaves from Gunpot Rd and passes through Bluff Hill's only remaining stand of native bush, connecting with the main walkway (35 minutes). Waihopai Walkway, along the banks of the Waihopai River, is only 10 minutes from the Youth Hostel.

There are several other walks; ask at the Visitors Information Centre or the DOC, and see the DOC booklet *Get Out & Walk – a guide to walking tracks in Southland*. The Museum & Art Gallery has a walking-tour leaflet for historical places around Invercargill.

### Tours

H&H (tel 82-419) offers a city sights tour whenever there are three people who want to go. It takes a couple of hours and you get a running commentary on all the historical, cultural and beauty spots of Invercargill. The tour leaves from the terminal on the corner of Don and Kelvin streets and costs $15.

Blue Star Taxis (tel 86-079) and Athole Bennie (tel 392-827, 86-091) offer tours for smaller groups. AB Mini Tours (tel 87-704) offers trips further afield, including farm visits, jet-boating, fishing and so on.

### Places to Stay

**Hostels** The world's southernmost *Youth Hostel* (tel 59-344) is at 122 North Rd, Waikiwi, about 3 km from the town centre. It costs $13 per night and sleeps 44. See the manager if you're interested in private hostel accommodation on Stewart Island.

The YMCA (tel 82-989) on Tay St doesn't have any accommodation, although it does have squash courts.

**Hotels & Motels** The *Montecillo Travel Hotel & Motel* (tel 82-503) at 240 Spey St is a friendly place with hotel and motel rooms. Including breakfast the hotel rooms are $44 for singles or $59/69 for the rooms without private facilities. The motel units cost $63 for two, without breakfast. The Montecillo is a straightforward but well-kept place conveniently close to the town centre. There are numerous other motels, typically from around $60.

The *Gerrard's Railway Hotel* (tel 83-406) is on the corner of Esk and Leven streets, opposite the railway station. It's a deliciously ornate 1896 building (with additions in 1907) which has recently been through a major renovation. It also houses one of the town's best restaurants. Single/double rooms with private facilities cost $65/69, B&B costs $47 for singles and $58 to $68 for doubles or twins, and there are some budget rooms with shared facilities for $38/49, breakfast included.

On Dee St, opposite the end of Don St, is the imposing old *Grand Hotel* (tel 88-059) where singles cost $47 to $70, depending on their size, and doubles or twins cost $76. The restaurant there is open every day. The *Kelvin Hotel* (tel 82-829) on Kelvin St in the town centre is the largest hotel in Invercargill. It's well kept but bland and costs a hefty $96/100 for singles/doubles.

**Camping & Cabins** The *Invercargill Caravan Park* (tel 88-787) is at the A&P Showgrounds on Victoria Ave off Dee St, only 1 km from the centre. It's closed during showtime but the rest of the year tent sites are $6 per person, or $8.50/15 for one/two people with power. They also have cabins at $12/22 and on-site caravans at $24 for two, all you supply is your bedding.

The *Coachman's Caravan Park* (tel 76-046) at 705 Tay St has sites for $6.50 per person or $16.50 for one or two persons with power. There are also cabins at $28 for two.

The *Beach Road Motor Camp* (tel 330-400), out towards Oreti Beach 8 km from the centre, has sites for $5 per person ($8 with power), cabins from $22 for two, and tourist flats at $35 for two.

### Places to Eat

Because Invercargill is the centre of an important fishing area there's lots of seafood for sale – particularly crayfish, cod, and the superb Bluff oysters for less than $3 a dozen. It's also the home of mutton birds. The local Maoris are allowed to collect them from small islands off Stewart Island at certain times of the year. They keep the best ones and sell the rest through the shops. But make sure you know how to cook them or they'll taste revolting!

**Snacks & Fast Food** Along Dee St and around the town centre there's the usual collection of fast food places and a number of sandwich places. *Nobles* at 47 Dee St serves pretty reasonable sandwiches in comfortable surroundings. It's open from 7 am to 4 pm Monday to Friday, but closes a little later on Fridays. *Joy's Gourmet Kitchen* at 122 Dee St has a good selection of salads, wholemeal goodies, sandwiches, quiches, wholemeal pizzas and budget hot roast meals. You can eat in or take away.

The best vegetarian/wholemeal/health food place in Invercargill is *Tillerman's*, upstairs at 16 Don St. It's quite a gathering spot locally and is open from 10 am to 3 pm Monday to Friday. It also opens from 5 to 7 pm on Fridays and then from 9.15 pm until late for coffees/teas and snacks.

Despite its plain appearance, *Moa's Restaurant* is something of a local institution and is open commendably long hours. It's at 142 Dee St and serves straightforward food in large quantities – this is the sort of place where the plate disappears under the steak and chips. Grills cost around $8 to $11 and lighter meals such as egg and chips cost $6 or $7. It's open from 9 am to 4 pm on Mondays and Tuesdays, 9 am to 11 pm on Wednesdays and Thursdays, 9 am to 1 am on Fridays, 11 am to 1 am on Saturdays, and from 11 am to 2 pm and 4.30 to 10 pm on Sundays.

There's the usual selection of fish & chip shops, including *Fresh Sea Foods*, a couple of doors from Moa's at 136 Dee St. It's open from 9 am to 8 pm every day, but opens a couple of hours later on Sundays. The food is straightforward and good value.

Further north up Dee St, about half-way to the YHA, there's a *Pizza Hut*, a *Kentucky Fried Chicken* and several other big drive-in takeaways. Next to the Pizza Hut, the *Willow* does Chinese takeaways, with a bargain lunch-time special for just $3.50. The takeaways counter is beside the fancier Chinese restaurant of the same name. *Enter the Dragon* at 107 Tay St is another Chinese takeaway although you can get burgers there too.

**Pub Food** Like Dunedin, there are plenty of pubs here and most of them serve food as well. The *Boulevard Cafe* in the Boulevard Hotel at 50 Tay St is a popular place, serving breakfast and brunch all day long, with pancakes or bacon & eggs for $5. Of course they serve lunch and dinner meals too, with plenty of seafood on the menu as well as steak, venison, roasts and the like, with main courses from about $12.50 to $20. It's open from 7.30 am to 8.30 pm Monday to Thursday and from 7.30 am to 9.30 pm on Fridays and Saturdays; it's closed on Sundays.

The *Avenal Homestead*, on the corner of Dee and Avenal streets, has the usual bars and a good restaurant, very much in the Cobb & Co mould. It's a modern, pleasant place with the standard pub food for $12 to $17. It's open for lunch every day except Saturdays and for dinner every night.

The licensed *Galaxy Family Restaurant* at the Waikiwi Family Inn is even more modern with its shiny, blinking-light space-age setting. The food, however, is more down to earth. All the regular pub fare is on the menu with main courses in the $11 to $14 bracket, including a trip to the salad bar. There's a children's menu for about $5. It's around the corner from Avenal Homestead, on Gimblett St, very close to the Youth Hostel.

**Restaurants** Most of the restaurants in Invercargill are pretty mundane. You could try the simple and straightforward *Ainos Steak House* at the Waikiwi Shopping Centre on Dee St, seven blocks north of the Youth Hostel. It's open for dinner every day except Sundays.

The *Willow* at 232 Dee St, next to the Pizza Hut, is an attractive licensed Chinese restaurant with six-course meals for $13 at lunch-time and around $20 to $24 in the evening. On Sunday there's a six-course 'family special' for $18 (children half price). A separate takeaways section is off to one side.

Back in the centre, *Gerrard's* at the Railway Hotel, opposite the railway station, is one local restaurant which does seem to have a good reputation. It's open every night; if you need a really flashy night out in Invercargill this could be the place.

**Entertainment**
There's not much entertainment in the town centre, which seems to close with a clang after 9 pm. You really need to get out to the suburbs to find anything happening at all, apart from the movies.

The weekend editions of the *Southland Times* will tell you what's on. The *Rafters Bar* at the Whitehouse Hotel is possibly the best place to go to, but it's right out at Lorneville, 8 km north of Waikiwi. There's a cover charge. The *Waikiwi Tavern*, on Gimblett St just off Dee St, is at least handy to the Youth

Top: Lake Te Anau (VB)
Left: Cruise on Milford Sound (JL)
Right: Deep Cove, Doubtful Sound (TC)

Top: Lanarch Castle, Dunedin (NK)
Bottom: Dunedin Railway Station (TC)

Hostel, and there's now a nightclub, *Lazers*, in the rear of the same large building. Other pubs with entertainment include the *Ascot Park Motor Hotel* on the corner of Tay St and Racecourse Rd and the *Southland Hotel* on Elles Rd.

### Getting There & Away

**Air** Air New Zealand (tel 44-737) has an office at 46 Esk St. It has daily direct flights to Dunedin, Christchurch, Auckland and Wellington although not all flights to Auckland and Wellington go direct. From these four cities there are connections to many other centres.

Ansett New Zealand (tel 44-644), at Invercargill Airport, has daily flights to and from Christchurch, Wellington, Palmerston North and Auckland, also with connections to other centres.

Flights to Stewart Island are made with Southern Air (tel 89-129). See the Stewart Island section for details.

In 1984 Invercargill had bad floods which caused immense destruction throughout the region, isolating it from the rest of New Zealand – and the world – for several weeks. The airport was completely flooded and there's a high water marker 2 metres above floor level in the terminal building. Despite extensive flood prevention measures there was a repeat performance in 1987 and again the airport was inundated, although this time only 1 metre or so. Air New Zealand flights were halted for weeks but flights for Stewart Island operated from the local race course.

**Bus** InterCity buses are based at the railway station (tel 81-939), behind the CPO in Leven St. There are daily bus services from Invercargill to Te Anau, Queenstown and Christchurch, with more frequent buses to Dunedin.

The Mt Cook/H&H bus depot (tel 82-419) is on the corner of Don and Kelvin streets. It has daily buses up the coast through Dunedin (3 hours), Christchurch (9 hours) and on to Picton (16 hours). The Picton bus connects with the ferry to Wellington. Other services include buses to and from Queenstown

(2½ hours) every day except Saturdays, and to Te Anau (2¾ hours) and Wanaka (5¼ hours) Monday to Friday. Mt Cook/H&H also has local services to Bluff, Gore and other centres further afield in Southland; see the Getting Around section for details.

**Train** The Southerner Christchurch-Dunedin-Invercargill train operates every day except Sundays, departing from each end of the line at around 8.50 am and arriving on the other end around 6.30 pm. It's about 3½ hours from Invercargill to Dunedin and 9½ hours to Christchurch.

**Car** See Dunedin to Invercargill, at the end of the Dunedin section, for details on the coastal road between the two cities, crossing the region known as the Catlins. Since this route is not covered by public buses, and light traffic makes it difficult for hitching, the best way to see this part of the country is if you have your own wheels.

**Hitching** Hitching between Dunedin and Invercargill is usually fairly simple and should only take about half a day. If you're on your way to Queenstown or Te Anau it gets steadily harder the further you go, and many people get stuck overnight in Lumsden. Without transport the coastal route between Dunedin and Invercargill is pretty hard – public transport is almost non-existent and there's little traffic for hitching. The same is true for the coast road heading west towards Te Anau.

### Getting Around

**Airport Transport** The airport is 2½ km from the centre and you can get there by taxi for around $9.

**Bus** Invercargill City Transport (tel 87-108) puts out a timetable with a colour-coded map of bus routes. Pick up a copy from the Visitors Information Centre. The buses run only from around 7 am to 6 pm Monday to Friday, or until around 9 or 10 pm on late shopping nights. There are no city buses on weekends. Local bus trips cost $1.20.

H&H operate a regular daily service to Bluff, including connections with the Stewart Island ferry. It also has local services to Gore, Riverton and other centres and to places further afield in Southland such as Te Anau, Wanaka and Queenstown.

# Stewart Island

Population 520
New Zealand is generally thought of as just two big islands – but actually there are lots of little-uns and one other fair size one slung right off the southern end of Invercargill – a sort of NZ Tierra del Fuego. Actually Stewart Island is not as inhospitable as that, but it most definitely is a get-away-from-it-all type of place. The miniscule population is congregated together, except for a few households on the western side of the island at Mason's Bay.

### History
There is all sorts of evidence that parts of Stewart Island were occupied by moa hunters as early as the 13th century. According to Polynesian mythology New Zealand was hauled up from the depths of the South Pacific Ocean by Maui who said 'Let us go out of sight of land and when we have quite lost sight of it, then let the anchor be dropped; but let it be very far off – quite out in the open sea'. One interpretation of this myth is that the North Island was a great flat fish caught by Maui; the South Island his canoe and Stewart Island the anchor – 'Te Punga o te Waka a Maui' being the legendary name for the latter. Much later the Maoris called it Rakiura – the island of the glowing sky.

The first Pakeha to come across Stewart Island was good old Captain Cook in 1770, who sailed around the eastern, southern and western coasts but could not make up his mind whether it was an island or a peninsula. Deciding it was part of the South Island mainland he called it Cape South. Several decades later this theory was disproved when

the sealing vessel *Pegasus* under the command of Captain Chase circumnavigated Stewart Island – presumably becoming the first European ship to do so. The island was named after William Stewart, first officer of the *Pegasus*, who charted the southern coast of the island in detail.

In June 1864 Stewart and the adjacent islands were bought from the Maoris for the sum of £6000 (about $12,000). Early industries consisted of sealing, timber milling, fish curing and ship building. The discovery of gold and tin towards the end of the 19th century also led to an increase in settlement but the rush didn't last long and today the island's economy is based on fishing – crayfish and cod – and tourism.

The people are hardy, independent, insular and suspicious of mainlanders, the law and bureaucracy. The weather is incredibly changeable – brilliant sunshine one minute, pouring rain the next. Conditions can be very muddy underfoot and you will need boots and waterproof clothing, but the temperature is much milder than you would expect.

Ann Pullen, a resident of the island, wrote to us since the last edition of this book and pointed out that the island's rainforest *is*, after all, more beautiful in the rain – and that mud is 'great character building stuff'!

### Orientation
Stewart Island is 64 km long and 40 km across, has less than 15 km of roads and its rocky coastline is incised by numerous inlets, the largest of these being Paterson. The highest point on the island is Mt Anglem at 980 metres. The principal settlement is Oban around Halfmoon Bay, with roads extending only a few km further out from there.

### Information
For information on tracks and tramping you can contact the DOC (tel 44-589) in the State Insurance Building on Don St, Invercargill, before you take off for the island. The Invercargill Visitors Information Service (tel 86-091) at 82 Dee St also has information on Stewart Island.

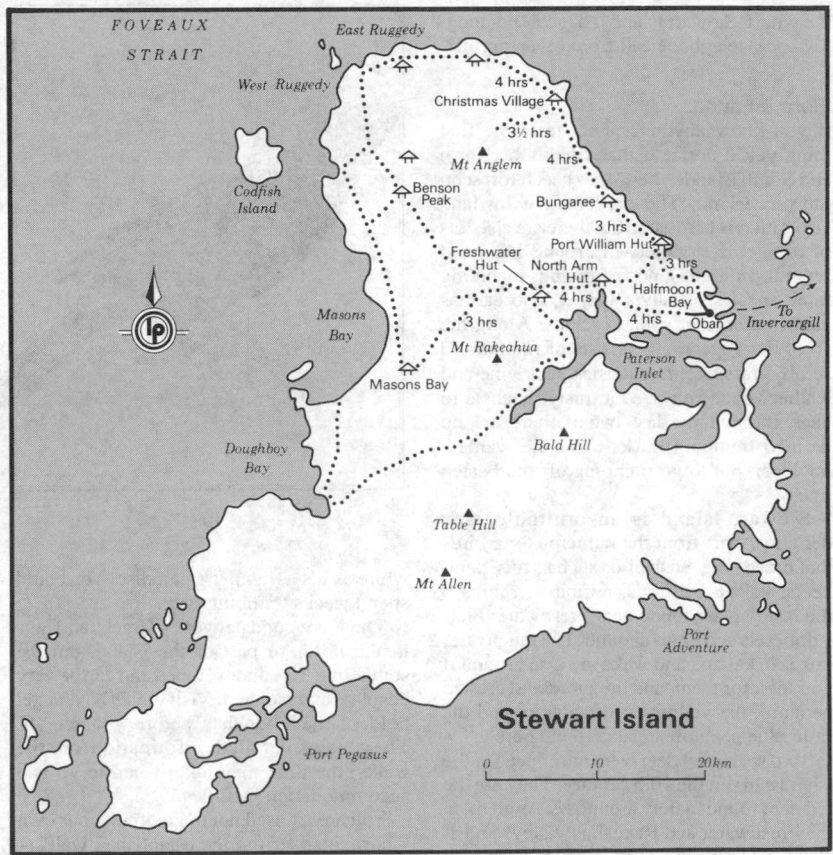

**FOVEAUX STRAIT**

East Ruggedy

West Ruggedy

4 hrs

Christmas Village

3½ hrs

Codfish Island

Mt Anglem

4 hrs

Benson Peak

Bungaree

3 hrs

Freshwater Hut

Port William Hut

North Arm Hut

3 hrs

Masons Bay

Halfmoon Bay

4 hrs

To Invercargill

Oban

4 hrs

3 hrs

Mt Rakeahua

Masons Bay

Paterson Inlet

Doughboy Bay

Bald Hill

Table Hill

Mt Allen

Port Adventure

**Stewart Island**

Port Pegasus

0   10   20km

On the island there's a DOC Visitors Centre (tel 391-130) beside the deer park on Main Rd in Halfmoon Bay. It's very close to both the Southern Air office (where you'll arrive if you come by plane) and the ferry wharf. In addition to much useful information on the island it has good displays on flora, fauna, walks and so on, and a summer activities programme in January. It publishes several handy cheap booklets including *Get Out & Walk – A Guide to Walking Tracks in Southland*; *Stewart Island*; *Stewart Island – Day Track & General Information* and *Stewart Island – Track & Hut Information*.

You can store gear at the DOC centre while you're walking.

There is a general store at Halfmoon Bay but as all food and commodities – including coal, meat and bread – have to be imported from the South Island, prices are high. The store is open from 9 am to 5 pm during the week and 10 am until noon on Saturdays and Sundays. Make sure you order bread, milk, eggs and newspapers in advance if you want them, because supplies are limited.

There is a post office where you can cash travellers' cheques. It's on Elgin Terrace, Halfmoon Bay, about 5 minutes walk from the wharf. Stewart Island is a local (not long-distance) telephone call from Invercargill.

### Flora & Fauna

If you know anything about trees the first thing you'll notice is that, unlike the North and South islands, there is no beech forest on Stewart Island. The predominant lowland vegetation is hardwood but there are also lots of tree ferns, a variety of ground ferns and several different kinds of orchid, including three species of lady's slipper, two earinas and a number of spider orchids. Along the coast the vegetation consists of muttonbird scrub, grass tree, tree daisies, jack vine and leatherwood. You need a trusty machete to hack through the last two if there are no defined tramping tracks! You are warned, however, not to go tramping off the beaten track.

Stewart Island is an ornithologist's delight. Apart from the numerous sea birds that breed here, bush birds such as tuis, parakeets, kakas, bellbirds, fernbirds, robins – the last two are found near Freshwater Flats – dotterels and kiwis abound. The much rarer kokako, kakapo and weka are also around if you look for them, and the Fiordland crested penguin, the yellow-eyed penguin, and the little blue penguin are also found here.

Two species of deer were introduced to the island early in the 20th century. They are the red deer found mainly around Mt Anglem, in the Freshwater and Rakeahua valleys and at Toi Toi Flat in the south-east, and the Virginia (whitetail) deer which inhabits the coastal areas of the island. Also introduced were brush-tailed possums, which are particularly numerous in the northern half of the island and rather destructive to the native bush. Stewart Island has lots of seals too.

### Walks

If you want to visit Stewart Island, plan on spending a few days there so you can enjoy the beaches, seals, rare bird and plant life. There are many walks on the island; although some take only a couple of hours, a day trip to Stewart Island is hardly worth-

Tui

while as it's a tramper's paradise. You could spend weeks tramping here.

There is a good network of tracks and huts in the northern part of the island, but the southern part is undeveloped and can be very desolate and isolated. Visit the DOC and get hold of their booklets before you set off. They have detailed information on the walks, the time they take, when to go and accommodation facilities.

You are advised not to go off on your own – particularly from the established walks – unless you have discussed your itinerary with someone beforehand. Foam rubber mattresses, camp ovens and billies are provided at each hut but you need to take food, sleeping bags, ground sheets, eating and cooking utensils, first-aid equipment and so on with you and, if you have them, a tent and portable gas stove may be useful as the huts can get packed out at certain times of the year. The stove is a useful insurance against finding wet firewood.

The first huts on the north-western circuit are about 4 to 5½ hours from Halfmoon Bay, and a lot of people just take the circuit to them. The track's well-defined and it's an easy walk, the major drawback being that it gets very crowded in the summer. There's a maximum stay of two nights in a hut. Hut fees for most huts on the island are $4 (children $2) per night. The tracks further away from Halfmoon Bay can be very muddy and quite steep in places.

## Museum & Other Attractions

The Rakiura Museum on Ayr St is no Victoria & Albert but it's worth a visit if you're interested in the history of the island. It's only open from 10.30 am to 1.30 pm on Mondays, Wednesdays and Fridays.

Also on Ayr St is a library which is open for even less time, from 2 to 3 pm on Wednesdays and 11 am to noon on Fridays. On your way to the Visitors Centre, drop into the deer park and check out the difference between red and whitetail deer. It's not far along Main Rd.

At Harrold Bay, about 3 km from town, is an old stone house built by Lewis Acker around 1835. It's one of the oldest buildings in New Zealand – probably the second-oldest after the famous Stone Store in Kerikeri which dates from 1832. You can look at it from the outside.

## Tours

In summer there are minibus tours around Halfmoon Bay, Horseshoe Bay and various other places. They're zippy little trips – only about an hour – because there really isn't very far you can drive on Stewart Island! There are also boat trips to Ulva Island (a great bird sanctuary), Ocean Beach, Port Adventure and Port William. Check with Stewart Island Travel (tel 391-269), or check the notice boards next to the store, for more detailed information. Fishing trips are other popular activities.

## Places to Stay

**Hostels** The *Shearwater Inn* (tel 391-114) in the centre of the township has both private and Associate Youth Hostel sections. In the hostel section, bunks are $12 and you provide your own sleeping bag; a hostel blanket will cost you an extra $3. Otherwise,

rooms (linen included) cost $28/46 for singles/doubles, or $20 per person in larger shared rooms. The inn has a restaurant serving breakfast and dinner, or you can cook your own meals, but it costs 50 cents for half an hour to use the hot plate. You can stay there with or without a YHA card.

**Hotels & Motels** A room at the *Rakiura Motel* (tel 391-096), 1½ km from the township, costs $80 per night for doubles. The *South Sea Hotel* (tel 391-059), close to the wharf, costs $56/85 for singles/doubles; there are also less expensive rooms for $28/45. The *Stewart Island Lodge* (tel 391-085) is much more expensive. Its four rooms all have private facilities and cost about $200 per person, including all meals.

**Camping & Cabins** There is a free camping site at Apple Bridge, Fern Tree Gully, but it's definitely basic, with a fireplace, wood and water supply and pit toilets only. It's about a half-hour walk from the wharf along Main Rd.

The *Horseshoe Haven* (tel 391-466), 4 km from Halfmoon Bay, has all the essentials and the sites cost $6 per person. An A-frame unit with bedding, pots, pans and crockery provided costs $35. There's also a bunkroom lodge for $13 per person.

The *Ferndale Carvan Park* (tel 391-176) at Halfmoon Bay has on-site caravans at $57 for two people – all you have to supply are towels.

**Homestays** An excellent alternative is to stay in one of the several homes on the island offering hostel-style accommodation at hostel (or lower) rates. Telephone after 5 pm to catch them at home.

Ann Pullen (tel 391-065) offers tramping-style accommodation in a small house behind the main house for $8 per night. It's very basic, but then the price is basic too, and it's a supremely friendly place to stay. You can leave extra gear here while you go off tramping. Bring your own sleeping bag and food.

A couple of other places offer very cheap

homestays. Michael Squires (tel 391-425) can accommodate up to four people in his 'house hostel'. The cost is $10; bring your own sleeping bag and food. With Andy and Jo Riksem (tel 391-230), you stay in the family home (they can accommodate up to five guests) and the nightly cost of $12 per person includes a cooked breakfast each morning! If you don't have your own bedding they will provide it for an extra $2.

The Youth Hostel in Invercargill can give you names of other people who offer private hostel-style accommodation on the island, usually for around the same prices. Or if all else fails you could just ask around, once you get to the island.

**Holiday Homes** Another option on Stewart Island is to hire a holiday home. There are several available. Stewart Island Travel (tel 391-269) has a couple for around $46 for two people, plus $13 each additional adult; families are especially welcome. Janette and Peter Goomes (tel Stewart Island 391-057, Invercargill 76-585) of Stewart Island Holiday Homes have two homes, each sleeping up to 10 people, about a 5 minute walk from the town. The cost is $55 per night for two plus $15 for each extra adult (children $7.50).

**Places to Eat**
There's not much choice of eating places on Stewart Island. It comes down to the *Travel Inn* tearoom or the *South Sea Hotel* where meals are available by prior arrangement. The *Shearwater Inn* has a restaurant where breakfast and dinner are served daily. You should expect prices to be higher than the mainland due to freight costs.

You can get basic necessities from the general store, buy fresh fish and crayfish from the locals (it's the main industry of the island so there should be no shortage), catch your own fish or bring food across from Invercargill and prepare meals yourself.

**Entertainment**
The only place to go for any nightlife here is the pub. The action will consist of bending the elbow, darts, eight-ball and maybe a brawl. Every now and again the fishermen get stuck into each other just for the hell of it.

**Getting There & Away**
**Air** Southern Air (tel 89-129) flies from Invercargill to Stewart Island for $63.50 one-way and $127 return (children half price). Two or more adults flying together get a discounted rate of $110.50 each for a return flight. They also have a student/YHA standby fare of $31.75 (return $63.50); you must present either a YHA or a student card. They like you to be at the airport 30 minutes before departure to see if there are any seats; it's a good idea to telephone ahead to see how many seats may be available before going out to the airport. Flights supposedly go three or four times a day and take 20 minutes to hop over the narrow strait, but in actual fact they put on as many flights as necessary. Sometimes they shuttle back and forth all day.

Southern Air sends a minibus once a day to pick up passengers from the Youth Hostel in Invercargill. Other than that, you'll have to make your own way to the airport. The bus from the airstrip to 'town' on Stewart Island is included in the airfare. The free baggage allowance is only 15 kg per person, which is very little if you're carrying camping or tramping gear – if you exceed 20 kg or so you'll be charged extra.

**Ferry** Stewart Island Charter Services (tel Bluff 378-376) operates a ferry from Bluff to Stewart Island for $34 each way (children 15 and under half price). There's also a YHA/student standby fare of $21 one way – to get this fare go down to the wharf, and if there's still extra space after all the booked passengers are on board, just present your YHA or student card and away you go.

There are usually departures two or three times a week – Tuesdays and Fridays during the winter and Mondays, Wednesdays and Fridays during the summer – but in summer they may go more frequently and during the Christmas holiday peak period they go daily.

# Chatham Islands

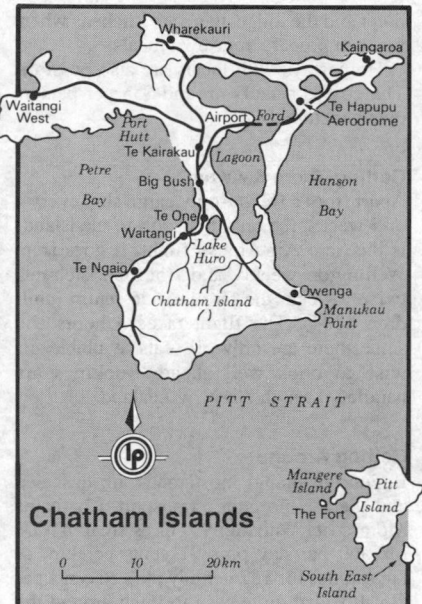

**Chatham Islands**

0          10          20 km

## Population 750

Way out in the Pacific, about 800 km east of Christchurch, the Chatham Islands are among the most remote parts of New Zealand. There are 10 islands in the group but apart from the 50 or so people on Pitt Island only Chatham Island is populated. It's a wild and attractive place, and very much off the beaten track.

### History

Chatham Island is renowned for being the last home of the Moriori, who were the pre-Maori or first Maori settlers depending on who you read. They are thought to have been here from the time of the first settlement of New Zealand, but with the arrival of Europeans things rapidly began to go wrong.

A British expedition first arrived at the island in 1791 and even that initial visit resulted in a clash, at aptly named Skirmish Bay. In the 1820s and 1830s European and American whalers began to arrive and then, in 1835, a Maori tribe was resettled in the Chathams. The impact on the peaceable Morioris was dramatic; their population crashed from around 2000 at the time of the first European arrival in 1791 to only about 100 in the 1860s. By the beginning of the 20th century there were just 12 full-blooded Moriois left. The last one died in 1933.

### Information

Waitangi is the only town on the islands. There are a couple of shops and a post office with savings bank facilities. The free *Chatham Island News & Views* carries the local news.

Information on the islands is available from Air New Zealand or, more particularly, from Safe Air Ltd (tel Blenheim 28-416), based at Blenheim Airport.

### Things to See & Do

The islands have plenty of fine beaches and it's a popular place for fishing and particu-

There are often extra sailings on public holidays. It's wise to book at least a few days ahead, especially in summer. In winter it's not so busy.

The crossing takes 2 to 2½ hours across Foveaux Strait, noted for its often stormy weather – it can be a rough trip, so take some seasickness pills with you. You'll see a lot of sea birds on the crossing.

To get to the ferry, catch an H&H bus (tel 82-419) to Bluff from the corner of Don and Kelvin streets, Invercargill. H&H buses connect with the ferry departures and arrivals.

### Getting Around

Rakiura Riders (tel 391-011) near the wharf rents motor scooters for about $15 per hour or $40 per day. A free tank of petrol is included with every hire, as are helmets and gloves; just be sure to bring your driving licence. Mountain bikes can also be hired in town, for around $2 per hour.

larly for catching crayfish. Crayfish are a major industry in the Chathams, and they're exported to North America. Birdwatching is another popular activity for visitors, with numerous rare and unusual birds to be seen. Scuba divers can explore the shipwrecks around the islands while trampers will also find interesting country to explore, particularly at the southern end of Chatham Island. Finally there's a small museum with Moriori artefacts in the council offices.

### Places to Stay

The *Hotel Chathams* (tel Waitangi 48) has single/double rooms for $45/50, or $35 per person for twin share rooms; meals are available.

The newer and more up-market *Chathams Lodge* (tel Waitangi 196) has single/double rooms for $66/78, or $106/150 per day including all meals (which you can also arrange separately). There's also a twin share rate of $38.50 per person, or $75 including all meals. The lodge hires out 4WDs and boats and can arrange a variety of activities including diving, fishing, boating, horse-riding and tramping.

The *Tuanui Motel* (tel Waitangi 150D) has rooms for $30 per person for a bed only or $60 per person including all meals; single meals can be arranged separately. Unlike the hotel and the lodge, there are kitchens where you can prepare your own meals.

Homestays with locals are also possible. The cost is usually around $55 per person, meals included.

### Getting There & Away

Apart from a freight-only cargo ship every 4 or 5 weeks, the only transport to the islands is the Safe Air Argosy flight. It goes from Wellington weekly and from Christchurch twice a week; the fare is $656 return (children $384). The flight takes 3 hours and since there are only 30 seats available it's wise to book well ahead. Bookings are handled through Air New Zealand.

### Getting Around

Beyond Waitangi most roads are unsealed and there is no public transport. Chathams Motors (tel Waitangi 93) hires small 4WDs for $60 per day plus 21 cents per km, or larger ones for $82 per day plus 26 cents per km. It's also quite easy to hitch around the island.

Air Chathams (tel Waitangi 126) operates a light aircraft for flightseeing and for trips to Pitt Island. It may be possible to hitch a ride with fishermen across to Pitt Island, but the seas are very rough.

# Index

## THANKS

Thanks to all the following people (apologies if we've mis-spelt your name):

Cosy Cat (NZ), Fullers (NZ), Terrace Travel (NZ), 435 Durham St Turret House (NZ), 71 Munster Rd Richardson (UK), Adam Coleman (NZ), Adrian P Tomlinson (UK), Alan Mavis, Alpine Rec., Canterbury Ltd, Andrew Griffiths, Angelika Watz (D), Ann Pullen, Anna Lena Zetterlund (C), Anne Braun-Elwert (NZ), Anne Johnston (Aus), Anthony Moston (NZ), Antonio Martin Vidal (Sp), Arthur Yap (S), Ashley King (NZ), Ashley V King (NZ), Aura Rose, B Blandford (NZ), B D Sweeney (Aus), Barbara Lewin (UK), Barbara Magnew (NZ), Barbara Todd (NZ), Bernd Klagge (D), Bob & Avis Avery (NZ), Boel Carlsson (Sw), Bridgitte James (UK), Brigitte Humpl (D), Britt Finkelmann (D), Bruno Belanger (C), C & W Conway (C), C A Moore (UK), C Power & J Sametz (C), C/O Mr Helm Wettig (Aus), Camille B Morin-Leisk (USA), Catherine Hankey (UK), Charlotte McNaughto (NZ), Chris Carver (UK), Chris Terrell (UK), Chris Warren (NZ), Christer Larsson, Christine Whitaker (US), Christoph Tiefenbacher (D), Cindy Butler (USA), Clarke Price (UK), Colin & Sarah Carey (NZ), Colin Partridge (UK), Cyril Locher (CH), D (UK), D Oatway (UK), Daniel Wagner (Aus), David Skarsgard (C), Delwyn MacDonald (NZ), Derek Tobias, Dexter Da Silva (J), Doug Cole (USA), Dr Claudia Schmidt (D), E M Spijkerbosch (NZ), Elaine McKiwon (USA), Elizabeth Capon (UK), Elizabeth Wyke (USA), Ellis McIntyre (NZ), Emma Goldsmith (Aus), Evelyn H deFrees (USA), F G Grover (NZ), Frances Gallagher (NZ), Gabor L Lovel (NZ), Gabor Lovei, George Ford, Gillian Ashworth (HK), Gordon Bonin (NZ), GP Schurr (NZ), Grant Montgomery (NZ), Grendon Sullivan (NZ), Greta Simmonds (NZ), Harriett Bryson (UK), Helen Apouchtine (C), Helen Dunn (NZ), Horace Macaulay (C), Hugh Harrop (UK), Huw Charles-Jones (NZ), Ian Compton (Aus), Ian Trafford (NZ), J & E Edwards (A), J Brynes (USA), J W Clark (NZ), Jackie Cozby (NZ), Jackie Gibbs (UK), Jamie Brind (UK), Jan Crawford (USA), Jane & Simon Robinson (NZ), J C Lenthal (Aus), Jean Thompson (NZ), Jenni & Rob Penderton (NZ), Jennifer Carri (USA), Jenny & Paul Wetton (UK), Jill Mogg, Jill Wainwright (NZ), Jim DellaGiacoma (Aus), Jim Gambling (Aus), Joan Sutherland (NZ), Joanne McTavish (NZ), Joe Doherty (Ir), Joe Richards (USA), Joelle Nicholson (NZ), John Cairns (NZ), John Channings (NZ), John Cross (USA), John Edwards (USA), John Fitzpatrick (Aus), John L King (UK), John Morrow (NZ), John Morton (NZ), John Rains (NZ), John Ramsay, Jon Etchells (UK), Josje Hebbes (Nl), Joy Lovinger (USA), Judith Butt (NZ), Judy Arday, Julia Selby (Aus), Julian Harris (Aus), Julian Haworth (NZ), Julie Bremner, Julie Nock (UK), Karen Alliott (UK), Kate Maehl (USA), Kay Watson (NZ), Keith Scott (NZ), Keren Searer (USA), Kerry Kitchen (NZ), Kim Skaya (NZ), Kurt W Nielsen (Dk), L V Astill (NZ), Lamar & Sally Hoover (NZ), Lawry & Sue Dixon (UK), Leon & Doreen Maitland (NZ), Lesley A Hopkins (Aus), Lesley Anne Gardiner (Aus), Liz Schafer (Aus), Lora Bickers (USA), Louise MacDonald (NZ), Lynda Chamberlain (NZ), Lynn Chadwick (Aus), Lynne Saintonge (C), M & D Pigneguy (NZ), M Roller (UK), Malcolm George (NZ), Maree Adams (NZ), Margaret Christensen (NZ), Margaret Kay (NZ), Maria Palazzolo (USA), Marianne Salzmann (NZ), Mario Busch (NZ), Marion Busch (NZ), Mark Duffy (USA), Mark Hutton (USA), Mary Kilgour (NZ), Mary Nicholson (NZ), Mary Reaney (UK), Matthew Dickins (Aus), Megan Dawson - Postbank (NZ), Mel & John Ainsworth (NZ), Michael Bridgman (NZ), Michael Sorensen (Dk), Mike & Louise Roberts (USA), Mike Nicholls (NZ), Mike Scwhab (NZ), Miles Dracup (Aus), Miss J Humphreys (UK), Miss L M Innes (UK), Mrs E Griffiths (Aus), Mrs Elspeth Jubin (UK), Mrs Gwen Pritchitt (UK), Mrs J E Orchard (UK), Mrs Maree Adams (NZ), Mrs S M Machellan (UK), Mrs Val Brannan (NZ), Ms A Colley (Aus), Multhaup & Appleton (NZ), Murray Davidson

462

(NZ), Murray Wilson (NZ), N Griffiths (NZ), Natalie Polvi (C), Neil Ross (NZ), Niculina Apetri (Dk), Nils Hgberg (Sw), Pamela Dudley (UK), Pat Frost Fullers Northld (NZ), Paul Johnson (USA), Paula Wagenbach, Per Elbaek (Dk), Peter & Kerry Kitchen (NZ), Peter Andeweg (Nl), Peter Attwell (NZ), Peter King (NZ), Peter Peck (Dk), Peter S Gillies (NZ), Peter Schuepbach (CH), R & M Schellkes (NZ), R U Rattur, R L White (NZ), Rachel Wynne (UK), Ray King (NZ), Rebecca Nash (Aus), RF & AS Passmore (NZ), Richard & Kelle Gutman (USA), Richard Blackburn (NZ), Rick Hellriegel (NZ), Ringway Ridges (NZ), Rob & Teresa Lilley (NZ), Robert Barr (Aus), Robert L St Martin (Aus), Robert McGregor, Robin Harman (NZ), Robin Liston (NZ), Rohan Collings (NZ), Rona McIntyre (UK), Rosanne Payne (NZ), Rosmarie North (NZ), Roy Carter (NZ), Ruth Kaufman (NZ), S & L Armitage (NZ), S & R Lewis, S Steenstrup (Aus), Sarah Feather (NZ), Shelley Attix (USA), Sidney Murdoch (NZ), Sim & Brian McGowan (NZ), Simon Pavlovich (NZ), Simon Rea, Steen K Rasmussen (Dk), Stefan Boldt (Dk), Stephan Stoelting (NZ), Stephen & Rosie Smith (NZ), Stephen Arndt, Stephen Diserens (Aus), Steven Turner (C), Steven Wheeler (UK), Sue Howard (NZ), Susan Hollsten (Sw) Tanger Kjellberg (Sw), Tannis C Hill (C), Tom Lanigan (Thai), Tony Beaulah (UK), Tony Searle (NZ), Tony Skeggs (Aus), Trish Reid (UK), Ulrike Stephen (NZ), Urs & Linda Honegger (CH), Vincent Baytion (NZ), W Bain (NZ), Wallace McNaul (Ir), Warwick Orchiston (NZ), Wombat Tahanga (Aus), Wombat Tahanga (USA), Yola Macken (NZ).

Aus - Australia, C - Canada, CH - Switzerland, Chi - China, D - West Germany, Dk - Denmark, HK - Hong Kong, Ir - Ireland, J - Japan, Nl - Netherlands, NZ - New Zealand, S - Singapore, Sp - Spain, Sw - Sweden, Thai - Thailand, UK - United Kingdom, USA - United States of America

# Guides to the Pacific

### Australia - a travel survival kit
The complete low-down on Down Under — home of Ayers Rock, the Great Barrier Reef, extraordinary animals, cosmopolitan cities, rain forests, beaches ... and Lonely Planet!

### Bushwalking in Australia
Two experienced and respected walkers give details of the best walks in every state, covering many different terrains and climates.

### Islands of Australia's Great Barrier Reef - a travel survival kit
The Great Barrier Reef is one of the wonders of the world — and one of the great travel destinations! Whether you're looking for a tropical island resort or a secluded island hideaway, this guide has all the facts you'll need.

### Tramping in New Zealand
Call it tramping, hiking, walking, bushwalking, or trekking — travelling by foot is the best way to explore New Zealand's natural beauty. Detailed descriptions of 20 walks of varying length and difficulty.

### Fiji - a travel survival kit
Whether you prefer to stay in camping grounds, international hotels, or something in-between, this comprehensive guide will help you to enjoy the beautiful Fijian archipelago.

### New Caledonia - a travel survival kit
This guide shows how to discover all that the idyllic islands of New Caledonia have to offer — from French colonial culture to traditional Melanesian life.

### Solomon Islands - a travel survival kit
The Solomon Islands are the best-kept secret of the Pacific. Discover remote tropical islands, jungle covered volcanoes and traditional Melanesian villages with this detailed guide.

### Tahiti & French Polynesia - a travel survival kit
Tahiti's reputation as an idyllic island paradise continues to enchant travellers ... and after you have explored Tahiti, more than 100 other islands await you across the crystal clear water.

### Rarotonga & the Cook Islands - a travel survival kit
Rarotonga and the Cook Islands have history, beauty and magic to rival the better-known islands of Hawaii and Tahiti, but the world has virtually passed them by.

### Papua New Guinea - a travel survival kit
With its coastal cities, villages perched beside mighty rivers, palm-fringed beaches and rushing mountain streams, Papua New Guinea promises memorable travel.

### Micronesia - a travel survival kit
The glorious beaches, lagoons and reefs of these 2100 islands would dazzle even the most jaded traveller. This guide has all the details on island-hopping across the north Pacific.

### Tonga - a travel survival kit
The only South Pacific country never to be colonised by Europeans, Tonga has also been ignored by tourists. The people of this far-flung island group offer some of the most sincere and unconditional hospitality in the world.

### Samoa - a travel survival kit
Two remarkably different countries, Western Samoa and American Samoa offer some wonderful island escapes, and Polynesian culture at its best..

*Also available:*
*Papua New Guinea* phrasebook.

# Lonely Planet Guidebooks

Lonely Planet guidebooks cover every accessible part of Asia as well as Australia, the Pacific, Central and South America, Africa, Eastern Europe, the Middle East and parts of North America. There are four main series: *travel survival kits*, covering a single country for a range of budgets; *shoestring* guides with compact information for low-budget travel in a major region; *walking* guides; and *phrasebooks*.

## Australia & the Pacific
Australia
Bushwalking in Australia
Fiji
Islands of Australia's Great Barrier Reef
Micronesia
New Zealand
Papua New Guinea
Papua New Guinea phrasebook
Rarotonga & the Cook Islands
Samoa
Solomon Islands
Tahiti & French Polynesia
Tonga
Tramping in New Zealand

## South-East Asia
Burma
Burmese phrasebook
Indonesia
Indonesia phrasebook
Malaysia, Singapore & Brunei
Philippines
Pilipino phrasebook
South-East Asia on a shoestring
Thailand
Thai phrasebook
Vietnam, Laos & Cambodia

## North-East Asia
China
Chinese phrasebook
Hong Kong, Macau & Canton
Japan
Japanese phrasebook
Korea
Korean phrasebook
North-East Asia on a shoestring
Taiwan
Tibet
Tibet phrasebook

## West Asia
Trekking in Turkey
Turkey
Turkish phrasebook
West Asia on a shoestring

## Indian Ocean
Madagascar & Comoros
Maldives & Islands of the East Indian Ocean
Mauritius, Réunion & Seychelles

# Mail Order

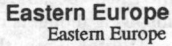

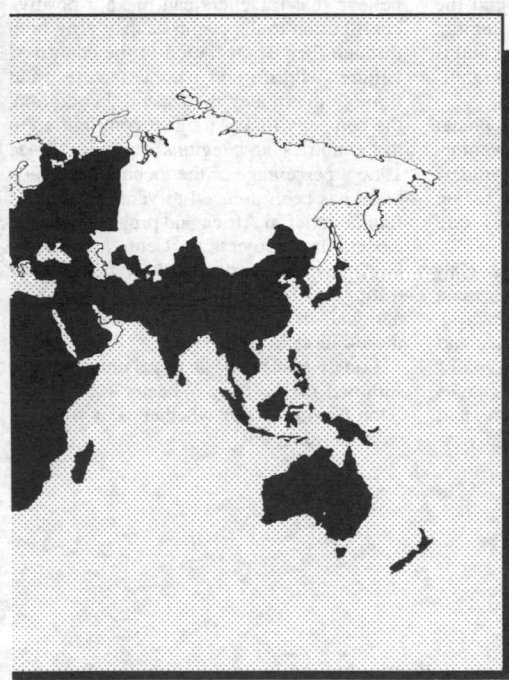

## Eastern Europe
Eastern Europe

## Indian Subcontinent
Bangladesh
India
Hindi/Urdu phrasebook
Karakoram Highway
Kashmir, Kadakh & Zanskar
Nepal
Nepal phrasebook
Pakistan
Sri Lanka
Sri Lanka phrasebook
Trekking in the Indian Himalaya
Trekking in the Nepal Himalaya

## Africa
Africa on a shoestring
Central Africa
East Africa
Swahili phrasebook
Morocco, Algeria & Tunisia
West Africa

## North America
Alaska
Canada
Hawaii

## Mexico
Baja California
Mexico

## South America
Argentina
Bolivia
Brazil
Brazilian phrasebook
Chile & Easter Island
Colombia
Ecuador & the Galapagos Islands
Peru
Quechua phrasebook
South America on a shoestring

## Middle East
Egypt & the Sudan
Egyptian Arabic phrasebook
Israel
Jordan & Syria
Yemen

## The Lonely Planet Story

Lonely Planet published its first book in 1973 in response to the numerous 'How did you do it?' questions Maureen and Tony Wheeler were asked after driving, bussing, hitching, sailing and railing their way from England to Australia.

Written at a kitchen table and hand collated, trimmed and stapled, *Across Asia on the Cheap* became an instant local bestseller, inspiring thoughts of another book.

Eighteen months in South-East Asia resulted in their second guide, *South-East Asia on a shoestring*, which they put together in a backstreet Chinese hotel in Singapore in 1975. The 'yellow bible' as it quickly became known to backpackers around the world, soon became *the* guide to the region. It has sold well over ½ million copies and is now in its 6th edition, still retaining its familiar yellow cover.

Today there are over 80 Lonely Planet titles – books that have that same adventurous approach to travel as those early guides; books that 'assume you know how to get your luggage off the carousel' as one reviewer put it.

Although Lonely Planet initially specialised in guides to Asia, they now cover most regions of the world, including the Pacific, South America, Africa, the Middle East and Eastern Europe. The list of *walking guides* and *phrasebooks* (for 'unusual' languages such as Quechua, Swahili, Nepalese and Egyptian Arabic) is also growing rapidly.

The emphasis continues to be on travel for independent travellers. Tony and Maureen still travel for several months of each year and play an active part in the writing, updating and quality control of Lonely Planet's guides.

They have been joined by over 50 authors, 40 staff – mainly editors, cartographers, & designers – at our office in Melbourne, Australia, and another 10 at our US office in Oakland, California. Travellers themselves also make a valuable contribution to the guides through the feedback we receive in thousands of letters each year.

The people at Lonely Planet strongly believe that travellers can make a positive contribution to the countries they visit, both through their appreciation of the countries' culture, wildlife and natural features, and through the money they spend. In addition, the company makes a direct contribution to the countries and regions it covers. Since 1986 a percentage of the income from each book has been donated to ventures such as famine relief in Africa; aid projects in India; agricultural projects in Central America; Greenpeace's efforts to halt French nuclear testing in the Pacific and Amnesty International. In 1990 $60,000 was donated to these causes.

Lonely Planet's basic travel philosophy is summed up in Tony Wheeler's comment, 'Don't worry about whether your trip will work out. Just go!'